Words in Blood,
Like Flowers

SUNY series in Contemporary Continental Philosophy

Dennis J. Schmidt, editor

Words in Blood, Like Flowers

Philosophy and Poetry, Music and Eros in Hölderlin, Nietzsche, and Heidegger

Babette E. Babich

STATE UNIVERSITY OF NEW YORK PRESS

Published by
State University of New York Press, Albany

Cover illustration: Dionysus detail. Attic red-figured amphora, 490 BCE.
Kleophrades Painter (500–490 BCE).
Staatliche Antikensammlung, Munich.

For information, address State University of New York Press
194 Washington Avenue, Suite 305, Albany, NY 12210-2384

Production by Diane Ganeles
Marketing by Susan M. Petrie

Library of Congress Cataloging-in-Publication Data

Babich, Babette E., 1956–
    Words in blood, like flowers : philosophy and poetry, music and eros in
Hölderlin, Nietzsche, and Heidegger / Babette E. Babich.
        p. cm. — (SUNY series in contemporary continental philosophy)
    Includes bibliographical references and index.
    ISBN 0-7914-6835-6 (hardcover : alk. paper). 0-7914-6836-4 (pbk. : alk. paper)
    1. Nietzsche, Friedrich Wilhelm, 1844–1900. 2. Heidegger, Martin, 1889–1976.
3. Hölderlin, Friedrich, 1770–1843. I. Title. II. Series.

B3317.B22 2006
193—dc22   2005029298

10 9 8 7 6 5 4 3 2 1

Contents

Preface

The title of this book, *Words in Blood, Like Flowers*, repeats the language and the passions of Friedrich Hölderlin and Friedrich Nietzsche. For it was Nietzsche who wrote of living with ideas as one lives with companions—as real as flesh and blood—and he spoke more forcefully of writing in blood, telling us that of everything written, his Zarathustra "loves" only "what one has written with one's blood. Write with blood and you will learn that blood is spirit" (Z, "Of Reading and Writing"). Hölderlin, in his poem *Bread and Wine*, uses the language of "words, like flowers" and writes variously, as only a poet can, of the "flowers" of the mouth and "the flowers of the heart."

Written, as we say, with one's heart, words in blood express the passion that for Heidegger belongs to philosophy at its inception as *thaumazein*, as *pathos* itself, which Heidegger understood as the key to the attunement [*Stimmung*] of philosophic astonishment, the sustained wonder or amazement that things are, that what is is as it is—and not otherwise. One can keep this wonder only in "authentic questioning," a questioning "that opens up its own source" (I, 6). In this self-rending tension, philosophy "never makes things easier but only more difficult" (I, 11). This same difficulty is the reason Heidegger thinks that philosophy might, indeed, "if we concern ourselves with it, do something *with us*" (I, 12).

Using the language of writing in blood, Nietzsche does not fail to underscore its Faustian implications, on the one hand in teasing, as Nietzsche liked to tease Goethe, on the other hand in all seriousness. If one writes in blood, one surrenders one's soul. But if these authors put themselves into what they write, we will see that they claim the same from the reader.

The conjunction between philosophy and poetry, not to mention music and eros, is a complicated one. And this limits, if it also constitutes, its appeal. For if the reading I propose between the poet Hölderlin and the philosophers Nietzsche and Heidegger will speak to some readers, it is just as obvious that this approach will not appeal to others. Here

I can have little to say as these other readers will be unlikely to have read even this far or if they do read further, will likely dip and pick, leaving out context and sidestepping all such complications as inherently belong to the themes of philosophy and poetry, music and eros in Hölderlin, Nietzsche, and Heidegger and so constitute the substance of this book.

To summarize the chapters to follow, I begin with a discussion of Heidegger and Nietzsche on philosophy, poetry, and love, including some everyday reflections on philosophical affairs. I then note Nietzsche's aphoristic style and the role of rhetoric in order to raise the question of how the spirit of music would account not only for the heart of Nietzsche's first book on tragedy but also for his singular insight into the sound of ancient Greek itself and his emphasis on language with respect to the sounds of its words, its meters and its rhythms, likewise articulated and exemplified (this similarity is no accident) in the beauty of Hölderlin's poetry. For Nietzsche had discovered nothing less than the "breath" or spirit of music in the words of Greek tragedy, which was also his testament to oral culture in antiquity. Yet this discovery, particularly as Nietzsche chose to illustrate its consequences for modern culture (a very classical, indeed classicist's programme, precisely in the spirit of Erwin Rohde, and contra Wilamowitz, as Karl Reinhardt would also attest, the same Reinhardt whose father had studied with Nietzsche in Basel and who had even urged his son to take up Nietzsche's cause precisely as a "classicist"), drew little resonance from his readers (be they specialists or not). This may have been the reason Nietzsche began with the same focus in *The Gay Science*, drawing on the example of the troubadour and yet another oral tradition of poetic or song composition.

I particularly attend to Nietzsche's life-long preoccupation with Pindar's poetic word: Become the one you are! Nietzsche hears this word in the enigmatic voice of conscience (GS §270), a creator's conscience, spoken with the utter innocence of the creator. "That one becomes what one is presupposes that one does not have the remotest idea what one is" (EH, "Why I am so Clever," §9). The philosophically reflexive point here, taken in connection with the resonant influence of poetry (that is: the heart "of what is *music* in it" [GS §373], to use Nietzsche's own language), underscores the inevitable limits of a reading that would reduce everything in Nietzsche (or in the Greeks) to prior sources, a project which not only disregards the transformations of style but excludes the same spirit of "music" as well as what Nietzsche regarded as historical reflection—a judgment on the critical sense of history Nietzsche had in common with Herbert Butterfield, a scientific historian in almost the same sense that Nietzsche was.

When Nietzsche reflects on his writing, he reflects on the Greek convention of the poetic muse or inspiration,"the idea that one is merely incarnation, merely mouthpiece" (EH, Z §3), as this idea inheres in the ecstatic essence of *Dichtung*. This is what works in or *through* him quite apart from his own will: "One hears, one does not seek; one takes, one does not ask who gives; a thought flashes up like lightning, with necessity, unfalteringly formed—I have never had any choice" (ibid.). In this fashion, the same Nietzsche who celebrates the primacy of the active artist above the passive spectator and who assumes the determining superiority of the wealthy (for Nietzsche, the rich are not merely consumers but those who impose their standards as "taste") is also careful to set the unconscious dynamic of poetic invention in place of the creative subject and contra the ideal of artistic genius.

Reflecting on the "phoenix of music" where he also tells us that "the whole of Zarathustra may perhaps be reckoned as music" (EH, Z §1), Nietzsche adverts to the singular achievements of his style: the "aphorism trembling with passion; eloquence become music" (EH, Z §6). For my part, I consider the metaphorical and literal expression of philosophy as music as this has come down to us from Heraclitus and Plato. A musical resonance works through Hölderlin's poetry where it is taken up in Nietzsche's most personal poem to the city of bridges and music: Venice itself. The same resonance works, so Theodor Adorno reads this resonance, as Hölderlin's voice recurs in Heidegger's paratactic expression. From the problem of the artist, Nietzsche turns to the question of the actor, thence to the question of the Jew, and ultimately to the question of woman. For Nietzsche, who always felt himself to have "the soul of a lover," the question of woman takes us to the eros of art as the illusion of the actor and thus the artist.

The concluding section of this book turns to Nietzsche's archaic reflections on chaos as well as Hölderlin's poetic call to a mindful consideration of the relation between nature and art (adumbrated, for the poet, in technological terms). This also includes a review of the judgments rendered by the advocates of art history and hermeneutic aesthetics regarding Heidegger on the origin of the work of art, which I consider with reference to contemporary sensibilities, with respect to the locus of the museum (I discuss Christo and New York's Central Park) and the question of conservation (the preservation of antiquities in Greek Arcadia as in Athens). The penultimate chapter offers a reading of Heidegger's politicizing of language between Germany and Greece and the last chapter considers Heidegger's intended legacy as he crafts his own self-oriented *Nachlaß* in his *Beiträge*, which he composes, so I argue, on the model of Nietzsche's *Will to Power*—an ironically unsuccessful ambition given the posthumous editorial interventions in the published version. After reviewing the consequences of such interventions, I read the *Beiträge* in relation to the technologically globalized world.

But reading alone will not be enough. The three authors mentioned, one poet and two philosophers, are unified voices inasmuch as they each invite (or compel) us to think. So we hear Hölderlin in his novel, *Hyperion, Or the Hermit in Greece*: "Poetry is the beginning and the end of philosophical knowledge."[1] But this is only because the "great saying, the εν διαφερον εαυτῳ (the one within itself differentiated) of Heraclitus, could be found only by a Greek, for it is the essence of Beauty, and before it was found, there was no philosophy" (StA 3, 81).

Beauty, for Hölderlin, is worth more than reason for philosophical thinking, as Schiller also argued in a still-Kantian modality. But what poetry does best it does in spite of us. And if Nietzsche and, in a different way, if Heidegger, too, can seek to borrow the thunder of poetry—that is, as already observed, poetic style and poetic rhetoric—it will be to take us beyond what we are convinced we already know. For one must, so Nietzsche argued, learn to think just as one must similarly learn to read. When Heidegger answers the reproof that his language is emptily tautological and hence unlikely to "get us anywhere" with meditative patience: "But we do not want to get anywhere. We would like only, for once, to get to just where we are already," (L, 190) we may be reminded of T.S. Eliot's ultimate exploration that finishes by allowing us "to arrive where we started / And know the place for the first time." Eliot's reflection towards the conclusion of the last of his *Four Quartets*, begins "With the drawing of this Love and the voice of this / Calling," and ends

> Through the unknown, unremembered gate
> When the last of earth left to discover
> Is that which was the beginning; [. . .]

For What Is To Come: More Soon—*Nächstens mehr*

The beginning, as the ancient Greeks said, is everything. Precisely for this reason Heidegger sought what he called "another beginning," a step back. Nietzsche sought to recall the innocence of things: the innocence of becoming or change, just as becoming is the enemy of every beginning. If Hölderlin turns to a reflection on the bowed course of life that is mortal life (and the sinking down or inclination that is mortal love), he could also write in his poem *The Rhein,* dedicated to his friend Isaak von Sinclair, "For as you began, so you will remain." [*Wie du anfiengst, wirst du bleiben.*] Here, Hölderlin emphasizes the very Greek insight that everything is already fully present at the start.

When Hölderlin writes *The Death of Empedocles* in three progressive versions, it is significant that in the last version, Empedocles does not simply take leave of life, sacrificing himself in death. The philosopher's leap into Etna is for the sake of another beginning, as love succeeds hate, and life succeeds death, in an eternal cycle. Transforming or perhaps consummating all syncretism between the life of Empedocles and the life of Christ, this recalls the vision of nature's reconciliation at the conclusion of *Hyperion.*

In the poet's later, elegiac voice, this is expressed analogically:

> . . . But reading, so to speak,
> As though in a script, men imitate
> Infinity and riches. Is simple heaven
> Rich, then? Surely like blossoms are
> Silvery clouds. Yet from there it is that dew and
> Moisture rain down. But when
> The blueness is extinguished, the simpleness,
> Then shines the pale hue that resembles marble, like ore,
> An indication of riches.[2]

In this fashion, the third version begins "you the most matured" [*ihr Gereiftesten*], invoking the most full or consummate—one is reminded of Nietzsche's image of ripened figs—"In you I'll recognize my new life's day."[3] In this way, when Pausanias entreats Empedocles to recall their bonds to one another, hoping that this love might be a means to hold him in life—and Hölderlin always regarded love, both mortal and immortal, as liberation, not confinement—Empedocles answers him: "But you must know, I am not yours/ No more than you are mine,/ Where you walk, I do not; my blossoming/ Elsewhere awaits me."[4] For Empedocles, this destiny was decided from the day he was born but he can also claim that this prefigured fate promises a transfigured resolution:

> Look up and dare to know it! what is One breaks up,
> Yet love in its bud does not die,
> And everywhere in bold, untrammeled joy,
> Unforced, the airy tree of life divides.[5]

If their different paths mean that Pausanias is to keep calmly to the joy of "Earth's drunken image" [*der Erde trunknes Bild*] and the

"perpetual round dance" [*der geschäfftge Reigentanz*] of human existence, and, from time to time, even to commemorate his friend at evening
[*und denk am Abend mein*], it is the philosopher's physical, bodily alteration that gives him the most intimate hint that his time has changed.
Thus he reflects that if he once pretended or aspired to an attunement
to a vision of higher "melodies" and sought to imitate them—are we
speaking of the poet or the philosopher?—it is now clear that "that was
all a jest!" [*es war ein Scherz!*] Thus transposed in a back-stretched
Heraclitean modality, what is transformed in Empedocles is nothing less
than his attunement: "More gravely now I hear you, voices of the gods."
[*Nun hör ich ernster euch, ihr Götterstimmen*].

If Nietzsche borrows Pindar's voice to call to himself and the friend
of youth: "become the one you are!," Hölderlin's Empedocles points to
a different transition, the transition that is nothing but the heart of
becoming, and a heart indeed that echoes Heraclitus: "I am not the one
I am, Pausanias," he says continuing: "And not for years may sojourn
here,/ Only a gleam, a glint that soon must pass,/ One note the lyre-
strings hold—"[6]

And yet we can scarcely forget that, again like Heraclitus, Empedocles
is the teacher of cosmic recurrence, of a return, as he says in one tone
to his young friend: "Go, and fear nothing. Everything recurs./ And
what's to come is already completed."[8] We hear these final words, in a
different, more reserved or careful tone addressed to his former teacher,
"Now leave me. When over there the light/ Of day goes down, you'll
see me once again."[9]

Calling to nature itself, the theme of recurrence is already to be
heard at the conclusion of Hölderlin's first book: "like spoiled fruits from
you, fall human beings, ah, let them perish, for so do they return again
to your root, . . . O tree of life" (StA 3, 159). The promise of a deeper,
Heraclitean, concord comforts Hyperion: "We too, we too are not parted,
Diotima, . . . Living tones are we, tuned together in thy harmony, Nature! who can rend this? who may tear lovers asunder? —"

The musical secret of tragedy echoes in this Empedoclean exchange
or counter-rhythm: "Like the quarrels of lovers are the dissonances of
the world, reconciliation is in the midst of strife and all that has been
divided finds itself again" (160). Nietzsche, of course, will reprise this
musical dissonance at the conclusion of his first book. For his part,
Hölderlin finds six syllables, seemingly to say the same again, to end his
novel— "*So dacht' ich. Nächstens mehr.*"

Acknowledgments

This book was written over the course of the last decade, and I have accumulated correspondingly numerous debts, personal and institutional. To begin with the most important personal acknowledgments, I am grateful to David B. Allison, for his gift of friendship and his wisdom, and to William J. Richardson for the power of his heart and mind, and I remain forever indebted to Patrick A. Heelan, for his joy and his mirth as well as for his kindness and his intelligence.

I owe thanks to my good friend Richard Cobb-Stevens and also to Alasdair MacIntyre whom I have admired for years. I am indebted to other friends who were helpful to me in the writing of this book, in particular, Annette Hornbacher and Anke Bennholdt-Thomsen, but above all to my long-time friend, Holger Schmid and to Heidi Byrnes for many conversations and for their help, *sine qua non*, with my efforts with the German language. I owe a debt to my friends and colleagues, Christa Davis Acampora, Keith Ansell-Pearson, Debra Bergoffen, Robert Bernasconi, Howard Caygill, John Cleary, Volker Gerhardt, Trish Glazebrook, Larry Hatab, Marcel Hénaff, Hans-Gerald Hödl, George Leiner, the irrepressible Al Lingis, Angèle Kremer-Marietti, Paul Miklowitz, Pina Moneta, Abraham Olivier, Martin Schönherr-Mann, Alan Schrift, Harald Seubert, Robin Small, Gary Shapiro, Eileen Sweeney, Jacques Taminiaux, and Paul van Tongeren. I am also grateful to the poet Josianne Alfonsi and to Stanley Aronowitz, Roger Berkowitz, Frank Boyle, Thomas Brobjer, Jeffrey Bussolini, Drucilla Cornell, Marcel Detienne, Stuart Elden, Nicole Fermon, Fred Harris, Marion Heinz, Duncan Large, Hugh Lloyd-Jones, Frederick Love, Gregory Moore, Jean-Michel Salanskis, George Steiner, Hubert Treiber, and Martin West, among others. I also honor the memory of my teachers Wolfgang Müller-Lauter and Hans-Georg Gadamer as well as my much admired colleagues, Dominique Janicaud and Reiner Schürmann.

I owe a special word of tribute to my good friend, Alexander Nehamas, and to my husband, Tracy B. Strong.

I gratefully acknowledge the institutional support provided by the Graduate School of Georgetown University for the writing of the final chapter in this book which was also part of the research project, *Hermeneutic and Phenomenological Approaches to the Philosophy of Science*, directed by Patrick A. Heelan, S.J., William A. Gaston Professor of Philosophy. In addition, I thank Professors Volker Gerhardt and Karl Schawelka for their support which led to the opportunities provided by my third Fulbright Fellowship to Germany, this time as Senior Fellow for research and lecturing at the Humboldt University in Berlin and the Bauhaus University in Weimar, 2004–2005. I am grateful to the Stiftung Weimarer Klassik und Kunstsammlung and to Dr. Rüdiger Schmidt-Grépaly, the director of the Kolleg Friedrich Nietzsche, for a fellowship invitation to give four public lectures in Weimar in the Fall of 2004, when I was also honored for contributions to international Nietzsche scholarship. I also express my gratitude to John C. Hollwitz, Academic Vice-President at Fordham University for much needed supplementary support during the Fall 2004 semester when I took a leave without pay. I thank the Deans of Fordham University for a course reduction from three courses to two courses for the Spring of 2005, a liberty which eased the many time demands involved with finishing the present volume.

With respect to the actual reality of making this work a book—and, as an editor myself, I have some sense of these complexities—I express my thanks to Jane Bunker, my generous editor at State University of New York Press. I am grateful for her wonderful intelligence, great good humor, and, above all, for her patience throughout. I also wish to thank Diane Ganeles, the managing editor, for her expert copyediting.

Earlier versions of some of the sections in this book have appeared as articles or chapters in the following places: "From the Ethical Alpha to the Linguistic Omega: Heidegger's Anti-Semitism and the Question of the Affinity Between Ancient Greek and German," *Joyful Wisdom: A Journal of Postmodern Ethics*, Vol. I (Fall 1994): 3–25; "The Poetic Construction of Nature: Hölderlin's Contribution to an Ethos of Nature and Art," *Soundings*, LXXVII/2 (Summer 1995): 263–277; "Nietzsche's *Chaos sive natura*: Evening Gold and the Dancing Star," *Portug. Revista filosofia*, 57/2 (2001): 225–245; "Nietzsche and Eros Between the Devil and God's Deep Blue Sea: The Erotic Valence of Art and the Artist as Actor—Jew—Woman," *Continental Philosophy Review*, 33 (2000): 159–188; "Between Hölderlin and Heidegger: Nietzsche's Transfiguration of Philosophy," *Nietzsche-Studien*, 29 (2000): 267–301; "*Mousikē technē*: The Philosophical Praxis of Music in Plato, Nietzsche, Heidegger"in Robert Burch and Massimo Verdicchio, eds., *Gesture and Word: Thinking Between Philosophy and Poetry* (London: Continuum, 2002), pp. 171–

10; 200–205; "Nietzsche's Imperative as a Friend's Encomium: On Becoming the One You Are, Ethics, and Blessing," *Nietzsche-Studien*, 33 (2003): 29–58; and "Heidegger Against the Editors: Nietzsche, Science, and the *Beiträge* as *Will to Power*," *Philosophy Today*, 47 (Winter 2003): 327–359.

Abbreviations

AC	*The Antichrist/The Anti-Christian*
B	*Beiträge/Contributions to Philosophy*
BGE	*Beyond Good and Evil*
BT	*The Birth of Tragedy*
EH	*Ecce Homo*
FS	*Frühe Schriften*
GA	*Gesamtausgabe*
GM	*On the Genealogy of Morals*
GS	*The Gay Science*
H	"Letter on Humanism"
I	*Introduction to Metaphysics*
HH	*Human, All Too Human: A Book for Free Spirits*
KdrV	*Kritik der reinen Vernunft/Critique of Pure Reason*
KGB	*Briefwechsel Kritische Gesamtausgabe*
KGW	*Kritische Gesamtausgabe*
KSA	*Kritische Studienausgabe*
L	"Language"
Meta.	*Metaphysics*
N. Eth.	*Nicomachean Ethics*
N1	*Nietzsche: Volume I: The Will to Power as Art*
N2	*Nietzsche: Volume II: The Eternal Recurrence of the Same*
N4	*Nietzsche: Volume IV: Nihilism*
NNS	*New Nietzsche Studies* [Journal]
NS	*Nietzsche-Studien* [Yearbook]
NL	"Nature of Language"
O	"Origin of the Work of Art"
PTG	*Philosophy in the Tragic Age of the Greeks*
RB	"The Relevance of the Beautiful"
Rep.	*Republic*
StA	*Stuttgarter Ausgabe*
SZ	*Sein und Zeit/Being and Time*
TI	*Twilight of the Idols*

TL	"On Truth and Lie in an Extra-Moral Sense"
UM	*Untimely Meditations*
W	*The Wanderer and his Shadow*
WP	*The Will to Power*
WL	"The Way to Language"
WT	*What Is Called Thinking?*
Z	*Thus Spoke Zarathustra*

References to frequently cited material from Nietzsche and Heidegger are given by title abbreviation in the body of the text. To avoid confusion with Nietzsche's *The Birth of Tragedy*, Heidegger's *Being and Time* is cited as SZ. In the case of citations from Nietzsche's works, I do not give references to page numbers in particular translations or editions of his works, but I instead refer to numbered paragraphs where Nietzsche himself uses these, or else to section titles as he provides these, for example, as in the case of *Thus Spoke Zarathustra*. This facilitates locating Nietzsche's texts in German or indeed in other translations. In the case of numbered prefaces (e.g., Nietzsche's "Attempt at a Self-Criticism" to his *The Birth of Tragedy*), references are made with lower case roman numerals, for example, BT ii. In the case of references cited in the text to translations from Nietzsche's *Nachlaß*, I refer to the KSA and FS by page number. Almost all citations follow the author's translation, and at times, the German is given either in the text or in the notes for the sake of scholarly clarity. I have consulted existing translations and these are listed in the bibliography.

German language sources include *Nietzsche Werke: Kritische Studienausgabe*, Giorgio Colli and Mazzino Montinari, eds. (Berlin: Walter de Gruyter, 1980). All citations from Nietzsche's unpublished works refer to the KSA edition when given in the text I list only the volume number, followed by the page number. In general, references to the *Frühe Schriften*, Hans Joachim Mette, ed. (Munich: Verlag C. H. Beck, 1994) [FS], the KGW, Kröner edition, and *Nietzsche Briefwechsel Kritische Gesamtausgabe* (Berlin: Walter de Gruyter, 1987ff.) are given in the notes to each chapter.

Illustrations

Philosophy, Philology, Poetry

1

꒰ꔛ꒱

Philosophy and the
Poetic Eros of Thought

If we trust Heidegger's own assessment at the end of his life,[1] as Gadamer has transmitted this to us, Nietzsche would be Heidegger's undoing. Nevertheless, Heidegger undertook to read Nietzsche in a way that remains a rarity to this day.[2] Completing Nietzsche's project at the "end of philosophy," Heidegger thinks the "other beginning."[3] But Heidegger's beginnings are known only in the flashing of the moment: as the first edge of the sun at the break of dawn or the wake of an eclipse.[4]

In his lecture courses, Heidegger took care to bracket then-contemporary presuppositions about Nietzsche, the very presuppositions that continue today. Not as a philosopher of life (and we note that past as well as more recent readings of Nietzsche and biology and even Nietzsche and the body continue to install him in the conceptual register of life or blood and thereby race) and not as a poet-philosopher, Nietzsche, for Heidegger, can tell us what philosophy can be.[5]

Philosophy, Love, and Wisdom:
Heidegger, Nietzsche, and the Erotic

If philosophy, as the "love of wisdom" involves thinking and if thought has knowledge as its object, then all human beings, to the extent that it is true that it is in the nature of the human to "love" or to search for knowledge, may be supposed to be philosophers at ground or *in nuce*. Thus Aristotle begins his *Metaphysics* with the assertion that "All men by nature desire to know" (Meta. 980a), an assertion that seemingly emphasizes the philosophical temperament as specifically humanizing, just as

3

Aristotle distinguishes human beings from plants and from animals in terms of the capacity for reflective thought. This humane confidence has often been used to obscure what Nietzsche regarded as the consummately undemocratic tenor of antiquity, a tenor corresponding to the paradoxically sublime forbearance of the noble vis-à-vis the common, the core of Nietzsche's notion of the "*pathos* of distance" (GM I:2).

For Nietzsche, the Greek ideal of nobility (or virtue) is as impossibly distant for us as is the ancient Greek understanding of slavery and its attendant contempt for necessary or life-essential labor, that is, in support of the life of the species.[6] In other words, ancient Greek conceptions of slavery are intrinsically foreign to our modern sensibility, to a lifestyle or "art of living" that willingly trades the hours of its day for material compensation, payable by the hour or still worse, as a career, in exchange for a secure salary (see GS §330). "The Greek philosopher," Nietzsche wrote, "went through life feeling secretly that there were far more slaves than one might think—namely that everyone who was not a philosopher was a slave" (GS §18). To comprehend this attitude of self-mastery, pursuing wisdom not for social rewards or for the sake of "earning a living," as the English idiom so tellingly has it, the philosopher has to be fundamentally genuine, in Heidegger's sense, foundationally real, and only in this ultimate sense, a true lover of wisdom.

This is the high foundational significance of "real" or "actual"—the meaning Heidegger gives to being a "real" poet: "provided, for example, there are poets only, but then: really poets, to the extent that there are thinkers only, but then: really thinkers. . . ."[7] Heidegger's emphasis here, "die Dichter *nur*" contrasts with Nietzsche's plainly poetic expression, only a fool, only a poet, "*nur Narr, nur Dichter.*" Thus as Nietzsche teases, the philosopher (even the genuine or real philosopher) turns out to be merely a lover of wisdom (a perpetual suitor, as the poet John Keats comforts—or curses—the swain frozen on an antique urn, "She cannot fade, though thou hast not thy bliss, Forever wilt thou love, and she be fair!"): an eternal seducer of wisdom, but an inconsummate, impotent failure just the same.

In a lecture presented in Normandy on the theme *What Is Philosophy?*, speaking ten years after the end of World War II, Heidegger shows himself to be a master of rhetoric, and, therefore, of diplomacy. In contrast to the usual characterizations of Heidegger's chauvinism, reserving the German language for philosophy and expressly excluding other languages, Heidegger here addresses his French audience beyond their own Gallic and Latinate heritage, reminding his listeners that when one invokes philosophy, whatever language one speaks, every scholar is in the province of ancient Greece. In this way, Heidegger tells us, all philosophers may be ranged within the legacy of that Greek thinker, presumably Heraclitus, who first coined "the word *philosophos* [φιλόσοφος]."[8]

The lover of wisdom is like the lover of anything, as Heidegger goes on in the same good scholastic fashion, retracing the hierarchical cadence of love well known to us after both Plato and Aristotle—"like *philarguros*, loving silver, like *philotomos*, loving honor."[9] Thus an "*aner philosophos* is *hos philei to sophon*, he who loves the *sophon*."[10] For Heidegger, such love, conceived as harmony, and accordingly understood in the cosmological fashion that Heraclitus speaks of the physical meaning of love, like Empedocles, is an accord with the *sophon*. This is the meaning of "*hen panta* (one is all)." Heidegger continues: "The *sophon* says—all being is in Being . . . being is Being."[11] This is the "that" of the wonder expressed in the Greek *thuamazein*—the sheer *that* that things are, which—as every student learns—is the beginning of philosophy in astonishment or wonder. But for Heidegger, the love of the *sophon* ("the being in Being") is from its inception, and almost immediately, lost. This radically sudden loss or eclipsed beginning is the lightning flash that, in the oldest conversion of metaphors, may be regarded as the ground tone resonating throughout the later Heidegger. In what Nietzsche calls the jealous and compensatory "vicariousness of the senses,"[12] this music barely begins to sound, that is to say: this lightning just flashes and is as quickly lost to senses of apprehension and to thought. Thus Heidegger calls for another beginning in thinking, a step back interior to philosophy itself. Philosophy is consequently already metaphysical at its inception, a striving (*orexis*): it becomes a sundered longing for the *sophon*. "Because the loving is no longer an original harmony with the *sophon* but is a particular striving towards the sophon, the loving of the *sophon* becomes '*philosophia*.' The striving is determined by Eros."[13] But ancient Greek *eros* and *philia* are two different (if always affine) things.

Heidegger therefore maintains that philosophy exemplifies a particular love, indeed a clearly erotic relation to thought.[14] And in his lecture course *What Is Called Thinking?*, he turns to Hölderlin to articulate the relation between love and thinking to trace the relation between thinking or philosophy and love. Reflecting on thought and poetry, Heidegger claims that poetry, as its own "standing in itself," must be seen "its own truth" in the "beauty" of its very word (WT, 19). This self-standing in the truth "does not exclude but on the contrary includes what we *think* in the poetic word" (Ibid.). Heidegger's reading of the poet's word turns it out of the center of one of Hölderlin's seductively intriguing poems, "Socrates and Alcibiades": "Who the deepest has *thought*, *loves* what is most alive" [*Wer das Tiefste* gedacht, liebt *das Lebendigste*].[15] The poet draws us to thinking and love, posing them side by side, as Heidegger observes: " *'thought'* and *'loves'* form the center of the line. Inclination [*Mögen*] reposes in thinking."[16] The alignment of love (the past of thinking and the present allure of love) betrays the sobriety (and self-sufficiency) ordinarily supposed for the life of thought.

"*Mögen*," for the Suabian Hölderlin as much as for Heidegger— love, for Heraclitus (and for Empedocles)—is a vulnerable and imperma- nent disposition, a harmony, which needs to be held, sustained, or tuned in being, or it vanishes. This vulnerability is key beyond the excitement associated with an attunement of any kind: "Once, however, in the beginning of Western thinking, the essence of language flashed in the light of Being—when once Heraclitus thought the Λόγος as his guiding word, thus to think in this word the Being of beings. But the lightning vanished abruptly. No one preserved its streak of light or the nearness of what it illuminates."[17] As the mark of loss, this reversed eclipse is an erotic figure. We begin, with Heidegger, by talking about philosophy, the love of wisdom. Just as quickly, we find ourselves talking about longing; betrayed in the same movement, we are talking about eros and this is never quite, if it is also never far from, the discourse of love.

This is the eros of philosophy that has Nietzsche commending Socrates as a sublime eroticist (TI, "The Problem of Socrates," §8, vgl. BT §13), and speaking, in advance of Wittgenstein, and this may be no accident, of the permeation of eros to the depths or else to the heights of the human soul (BGE §75), the same eros that was given poison to drink: crippled but not killed by the church (BGE §168).

Numerous commentators, including Luce Irigaray, Jean-Luc Nancy, and Giorgio Agamben have undertaken to write on (and often enough, on the impossibility of) Heidegger and the subject of love. Recently, George Steiner has even installed Heidegger in the place of Peter Abelard in the lover's square opposed to Hannah Arendt's Heloise (a disquieting constellation, one might say, and in more than one sense).[18] Yet this last construction reminds us of the old claim that philosophy begins in gossip (another way to translate the famous first line of Aristotle's *Metaphysics*). And talking about gossip—or about love affairs in Heidegger's case—the theme of Heidegger and eros is eminently seductive. Confirming this dimension, Heidegger himself instigates the arch erotic move of evasion, the master's move that like Socrates' own gambit, assures his lasting allure. Declaring, as I am told that Heidegger declares, and I am happy to take it on the purest faith,[19] that "the essence of eros is nothing erotic," Heidegger would outdo even Nietzsche for sheer provocation.

Agamben too has a lover's "complaint" about Heidegger and love. Limiting his concern to Heidegger's *Being and Time*, Agamben draws attention to Heidegger's seeming failure to mention love (just as

Heidegger fails, quite fatally for Sartre one might remember, to talk about beer, or just as cataclysmically for Irigaray, to mention air). Agamben has to qualify the claim with reference to Heidegger's invocation of the terminology of Pascal and Augustine (as most other such claims might also be qualified—this is the same Heidegger who begins by talking about nothing only to discover Being or, beginning with Being, to advance to thinking about nothing, quite differently than Alain Badiou's important valorization of the same).

Given, so Agamben claims, Heidegger's familiarity with Max Scheler's views on the preeminence of love (and hate) and considering (this is Agamben's trump card) the circumstantial romantic involvement of Heidegger and Arendt, attested in a backwards look from a letter Heidegger wrote to Arendt later in life, Agamben nevertheless has his satisfaction on just these terms. For Agamben, the very "writing of *Being and Time*" took "place under the sign of love."[20] If Luce Irigaray's reading in *Heidegger and the Forgetting of Air* retains the elevated tone of a Derrida by comparison—and despite or better said owing to the distractions of her Lacanian formation—by gentle or literary contrast with Irigaray's philosophic inquiry, George Steiner's reading raises the question of a traditionally redemptive romantic entanglement.[21] The stakes of this redemption correspond to what Steiner happily—or unhappily—calls the *Lessons of the Masters* (he took the English title reluctantly, so he assures us in his introduction).

Steiner's "lessons" are offered beyond the reality of sexual harassment—he has no patience with the language and imputations of unwanted attentions (how could there be anything but mutuality here, albeit upon on a clearly unequal level, Steiner seems to ask), nor does he have any time to consider the possibility of less than gentle consequences of such mismatched seduction (again, on both sides). The masters never want to be masters at this level: this is the chance to return to the Shropshire of their remembered or unfulfilled youth. And to be sure, for such literal-minded thinkers of the old school, what the media calls "sexual harassment" is a lame word for the dynamic of intellectual betrayal, frustrated hope, and wronged innocence that teachers of a past generation can never imagine. Never, never ever.

Teaching—to paraphrase Nietzsche—is so erotic. But it is essential, if only for the lovers' ideal of fantasized reciprocity (as Lacan would mock us), to ask: for whom? Whose eros is this if it is not the master's erotic ideal: for we are not talking about a student playground, youth on youth.

Nietzsche stood square in the company of the masters—professors, teachers. He did not, so he assured Lou in a disarmingly innocent protestation of his "intentions," merely want someone to act as his secretary and practical assistant in household affairs, he wanted a—she could be his—pupil. And Arendt was Heidegger's student. It is worth pausing a moment to ask ourselves why we persistently call Lou Salomé by her first name, just where we do not refer to Nietzsche as Friedrich (forget Fritz or Freddy), or why Arendt is almost always emphatically *Hannah* Arendt and Heidegger only *Martin* in the context of a love story? The paradigmatic love story for academic masters, as Steiner recalls this account, is that of Heloise (had she a surname?) and one Peter Abelard, an unusually gifted troubadour and on this account quite successful with all the women who heard him, as Heloise would later accuse in one of her letters. Maybe we are all of us vicarious masters, in Steiner's phrase, and thus we, male or female, assume the right of speaking on a first name basis whenever we speak of women. Indeed, we extend this intimacy to women we are not supposed to like, thus we call Nietzsche's sister Elisabeth, as we name Heidegger's wife Elfriede, or Wagner's wife Cosima or his daughter Winifried.

But Nietzsche challenges philosophers as such, just because what characterizes Nietzsche's understanding of philosophy is precisely the notion of command. Thus he routinely tells philosophers what they should do, as he famously distinguishes between the tractable, scientific laborer and the philosophical legislator or ruler, just as he saw himself as philosopher rather than philologist alone. If Nietzsche was correct to upbraid philosophers in this case, criticizing them for what he diagnosed as their "lack of love,"[22] a point addressing less the philosophers' innocence or their deficiencies in matters erotic (as sex-manual mad or just gender scholars have assumed) than the philosophers' lack of critical concern with the very "question" of love. The philosopher simply assumes that he (it is always a he)[23] simply knows what love is. But Nietzsche sought to raise questions where one usually does not think to do so (he regarded this as the determinative characteristic of critique and thereby, and this was the same for Nietzsche, of science).

Pastor's son that he was, Nietzsche called attention to the philosophical and widespread conviction concerning the nature of love. Worse than Augustine's question concerning the nature of time, everyone knows—asked or unasked—what love is, and everyone knows that love is desirable (this is Plato's ironic edge, conveyed in the words of two hired lovers, both male and female: equally contracted and duly paid for the pleasure of their beautiful speeches, because the art of speaking well was thought by the ancients to be the most alluring of all, as Nietzsche reminds us [cf. GS §80]. Thus Plato gives us Diotima's remembered teaching in the *Symposium* and details the triangular constellation of Lysias's written seducer's speech in the *Phaedrus*). Much more, as

Nietzsche goes on to deepen his challenge to this presumption, everyone knows that a god of love—and here Nietzsche turns ugly—must correspond to a *higher* divinity than any other god before him. Exactly how this divine evolution might advance (GS §140), and even pondering what a god of love, exigently requiring love (GS §141), would have to learn about love (BGE §142), Nietzsche argues that our convictions, already knowing as we do, just might be unfounded (GS §307). As Descartes critiques the common conviction concerning "good sense," whereby "everyone thinks himself so abundantly provided with it"[24] that one also assumes oneself entitled to forego the acquisition of "rules" for the direction of thought, so too, we tend to forget that we need to learn how to love things in general (GS §334), be they musical, artistic, or corporeal, whether our love is the love of words (philology) or wisdom (philosophy).

Despite Agamben's assertions, and as Irigaray has noticed (and Steiner follows her, if to be sure, without adverting to her lead), Heidegger himself inquires about love in his discussion of philosophy, even in *Being and Time*, if only indirectly. Later, and inspired by Nietzsche, Heidegger will observe that in the philosopher's love of the *sophon*—that is, for Heidegger: being in Being—the disposition of love turns to desire from the start. Love in the process, this is the legacy of formal indication, obscures the character of this solicitude. Failing the exigent reticence of love, the philosopher becomes a scholar, aspiring to wisdom. Worse (in what Heidegger called "cybernetics" and what would today be called "cognitive science"), the philosopher can become a man of science, dedicated to the calculation of practical knowledge, a calculation of security that is for Heidegger (as it would also have been for Nietzsche) no different from the calculation of the man of faith.[25]

The Philosopher as Poet

The Nietzsche who wrote a handbook of poetry also wrote poems, just as the Nietzsche who celebrated music above all, also composed, and, perhaps most importantly, also *played* music.[26] If it is true that Nietzsche's well-attested gift for musical improvisation has rarely been considered (and such a consideration would be challenging indeed), his compositions have been judged harshly, from Nietzsche's contemporary, the composer Hans von Bülow to Cosima Wagner to Georges Liébert.[27] And his poetry would seem to present a similar case. If, as we shall see in the chapter to follow, Nietzsche borrowed the title for the poems that introduce *The Gay Science,* his "Prelude in German Rhymes" from no one less than Goethe ("Scherz, List, und Rache"), his efforts here repeat the handbook of the troubadours' guild, the aristocratic singers' repertory of poetic form as a kind of poetic or literary exercise. I will argue that *The Gay Science* as a whole can be seen from this perspective. If this case can be made, it nonetheless remains difficult to draw Nietzsche's thinking out of his poetry. Well in advance of his auto-bibliography, *Ecce Homo: How One Becomes What One Is*, Nietzsche proposes his own self-summary under the same inscription in the set of rhymes introducing *The Gay Science*:

> *Ecce Homo*.
> Yes! I know now whence I came!
> Unsatiated like a flame
> my glowing ember squanders me
> Light to all on which I seize
> ashen everything I leave:
> Flame am I most certainly. (GS "Prelude," 62)

Thus the same Nietzsche who was to be charmed by a published comparison between himself and "dynamite"[28]—only consider the late-nineteenth-century force of this imagery!—had already compared himself to light, to burning flame (deploying an image used in the English Shelley's concluding stanza to his "Ode to the West Wind"—"Scatter as from an unextinguish'd hearth, / Ashes and sparks, my words among mankind!"). And the same Nietzsche also wrote "My Roses" (*wollt ihr meine Rosen pflücken*), a poem of inspired—and erotic—ambiguity, as well as the magical "Sils-Maria" in the 1887 appended *Songs of Prince Vogelfrei* (a series likewise dedicated to Goethe), as well as the self-ironic "Poet's Calling" (and with this last song, one surely has Nietzsche's blessing for calling him a tick-tock poet).

Martin Heidegger's poetry is a different affair to the extent that it has been read as part of his philosophy. This difference does not make Heidegger better—or worse—than Nietzsche as a poet. But it does mean that to read Heidegger, one does well to attend to his poems.

William J. Richardson thus begins his masterly overview of Heidegger's work, *Through Phenomenology to Thought*, with Heidegger's poem "Eventide over Reichenau" [*Abendgang auf der Reichnau*]. Echoing Hölderlin's *Bread and Wine*, as Hölderlin calls to Heinse's earlier poem to the night, it is significant to observe that this may be counted as Heidegger's own *Abendlied*—or *sirenas*, to use Nietzsche's classifying translation of the forms of troubadour song.[29] Richardson's commentary on this poem is keenly insightful and it recurs in an important fashion in Richardson's later reflections on Heidegger.[30] If most readers of Heidegger's poetry have been literary scholars, as George Steiner will go on to confirm, the value of this poetry for his thinking, as Richardson's analysis shows, is plain for philosophy.

Robert Bernasconi similarly reads Heidegger's poetry as articulating the said/unsaid,[31] adverting to Heidegger's politically impossible silence in much the same way, as does Steiner, and as I too have reflected upon this same silence, under the sign of "a language whose words have already broken."[32] I find it essential here to read Bernasconi's focus on this interrupted speech as a *musical* attention. In the "space" of such a music, listening to Heidegger's silence, one must also attend to the articulation of the needful connection between saying and thinking, so that for his own part, as Heidegger reads Parmenides he invokes a paratactically musical reading, in the acoustic dimensionality of the punctuation marks Heidegger adds for our eyes, visually, literally, transposing a voiced break (one which can only be heard in ancient Greek): "saying speaks where there are no words, in the fields between the words which the colons indicate" (WT, 186). This is the silence that speaks between the words, between the lines: echoing as the unsaid in what is said.

Bernasconi takes the inspiration for his reading of Heidegger's poem on language, "Sprache," by means of a recollection of the poem-question overheard in Heidegger's reading of another poet, Stefan George,[33] who wrote himself of the failing of the word as word: "where word breaks off, no thing may be."

Heidegger's question turns in Bernasconi's reading on the question of the word's return: "when will words again be words?"[34] Bernasconi's invocation of Heidegger's reply echoes only in the highest tonality: "when they bear us back to the place of ancient owning [*uralter Eignis*] where the ringing of stillness calls."[35] Heidegger's poetic words are set into the philosophical substance of his thinking. A musical reading of his thought entails that we seek to hear what is said/unsaid in these words.

The question of language and translation is at issue for us, precisely as English language readers. The translation of *uralter Eignis*, "ancient owning" is a fine and beautiful rendering—and yet it does not invite us to hear what Heidegger says, *not* because these words mis-take Heidegger's language, but because we cannot hear his meaning in this. To read Heidegger, to read Nietzsche, to read Hölderlin, we have to read German.[36] And like any language, a foreign language can only be mastered for us, for English-speaking readers, in order to return us once again and only not to the foreign language as such but to what is our own, to what is native to us—as both the poet Hölderlin and the linguist philosopher Wilhelm von Humboldt had differently emphasized, echoing for their part the spirit of eighteenth-century hermeneutic reflection.[37] Given this poetic and hermeneutic limitation, to read Heidegger's "Sprache," to

read the poetic word *uralter Eignis,* we would have to be able to catch
a resonant, metonymic reference to the penumbra of sounding words
that echo in the word as word: *eignen* [fit, suit, attempt] as much as
eigen [own, ownmost] and *Ereignis* [event, happening, occurrence]. Do
we have this capacity? Ought one to hear *Eigentlichkeit* [authenticity] as
Eignis in Heidegger's 1972 poem as it may, perhaps—I do not know if
this is true—recall the key word of his 1927 masterpiece?

In a personal letter, Reiner Schürmann noted the difficulty reported by English readers reading Heidegger on language, as on poetry
and thought. Schürmann suggested that we might do well to return to
reflecting upon the indispensability of a critical familiarity with German.
This familiarity resonates with Heidegger's recommendation that one
first of all read Greek, which for many of us can mean that we need to
begin to learn Greek. Here Schürmann invoked the results of linguistic
research as "substantiating" Heidegger's nationalistically irritating (and
politically unsettling) claim for a supposed and philosophic affinity proper
to the German—as to the Greek.[38]

Nietzsche as Thinker

We have already noted that Heidegger began his lecture course in the
1930s by underscoring Nietzsche's relevance as a philosopher *tout court*—
and not a poet or a "life-philosopher" and, most radically, emphatically
not as promulgator of racist or "biological" teachings."[39] What Nietzsche
teaches us about thinking, about "thoughtlessness," Heidegger finds in
Nietzsche's "simple, because thoughtful words, 'The wasteland grows' "
(WT, 29). *Die Wüste wächst.* And Heidegger emphasizes Nietzsche's
next reflection on the consequences of nihilism, "Woe to him who hides
wastelands within" (29). Not a matter of negative judgment or pessimism, it is "that which gives us food for thought, which is what wants
to be thought about" (30). In addition to somber affairs, such as death
as one had since *Being and Time,* all-too-typically (and for Heidegger,
all-too-journalistically) associated with his thinking, Heidegger wrote that
lightness and love: "and beautiful and mysterious and gracious things
give us food for thought" (Ibid.). In all that belongs to be thought
about things as such, "what is most thought provoking—especially when
it is man's highest concern—may well be also what is most dangerous.
Or. . . ." Here Heidegger interrupts himself in a Suabian voice, different
from the more rhetorically stylized way that Nietzsche interrupts himself
(these are Nietzsche's very deliberate *Gedankenstriche*). By means of this
elevated, questioning use of "*Oder,*" Heidegger invites us to think back
upon what is said, reflecting upon our own assumptions: "Or do we

imagine that a man could even in small ways encounter the essence of truth, the essence of beauty, the essence of grace—*apart from danger?*" (31, emphasis added). If it is to think about what provokes thoughtfulness with respect to the range of what is dangerous to be thought about—from truth to love, beauty, and grace—to think about such thinking invites reflection on danger itself, on "the Danger" as such: it is to engage in thinking about danger. Here, Heidegger's reflections present Nietzsche as the ultimately dangerous thinker: "I am no man," we again recall Nietzsche as writing, "I am dynamite" (EH, "Why I Am a Destiny," 1).

There is an important sense in which, unlike Hölderlin or Pindar or any other poet, but like Kant, and as a philosopher, even as Nietzsche claims to invert Plato, Nietzsche remains in thrall to Plato just as Heidegger says, almost as Nietzsche contends, and thereby to Aristotle. In this manner, Nietzsche turns within the orbit of Western metaphysics as the culmination of Western thought.

What is important to observe about this Heideggerian compulsion is that it is no kind of error as it is also nothing like a mistake that could (or should) be corrected. Western metaphysics at its end is a matter of perspective. That is, thought itself, in the Western tradition, taken with the darkness of nihilism's unthinking refusal or, otherwise said, the light openness of mystery, as critical rationality and sensible, reflective understanding, *thought itself* is nevertheless, with everything at its disposal, unable to overcome this constriction. Heidegger never abandons this insight into what is called "thinking." These are the complexities of thought as Heidegger calls for thinking in the critical terms of Nietzsche's challenge to Western reason or nihilism.

Heidegger cites Nietzsche's prophecy: "The wasteland grows . . . ," and for Heidegger, these words express the philosopher's heart ("Nietzsche put all that he knew" into them) (WT, 51).[40] With this citation, as he repeats it in *What Is Called Thinking?*, Heidegger commands the seduction of a prophecy drawn from Nietzsche's sardonic (more than a few scholars have ventured their explanations of the reasons Nietzsche had for adding this) fourth part to the book that the present author, with all due caution, cannot but regard as Nietzsche's Trojan horse, that is, his most dangerous gift to the reader, indeed, a book that destroys as it gives: *Thus Spoke Zarathustra: A Book for All and None.* Heidegger will make this the key to his esoteric reading of Nietzsche, a key he takes from Nietzsche himself. Thus, "Nietzsche, the thinker, hints at the secret fittingness of his thought in this manner" as he inscribes it in the most obvious place—that is the prime esoteric locus—in the very subtitle of his most famous book, "a subtitle which runs: *A Book for Everyone and*

No One" (WT, 50). But it is for just this reason that Heidegger will later remind us that "this too remains for us to be learned, namely, to read a book such as Nietzsche's *Thus Spoke Zarathustra* in the same rigorous fashion as one of Aristotle's treatises" (Ibid., 70).[41]

For Heidegger, "In the realm of essential thinking, Nietzsche sees the necessity of a going beyond [*Übergang*] with greater clarity than any before him" (WT, 57). Reading Nietzsche's thinking, it is not only essential that we "refer everything in his thought that is still unthought back to its originary truth" (Ibid., 54), but much more than that, Heidegger argues, we are to see Nietzsche as the one thinker who recognizes that in the history of Western man something is coming to an end. This transition, as we have already cited it, is named as the danger, a word borrowed from Hölderlin.[42] It appears in "Die Gefahr," a title figuring with *Das Gestell* as one of the lectures to the Club of Bremen, a term included in the unpublished opus of the *Beiträge* and familiar to us from the conclusion to his published essay, *The Question Concerning Technology*.[43] This danger today is the totalizing domination of Western, that is, perfectly technological humanity as the measure and definition of all that is, and it is what Heidegger names the "end" of philosophy—in a very different sense than the oddly Hegelian sense intended by Francis Fukuyama when he speaks of the "end" of history. For Heidegger, the end of philosophy "proves to be the triumph of the manipulable arrangement of the scientifico-technological world and of the social order proper to this world."[44] It is in this humanistic context that Heidegger recalls Nietzsche's anti-philosophical (arch-philosophical) definition of the human as (the non-exclusively) rational and (not specifically) political animal. "The human being," as Nietzsche defines humanity, and as Heidegger quotes him, "is the *always yet undetermined animal*" (WT, 59; BGE §62). Citing the limits of the physical and psychological sciences, as the limits of cosmology and metaphysics, such an undetermined being must find "a passage beyond himself," and "for this reason the bridge must be found to that nature by which the human being heretofore can be the *surpassing* of his former and last nature" (WT, 59). This bridge is the *Übermensch*, read not in terms of race (even Heidegger's original lectures on Nietzsche are unwaveringly clear in their opposition to the error of reading the biological doctrines of National Socialism back into Nietzsche) but sheer, active transcendence.

Nietzsche's critique of subjectivity and therewith his critique of intentionality—the knowing consciousness of the knower who knows, as this may be addressed to Aristotle, Descartes, Kant, but also, *avant la lettre*, Husserl—addresses language in the poetic sense so important for

Heidegger. Language is thus what speaks us: thoughts come when they—and not the thinking subject—are moved to come: "One hears, one does not seek; one takes one does not ask" (EH, Z §3). As Nietzsche declared of himself and his own compositional craft and powers in his *Ecce Homo*, reflecting upon his inspired way of writing in *Thus Spoke Zarathustra*, "I have never had any choice," choosing the subjective *I* quite deliberately in opposition to classical, thinking subjectivity. As the supposedly most radical and, popularly, as the most individually free thinker of our time, for Heidegger, Nietzsche "neither made nor chose his way himself, no more than any other thinker ever did. He is sent on his way" (WT, 95; 46). As thinker of thinking, thinking what is called (or calls, sends us to) thinking, Nietzsche's reflection on subjectivity as he questions the notion of the subject is the patent reason Heidegger engages Nietzsche as he does in *What Is Called Thinking?*

As in the associative couple *Denken/Dichten*, thinking becomes a kind of poetizing. With Nietzsche's observation—that a thought comes when it wants—thinking becomes a species of the same kind of enthusiasm or inspiration that is poetry and which, for Heidegger, works to transform thought as *Dichtung*. This way of conceiving thought yields a kind of love or crossover, an affinity between thinking and poetry: "a secret kinship."

The Relation Between the Poetry and Music/Silence of Language

Unlike Nietzsche, Heidegger is not typically regarded as a poet but he is also not typically denied the title of philosopher, if his rank as a philosopher has been the subject of ongoing dispute owing to his style, famously regarded as unclear, if it is also plain that this dispute owes at least as much to his politics.

I argue, together with George Steiner as it turns out, that if we attend to the music (or "style") of Heidegger's writing, the claim that Heidegger's writing is unclear[45] loses its force. To read Heidegger as a poet is to take Heidegger's musical style as relevant for what he says. In this sense, what determines whether we can hear what he says or merely find it unclear or "badly" done depends in turn upon whether we have (or can develop) an ear for that same writing style.

As thinker, Heidegger is consigned to use language to understand the essence of poetry and language and thought, as of being itself. But the philosopher as writer is subject to the readings of the critics and their judgment has been harsh if intriguingly subject to a self-overcoming or reflective return. Hence it is important that although in 1988 Steiner was able to observe of Heidegger's expressive gifts: "Words failed Heidegger and, at a pivotal stage in his life and work, he failed them,"[46] almost a decade and a half later Steiner has turned, as he has written to the present author, to a study of those very words: Heidegger's poetry. Already in 1991, Steiner had underscored the matter of Heidegger's style as Heidegger's voice, and below I return to the question of this voice in an exactly modern musical mode.

Steiner's emphasis is both strikingly literal and instructively phenomenological (if it is also posed contra Derrida), and in the spirit of Nietzsche's philological style (a style Steiner for his part does not attribute to Nietzsche). Thus Steiner highlights the "central *orality* in Heidegger's teaching and concept of the enterprise of serious thought,"[47] explaining this diction as that of a specifically poetic or lyrical kind: "I have found that passages in Heidegger which are opaque to the reading eye and stony on the page come to more intelligible life, take on a logic of an almost musical kind *when they are read aloud.*"[48]

It is Heidegger as poet who writes in "The Way to Language," "Language speaks by saying, this is, by showing. What it says wells up from the formerly spoken and so far still unspoken saying which pervades the design of language. Language speaks in that it, as showing, reaching into all regions of presences, summons from them whatever is present to appear and to fade."[49]

Heidegger is aware that such a "gnomic" formula as his pronouncement that "Language itself is language,"[50] leaves him open to the charge of Anglo-analytic vagueness. "The understanding that is schooled in logic, thinking of everything in terms of calculation and hence usually overbearing, calls this proposition an empty tautology. Merely to say the identical thing twice—language is language—how is that supposed to get us anywhere?" (L, 190). Heidegger answers this simple question with disarming intensification, that is, still more simplicity. We have seen that he concurs, in an unsettling admission for philosophy used to supporting the progress ideal of rationality and the pragmatic ambitions of scientific technicity, "but we do not want to get anywhere." For Heidegger, the passion for novelty and the latest discoveries are distracting tendencies of the modern era and irrelevant to thought itself, especially philosophy. Thus Heidegger concludes with an equally gnomic declaration that has already compelled us to question its significance: "We would like only, for once, to get to just where we are already" (Ibid.).

An advocate of releasement [*Gelassenheit*] and therefore pleading the liberating *uselessness* of philosophy—" 'You can't do anything with philosophy' "—Heidegger nevertheless could expect philosophy to have the highest advantage: "granted that *we* cannot do anything with philosophy, might not philosophy, if we concern ourselves with it, do something *with us*?"[51]

In this sense, and beyond the reproofs of Theodor Adorno's "jargon" but also beyond the charge widespread in analytic circles of his endemic obscurantism, Heidegger's wordplay opposes both the received sense of philosophy and the received use of language as a mere playing. As poet, Heidegger is just and only and no more than a poet through whom what is said is said. To this extent, what Heidegger writes is without gain, profit, or advantage, and that *indigence*—to use Richardson's language[52]—is a simplicity in its purest sense: beyond value, yet more crucially beyond valuing. Thus Heidegger suggests that rather than attempting to attain to something *by means of* or *with* philosophy—doing things with words, or "doing" philosophy or theory in the pragmatic or praxical sense—we might rather and like Nietzsche, make the effort to risk or to dare to suffer that philosophy *do* "something *with us*." This, as I read it, is the meaning of Heideggerian *Gelassenheit*.

In Nietzsche's case, to regard Nietzsche as Heidegger proposed to do, that is, to read him as a thinker in the most rigorous sense, is to read his critical writing on thinking as a critique of logic and scientific rationality. Such a critique examines the rational foundations of logic and rationality itself as a means of knowing the world to be known. Such a radical critique is thereby turned upon reason itself as a means of knowing the knower. In this way, Nietzsche's thinking offers a critique of reason: simply or purely and as such.

And it is in this rigorously Kantian sense that we are also to understand Nietzsche's avowed ambition to doubt more radically than Descartes a part of Nietzsche's critique of the subject.[53] But when and if we can understand Nietzsche as going beyond his predecessors in this fashion, as more critical than those very critical thinkers who came before him, we may well find ourselves as frustrated as Heidegger found himself at the end of his life.[54] In this way, Nietzsche's project thus destroys not only the historical past of philosophy, not only its representation of itself to itself, but the very project of thought itself.

In the most rigorously self-conscious sense of critique, a sense that was enhanced and not weakened by the lack of scholarly resonance with his critical work, Nietzsche took his scholarly point of departure from the critical proposition that an instrument of criticism (rationality) cannot as such be turned upon itself. This is the critique of critique as Nietzsche dares to pose this question against scientific reflection itself. If what you are doing is fundamentally reflexive, *critical* thinking, the result turns out to be an unsustainable project on its own reflexive, fully critical terms. Philosophy in this sense reaches an end: it goes aground—an all-too-Nietzschean shipwreck.

If one thus regards Nietzsche's consummation of Western metaphysics less as a metaphysics, as Heidegger's interpreters have been all-too-literally inclined to do, than as a critique of the subject, the same critique of humanism that Heidegger shared with Nietzsche, together with his critique of the physical world and the ideal/illusory world, one finds once again, and on Heidegger's terms, that Nietzsche's thinking includes philosophy on every level, beyond ontology to the thought of thought itself. Beyond Heidegger, if indeed beyond most Nietzsche interpretation to date, this is the Nietzsche that still calls to be read.

What follows is an attempt at such a beginning, a reading still underway inasmuch as a Heideggerian guideline is one that seeks to keep the question of reading in mind precisely as a question. In the case of Nietzsche, this requires attention to the elusive and esoteric project of attending to the acoustic echo of the soul of ancient music in the text of ancient Greek lyric poetry as he himself had linked it to his recommendations for the culture of the future.

2

⌦

Philology and Aphoristic Style

Rhetoric, Sources, and Writing in Blood

Writing in blood, one wants not to be read but to be learnt by heart.

—*Zarathustra*

Nietzsche's scholarly training was in the field of ancient philology, or classics, which he embraced not merely with a theoretical passion but with characteristic expressive or articulative genius. Together with Luther and Goethe, Nietzsche is regarded as one of the best writers in the German language. If his writing style manifestly makes a great deal of difference to the way we read him, it also makes him no easier to read and it is important to point out that Nietzsche's philosophical bent, his passion for saying very complex things, only compounds the challenge.

I will speak of Nietzsche's aphorisms but, as we shall see, it will not do to begin there. Thus I first review Nietzsche's rhetorical style in connection with the question of scholarship, particularly contemporary source scholarship and the history of ideas.

Nietzsche's Rhetorical Style: On Rhetoric and Reading

Famously and dramatically, Nietzsche declared himself born for "the day after tomorrow"—a claim that has been heard to imply that those who would ultimately have ears for his philosophy have yet to be born. The same seductive claim has been taken to imply that current readers might fit the bill. If Nietzsche was poorly received in his own era (a claim that should perhaps be taken with a grain of salt, if only because Nietzsche himself makes this writerly complaint about his readership), it seems that he was fated to be understood by a later generation and we are those destined to hear him.

His popularity today supports such a conclusion. Rare among philosophical authors, Nietzsche appeals to an astonishing range of academic readers, within and apart from philosophy, but also (and this is not an unmixed blessing) extending beyond the scholarly professions to the journalistic talents (and these are not to be imagined as being limited to journalists) Nietzsche, like Heidegger, could not abide. Moreover, his predictions—in cultural but above all in political and even historical domains ("there will be wars . . .")—seem so accurate that philosophical, political, psychological, or sociological and anthropological theorists have turned to Nietzsche as the source for so many (and so very) literal cues to the present day, transforming him into a kind of latter-day Nostradamus in the process. If Nietzsche would call upon the quality of *"suspicion"*[1] in the first section of the 1886 preface to *Human, All Too Human*, it was to avoid just such scholarly credulity. But the same critical qualities Nietzsche called for are rare. Dancing not in the "chains" of stylistic rigor (to recall the image Nietzsche used to capture the contradictory demands of Greek style for his students of classical rhetoric), but rather introducing a Dionysiac play with question marks, bringing writerly style to philosophy in the process, Nietzsche did not, as is so often assumed, call for a "light" philosophy, an easier, more affably "gay" approach to philosophy. Indeed, readers as careful as Heidegger have found that Nietzsche's rendezvous of questions makes philosophy yet more difficult: daring the abyss, daring a new infinite, such a philosophy embraces the open horizon of risks and challenges.

Nor is this roundelay of question marks and ideas learnable. Nietzsche's unremitting and professionally unsettling condemnation of the scholar is the scholar's creative distance from the subject of his analysis. Taken as expert, respected as *canonic* authorities on those whose work they would never be expected to equal, scholars routinely read Goethe without having to "be" Goethe, never mind Raphael or Beethoven (as Nietzsche similarly invokes theoretical parallels to the artist and the musician). In philosophy, this will mean that one reads Kant yet without having (and without supposing that one needs) to have the ability to think as Kant thought, much less to go beyond him (as we began by emphasizing that Nietzsche would mean to do). But what about Nietzsche and what about Nietzsche scholarship? Do we have to "be" or to measure ourselves against Nietzsche? Does Nietzsche's challenge, that the scholar invariably falls short of the object of scholarship, hold with regard to his own writings? How hard is it to read *Zarathustra*? Have we not had book after book of the kind that instructs us on the matter of "what Nietzsche really said"? And even where one does not mean to be a scholar of his thought, Nietzsche appears to be a universal personal hero, coffee-mug personality, refrigerator magnet, plush toy, or rag doll. Surely in the case of Nietzsche, so it seems, the challenge seems out of place.

Exclaiming with personal pronouns in his writing, You! he calls out to the reader, are to become the one you are! I!—he proclaims of himself, Luther-style—I have never had any choice! We! he flatters—and abuses—the reader, we knowing ones, we fear—and we want to overcome our fear, and, finally: we fly! But the reader, any reader—that means you, that means the present author, that means that all of us, *as readers*—are advised to be on our guard, to beware. The seductiveness of this style is utterly non-spontaneous, all of it deliberate calculation on Nietzsche's part.

David B. Allison has highlighted this style in terms of the arresting quality of its deeply personal appeal: "Nietzsche writes exclusively for you. Not at you, but for you. For you, the reader. Only you."[2] And Nietzsche himself analyses the direct address of such a writing style:—to you, "only you,"—educing the model of the Bible as the paradigmatic book of books, a book for all the world, *Allerweltsbücher*.[3] As Nietzsche underscores this point in *Human, All Too Human*, the Bible is a book written to include *everyone*. Precisely *as* the word of God, the Bible is a highly personal, democratically inclusive text, not only addressed directly to the reader but expressed in a style that seems to reflect the reader's own and most intimate wishes.

Referring to the New Testament, Nietzsche here remarks upon the consummately stylistic accomplishments of the text. For Nietzsche,

> a perspicacious man can learn from it all the expedients by which a book can be made into a universal book, a friend of everyone, and especially that master expedient of representing everything as having already been discovered, with nothing still on the way and as yet uncertain. All influential books try to leave behind this kind of impression: the impression that the widest spiritual and psychical horizon has here been circumscribed and that every star visible now or in the future will have to revolve around what shines here. (HH II §98)

Nor is Nietzsche the only one to take a leaf from the book of books. Wagner, too, for Nietzsche, would have elements of this same all-inclusive and all-comprehending or universal or "true friend's" style, as Allison has highlighted this intimate stylistic achievement in Nietzsche[4] and as others have also explored this same (and not coincidentally religious) theme of friendship.[5] For his part, Nietzsche finds the vehicle for this same fond comfort (glad tidings) in written form and substance in his own *Thus Spoke Zarathustra*, planned as a masterpiece and sent out to a world that had thus far failed to respond (in the way that Nietzsche wished a response) to his earlier offerings.

For Nietzsche, as we recall the model of stylistic concision, as he expressed it: his own writing would embody such a style, in contrast with the reigning (and still enduring) German bombast in popular expression and its scholarly variations.[6] In a section entitled "Rare Feasts" in *The Wanderer and His Shadow*, Nietzsche writes a self-admiring word of encouragement to his reader: "Pithy compactness, reposefulness and maturity—where you find these qualities in an author stop and celebrate a long feast in the midst of the wilderness: it will be a long time before you experience such a sense of well-being again" (HH, W §108). Just as he would celebrate the ideal of Greek style as extreme constraint and extreme freedom, "dancing in chains"[7] as we have seen, so Nietzsche asserts Sallust, a Roman icon of laconicism, as the occasion for his own stylistic inspiration.[8]

Whether modeled on Sallust or whether drawn from the Bible itself, what we call Nietzsche's "style" is anything but accidental. And given the rhetorical mastery of Nietzsche's "style," the current and ongoing appeal of his writing is not solely a result of the sensitivity of our contemporary response to his voice. The question of style here is the question of rhetorical efficacy. How does this text work as it does? How does Nietzsche *do* what he does with his writing?

Unobtrusively self-promoting, Nietzsche ultimately and effectively persuades his readers to appropriate his views (and what else is persuasion?) while yet discouraging such an appropriation (restriction is the best seduction to this end), *telling* his readers *not* to follow him but much rather urging them to find their *own way* instead. Yet, and of course, following his prescriptions, using his metaphors and self-assessments, taking over his examples and repeating his analyses, Nietzsche's readers discover their own best voice in words taken from Nietzsche.

Very carefully calculated, Nietzsche's style is the product of an accomplished literary art. This methodic calculation or textual work is the secret of poetry—as the poets themselves have told us, not only Edgar Allan Poe but also Friedrich Hölderlin and Paul Valèry, T. S. Eliot, Wallace Stevens, Mark Twain, and so on. Poetry, we learn, is rather less subjective expression and sentiment than exigence and law; poetry, of all things, is rule. So far from the unguarded impetuosity of expression ordinarily attributed to his writing style, Nietzsche spent every possible moment rehearsing this poetic craft.

From his scholarly beginning as a teacher and a writer, Nietzsche brought this same understanding of rhetorical style to bear on the question of what would be required in order to begin to say very complicated things: complex in themselves and given his readers and given the way readers read. Such a reader-directed and self-deconstructive style[9] is evident not only in the books Nietzsche prepared for publication but it may also be seen, and this should not be a surprise, in the drafts of the letters he prepared for his correspondents.[10] It is thus clear that Nietzsche had achieved not only a *theoretical* but also and remarkably—for this accession is the exception among scholars—a *practical* mastery of the art of written composition or style.[11] This mastery, as already noted, does not necessarily make Nietzsche easier to read if only because much more is going on in his texts than is manifest at a first encounter, or even after many such encounters. In part this has to do with Nietzsche; in part this has to do with his audience.

Style and the Problem of Scholarship and Its Sources

It is more than tempting to say that Nietzsche has the art of style "down to a science." The "science" in question however is not quite a figure of speech (as we shall explore it with reference to *The Gay Science*), just as it was more than a metaphor for the Nietzsche who emphasized his own task as the project of raising the question of science as a question—for the very "first time," as he carefully, critically emphasized this question. So too he also underscored the significance of his writing style in the same locus. To raise the question of what Nietzsche then called the problem of science takes us too far and too fast at this point. For if I have argued that from his earliest to his latest writings, Nietzsche was always and very literally preoccupied with the question of science (which for him included philology as much as it included physics) and if this concern must be seen neither as a literary metaphor nor as literature but rather as a philosophical concern and ultimately as laying the foundation for what might be regarded as a genuine (because critical) *philosophy of science*, there remains the stylistic question of poetry and that is, as we shall see, Nietzsche's "gay science."

Apart from Heidegger, and with certain exceptions, the vast majority of Nietzsche's readers have been more concerned with the fortunes of morality and the death of god and the question of Nietzsche's literal intentions with regard to his doctrine of the eternal return of the same than with the epistemological discontents or "question" of science, a science gaily poetic or otherwise. If this is changing, it is not ultimately clear that the change constitutes a move in the direction of the greater critical focus Heidegger had rightly identified as essential to reading Nietzsche. As knowers, Nietzsche tells us, we need a certain and constant self-critique. And yet—and this remains the greatest obstacle for an analytic approach to philosophy (much more than just an analytic reading of Nietzsche)— it is precisely as "knowers" that such a critique eludes us (BGE §i).

In the well-known essay, "On Truth and Lie in an Extra-Moral Sense," Nietzsche describes the extramoral (i.e., beyond blame and ethical fault, and which turns into the dominion of what lies beyond good and evil) as the logical matter of truth, metaphorical reference, and even more precisely, the relation between truth and lie in a perspectivally, observational, all-too-eco-physiological sense.[12] Nietzsche's commentators, especially the analytically trained among them, can be inclined to side-step the logical question of truth and lie, on the assumption that Nietzsche knew little logic and less science. Thus one brackets Nietzsche's references to the empirical domain of perceptual observation or human physiology to talk instead about the all-too-fluid concept of the "body," just as an earlier generation (Merleau-Ponty-inspired, Bataille-inspired), might have been inclined to speak of the earth, to speak of "flesh" or else, still more recently, one will speak of cognitive metaphor or, this is most common, one skips over the question of truth altogether in order to concentrate on moraline discoveries.

It is relevant to note that this "moralizing" tendency is today exacerbated by a new "positivism" in Nietzsche scholarship, increasingly focused upon the literally reductive terms of a hunt for Nietzsche's own sources. Thus source scholarship has unraveled some of the sources of Nietzsche's "On Truth and Lie" (notably and to wit: Gustav Gerber's *Die Sprache als Kunst* [*Language as Art*], a rich compendium of sources and reference contexts).[13] Yet we recall that Nietzsche himself reviews the presumptions at work in the same, all-too-modern ideal of originality in his *Philosophy in the Tragic Age of the Greeks*, criticizing the very notion of "original" sources in terms of an importantly hermeneutic contextualization of neighboring influences. As Nietzsche argued on behalf of antiquity, as we might here attempt to argue in parallel on his own behalf, originality as such was not and could not be at issue, and only and exactly because the question of such a reduction to the creator misses the point (this is the force of Nietzsche's early lectures on Homer and philology and the *agon*).

For Nietzsche, the "genius" of the Greeks was importantly, irreducibly mimetic. Taking over the discoveries of others, Nietzsche tells us that the Greeks were uncommonly gifted in "the art of fruitful learning" (KSA 1, 806). This same art of productive learning presupposes proper inception or timing. Thus Nietzsche writes, "the Greeks had understood how to begin at the right time" (Ibid., 805). By pointing to the importance of inceptive poise, Nietzsche is able to concede "how much the Greeks found in oriental foreign lands" (Ibid.), underscoring the "foolishness" of attributing an "autochthonous formation" to the Greeks. Like many ancient peoples, the Greeks excelled in appropriating alien forms of life as their own: "they advanced as they did because where another people had abandoned a spear, they knew how to take it up and cast it further. In the art of fruitful learning, they command admiration" (Ibid.). We shall later see that Nietzsche here echoes both Wilhelm von Humboldt's insights into language as well as Hölderlin's reflections on the relationship between the native and the foreign.

To this extent, what Nietzsche says on truth and lie is what source scholarship has "uncovered" as a glossed engagement with Gerber's handbook of rhetoric, *Kunst der Sprache* [*The Art of Language*].[14] Yet it is important to emphasize that Nietzsche does not simply restate Gerber's project, as scholars of contemporary philology, tracing the doxography of Nietzsche's own texts, claim. It is important to emphasize the scholarly sophistication Nietzsche supposed to belong to the rigorous science of philology. For the dogmatic impetus, the spirit of this doxographical research presupposes an original text, a first text never given as such in the past and a "text" which may not be found in the present.

It is still more imperative to note the classic difference between exemplary texts and models, as between exemplars and edifying discourses. Hence this same source-critical obsession with the ideal (whatever we might think with Nietzsche about the reality) of originality never even touches what David Allison would designate as the "cheap ontic" question of everyday, merely mechanical reproduction. At this level, scholars, scribes, and authors are and have always been copyists—as Nietzsche was, as Heidegger was. It is an artifact of contemporary technology that we need to be reminded that such copying does not quite perfect the art of plagiarism nor is it inevitably evidence of derivative thinking (in Nietzsche's case, as in the case of the Greeks and their influence, exactly the contrary holds).

Where former generations of scholars copied their sources by hand, learning them by heart, as Nietzsche did, allusions, such as Nietzsche's own, indeed and particularly in his unpublished and personal notes, could be taken for granted unless one had, as in the case of Wilamowitz's scathing review of *The Birth of Tragedy*, didactic occasion to do otherwise. Yet it remains to the point to note that Wilamowitz himself is awash in uncited or unreferenced allusions: for it is the case that these allusions, then as now, do the work of scholarly one-upmanship.[15] Thus Nietzsche himself would speak of the exoteric and the esoteric domains (and where would Straussians be without such distinctions?)

It is hard to parse the same allusions today just because we not only read less and less but we also presume upon a common stock of references that diminishes daily. When we research sources (and the point of source scholarship emphasizes that we need to do this because our common stock is as lean as it is) we tend to photocopy the texts in question, double page by double page and in an age of electronic and downloadable texts, we print them out, texts of whatever length, with a single keystroke—so that it can happen that we may never have seen—much less have actually taken the time to "read"—the original itself. Some elements of this growing cultural distance may stand behind the difficulty we have in comprehending what Nietzsche meant by the "exemplar" (or still resonant in the French sensibility to the text that echoes in the word *formation*).

To take the perfectly *exemplary* case of "truth and lie," Nietzsche does not merely advert to the artistic potential of Gerber's *Language as Art* as much as he seeks to push the question of truth and lie in language, importantly enough, taking the same question of language, truth, and knowledge in the tradition of language philosophy derived in turn from Wilhelm von Humboldt, just as Gerber himself would continue to raise the further epistemological question of language and science, publishing *Die Sprache und das Erkennen* [*Language and Knowing*] in 1884.[16]

It is on the terms of this longer tradition of *language philosophy* that Nietzsche goes on to raise the arch-philosophical (even analytically philosophical) question in Austin's (or in Wittgenstein's) terminology as the question of how we do things with language, and Nietzsche further extends this question in a direction of particular importance as Heidegger came to hear the question. Thus Nietzsche goes further than Austin, Wittgenstein, or Stanley Cavell (*pace* all Cavellians) to raise the question of how language (and thus philosophy) might do things "with"[17] or to the speaker. Taking this dimensionality in yet another direction, Josef Simon has argued that Nietzsche poses his own analysis of language in the all-too-philosophically familiar terms of a discussion of valid and invalid statements, as a reflection on the context of the critical possibility of knowledge as such.[18]

The epistemological question of the critical possibility of knowledge is Gerber's concern in his foreword to the later single-volume edition of his book, published as *Die Sprache als Kunst* [*Language as Art*] in 1884, where Gerber appeals to Kant's critical philosophy to conceptualize his own "critique of language," naming it a "Critique of Impure Reason" [*Kritik der unreinen Vernunft*]. With a comparable allusion to Kant's critical philosophy in the second volume of the 1871 edition, Gerber had already exemplified a hierarchy of dependencies, moving from Kant to Lange, to Hegel, to Spinoza, to Kuno Fischer. Today's source scholarship might have sought to raise the question of the critical possibility of knowledge on the terms of language and its timeliness, both grammatical and metaphorical, but instead this same string of references has been used to argue source-questions alone. Hence we learn that Nietzsche's familiarity with *all* these authors may be traced back to Gerber—and it is worth reflecting on the significance of this reductive passion. Thus there is here in Nietzsche-Gerber, Nietzsche-Lichtenberg, an uncannily exact parallel with the Nietzsche-Kant question (where, barely decades ago now, one might have learned that Nietzsche took his Kant secondhand from Lange) where, more typically, we are instructed that Nietzsche had his knowledge of Kant from Schopenhauer (one would wonder why Wagner would not be a contender: the Wagnerians themselves have no trouble maintaining that Wagner was well able to read *both* Schopenhauer *and* Kant on his own, a scholarly achievement stubbornly denied Nietzsche).[19] Manifestly enough, the continuing problem with the difficult if related question of Nietzsche's reading of Kant is all about the radicality of Nietzsche's reading and philosophic thinking. It is unsurprising that just this reading has been rejected by those who regard Kant as a foundational source of reason but not critique, that is, heaven forfend! not *radical* critique.

Whatever one may say regarding the inspiration that leads source scholars to suppose themselves to have uncovered the derivative qualities of Nietzsche's philosophic ideas, often wholly on the strikingly positivist or literalist basis of a library record or the presence of a book in his personal library, or the annotations in the same, I have already emphasized that those who mean to read Nietzsche on philosophical terms have almost uniformly been inclined to disparage his claims on truth and lie and to disregard (or to correct, which is the same thing) his reflections on the possibility of knowledge, or to dismiss his cosmological or his ecological theories or his judgments on the quality of scientific theory (from Darwin to Boscovich and Democritus to the physio-psychology of diet).[20] Indeed, typical of Nietzsche scholarship *on both sides* of the so-called analytic-continental divide has been an attention to Nietzsche's powers of "invention," where Nietzsche is thought not only to have invented a conception of life "as literature"[21]—to use the convention favored by both Alexander Nehamas and Michel Foucault—but to have "invented" entire subject areas such as the "pre-Socratics,"[22] including the very idea (that is: the dynamic constellation) of Dionysus himself in the birth of "tragedy."[23] Thus it rather conveniently turns out that Nietzsche was not only derivative *as* a thinker but also and simultaneously radically creative or "inventive" as well.

Accordingly, so the reasoning seems to go, assuming that Nietzsche was able to fabricate or "invent" whole vistas of fictive conventions, like pre-Platonic philosophy or the idea of the Dionysian, he can also be said to have invented a vision of truth, a vision of science, and even a vision of what physicists do (described with a word from his own discipline as an "interpretation" of, rather than a given "fact" about, the world [BGE §22]). When Nietzsche remarks that "maybe it has begun to dawn on five or six minds that physics too is no more than an interpretation and arrangement of the world" (BGE §14), identifying a certain scientific methodology (simplicity) as a deliberate articulation of the "greatest possible stupidity"[24] and goes on to then criticize the "prejudices" of science or the "crudity and naïveté" of calculative scientific convention (GS §123 and §373), or else when Nietzsche debunks the Enlightenment conviction concerning the opposition between *logos* and myth, declaring that the "biggest myth is the myth of knowledge" (KSA 13, 141), Nietzsche's claims, so we are constantly assured by his most analytic interpreters as well as (and we should not miss the parallel here) by his philological readers and his literary interpreters, are not to be received as philosophically earnest propositions.

In this way, and as a kind of clearing of the conceptual air, recent interpretive trends tend increasingly to suggest that *whatever* Nietzsche was doing (be it the stuff of rhetoric or cultural criticism or "therapy" or just and *merely* playing parodically with our own all-too-earnest approach to scholarship), it wasn't/isn't philosophy. Thus one has argued that Nietzsche was a child of his times—limited by the thermodynamics of his day or else by biological and health sciences (superstitions and non-science) of his era. One ate graham crackers (and cereals) at the turn of the century to avoid the sickness with which Nietzsche himself was infamously afflicted (onanism, or "self-abuse" and its then-presumed resultant physiological enervation, depletion, or "decadence"). Today one eats bran (and flaxseed and other dietary fiber) to avoid the intestinal afflictions with which Nietzsche was also deeply concerned for his own part, and as his contemporaries had observed, not altogether kindly, with good reason.[25] There are problems with the uncritically presentist limitations of such perspectives. But here I am less concerned with such Whiggish[26] tendencies (and these are almost unavoidable in the project of the history of ideas) than I am interested in the consequences of such a historical review (not retrieve) for a possible understanding of the relevance of Nietzsche's philosophical perspective for the philosophy of those same sciences of his day, and hence, *ceteris paribus*, for our own contemporary understanding of science. Here what is at issue is the corollary that is so often drawn from such Whiggish reflections as this bears more generally on the representation of Nietzsche "as" philosopher in any appropriate sense.

The implicit and explicit claim here is that we today need not, given current advanced knowledge (be it of philosophy, science, history, classical philology, literature), take Nietzsche at his word on anything— particularly when he stylizes what he says as he does. Hence (analytic) philosophers (and classicists and other scholars) are not to worry. Even if Nietzsche appears to be talking about philosophy (classics, aesthetics, history, science, etc.), we are not to mind him: he's only playing (experimenting) with ideas—but laying no justifiable claim to the scholar's mantle. In particular, this typically "deflationary" (i.e., analytic)[27] interpretive tendency characterizes current studies of Nietzsche's "rhetoric" and style (although, and to be sure, contemporary conceptions of rhetoric and Nietzsche's own formative specialization in the classical tradition of ancient Greek and Roman rhetoric engage importantly different arenas).[28] By contrast with these recent influential trends, I have sought to argue that precisely via Nietzsche's style—that is, by means of what Nietzsche could "do" with words—Nietzsche stakes a very special and to date still rarely engaged but nevertheless precisely *philosophical* claim.

Nietzsche's Aphorisms: Writing in Blood

The aphorism seems to cut philosophy down to size—bite size. The form has its historical inception in the ἀφορισμοί of Hippocrates. These were maxims in place of a handbook or physician's manual, for the physician who would have no time to consult one in the field: "Life is short, art long, opportunity fleeting. . . ."[29] But accessibility here is also the danger. This brevity (and this is the ingeniousness of the structured design) is why the aphorism can be remembered; above all, this same brevity is the reason the aphorism can be understood. Short, one is able to *get* the point.

This is the beauty of the quick take. Quickly read, like the cold baths Nietzsche suggested as the best way to face the prospect of nothing so seemingly unobtrusive as a letter (and it is the experience of email, especially of checking email, that underlines the value of Nietzsche's sense of violation), the same tactical concision corresponds to Nietzsche's vanity (and this it would be foolhardy to deny).

Nietzsche expresses this ambitious presumption in *Thus Spoke Zarathustra*, as he speaks of writing in blood: "Anyone who writes in blood and sayings does not want to be read but learnt by heart" (Z, "On Reading and Writing"). More emphatically still, Nietzsche affirms his "ambition" to say in the aphorism what others say—he interrupts himself to sharpen his point, as he so often does, with a thought-slash, a *Gedankenstrich*: "—what everyone else *does not say* in a book . . ." (TI, "Expeditions" §51).

Unlike Hume, unlike Kant, unlike Heidegger (in spite of his best efforts to imitate Nietzsche), Nietzsche writes—or, as he says: he composes, this is, he casts—aphorisms. And if Wittgenstein also wrote in aphorisms, the title numbers betray what reading between the two can also tell us: Nietzsche is more readable by half and again. This accessibility will be what is in question and what is at stake in what follows.

For the sake of a review of the complexity of the aphorism as a self-elaborating form of self-deconstruction, used as Nietzsche uses it to implicate the reader in the reading and simultaneously, formulaically, and perhaps all-too comfortably (we will return to this point at the end) also to absolve himself as author, we consider Nietzsche's own prefatory comment on the way an aphorism functions just because it reflects his prescription for reading his aphorisms where he discusses this at the end of his preface to *On the Genealogy of Morals*.[30] At the same time, it is worth noting, in advance, that part of the difficulty in reading Nietzsche's aphorisms is the problem of identification. Patently, not everything Nietzsche wrote was an aphorism. And this is a problem that has called forth nothing less than a valuably, instructively hermeneutic engagement on the part of traditionally analytic philosophers.[31] Epigraph or aphorism, that was the question for John Wilcox and Maudemane Clark. It did not help the task of exegesis that the dubious epigraph was seductive enough that it could not be overlooked: "Untroubled, mocking, violent—thus will wisdom have us: she is a woman, she always loves only a warrior.—*Thus Spoke Zarathustra*" (GM III, "Epigraph").

Beyond the analytic quandary (and, in the case of Wilcox and Clark, duly accurate resolution of the problem) of locating the aphorism to which Nietzsche refers in this problematic case, let us review Nietzsche's words both at the beginning of and at conclusion to his preface to *On the Genealogy of Morals*.[32] To start with, Nietzsche writes that it is as readers, that is, as scholars, that we remain "unknown to ourselves" and this is inevitably the case because "we have never sought ourselves" (GM i). At the end of the preface, the reader is again upbraided on what can be seen to be the same terms (note that this aggression is featured in the preface, a locus which, if we have managed already in advance of the work to forget its subtitle—*A Polemic*—might have seemed a poor position for an author to show his teeth). Challenging the reader who finds his writing "difficult to understand,"[33] Nietzsche retorts that his texts are "clear enough, presuming what I presume: that one has first read my early writing and without sparing oneself a few pains in the process" (GM §viii). The authoritative claim is not only one that blames the reader but audaciously encourages still further reading—not only of the text at hand but everything else the author wrote previously.

The problem, as Nietzsche analyzes the problem of the readers (readers, he would always complain, that although constantly sought out by this author, were nonetheless never to be found) is that the aphorism is not taken seriously enough. Note the compound complexity of this complaint: if the allure of the aphorism lies in its brevity and if the beauty of brief things is that one take them fast and light, like a witticism or a clever saying, Nietzsche's prescription to us is to take his aphorisms *seriously*, as good medicine: and that is also to say, as philosophy.

This dissonant dimension echoes in Nietzsche's concluding word in his prefatory reflection on reading in his *On the Genealogy of Morals*, where he also proposes a metaphor for reading that is usually reserved for religious texts—sweet as honey, such texts are to be eaten[34]—we are told that the way to understand his writings will be to chew them over, to turn them over in ourselves, in our mouths, ruminating again and again, *das Wiederkäuen* (GM §viii).

But such rumination fails us and we hastily pass over passage after passage, spurred on as often as not by well-meaning introductory works by noted scholars or on the encouraging advice of helpful translators. One is advised to read Nietzsche until one finds a passage one likes, then look for another, and so on, just as one might surf the internet, moving from link to link, until one finds something vaguely worthy of being "bookmarked" as a "favorite" or else, for another example in a market economy like our own, as one might take a tour through a shopping mall or vacation spot. By contrast with such "searching and finding," to use metaphors borrowed from the scholarly disaster that is an electronic or searchable text, Nietzsche instructs that "an aphorism consummately coined and molded, is not yet 'deciphered' in that it is read out; much rather has the interpretation first to begin" (GM §viii). And it is not enough simply to begin to interpret. The *hermeneutic work* of reading is required: what is needed is "art of interpretation" (Ibid.).

The task of so interpreting Nietzsche's aphorism thus requires a commentary—indeed, a commentary that would otherwise be matched to what others say or fail to say "in a book." Nor do we lack an illustration of what such a commentary would look like. Nietzsche offers an example of such a reading using the musical model of a coda. Note again that this is not simply prescribed or recommended on Nietzsche's part as a task for the reader to accomplish as he or she will. Instead—and this is the point—an example is provided in an elaborate form, going so far as to begin with a resumé (the scholar's nutshell) at the beginning of the last part of the *Geneaology*, just where the author tells us to find it at the conclusion of his preface: "In the third essay of this book, I offer an exemplar of that which I name 'interpretation' in such a case:—at the start of this essay is an aphorism, to which the essay itself is the commentary" (Ibid.).

The Nietzschean aphorism can be as short as a sentence or part of a longer paragraph, such as the one that begins very famously: "Assuming it given, that truth is a woman . . ."—a word including its consequent reflection on philosophers and dogma.[35] And the aphorism can be very long indeed, as can be seen especially in the case of *Human, All Too Human* but also elsewhere, indeed particularly in *Thus Spoke Zarathustra*, if read not as a novel of aphorisms but as a single aphorism in symphonic variation. If brevity is the prime characteristic of the aphorism, it is not the only one, at least not in Nietzsche's case.

For the point above is that the aphorism elaborated in GM III, §1 is one that resumes itself in its own recapitulation, an elaboration of which extends to the author's own commentary on it in the third part of the book as a whole. In this latter case, we have to do with an aphorism within an aphorism (indeed, and of course, in a book of aphorisms). This recapitulation is found at the end of the aphorism that seems to challenge and confirm the working power of Nietzsche's aphoristic style, where he poses the question, "What are the meaning of ascetic ideals?" two-thirds of the way into a book on the generation of those same ideals: One doesn't get it? Is it still unclear? (The question replays an earlier question as we recall: GM I, especially §8 and §9.) The answer given is not coincidentally adapted from the dancing master or the conductor: Shall we take it from the top? *Da Capo!*

In this way, the same first section that begins with the question, "What is the meaning of ascetic ideals?" answers its own question by emphasizing the problem of understanding and the need to begin a reflection. The task of learning to read, like learning to think, is the kind of thing that, as Nietzsche was fond of emphasizing, needs, like loving, to be learnt. In this sense, the aphoristic structure of the first section stands to part 3 of *On the Genealogy of Morals* as the preface suggests it does. It is a section that announces itself as problematic and bears out the need for the commentary or exegesis in the subsequent sections and, although we cannot pursue this question further here, that commentary is also one that can be tracked or hermeneutically traced. What makes this problematic is that this same hermeneutic art is "something that has been unlearned most thoroughly nowadays" (GM viii).

Aphorisms and the Art of Reading the Reader

The aphorism as self-contained, as self-referring, as something that can and should be read over and over (accordingly a word that can be carried beyond the text), has to be read both in itself and against itself. As a word, aphorism has the roots, as Liddell and Scott remind us, ἀφ–/ἀπ- from, off, away; ὁρίζω: to divide, to set apart, separate as a boundary. Hence and substantively, the essence of aphorism is almost preternaturally phenomenological. Nor has this gone without remark: one author observes the word itself means "formal 'de-limitation' and simultaneously substantively something 'manifestly removed from its usual horizon.' "[36] In this way, the aphorism presupposes or better said, and this is why Nietzsche favored it as a stylistic form, it *accomplishes*, achieves, or effects an *epoché* or bracketing of the phenomenon.

Nietzsche's aphorisms thus read themselves into the reader and what is intriguing about his stylization of this form is that they do this in spite of the reader's prejudices and more often than not *because* of these: playing with such readerly convictions and turning them inside out. An example of this reader-involved efficacity is Nietzsche's discussion of Jewish morality in the first part of *On the Genealogy of Morals* (GM I §7).

Reading the working of this particular aphorism in this way, its tactical tempo only increases in its intensity—a plainly seductive appeal which draws in and plays to the prejudices of the anti-Semite. A related tactic and tempo is at work from the start in *On the Genealogy of Morals* as Nietzsche orients his reflections on the genealogical provenance of morality to the scientific ears and utilitarian sensibility of what he called the "English psychologists" (GM I §1) while the very Darwinian oblivion of mechanical habit and sociocultural reinforcement is exactly under fire. Here, in GM I §7 the text is directed to and hence it begins by appealing to the most typical prejudices of all-too-Christian anti-Semitism.

The anti-Semite is educed into and seduced into the text, as Nietzsche's word seems to be expressed as a defense of a "lordly" or "noble" Greco-Roman past, posed against Jewish antiquity. Thus one reads that everything that has ever been done against the historical phantasm or "ideal" of the "noble" fades into inconsequentiality compared with what "the *Jews* have done against them" (GM I §7). The doubling of the aphoristic stylizing of this text (I have elsewhere called it the barb of his style not to refer to Derrida's spurs but rather to underline the "fisher of men" language of Nietzsche's texts as fish hooks) turns the reader's conviction against the reader himself or herself, a recoil that is all the more effective the more deeply anti-Semitic the reader and exactly in the course of reading. Indeed, as he or she continues to read, the anti-Semite will have no choice but either to stop in the middle of the text or to read by skipping about in the text.

Identifying the Jew as the one who inverts the "aristocratic value equation" turning over the noble self-sufficiency of strength, confidence, and joy ("good = noble = powerful = beautiful = happy = beloved of God" [GMI §7]) by means of the alchemy not of love but of the most "abysmal hatred," Nietzsche transcribes the equation into the now-dissonantly Christian litany of the indemnification of the disenfranchised as we recognize this message from the Sermon on the Mount (Mt. 5: 1–13). The new equation of Jewish revaluation is later elaborated as *ressentiment*. Into the mouth of this Jewish revaluation Nietzsche sets nothing other than (plain) Christian values: "the wretched alone are the good, the poor, powerless, lowly alone are the good; the suffering, deprived, sick, ugly alone are pious, alone are blessed by God . . ." (Ibid.). Nietzsche thus articulates the newly revalued equation as a re-weighting of the original values of strength (the "lordly" or noble values of antiquity) not in order to conclude nostalgically for a return to such pristine values but for the sake of an elaboration of the consequences of this genesis: ". . . One knows *who* appropriated the legacy of this Jewish revaluation . . ." (Ibid.).

The reversal of the aphorism already occurs in the double ellipsis *included* in Nietzsche's own text. Nietzsche thus draws the anti-Semitic reader into the text, only to turn his or her reflections contra the last consequences of the same reader's convictions. It now transpires that the anti-Semite is himself or herself a Jew and everything turns out to be coordinately on the way to becoming "Judaized, Christianized"—and for good, socialist, and atheistic measure, Nietzsche includes an allusion to the "people" as well (GM I §9). "What do words matter?" (GM I §9), Nietzsche asks with regard to the title of Christian or Jew and as he will later remind us in his *Anti-Christian* that the Christian is and can be nothing other than a Jew of a more catholic or encompassing "confession" (AC §44).

For the sake of the reader who might be "incapable of seeing something that required two thousand years to achieve victory" (GM I §8), Nietzsche repeats the redoubling emphasis in his next section with an agonized reflection on the working of revenge and *ressentiment* in religion and moral values. Describing such "a grand politics of revenge"— and recollecting as we shall detail below the spiritual danger of "grand politics" in *Human, All Too Human*—Nietzsche argues that Israel itself has to "deny the active instrument of its revenge before all the world as its mortal enemy and nail it to the cross" (GM I §8). This denial ensures

that "the opponents of Israel" swallow the bait, precisely as they are
defined in reactive terms by contrast with Israel. Nietzsche's text plays to
the reader's anti-Semitism (conscious or not), and convicts the reader on
the very same terms.[37]

The Nietzschean aphorism goes beyond the dynamic of an author
who can write against the prejudices of anti-Semitic conviction exposing
the Semite within, the self-loathing of prejudice against the other as it
betrays us in ourselves. Nietzsche thus needs a doubled reading, an
acroamatic or discursive or listening reflection—that is to say that Nietzsche
needs, as he asks for it, "ears" for his words.[38] In the same way Nietzsche
insinuates a dialogical dimension into the text and the reader has to attend
to this acoustic dimension in order to engage the text critically.

To take a further example, consider what might at first glance
seem the incidental aphorism that relates the contest between memory
and pride. "I have done that,' says my memory. 'I cannot have done
that'—says my pride, and remains adamant. At last—memory yields"
(BGE §68).

The reflex here turns on the balance of pride and memory and in
particular on the conviction that the one belongs to a primary (and more
objective) and the other to a secondary (and more subjective) mental
order. The ultimate primacy of what had appeared to be the secondary
faculty of pride, the corrigible, sheerly subjective faculty, supplants and
corrects the (objective) faculty of memory. Between memory and pride,
Nietzsche's teasing point contra objectivity is that memory itself defers
to pride's desire in recollection.

A similar dynamic is at work in a longer aphorism, entitled "Grand
Politics and Their Costs," Nietzsche observes that from the moment a
people begins to preoccupy itself with war (be it for defense or con-
quest), "a great number of the most leading talents are sacrificed upon
the 'Altar of the Fatherland' or national honor, where other spheres of
action had formerly been open to the talents now absorbed by the political" (HH I: §481). This spiritual impoverishment is the wastage of
nihilism. In complete accord with Plato (and subsequently both Jacques
Rancière *and* Pierre Bourdieu),[39] Nietzsche links politics and greed as
indissoluble. A *Nachlaß* note reflects the widespread character and tendencies of his age: "Here the ghostly finger of the spiritualists, there the
mathematical-magical conjurer, then the brain-wasting cult of music, there
the re-awakened vulgarities of the persecution of the Jews—mark the
universal training in hatred" (KSA 9, 213).

A comparable political and cultural anxiety is at work where
Nietzsche writes: "It is a costly affair to come to power: power *makes us*
stupid. . . . Politics devours all seriousness for actually intellectual things,

Deutschland, Deutschland über alles, I fear, was the end of German philosophy" (TI, *What the Germans Lack* §1).

This provocative backwards and forwards, damned if one does and
damned if one does not, is the essence of the philosophical aphorism. The
conclusion, like the related premises invoked by association, is alluded to
but not given and in fact only alluded to *in potentia*: the resolution of an
aphorism is not fixed and can always change: the shifting reference in part
accounts for Nietzsche's apparent mutability in meaning from reading to
reading. And the same mutability seems in turn to justify multifarious and
even racist, fascist, dangerously criminal readings.

The problem of understanding the persistence of Nietzsche's political sentiments as they manifestly persist from *Human, All Too Human* to
Twilight of the Idols is thus, if we hear Nietzsche's words, to be located
not in the dissonance of Nietzsche's texts but on the side of our readerly
"convictions": "*adventavit asinus*" (BGE §8; cf. "the great stupidity
which we are" §231).

But such a reflection hardly resolves our problem and can only return us to the question of Nietzsche's style as an effective or *working* style.
Was Nietzsche then exactly and ultimately responsible *for not* having written in such a way that it would be impossible to take him amiss? If he
could do so much with words, with his rhetorical mastery, why not secure
his words against malicious appropriation? This ethical question corresponds to Nietzsche's own questioning challenge against Christian stylistics,
against the pastiche style and aura of the New Testament: "It was a piece
of subtle refinement that God learned Greek when he wanted to become
a writer—and that he did not learn it better" (BGE §121). Perhaps Nietzsche,
who was associated, at least from the British side, with both World Wars (like
Hölderlin, Nietzsche's *Thus Spoke Zarathustra* was published in soldiers'
editions, for the "field"), should have learnt his own rhetorical polishing of
his German language style much "better" than he did.

Given all that Nietzsche could with do words it is also true that his
achievements in this domain are far too limited both socially and politically, just as so many scholars have rightfully observed.[40] Yet, in the end,
perhaps what is important is not that Nietzsche's words failed to arrest
world history in advance, or indeed that all his longing failed to bring
back the Greece of the past, even in the form of a rebirth of the tragic
art. As much as he sought to change the world in his writing and from
the start, it is perhaps more important and salutary to recall that he
himself knew the limitations of his efforts and would express himself in
this impotence in ever more impatient fashion (in letters and postcards
to friends) for the rest of his life. And in one of his last notes he vainly
declares, "I am having all anti-Semites shot."

3

∿ᴐᴄ∾

The Birth of Tragedy

Lyric Poetry and the Music of Words

The stylistic role of music in *The Birth of Tragedy*[1] presupposes the relation Nietzsche had uncovered between "music and words" in his theory of meter and rhythm in ancient Greek.[2] This is Nietzsche's *architectonically*[3] *quantitative*, measured and timed, theory of words and music for his courses on rhythm and meter as well as his discussion of tragedy and music in his first book.[4] A recollection of the meaning of the spirit of music also reviews the logical questions of metaphor and truth and invites a parallel with *The Gay Science* with regard to language and the alchemical art of love, likewise in terms of both music and science.

This inquiry entails the purely philosophical questions of knowledge and truth yet the discussion to follow takes its point of departure from classical philology, reviewing what Nietzsche himself held to have been his most scientific "discovery" on the terms of his own discipline: a discovery never disputed by Nietzsche's arch-critic, Ulrich von Wilamowitz-Möllendorff. Indeed, and although we have become accustomed to view Nietzsche as the perfect embodiment of the academic outsider, his discovery is now taken as the standard in his field (so standard as to be received without fanfare or routine acknowledgment as such).[5]

What was that discovery?

Music and Words: The Influence of Modern Culture

I. On Modern Stress and the Language of Ancient Greece

Nietzsche had argued against the accent-based or stressed theory of Greek prosody that was the "received view" in nineteenth-century philology. Recent assessments (Bornmann, Pöschl, Fietz, Porter)[6] consistently observe that the substance of Nietzsche's claim has since been vindicated. But Nietzsche's point contra the infamous ictus remains as difficult to understand (or to prove) as it is to criticize (or refute). Because we so deploy stress in modern Western languages (as we do in our music) that emphatic syncopation constitutes our very notion of metered rhythm (we need to "keep time"—to use Shakespeare's language: we need the aid of a metronome), we can hardly imagine alternatives in contemporary languages, so that the example of Japanese, as suggested by Devine and Stephens in their book, *The Prosody of Greek Speech*,[7] is still too exotic for most readers. And many readers will likewise find Porter's differentiation between rhythm and meter in his discussion of the ictus[8] of limited help.

The stressed character of modern speech as Nietzsche complains of the "decline into Latin vocalism" (and Porter cites but does not elaborate upon this judgment),[9] separates us by what Nietzsche also repeatedly underscores as an unbridgeable abyss from the measures of, that is, the *sound* of (or the *music* of) ancient Greek. It is the unknowability of this gulf that Nietzsche never fails to emphasize, precisely as a philologist, that is, for all-too scholarly, exactly "scientific" reasons. It is the same unbridgeable gap (precisely named as unbridgeable) that alienates (or frustrates) other scholars who claim to know better (and who have made this claim in handbooks detailing ancient Greek prosody/pronunciation).[10]

Apart from the issues of artistic expression, already to say that ancient Greek prose was uncontrivedly poetic, as Nietzsche emphasized, and to say that this poetry was advanced by way of a musical tact utterly unlike either that of modern poetry or indeed that of modern music (lacking stress but also lacking harmony as Nietzsche reminds us) is to say a great deal if it cannot tell us how it *would have* sounded for our own ineluctably stress-keyed ears, that is—and this is the point here—provided our stress-attuned ears could have heard it at all.

II. Modernity and Music

What does it mean to speak of *The Birth of Tragedy Out of the Spirit of Music*? How does tragedy come into being out of music? Nietzsche intends the language of "birth" as literally as one can in such a context[11] and assuming one has "ears" to hear that literality. But how can music

give "birth" to anything? How do the "brothers" Apollo and Dionysus
play the role of co-progenitors? This question will be considered below
(if I cannot promise a resolution here) but Nietzsche's provocative language goes further as we recall Nietzsche's youthful reflection on the
crossover of the metaphors for light and sound,[12] noting the poetic
transference of the metaphors of vision—the eyes—to those of hearing—
the ears—, a transfer that the Helmholtzian[13] Nietzsche liked to note as
operative on the level of the senses as well (cf., contemporary theories of
synaesthesia). To give this another expression here: as poets speak, mixing the metaphors of one sense into those of another,[14] so our bodies
transfer (or mix) the impulses from one sense, apprehending the one
sensation on the terms of another. Nietzsche's talk of "hearing with one's
eyes" in *Thus Spoke Zarathustra* reflects this same early emphasis. But what
does it mean and how do metaphors work in this connection? This is the
epistemological or philosophical connection Nietzsche heard between the
spirit of music (poetry) and the science of words (philology).

The Nietzsche who will come to teach us so much about genealogy, a tradition he had learnt in turn from his own teachers (such as Otto
Jahn, who also used the language of genealogy, as well as Friedrich
Ritschl, and as Nietzsche drew upon a general formation following the
ideal [and inevitably idealized] example of Friedrich August Wolf), begins *The Birth of Tragedy Out of the Spirit of Music* by articulating the
natal genesis and perfect pedigree of an art form requiring the prudential
judgment of two different creative impulses (indeed, and, as noted previously, no less than two different *fathers*, recollecting Nietzsche's language of a "fraternal union" [BT §§21, 22, 24; cf. BT §4]). Its author
intended to provide a "contribution" to the "science" or philosophical
discipline "of aesthetics" (BT §1),[15] which Nietzsche expressed in the
terms of the school tradition of the same, thus including Aristotle (BT
§§6, 7, 14, 22) and Plato (BT §§12,13, 14) as well as Lessing (BT §§8,
11, 15), Schiller (BT §§3, 5, 7, 8, 20), Schlegel (BT §4), in addition to
Schopenhauer (BT §§1, 5, 16, 19, 20) and Kant (BT §§18, 19).

The science of aesthetics, as Nietzsche named it, going back to
Baumgarten and Kant, is the science of sensual judgment: the power of
engendering (this creative dimension of the aesthetic will be Nietzsche's
special emphasis), and *responding* to artistic representation, Nietzsche
invokes a context directed to a hermeneutic clarification of our tendency
to *theorize* the subject matter of what he calls "*poesie*":

For a genuine poet, metaphor is not a rhetorical figure, but an
image which stands in the place of something else, which it
genuinely beholds in place of a concept. The character is for him
not a whole composed out of particular components, but an

intensely alive person, distinguished from the vision, otherwise
identical, of a painter only by the fact that it [diachronically] goes
on living and acting. How is it that Homer's images are so much
more vivid than those of any other poet? Because he visualizes
that much more vividly. We speak so abstractly of poetry to the
same extent that we tend to be such *bad* poets. (BT §8)

The reference to poetry and painting here shows that even where
Nietzsche fails to invoke the aesthetic tradition by name, he makes allusion to it. Here he refers to Lessing as well as the tradition of classical
criticism dating from antiquity addressed to the relation between depiction in words and images, painting and poetry. And in this same aesthetic
reflection, Nietzsche emphasizes the working (the *energeia* in Wilhelm
von Humboldt's language) of metaphor.

This same philologist's hermeneutic account of metaphor recurs in
Nietzsche's genealogy of value terms, particularly of religious value and
practice. Thus he explains in *On the Genealogy of Morals*, "all the concepts of ancient man were incredibly crude, coarse, external, narrow,
straightforward, and in particular *unsymbolical* in meaning to a degree
that we can scarcely conceive" (GM I §6).[16] The attributes of purity and
impurity of spirit (and heart) were metaphorical attributions: terminological accretions taken in place of truth.

The challenge of metaphor is the question of literality and that is
to say, the question of truth and lie. From start to finish, Nietzsche
approaches the question of metaphor on epistemological terms, exactly
those terms (Cartesian certainty) that are determinative for modern theories of knowledge, and this emphasis has inspired analytic-style readings of
Nietzsche preoccupied by the question of metaphor in Nietzsche (comparable only to the preoccupations of literary scholars following Paul de Man
and Philipe Lacoue-Labarthe).[17] This metaphoric focus is evident in
Nietzsche's unpublished *Philosophy in the Tragic Age of the Greeks*, where
he remarks that given (as Nietzsche always assumed as given) the revolu-
tionary advances of modernity in the wake of Kant's critical philosophy,
the psychologism of the Parmenidean vision (deriving "absolute being
from a subjective concept") becomes so unsustainable as to require "reck-
less ignorance." Challenging the philosophical conceptualizations of those
"badly taught theologians who would like to play philosopher" (his reference here is primarily to Hegel), Nietzsche declares,

the concept of Being! As though it did not already reveal its
poorest empirical origins in the etymology of the word! For *esse*
means fundamentally merely "to breathe": if man uses it of all

other things, he consequently projects his own conviction that he breathes and lives, by means of a metaphor, that is, by means of something non-logical, projected upon other things and conceiving their existence as breathing in accord with an analogy to humanity. The original meaning of the word was swiftly blurred: enough, however, remains that by way of analogy with his own existence [*Dasein*], the human is able to represent the existence of other things [*Dasein andrer Dinge*], that is to say anthropomorphically and in any case via a non-logical transference. Yet even for the human himself, ergo apart from such a transference, the proposition, "I breathe, therefore there is being [*Sein*]" is wholly insufficient: and the same objection holds against it as likewise holds against *ambulo, ergo sum oder ergo est* [I walk, therefore I am *or* therefore it is (existent being)]. (PTG §11)

Bracketing the question of Nietzsche's sympathy for Kant together with his aversion to Hegel (both of which are evident in this section), note the dynamic role of metaphor.

A Humboldtian preoccupation with energetic power characterizes Nietzsche's thinking on metaphor (and scholars like Martin Heidegger and the late Jacques Derrida have followed his example in their reflections on translation). The active leaping over that is metaphor is the transfer from one sphere to another, all the while (and this subliminal perdurance is essential to Nietzsche's theory of knowledge and his critique of the subject/self-consciousness) simultaneously forgetting (and this forgetfulness, as Nietzsche emphasizes, is key) that one has made any transfer at all.

In a metaphor one searches in vain for any trace of comparison, explicit analogy, or positively critical "as if." Thus we recall the *locus classicus* of Nietzsche's discussion of truth and metaphor, "On Truth and Lie in an Extra-Moral Sense." It is here that Nietzsche asks the epistemological question relevant to language in general: "do things match their designations? Is language the adequate expression of all realities?" [*decken sich die Bezeichnungen und die Dinge? Ist die Sprache der adäquate Ausdruck aller Realitäten?*] (TL 1, KSA 1, p. 879). The answer to this question is manifestly negative: "If he will not content himself with truth in the form of tautology, i.e., with empty husks, he will always trade with illusions in place of truths." [*Wenn er sich nicht mit der Wahrheit in der Form der Tautologie d. h. mit leeren Hülsen begnügen will, so wird er ewig Illusionen für Wahrheiten einhandeln*] (Ibid.). Apart from such empty shells, apart from the triumphant utility of knowing that "A = A," as Nietzsche declares,[18] one is condemned to deploy illusions in place of truths. And this is inevitably so because, for the philologist Nietzsche, metaphor starts at the level of the word.

Language is, as it were, metaphor all the way down. Put all the languages together, Nietzsche suggests—replaying the biblical account of the tower of Babel as a symbol for the Fall that was also a failure to attain to the fruit of the tree of knowledge itself—and one sees that with regard to "words what matters is never truth, never the adequate expression, for otherwise there would not be so many languages" (TL 1, KSA 1, 879).

For Nietzsche (as for Kant), the noumenon (and like Kant, Nietzsche, will always use the convention of an indeterminate X), the thing in itself, apart from its apparent, phenomenal relation to us, simply cannot be known:

> We believe that we have knowledge of the things themselves [*den Dingen selbst*] when we speak of trees, colors, snow and flowers, whereas we possess only meaphors of things which correspond in absolutely no way [*ganz und gar nicht*] to the original essences [*Wesenheiten*]. As the tone appears as a sand-figure, so the mysterious X of the thing in itself [*des Dings an sich*] now appears as a nervous stimulus, then as image, and finally as sound. (Ibid.)

For this reason, Nietzsche continued to emphasize the relevance of this insight for the entire cognitive enterprise: "the entire material in and with which the man of truth, the researcher, the philosopher works and constructs, is drawn, if not from cloud-cuckoo-land, then certainly in no case from the essence of things [*dem Wesen der Dinge*]" (Ibid.).

If today's researchers have learned the trick of sidestepping the issue, leaving aside the question of the knowledge of truth as such, rather like Heidegger's question of being or his talk of the history of metaphysics, it is because a reflection on the nature of consciousness brackets the question of the knowledge of the world as such and in itself altogether. It seems to us that we are successful in this because our instruments can be turned on our own consciousness (or, better said, what we take to be the measureable locus of the same). But Nietzsche's problem is not thereby solved: for what remains is the problem of metaphor and it is the veritable problem of analogy as such. Indeed and accordingly Nietzsche would use the terminus "*Analogieschluß*" to *define* metaphor.

Other theories of metaphor, especially cognitive theories, depart not from this physical, sensual understanding of the work of metaphor (as *metaphora*), but rather from a philosophical view (as opposed to a linguistic point of view). It is essential to note that Nietzsche articulates the question of metaphor neither philologically nor psychologically (though he always draws upon the terms of both) but epistemologically, in the direct lineage of Aristotle and Kant. More in line with Hume and Kant than with Schopenhauer in this case, Nietzsche writes, "A sensed stimulus and a glance at a movement, linked together, first yield causality as an empirical principle: two things, namely a specific sensation and a specific visual image always appear together: that the one is the cause of the other is metaphor borrowed from *will* and *act*: an analogical inference" (KSA 7, 483).

However much we may wish to abstract from metaphorical language, we can have "*no genuine knowing without metaphor*" (Nietzsche's emphasis, KSA 7, 491). Nor is there an escape from this devil's circle. Thus truth, as we have already noted for Nietzsche, is a "forgotten metaphor, i.e., a metaphor of which it has been forgotten that it is one" (7, 492). At issue is the question of justification; what is at stake is knowledge.

For Nietzsche, metaphor is above all an epistemological figure, here metonymically expressed in Kantian terms as a "synthetic judgment" (KSA 7, 496). A "synthetic judgment," as Nietzsche further details this same figure, "describes a thing according to its consequences, which means *essence* and *consequences* are *identified*, which means a *metonymy*. . . . which means it is a false equation" (Ibid.). This functions because of the nature of language itself: "the *is* in the synthetic judgement is false, it contains a transference: two different spheres, between which there can never be an equation, are posed alongside one another. We live and think amidst nothing but sheer effects of the the *unlogical*, in non-knowing and in false-knowing [*Nichtwissen und Falschwissen*]" (Ibid.).

Raising the question of the *genealogy of logic*, as Nietzsche does in his essay on philosophy in the tragic age of the Greeks, and as he expresses the same query at the very beginning of his *Menschliches, Allzumenschliches*, paralleling the point we have already noted previously in his reflections on the vivid literality of the ancient poet in *The Birth of Tragedy*, logic turns out to be derived from myth, born of the non-logical, the illogical. If Nietzsche's observation differs not at all from standard accounts of the history of philosophy—reconstructions tracing the history of intellection from mythic to rational thought—Nietzsche undertakes to question just this generative account as a supposed evolution: "*Origin of the Logical*. How did logic come into existence in the human head? Certainly out of illogic" (GS §111). And from beginning to end, Nietzsche's question remains the same: *how is it possible* to derive rationality on the basis of myth? In other words: how do we arrive at truth when we begin with lie? How does logic evolve from myth? Thus the question at the start of Nietzsche's *Human, All Too Human* recalls a Cartesian modality: "how can something originate in its opposite, for example: rationality out of irrationality, the sentient in the dead, logic out of illogic, disinterested contemplation out of covetous desire, living for others in egoism, truth out of errors?" (HH I §1). Nietzsche's catalogue of opposites repeats the same epistemological concerns that would always intrigue him, along with his studies of the birth of the tragic work of art (poetry) in musical song (lyrical poetry). He continued to pursue these same questions throughout his work, including *The Genealogy of Morals,* his famous critique of the subject (and thereby of subjectivity itself), taking it still further as he mounts what is still today the most radically empirical (or scientific) critique of empirical knowledge (cf. KSA 13, 257).[19]

If some might find these theoretical reflections only obliquely relevant to the theme of classical philology and music in Nietzsche, they constitute only a small part of the full scope of Nietzsche's own understanding of his explorations. Thus his reflections on this question integrate the question of science (*as* a question, as he would emphasize it in 1886) in addition to the physiological, psychological, and culture-theoretical ramifications of his critique of the subject and of society. Here, these preliminary reflections permit us to turn to Nietzsche's philological beginnings in his study of *The Birth of Tragedy,* including the question of ancient Greek music drama: lyric poetry and tragedy in terms of their aesthetic origins.

The Origin of Music in Ancient Greek *Musikē*

To understand Nietzsche's reflections on the spirit of music in terms of the elusive aspects of his theory of quantitative or timed measure (rather than voice stress), Nietzsche emphasized that we differ from the ancients in our understanding of music and warned against the easy, because intuitive or instinctual, tendency to conflate the modern with the ancient concept of music. Rather than an advocate of a subjective or empathic approach to antiquity, Nietzsche was its most stiff-necked opponent. If Nietzsche drew upon his own affinity for the modern music of his own times for the sake of his studies of ancient music, he never let himself forget the differences between modern and ancient conceptions of "music."[20]

Thrasybulos Georgiades, whom I invoke again in a later chapter on the specifically musical practice of philosophy, emphasizes Nietzsche's observations by first noting that the "Western verse line is not a musical but rather a linguistic form." By contrast, the "musical-rhythmic structure of the ancient Greek verse line reflected the music of the language as it was both a linguistic and simultaneously a musical reality."[21] A musicologist, Georgiades goes on to offer a musical illustration of this point and invokes the succession of accents ordinarily heard in the language of the German phrase, "Das Wandern ist des Müllers Lust," marking the accents:

/   /   /   /
Das Wandern ist des Müllers Lust

Although as Georgiades points out, in Western languages, "the accents" proceeding from spoken "language" (indicated in the German text cited) are "binding for the music" or musical setting of the text, it is important that this linguistic accenting does not determine "all aspects of the musical rhyme." As a result, the phrase can be set to music in various ways (Georgiades offers several examples to illustrate these possibilities). By contrast, "the ancient Greek verse line behaved differently. Here the musical rhythm was contained within the language itself. The musical rhythmic structure was completely determined by the language. There was no room for an independent musical-rhythmic setting: nothing could be added or changed."[22] To illustrate this point, Georgiades compares the emphatically flexible linguistic accenting of the aforementioned array of musical instanciations with the analogous accenting of the first verse line of Pindar's first "Olympian Ode":

˘ — — ˘ ˘ — ˘ — — ˘ — ˘ ˘ — —
Ἄριστον μεν ὕδωρ, ὁ δε χρυσος αἰσθομενον πυρ

Georgiades observes that the "ancient Greek word comprised within itself a firm musical component. It had an intrinsic musical will." As he further explains, because "individual syllables could be neither extended nor abbreviated,"[23] the Greek language was expressed in consummate, completed time. "The rhythmic principle of antiquity is based not on the distinction between the organization of time (the measure, system of accents) and its filling in (with various note values) but rather on intrinsically filled-in time."[24] For this reason, both Georgiades and Nietzsche are able to affirm quite literally that in ancient Greek, music and "poetic" speech was indistinguishable from "prose" speech, or to put it another way, as Nietzsche expressed it, "ordinary," everyday language was the vehicle of poetry.

The development of prose out of music separates music and text—it is no accident that this begins with the institution of writing whereby the text is liberated from its originally poetic (and hence musical) expression in the full measure of time.[25] As Nietzsche argued in *The Birth of*

Tragedy, the rule of Socratic reason presides over the death of tragedy. In his lecture notes, the rational predominance of the logical over the mythic will reflect the same shift in the case of musical rhythm: "the more the sensibility for natural causality took the place of magical causes, the more rhythm recedes" (FS 5, p. 374).

The start of Nietzsche's *Thus Spoke Zarathustra* invokes this same musical and poetic loss, where Zarathustra thunders: "There they stand (he said to his heart), there they laugh: they do not understand me, I am not the mouth for these ears. Must one first shatter their ears to teach them to hear with their eyes?"[26] I have been suggesting that we take this suggestion literally—but how are we to take such talk seriously—let alone literally? And what has become of metaphor?

We read Nietzsche's language of "hearing" with one's eyes, like his talk of a "musician's book" like his expression of "eye-persons,"[27] as manifold instances of figurative language, that is, mere metaphors: like the poet's convention of holding discourse with one's heart. But as Gerber in *The Art of Language*[28] expresses it (but also as the longer tradition of rhetoric would have already taught Nietzsche, as it had likewise taught Gerber), there *is* only metaphor. To take the word for the thing always demands more than language can give.

What does this mean for us as we seek to read Nietzsche? Beyond the art of language, beyond sheer metaphoricity, the diachronic consistency of Nietzsche's challenge to our "eyes" and our "ears" (limiting our biographical conviction to the textual level), adumbrates his earliest insight as philologist.[29] Here, I shall attempt to retrace the dense interconnections of Nietzsche's enduring preoccupations in the complex whole that is Nietzsche's thought, especially as we encounter it, that is: not as he conceived his work (in its psychological inception and ramifications) but as expressed in his writing.

In his first academically disastrous book (savagely reviewed by a junior classman, first shocking and then ignored by his teacher, Ritschl, and subsequently by everyone else in his own field of classics), Nietzsche had argued that the written visual marks preserved from the past also preserve the reconstructable trace of sound—the spirit of music—and are thus an exactly archaeological record of ancient Greek music drama. In ancient Greek (written in a *phonetically voiced* alphabet and time-structured in meter and rhyme and without stress), we have nothing less significant for Nietzsche's conception of what he called the "spirit of music" than virtual "recordings"—the texts of the past offer a *readable* repository of sound in the written word, given the tradition of folk song as it may be traced in lyric poetry.

Of course, and obviously, patently enough, we have no aural recordings and so nothing like what might be unimpeachably taken to be empirical evidence of the sound of Greek or the music to be heard in ancient Greek tragedy, hence we have only the barest part of what would be needed to understand it. Yet it is exactly this point that can be misunderstood. It is not Nietzsche's claim (and if he is right, it is not the case) that what has gone missing are the corresponding musical notes to the tragic poems (like the vowels in Hebrew, these would be conventions added only for a later—"more decadent" time, to use Nietzschean language). Instead, what we lack is the speech culture of archaic Greece. Nietzsche's early studies of Greek rhythm and meter and his convicted claim in his notes and in his letters that he had made a signal and radical discovery in this regard were oriented toward nothing less than the reconstruction of just this possibility and to this extent must be accounted the fundamental antecedent schema of *The Birth of Tragedy* itself and would hence constitute nothing less than the justification of the language of Nietzsche's subtitle *Out of the Spirit of Music*.

Nietzsche's argument was that we needed to "learn" to read *not* as moderns read, "with our eyes,"[30] but rather with our ears (as the ancients heard what was read, as they also "saw" the measures of their music stamped out in the steps of the dance).[31] Thus his first book invites us to listen and attend to the measure and the rhythm of the tragic text, phonetically, literally (especially attending to its originations in the folk song). The spirit of this music is the music that can be "heard" as derived from the temporal measures, Nietzsche argued, evident in the song tradition of ancient lyric poetry and perceivable in its performance in dance.

If all we have of the music of antiquity today are the rudiments preserved in lyric poetry, Nietzsche was correspondingly drastic about the limitations of the former. "We stand in a field of shards"(FS 5, p. 385), he wrote. What Nietzsche found in the metrical tradition of folk song and lyric poetry, was the musical key to the tragic dramas of antiquity. Once distinguished from its all-too-modern literary rendering as *subjective* expression—a fatal solecism as Nietzsche regarded it—the folk voice (the veritable mouth of the people: this is the song of language itself) resonant in lyric poetry resounded further as the very *music* of tragedy, and its objective capacity was what allowed for mimetic transfiguration. However counterintuitive it is to us, this was a theatre without spectators, a chorus, and a poet-composer that was not apart from the audience. And to comprehend this is to begin to grasp the ecstatic power of music in which "there was fundamentally no opposition between public and chorus; the whole is just one sublime chorus . . ." (BT §8). But to see this, as Nietzsche noted, requires more than "just one simile."

By means of this same poetic, metered opposition referring to his original philological discovery, Nietzsche claimed that he had "indicated the only possible relation between poetry and music, between word and tone" (BT §6).[32] Accordingly, he would argue that text itself *constituted* the music in question: "whoever hears or speaks today of Aeschylus, Sophocles, Euripides inevitably thinks of them most immediately as literary poets, for one has come to know them from *books*, whether in the original or in translation. But this is roughly as if one were to speak of *Tannhäuser*, intending and understanding no more than the libretto. These individuals should be described *not* as librettists but much rather as composers of opera" (KSA 7, 9). Tragedy was always conveyed via music—"the entire ancient art of poetry and music are born from the folksong" (KSA 1, 529). And this was more than a matter of accompaniment but its very articulation (or "spirit" as Nietzsche expressed it).[33] Traditionally, as Nietzsche emphasized and as most scholars likewise affirm, ancient Greek music was vocal rather than instrumental. In this sense, those scholars who simply identify the Dionysian with the instrumental and the Apollonian with the vocal may overlook the very Nietzschean point of this text.[34] For the loss of that same musical spirit corresponds to nothing less than the transformation of the oral culture of Greece (an orality that goes hand in glove with the literal phonetic function of the letter as a means for preserving sound) to the culture of the text and takes its point of departure from nothing less than its independence from the resonant sound of the culture that it at first preserves (as the spirit of the text) and then displaces (as the letter) of that same culture. Thus the tragic tone-drama could only suffer its own death at its own hand, which subtext (the death of the tragic art form) was of course the explicit subject of *The Birth of Tragedy* (BT §1, BT §11),[35] a death then that would have everything to do with the new domination of reason, the written word (*logos*) as opposed to the spoken word (*mythos*). Nietzsche's dream, of course, beyond his recollection of the birth and death of the tragic art form, was to see a rebirth of the same, possibly by way of Wagner (an association that has Nietzsche seeking to instruct Wagner, the virtuoso musician, by object lesson in his first book—an empty endeavor, given both Wagner's need (*and capacity*) for such instruction,[36] and vain too and in more than one sense on Nietzsche's own part).

It is the death of the spirit of tragic music that is consummate in our day. Thus, reading the texts of ancient tragedy, we are limited to what we *see*. We lack the ability to *hear* with our eyes, that is, to use the only metaphor that remains for us as a people of the book: we cannot "sight-read" ancient Greek music-drama. To illustrate this point, Nietzsche has recourse to periods in the Middle Ages when taste and convention had fallen into such disparity that one composed music with "visual aids," as it were, composing for the eye rather than for the ear. The consequently "illuminated" scores went to the color-book—or Power Point presentation—extreme of matching "notes to something's color: like green in the case of plants, or purple for vineyard fields" (KSA 1, 517). With regard to the spoken texts of ancient music drama, and like the medieval scholiast so charmingly absorbed by color, we are limited to the signs we *scan* rather than *hear* with our eyes.

This point may be compared to the difference between a musician's reading of a musical score and a non-musician reader of the same score. Reading a score, the musically trained reader *hears—and can sing* (and this emphasis is one Nietzsche makes and it will be important for his later self-remonstration: "*it should have sung*, this new soul")—what the other only sees. Just to this degree and for this very reason, Nietzsche declared, "we are condemned to misprision regarding Pindar, Aeschylus, and Sophocles" (KSA 1, 517). Our modern lack of the musical spirit of the text remains the fundamental obstacle to understanding ancient tragedy.

In addition to highlighting this literal musicality, Nietzsche also uses the same musical focus to oppose his study of tragedy to Aristotle on two counts: first refusing the myth of the myth (and that means, of course, the plot) and, second, refusing the function and expression of anagnorisis in terms of the audience's cathartic response or edificational benefit. Beyond the "therapy" of the theatre, the discharge or purification attributed to the experience of tragic sentiment, if also to illustrate the working dynamism of such a supposed and salutary benefit, Nietzsche invoked the example of the profoundly sensible pleasure that is the effect of musical dissonance to explicate the artistic comforts or the aesthetic joy of tragedy.

It is a parallel point that the philologist's tools Nietzsche used to explore antiquity will be the same tools he brings to every problem. Where in his early writings he uses the tools of philology—stylistic tools for reading in order to focus on the problem of the lyric artist—to make this same point, his later writing will play upon the words themselves: using provocative etymologies, as a genealogy of terminological assessments to different effect. One may thus find a parallel to his discussion of the lyric poet in *The Birth of Tragedy* in his discussion of the "noble" (or also of the "slave") in *On the Genealogy of Morals*. Hence it is important, essentially so, that Nietzsche's "genealogy" is anything but a literal retrieve of supposedly historical facts (there never was such an antique era) and even less an expression of Nietzsche's own fantasies or personal desires.[37] Instead, Nietzsche's rhetorical "polemic" on the origins of morality details the consequences of an *etymological* analysis—taken word for word. Thus he writes, "The signpost to the *right* road was for me the question: what was the real etymological significance of the designation 'good' coined in the various languages" (GM I §4). Accordingly, Nietzsche titles his beginning reflections in *On the Genealogy of Morals* with the contrast of terminological pairs outlining the heritage or linguistic fortunes of what is called *good*: that is, and of course, " 'Good and Evil'/ 'Good and Bad.' "

Nietzsche's musical (Apollinian-Dionysian) insight into the *Birth of Tragedy*—opposing an empathically epistemic (Aristotelian) interpretation of the subliminally cathartic comfort of pure dissonance (tragic or musical drama)—yielded a first book that was effectively overlooked. And Nietzsche famously protested this lack of influence. Thus he could complain, in reference to his first book: "every *purely scientific book* is condemned to live a lowly existence among the lowly, and finally to be crucified never to rise again" (MM I §98).

On Classical Texts: For Philological Regents and Philosophical Kings

As "educator," writing for his "best" readers, Nietzsche would again and again elaborate the limits of the rhetorical directionality of writing as the question of reading and the related necessity of *learning* to read. This didactic, writerly project was expressly, explicitly exoteric, related to the concern to communicate in general, and that is to say, as tailored to individual contexts. By contrast, the esoteric or internal problem of philology would be the problem of writerly-readerly reciprocity: the problem of right readers. For Nietzsche, always archaic in his sensibilities, like was required to know (or even to *begin* to *recognize*) like. And for his fellow philologists, Nietzsche remarks in a note in *The Gay Science*, the disciplinary project of philology as an enterprise, the conservation of "great" books—no matter how these are defined—underscores what Nietzsche confesses as philology's ultimate doctrine of faith. This is the conviction "that there is no lack of those rare human beings (*even if one does not see them*) who really know how to use such valuable books—presumably those who write, or could write, books of the same type." And using a handily emphatic trope, Nietzsche repeats his claim: "I mean that philology presupposes a noble faith—that for the sake of a few noble human beings, *who always "will come" but are never there*, a very large amount of fastidious and even dirty work needs to be done first: all of it is work *in usum Delphinorum*" (GS §102, my emphasis).

The relevance of Nietzsche's "*in usum Delphinorum*"—a variation of *ad usum Delphini*—has not received the attention it deserves, presuming (as one ought to presume) that one needs more than Kaufmann's gloss. Nietzsche's allusion was, of course, to the archetypically paternalistic project of creating special editions of Greek or Roman classic texts destined "for the use of the Dauphin."[38] What is important here is that the practical impetus and cultural character of the classicist's philological guild remains indebted to this same solicitous project. *This* was Nietzsche's point in inserting just this invocation here in his own text. The same solicitude continues to animate the high tone with which we speak today of the so-called great books. If the "political" connection between this standard philological convention and Nietzsche's ideal educator has not, to my knowledge, been explored (even by those who discuss Nietzsche in this same context), it manifestly has everything to do with the class distinctions associated with a classical education.

Nietzsche's point is that the ultimate aim of philology is to generate "tidied up" source matter, undertaken in anticipation of a very valued, indeed "noble" reader, a particular reader who *needs*, in the sense that the Dauphin had needed, to be protected from the sullying (questionable, misleading, erroneous) aspects of this same *source* material. Regarded with all the presumption of a duly vested member of the philologist's guild, the "Dauphin" now corresponds to future philologists: the scholars who are to come.[39] These are the precious "future readers" who are to be protected from the less edifying aspects of classical literature. But what Nietzsche does not forget (and what, oddly enough, today's classicists seem not to have fully grasped, ignoring, as classical *historians*, precisely what Nietzsche named a historical sensibility) is that the "texts" engendered for the scholars of the future are not (and never do *become* or turn into) original works.[40]

Conventionalized restorations, authoritative editions are *prepared texts* (and, so some critics will argue: expurgated or bowdlerized in the process, going in different directions depending upon whether the critic in question follows Vico or Dilthey, or even Butterfield). Such texts are produced, this is the hermeneutic point of Nietzsche's "philologist's complaint," for very particular eyes. But whose eyes? If we no longer have the moral justification or imperative for such an edifying project— if only because there are no Dauphins today and if only because fashions have changed and if only because the current balding Kings of France (to use Russell's reference on reference) either do not exist (exoteric) or are unhonored as such (they are too young to have lost their hair as yet: this would be the esoteric point)—the results continue to live on in the methods of today's classical philology and source scholarship.[41]

Given the presuppositions of his philological assumptions, claiming his works as written "for the future," Nietzsche offers us a painful rumination on the damnation of the author and thus a reflection of what he senses as his own destiny. In this way, it is important to recall that *The Gay Science* is a text written in the wake of Nietzsche's recognition of the failure of his first book. Thus embittered, but making yet another attempt, alluding to another textual tradition won from a legacy of living song, Nietzsche expresses the philologist's labor as utterly pointless. In other words, Nietzsche perceived himself as writing in the hope of those "who always 'will come' but are never there." The ideal and best readers are *always* (permanently) in the future, he claims, and he claims that the presuppositions of the discipline require this conviction despite the recalcitrant fact that there are no (and that there never have been) instances of such readers apart from the authors themselves, that is, "those who write, or could write, books of the same type" (GS 102). But what writer does not write for such ideal readers, however imaginary they may be, and what writer does not fail to recognize their absence? Certainly not Hölderlin who wrote in his *Brot und Wein* with a passion only a poet's voice could evoke, "Ah, my friend! we have come too late." [*Aber Freund! wir kommen zu spät.*]

Like the philologist, for Nietzsche, the writer's hope will turn out to be a matter of vanity: vain in more than one sense. As Nietzsche looks back on his own writing in *Ecce Homo,* he claims "My time has not yet come, some are born posthumously" (EH, "Why I Write Such Excellent Books," §1). Nietzsche's reflection in this context is self-laceratingly consistent. It would have to be odd, self-contradictory, to expect that his works be understood. That his readers have ears (and here he claims the metaphor of *having hands*) for his writings is an expectation that would go against the constitutional requirements needed in order to understand a book at all or in the first place (or even, but these are different things: to understand an author), as interpretive preconditions whose importance and indispensability he had always presupposed.

In a pre-Gadamerian, hermeneutic fashion, Nietzsche would attempt to articulate not the author's understanding better than the author's self-understanding but the inevitable projection of *one's* understanding of oneself and of the text into what one calls the "interpretation"—under which interpretation Nietzsche's text can only disappear (cf. BGE §38). From the outset, Nietzsche imposed upon himself the task of both underlining what such contextually perspectival limitations meant for philosophy and for reading (that is the work of science or scholarship), and he did this for the sake of his readers as well as for the sake of exceeding these same limitations.

A note he writes emphasizes this complexity and ties it to the fruit of his earliest insight regarding the unheard but not for that unhearable (one can learn to read, and this meant for Nietzsche that one can learn to hear the) music of the text: "Our eyes hear much more keenly than our ears: we have better taste and understanding when we read than when we listen—in the case both of books and music" (KSA 10, 103).[42] That is, given the purity of a musical score in advance of any realization for the ear—given the stilled musical resonance of ancient texts—we still have an opportunity for conceptualizing and thus for "hearing" both ancient and contemporary musical texts, provided only we have taken pains to *learn*, as Nietzsche constantly emphasizes the pain of learning, the *art of reading*.

In this sense, we can understand Nietzsche's short aphorism, "A Word of Comfort for a Musician," in *The Gay Science*, an aphorism including the included quotation marks of a word overheard from an extern's point of view, and hence voiced from an esoteric perspective:

> "Your life does not reach men's ears; your life is silent for them, and all the subtleties of its melody, all the tender resolutions about following or going ahead remain hidden from them. True, you do not approach on a broad highway with regimental music, but that does not give these good people any right to say that your life lacks music. Let those who have ears, hear." (GS §234)

The acoustic image invokes Nietzsche's charmingly fetishistic pre-occupation with his own small ears,[43] as Lou Salomé tells us and as Nietzsche tells us in his own verse—"Du hast kleine Ohren, Du hast meine Ohren" (KSA 6, 398)—a passion echoed in his lifelong invective against the long ears of those he found all-too present (and all-too deaf).

4

~~~~~~

Nietzsche's "Gay Science"

Poetry and Love, Science and Music

In his notes from Basel, as early as 1869, Nietzsche had paralleled the musical culture of ancient Greece and the song culture of medieval Europe precisely for the sake of an understanding of Greek lyric poetry and tragedy. Thus, as we have seen, Nietzsche could declare that "for the Greeks, text and music were so intimately joined that without exception one and the same artist created both of them." He further observed that the marriage of text and music was "hardly a rarity: think of the troubadours, the Minnesänger, and even the guild of Meistersingers" (FS 5, 308; cf. 367).

Laughter and Song: On Tragic "Science" and "Gay Scholarship"

In *The Gay Science* Nietzsche elaborates the troubadour's art—or science—of song.[1] *The Birth of Tragedy* and *The Gay Science* have commonalities in addition to music. Both were reissued in later editions. In the case of *The Birth of Tragedy*, the later edition would feature a new subtitle as well as a self-critical preface emphasizing the preeminence of science as the veritable core or focus of the book. In the case of *The Gay Science*, the 1887 title page substitutes a comic rhyme in place of the 1882 epigraph from Emerson and (like the later-added fourth book supplement to *Thus Spoke Zarathustra*), appends an additional, fifth book, polished with a further cycle of songs,—*Lieder des Prinzen Vogelfrei*[2]—invoking at once the knightly as well as the chastely[3] erotic character of the troubadour (and recurring in the arch allusions of Nietzsche's *Ecce Homo*).

A good many readers have underscored the preeminence of the art of laughter of the text: apotheosizing Nietzsche as the philosopher who teaches us to laugh. But an emphasis upon the parodic art of laughter tends to obscure the serious claims of Nietzsche's 'gay' science. Nietzsche himself decries the "vanity" of then-contemporary scholars incensed by his use of the "word 'science' "—a pique that not has quite played itself out—and their complaint: " 'gay' it may be but it is certainly not 'science' " (KSA 12, 149). Their objection manifestly touched a nerve, for Nietzsche had intended, so he would claim, to articulate a profoundly "serious" science (GS §382). Deeply serious, Nietzsche's "gay" science would be gay out of profundity—just as the ancient Greeks had discovered the art of drawing their delight in the surfaces of things, their gay "superficiality," from the depths of tragic wisdom (GS §iv).

From the start, Nietzsche understood his joyful science to go beyond the fun of mockery and "light feet." Invoking the troubadours' art of song,[4] *The Gay Science* might be regarded as a handbook to the art of poetry, as Nietzsche plays on the notion of *vademecum* in the series of short poems that made up his " 'Joke, Cunning, and Revenge': Prelude in German Rhymes," a title alluding to Goethe's *Scherz, List, und Rache*, by way of a contemporary musical setting.[5] In this sense, *The Gay Science* explicates the science of philology as much as it exemplifies the musical art of poetic composition. But this will also mean that one might say, as Heidegger argued in a different tonality in his Nietzsche lectures, that *The Gay Science* may properly be regarded as Nietzsche's most *scientific* work.

Provençal Song, Mirth, and Poetic Language

As we know from the quotation marks in the subtitle Nietzsche added to the second edition of *Die fröhliche Wissenschaft*, the language of *"la gaya scienza"* is not Nietzsche's. Indeed, in his notes, Nietzsche will reprove the blindness of his academic readers beyond their "misunderstanding of cheerfulness" [*Heiterkeit*]. Indeed and starting with "the title" itself, Nietzsche sniffed, "most scholars forgot its Provençal meaning."[6]

From Provence to the Occitan, one of Nietzsche's *Nachlaß* drafts, *Gai Saber*, begins with an address to "the mistral."[7] This is the troubadour's art (or technic) of poetic song, an art at once secret,[8] anonymous and thus non-subjective,[9] but also including disputation[10] and comprising, perhaps above all, the important ideal of action (and *pathos*) at a distance: *l'amour lointain*. Nietzsche's exploration of the noble art of poetic song[11] is intriguing enough to compel attention. Detailing these song forms in his notes as he does,[12] Nietzsche also seems to have framed some of his own poetic efforts in this tradition. To take an obvious instance, the appendix of songs added to *The Gay Science* in 1887 includes a dance song entitled, "To the Mistral," to be heard together with Nietzsche's praise of the south and affirming Nietzsche's love of Dame Truth herself [*Im Süden*]. Even more, as one literary scholar has reminded us in his reflections on the origins of the *"gay saber,"* the playful context of laughter—"hilarity"—and the joy of play is as central to the same medieval tradition of vernacular (as opposed to sacred) song as it is to Nietzsche's *The Gay Science*.[13] *The Gay Science* begins with just such a reference to gaiety as such as it also recollects the focus of Nietzsche's first book on musical poetry, *The Birth of Tragedy*, " 'Not only laughter and gay wisdom but the tragic too, with all its sublime unreason, belongs among the means and necessities of the preservation of the species' " (GS §1).

Nevertheless a focus on the art of the troubadour as key to Nietzsche's "gay" science inevitably takes the interpreter in a single direction. As the art of contest in poetic song and given Nietzsche's courtly allusions to Goethe as noted previously or else, and more patently, to Wagner, it is important to explore the tradition of the troubadour. Indeed, one might even be inspired to go still further afield to a plausible connection with Frédéric Mistral, the Occitan poet who popularized the inventive Provençal tradition of poetry, and who was a contemporary of Nietzsche's day.[14]

But we should also move slowly here—not just for reasons of philological care (Nietzsche's *lento*). Hence if the clearly erotic undercurrent (along with the recurrent focus on shame in *The Gay Science*—we recall that Nietzsche concludes both books 2 and 3 on the note of shame: "as long as you are in any way *ashamed* of yourselves, you do not yet belong to us" [GS §107] and, again, "*What is the seal of liberation?* No longer to be ashamed before oneself" [GS §275, see also §273 and §274]) cannot ultimately legitimate the assertion of Nietzsche's homosexuality,[15] a similar restraint is also essential in this case. If Nietzsche himself claims the reference to the troubadours for his own part (and to this extent, the current reading is not speculation), the riddle of *The Gay Science* hardly reduces to this.

We need more than a recollection of the Provençal character and atmosphere of the troubadour in order to understand Nietzsche's conception of a joyful science, even if, given the element of a complex and "involuntary parody" (GS §382), the spirit of the Occitan certainly helps, especially where Nietzsche adverts to dissonance throughout (betraying the disquiet of the mistral wind as well as its seasonal relief). For nothing less than a critique of science is essential for an understanding of the ideal of Nietzsche's gay science. As we have already seen in the first chapter above, a reflection on ancient Greek music drama had occupied Nietzsche's first concerns with the general question of what he would retrospectively call the "problem of science" in his 1886 reflections on his first book, *The Birth of Tragedy*. This object of Nietzsche's scientific or rigorously scholarly concern was Nietzsche's declared discovery of the birth of tragedy in the folk song, in lyric poetry—read and heard in the music of the Greek lyric word (BT §§5, 17, etc.).

Seen from this perspective, *The Gay Science* tells us Nietzsche's life work in terms of his scholarly achievements as well as his own deployment of the same: putting this "science" to work on his own behalf and taking this as far as the consummate promise of his troubadour's (and even Catharist) ideal of self-overcoming. This is the context of impossible love, the condemnation "never to love," as that intimate disappointment in which David B. Allison quotes Nietzsche's resolution to effect his own healing transfiguration.[16] If the "gay science" is a handbook of song, it prefigures what Allison has delicately analyzed as what will become Nietzsche's recipe for inventing "the alchemical trick for transforming this—muck [*Kothe*] into gold."[17] If Nietzsche's self-therapy works for the love of a woman, for Lou, as Allison argues, it is because the alchemical transformation consummates *amor fati*—loving life, real life, not just "warts and all," but exactly including as intimately necessary to life, the whole gamut of illness and suffering, misrecognition and disappointment, as well as death, constituting a patent catalog of the all-too real horrors of ancient tragedy.

For Nietzsche's "gay science" is a passionate, fully joyful science. But to say this is also to say that a gay science is a *dedicated science*: scientific "all the way down." This is a science including the most painful and troubling insights, daring, to use Nietzsche's language here, every ultimate or "last consequence" (BGE §22; KSA 13, 257). Doubting as well as Montaigne, more radical than Descartes, and still more critical than Kant or Schopenhauer, dispensing with Spinoza's and with Hegel's (but also with Darwin's and even Newton's) faith, Nietzsche's joyful, *newly* joyful, scientist carries "the *will* henceforth to question further, more deeply, stringently, harshly, cruelly, and quietly than one had questioned heretofore" (GS §iii). Even confidence in life itself, as a value, of course, but also as such, now "becomes a *problem*." The result is a new kind of love and a new kind of joy, a new passion, a "new happiness."

The commitment of a joyful science includes body and mind (Descartes), just because Nietzsche does not distinguish these any more than he distinguishes between soul and spirit (Kant and Hegel). The reference to the body derives from Nietzsche's experience of suffering as an adventure in transmutation. This transfigured suffering or pain he calls "convalescence," reminding us of the influence of the body and its milieu—interior and exterior, physiological and ecological—in the purest aspirations of reason. Like Montaigne, again, if also, again, playing off Spinoza and Leibniz, Nietzsche invokes the need for self-questioning and for self-experimentation precisely with an eye to the importance of physiological influences as these may be found on every level of thought, finally pronouncing philosophy nothing but an "interpretation" and "misunderstanding" of the body (GS §ii). As a philosopher in the fashion of the gay science, you can play or "experiment" with yourself in your own thinking, you can be the phenomenologist of yourself, varying the effects of health, illness, convalescence, or the persistence of illness and pain on thought itself. For neither science, nor scholarship, nor philosophy, Nietzsche tells us, has ever been "about 'truth' " (Ibid.). Each of these occupations, as Nietzsche tells us, has always had some other motivation or aim in mind, for example, "health, future, growth, power, life . . ." (Ibid.). Acknowledging the passions of knowledge heretofore, Nietzsche is at pains to argue that the ideal of objectivity is a delusion either of self-deceiving idealism or a calculated mendacity. Belief in such an ideal is the default of science altogether. In its place, Nietzsche argues against both the idea and the ideal of pure science, dedicated to sheer knowledge as if knowing should be its own end (GS §23), as he also argues against knowledge for gain and profit.[18] In every case, his reference point is the *noble* (cf. D §308 and BGE §212) ideal of *la gaya scienza*. Contra the idealistic convictions of the "will to truth," to "truth at any price," Nietzsche dares the proposition that truth, once "laid bare," no longer remains true (GS §iv). A gay science will *need* to know itself as art.

Reflecting on the title of Nietzsche's *Die fröhliche Wissenschaft*, Martin Heidegger has emphasized that metonymically tuned with *Wissenschaft*, science, the word *fröhliche*, happy or gay, light or joyful, evokes *Leidenschaft*, passion.[19] In this way, Heidegger argues, Nietzsche's passionate, joyful science can be opposed to the dusty scholarship for the sake of assonance, let us call it the "grey science," of his peers.[20] This same claim supports the surmise that like *Beyond Good and Evil* and *Twilight of the Idols*, Nietzsche's joyful science was intended as a challenge to Wilamowitz (and thence contra philology as the discipline that had excluded Nietzsche's contributions).

The test of Nietzsche's joyful science, *amor fati*, finds its planned—and executed—exemplification in *Thus Spoke Zarathustra*, as well as in the retrospective song cycle appended to the later-written fifth book of *The Gay Science*.[21] In this experimental fashion, in this very scientific way, the promise articulated on behalf of music in *The Birth of Tragedy* might finally be fulfilled, as his reflections in *Beyond Good and Evil* and *Ecce Homo* suggest. If the "spirit of science" [*der Geist der Wissenschaft*] and techno-mechanical progress could be shown to have the power to vanquish myth (even if only with a myth of its own) and poetry (even if only with poetry of its own),[22] the "spirit of music" might be thought—this remains Nietzsche's finest hope, it is his philosophical music of the future—to have retained the power to give birth once again to tragedy. Such a rebirth compels us to seek out the "spirit of science" precisely in terms of its antagonistic opposition to music's power of mythical creativity.[23]

As preserved in written form, like Homer's epic song, like Greek musical tragedy, *la gaya scienza* corresponds to the textual fusion of oral traditions—composition, transmission, performance—in the now-frozen poems of the troubadours. It is important, as with the ancient tradition of epic poetry, that the knightly art of poetry, the *gai saber* as it was recorded in the fourteenth century,[24] presumed a much older tradition dating back to the twelfth or eleventh century.[25] In a parallel fashion, Nietzsche's discovery had been that the musical tradition of the folk song gave birth to the archetypical Greek tragic art form, a genealogy that was for Nietzsche to be descried in the rhythmic structures that he called the music of lyric poetry.

The "spirit of music" gives birth to tragedy, the tragic art and knowledge that is ultimately the metaphysical comfort of the artist (BT §25).[26] In *The Gay Science*, Nietzsche articulates this "metaphysical" comfort as the distance and light of art (GS §339). By contrast with such a metaphysical or musical comfort, the comfort of "the spirit of science" is a physical one: "eine irdische Consonanz" (BT §17). In *The Gay Science*, Nietzsche will analyze this saving grace and working functionality as the reason we, too, remain "still pious" (GS §344). Astonishing in its patent, empirical, but insuperably contingent success, what "holds up" (GS §46) in science as the (technological) scientific solution to life is the gift of a deus ex machina, as Nietzsche clarifies the vision of Prometheus for us (GS §300), the "God of the machines and the foundries" (BT §17), put to work on behalf of a "higher" egoism, confident in the "world's correction through knowing," and of the viability of a "life guided by science" (Ibid.) but above all, capable of concentrating the individual within the most restrictive sphere of problem solving (the scientific method).

To illuminate the point of Nietzsche's allusion here, if Goethe's own Faust had been locked together with the spirit of the Earth so densely summoned forth at the start and compelled to turn within the same circle, he might well have declared, in advance of the whole tragedy, I *and* II, "Ich will dich: du bist werth erkannt zu werden" (BT §17; cf. GS §1). For Nietzsche, as for the rest of us, the method at work—stipulation, mechanism, and above all delimitation, that is, the working practice of method *as such*—is the key to the modern scientific age. The same methodification is also the means whereby science becomes art, but to say this is also to say that science departs from theory alone, from its metaphysical heaven or perfection, to become practicable and livable, viable, as such.[27] Nietzsche's Zarathustra thus teaches loyalty to the earth.

However effective they are (and they are very effective as Nietzsche underscores), the expression of natural laws in human relations or numerical formulae (GS §246) remains a metaphorical convention: a Protagorean conventionalism Nietzsche famously compares to a deaf person's visually metaphorical judgment of the acoustic quality of music on the basis of Chladni sand/sound figures (GS §373)—an image that gave Nietzsche proof of the veritably metaphorical convertibility of sound and light in wave forms or vibrations, or "Schwingungen," as Nietzsche triumphantly declared (KSA 7, 164)—and today we might reimagine the Chladni metaphor as the "music" of a digital music file printed as binary character text—or else, and more elliptically, as the visual "musicality" of the gleaming refraction surface of a music CD hung as a light-catcher. The full context here is as follows: "The *human being* as the measure of things is similarly the basic concept of science. Every law of nature is ultimately a sum of anthropological relations. Especially number: the quantitative reduction of every law, their expression in numerical formulas is a μεταφορά, as someone one who lacks the ability to hear judges music and tonality according to the Chladni sound patterns" (KSA 7, 494; cf. 445).

In this way, when Nietzsche first sets up the opposition between art and science in terms of music and myth—that is: in distinction to logic and calculative advantage—what is at issue is a proportionate achievement. As Nietzsche had argued in his first book, both art *and* science are ordered to life. Art seeks to harmonize dissonance, resolving it by transfiguration—not by elimination but by way of musical incorporation: "a becoming-human of dissonance" (BT §25, cf. §24). By contrast, especially in the guise of the technological science of modernity, as it begins with Socrates and the promise of logic and truth, mechanical or physical science effectively corrects or improves the world. In this fasion, science substitutes an earthly consonance in place of the elusive promise of the tragic art, or music, which for its part offers no solutions to mortal problems (this is tragedy), only beautiful concinnities as I have called Nietzsche's harmonies (this is the art of music).

For Nietzsche, a focus on science may not be distinguished from aesthetics (art) as we have already seen nor indeed from ethics (morality).

Nietzsche opposes, first, the failure of music in such a scientifically improved world; second, the self-deceiving truth of earthly consonance with respect to its own illusions (this would be a "lack" of science, beyond the praise for the probity of the thinker that compels him to turn to science [GS §335]; this would be "the good, stupid will to 'believe,'" which Nietzsche challenges as a "lack of philology," that is, "the lack of suspicion and patience . . ." [BGE §192]).

When "'modern scientific'" rationality (GS §358) turns its eye on suffering, it conceives and so reduces suffering to a "problem" to be solved (KSA 1, 394). There is a whole skein of difficulties here for Nietzsche, beginning with the question of the nature and extent of suffering (psychic or physical, cultural or historical) and including the quality and character of comfort and relief. The compassionate and tragic element will always be important for Nietzsche, a sensitive pathos he shared with Schopenhauer. But beyond Schopenhauer, Nietzsche would also argue that the problem of suffering eludes ameliorating reduction for the very reason that a solution to the problem of suffering also and inevitably elides the whole fateful range of what belongs to suffering (GS §338, 318). This is a complex point and it does not mean that Nietzsche was in favor of passively enduring much less inflicting suffering. But to strip off the multilayered, complex covering of truth (that is, its illusions) is *also* to dissolve what is true (GS §iv) in the same way that Rome as an empire came to dominate its world, to use Nietzsche's example of cultural supremacy (for a contemporary example, we can think of what we call "globalism"). Imperial Rome blithely obliterated the traces of its past (better said, the past of its predecessors) without the slightest inkling of bad conscience: "brushing off the dust on the wings of the moment of the historical butterfly" (GS §83). In one's own life, this layered and interwoven complexity is the inscrutability and that is exactly to say the *meaning* of suffering (GS §318). More critically, it is the problem of the meaning and significance of suffering for another (this is the problem of "other pains," as it were [GS §338]). In this reflection, key to the notion of the eternal return, Nietzsche touches upon the deep relation of suffering to happiness as well as everything that suffering necessitates and makes possible (Ibid.). This complex problem is Nietzsche's great challenge to contemporary expressions of care ethics or the ethics of compassion as Nietzsche would speak of the higher ethic of friendship (KSA 8, 333); it is his intriguing and still-untapped contribution to understanding Heidegger's notion of care in the elusive reflection contra pity (*Mitleid*) that would teach what Nietzsche names *Mitfreude* (GS §338).

Nietzsche's gay science of morality is complicated precisely because he is interested less in promulgating a moral theory than in questioning the presumptions of the same. For Nietzsche, questioning is the most important element in science (GS §2, §375) and what Nietzsche confesses as his personal "injustice" is his very scientific conviction that everyone must somehow, ultimately *have to have* this "Lust des Fragens" (GS §2). In Kantian terms, Nietzsche permitted himself to believe that everyone was in some measure possessed by a passion for questioning "at any price" (GS §344).

Science and *Leidenschaft*

Reviewing the motivations of established scholarship, that is, a job, a career, dusty and bored with itself ("lacking anything better to do"), the "scientific drive" of traditional, grey scientists turns out to be nothing but "their boredom" (GS §123).[28] By contrast what Nietzsche calls "the passion of the knowledge seeker" is a very erotic drive: a drive for possession. This is acquisitive to the point of abandon, "yearning for undiscovered worlds and seas" (GS §302), completely lacking selflessness, lacking disinterest, and in place of the ideal of scholarly detachment, "an all-desiring self that would like, as it were, to see with the eyes and seize with the hands of many individuals—a self that would like to bring back the entire past, that wants to lose nothing it could possibly possess!" (GS §249). So far from science's celebrated objectivity and neutrality (GS §351), "the great *passion* of the knowledge seeker" is a matter of intimate and absolute or utter cupidity (GS §249, §345). As Nietzsche regarded this passionate drive from the perspective of "nobility" (GS §3), the archaic quality of Nietzsche's joyful passion is ineluctably alien to modern sensibilities—if simply and fundamentally because (and this is what Nietzsche always understood by the ideal of nobility) the cupidity or desire of gay science is a non-venal one (GS §330).[29]

Both science and art draw upon the same creative powers, both are directed to the purpose of life, and most importantly for Nietzsche, both are illusions. Denying a Platonic world of noumenal truth, there is for Nietzsche only nominal truth (GS §58)—sheer illusion—but no noumenon. Indeed what is key to Nietzsche's inversion of Plato/Kant (i.e., Christianity), is that without the noumenal, there is no phenomenal world; without metaphysics, no physics. The world is mere will to power, chaos, and nothing besides (GS §109). The only truth is illusion, and there is no truth beyond illusion. But this is Schopenhauer's world, not Kant's. To make any headway with this, one needs a non-Western logic, the logic of the veil of Maya. But to say this, for the Nietzsche who always remains a scientist, ultimately means that one is grateful to art. In the context of this non-Western logic, the critical distance Nietzsche maintains with respect to Buddhism may well correspond to his rigorously preserved "scientific" attitude (see GS §§78, 299, 301, 339).

But what is science? Science is routinely presumed to be a matter of method (and quantifying analysis) and it was exactly the character of science as method that Nietzsche had in mind. Hence in the context of his early (and later) reflections, when Nietzsche proposed to examine "the problem of science," what he means by science presupposes its broadest sense because what he wanted to address was nothing less than the specifically *scientific* character of science. For this reason too, Nietzsche's talk of science with regard to aesthetics and ancient philology (i.e., in his book on tragedy) inevitably exceeded aesthetic philology in its scope and works and brought Nietzsche to speak of logic, rationality, and even of the mechanized way of life of modernity, in order to speak, in the classical mode, of the contemporary possibilities of Western culture.

It is the meaning of science that remains problematic here. And very few scholars have adverted to the problems of the compound construction of a "gay science." Among the few who do so, Heidegger asks "What does *gay science* mean?" reminding us with this question that Nietzsche's "science [*Wissenschaft*] is not a collective noun for the sciences as we find them today, with all their paraphernalia in the shape they assumed during the course of the last century" (N2, 20). Heidegger thus contrasts Nietzsche's conception of a gay science to the nineteenth-century ideal of the positive, measuring, or technologically defined sciences.[30] The point is not that Nietzsche opposes positive science but rather that such positive, or technologically defined sciences are immoderate precisely at this point for they have seduced themselves into taking their own axioms as demonstrated truths. By contrast with modern science and its calculative technologies (where physics is *the* paradigmatic science), the passion of Nietzsche's *fröhliche Wissenschaft* "resounds" like "the passion of a well-grounded mastery over the things that confront us and over our own way of responding to what confronts us, positing all these things in magnificent and essential goals" (N2, 20). In order to make some headway with the question of this passion for knowledge, a gay science, as already suggested, needs the art of love. And the erotic art must be learned, so Nietzsche argues, exactly as we "learn" to love anything at all.

Nietzsche's example for such learning is music itself: the cultivated love that is, like every other art of love, an acquired passion (GS §334). Indeed, for Nietzsche, only such a cultivated passion for knowledge has a justifiable claim to the title of science. In this sense, a supposed science of music apart from the art of music, apart from "what is music in it" (GS §373), would not be merely abstract. Blind and empty, a tone-deaf musical science would not be a science worthy of the name (GS §374).

The Music of the Gay Science and the Meaning of *Wissenschaft*

Science, regarded as a "symptom of life," Nietzsche argued, could well constitute a "subtle form of self-defense against the truth" (BT §ii). Suggesting that truth (and the will to truth) might be less than salutary, Nietzsche opposes both Socratic rationality (better living through science) and Christianity (truth saves). For the same reason, the task of presenting "*the problem of science itself,* science considered for the first time as problematic, as questionable" (Ibid.) exposes the thinker to the danger of truth. We recall Nietzsche's description of his own first book's grappling with what he called a "problem with horns" (Ibid.). Ignoring the focus on science as problematic, scholars have routinely argued that Nietzsche's attempt "to view science through the lens of the artist and art through that of life" was not addressed to what we take to be science today, not natural science, not *real* science.[31]

Walter Kaufmann (whose influence in an English-speaking context as Nietsche's translator—like that of R. J. Hollingdale's—can hardly be overemphasized) has assured us that the science in Nietzsche's *The Gay Science* has nothing to do with *science* per se but rather and only refers to the troubadour's art, just as earlier noted. And it is quite clear that Kaufmann is not uncovering an obscure detail but one Nietzsche himself emphasizes not only indirectly but on the title page to the second edition as well as in his later writings and throughout his *Nachlaß* notes (complete, as we have already seen, with schematizations of the song forms). Indeed, if anything, Kaufmann's gloss tells us *less* than Nietzsche does. For *The Gay Science* manifestly refers to the troubadour's art. But what art of song was that to be for Nietzsche? Was that the art of the famous Jaufré Raudel (c. 1125–1128) or Guiraut Riquier, the so-called last of the troubadours?[32] Was it the lyre song of Homer's Achilles? Or Pindar's "crown"[33] of song? Or Machiavelli's musical art? Or are we merely speaking of Orpheus? Or Wagner? Or, and this solution is still the favorite amongst most readers, are we speaking of Nietzsche himself, when he claimed that one *should* range his Zarathustra under the rubric of music, and given the portents of his concluding *incipit* in *The Gay Science*? At the very least, it would seem that Nietzsche aligns the gay science, as the art of the troubadour, with the ancient musical art of tragedy, as Nietzsche sings himself the song of his songs—and including the troubadour's *serenas* or evensong, or, given the context of music and Venice, his *planctus* or *planh* in his *Ecce Homo*.[34]

For Nietzsche, as for any German, both in his day and our own, the term *Wissenschaft* or science applies as much to historical studies of ancient philology as to the natural sciences. Where the problem of science qua science, that is, the problem of the scientificity of science, also corresponds to the logical problem of reflexivity, the general problem of science as such—both natural (and phenomenological) and philological (and hermeneutical)—calls for critical reflection. Nietzsche had argued that science as such (including the natural, physical sciences, as well as mathematics and logic) cannot be critically conceived (or founded) on its own ground nor indeed (and this was Nietzsche's most esoteric point as a hermeneutic of hermeneutics) can philology be so founded. It was because he wrote as a philological scholar, as a *scientist*, by his own perfectly rigorous definition of the term, that Nietzsche could regard his methodological considerations as directly relevant to the "problem of science."

We may note that in distinction to the narrow focus of the English *science*, the inclusiveness of the German *Wissenschaft* illuminates the parallels between Nietzsche's self-critique and Kant's expression of metaphysics in terms of a science of the future (as a future metaphysics).[35] Again, it is important to affirm that the present author is well able, as others seemingly are not, to assume that Nietzsche had "read" Kant.[36] For Nietzsche, accordingly, and as he writes in *The Birth of Tragedy*, the achievement of Kant's critical philosophy, a tradition of critique culminating in Schopenhauer, the same critical tradition that continues in Adorno and Horkheimer,[37] was to engage what Nietzsche regarded as the logical contradictions of the logical optimism of modern science.[38] This logical optimism is the positivist confidence that knowledge is both possible (in theory) and attainable (in practice). We still subscribe to the same optimism in our ongoing conviction that "all the riddles of the universe can be known and fathomed" (BT §18), and thus we faithfully denounce as anti-scientific and willfully obscure anyone who challenges this scientistic conviction.

Yet here the question of the meaning of *Wissenschaft* for Nietzsche (as for Kant, Hegel, and even Goethe but also Marx, Freud, Dilthey, Weber, Husserl, Heidegger, et al.) remains elusive. For if the *fröhlich* in the title of *Die fröhliche Wissenschaft* has required our attention, taking us to passion (with Heidegger) but also taking us to a willingness to dance over the abyss of unreciprocated or failed love or the dark neediness of the soul (with Allison), and ultimately to Nietzsche's own concerns as he summarizes these for us, daring the dangerous play of experimental questioning (GS §374), the meaning of *Wissenschaft* turns out to be similarly complicated. It is worth asking, again, what Nietzsche means by "science," be it "gay" or otherwise?

Intriguingly, although it is routinely observed that the German term *Wissenschaft* and the English word for *science* ought to be distinguished, commentators tend not to explicate the difference in question. I have elsewhere explored this point in greater detail, but here it is worth recalling that a differentiation between these terms is important as is the recollection that beyond such definitions, each word also carries with it its own penumbra of meaning and substitutions, articulating on each side a divergent range of associations, both metonymic and metaphorical.[39]

Dating from the fourteenth century, the term *Wissenschaft* was coined in German for the needs of a theological and mystical context in order to translate the Latin *sciens, scientia,* terms given as *science* in English, and related to *scire,* to know, *scindere,* to cut or divide. Key here in understanding *Wissenschaft* are the set of associations of the root terms, in particular the powerful etymological array via *wissen* linked to the Old High German *wizzan* and Old Saxon *wita* but also the English *wit* and *wot* and thence to the Sanskrit *vēda* and the ancient Greek οἶδα as well as the Latin, *videre.* As a philologist, Nietzsche was characteristically conscious of this root connection between vision and scientific knowledge—hence his focus on the ocular tendency of science in general—but especially natural science. See the following note: "Science aims *to interpret the same phenomenon through different senses* and to reduce everything to the most *exact* sense: the optical. Thus do we learn to understand the senses—the darker are illuminated by the lighter" (KSA 11, 114). And it might be worth investigating the degree to which this ocular conception inspired both his focus on what he called the "science of aesthetics" in his first book, his emphasis upon the importance of the haptic sense in the physical sciences (cf. TI, " 'Reason' in Philosophy," §3), and his special attention to the sense of "taste," a focus he earlier played back to its etymological association with wisdom as such: "The Greek word that signifies 'wise' etymologically belongs to *sapio,* I taste, *sapiens,* the one who tastes, *sisyphos,* the man of the keenest taste; a keen ability to distinguish and to recognize thus constitutes for folk consciousness, the authentic philosophical art" (KSA 1, 813). Whether deliberate or not, Nietzsche's example is in remarkable parallel with David Hume's reflections on aesthetic taste.[40]

Importantly however—and Heidegger makes much of this—it is only since the eighteenth century that the current meaning of the sciences (that is: as opposed to and as distinct from the arts) can be dated. If it can be argued that the meanings of *Wissenschaft* and *science* now and increasingly tend to coincide, *Wissenschaft,* as we have seen that Heidegger has also emphasized, yet remains unquestionably broader, as it corresponds to the collective pursuit of knowledge kinds. This collectivity is the meaning of *-schaft,* analogous to the suffix *-ship,* as in *scholarship* (a word that only partially renders *Wissenschaft*).[41] As the noun corresponding to *wissen, Wissenschaft* also retains the connotations of the "ways" or conduits of knowing, ways that can still be heard in English with the archaic *wis* (to show the way, to instruct) or *wist* (to know).

Reviewing the above definitions, it is plain that although Nietzsche's identification of himself as a "scientific" practitioner may still strike a contemporary English speaker as sufficiently non-idiomatic to call forth at least a footnote (if not whole books on source scholarship) designed to explain the problem away, remanding it to the conventionality of the history of ideas and influences, his identification of his research interests as "scientific" would be routine in contemporary German usage. But this is exactly not to say that all Nietzsche was talking about was his own disciplinary field of ancient Greek philology. For Nietzsche, as should now be clear, what made his own discipline scientific was what made any discipline scientific.

The problem is not at issue in German readings of Nietzsche (though there remains a related problem in German contributions to epistemology and the philosophy of science to just the degree that these fields continue to be received as Anglo-Saxon disciplines). The problem is in understanding Nietzsche's references. And the problem is the problem of equivocation. For in spite of all the well-known rigor of the study of classics, we can only be hard pressed to see classics as a "science" per se. For this reason, when Nietzsche, a classicist, speaks of himself as advancing science, we do not quite take his reference except by putatively broadening his claim to an assertion about "scholarship" in general, but by which we mean literature, in fact, and particularly, classical philology, and then, following Wilamowitz's academically devastating critique of Nietzsche's supposed innovations, not even that.

Nietzsche poses the question of science not as a resoluble but much rather as a critical problem. As a critical project, Nietzsche adverts to the stubborn difficulty of putting science in question—the difficulty of questioning what is ordinarily unquestionable. Science, indeed, as presumptive authority and as "method" is ordinarily the ground or foundation for critical questioning. For this same critical reason, Nietzsche holds that the project of raising "the problem of science itself . . . as a problem, as questionable" (BT §ii) was a task to be accomplished over time, not merely a point to be made, or a problem to be remedied.

If Nietzsche liked to assert that he aspired to a more radical doubt than Descartes (KSA 11, 640–641), and if Nietzsche was surely more critical than Kant in calling for the key reflex of the critical project to be turned against itself (GS §357; cf. BGE §11), Nietzsche nonetheless differs from the Enlightenment project of philosophical modernity in general. Thus Nietzsche *does not* exclude his own deliberately provocative solution as a problem at the limit of critical reflection. Instead, Nietzsche presupposes an unrelenting self-critique, precisely for the sake of science and this is why Nietzsche's reflection continues to matter for the sake of any possible philosophy of science that may be able to come forth as a science.

Self-criticism, critique of one's tacit assumptions, has to be a constant attendant to philosophical critique but—and Nietzsche is just as quick to remind us of this—where are we to position ourselves for the sake of such self-critique? Raising the question of the subject, challenging that there is nothing that thinks, the Archimedean standpoint provided by the Cartesian thinking subject is suspended where it emerges: in the middle of nowhere, and this is, if it is nothing else, a questionable foundation. The result is the giddiness Nietzsche claims endemic to the modern era, an era without definable up and down (and the orienting disposition of the same to above and below), without belief in God (cf. GS §125), and increasingly lacking even the firm foundation of the ultimacy of the human subject.

Gay Science: Passion, Vocation, Music

As a *Leidenschaft* in Heidegger's sense, Nietzsche's science opposes the usual conception of either science or scholarship, even and perhaps especially philosophy, (even if, as Nietzsche remarks, philosophy is the discipline named for love or passion). As already emphasized, Nietzsche's gay science is not just relevant to science in general but exactly opposed to the nineteenth-century ideal of the positive, measuring, calculative, or technologically defined sciences.[42]

If this were an armchair problem of the classically metaphysical kind we could let it go at that: as a puzzle of the ordinary Kuhnian kind—science as Popperian problem solving. But because the problem is the problem of science as the "theory of the real" (see GS §57), we have been attempting to take it by its figurative horns, in the very spirit of Nietzsche's own metaphorical invocation of the Cretan art of bull dancing (BT §ii). The "horns" of this dilemma may also remind us of Nietzsche's polemical language in his preface to *Beyond Good and Evil*, whereby all of us, as philosophers and as scientists/philologists, conceived as impotent, or at least as inconsequential, suitors of the truth, are also crowned with all the allusions to the liar that are inevitable with reference to Nietzsche or even, thinking of Ariadne, to Theseus himself. But here, our ambition is more sober than trivial matters of scholarly pride, or what Nietzsche called "scientific pedantry." An unquestioning inattention to modern science and technology continues to rule in modern confidence, that is, in what Nietzsche called our "convictions."

For Nietzsche, we explain (or as he takes care to specify, we "de-scribe" [GS §112]) everything with reference to ourselves and our own motivational intentionality, consequently and inevitably, here Nietzsche goes beyond *both* Kant and Schopenhauer, we fashion (or invent) the very concept of a cause (GS §112; cf. GS §357) and thereby misconstrue both the world *and* ourselves in a single blow.[43] Nietzsche's critical reflections on science may be summarized as the critical reflexive question of science raised in terms of the conditions of any possibility of knowing, that is to say: looking at science itself as a problem, *scientifically*, and that is, again, from the perspective of art and life. Like the sand patterns of the Chladni sound figures that so captivated Nietzsche's imagination,[44] the question of science can be raised in terms of music, not only in terms of the troubadour's musical art but also in terms of its remainder. This is music's ineffable residue, sedimented in the words that still remain to be sung.[45]

In *The Gay Science*, Nietzsche outlines a critical revision of the standard genealogy of science out of the spirit of myth and magic and alchemy as he also finds science modeled on the occluded paradigm of religion (GS §300; GM III, 25). Nietzsche does not merely parallel science and religion in terms of both faith and ultimate goals, that is, piety and metaphysics (GS §344) but earlier, in a rarely remarked upon aphoristic tour de force, Nietzsche plays between science and religion and the prejudices proper to both. Thus Nietzsche tells a parable to explain (and not quite to denounce)[46] an earlier era's wholly scientific (one thinks of the Jesuit scholar, Robert Bellarmine's) resistance to Galileo and to Copernicus and so on. In the very way that the noble passion of love (the purity of the lover, the same purity that forgives even the visceral vigor of lust itself, as Nietzsche notes [GS §62]) would be dis-inclined to wish or to be asked to imagine the inner guts of the beloved, the whole network of tissue and blood and nerves in all their glistening truth, so the believer would have had, in times gone by, a similar lover's horror with respect to the divine sensorium. In earlier, more religiously (as opposed to more scientifically) pious times, one recoiled from the viewpoint that would reveal the beloved: the cosmos and thus God himself, laid bare by the incursions of telescopes and astronomical theory: "In everything that was said about nature by astronomers, geologists, physiologists, and doctors, he saw an intrusion on his choicest property and thus an assault—and a shameless one on the part of the attacker" (GS §59). We see here the sensitivity of Nietzsche's rhetorical style at work: beginning where "all the world" knows its way around and knows all about (namely: about love and love affairs, think of the philosophers of sex and love), Nietzsche's parable takes the reader to a more esoteric insight, namely into scientific cosmology itself and the trajectories of its historical contextuality and thence to the philosophy of science as such.

For the sake of the philosophical question of truth and logical rationality, Nietzsche raises the question of science as the question of the measure of the world of real—not ideal (GS §57)—things. For Nietzsche, just as one cuts away the metaphysical domain of the noumenal, real/ideal world and loses the phenomenal world in the same process, the clarification of the human being in modern scientific, evolutionary, and physiological terms also works to eliminate the pure possibility of knowledge as such. If what works in us are tissues and cells, genes and evolutionary history, associations and habits, then we cannot speak of knowledge, and certainly not "reality." The problem is worse than a Kantian conceptual scheme, space-time, causality, et cetera, the problem is the in-mixture of ecology, physiology, and electrochemical processes. Thus Nietzsche can conclude: "There is for us no 'reality' . . ." (GS §57). When, in the subsequent section, Nietzsche goes on to detail his radical nominalism he is not merely invoking the sovereignty of human invention but its impotence. Thus he declares his conviction, "that unspeakably more lies in what things are called than in what they are" (GS §58). This is complicated as it begins in arbitrary convention but ends in something even more durable than habit as there is also (and there are entire sciences like philology but also, like anthropology and the other "human" sciences that seek to adumbrate Nietzsche's insight here) a natural history of conventions or habits. Thus he reflects that "appearance from the very start almost becomes essence and works as such" (Ibid.). But cutting through all of this is itself a proof of its efficacy and origin and above all, "it is, we should not forget, enough to create new names and estimates and probabilities in order to create new 'things' in the long run" (Ibid.). This poetic creativity is the ultimate meaning of the troubadour's art (*trobar*, an etymologically disputed term, meaning invention but also related to tropes and their variations)[47] as a science (GS §335): it is the heart of what Nietzsche called *"la gai saber."*

For Nietzsche, "all of life is based on semblance, art, deception, points of view, and the necessity of perspectives and error" (BT §v).[48] Nietzsche saw that the critical self-immolation of knowledge ("the truth that one is eternally condemned to untruth" [KSA 1, 760]) at the limit of the critical philosophic enterprise is to be combined with the sober notion that insight into illusion does not abrogate it and, above all, such insight does not mean that illusion lacks effective or operative power. To the contrary, "from every point of view," Nietzsche argued, "the *erroneousness* of the world in which we live is the surest and the firmest thing we can get our eyes on" (BGE §34; cf. GS §§111, 112). Nor, as we have traced the etymology of *Wissenschaft*,[48] is this visual metaphor an incidental one here. For Nietzsche, to regard the body as a complexly knowing instrumentarium, widely keyed to all its senses and not restricted to sight alone, is to understand the body itself as mind, that is, not as opposed to the mind, and not imagined as a Cartesian or Lockean adjunct to the mind, but, writ large and veritably Hobbesian (if beyond Hobbes), a "grand reason, a plurality with one sensibility, a war and a peace."[49]

As "physician of culture," the philosopher is to be an artist of science, a composer of reflective thought, refusing the calculations of science as the thickness deadly to the "music" of life (GS §372; 373). Refusing such calculations, the gay science promotes a more musical, more passionate science. In this way, the "only" help for science turns out to be not more science or better scientific understanding but the therapeutic resources and risks of art.[50] The goal is not a more charming, comic, or "light" science but, much rather—and much more—a science worthy of the name, if perhaps for the first time: a gay science with the courage truly to question (GS §§345, 346, 351) resisting what Nietzsche analyzes as the always latent tendency of degraded and ordinary science, "grey science," I have been calling it, to rigidify into either the damning exclusions of dogma, "You must be mistaken! Where have you left your senses! This *dare not* be the truth!" (GS §25), or empty and mindless problem solving ("an exercise in arithmetic and an indoor diversion for mathematicians" [GS §373]).

What Nietzsche means by thinking in the critical service of science (as the artful "mastery" of this same, newly gay science) can only be expressed in its contextual connections to topics in other kinds of philosophic reflection traditionally regarded as distinct. One allies laughter and wisdom, rejoining art and science because, for Nietzsche, the problem of science corresponds to the problem of art and life.

It is for this reason that one always misses the point when one declares that Nietzsche is "against" (or "for") science. Instead, Nietzsche's interpretive touchstone contrasts what affirms mortal life on this earth with what denies that life. But because mortal life includes sickness, decay, and death, this tragic perspective opposes the nihilism (be it mystico-religious or rational-scientific) that would seek, as does religion, to redeem or else, as does science, to improve life because *both* perspectives turn out to *deny* mortality (suffering, frustration, death—an emphasis common to the troubadours as well as ancient Greek music drama or tragedy and, indeed, opera).

Like the problem of suffering, Nietzsche's philosophy of science addresses the problem of mortal life without seeking to solve it. For

Nietzsche, "knowledge and becoming" (truth and life) mutually and incorrigibly exclude each other (KSA 12, 382; cf. 312). Thus to say that "our art is the reflection of *desperate knowledge*" (KSA 7, 476) is to set art and knowledge on the same level and for this same reason, both art and knowledge can be used either against life or in the service of life (and we recall that "life" is the "woman" of Nietzsche's troubadour song in *Thus Spoke Zarathustra* [see too GS §229]). But when Nietzsche writes in *The Gay Science* that "*science* can serve either goal" (GS §12), he cannot be articulating a traditionally naïve expression of science's celebrated neutrality, as we have seen. Instead, and precisely as a logical or theoretical project, science is the kind of art or illusion (or convention) that remains inherently nihilistic. Because science (as such) is not objectively neutral, science must *always* be critically reviewed not on its own basis (we have noted that science is not and cannot be in a position to do this) but rather on the ground of what makes science possible, and that is what Nietzsche originally named the "light" of art.

It is art that gives us perspective on things (GS §339) just as art teaches us to regard them from the proper distance (GS §107). This is the perspectival knowledge proper to the art (or science as Nietzsche would say) of rhetoric. That same framing optic—or perspective prism, to use a Goethean metaphor for Nietzsche's own approach to science— focuses on life in its complexity, regarded in such a way that it can be seen in all its shifting complexity. "At times we need to have a rest from ourselves," he writes, a pause gained "by looking at and down at ourselves and from an artistic distance, laughing *at* ourselves or crying *at* ourselves; we have to discover the hero no less than the fool in our passion for knowledge; we must now and then be pleased with our folly in order to be able to remain pleased by our wisdom" (GS §107).

This artful joy (or gaiety) is what Nietzsche encourages us to learn from "the artists," and to learn this in the same manner and with the same expectations with which we learn from doctors and pharmacists how best to down a bitter drink: by thinning it, to diffuse or veil it, or by mixing sugar and wine into the potion (GS §299). The bitter potion stays bitter, but it can be drunk. Art has at its disposal a variety of means for *making* things beautiful, alluring, and desirable, precisely when they aren't— for "in themselves, they never are" (Ibid.). Here Nietzsche calls upon us to be wiser than, to go further than, the artist who forgets his magic at the point where his art leaves off: "We however want to be the poets of our lives, and first of all in the smallest and most everyday way" (Ibid.).

As "the actual poets and authors of life," this poetizing would extend to a benediction of life, as it is, *amor fati*. Promising to bless life,

Nietzsche made this his own Saint January resolution of the great year of eternity: "I want to learn more and more how to see what is necessary in things as what is beautiful in them—thus I will be one of those who make things beautiful" (GS §276). This alliance of science (necessity) and art (creativity) is the art of living and it is the practical achievement of Nietzsche's joyful science.

5

❧

Pindar's Becoming

Translating the Imperatives of Praise

Become the One You Are:[1]
Philology and Philosophy Between Nietzsche and Pindar

Nietzsche's aphoristic injunction—*Become the one you are*—has been identified as a mistranslation of a line from Pindar's second "Pythian Ode" (72), Γένοιο οἷος ἔσσι μαθών.[2] The phrase in question is troublesome even in routine translation,[3] but—and this elision is the problem—Nietzsche's version leaves out μαθών—having learned.[4]

If Pindar's verse is difficult to translate (as indeed it is), there is no shortage of standard and standardizing translations. Thus William H. Race's 1997 translation, "Become such as you are, having learned what that is"[5] offers concision in contrast with the nuances of Sandys' fifteen-word version: "Be true to thyself now that thou hast learnt what manner of man thou art."[6] Similarly spare, Barbara Fowler's disarmingly straightforward, literary translation gives us: "Be what you know you are."[7]

Extended readings of the line in question have always been in contextualizing translation to highlight the didactic emphasis. Thus R. W. B. Burton argues that Pindar's phrase serves as a supplemental encomium directed to Hieron, the champion mule charioteer, just where Hieron himself epitomized a "Dorian aristocrat." The word of praise corresponds to what it is to be noble: "The poet holds up to Hieron a mirror in which he may look and know himself, urging him to be what he is, one of the ἄνδρες ἀγαθοί."[8] For Burton, the point is to serve as

75

a chiding reference to the "proverbially wise" judgment of Rhadamanthus whereby it can be claimed as the counter-to-the-ideal horn of an imperative's yoke: "the king [Hieron] . . . has for the moment fallen short of the ideal of wisdom." In this way Pindar's imperative becomes an exactly counterfactual plea, urging Hieron to live up to his own better potential:[9] "Colloquially then, γένοι᾽ οἷος ἐσσὶ μαθών could be translated 'be your age.' "[10] Using context to reduce the rendering to a record three words, it is the didactic ethos that here retains the tension of the imperative.

More fluidly, more ambivalently, Alexander Nehamas translates: "Having learned, become who you are."[11] Nehamas's version is remarkably similar in its English to Friedrich Hölderlin's rendering in German with its emphasis on experience. In the same way, Heidegger emphasizes observance or measure in reading Hölderlin. But the question still remains: Why would Nietzsche—of all authors—neglect the reference to experience or learning or knowledge that would make explicit the implicit project heard in the "not yet" that serves as the unspoken (and unneeded) anacoluthon—become the one you are [not yet]—the one you can be—*in potentia*? Becoming, after all, is all about possibility. Why did Nietzsche, who knew more than a little Greek and rather a lot about the working of didactic rhetoric and its possibilities,[12] not add the edge of poised promise: and, by so doing, hold and maintain the measured guideline of "learning" first and foremost?

For reasons of such disputed precision and comprehension, tracing the Pindarian origins of Nietzsche's imperative seems not to advance our understanding of Nietzsche's formulation of the same imperative. The thoroughly received perspective on this matter has assembled good textual grounds for the claim that Nietzsche mis-takes and accordingly misrepresents Pindar.[13]

The trouble with—despite the undeniable fun of—finding Nietzsche mistaken, as the great and enduring trouble with Nietzsche's *Birth of Tragedy* (see Ulrich von Wilamowitz-Möllendorff's 1872 critique,[14] and see too its Lacan-inspired reprise in James I. Porter's two books on Nietzsche and philology),[15] is the problem of scholarship. As we have seen, this problem is to be taken literally as what Nietzsche named "the *problem* of science" [*das* Problem *der Wissenschaft*] (BT ii).[16] Throughout his writing, Nietzsche challenges and champions the scientific ideal over the course of his own scholar's lifetime of what he perceived as scholarly disenfranchisement: "Zarathustra is no scholar"—Nietzsche declares and mocks the sheepish source and accuracy of such a judgment, "A sheep came and ate the ivy off my head as I slept" (Z, "On the Scholars").[17] The problem of science (or scholarship) in question is not unrelated to the problem of the supposed correctness or accuracy of Heidegger's etymologies.[18]

But to attack the academic accuracy of such readings is already to substitute another perspective and another problem in the place of the original problem. Thus literalist and supposedly empiricist objections abandon the original paradox with which they begin. One notes that Nietzsche's imperative does not translate Pindar's poetic injunction. Such an assertion claims no more than access to a dictionary yet ignores the larger question of attested obscurity in Pindar's poetry,[19] as well as the critical question of what it would mean to claim accuracy in translation. Nor indeed does it raise the question of the relevance of these two questions (i.e., the poetic meaning of Pindar's word and the truth of translation), the one for the other. One assumes that Nietzsche's phrase is a purported translation of the ordinary kind, and finds Nietzsche insufficient as such. Yet the problem of the meaning of Nietzsche's strange command, now further burdened with the reproof of error or untruth, remains as unilluminated as ever. Typical in analytically styled approaches to philosophy and particularly to reading Nietzsche, but also in traditional approaches to classics, it is implied that there is a path of reading a text that would/could avoid error, a path that avoids untruth, the same path that Nietzsche himself, we are given to believe, could have, or better, *ought* to have followed. Nietzsche's many reflections on interpretation contest the theoretical presumption that underlies this conviction.

Wie Du Anfiengst:
Nietzsche, Hölderlin, and the German Tradition of Translation

Here it is helpful to situate Nietzsche's reading of Pindar with reference to Nietzsche's reception or response to Hölderlin, another poet likewise influenced by Pindar and the whole of antiquity, but who sought in particular to capture the harmonious tension or constrastive variety of Pindar's celebrated ποικιλία."[20]

Nietzsche's recollection of Pindar should thus be seen in the context of a pre-existing tradition of German translation of classical and other languages, particularly Greek. This was a tradition of linguistic exchange, complicated as a "calculated misprision."[21] Evident in Hölderlin, this same tradition recurs in Nietzsche's reflection on the translation of such things as rhythm from language to language (BGE §28) as well as in Heidegger, a tradition that (in addition to Hölderlin as we note here) might well provide the context in which Heidegger urges us to tell him what we think of translation in order that he, in turn, might tell us who we are.[22]

Reviewing the traditional context of translation, one scholar reminds us that with Luther's Bible, *"the book which established written German is a translation."*[23] Recall Wilhelm von Humboldt's reflection on translation, reminiscent of—and fairly contemporary with—Hölderlin's expression in his own (more famous) letter to Böhlendorff on near or national sobriety and foreign fire. Reflecting upon the same appropriate/ appropriative relation between one's own language and the foreign, von Humboldt muses that "every translator will always come to grief on one of these two rocks: either to the detriment of national taste and language, sticking too closely to the original, or to the detriment of the original, keeping too close to the peculiarity of his nation."[24]

An exactly extreme (this is Voss's legacy to Hölderlin, and thence to Nietzsche and so on) preoccupation with translation characterizes German thinking. It may be argued that we overlook this tradition, its Hölderlinian turn and express context, at the risk of failing to see not only the sense of Heidegger's comment on Hölderlin in that same tradition but also what Nietzsche's sparely framed parsing of Pindar in a friendly (if also, as we see now, all-too-German) context, can gain for us precisely as seekers or lovers of knowledge.

The key to Nietzsche's encomium or imperative word to us, *Become the one you are*, is Nietzsche's 1873 citation of a poem by Hölderlin reflecting the same archaic circuit of life, recurrent we might even say, as *amor fati*.

> "A mystery are those of pure origin
> Even song may hardly unveil it
> For as you began, so will you remain,
> And much as need can effect,
> And breeding, still greater power
> Adheres to your birth
> And the ray of light
> That meets the newborn infant." Hölderlin.[25]

Hölderlin's poem begins with mystery and contains the provocative and very Pindarian claim, that "as you begin, so shall you remain [*Wie du anfingst, wirst du bleiben*]. The poem, one of only two quoted from Hölderlin at length in the later notebooks,[26] highlights Nietzsche's reflection, not as the problem of the self but of becoming. The focus is a matter of fate and conscientious, consummation or fulfillment. The task is to catch oneself in the act of being, the moment of illumination, the birth of recognition. As Hölderlin translates Pindar's Pyth. 2, 72, "Werde welcher du bist erfahren"[27]—"become what you have been learned," what you have undergone—the emphasis on learning returns attention to experience: one is to become what one has lived through and which one has only come to know in this transit. For Nietzsche, thought is bound to the truth of origins as the truth of genealogy. Thus this imperative poses the question of the perplexing nature of the subject of consciousness as the nature of the subject itself. Who are we, really? What in us really wants truth? What is the truth of the self?

And even the power of poetry, which Hölderlin named song, can barely prise the mystery of the subject: "As you began, so will you remain." Hölderlin continues: "As much as need can effect / And breeding, still greater power / Adheres to your birth," words that frame Nietzsche's own. The reference to *Zucht*, breeding, formation or *Bildung*, emphasizes not a Nazi allusion to race or to blood, but the Nietzschean sense of *Werden* here poised in coincident contrast with Hölderlinian and Heraclitean *Vergehen*.

Nietzsche's expression entails the elided sense of rule ("Du sollst der werden") and measure ("Wie man wird . . ."). In this sense, to become the one you are is to have found in the course of life, in living or becoming, an answer to the one thing that is said to be needful: the task of giving style to one's character, as a self-appropriation that is only a return. Needfulness and what is needed, the whole of one's beginning, means that one can only keep true to one's start, or as Hölderlin also reflects, "But not for nothing does / our arc return us whence we began" [*Doch es kehret umsonst nicht / Unser Bogen, woher er kommt.*][28]

To keep true to one's origins, as a self-appropriative return to oneself, it is not sufficient, as Nehamas suggests, that one "identify oneself with all of one's actions."[29] Indeed, as Nehamas reads Nietzsche, the task will be "to give style to one's character" but this is interpreted as identifying with (or *being*) becoming. And because, for Nehamas, such identification, such being, is ineliminably a matter of invention or fiction, any paradox in Nietzsche's imperative may be reduced to a literal matter of literature as such.

This project, reading one's life as (self-invented) literature, is in Nehamas's case a matter of reading Nietzsche's life as Nietzsche indeed urges us to read it in *Ecce Homo*, as an achieved and "perfect unity," a unity achieved, so Nehamas argues, by the expedient of writing, as Nietzsche did write, "a great number of good books that exhibit great apparent inconsistency but that can also be seen as deeply continuous with one another."[30] In this way, not only will Nietzsche's writing express his style but the very range of his books can trace the development of this same style, and I agree that there is a great deal of truth in this. But because this is a reductive tactic, that is, not only incidentally analytic, there is also not a little error, because, on most interpretations, this same vision of self-invention slides into an identification of Nietzsche that precisely "mistakes" him with what he is not (this is the sense in which Nietzsche writes in this same context and this same locus: "I am one thing, my writings are another"). Thus the ideal of *Life as Literature* can become a practical project of Foucaultian self-cultivation and this turns, almost inevitably, into *The Art of Living*.

Thus Zarathustra tells himself, himself: Zarathustra holds discourse with himself, just as Nietzsche will do in *Ecce Homo*. To return to Nietzsche's imperative is to return to a specific reflection on the same reflexive paradox of the command to become—not to be, and not quite to identify with—what you are. For this command does not insist that we discover or "find" ourselves where Nietzsche's happily celebrated (but by commentators often unreflected) critique of the subject highlights the very unknown heart of our fantasy image of our "selves."

Asking us to place a question mark behind ourselves as behind our convictions, an objection poised here as much against any possible reader as against himself, Nietzsche reminds us that precisely as seekers of knowledge we remain irretrievably unknown to ourselves, irretrievably because our search for knowledge is turned outward. The philologist Nietzsche is (and remains) reflected in his effort to include his own preoccupations as part of the task of interpretation—on pain of presentism or what Nietzsche named a "failure of philology" (BGE §47).

For philosophers such as ourselves, the last place we are inclined to place a question mark is after ourselves. And in our confidence in the critical search for truth we find a parallel lack or failure of critique. Thus a failure to search for truth is a word for that (self/subject) which is furthest from our minds, which is not the object of self-critical questioning or doubt. And to be fair: this is the problem of the subject as it is posed in Nietzsche's reflexive critique. We are poorly placed to raise the question of our own nature: even if we were, even if we could be, of a mind to do so. We cannot jump over our own shadow: we cannot get behind our own skin, behind ourselves, because of all the nearest and closest things that, as Heidegger points out, are distant from us due precisely to such proximity: *what* we are is most alien to us. For this and related reasons, Nietzsche's "become what you are" or *Werde der du bist* is not and cannot be about the cult—culture—cultivation—of the self, because it is ultimately not about the self at all,[31] neither ascetic self-transformation (or care) nor aggrandizement, but it is about being. The imperative urges an inevitable consummation—*Du wirst es jedenfalls* (KSA 9, 504).

Nietzsche's expression of Pindar's exact, archaic ideal, *Become what you are*, remains incorrigibly paradoxical. In its concision, it is extraordinarily intuitive: counter-intuitively intuitive. The invitation to become what one is is an encomium, praising not one's human potential or possibility for being but what is already a consummate, measured achievement (if not for that a "conscious" one): thus it is one's *conscience* that says: "Become the one you are!" (GS §270). As an encomium, Nietzsche's imperative is a return: its action is not upon or for the future but the past. One is called to come to oneself by way of a return or a recognition consonant with what Nietzsche calls the eternal return of reflection or *amor fati*. And the enduring or ineliminable paradox and intuitive problem, as Nietzsche writes, in a context related to the futural dynamic of the eternal return, is that *you will* do so in any event: *Du wirst es jedenfalls.*

We may thus emphasize the transformed problem of such an encomium/imperative in this context of inevitability where not only are you (already) what you are but where what you are called to become is ominously that which you, in any event, will do. Thus to become the one you are requires more than an "identification" with yourself and more than an acceptance of yourself à la new age thinking or postmodern Nietzscheanism, the last thought to be increasingly passé but all-too common, but rather the reflection of *amor fati* that is the eternal return of the same.

As encomium, the words *Werde, der du bist* are words of valediction that also count as a patent *memento mori* and hence as something of a cliché (or "Gemeingut," as a German friend would say). A gravestone inscription on display at the Musée d'Unterlinden in Colmar can illustrate this point. Among other monuments of the same kind arrayed along the walls around the enclosed garden, one finds a 1604 gravestone written in the local German dialect, "Gedench an wer du bist / und auch wirst werden."[32] Here, the idea is that the reader (passerby) would do well to contemplate his or her own mortal prospects. In *Thus Spoke Zarathustra*, there is a similarly recollective use of the same words as a warning of Zarathustra's destiny, where Zarathustra's animals assert their knowledge of Zarathustra: "who you are and must become . . ." (Z, III, "On the Convalescent").

The very valedictory fashion in which this imperative appears in Nietzsche's letters to Rohde in the Autumn of 1867 as a young artillery officer, enlisted for his year of military service in Leipzig,[33] takes our reflections back to Pindar. Toward the conclusion of his November 3 letter, Nietzsche recalls the farewell party where, along with a few others, Nietzsche and Rohde had erected a monument they had christened "Nirwana" and inscribed with the words γένοι οἷος ἐσσί. Nietzsche writes, "If to close, I refer these words to you as well, dear friend, so might they include the best of what I bear for you in my heart . . . I shall look back with joy and pride upon a time when I won a friend οἷος ἐσσί."[34] Nine years later, Nietzsche notes, "Become the one that you are: that is a cry that is *always* only to be permitted among rare human beings, yet utterly superfluous for the rarest of those rare beings."[35]

Nietzsche's praise of his friend, οἶος ἐσσὶ, as he specifically articulates this in his letter to Rohde, expresses the same sentiment as Rimbaud's "I is an other" [*Je est un autre*], reading Nietzsche's reflections on one's own self-distanced subjectivity in the mode of critique "—you are always a different person [*du bist immer ein Anderer*]—" (GS §307).

As I read it, it is in this sense that one should understand Nietzsche's aphorism noted in quotation marks in *The Gay Science*, "What does your conscience say?—'You should become the one you are' " [*Was sagt dein Gewissen?—'Du sollst der werden, der du bist.'*] (GS §270). In this same spirit Nietzsche writes to himself as author in the mode of self-formation that he will patent as his own in *Ecce Homo*: "Become more and more the one that you are—the teacher and fashioner of yourself" (KSA 9, 555).[36] And in the first section of the fourth part of *Thus Spoke Zarathustra*, we hear a similarly self-creative, literally educing reflection: "For I am *he*, from the heart and from the beginning, drawing, drawing toward me, drawing up to me, raising up, a drawer, a trainer, and a taskmaster who once bade himself, and not in vain: 'Become what you are!' " ("The Honey Offering").

The archaic phrasing alluding to Pindar's Greek in Nietzsche's letter to Rohde also recurs in *Thus Spoke Zarathustra* on no theme other than friendship in the section entitled "On the Friend" [*Vom Freunde*].[37] There Nietzsche reflects on the relation the hermit bears for himself as the relation to the self's other. For such, between the self that is my own, that is: the self with whom thought holds its own discourse, the friend is "always the third person: the third is the cork that prevents the conversation of the two from sinking into the depths" (Z, "On the Friend"). The associative allusion to Pindar's Pythian II recurs here in Zarathustra as well—for Pindar characterizes the poem he sends to Hieron as a bonus offering, (the so-called Castor song): "This song is being sent like Phoenician merchandise across the grey sea" (Pyth. 2, 68). Such corks, indicating the locus of sunken goods, insured against loss. Thus Pindar's poem promises to weather untutored fancy, floating above both slander and flattery.

> just as when the rest of the tackle labors
> in the depths of the sea, like a cork I shall go undipped
> over the surface of the brine. (2, 70)

In this way, the reflective voice, the transcendent balance of light feet, turns out to be the gift of friendship and it is that which takes us back to the word of praise or encomium. Because such buoyancy requires the judgment of a Rhadamanthus, there is a reticent solicitude in the warning that one refrain from presenting oneself carelessly, but this is also to say, that one is urged to take care with one's care of one's self for the sake of the friend, masked and groomed, made beautiful. One is *not* to show oneself before one's friend ungroomed or uncultivated. "Should it be an honor to the friend that you give yourself to him as you are?" This solicitude corresponds to one's reverence for and responsibility to the friend: "You cannot groom yourself too beautifully for your friend: for you shall be to him an arrow and a longing for the overman."

It is not simply that all Nietzsche's efforts for the sake of the friend were to fall short of lasting friendship. His note in *Ecce Homo*, using a fisherman's metaphor for his writing and complaining that there were "no fish" to catch (EH, "Prelude to a Philosophy of the Future," §1) recalls his early letter to Rohde, affirming the importance of writing only for those related to one in spirit and thus only to those able to understand one's writing. Such fishhooks are *selective* ventures, and it is with regard to this selectivity that Nietzsche asks, "Perhaps I know as much as anyone else about fishing?" (Ibid.) Ergo and as if to compound the problem of the friend, and in the same way as, at the end of his life, Nietzsche could seek to become *both* father and mother to himself, it can be argued that in the end he also sought to be his own best friend:[38] the same vocative address that draws us so intimately into his text is an address that turns back upon the author himself, to seek out and to find only his own ear.

Returning to the textual, archaic context of the commandment Nietzsche used first to hail his friend and later to greet himself, we do well to ask what the words (themselves and alone) might mean. We may analyze the reflex of what this imperative commands as such: Become the one you are. *You*—that one that you are—that *x*, *become* the very one that you are—that *x*. Because ordinary logic would fail us here, yielding little more than, or at a solecistic, grammatological best, nothing but a tautology, we can note a quasi-zen tension between becoming (future or anterior protention) and finished or perfected presence.

This is the same paradox in force in the classic locus of this imperative, in standard literary or classical analyses of Pindar's Pyth. 2, 72, where the same koan-like asseveration seems to hold and to parse it commentators allude to a skein of intrigues and resentment. We are told that the phrase is a tease, a rhetorical ploy, a piece of flattery, proffered rather limpingly, after the work of the poem had been completed (where, attesting to the problem of naming it a *Pythian Ode* and so placing it altogether, the ode itself was not the "official" victory poem but only secondarily commissioned). After bidding farewell to Hieron as the addressee of the poem, we now hear a coda, likewise addressed to Hieron, greeting him at the start of what is thus a new poem. *Become what you are*. Otherwise said, reversing the order of the phrase to reflect its context: Now that you have learned (what manner of man thou art), become the one you are. In this context, the expressed imperative begins a series of contrasts contra flattery, contra rhetoric, contra poor judgment, contra bad poets. Hieron, the noble born, and hence consummate, athlete, is urged to become worthy of the measure of his achievements—in contrast with, so the play of words or implied tone: the imminent danger of falling short of the same nonetheless enduring measure.

I add the last words above: *the same, nonetheless enduring measure*, to emphasize what is essential in Pindar's gratuitous reflection, the so-called Castor song, or Phoenician addendum and what most commentators, from Burton to Most, tend to overlook. Such supplementary musings are not a rebuke nor do they work as flattery, as flattery is currently understood. Pindar's Greek nationality, his heritage and his language, is itself part of the interpretive problem. As Alasdair MacIntyre, tracing the deadened aura of virtue, underscoring its shadow in the modern, post-enlightened world, has sought to remind us: if Nestor's rebuke to Agamemnon in Homer's *Iliad* urges a course of action adverting to an excellence (*agathos*) without however at the same time contending that any course of action could really (potentially) abrogate that same excellence or position,[39] the very least to be concluded is surely that neither Homer nor Pindar offer us hypothetical or practical much less categorical imperatives. Hieron is urged to become the one he is: a tautological urging. The recollection of the childish aesthetic misjudgment is contrasted with the judgment of wisdom, Rhadamanthus, and the scope of being is only seen from the perspective of the whole.

Ethics and Time: Stamping Becoming in the Likeness of Being

"Become the one you are" seems to be the imperative of authenticity itself. As a word of praise, it commands both potential being and the consummation of time. This is so in Pindar as in Hölderlin. Likewise, in Nietzsche, it is not a word directed to mere being, nor indeed to personality (however disappointing this may be to fans of modern sports competitions or self-improvement, Pindar does not encourage Hieron, recollecting his achievements, to live up to them or to be himself, or to "act his age" as Burton renders it, but just and only to conform to his way of being in time). This imperative word of just praise is an authentic encomium. It lauds Hieron as an appeal only to come into his own precisely by recognizing it.

It is, by contrast, *prudential* advice that commands: become honest, because that is *not* what you are or because it is what you are at risk of losing (and because honesty ensures felicity, or else because it is commanded "Thou shalt not lie," or else because to do otherwise violates reason itself, and hence you qua rational, inevitably wish to be honest, to add the suppressed premise of any assertoric practical syllogism), become righteous just because as it now stands, you fall short (or may come to fall short) of righteousness! Such recommendations or urgings are meaningful because the logic of becoming here is consonant with practical reason and the practical possibility of self-invention, of self-transformation.[40] It lies in the power of mortal beings to undertake activities that transform them, remaking themselves or acquiring another nature by learning (or Aristotelian habituation), thus overcoming themselves in terms of former limitations, remade in the light of a new ideal. Thus one can be asked to seek oneself (when it is assumed that until now one has not sought oneself), and some readings would have Nietzsche say, through the mouth of certain readings of Zarathustra, that one can also be called to transcend oneself, thus is one invited to *become* an *Übermensch*.[41] Thus, we might be tempted to rename the subtitle to Nietzsche's *Ecce Homo*: "How To Be What You Are.—How to Be Yourself." The endorsement: "Be yourself" seems to offer only encouragement and affirmation, only consent. It would thus also appear on this reading that Nietzsche's "will to power" is exactly a will to self-assertion, or acceptance, giving credence to the historical legacy of this notion throughout the fascist instaurations of the last century and continuing on in our own materialist egoism or current cult of the self: Be yourself, be what you are, or, more gently, follow your bliss . . .

But acceptance, be it of fate or the self, if we are to learn nothing else from Schopenhauer or from the Stoic tradition, requires an abnegation of the will and Nietzsche puts his command differently. And even here we can draw from Zarathustra for understanding: *Nothing can be required*—what *would be madness* would be to imagine that the will *can* willingly cease to be what it is or *become* non-willing. To become the one you are, so he tells us, will require that you turn your own will upon itself. If the will cannot will against its own nature, if willing cannot become nonwilling, if the will is powerless against time and its "it was," like the stone fact that shatters the steel force of will, the will is exactly not powerless on will as the durable course of *ressentiment* alone would prove.

Teaching the will to will backward as Nietzsche proposes to do, turns it back not upon the past but precisely back upon what is immediately, consummately present: thus it turns the whole of will, desire, or ambition, back into what is *already* what it is. It is for this reason that Nietzsche promises to explain *how* one becomes what one is. This is a practical philosophy and in this poetic word of praise lies perhaps the heart of Nietzsche's ethics.

And yet, as philosophers, we ask if one is only to become the one one is, without regretting or resenting oneself, without wishing to remake or redeem oneself, is it not true that one has already accomplished

the task: a perfect *fait accompli*? Nietzsche's paradox of time and destiny—that is *amor fati*—in the light of the teaching of the eternal return,
remains because it is not a vicious but an exactly perfect or perfected
paradox: a paradox delightfully, deliciously full of possibility: an already
achieved or "standing" paradox.

And yet, to return to the contradiction with which we began, given
that you are what you are anyway, where do we locate becoming? Following Parmenides, we may not identify (reconcile or equate) being and
becoming.[42] To stamp becoming in the image of being seems to set
becoming above being: the ideal is the ideal of organic Romanticism:
Werden im vergehen, of flux, or, as Nietzsche famously expresses the lived
meaning of becoming for philosophic sensibilities: in terms of organic,
very bodily, very visceral, very physical, and very limited life, that is, in
terms of a serial course of growth, procreation, death, all characterized,
above all, by suffering. Thus we can anticipate Nietzsche's rhetorical
preoccupation with suffering and pain, in life and in love, inextricably
bound together.

For these and other reasons, the call to become the one you are
remains a hollow or empty imperative. If the goal, say, is only to arrive
where we already are (as Martin Heidegger argues as the teacher of
hidden or concealed truth, *aletheia*), surely we might dispense with the
imperative form. This dispensation takes us right back to the self-inventive
literature of writing the story of one's own life. Yet for Heidegger,
following both Hölderlin and Nietzsche and, in his own time, following
Pindar's own recognition, the point is that this—merely to be the one
you are—is precisely not given as such, nor is its consummation automatic for mortal beings, always at odds with what we are. This is the war
of memory and desire against the past and hoped for future. This is what
Nietzsche means by *ressentiment* or rancor, this is a war of the self with
itself, with what one has become, with what one has done. For we can,
and we do, fall short in being. We can fail in becoming what we are,
despite the fact that we do become what we are in any case, because we
can fail on the level of becoming itself as creatures of implacable resentment. This contrast is what Allison hears in his account of the eternal
return of the same.[43] Likewise, it is here that Nehamas's suggestion: to
be becoming, properly comes into its own—not as an identification with
becoming but precisely as being (being in) the flux itself, the flow of life,
that is that part of life that is a thing apart from literature, beyond the
reductive reasonableness of identification. The functioning of grammar
and the meaning of words and their logical implications is not enough
to save us from being unknown to ourselves, not only because, as already
mentioned, we have never thought to seek ourselves but because it may

well be that we are blocked from seeking ourselves. In any case, we presume upon without questioning ourselves, even when we question God, the world, and those around us. Hence even when we doubt, even when we doubt ourselves, we do not put ourselves in question. Wherever would we stand, where would we have to place ourselves with respect to ourselves to pose such a question?

How *does* one become, as Nietzsche says, what one is? Moreover, why is an account of this doing and this becoming of any relevance, especially if this is what one will in any case do? If we are to read Nietzsche's account in its most articulate locus we will need to reread *Ecce Homo*. Bearing the subtitle of our current question, *How One Becomes What One Is*, reading his epigraph as a key to the text, we have a book relating Nietzsche's story of himself, which he recounts—so he tells us—to no one but himself alone "and so I tell myself myself."

This is the story he tells "on this perfect day, when everything has become ripe and not only the grapes are growing brown, a ray of sunlight has fallen onto my life: I looked behind me, I looked before me, never have I seen so many and such good things together" (EH, "Epigraph").

Despite its title, because of its subtitle and because of the paradox of its thesis ("I am one thing," Nietzsche declares, "my writings are another" [EH, "Why I Write Such Excellent Books," §1), *Ecce Homo* is not a biography. How are we, who know Nietzsche *only* through his books, who cannot but imagine his being exhausted in his writing, to understand this invitation (this prohibition) to and against the man? How is he to be one thing, his writings another, *precisely for us*, precisely for the reader who cannot know him as a man, as a human being, apart from his writings? Who is the Nietzsche we are warned against mistaking, here taking him in the wrong fashion, in a book that perpetrates what would appear to be this very mistake by giving an account of the man himself, so wise, so clever, and so on? This is a book about Nietzsche's books, recounting the conditions of, the genesis of, Nietzsche's writings and what we read about his person always remains ordered to this. Hence Nietzsche offers an account—a recounting—of his own books.

Who is Nietzsche, who can he be for us, late-born in fact not ethos, who can never know him? How else could he have come to become what he is than what he tells us? What else is there? Indeed, and in an extraordinary measure, *Ecce Homo* is all about Nietzsche's books, if it is also true (and this is the deepest sense of Nehamas's important insight) that Nietzsche himself seemed to think of himself in terms of his books—his best present for Cosima Wagner was a *preface* to a not yet written book. This was the most seductive gift Nietzsche could imagine, as Allison recollects in *Reading the New Nietzsche*. And Nietzsche would return to his published books to rewrite his prefaces, completely reworking the influence of his works in the process, such as his "Attempt at a Self-Criticism," and so on. Books rather than children, Nietzsche proposed, as he famously regarded the creative disjunction between the two as an exclusive one: books or children, not both. In this way, Nietzsche means what he says when he calls Zarathustra his son.

In this esoteric manner, *Ecce Homo* will not be the story of Nietzsche's life but rather of the books he writes: the adventure of the development of his reflections on those texts and into other texts. To become the one you are is to become what at the end of the day Nietzsche found himself to be at forty-four years of age, having composed all these—so many and such good—books: *The Birth of Tragedy*, his *Untimely Meditations, Human, All Too Human, Daybreak, The Gay Science, Thus Spoke Zarathustra, Beyond Good and Evil, On the Genealogy of Morals, Twilight of the Idols, The Wagner Case. . . .*

Ecce Homo is an *auto-biblio-graphy.* As Sarah Kofman reminds us at the start of *Explosions,* her two-volume study based on her lecture courses on *Ecce Homo,* this was a book deliberately written as a bibliographical testament.[44] For patently venal reasons, on Kofman's account of it, Nietzsche wrote to satisfy a publisher's requirements and thus he justifies a new publication of nothing but a row of already published books, such a new publication was needed in turn to satisfy an author's wish, lacking readers in the wake of the then-extant editions of his work and hoping for the future to offer new editions to a world of readers ever new. As Kofman argues, it was where and because no other candidate could be found to offer such a retrospective review and summary of Nietzsche's works to appease such a publisher's demands, in advance of reissuing a new edition of those same works, that Nietzsche himself wrote his own overview and thus meant to provide what everyone else evidently lacked the intellectual insight and the courage to have done or to do. Thus Nietzsche, as Kofman puts it in so many words, wrote his own cummulative summary of his oeuvre, composing in the process what might be called in a perfect literary mode, an "*over-book.*" Thus the plausibility of Nehamas's thesis that such a reflex can only be about a life (lived) as literature.

Nietzsche further confounds the issue here by writing, "I am one thing, my writings are another." And, above all, just to be sure that we do not miss the reference, we are invited to read this as an invitation to come to know the man, the author himself—*ecce homo.* Thus it is that we are likewise asked to refrain from mistaking the one with the other. By his works, as any good pastor's son would know, we, his readers, shall know him. Thus he calls, "*Listen to me! For I am thus and thus! Do not, above all, confound me with what I am not*" (EH, "Foreword," §i).

Becoming and *Bildung*

Nietzsche's own expression of the need to give style to one's character entails the exactly, rigorously cosmological interpretation of the doctrine of the eternal return in its strongest and most literal determinist and statistical form. As in the description of the collision of time in the Gateway of the present moment or *Augenblick* in *Thus Spoke Zarathustra* (have not all things been and must not all things recur: " 'Must not whatever can run its course of all things, have already run along that lane? Must not whatever can happen of all things, have already happened, been done, and gone by?' " [Z III, "On the Vision and the Riddle," §2], as in the original context of the phrase, "You will do so in any case" [*du wirst es jedenfalls*] [KSA 9, 504], it can be seen that Nietzsche's teaching declares itself as an assertoric statement or descriptive account. What is at stake in the so-called cosmological (or theoretically strong) articulation of the eternal return is the force of the by no means separate (or weaker) "moral" (or performative) imperative that is the resultant of the thought of the eternal return, "My teaching says: so live, that you must wish to live again is the task—you will do so in any case. . . . Eternity reigns."[45] In the teaching of the eternal return of the same, as the insight of the moment, Nietzsche presents the whole and singular blessing of a life as a whole, as it can be seen forward and backward, bound to iron necessity or chance. Without everything just as it was, with nothing altered and holding nothing alterable, nothing at all—not even the most transient, ecstatic moment of happiness or joy—*can* have been.

Causality works forward in this kind of passionate affirmation only by working backward like the ray of sunlight Nietzsche sees shining on his life: "I looked backward, I looked forward, never did I see so many and such good things at once." Nietzsche's account, telling his life to himself, thus *works* upon his life as a word of praise. This praise or affirmation transfigures the glance, transfiguring what *was* into what *was willed as such*, which is the meaning of what it is to will backward, declaring: "*how could I fail to be thankful to my life?*"

To *become* what one is, one must take over one's own life as an invention; even more importantly and at the same time, one must learn love.[46] The need for love, for learning how to love, and an active erotic deed or lived passion or expressed, articulated desire expresses the importance of what Nietzsche calls benediction or yes-saying. To learn love is to learn to bless and this love has an extraordinary mien: as human as divine.[47]

The benediction that is such a word of praise is the affirmation of the great and the small, "a yes-saying without reserve: to suffering itself, to guilt itself, to the most questionable and strangest in existence itself." For Nietzsche, such a comprehensive yes-saying is needed for reasons of actual and physical reality. Its necessity is a matter of pure fact: simply because "nothing that is can be subtracted, nothing is dispensable" (EH, "The Birth of Tragedy," §2).

To say that "nothing can be subtracted" is a *selectively inclusive* encomium. It does not mean that there is or was or will be "no suffering," no guilt, nothing strange and questionable or that there are no painful or inhumane things inflicted or suffered but—this is the meaning of fate—that everything about what is is necessary or needful. What is required or needful is everything, where everything is necessarily and fatefully contingent upon exactly what is and has been as it was. This is everything that preceded, accompanies, *and* succeeds each moment. Ergo, so Nietzsche argued in a beautifully, elegantly Goethean modality, reprising the whole of Faust in a single question: if, in a single tremendous disposition or if in the happiness of a moment, one were willing to affirm or to bless even one joyous fruition, one inevitably wills everything that has been as necessary, prerequisite, for the moment itself to be at all, and one wills, one commands what will be in the selfsame moment.

Reflecting the knotted interpenetration of everything that is, where "nothing is self-sufficient, neither ourselves nor things," Nietzsche notes that the "first question is by no means whether we are satisfied with ourselves, but whether we are satisfied with anything at all. Assuming we affirm a single moment, we affirm not only ourselves but all existence" (KSA 11, 307).[48] Echoing the *Saitenspiel* that is the full soul trembling like a strung chord sounding with happiness, Nietzsche notes that "all eternities were needed to produce this one event—and in just this moment of yes-saying all eternity was called good, redeemed, justified, and affirmed" (KSA 12, 308).

Thus Nietzsche retrospectively describes his own Zarathustra as "*yes-saying* to the point of justifying, of redeeming even the entire past" (EH, "Thus Spoke Zarathustra," §8). As he praises in this way, he is able to bring together into one "what is fragment and riddle and dreadful chance." The lean time and the wreckage of life, the failures and the humiliations are as necessary as the full and perfect moment of time, as the consummate turning of life. The stumbling move must be caught, not denied or named an error or an illusion; rather has it to be both blessed *and* turned into the balance. But, on all realistic terms, the times of difficulty are the times that are hardest to hold, hardest to yearn for, hardest to keep.

The key to both suffering and joy is not about staying the moment (to repeat Goethe's poetic formula for honoring the moment in a frozen tribute to its beauty) but letting it go. Thus we hear Nietzsche's strangest language in the face of suffering. Faced with the prospect of pain and in the face of loss, Nietzsche speaks of *sacrifice* and *gift*.

It is the idea of sacrifice that remains as the most troubling part of what Nietzsche's teaching of the eternal return of the same entails on the level of true misery, real horror, genuine and not merely academic suffering. This is the meaning of his imperative to become the one you are, as what you will, in any case, do. Not a quietism, Nietzsche emphasizes the ineluctable necessity of becoming together with the impossibility of eliminating pain. There is no way to a philosophy that makes it possible, in Theodor Adorno's words, to "write poetry" in the wake of Auschwitz—which does not mean that Paul Celan or René Char did not write such "poetry." One wants a way beyond the moral justification of duty, a way that would teach one to see the future and transform it, and what Nietzsche offers in place of the dutiful ideal that commands us to frame an imperative for our philosophizing such that it would be impossible to permit inhumanity on the order of the Holocaust (or dare we say, on the order of the utter oblivion and neglect of even the word for the cruelties perpetrated in the name of revenge in bombing Afghanistan and the once and future Gulf War (now going on [and on] in Iraq) is a philosophy that, in advance of all external events, all contingent brutality, would enjoin us always to act in the love of our neighbor or the hope of eternal salvation. We already have such a philosophic foundation in the Scriptures, this is well known, and we have a philosophic formulation of such a command already before Levinas in Immanuel Kant's uncanny invention of a categorical imperative that would *avant la lettre* or apart from the Bible itself nonetheless enjoin its most stringent commandments, grounded not on faith but reason. Denying reason to make room for faith, one sets aside a philosopher's rule for the sake of the gold of the living Word. Nietzsche wants something other than the imperative rule of righteousness because one cannot separate the self-gratifying succor of reason at its own service from the ideal of salvation, be it through pure, triumphant reason in practice, or, reason denied, be it achieved through faith.

Contra the ethical imperative (which Nietzsche claims "reeks of cruelty," echoing Jacques Lacan's all-too-clever alliance of Kant with Sade), Nietzsche offers an affirmation that redeems the innocence of becoming. This is the teaching of the eternal return of the same and it is something commentators find seemingly more cruel: an affirmation of pain and violence as not only inevitable but necessary, of age and death and change all as necessary and as a reconstitution of the becoming that brings such change, absolved in itself as innocent, without fault. Commentators have supposed that the sheer promulgation of the doctrine of the eternal return of the same affirms every event in history. Reflecting on oneself, one is immediately called to a reflection on the destiny of the universe. No wonder Nietzsche calls us "beings who play with stars" (KSA 12, 40).

Nevertheless, what the eternal return of the same teaches is that you, you *yourself,* will return, as Nietzsche's Zarathustra famously emphasizes "—not to a new life or a better life or a similar life . . . [but] this identical and selfsame life" (Z, III, "The Convalescent").

Nietzsche's imperative commands us to affirm not the past of others (a morally questionable preoccupation from the perspective of the Nietzsche who would find such a concern to be as reactive as a preoccupation with deploring, pitying, mocking, or indeed, denouncing the past of others), as a generic historical past, but much rather and exactly the past that is our own—that is your life as you have lived it—the past as it bears on that part of being about which only we have and can have as our concern, our affirmation, and our denial.

And, to be sure, we are brought to the depths of despair less on the manifold accounts of the inhumanity inflicted by human beings upon other human beings, or even as wrought against non-human, but living beings in general, or against the earth itself, than by a reflection on ourselves, in all our pettiness and all our much-esteemed value for and to ourselves.

In our "loneliest loneliness" we are affected by ourselves (our most alone aloneness) and this is not quite the thought of Hiroshima, not Auschwitz, not the firebombing of cities, Dresden, London, Baghdad, not the violence of African and South American warlords against their own peoples, not the Athenian holocaust of the island-dwellers of Melos, not the fall of Nineveh. Much rather what we mourn is the smallest of all such horrors as we reflect on ourselves. We look backward and forward on the ground of such remembered pain, and in Robert Burns's words, *we doubt, 'an fear.* To teach the eternal return of the same, to teach *amor fati,* is to teach us to let such doubts and terrors be for ourselves.

The doctrine of the eternal return does not teach us to say of Golgotha, once again! or of Waterloo, once again! or, once again! the fall of twin skyscrapers shaken down to Manhattan's famously unshakeable bedrock: you take yourself out of history with such an affirmation, but for Nietzsche, as the hourglass of existence is turned, your bit of life goes with it, among all the other bits of dust. Moral objections are born from the all-too comfortable conviction that such a yes-saying is not about our bit of dust but all the names of history—a moralizing justification that preserves (as Nietzsche teaches us, this is the working of *ressentiment*) our more immediate fears.

If good things are often little enough as we see them in our own lives, the point of *amor fati* is to love life on this earth as it is, rather than

for the sake of a future redemption.[49] Thus Nietzsche's New Year's resolution, expressed in what would originally have been the concluding
book of *The Gay Science*, was a universal affirmation, blessing life.

If Nietzsche, despite his creative reminiscences to the contrary, did
not begin his inquiry into *The Birth of Tragedy Out of the Spirit of Music*
as a conscious exploration of the erotic dimension of tragedy (this was
the very unsubtle criticism made by Wilamowitz in his review of
Nietzsche's first book),[50] he certainly concluded his lifelong investigation
into the tragic in this fashion. Thus he declared the "Dionysian
phenomenon . . . as a means to understanding the older Hellenic instinct,
an instinct still exuberant and even overflowing: it is explicable only as
an excess of energy" (TI, "What I Owe the Greeks," §4). The Dionysian,
the erotic dimension, is Nietzsche's "triumphant Yes to life beyond death
and change: *true* life as collective continuation of life, through procreation, through the mysteries of sexuality" (Ibid.). Nietzsche's now eroti-
cized consciousness of the tragic insight colors both the affirmative and
the reactive dispositions of abundance and need. Whatever is replete with
overflowing energy cannot be conserved—this is the economy of expenditure or expression: affirmation. The will to power that is a capacity for
expression can only be given out without reserve.

By capacitative contrast with such overflowing abundance, the
modern impotence of fear seeks to preserve or save itself, to keep itself
in reserve. Such a conservative impulse cannot imagine (and can *never*
believe) that such overflowing power, such great health, "one does not
merely have, but also acquires continually, and must acquire because one
gives it up again and again, and must give it up" (GS §382). The will
lacking power is the will to power that does (and can do) nothing but
conserve itself in the power it lacks, already played out, already without
reserve. This is the dynamic difference between the will to expend and
the will to save. If one cannot spend more than one has, expenditure
remains at stake. Like any economy of the body and its health/sickness,
an erotic economy is an economy of expenditure. Bataille and later
Klossowski and Blanchot as well as Deleuze will make more of this bodily
economy seen from the perspective of what Nietzsche calls the Dionysian.
Here, the decadent or nihilistic desire for power is bound to failure.
Where, as Nietzsche continually repeats from the end of his *Genealogy of
Morals* through his *Antichrist* (or *The Anti Christian*), the nihilistic,
played out, or decadent will is an exactly grasping will *to* (acquire) power;
in contrast with such a needy will, power, positive and flourishing power
can *only* be maintained if continually spent, lost, expressed. The course
of desire sacrificed is the eternal return of the same.

If one thereby changes nothing (this is what it means to speak of
illusion), the point will be that in the transformative insight that is the

gift of such joy, one *wants* to change nothing. Taking one's life as it has been, Nietzsche's idealizing commandment to become what you are, the friendly word of praise to yourself, encouraging, celebrating, blessing yourself as you have become yourself is thus a sheer or transparent or even—for it makes no difference to the Nietzsche who never relinquishes his earliest insights into the coordination of truth and lie—an *illusory* gilding of the life you have been given and as you have found yourself in living it.

What would be error in such an illusion (what would be unmeasured, immoderate), would be to calculate this end as a goal, however obliquely. One can calculate (so Nietzsche reflects on the moral inspirations of dieting) to undertake particular restrictions for the sake of a return to a more expansive condition of life. But exactly such practical purposiveness is at odds with Nietzsche's word.

Does this give us a way to effect the impossible alchemy Nietzsche proposed to himself as his own task in *The Gay Science*—to make things beautiful, and hence to make them lovable, exactly *when they are not?* For the sake of the love of things *as they are* (fate or destiny), Nietzsche's practical aesthetics invites us to work the magic of art, as the artist does, to *make* things beautiful *when they are not*—the means for this is an artistic intoxication or love, winning a consecration or blessing of what is our own.

More than a word contra humanity, as supposed readings of the overman suggest, and much more than a charge to a superhuman spirit, or divine conscience within, Nietzsche, like Kant before him, sought blessing apart from faith. If this was a purely rational exercise for Kant, it acquired an all too real urgency for Nietzsche on the cusp of what would become the most violent century in the spirit of technoscientific rationality. Heidegger abandoned this project in the life of the world to come with his retrospective reflection, *Only a god can save us.* Nietzsche's already fulfilled, already consummate friend's imperative, spoken to yourself, as a friend would speak: become what you are, takes the measure thereby of divine blessing as the perfection of finite life. This consummate imperative was Pindar's word of praise, as we have seen that Nietzsche repeated it to himself as he had called out to the friend of his youth, οἷος ἐσσί.

Music, Pain, Eros

6

⁖

Philosophy as Music

As articulated in Socrates' deathbed confessions—as Plato frames this wonderfully literal conceit—the idea of μουσική, that is, the art or practical technique of music included philosophy among the broad range of the arts guided not only by the attunement of Apollo's lyre, said to have been teacher of the muses, but also the wild dance and intoxication linked with Dionysos (and thereby, so it is said, to the irrational temperament of the aulos or reed pipe).[1] If Socrates adds a hymn to Apollo and substitutes Aesop in the place of Dionysos as a supplement to his practical life of philosophizing, his original conviction that music *included* philosophy, as a technical or practical musical modality, was not exceptional in ancient Greek culture.

And in philosophy itself, the metaphors of music are not lacking: the pre-Platonic philosophers use musical language to the extent that the Rumi-intoxicated classicist Peter Kingsley can call attention to the "sound" of the syrinx in Parmenides' haunting description of the chariot wheels that take him on his journey "beyond the gates," carrying him to an endpoint Kingsley teases his reader as bearing similarities to the mouth of chaos: the gaping of the gates to which the goddess leads Parmenides.[2] In the heady wake of Parmenides' wild allusions, Heraclitus speaks far more clearly of the hidden attunement or backstretched connection that is, as Socrates too would claim, the secret of harmonious variance. Still more literally, if no less mystically, Pythagoras held that both mathematics and philosophy derive from the structural nature of music. And with the same regulative measure that follows an understanding of the political/ethical effects of musical tuning, Plato could erect an ideal city on the same well-tempered measure as a foundation and Aristotle could invoke the ethical ideal of musical harmony (N. Eth. 1131a–1134b).

In the illustrations to follow, including a reading of Plato's myth of the Socrates who made music, Nietzsche's aphorisms, and Heidegger's language of paratactical silences, I suggest that the practical art of *hearing*—with our eyes—in a philosophic mode presupposes not only the author's but the reader's discursive art of musical attention. The philosopher is called upon to be more than a mantic Hermes, bringing the story of the demon's message to Socrates' secret attention. Instead, an acroamatic, inherently mutual, or dialogical, hermeneutic is called for: a hearing attunement on the part of the speaker/listener who is, at least as Nietzsche dreams of such a listener, one for whom listening has become a practiced art: the art of discourse or Hölderlin's *Gespräch*, related to but not the same as what Gadamer unassumingly called conversation. Such a *musical ethos*—if we may recall the radicality of Georgiades' suggestion—might inaugurate a musical society.[3] So this works in conversation, for the said—and the unsaid. But how to bring the ear into reading? How is the reader to hear but also play and engage Nietzsche's questioning of the value of truth, the order of moral value? What tact, what discursive rhythm is involved with Heidegger's invitation to take Nietzsche's invitation to overcoming still further, inaugurating a "new beginning," "a step back,"—"thinking"?

The Muses as the Origin of Music in Ancient Greek μουσική

According to Liddell and Scott's *Greek-English Lexicon*, μουσική is as "*any art over which the Muses presided*, esp. *music or lyric poetry*."[4] For Homer, the art of the Muse embraced the broadest range of the fine arts as eloquence or cultivation in general. Thus the appellation *musical* [μουσικός] characterized one "skilled in music," as well as, and more "generally, *a votary of the Muses, a man of letters and accomplishment, a scholar*."[5] Giovanni Comotti's *Music in Greek and Roman Culture* recalls the scope of these dictionary entries in his elaboration of the broad meaning of music:

> in the fourth and fifth centuries B.C., the phrase *mousikos aner* would be used to indicate an educated man, able to comprehend poetic language in its entirety. The unity of poetry, melody, and gesture in archaic and classical culture made the rhythmic-melodic expression contingent on the demands of the verbal text. The simultaneous presence of music, dance, and word in almost all forms of communication suggests also the existence of a widespread musical culture among the Greek peoples from the remotest times.[6]

In musicology and, as we have already seen, in clear connection with its relevance for philosophy, Georgiades underscores the difference this breadth makes for our understanding of music in Ancient Greece: both prose language and poetry derive from the exactly, comprehensively musical complex of "*musikē*."[7] This musical complex is what makes it possible to understand the otherwise irremediably paradoxical, or at best metaphorical, meaning of *musikē* as Georgiades affirms its formative and literally ethical sense. As we saw in connection with Nietzsche's reflections on the musical prosody of ancient Greek, what Georgiades regards as the "ethical functionality" of ancient Greek is more than a metaphor of Plato's imagination (or Pythagoras, before Plato, and Aristotle afterward). The difficulty that we have with respect to antiquity as modern readers extends to our acoustic sensibilities as well, this Nietzsche named the "acoustic illusion" that where one hears nothing, there is nothing to be heard (EH, "Why I Write Such Good Books," §1). As Nietzsche writes to his teacher, Ritschl, the scientific or scholarly key to a sensibility to the music of antiquity will be to resist the tendency to think that one can empathize with the spirit of antiquity (KGB 3, 173), and to the same extent Nietzsche will constantly emphasize the need to learn how to hear (GS §334, cf. KSA 7, 57).

Dramatizing something of this distance, Comotti's book includes a photograph that virtually captures the specific difference that may be heard between *musikē* and modern music. This bronze figure of poetic, melodic, and gestural unity, a statuette from Heraklion's Achaeological Museum, represents a singing phorminx player. The pose—Nietzsche would have said, the mimetic pose, the miming gesture—of this small bronze (700 BC) is reminiscent of pre-Greek Cycladic culture found in the singularly liquid marble harmony of the well-known example of Cycladic Art: a seated figure playing an angular harp (ca. 2800–2700 BC).

It is significant that both Martin West and Warren Anderson have identified such seated harp players are identified as male figurines. Why so? Note that here it is not my concern to argue a gender-theoretical or feminist line. Hence, my question does not suppose that the figures in question "might" ("could") *represent* female players (the scholars who codify the conventions used to identify such statues have determined that these figures represent male harpists). Here, I advert to nothing but the stylization of form as such, iconic in these two figures. The harmony of the composition strikingly streamlines identification (one way or the other), highlighting the *conventionality* of convention or scholarly identification. As an embodiment of the consummate stylization that is style itself, not only the sex but also the distinguishing humanity of the Cycladic figure disappear in the organic form of a body in perfect harmony with the triangled arc of the harp as a player playing "the song itself" (cf. Rep. 531a–532c). The theme of physical analogy or harmony between sculpture and music is the architectural foundation of the music of philosophy and, to speak with Nietzsche, of the music of music, the music of life.

Now, and as we have already seen, for Georgiades, *musikē* articulates the *Eigenart*, that is, the *essence* of the work in particular. It is for this reason that he can emphasise that in its grammatical form, *musikē* is not substantive but primordially or prototypically adjectival, corresponding to the muses: "It means 'musist,' 'corresponding to the Muses.' "[8] In this way the ancient Greek conception of music varies with particular works and because music also articulates itself as an activity in play, music in its very primordial essence can never be a finished, objective, or fixedly given work. Thus Georgiades can emphasize that a classical "musical" "education" presupposes "musical activity," and Nietzsche invokes the multidimensionality of this same musical education.[9] If we are to believe Georgiades, we may also say that this dynamic dimensionality reflects the unique character of the Greek language.

But to say this is to emphasize, as Nietzsche did, an insurmountable conflict between the ancient conception of music and our contemporary understanding of music, an understanding, which, like our contemporary concept of art, refers to a world *apart from* the everyday.[10] Thus Georgiades reminds us that an intrinsically Western perspective "presupposes the field of tension which formed between the word and art, between language and music."[11] Because art and truth formed "an indissoluble unit" for the ancient Greek, to translate μουσική "simply as music," would be a serious mistake.[12] Indeed, it "cannot even be termed 'art' in our sense."[13] Even for otherwise-minded scholars such as Warren Anderson, the modern word *music* should not be used "to render *mousikē*." As Anderson clarifies further, "[t]he Greek term designates here the oral training in poetry—sung to lyre accompaniment or recited without it—that had for so long been the means of transmitting the values and precepts of Greek culture."[14] *Musikē* corresponds to the entire cultural scope of such training.

The modern tendency to reduce music to the "organised" art of sound obscures the equiprimordial sense in which *musikē* could be regarded, as Nietzsche saw it, as the enabling element of intellectual or spiritual as well as aesthetic and physical education and in which *musikē* figures as the determining force of both individual and societal character [*ethos*].[15] Yet the ethical character of *musikē* works *because* of the literally musical linguistic difference Georgiades constantly emphasizes between the language of archaic Greece and contemporary Western languages.

The fundamental musicality of antique Greek resides in the tonic interval of fixed time: long or short, that is also what Georgiades names its static character (its *masked* dimension, paralleling the fixed expression of the masks of ancient Greek theatre). Most musicological studies of antiquity recognize this connection. Nevertheless, and as a recent compilation centering on nothing but the historical record of ancient Greek musical notation makes clear,[16] the tendency even in such newer studies continues to represent music in antiquity as comparable to music in contemporary contexts. This is music as independent form or as an ("absolutely") distinguishable accompaniment to a text. But this representation may be more than presentist but too occidental a conception, as Martin West himself is careful to remind us.[17] Indeed and even more so than in the case of postmodern music,[18] it may turn out that we need all the resources of ethnomusicology to approach the ancient Greeks just because their music is not merely non-Western but ultimately silent for us or only available after a great effort on our part, especially assuming we take Nietzsche's suggestions to heart.

As we have seen at the start, Georgiades has emphasized that ancient Greek was expressed in consummate, completed time.[19] "The rhythmic principle of antiquity is based not on the distinction between the organization of time (the measure, system of accents) and its filling in (with various note values), but rather on intrinsically filled-in time."[20] For this reason, both Georgiades and Nietzsche would maintain that music inveigled ordinary discourse in ancient Greek culture.[21]

In his lecture on "Greek Music-Drama," clarifying and thereby highlighting the alien spectacle that an ancient Greek tragic production would have been for the modern guest, Nietzsche initially describes the actors as so weighed down by the ungainly, immense painted masks and thickly padded costumes of the actors that "they could hardly move" (KSA 1, 519). Encumbered in such a physical fashion, they simultaneously bore an enormous artistic weight: "in order to make themselves heard by a mass of spectators, 20,000 strong, they had to speak and sing in their strongest voice through the mask's wide-open mouth," delivering "some 1600" verses over the course of "ten-hours" (Ibid., 520). The ideal of a clear presentation was central in all this because the competitive exercise was all about a performance in the face "of a public that inexorably punished every extravagant tone and every incorrect accent" (Ibid.). For Nietzsche, this unswerving exactitude was the reason he could argue for the absence of harmony in its contemporary musical sense: "choral song was distinct from solo song only by the number of voices" (Ibid., 530). "The primary exigence was that one understand the content rendered in song" and "when one really comprehends a Pindarian or

Aeschylean choral song with its daring metaphors and conceptual leaps, it assumes an astonishing art of execution and at the same time the most extreme character of musical accentuation and rhythmicality" (Ibid.). In addition to the parallelism of this musical-rhythmical periodic construction, Nietzsche points to its simultaneous adumbration in orchestral dancing [*Orchestik*]. What this meant then for the Nietzsche who thereby resolves the imperative ideal that music subordinates words to melody is found in the dynamically broadened context of ancient Greek music-drama in its lived performance practice: "As the music intensifies the effect of the poetry, so the orchestral dancing articulated the music. Hence the poet, in addition to being a tone-poet, had also to become a creative choreographer" (Ibid.).

This selfsame unity of practice was reflected in those aspects of the tragic poet's compositions that could not be sung. For Nietzsche, however, even these would have to be regarded as a "part recitative" (KSA 1, 530). Rather than any kind of duality between music and the dramatic word, "the ruling influence of music held dominion even in language" (Ibid., 531).

Nietzsche merely sought to render the most abstruse aspects of antiquity present to his listeners in the best nineteenth-century classicist's sense of *Vergegenwärtigung*. Georgiades goes further because, for him, the speaking subject was engaged not only as a speaker but always also as himself an active listener and vice versa. From this he drew a specifically philosophical and ethical conclusion, arguing that ancient Greek presupposed a community and possessed a community-building power nearly impossible to imagine today. For Georgiades, this implies a fundamental ethic of responsibility that encourages his assertion that the working power of a Hitler would not have been possible in Ancient Greece.[22] For my part here, I cannot maintain that I know whether or not this is correct, and, manifestly, it would be difficult, if not impossible, to imagine how his assertion would be confirmed (or, to be sure, contested).

Neither Socrates, nor Nietzsche, nor in the end Heidegger (although he was perhaps most sensitive to the imperative need for such a recollection) have been able to restore the loss of the full power of music in language. Heidegger thought it was enough to stop in silence. Most of us have learnt that such silence falls short, which shortfall does not mean that today's scholars—and this includes the present author—can lay claim to the final word.

Philosophy as Highest Music: The Technical Case of Socrates

Pythagoras's esoteric, exactly allopathic, conception of a musical harmony between world and soul renders music the soul of philosophy.[23] In

his *Republic*, Plato agreed with traditional wisdom concerning the consequences of any changes to the musical modulation of the state: "when
the modes of music change, the fundamental laws of the state always
change with them" (Rep. 4.424c).[24] Where writing (just because it is
writing) underlines what is no longer a universal practice,[25] Plato's expression of philosophy as a kind of music invokes a precisely traditional,
culturally Greek conception of music. As the love of wisdom or theory,
philosophy installs itself precisely in the place of music as the highest or
noblest kind of music. And it is in this same correspondent, musical
company that the idea of the musical practice or ethos of philosophy is
more than a matter of metaphor.

In apparent tension with the negative judgment on music rendered
by the *Republic*, the question of the right relation between music and
philosophy is addressed in the *Phaedo*, the locus of the question with
which we began regarding the primacy of philosophy over poetry or
music. The ethos of music represented both the very Pythagorean possibility of harmonious resonance of soul and world as well as, and especially in its more popular modes, posing the most effective threat to the
rational dominion of the soul. Music in its breadth could be regarded as
constituting a vital danger to philosophy (as the highest music beyond
popular music and poetry) and consequently the practice of music threat-
ened Plato's Socratic ideal of philosophy as the project of conceiving and
living a well-ordered or examined or good life. As the greatest of erotics,
to use Nietzsche's language, a seductively ironic Socrates left the world
nothing but music without a text, naming philosophy the highest kind of
music in a teasing gesture that closes off the rest of what had been ancient
music—and it is for this reason that Nietzsche always links Socrates, along
with Euripides, to the death of tragedy.[26]

Socrates, the amateur sleuth of the good, pretending incompetence and distraction as a ruse to convert (convict) his interlocutors (a
contemporary model would be television's Lt. Columbo), was notoriously fond of seemingly vulgar and simple allusions and oaths, as well as
banausic and pedestrian examples. We all know that the immortality of
the soul is the theme of the *Phaedo*, where Socrates recounts his eleventh-
hour musical exercises. And soul or not: the dialogue is all about the
body—beginning (and ending) with strikingly graphic references and
physical descriptions. The pathos of the body includes pain and feeling,
especially erotic feeling. Thus the dialogue begins with Socrates sending
away his wife, to spare himself (we are told) the unseemly sounds of her
anguish. Scholars are quick to advert to the typically ironic foreshadow-
ing of the later lamentation of Socrates' manly disciples at the dialogue's
conclusion, ignoring the relevant detail of Xanthippe's tacitly intimate
support of his last earthly night, which she spends with him (the dialogue

begins with his male friends waiting impatiently for morning light for his jailors to admit them; Xanthippe is already within and is sent away, with the women of her household, when the men enter).[27] In the same bodily context (and it is the same metaphor within a Platonic context), Socrates' fetters are loosened and Plato offers us the sight of Socrates rubbing his legs (a dissonantly homely image, not unlike the paradoxical picture of Heraclitus surprised by his admirers with his back to the kitchen stove). Socrates here remarks on the very Greek tension between pain and pleasure, and this resonantly erotic detail, by analogy, is likened to his death to come. We are further offered so many details of Socrates' death that it is possible to reconstruct the ancient aetiological understanding of herbal pharmaceuticals, and we here refrain from commenting on the typically scholarly blush that accompanies any reference to the precise place where the poison rises to call forth Socrates' last words, referring to a debt: a rooster to be paid to Asklepius, god of healing.

In this confessional context, Socrates reports that all his life he was persistently visited with the same unusual dream figure, repeatedly uttering an imperative caution. The oneiric warning never varied: "make music" (*Phaedo* 61a).[28] Throughout his life Socrates had always assumed that because philosophy itself represented the apex or culmination (*hē megistē mousikē*) of the musical arts (*Phaedo* 61a), for his part, so he supposed, he had *always already* been in compliance with the dream's command, dedicated as he was to philosophy. But the recurrence of the dream remained a perplexity for him and the circumstance of his death-sentence brought him to rethink his lifelong interpretation of philosophy as music in the highest sense. And in an ironic gesture of superstitious appeasement that does not accidentally recall the pious preoccupations of Cephalus in the *Republic*—where Plato subjects music to the most stringent regulations—Socrates affirms that he casually turned to practice "music in the commonly accepted sense," composing a hymn of praise to Apollo, together with a few common verses (construed from Aesop's fables).[29] As the parallel with the *Republic* suggests, it is not difficult to extend this observation of Socrates' very musical achievement to the composition of the dialogue as playing "the song itself," as Ernest McClain has done much more esoterically.[30]

To take the Socrates of Plato's *Phaedo* at his word is to invert the order of indebtedness that is the pattern of its final irony. There is no challenge to the conception of philosophy as the highest music in the ultimate recourse to everyday musical kinds. Indeed, the triumphant point of the conclusion is reinforced by the lyre lessons West tells us Socrates takes at the end of his life, because, as West also tells us, like champagne to us, for the Greek, "Music is constantly associated with celebration."[31] Given the Platonic representation of the body as the prisonhouse of the soul, Socrates' causal reflection on the relation between pain and pleasure at the moment of his preliminary liberation from his fetters at the start of the dialogue foreshadows the ultimate Platonic ideal of liberation from the illusions of earthly life. And we find a similar parallel, again, between the vulgar practice of music, sacrificed by way of expiation to the noble healer god, Apollo, as the dream god, leader of the Muses, *Musagetes*,[32] and the rooster Socrates asks Crito to sacrifice to the folk god of healing, Asklepius.[33]

Confessing a vain conviction in precise accord with Greek tradition, Socrates appeals to the popular practice of music. Thereby he exploits an exoteric image for the sake of his most consistent account of the priority of soul or pure form over body or sullying matter. But if we have learnt nothing else from Freud, it is the secret of the secret as confessed or betrayed in such an overtly provocative manner. And we wait for the second master of suspicion to hear Nietzsche wondering about the character of a Socrates who might have lived a life not dedicated to philosophy as the highest music but to the breadth of music as such.

The Thinker's Concinnity:
Nietzschean Discrimination and Nietzsche's Aphorisms

Nietzsche may well be the philosopher most often associated with music and, as Ernst Bertram has argued and Curt Paul Janz has demonstrated at length, Nietzsche's life was bound up with music.[34] This is a literal claim in the case of the Nietzsche, who played piano with a passion and performative skill that captivated most of his contemporaries.

Today we are surrounded by the technologies of musical reproduction: television, radio, on planes, in cars, elevators, waiting rooms, and personal or portable music systems, ipods and other mp3 players, cellphones and organizers, as well as home "theatre"—in the sense of the total artwork of a surround-sound set up or system—all such means of musical reproduction are seemingly ubiquitous. This was not so in Nietzsche's day but that is, of course, not to say that there was less music. In particular, Nietzsche's involvement with music was an active one, playing, interpreting or else composing. Thus when Nietzsche suggests that we take his texts as his musical legacy to us, his meaning is less metaphorical than one would otherwise imagine. Indeed, Nietzsche's convictions in this regard were so deep and so early that he designed a title page vignette for his first book, commissioning a woodcut engraving of Beethoven's Prometheus. As we have seen previously, in Nietzsche's eyes, his first book was to have been a literal contribution to music.

The Birth of Tragedy is one thing. But how should we read Nietzsche's *Thus Spoke Zarathustra* as music? How do we begin to parse this un-book as a book of parables, modeled on the Bible, as so many commentators have informed us? Are the gospels a kind of music too, or, more dangerously ironic than Socrates' Aesop, has Nietzsche merely set the New Testament in (much-too-free) verse? Or, as more than one commentator has told us, is Nietzsche's *Zarathustra* not much rather modeled on Wagner's Ring?[35] To give the question of the self-declared musicality of Nietzsche's texts another edge, how do we read Nietzsche's claim in his self-criticism of his first book, as this descriptive assertion could catch the exactly poetic sensibilities of Stefan George: "it should have *sung*, this 'new soul'—and not spoken!" (BT iii).

To answer these questions I have elsewhere had recourse to a borrowed metaphor, in the somewhat conceptually dissonant term, *concinnity*.[36] I take the term in its very harmonic musical sense, largely affine to the sense of the Latin *concinnitas* as rhythmically attuned diction. Rhetorical concinnity resounds in the well-rounded or happy phrase. The derivatively architectural sense of concinnity belongs to or is part of the original term employed by Cicero and Seneca to indicate the successful musicality of expression. But where one may speak of music as liquid architecture and where Nietzsche insisted on architectural resonances to describe his definition of the *grand style*, the term *concinnity* evokes its own architectonics in addition to its rhetorically musical dimensionality.[37] This properly architectural significance originates with Alberti's definition of concinnity as the coordinate harmonization of naturally divergent or contrasting parts.[38]

The need for such musicality in reading (and thought) is not figurative (or allegorical and so able to be conceived as an isolated interpretive turn) but a literal (i.e., textually explicit) requirement. Indeed, a musical reading is ultimately, tropologically, a fundamental prerequisite for a resonant hermeneutic of the aphorism written, as Nietzsche writes, and he declares that he so writes, in a reader-ironizing counterpoint. And on Nietzsche's author's or compositional side, such a musical or aphoristic style supports or enables an account of the world without truth, without event, without remainder.

For the reader's part, a specifically musical attunement will be needed just to follow (to read) Nietzsche in his textual ventures. Without a musical reading, Nietzsche offers only contradictions and logical infelicities—at best a kind of poetry for philosophers with a taste for it, at worst, sheer nonsense. Nietzsche quite literally plays philosophical perspectives upon philosophical perspectives, conceptual scheme upon conceptual scheme.

Yet most immediately relevant because most pernicious, the same musical character also quite deliberately (as we have seen previously), quite complicitly, renders his text liable to misunderstanding through simplistic or shortsighted or flattened and consequently inadequate readings. Mis- or short readings exemplify the connection between the aesthetic nihilism that inheres in the pathos of truth and the interpretive truth of truth, the truth of illusion, or the truth of the world as will to power.[39]

The elusiveness of Nietzsche's style derives from the specifically Heraclitean—and intrinsically musical—tension of his aphorisms. In virtue of this literally compositional tension, the aphorism can—and must—be read against itself. In other words, the music of Nietzsche's aphoristically composed text inevitably plays upon both sides of the listening/reading dynamic. The advantage of what I call a "concinnous" or musical reading is manifestly useful for the interpretation of any aphorism, any rhyme, any joke—but such a musical reading is indispensable in the case of Nietzsche's aphorisms. Falling short of the aphorism's music, deaf to the resonance of the text, the prosaic reader, like Socrates' uncomprehending vision of the music of tragedy, not only fails to "get it" as we say, but as a failure unawares, such an error is thus incorrigible.

This does not mean that Nietzsche will not be understood: it turns out that it is no kind of philosophic achievement to "get" a sense of Nietzsche's meaning—in contrast, say, as the scholar Erich Heller years ago first noted, with Kant. Despite Nietzsche's constant anxiety regarding his posthumous reception, not only does he seem to be read today, with readers far beyond those claimed by most philosophic authors, but it also seems to be a simple matter to understand or at least to read Nietzsche. And to be sure there is truth in this commonsense judgment. As we have already noted, every Nietzschean aphorism has several points to spare. This characteristically Nietzschean excess tends to guarantee that any reader, whatever their level of hermeneutic, philological, or philosophical competence, may rightly presume at least a partial notion of the text. Nietzsche's esotericism is not exclusive: it works by including—thus Martin Heidegger shakes his head in aggravation and annoyance and a *Book for Everyone* becomes a *Book for No One.* Such an esoteric style is articulated by means of the aphorism that, precisely in its musical expression, distinguishes readers and readings by making the distinction one that functions or works on the reader's part. This is also why, throughout the course of his life, Nietzsche hoped that he might nonetheless "fish" for the right readers using the "hooks" of his writing to do so (EH, "Prelude to a Philosophy of the Future," §1; cf. KGB 3, 166).

The musical dimensionality of Nietzsche's aphoristic style is consequently capable of instigating an ironic reversal or provocative inversion of best intentions (this is the reflective core of esoteric Protestantism). Thus, bristling in a forest of related aphorisms in *Beyond Good and Evil*, Nietzsche warns, "He who fights with monsters should look to it that he himself does not become a monster. And when you gaze long into an abyss, the abyss gazes into you" (BGE §146). [*Wer mit Ungeheuern kämpft, mag zusehn, dass er nicht dabei zum Ungeheuer wird. Und wenn du lange in einen Abgrund blickst, blickt der Abgrund auch in dich hinein* (KSA 5, 98)]. Without hearing its resonantly rhetorical "English," without a specifically attuned or "musical" reading, the reader may indeed catch Nietzsche's reference to monsters *and* the danger of the abyss while still missing his emphatic melancholy. To take Nietzsche's words flatly or atomistically, as logically ranged terms and not as the reticulated elements of a provocatively framed aphorism, is to obscure their inherent backward (and rhythmically musical) reflex. And it is no accident that a number of readers offer interpretations assuming that the monstrosity of the abyss is a specific or accidental and hence avoidable enemy and that the point of the statement is tactical avoidance rather than a word confessing the inevitable entanglement of engaging corruption or evil. The threat of the abyss thus becomes yet another threat to modernity, a thing to be banished with the light, a monster lurking in the closet, a fault to be paved or smoothed over with the landfill of "values." But for Nietzsche—and this is the Kantian dimension that would most intrigue Heidegger—the knower's confrontation with the abyss inevitably admits the abyss in the knower. All engagement is relational. Like the backward and forward relationality of Nietzsche's reconstruction of the human subject poised by and not merely posing the object of judgment, there is a coordinating movement inherent in the progress of verse and music. Correspondingly, and this is important, a musical reading is impossible unless the reader holds with—as one must when listening to (reading) a poem or a piece of music—the beginning through to the end.[40]

A similar interpretive dynamic accounts for the typically flattened reading of the warrior's maxim listed at the start of *Twilight of the Idols*: "From the military school of life," and which continues "—What does not kill me makes me stronger" (TI, "Arrows and Maxims"). Here, the prose or routine reading overshoots the emphatic prelude as context: one reads Nietzsche's contention as literal, literally prosaic truism. Nietzsche, one takes it, says the same thing as any military or personal sports trainer might say: what doesn't kill one, makes one stronger. This too includes a challenge against the declaration. And the title of the maxim, the one for whom such a personal rule might be supposed, offers a backward echo: from such a perspective on strength and intensification, but also compulsion, blind loyalty, and humiliation, it is said, and said from within a military mode, that what doesn't do one in, leaves one better off or makes one stronger. Or so the tired veteran hears the tale told from Pericles' Athens to Lincoln's Gettysburg and still today in everyman's army. Nor is it untrue as such, rather it is only and exactly half true, just as to be half-dead is also to be half-alive. On matters military, Archilochus reclining on his spear to drink—in a dialectic reflection poised with this very posture—muses on the attunement of two truths held in balance. For the first: "Some Saian sports my splendid shield: / I had to leave it in a wood, / but saved my skin. Well I don't care— / I'll get another just as good."[41] What is then usually rendered in helpful translation as living to fight another day, promises another kind of restitution or payback. The more suitable "leaving-present"[42] Archilochus threatens for his future return can only be dealt from a mercenary's perspective—beyond the "military school of life." Nietzsche's *Kriegschule des Lebens* captures the brutality of the training ground from the vantage point of an irony that goes beyond it.

For another example, in a provocatively brief declaration, a two point epigram is offered against the iconic image of truth: " 'All truth is simple.'—Is that not a compound lie?—" (TI, "Arrows and Maxims"). In this case, the epigram undoes itself overtly, but here, as it may be claimed in every Nietzschean stylistic case, without dissolving the original contrast. And it is this original contrast that matters.

Taking up the musical sense of the aphorism keeps both its subject matter and its development as parts of a whole. Thus positions, statements at variance with one another are not simple contra*dictions* but contra*puntal* (the terminological contrast need not be taken literally but can be read metaphorically here, as "music"), balanced exactly in their opposition in the backstretched connection Heraclitus long ago compared to that found in the (philosophic) bow of life and the (musical) lyre.

Nietzsche named music the intimation that perhaps the solution to the suffering of existence was not its redemption (religion) or alleviation (modern science) but its intensification, in the *Rausch*, the intoxicated play of the Dionysian, standing as the frozen music of the grand style, a name for a life ventured or vaulted in time.

We have seen that like Hölderlin on whom he was dependent for so many things, Nietzsche too underscored the meaning of tragedy as joy. Borrowed from Hölderlin, it is this solution that Nietzsche articulates throughout *The Birth of Tragedy*, especially in the second half of the book, the part that is usually read in terms of its associations with and hence its debts to Wagner and rather less, but more importantly as it should be read, in aesthetic terms. On these terms, Nietzsche challenges Aristotle's understanding of the pleasure of the tragic work of art. In a two-line poem to "Sophocles," we hear Hölderlin's insight: "Many have sought, but in vain, with joy to express the most joyful, here, finally, it speaks itself out in sorrow to me." [*Viele versuchten umsonst, das Freudigste freudig zu sagen, / Hier spricht endlich es mir, hier in der Trauer sich aus.*] This poem to the genius of tragedy illuminates Nietzsche's conclusion to his first book. But Nietzsche shows how this joy, this poet's joy, can work—and it will do to hear Beethoven just as Nietzsche writes to Wagner in the first preface to *The Birth of Tragedy*, in order to hear what our eyes tell us in the vignette Nietzsche includes of *Prometheus Unbound*. It is music that Nietzsche brings to illustrate how tragedy can work on us, "with joy to say the most joyful."

This is why Nietzsche has recourse to the example of musical dissonance and this dissonance shows us experientially the pleasure of the tragic work of art that is not a melodrama of modern dramatic tragedy and not the purgative expression of grief and fear. Tragic sorrows can work as joy because Nietzsche finds their counterpart in the structure of music, exactly in the dynamics of musical dissonance. Not metaphorically, but literally, in dissonance, the greatest pleasure of music, Nietzsche finds Hölderlin's joy—a joy that is more Beethoven if it is still Wagner, a joy that is Bruch and a joy that might have been consummate for Nietzsche in Mahler or Messaien.

The Special Case for Heidegger's Musical Style: Blessing Muses

If I have argued that what Nietzsche calls "reading with one's ears" (and I name concinnity) is indispensable for reading Nietzsche, I have also argued that a philosophical reading of the Heidegger who links poetry with thinking must be no less musically accented.[43] So much follows as well from Steiner's reading of Heidegger's poetic voice.[44]

Where Heidegger invokes the nearness of thinking and poetry, the saying or ringing of the same that is said in silence is the inherently musical silence of Heidegger's favorite emphasis: the caesura. And this is the key to the musical serialism of Heidegger's style. Such a musical reading may enable us to go beyond both the seductive resonance of Heidegger's text (as Steiner, as we have already seen in chapter 1, sensitively characterizes its esoteric dimension, following Löwith and Arendt but also echoing Gadamer) as well as its well-publicized cognitive opacity.

The musical cadence of Heidegger's philosophic expression, reflecting and keyed to a rhythm of instigative and recuperative concepts, is an integrally stylistic aspect of Heidegger's thinking. The same rhythm tunes the "musical" attention essential to his thought. I shall later return to the claim that precisely as musically styled, Heidegger's text counters the mesmeric aspect Steiner calls the dark side of Heidegger's "orality."[45] This musical energy of Heidegger's thought may be heard not just by listening to recordings of the aged Heidegger speaking but, as Steiner underlines and as he for his own part confirms, simply by reading the text out loud.

Apart from attending to the "musical logic" of Heidegger's writing style,[46] Steiner adverts to what he regards as the lack of a literally specific musical reference as a "tactical," "damaging" deficiency in Heidegger's text.[47] Recalling (but not invoking) the Augustinian example of musical experience (and the character of time), where "immediacy, recollection, and anticipation are often inextricably fused," to illustrate Heidegger's conceptions of (human) being and of (human) temporality, Steiner's initial reading conjoins the experience and the meaning of, the essence of, music: "In music being and meaning are inextricable. They deny paraphrase. But they are, and our experience of this 'essentiality' is as certain as any in human awareness."[48] Yet this music, as Steiner himself underscores, all the while contesting it, is not lacking in fact.

In its dynamic design, Heidegger's text *works* both in anticipation and in return, projecting, catching or recollecting what is deliberately, provocatively let fall by the spoken cadence of the text.[49] Such "music" adumbrates the textual work of Heidegger's philosophic world. If the musicality of Heidegger's text is not exactly not his "life" as music was Nietzsche's life, nevertheless it characterizes Heidegger's style.[50] Thus the musicality of both Heidegger's and Nietzsche's texts embody the specifically resonant ethos of philosophy, as a musical ethics for philosophers *in artibus*, where just this last relation or affinity constitutes the precondition for any kind of answering harmony.

Indeed, indeed. But what of music as such, real music? Is this no more than a metaphor for philosophers, as Plato first tells us, the same Plato who dutifully destroyed his compositions for the sake of the "higher" music making that is philosophy? Am I not a similarly dutiful acolyte in the school of Socrates, reviewing the music of philosophy by way of an analogy with the music of music, the "highest" music, the Platonic "tuning" of the soul? Are these not toneless, even dead words? What about *real* music? What ringing sounds in Heidegger's silence? Is it Cage's Piano Concerto played on the radio—and not even as a concert performance—for the ears of a mystified but therefore captivated Adorno (and much can be said of this exigent frustration of Adorno's relation to postmodern music and even to jazz)? Can one use the metaphor of silence to speak not only of language, as Heidegger does, but also of music? At least one scholar has made the argument that Cage, for example, offers us the way to "hear" Heidegger's peal of stillness: "the snow that soundlessly strikes the window late in the day when the vesper bell rings"?[51] Manifestly the side of common sense works against Heidegger's expression of language (and I have now extended it to include music) as "ringing silence" and yet it is important to note that for all the Doric spareness of his style, Heidegger had already adverted to the problems of defining language in this fashion. At the beginning of his essay on "Language," Heidegger adverts to the commonplace quality of this problematic, by conceding that to talk about language is "presumably still worse than to write about silence" (L, 190). How is it possible to hear the restrained music of a speaking and a thinking that bids us above all to the reserved, anticipatory restraint that as "aesthetic hearing holds back its own saying"? And we need to ask because for Heidegger, "hearing keeps itself in the listening by which it remains appropriated to the peal of stillness" (L, 209).

Reading the Stylistic Strategies of Cadence: *Being and Time* and *What is Called Thinking?*

Heidegger's style is characterized by its clearly didactic structure: proposition, intensification, and recuperation (which we know as *retrieve*). Advancing a particular position or interpretation against the tradition (this is the moment of a provocatively charged or audacious *anticipation*), Heidegger draws out or intensifies the paradoxes of his own position (this is its deliberate falling out). Thus again, "to talk about language is presumably even worse than to write about silence" (L, 190). Precisely for the benefit of the reader's reflection, the working cadences of this deliberately emphatic admission intensifies the text. This moment in turn develops a convicted or properly hermeneutic recollection or return, which Heidegger calls "retrieve." In this triple stylistic turning, prelude, cadenced conviction, and return, the anticipation, work, and resolution of Heidegger's expression is plainly announced in his own text.

Where Heidegger poses his claim and then lets it fall, even heightening its fall, Heidegger addresses what is troublesome for a reader's expectations. Continuing to intensify or push the tradition-specific dissonance of his own pronouncement (contra anticipations, Gadamerian prejudice, Nietzschean convictions), Heidegger's elaborating intensification (or cadence) carries the first assertion to an extreme (and not only, as Jacques Lacan might have said, so that there will be no mistake about it). Finally, we can see the sense of what Heidegger calls the "retrieve," recuperating the thusly charged and now elaborated expression for his own thought. This last recuperation returns the project in the direction

of the tonality to be heard, apart from but also through the ambiguity
of language or thoughtful expression.

To illustrate the rhythmic textual or musical moments of anticipation, intensification, and return, I refer to the very last section of Division I of *Being and Time*[52] just because the section reviews truth, which
is not incidentally the most important conception in the Western intellectual (philosophic and scientific) tradition: "The Kind of Being which
Truth possesses, and the Presupposition of Truth" (SZ, 269). Here,
Heidegger had already, in the context of the tradition and the phenomenological hermeneutic articulation of truth, explained truth as un-
coveredness (ἀλήθεια). Thus, in summary, "Da-sein, as constituted by
dis-closedness, is essentially in the truth" (Ibid.). The anticipatory provocation in this concluding summary is already prepared and is thus highlighted: " '*There is*' truth only in so far as Da-sein *i s and so long as Da-sein
i s.*" (Ibid.) This provocative assertion means, Heidegger explains, "that
entities are un-covered only when Da-sein *is* and only so long as Da-sein
is" (Ibid.). Readers with an understanding of truth as a coordinate function (or correspondence) between knower and the known are thus confronted with Heidegger's intensification of his analysis of truth, advancing
the full implications of the claim that, as Heidegger had earlier expressed
it, entities discovered in the world would in this sense only be "uncovered" for Da-sein as being in truth "in a secondary sense," while
"what is primarily 'true'—that is un-covering—is Da-sein" (SZ, 263).
This claim now resounds in all its dissonance for the ear of a traditional
sensibility to the received meaning of truth, especially scientific truth.
The intensification carries Heidegger's Kantian investigation of truth to
the ontically current order of scientific discourse. Just because this resonance will be especially important in the so-called later Heidegger, it is
important to note that the cadence here resounds against the whole
philosophic/scientific tradition of the value of theoretical truth and of its
ontological locus as perdurant in time:

> Newton's laws, the principle of contradiction, any truth what-
> ever—these are true only as long as Da-sein *is*; and only as long
> as Da-sein is. Before there was any Da-sein, there was no truth;
> nor will there be any after Da-sein is no more. For in such a
> case, truth as un-coveredness . . . *cannot* be. Before Newton's
> laws were discovered, they were not "true." (SZ, 269)

This remarkable cadence (a cadence as it falls out against the metaphysical ideal of objective, out-there-now, real truth) is however recuperated

or given an ameliorative interpretation by an almost immediate return, where Heidegger observes that nothing concerning the falsity of these same laws follows from such a reserve concerning their truth. Thus to say that in advance of their discovery, Newton's laws "were not 'true' " does not claim that they were false once upon a time. Such a proposition or claim would belong to the same accounting or register of formal truth and Heidegger means to go beyond this register.

Using the same turns against the reader's expectations and the scholar's assumptions, Heidegger had earlier adumbrated the meaning of the claim that Being is *given* with Da-sein: "only as long as Da-sein *is* . . . 'is there' Being" (SZ, 255). That this is an ontological and exactly not an ontic claim is recollected in two parenthetic moves: "Being (that is: not entities) is dependent upon the understanding of Being; that is to say Reality (that is: not the Real) is dependent upon care" (Ibid.). And Heidegger employs the same redemptive, cautionary strategy: "To say that in advance of Newton his laws were neither true nor false, cannot signify that before him there were no such entities as have been uncovered and pointed out by means of those laws" (SZ, 269). What this conviction suggests in terms of scientific discovery and understanding is now simply that "through Newton the laws became true; and with them, entities became accessible in themselves to Da-sein" (Ibid.). Thus the disclosure yielded by Newton's scientific discoveries illuminates the domain of physics as the lighting up of the kind of understanding that the poet Milton could celebrate and because "once entities have been uncovered, they show themselves precisely as entities which beforehand already were. Such uncovering is the kind of being that belongs to 'truth' " (Ibid.).

To read this passage, we need a musical reading that does not revert to thinking the truth of what is "out there"—divorced from and apart from the knower, understood above all as perdurant both anterior to and subsequent to discovery. Such a divine notion of the truth (what was, is, and shall be) has nothing to do with the positive qua precisely contingent and positional disclosure of Da-sein's truth in "Reality," where for Heidegger, "*all truth is relative to Da-sein's Being*" (SZ, 270). Because of the nature of truth, this relationality is phenomenological in Kant's sense: it is not reducible to the claim that truth is "subjective." Truth is rather what enables an encounter "with the entitites themselves." Neither is this to be reduced to the suggestion that Da-sein engenders truth. For Heidegger, "truth is only in so far as Da-sein is," and given truth's equiprimordiality of Being, "Being (not entities) is something which there is only in so far as truth is" (SZ, 272).

Where Heidegger invokes the nearness of thinking and poetry, the saying or ringing of the same that is said in silence may now be recognized as the inherently musical silence of the cæsura Heidegger adapts from Hölderlin in a precisely archaic or Greek dimensionality. It is no accident that Heidegger links silence with speech in its most ethical dimension. Thus the later lecture course *Was heißt Denken?* not only offers an acoustic resonance in the German of the title, an allusiveness that cannot be heard in the English, *What Is Called Thinking?*, but exemplifies the work's stylistic advance. It also turns reflexively on a reading of Nietzsche, where Heidegger writes (in a fashion that was to inspire Derrida's stylistic appropriation of the same trope), "We ask: what is called thinking—and we talk about Nietzsche."[53]

Beyond what Heidegger names "one-track [or academic] thinking" [*eingleisige Denken*]—Heidegger's style of writing is sustainedly pedagogic. Thus our reading of the musical dynamic of Heidegger's argument provokes as the effect of a deliberate shock. This is the didactic dynamic of a claim dropped contrary to expectations, clashing with ordinary philosophic assumptions. It is well known that Heidegger's scholastic strategy famously backfires (it leads, at one extreme, to frustration and, at another and more consequent extreme, to violent denunciation), and yet I argue here that it can also teach the forbearance that we need, after Nietzsche, for the sake of the poetic renunciation that Stefan George invokes in order to say what Hölderlin meant by observance. The three-point strategy (provocation or prelude, intensification or conviction, return) works against what Heidegger regards as the ordinary tendency of scholarly thickness: one-sidedly dogmatic statements heard and perceived as such by thinkers locked into "one-track thinking." In this serially musical strategy, Heidegger does more than remind us that we need (as Nietzsche likewise emphasised that we need) to *learn* to think.

The pronouncement that "we are still not thinking" (WT, 35) is not "tuned to a key of melancholy and despair"—even if it is not a piece of optimism. If the assertion nevertheless *seems* "tuned in a negative and pessimistic key" (Ibid.), Heidegger argues that this appearance results from the present circumstance of the failure of thinking. This turns Heidegger from an attention to the keynote to the character or resonant "way in which it [this tuning] speaks." Here Heidegger's musical allusion is overt: " 'Way' here means melody, the ring and tone, which is not just a matter of how the saying sounds" (Ibid., 37).

Reflecting on the paratactic framing of Parmenides' gnomon— "needful: the saying also thinking too: being: to be" (WT, 182). Heidegger illuminates this same ringing silence: "We call the word order of the saying paratactic in the widest sense. . . . For the saying *speaks* where there are no words, in the field between the words which the colons indicate" (WT, 186).

For Theodor Adorno, what Heidegger here invokes as the paratactic character of philosophic discourse at the origin of logical reasoning itself captures the modern essence of atonal music. But for Adorno this essence resonates in Hölderlin's poetry. Thus Adorno writes, "Hölderlin's method, steeled by contact with the Greek, is not devoid of boldly formed hypotactic constructions, parataxes are noticeable as elaborate disturbances that deviate from the logical hierarchy of subordinating syntax. Hölderlin is irresistibly drawn to forms of this sort. The transformation of language into a concatenation, the elements of which combine in a manner different from that of judgment, is a musical one."[54]

This paratactic approach now affords us another musical style, the *serial* modernism of Heidegger's reflections on the participial construction of "blossoming," taking blossoming together with flowing, being together to catch the mutual relation, the backward/forward *movement* of the participial form as musical. Once serialism is counted in place of the paratactic tact of Heidegger's reading of Parmenides, the answer to what is called thinking may be sounded forth: "Thinking means: letting-lie-before-us and so taking-to-heart also: beings in being" (WT, 224). And so taking-to-heart also, also.

As an atypical tonality, a musical serialism in Heidegger's philosophical voice teaches us to interrupt our own always "already-knowing." In this interruption, we are literally compelled to take a step back, turn to another beginning, and in this way, but only as a sheer and fading possibility, we may yet come to hear Heidegger's resonant word, as the *melos* of the appropriative event.

"Saying" for Heidegger "is the mode in which Appropriation speaks" (WT, 266). Saying speaks in every word, saying speaks in silence, and most particularly as the event of Appropriation, as what catches us up, as *Ereignis*, in the *melos* of the song that in "saying speaks." Expressing the way in which we might be so appropriated as the *melos* of *Ereignis*, "the melodic mode, the song which says something in the singing" is the frame of song, arraigned as what lets be, what "lauds," all present beings, allowing "them into their own, their nature" (Ibid.).

Silence can be the kind of attunement in its ringing, its tolling knell or breath, that holds itself out, not sounding what it already knows but seeking an attending, listening word in reply. Such an attunement attends to language, to nature itself, or philosophy. For to say, as Hölderlin says, that "soon we shall be song" proposes the possibility of a musical hearing, the song of praise or wonder that is the sounding shock of wonder: the ringing silence or dazzled mien of philosophic thought broken open at its inception.

7

⌒⌒⌒

Songs of the Sun

Hölderlin in Venice

*B*eyond *the limits of literary and historical accounts of Hölderlin's influence on Nietzsche, which we have already begun to explore with regard to Nietzsche's sensibility to music and sound as well as with regard to the originally archaic meaning of music, it is important to review the musical dimension of Hölderlin's influence on Nietzsche, especially given Hölderlin's own attunement to the dimension of sound.*

Pindar's Shining Paean: Memory and Metaphor

In 1864 (April/May), Nietzsche cites a crucial poem from Hölderlin in his early philological notebooks, a citation followed by two shorter verses from Goethe.[1] Reflecting on the locus of Pindar's metonymic image of the lambent paean (entitled "*Nachtrag* zu der Stelle 'παιὰν δὲ λάμπει,'" [FS 2, 398]), the entry as a whole explores a motif that would occupy Nietzsche's greater creative powers throughout his life. In this case, the compound figure exemplifies the mutually inveigling metaphors of light and sound, the one coloring the other. Nietzsche's treatment of this theme here also included a reference to the sounding wonder of Memnon's statue at sunrise,[2] a mythic figure he later invokes to explain the power of tragic drama as a reversed penumbra of lucid beauty cast like a veil over what he never fails to describe as a "glance into the abyss." The later reference, given in *The Birth of Tragedy*, begins with a subtle and wonderful allusion to tragic dance ("the greatest strength remains merely potential, betrayed in the flexibility and abundance of movement" [BT §9]) and addresses the paradox of tragic insight and dark terror: "the Hellenic poet touches the sublime and terrible Memnon's Column of myth like a sunbeam, so that it suddenly begins to sound—in Sophoclean melodies" (Ibid.).

Beyond the wondrous vision of a sunbeam attuned to the resonant frequency of an Egyptian monument of an unknown order, Nietzsche's early 1864 study explored the metaphoric attunement of the senses: "closely related one to another in an affine manner, like smell and taste," he writes, "are the senses of sight and hearing" (FS 2, 398). Tracing this similarity to the common transmission of light and sound ("through oscillations," or as waves), Nietzsche focuses on this affinity as it appears in folk myth and poetry, illustrating the sensible resonance of light and sound. In the poetic tradition, the metaphors for the one enhance rather than contradict the other and because of this resonant coincidence, Nietzsche recalls Apollo as "a divinity of light and a sungod and, at the same time, as the discoverer and lord of tone" (Ibid.).

Declaring that "it was altogether in the Greek spirit that Hölderlin sung" (FS 2, 398), Nietzsche goes on to cite Hölderlin's "Sonnenuntergang," and it is essential to repeat this in German to illustrate its acoustic influence on Nietzsche:[3]

> *Wo bist du? trunken dämmert die Seele mir*
> *Von aller deiner Wonne; denn eben ist's,*
> *Daß ich gelauscht, wie, goldner Töne*
> *Voll, der entzückende Sonnenjüngling*
> *Sein Abendlied auf himmlischer Leyer spielt';*
> *Es tönten rings die Wälder und Hügel nach . . .* *

Goethe, as Nietzsche observes, also mixes or plays the terms for one sense into those of the other: "A similar intuition is evident when the sage reports that the sun rises with a great sound in the early morning, or as Goethe says: *Clear to spirit ear rebounding / knell of day's renewal sounding*" (FS 2, 398).[4]

Without meaning to deny the crucial influence of Goethe on Nietzsche's thinking,[5] my claim here will be that in contrast with Goethe's exemplary value for Nietzsche, Hölderlin's role in Nietzsche's thinking

---

*Where are you? Dazzled, drunken my soul grows faint / And dark with so much gladness; for even now / I listened while, too rich in golden / Sounds, the enraptured youth, the sun-god / Intones his evening hymn on a heavenly lyre; All round the hills and forests re-echoed it . . .

and writing echoes far beyond Nietzsche's early reflection on the resonances of light and sound.[6] A jubilant expression of the soul's intoxication, a tribute of longing for a vanished god (the elided ellipsis continues: "Doch fern ist er zu frommen Völkern, / die ihn noch ehren, hinweggegangen"*), Hölderlin's song to Apollo anticipates Nietzsche's description of the beautiful dream-birth of Apollinian vision, and both Hölderlin and Nietzsche pair music with the comfort of the dream.[7] The sustained resonance of this early encounter with Hölderlin continues throughout Nietzsche's life, articulated by a patently acoustic or musical influence. The golden tone of the setting sun in Hölderlin's poem resounds throughout the spirit and the substance of Nietzsche's poem to Venice in *Ecce Homo*, reflecting the image and locus of music but also giving Nietzsche's most arresting poetic voice to the soul's pain and its song as it calls to be heard.[8]

Nietzsche's youthful exercise lists almost the whole of Hölderlin's *Sonnenuntergang*.[9] Like the first ray of sunlight tuning Memnon's mythic statue, I argue that Hölderlin's poem had a profound influence on Nietzsche. In this sense, Hölderlin's poem would remain with him until Nietzsche drew on this memory in the best poem he would ever write, composed less to address the golden glory of the setting sun, calling over Hölderlin's wooded hills (although the time of day is not far distant), but a song to the magic of the violet, bronzed night of the Italian city of bridges.[10] The first song was sung as an echo to recall an imaginary friend, as the poet Hölderlin was supposed in the place of such a friend in Nietzsche's seventeenth year; the later song would be sung in the wake of the death of Nietzsche's one-time patron and one-time friend, the musician and poet, Richard Wagner.

We hear and read the connection between Hölderlin and Nietzsche in the drunken, shadowed, glimmering of the soul in Nietzsche's Venetian poem, offering a nearly verbatim tonal recall of Hölderlin's song to the setting sun.

Nietzsche's song, which is plainly an evening song, what Nietzsche classified in his notes as the troubadour's *serenas*, is also, just as plainly in the present context, his *planh*, or *planctus*, that is, a song of mourning and melancholy, evening lights, and music

> *An der Brücke stand*
> *jüngst ich in brauner Nacht.*
> *Fernher kam Gesang:*

---

*Though far from here—to pious nations / Who still revere him—by now he's journeyed.

> *goldener Tropfen quoll's*
> *über die zitternde Fläche weg.*
> *Gondeln, Lichter, Musik—*
> *trunken schwamm's in die Dämmrung hinaus ...*
>   *Meine Seele, ein Saitenspiel,*
> *sang sich, unsichtbar berührt,*
> *heimlich ein Gondellied dazu,*
> *zitternd vor bunter Seligkeit.*
> *—Hörte Jemand ihr zu?* *

Seen in the light of Hölderlin's *Sonnenuntergang*, Nietzsche's Venetian poem offers a glimpse into the Nietzsche who so often turned his writing as a foil to deflect the reader's reflections back upon the reader. Nietzsche's Venice poem opens into the soul's own converse with itself, an exposition that continues until its final reversal, marked with a caesura, here halting on an open note, and changing direction with its last, unfinished word: "Hörte Jemand ihr zu?" . . . [—Was anyone listening?]. Echoing Hölderlin, reflecting the watcher, overhearing and overseeing distant drops of darkly shimmering gold, Nietzsche recalls the Stendhalian promise of the happiness he always imagined to lie just beyond his grasp, like his frustrated reception as a philosopher, or as a musician—a happiness waiting like a wanted friend, somewhere in the distance. An outsider, by default, the watcher on the bridge listens to a song from afar, gives no sign of his sense of isolation or of his responsiveness, and closes with the melancholy echo, is anyone listening?

After "Wo bist Du?" [Where are you?], the conclusion of Hölderlin's first line, "trunken dämmert die Seele mir" [drunken, glimmered my soul], reappears in Nietzsche's conclusion to his first strophe: "trunken schwamm's in die Dämmrung hinaus . . ." [drunken it swam out into the gloom . . .]. The golden sound of sunset[11] is the sound of transfigured light, changing to evening twilight and to night, echoing in the brown and burnished dark. In its place and its time at the end of day, Nietzsche's song in the city of bridges reprises the occasion of Hölderlin's tone-setting answer to the deep resonance of the sunset and the image now heard in Venice, replying, calling again for an echoing song.

---

*Lately I stood at the bridge / in the brown night / From afar there came a song; / a golden drop, it swelled / across the trembling surface. / Gondolas, lights, music—// drunken it swam out into the gloom ... / My soul, a stringed instrument, / invisibly touched, sang to itself / secretly a gondola song, / trembling with sparkling blessedness. /—Was anyone listening? (EH, "Why I am So Clever," 7).

We hear not merely the same sonorities in the words of the two distant poems: Hölderlin's "goldner Töne / Voll," [in golden tones / Full] in Nietzsche's "goldener Tropfen quoll's" [golden drops, it swelled]—or the same play of words and meaning—[*himmlische/Seligkeit*], [*gelauscht/zitternd*]—which resonant echo would be sufficient to suggest that Nietzsche had at least kept the memory of this poem at the heart of a life of thinking on music, but much more the flow and the structure of the cited fragment bears comparison to the directed structure of Nietzsche's poem. Hölderlin writes,

> *... denn eben ist's,*
> *Daß ich gelauscht, wie, goldner Töne*
> *Voll, der entzückende Sonnenjüngling*
> *Sein Abendlied auf himmlischer Leyer spielt;* *

In darker, browner evening,[12] the same lyre play of Apollo's golden youth is transformed for Nietzsche into his very soul: "An der Brücke stand/jüngst ich in brauner Nacht."** The song heard from afar, *Fernher kam Gesang*, recollects Hölderlin's song as the echo of the swelling soul, trembling in its intoxication, now in a more liquid resonance in Nietzsche's fluid play of sound and golden droplets and the distant cradles of magical gondolas gliding beyond sight in the twilight:

> *goldener Tropfen quoll's*
> *über die zitternde Fläche weg.*
> *Gondeln, Lichter, Musik—*
> *trunken schwamm's in die Dämmrung hinaus ...*

Nietzsche's entire soul resonates in attuned response to the golden drops welling on the surface, the gondolas, lights, and the music of the evening:

> *Meine Seele, ein Saitenspiel,*
> *sang sich, unsichtbar berührt,*
> *heimlich ein Gondellied dazu,*
> *zitternd vor bunter Seligkeit.****

---

*... for even now / I listened while, too rich in golden / Sounds, the enraptured youth, the sun-god / Intones his evening hymn on a heavenly lyre;

**Lately I stood at the bridge / in the brown night

***My soul, a stringed instrument / invisibly touched, sang to itself, / secretly a gondola song / trembling with sparkling blessedness.

In this way, the most significant gondola song, answering more than the calls along the distant corridors of Venetian canals, would be the song between Hölderlin's poem to the crown of the day and Nietzsche's twilight song, answered in brown velvet. Like Nietzsche's image of the voices echoing from proximities that may only resound from mountaintop to mountaintop, which Heidegger later appropriated to exemplify the nearness of greatness, Hölderlin's call resounds in Nietzsche's soul. Thus we hear two poetic voices. "Wo bist Du? . . ." [Where are you?] calls forth an answering song from Nietzsche leaning on his bridge in Venice, in the southern night of his own soul—*ein Saitenspiel,* a playing of strings, as Nietzsche names the accord of his soul—singing a gondola song in reply to the one heard—in the remembered tone, poised above the night waters of Venice on the bridge of life itself (in the pensive wake of Wagner's still-present death)[13] thus calling for a reply in turn "—Hörte jemand ihr zu? . . ." [—Was there anyone to hear it?]

Where Hölderlin and Nietzsche and Heidegger invoke the ideals of feast, celebration, and joy in precise connection with thinking or philosophy, Nietzsche's transfiguration of philosophy as a festival of thought (or art) plays between Hölderlin and Heidegger. This complex constellation as the dynamic play of affinity and influence regarding the manner in which Nietzsche's own writing (his "poetic" style), has been seen, after one hundred years of complex and changing reception, to have transformed not only the literary possibilities of philosophic expression but the critical basis and essence of philosophy itself and therewith, again, and only perhaps, the potential of what may be thought philosophy.

Influence and Interpretation

The musical resonances we have found here make it plain that Hölderlin's mark on Nietzsche was thus both brighter and more complex than Cosima Wagner's differently inspired report.[14] Writing what this author regards as his most beautiful poem in Hölderlin's own tone, after a poem Nietzsche had first inscribed in his early notes, a poetic recollection that he almost certainly knew by heart, we also know that he went so far as to pattern what he called his greatest work on Hölderlin's fragments for the tragic drama, *The Death of Empedocles.*[15] But for the scholar—particularly for one entranced with reducing Nietzsche to his "sources" or to tracing out the serial frequencies of a search-string, conducted with the aid of electronic resources (colligating the resources of more "memory" than coherence)—Nietzsche seems to disappoint this same influence, a disappointment that may explain the limitations of today's source scholarship on Nietzsche and Hölderlin.[16]

For Nietzsche compromises Hölderlin in his notes about him—the way Nietzsche compromises everyone and everything, very like Heidegger's notorious obscuring of the received line on the history of philosophy in favor of his own reading. An intriguing aspect of Nietzsche's protean style permits him to give the lie to his own posturing bravado as he speaks it (and for a man who comes to an end in a putative madness so many name similar to Hölderlin's own surmised destiny, this is exactly an excess of identification), reprising his early allusion to the spirit of Hölderlin's paean to the music of antiquity as late as *Ecce Homo*.

We have already in an earlier context referred to Nietzsche's pretended "enthusiasm" (the text in question was a school assignment) for his *Lieblingsdichter* (October, 1861). This affection was expressed in the classicist's traditional exercise (a practice in paedogic formation that can be traced back to its roots in Roman rhetoric), writing a fictitious letter to a fictitious friend (which fictitious letter, in the regular or standard mode of fictitious letters of the genre, Nietzsche appropriated from another source to begin with). As noted in chapter 1 above, Nietzsche's dependence on handbooks and other source studies of rhetoric was by no means limited to his school days, as recent explorations of the importance for Nietzsche's lectures on the rhetoric of Gustav Gerber's handbook on the art of speech have made clear. In the same context, we recall that the charge that Greece was less than original was well known in Nietzsche's times (and novel ideas are hardly in short supply—as the overburdened shelves at the Bureau of Patents would attest). For Nietzsche, as noted previously, the modern ethos of original and creative genius is misleading. Hence, to understand the usual thing that was philosophy in ancient Greece, Nietzsche referred to the very Greek ideal of culture ("Go get yourself a culture, only then will you find out what philosophy can and will do" [PTG §2]). Nietzsche's attention to the singularly Greek capacity for learning was coupled with a reflection on timeliness. For Nietzsche "at the peak of mature manhood, as pursuit springing from the ardent joyousness of courageous and victorious maturity, at such a period of their culture, the Greeks engaged in philosophy, and this teaches us not only what philosophy is and does, but also gives us information about the Greeks themselves" (PTG §1). This character makes all the difference in what would become "Greek" philosophy. For as well known as it was that the "Greeks were able to find and learn" (ibid.) a great deal from others, what Nietzsche challenged was the inevitability of merely derivative stature in consequence. Against the awkward search for philosophical origins, Nietzsche contended that the most developed or "highest levels counted in all things." From this perspective, that is, original or not, the Greeks were nonetheless the originators of "the archetypes of philosophic thought. No philosophic mind has made an essential contribution to them since" (PTG §1).

Here, with the *thumos* of a seventeen-year-old, Nietzsche would betray not only an absorbing passion but a self-righteous, self-identifying, and thereby it is to be thought, self-transfiguring reading of Hölderlin.[17] Nietzsche's sympathy for Hölderlin's poetry and the famed *Hyperion*,[18] including Hölderlin's less well-known drafts for a tragedy on what Nietzsche called the "divine" death of Empedocles (in many senses the basis for Nietzsche's *Thus Spoke Zarathustra*), is clear and manifest by reason of this same transparency, as numerous studies have attested.[19] The same affinity suggests that Hölderlin's relationship to antiquity, including Sophocles and Pindar, taken together with a noble and tragic sensibility vis-à-vis the modern, recurs in Nietzsche's philological formation quite apart from his insightful polemic against the standard account of Hölderlin's unclarity and his disqualifying, quite disreputable, non-bourgeois madness.

Today we are able to celebrate Hölderlin not merely as perhaps the most profound of poets, but thanks to Heidegger and, so I have been arguing, ultimately, thanks to Nietzsche as well, precisely from a philosophical perspective. From a historically analytic perspective, Dieter Henrich's contributions to this philosophic reading are to be set along side others taking a more traditionally continental approach, such as Vèronique Foti and Dennis Schmidt. But this was not always so. Hence in Nietzsche's day, that is to say, when there is any judgment at all, the then-standard scholarly judgment of Hölderlin's poetry condemned it as obscure—as Nietzsche's teacher Koberstein condemned Nietzsche's choice—in the same way and for the same reason that Heidegger's philosophy continues today to be popularly condemned. Similarly, Hölderlin's interest in antiquity (together with his pantheism) was rejected as less than properly or decently "German"—or, in a historical solecism, relegated to the excesses and enthusiasms of romanticism.

In this way, Nietzsche's cribbed school letter outlines a plan Nietzsche does not abandon notwithstanding its derivative origins and despite his teacher's critique (which Nietzsche never directly challenges). Taking this project further, it became "David Strauss, Confessor and Writer," the first of Nietzsche's *Untimely Meditations* (each of which, we recall, and not only the essay on Schopenhauer, may be counted as reprising the formative influence of his elective and affective "educators," his "Erziehern" [UM I §2]). Here inverting the aesthetic claim against Hölderlin by showing its unthinking basis, Nietzsche outlines an early genealogy of what he will later name *ressentiment*, claiming that such critical denigration, as he will always claim and especially in his own regard, can reflect a failure to comprehend (the whole of) an author's work. To understand Hölderlin (Nietzsche), to be able to talk about Hölderlin's (or Nietzsche's own) work, one needs to have read the whole of it, a hermeneutically philological prerequisite as Nietzsche liked to emphasize. Judging criticism in the spirit of inadequate reading in this fashion, Nietzsche identified a plain-minded barbarism in the negative judgments commonly made of Hölderlin, culminating in Friedrich Vischer's condescending account of the poet. Against Vischer, who had condescendingly suggested that what was "tragically" lacking in Hölderlin was a "sense of humor,"[20] Nietzsche argued that what defines the philistine turns out to be nothing less than a mocking sense of humor: the *cultured* barbarian captures the essence of philistinism itself. This many readers will reject if only because this is not the laughing Nietzsche they know: the Nietzsche who "teaches" us to laugh at everything, as so many commentators have told us, the Nietzsche who, shades of Vischer himself, brings "a sense of humor to philosophy."[21]

Beyond his mockery, Nietzsche also shared the same sobriety with Hölderlin, especially with regard to the past. Nietzsche identified cultural philistinism as characteristic of contemporary German culture. By contrast with contemporary culture, this distant fantasy was Greece: here is what was and here is what is, and—far more than historical methods and more critical than historical accuracies—what *can* be lies shattered in the shadowy hiatus of thick and unthinking barbarism in the between that endures beyond the mere separation of time.

Vischer's negative judgment of Hölderlin endured until fairly recently.[22] Nor is it the case that this judgment simply vanished with Norbert von Hellingrath's publication of the late work of so-called madness, though, and to be sure, it began to change with the Stefan George circle (if this change swung toward the Charybdis of all-too-excessive German Nazi alliance), or, to name the philosophers Wilhelm Dilthey (who called Hölderlin a "visionary") or Karl Jaspers (as the philosophical and scientifico-medical counterpart to Stefan Zweig, exemplifying the lasting influence of psychoanalytic judgment, today derived at one extreme from Jacques Lacan by Jean Laplanche, originally, for Zweig and Jaspers, drawn from Freud and Jung). Today the luster or *frisson* of poetic madness continues to be taken for granted as Hölderlin's distinguishing characteristic. Still evident in both Hölderlin and Nietzsche studies, such a romanticism of romanticism would mean that Hölderlin would bear the heroic mark of mantic, that is, *divine* enthusiasm: "When one lives thus among gods, one's words are no longer understood by men."[23] Scholars ranging from Albert Lange to Ernst Cassirer to Georg Lukàcs, would continue (and this tendency continues, gently enough, in David Krell and others) to fit Hölderlin into the quasi-divine (and given Socrates' discussion in the *Apology* and in the *Phaedo*: within the very philosophically respectable) lineage of madness.

The association with Nazism is the most pernicious among such persistent currents. Among other things, it is claimed that Hölderlin's hymn "Germania" was subjected to certain elisions in order to be useful in a time of war.[24] If Heidegger never made such an elision, his apostrophizing of Hölderlin's essence and rank, "Dichter des Deutschen," is nonetheless routinely read as if Heidegger were expressing a typical party or Nazi enthusiasm for the poet.[25] Second only to Nietzsche,[26] Heidegger was one of the first scholars or philosopers to regard Hölderlin as poet without coordinately reducing his poetry (but as pathology or as divine characteristic) to madness. For Heidegger, and *schlechthin*, Hölderlin is the "*Dichter des Dichters*"—even if naming him as such arraigns him not only with Goethe and Schiller, Klopstock and Heine, Rilke and Benn, but above them all, as a poet's poet: a prince of the veritable word. Heidegger's reading, it may be said, ultimately made all the difference for Hölderlin's reception.[27]

For what von Hellingrath's Promethean venture had done was to dislodge Hölderlin's oeuvre from the guarded reserves and the critical esteem of his more conservative editors (and of scholars like Nietzsche's own teacher and others from Vischer onward), setting a new aspect of the poet before a new generation of war-sober eyes and revitalized judgment.[28] In this way, like Gadamer before him, Eckhart Förster recalls Heidegger's priority in Hölderlin's scholarly reception (which, to be sure, is to the great advantage of an English-language audience). Citing Nietzsche as the "philosopher who set the stage for the Hölderlin renaissance in our century,"[29] Förster confirms the importance for Heidegger of von Hellingrath's edition as "an earthquake,"[30] in Heidegger's words (these are the same words Stefan Zweig employs, recalling not only Nietzsche's own description of Hölderlin's *Hyperion* as a turbulent wave crashing over him,[31] but Hölderlin's own account of the self-transformation effected by his sojourn in Bordeaux: "and as it is said of the heroes, so I may say that Apollo struck me"). Förster is thus able to situate the critical and "perhaps unique" importance of Heidegger's reception of Hölderlin. Beginning with his 1934–1935 lecture courses (held directly in the wake of Heidegger's failed debut as Nazi rector), Förster writes that Heidegger "entered into a dialogue with the poet that continued throughout his life," whereby "Hölderlin represents the alternative to the entire metaphysical tradition that reaches its peak in Hegel's system."[32] In specific and contrasting focus, Henrich's interpretive project opposes Heidegger's reading, both as an account of his poetry and as philosophy, reclaiming Hölderlin, at least in theory, and qua theorist, to be installed within the frame of idealist philosophy, vis-à-vis Kant, Hegel (and Schelling), and Fichte (Schiller and Goethe, as much Reinhold as Maimon). In this way, Henrich proposes that we understand Hölderlin from the perspective of idealist philosophy, hearing his poetry under the same constraints. It is hardly any wonder that Henrich refuses the poet a voice in his interpretive text, that is, Henrich cites Hölderlin himself as sparingly as possible, just where the poet's own words might have opposed the same reductive claim.

Nietzsche and Hölderlin:
The Ground of Empedocles and the Tragic Ideal

Nietzsche stands between Hölderlin's archaicizing and metaphorical invocation of the forgotten deities of Greece and Heidegger's politically charged assertion of the essential relation between Germany and Greece. For Heidegger, this affinity is found (as Heidegger ultimately finds everything) in language. But this connection is hardly unique either to Hölderlin or Heidegger and other perspectives have identified this special relationship in terms of the "tyranny" of Greece over Germany (as in the title of Eliza M. Butler's still indispensable book) or more commonly described in terms of a Germanic "nostalgia" for Greece (as Jacques Taminiaux offers a considered and careful philosophical reprise of the classicism of German idealism and thought at the turn of the century that irrevocably links the fortunes of the nineteenth to the eighteenth century).[33]

The contrast between other national approaches to the legacy that is Greece and the special privilege that is Germany betrays the primacy of interpretation over philosophy. Such readings have increasingly been expressed politically.[34] In this way the scholarly *is* the political and one betrays one's orientation by one's choice of the "heroes" one makes one's own—to invoke the language used in certain readings of Heidegger's lamentable politics. In this same politicization, we can retrace the moralistic tone of recent debates on the national or the proper.[35]

These debates seem to be intended to remind the reader that Heidegger's focus on the specifically, identifiably, regionally German in Hölderlin's poetry was for its part and in its time nothing other than a massively unhappy emphasis, that is: a historically fatal mistake.[36] The associative play governing all such national namings and alliances need not (cannot) interest us here, nor indeed the question of whether it is (or could be) correct to trace the origins of Greece to the Orient (or substitutable Egyptian/African)[37] but instead to note that the key to such a reading seeks to establish not merely that the Greeks are "foreign" to us, as Hölderlin already wrote, but utterly and (polemically presented as Hölderlin's insight into the orientalism of Greek antiquity) precisely "other."[38] Nor would I seek, in a context including Nietzsche as much as Hölderlin and Heidegger, to argue against this radical difference exactly as the Hölderlinian difference between what is one's own and what is foreign as it is expressed in the Heideggerian context of open appropriation. This is the challenge of culture from Goethe to Hölderlin to Nietzsche to Heidegger. It is a resonant echo from Pindar to be heard as a tension between Hölderlin and Nietzsche, coming to be what one is, at the end of an unlikely and longer day, as a coming home that can only be mediated as remembrance, as and through what is foreign because, as Heidegger draws out these reflections, what is most one's own remains what is most alien in exactly the passage he named "Ereignis."

The issue at stake in the contrast between what Heidegger recalls that Hölderlin named " 'the holy pathos' and the 'Occidental Junonian sobriety of representational skill' in the essence of the Greeks" is the contrast between Heidegger's concept of *Rausch* and what Nietzsche named the grand (because political) style. But it is important to add Hölderlin's own reflective word to an account that is so dependent upon the poet's dense and provocative word just because for Hölderlin, as much as for Pindar, one *may not* freely dispose of what is most one's own.

To articulate the relation between thinkers such as Nietzsche and Heidegger, we can take Hölderlin to mean that the disposition over one's own is obstructed and, to gain some purchase here, we are to turn to what is foreign. But and exactly for the Germans, in Nietzsche's extraordinary expression: "all bridges are broken" (KSA 11, 678). To my mind, the new prospect of the modern world (under the aegis of globalism) suggests that the same shattered prospect holds for the French, as for the English, and must even be assumed for Americans, despite the melting pot mythology, as well. The remedy, if there is to be one, might lie in the "almost" that must be counted in the place of so much in life. It is only *after* "we have almost lost our tongue in foreign lands" (Hölderlin, "Mnemosyne"), that we can begin to return to or read a sense back into the poet's imperative suggestion that the "Greeks are not really master of the holy pathos, since it is innate in them," but are rather those who dispose magisterially over the "*Junonian sobriety*" to the very extent that they *made* it over or assumed it into their orbit. But to appropriate what Nietzsche called "the rainbow bridges of concepts" (KSA 11, 678)—that is, both fantasy and saturnalia between foreign lands of thought—one must go beyond the passion for thinking he casually mocks as the will to "ghostlikeness" [*Geisterhaftigkeit*] (Ibid.). Thus Nietzsche describes scholars as "Hellenizing specters" [*gräcisirende Gespenster*], while adding as his own redemptive transfiguration of the scholarly, indeed scientific spirit: "but some day, we may hope, also with our own body!" (Ibid., 679). Beyond mind and body, the same transfiguration would also be the key to divine happiness: one must come to oneself, not as a homecoming but as a re-cognition of the foreign that inheres in one's own heart and history.[39]

Where Nietzsche begins his preface to *On the Genealogy of Morals* with the claim that we are strangers to ourselves and concludes with a reflection on the urgency of learning to read (as he elsewhere reminds us of the necessity of *learning* to think and to love), Hölderlin explains that "what is one's own must be learned as thoroughly as what is foreign. For that reason the Greeks are indispensable to us. But precisely in what is our own, in what is our national gift, we will not be able to keep pace with them, since . . . the free employment of what is one's own is most difficult."[40] Nietzsche's effort to approximate the problem of "the free employment of what is one's own" lies in his work, patently traced though the lines of the self-reflected lineage of an author's self-becoming, that is, his *Ecce Homo: How One Becomes What One Is.*[41]

Nevertheless, it is obvious that the prejudice in question contra Germany (and its historical equation with Nazism) and antiquity (called Greece) is the same as the "prejudice" or "convicted" thinking of the nineteenth-century academic response to Hölderlin that had judged him, as he had been in Nietzsche's then-contemporary response to this judg-ment, qua all-too-Greek, and hence: qua insufficiently German, far too strange and—here we recognize once again the Cartesian bugbear en-demic to both poetry *and* philosophy—insufficiently "clear."

I have already observed that Nietzsche's response to this critique was delayed until the *Untimely Meditations*. Nietzsche's response then coincides with a convergent reference to the point of Hölderlin's own letter to Böhlendorff between what is one's own and what is foreign, the difference between what is achieved with ease or grace and what can only be won in a rain of fire, kissed by language—as Bettina von Arnim's enthusiasm expressed the medium of Hölderlin's poetic vocation as the very elemental fire of antiquity. Bathed in fire, standing poet's head drenched in aitherial lightening, the Greek attains (this is the tension tensed within itself, the one in itself differentiated, that is, the *Vermächtnis* contrasting the oriental [*a-orgic*, nature] with the Western European [*org-anic*]) that is its own nature in the play (or fire) of the word. Nietzsche discovers the same tension in the very different, still affine names of the gods Dionysus/Apollo and the poets Archilochus/Homer in the oppositional, lyric/epic dynamic of *The Birth of Tragedy.*[42]

Heidegger, like Nietzsche, uncovers the most dissonant terms to convey the legacy of ancient Greece and its poets, which he explicitly appropriated from Hölderlin in his reading of the strange and the uncanny in Hölderlin's translation of Sophocles' *Antigone*. And thus, if only for this reason, the recent tactic of rereading the postmodern conception of (Levinasian/Derridean) difference or alterity against Heidegger's concern for the foreign and the distant cannot be expected to work against the one whose most enduring achievement was to teach a generation of scholars "to think"—an extraordinary legacy, as our own generation is beginning to mark its absence.

But this means that Heidegger's language-referred effort to trace the relationship between Germany and Greece has more in common with Nietzsche's tragic sensibility contra the standard review of the reception of antiquity than has previously been conceded—given the antagonism scholars continue to install between Heidegger and Nietzsche, as a chasm separating the one philosopher who engages Nietzsche for philosophy (and not merely for and as an exegesis of his thought).

For Heidegger, for Nietzsche, as for Hölderlin, the Greek is not imagined proximately German (the banality of saying the same) as much as the Greek is utterly distant from the German. Thus the modern is charged to come to win itself by an effort to approach the foreign, to track, and so to measure antiquity with the sense of a prior eclipse or disappointment in Heidegger and echoing in Hölderlin's double and complex sense of the elusive challenge of archaic measure, ". . . nie treff ich, wie ich wünsche, / Das Maas . . ." [. . . Much though I wish to, never / I strike the right measure . . .][43] Already echoed in Nietzsche, and already found in Heidegger's response to Hölderlin, Philippe Lacoue-Labarthe reminds us of this double reflex.[44] This "oriental Greece, if you will, always tempted in the direction of what Hölderlin calls the *aorgic* in order to distinguish it from the *organic*. . . . is finally what continues to haunt the German imaginary up to our time, and what will at any rate traverse the whole of the text of philosophy from Hegel to Heidegger."[45] And with this, with "the Greece Hölderlin invents" to use Lacoue-Labarthe's expression, we are returned to our reflection on Nietzsche and the tragic mode of antiquity.

Nietzsche and Empedocles: The Philosopher as Lawgiver

The perspective Nietzsche adopts is as little tied to historical references as the many nominal references characterizing the style and course of his discourse. This illustrates less Nietzsche's particular and personalized imprecision (as his critics charge) than the very critical purpose and point of his own historical, all-too-philological (we would say all-too-scientific or all-too-scholarly) emphases. It is no accident that Nietzsche sets the claim to any other emphasis than such a critical *and* questioning, openly "scientific" emphasis—that is, what Eugen Fink characterizes in Nietzsche's own case by saying that Nietzsche's "enlightenment is enlightened about itself,"[46] enlightenedly "scientific" about its own "scientificity,"[47]—as the confirming demonstration of what Nietzsche called a failure of or "*lack* of philology.*" Once more, one misses the point if one charges that Nietzsche gets things wrong.[48] Of course he does. The point remains in Nietzsche's assertion of the veritable impossibility that it would be to get them right. This is not a conclusion, philological or otherwise, but the beginning of a problem for philosophy and for the task of understanding Nietzsche's thought. The key here is not the issue of error (what is wrong with being mistaken? Nietzsche asks again and again). Not getting things "wrong," not being in error, Nietzsche's problem with his own profession was what he repeatedly decried as a "lack" of philology. For him, that failure bespeaks a lack of scientific exigence. This lack of scholarship is the conviction that one has settled a scholarly question once and for all. In its place, Nietzsche called for questioning: the *scientific* critique of all such confidences, not just the ones an all-too, still-too fashionable rationality deems nonsense.

This critical contention against the security of knowledge, challenging the conviction that one has a right (any right) answer, is the substance of Nietzsche's critical epistemology, the same epistemology that Nietzsche scholarship, be it German or American or French, not to mention mainstream philosophy, continues to ignore by reducing Nietzsche to a *mostly moral* thinker. For the sake of their insight into the essence of being as existence (that is, nature as such) as well as for correlevant ancient teachings, Nietzsche would invoke the names of Empedocles and Heraclitus. Nietzsche's cardinal opposition to reigning convention, denouncing "this illusion of 'Greek cheerfulness' " in "Socrates and Greek Tragedy," puts the point on his own teasing counterreflection, "as if there had never been a sixth century with its birth of tragedy, its mysteries, its Empedocles and Heraclitus, indeed, as if the great artwork of the time were unavailable, each of which—in its own way—cannot be explained on the basis of such a senile, slavish delight in existence and cheerfulness but imply something utterly alien" (KSA 1, 603).

Nietzsche's artistic account of the nature of understanding (i.e., the Nietzschean illusion of knowledge) constitutes his very apostrophic and specifically antagonistic or polemical history of philosophy, for example: "From Thales to Socrates—nothing but transferences of man onto nature—the immense shadow play of man upon nature, as if upon the mountains!" (KSA 7, 462).

Paralleling Nietzsche's Heraclitus with Nietzsche's "Empedokles" (Nietzsche uses Hölderlin's orthography here), it may be objected, in good philological exactitude, that Nietzsche only highlights Heraclitus's basic misanthropy, in careful contrast with Empedokles'/Zarathustra's popular devotion to the people, toward the end of—or in a Hölderlinian modality—*for the sake of* a higher reconcilation with the world of nature and in a still greater context, with time or the divine (Hölderlin's Kronos and Hölderlin's Kronion, Saturn and Jupiter, as we shall see later). But, and again, it is Nietzsche's circumspect context that must be considered with reference to clarifying this coordinate connection. Hence Nietzsche writes, "*[m]astery of the knowledge drive*—or the strengthening of that which is mythical, mystical, and artistic (Heraclitus, Empedokles, Anaximander). Legislation by *greatness*" (KSA 7, 462). And again, he lists: "Empedocles Love and Hate in Greece" with "Heraclitus. Cosmodicy of Art" adding, "Democritus and Pythagoreans. Natural science and metaphysics" (KSA 7, 526). In this way, Nietzsche regards both Heraclitus and Empedocles as lawgivers and as artists of the mystical, of the mythical (and, Nietzsche affirms, in Empedocles' case: of the magical). Nietzsche's politics turns on the questions of myth, magic, and mysticism. And if one is to understand Nietzsche's notion of artistry in a political context (the question of style, especially the "grand style"), it will be by way of such a mystical expression.

Beyond Nietzsche's associative reading between the names of Heraclitus and Empedocles, scholars have reflected on the implications of Hölderlin's Empedocles for Nietzsche's thinking, especially for the figure of Zarathustra.[49] Nietzsche's Zarathustra, including his versions or drafts for the same in his notes, echoes both the character and function of Hölderlin's Empedocles, not merely with reference to the historical philosopher but as a creative, literary, and dramatic venture or "work." This works both as a guise—Nietzsche's *Thus Spoke Zarathustra* conceived and presented as a masterwork (as Nietzsche proposed the text as a calculated or parodic work), was also conceived esoterically, as a kind of Trojan horse one might say, so that in a parallel with the grandest spirit of *ressentiment*-driven duplicity, as an aesthetic triumph of the same ascetic idealism, "all the world would swallow just this bait" (GM I §9). Yet prior to such an ironic stylistic achievement, we can recall Nietzsche's query in his *Untimely Meditations,* answers Schopenhauer's pessimism with Goethe: " 'Do you affirm this existence in the depths of your heart? Is it sufficient for you? Would you be its advocate, its redeemer? For you have only to pronounce a single heartfelt Yes!—and life, though it faces such heavy accusations, shall go free.' "[50] Thus Nietzshe is able to advance the sacrificial moment beyond this life as enacted by "Empedokles" as both spiritual answer and corporeal refutation.

With Empedocles, Nietzsche evokes Zarathustra's deepest insight set alongside his heaviest thought. Likewise, Nietzsche describes the tragic countenance and comportment of Anaximander as Empedokles' own exemplar: "He lived as he wrote, spoke as magnificently as he clothed himself, he raised his hand and placed his foot, as if this existence were a tragedy in which he was born to play the hero. He was Empedocles' great paragon in all this" (KSA 1, 821).[51] And Nietzsche offers a description of Zarathustra's manner that similarly embraces Zarathustra in the idealized light of his own inventor: "Empedocles is the pure tragic human being. His leap into Etna—the knowledge drive! He longed for art and found only knowledge. But knowledge creates Fausts" (KSA 7, 118). Later, Nietzsche would extend this same tragic projection of the transformation of art conceived throughout his philosophy and via his Zarathustra project beyond the limits of the sacrificial death of Empedocles. In addition to the project of the ascetic ideal in science ("knowing without measure and limit"), Nietzsche observes in a manner remininscent of his later incantation of the life-affirming urgency of art as a shield in the face of the deadly efficacy of truth: "This drive must generate art, indeed, as healer."[52] A similarly aesthetic reference is evident in Nietzsche's own careful association of Empedocles as rhetorician and the speeches and the task of conversion or persuasion ascribed to Zarathustra.[53]

I have suggested that Nietzsche's association of Heraclitus and Empedocles be understood in terms of his own apostrophic but philologically dictated history of ancient thinkers. This classicist's perspective is important because in his notes or studies, from early to late, Nietzsche rarely presents a single pre-Socratic name out of context—and this is a significant difference again to the published declarations where Nietzsche, like Hegel, noisily professes his own affinity for Heraclitus.

Otherwise, Nietzsche exemplifies a careful philological concern to trace the names of antiquity as they are given to us, in citation and report, in terms of influence, a dedication that took every bit of Nietzsche's philological formation, ultimately as articulated for the sake of philology (today's classics) and thence to philosophy. Not to abandon the disipline of philology for the liberties of philosophy as some less careful readings can conclude, Nietzsche much rather sought to raise critical questions in that same tradition and thus to represent "the ancient philosophers, the Eleatics, Heraclitus, Empedocles, as the tragic philosophers" (KSA 7, 118). Thus, no more than his first book on tragedy, Nietzsche's unpublished study of *Philosophy in the Tragic Age of the Greeks* does not amount to a refusal of his first formation but constitutes the heart of his contributions to that same science of reading (discovering) (the archaeology of) the Greece of Antiquity.

Recent readings recast Nietzsche's philological achievements by measuring what counts (in exactly the same disciplinary esteem) as measured by what is apprised as "good," "scholarly work."[54] As a result, Nietzsche's name can fail even to be mentioned in passing in studies bearing exactly on areas where his work might seem to be of some value for philology, if only by contrast.[55]

It is the difference made by one's scholarly formation that is crucial here. For we have been attempting to raise the question of the relationship between philosophy and poetry as unequal offspring of the spirit of music. And whenever the question is raised, we must also remember that the univocal answer uttered from the side of criticism is a claim that refuses philosophy any purchase on (any reflective rights concerning) poetry, while claiming that the origins of this same disqualification derives from philosophy alone, stamped out in the imprint or tread of, Plato. Thus its literary advocates inform the philosopher that the meaning of poetry is to be found nowhere but in the poem, which in turn turns out to be exactly—or nowhere else but only—where the critic finds it for us.

Claiming that philosophy means to vanquish poetry, as literary criticism cries again and again against the wolf of philosophical critique, is to exclude the judgment, the perspective of the philosopher in advance (which preemptive strike seems ironically, tactically, retrospectively necessary, for whenever the philosopher does manage to speak, the rest of criticism is henceforth conducted on its terms or else—and this is the same—it is preoccupied with refutation: to wit Heidegger's interpretation of Hölderlin in both German and French as well as Anglophone criticism). For the professional ambition of literary criticism, admissible concourse is only to be between poets and explicators of poetry for the sake of exegesis, criticism, theory. Except, of course, and this is a grievous weakness, like the philosophers, the poets themselves do not speak as critics, and when they do, as Hölderlin does, speaking the language of theory, their words are regarded as matching what the critic can say and are ultimately reclaimed as still in need of this same reading and so subject to the authority of the critic's discipline.[56]

8

⤫

On Pain and Tragic Joy

Nietzsche and Hölderlin

As we saw at the start, Nietzsche proposes to understand the archaic nature of tragedy as a poetic and musical art. But at the same time he emphasizes that what is "tragic in tragedy is comprehending the world from the point of view of suffering" (KSA 8, 105). The Dionysian tragic myth is summarized in music. In this, as we have seen, Nietzsche's inspiration was Hölderlin, who had earlier found the secret of joy in the mystery of tragedy: "joyously to say the most joyful,"[1] and the tragic is the counter-tone to every word that speaks of mild air, soft breezes, the tension between abundance and loss corresponding to the poet's capacity for pain as he reflects on himself, as on his native land: *". . . Drum bleibe diß. Ein Sohn der Erde/Schein' ich; zu lieben gemacht, zu leiden."*[*][2]

Nietzsche made the tension between pain and beauty the keystone to his *The Birth of Tragedy* and the influence of Hölderlin's *Hyperion, or the Hermit in Greece*, arguably begins here, a dark influence that will culminate in Nietzsche's *Thus Spoke Zarathustra*. Indeed, in the third section of his book on tragedy, Nietzsche first cites and then goes on to offer an extended reflection on the words that served Hölderlin as motto to the second volume of *Hyperion*:

---

[*]"So be it, then. A son of Earth / I seem; and made: to love, to suffer. . . ."

μη φυναι, τον απαντα νικα λογον. το δ'επει φανη βηναι χειϑεν,
οϑεν περ ηχει, ιπολυ δευτερον ως ταγιστα. —Sophocles*[3]

Hölderlin's own context elucidates an Empedoclean resolution, the play of love and joy—the sweet-bitter, of Sappho's *glukupikron*—and concludes with the rending that drives harmonies apart only to be reconciled in Hölderlin's favorite Empedoclean image, like the quarrels between lovers. At the conclusion of this chapter, we return to Hölderlin's recourse to music as an expression of erotic harmony: "Living tones are we, tuned together in your harmonies, Nature! Who then can sunder? Who can separate lovers?" In this context of harmony and dissonance, to speak of lovers is also to invoke literally musical intervals.[4]

Scientific Vivisection and the Feminization of Pain

If it is tempting to think of Nietzsche as a philosopher of laughter, it is perhaps even easier to imagine the man who lived a life accompanied by persistent illness, debilitating disabilities, all aggravated by pain, as a philosopher of pain.[5] At the same time, however, he is not to be thought a philosopher of Pythagorean, Epicurean, or even Schopenhauerian sensibilities on the matter or question of pain. Even less is he to be conceived as a philosopher on the more routine level of modern analytic philosophy's (somehow "insensitive") reflections on the problem of what we might call, to risk an awkward parallel, "other pains."

Despite his, perhaps because of his, complex understanding of pain, Nietzsche is inclined to petty provocations on the subject. And he has a number of these. Indeed, he might be compared to the Marquis de Sade or else and for a more contemporary example, with Georges Bataille for the frequency with which he has recourse to images of cruelty, indeed, and the parallel continues, often in salacious terms, especially in *On the Genealogy of Morals*. We are, reading Nietzsche on such themes, disturbed less philosophically, I will suggest, though this is surely also at work, than by the dissonance of his allusions, catching us up in our own more or less non-philosophical prejudices concerning both pain *and* empathy. Hence the deliberately contentious point of his collocation of comparisons (opposing scientific perspectives) can be all too easily overlooked in our politically enlightened horror or "better-knowing" contemplation and our corresponding urge to overspring its content:

---

*Not to be born is best, past all prizing, best; but, when a man has seen the light, this is next best by far, that with all speed he should go thither, whence he hath come.

Perhaps at the time, pain did not hurt as much as it does today, at least a physician might draw this conclusion who has treated Negroes (taking these as representative of prehistoric humanity) for serious cases of internal inflammation; such inflammation would drive even the best organized European almost to despair [*Nietzsche, as we recall, had an intimate knowledge not only of such inflammation but also of the social and outward manifestations of pain*]—but in the case of Negroes this does *not* happen. (In fact, the curve of human capacity for pain seems to fall off relatively abruptly, once one passes the upper ten thousand or ten million of high culture [*Übercultur*]; and I have no doubt that in comparison with a *single* painful night undergone by one hysterical little cultured lady, the *total* suffering of all the animals questioned in the interests of scientific research by means of the knife simply does not enter into the balance. (GM II §7)

This aphorism appears in the context of the second part of *On the Genealogy of Morals*, the same part that begins with questions of punishment and selective breeding, promises and rights. Nietzsche's reference to vivisection, it is important to note, largely replays Kant's very influential juridical model of experimental scientific inquiry.[6] It is here that Nietzsche most memorably attributes nothing less than the invention of human culture itself (or its more interesting variations) to what he calls the *mnemotechnics* [*Mnemotechnik*] of pain. Pain, in conflict and oppression, is the engine of *ressentiment*. As the emblem and proof of the ascetic ideal, pain is also perhaps the most recognizable instrument of self-creation. Presuming upon scientific conventions, Nietzsche proposes at the same time to challenge the scientistic *convictions* of nineteenth-century neuroscience. In this challenge, the complex detail of Nietzsche's description of pain underscores the elusiveness of sensibility and the impossibility of sentiment.

For we *do not* and we *can never* feel another's pain, although at the same time (and this is why Nietzsche's counter-question to the challenge of theodicy works as it does), we *can* know the pain of the other by exactly direct perception (we can feel *that* they suffer) while at the same time we can also disregard the pain of the other. The advantage of the *Bildungsweibchen*, that is, the cultivated or "cultured little lady" (today she would perhaps correspond to a lady of standing in the social register), is precisely that this nineteenth-century invention can reach for the smelling salts: she can faint or threaten to do so, she can sigh, beat her breast, and in general make enough fuss about it that one adverts to her indisposition, even if only under the sign of the dismissive word "hysteria."

In our interactions with one another, at any level of society, the same games continue in different, more contemporary guises. We tend, in our own estimation of it, to downplay another person's pain even as we acknowledge a declared expression of pain with sympathy. We note it without altogether believing it, wondering if, perhaps, it is not quite so bad, if perhaps "one" might not be overdoing it. Because the other is well aware of this discounting, there is, in truth, a tendency to exaggeration but less to mislead than to persuade and this dynamic feeds the cultivated drama of headaches and the communication of social pains. And so we have a script that we use not only in public but also intimate contexts—and this clichéd constellation is hardly an accident: I really, really have a headache, my head is splitting, I am dying. Complete with pantomime, the play would not be out of place for Nietzsche's society lady.

To review the further point regarding other races and other species, precisely on the Victorian continuum invoked by the deliberately denigrating reference to the "hysterical little cultured lady," driven as she is by nature, today in the form of what we call hormones (and psychiatrists continue to characterize women with reference to hysteria and the only organ that matters to science, as Simone de Beauvoir quotes this judgment, "*Tota mulier in utero*," "woman is a womb"),[7] Nietzsche's diminishing references to Negroes and animals continue the analogy. Forgive me for these examples, but it is important to consider the slaughterhouse workers who harry and bludgeon, and finally bleed out the life blood of tens or hundreds of thousands[8] of animals: cattle, horses, pigs, sheep, without counting chickens, ducks, geese, et cetera, transforming them from breathing, conscious and bellowing, crying[9] beings to bloodless[10] meat—that bloodlessness is the reason animals are exsanguinated: deliberately bled to death—on an unimaginably massive scale in automated processing plants,[11] or of the hunters (fishers on their off-season) who systematically club every baby seal in sight, skinning them, sometimes alive, in the view of their consternated mothers, or of the dog butchers who slowly strangle and beat dogs to death for the sake of ensuring maximum agony (as it is precisely the animal's pain that is believed to improve the benefits of the meat for the sexual debilities of aging men), or modern vivisectionists who work in research labs in the university (*our* universities) and industry, or workers who "put animals down," often by gassing them en masse, or else by painful injection (expense and time constraints dictate this) on the scale that is the daily business of animal shelters of whatever kind, et cetera. The individuals who systematically kill animals (a process that involves deprivation and suffering from start to end and is enacted nearly always more brutally than not) in the course of their everyday occupation are hardly unaware of the pain they inflict in what they do, but they are inured to it, they "disattend."

Manifestly, we can know another's pain cognitively, as the preceding, all-too offensive examples plainly illustrate, if it is also true that we can always discount our empathic understanding. That we can directly apprehend another's suffering Nietzsche does not deny: hence his recognition of the priority of conceptual, consciously represented agony *above* real or bodily torture. Nietzsche's image would apply to no one better, no one less literally than the late Susan Sontag, among many others. The pain of the other is an inherently feminine pain, or better said, it becomes *feminized* pain. This is the pain that is the trivialized hysteria of the lady of culture or learning—to rename the translator's "bluestocking" from an earlier generation, for, make no mistake about it, we are of course talking about academics. These are the same educated women that Nietzsche always accused of reproductive disfunctionality all while celebrating his own: books or children, but not both, he would write.

The pain of animals, the pain of a woman, the pain of non-Europeans, the all-too-Aristotelian dimensions of Nietzsche's comparative scale traces the problem of "other" pains: pains that are conspicuously not our own. But all this is exactly not the same as to say that we feel what others feel *as* they do. This means that we do not feel the other's pain *as* we feel our own pain, even if our feeling appropriation of another's pain can be the keenest felt occasion of personal anguish (one thinks of battle companions, a sensibility to a fallen comrade that since antiquity has been compared to the pain of lovers or the pain of the mother in the face of her child's suffering). For in these cases, the agony is our own and in sympathy we wince within. But as we wince for the other, we wince for ourselves: in the grip of sympathy (note the haptic image), we feel their pain *as* our own and this is why so many of us simply turn away from or block out the sight of cruelty—particularly the horrifyingly brutal images of the same animal slaughter on which, of course, our civilized lifestyles depend: in nearly innumerable ways, we eat and we drink, we wear and are shod with, we sleep upon, and we play with the artifacts of death.[12]

More than our own existence and even more than death, our pain is our own even when we are able to transcend our own pain in spirit or in the soldierly fortitude practiced by the young Nietzsche. As already noted in an earlier chapter, we recall that after Nietzsche suffered his famous injury while mounting his horse for a military exercise, he would continue to complete the morning exercise, riding without giving a sign of pain and not adverting to his injury, even after dismounting, looking to his horse, and continuing in this routine fashion until finally collapsing later in the day. The "nobility" of his personal comportment, as Nietzsche doubtless imagined his conduct, condemned him to a wound that would abscess, eventually to require surgery and which subsequently took *months* for recovery. The persistence of injury, the worsening of a wound one does not attend to, is to the point here. Like one's own shadow, Nietzsche spoke of his more chronic, systemic pain as his "dog" (GS §312), for pain transcended (or temporarily forgotten) is not conquered: pain is loyal even without our attention to it, like a dog. Reciprocally, we can add, even when a pain has vanished, the mind goes looking for it, as Leo Tolstoi's character, Ivan Illich, does this in the course of his illness. But as pain and sympathy refer us to ourselves, this same singularizing isolation also means that what we lack with respect to the pain of others is not the apprehension of those pains but ultimate respect, as Levinas for his own and quite different part has turned this key point into an entire philosophy. In place of the *awe* that might be the appropriate complement to ignorance (rather than pity and not sympathy for another's suffering), in a move Nietzsche repeatedly analyzes even where our moral rule would commend such a high regard in our feelings and in our own minds, we answer the imperative command of perceived suffering by *diminishing* the other's pain, and thus we block our apprehension of it. In consequence, we reduce it not merely to a cognitive or intuited estimation but instead to nothing more than our own feeling.

But this is also to say that from our own vantage point we are well able to degrade the suffering of others to greater or indeed to lesser degrees of insubstantiality. For Nietzsche, we are inclined to imagine that what *we* feel, the other feels as well. Hence, he calls attention to our propensity to suppose that "where we feel nothing, (it seems!) nothing exists" (KSA 9, 470; cf. 12, 81). Pointing to the ancient traditions that paired festivals with suffering, Nietzsche would argue that the celebratory pleasure associated with the very sight of suffering that continued not only into medieval times but into the New World (stocks, public hangings, etc., even traffic jams at the scene of an accident have an element of this *Schadenfreude*) betrays much more than the exhilaration that "it isn't me" but a dark and deeply loaded and very human pleasure in seeing suffering but also in *making* suffer. Nietzsche analyzes this pleasure in *On the Genealogy of Morals* as the prime motivation behind the ancient institution of punishment, a motivation that persists in the modern as well (and not deterrence and not "correction," despite the fact that we prefer to name houses of punishment in this way). But feeling no pain for one's part, and without investment in the pain of the other— the objectivity of the experimental scientist that can also be named schizophrenia—one can go so far as to claim that certain human beings, and all animals, "feel" less pain, as Nietzsche recounts it, or indeed no pain at all.

Nietzsche's example invokes the contrast of animals subjected to the institutional torture that had begun in the archetypically "scientific" enlightenment of the nineteenth century and Claude Bernard's almost single-handed invention of the practice of vivisection in medicine—all for the timeless good and pointless (*because* pure) aims of science. Bernard, who is known today not for his grisly operations but for the inner environmental theorization of the organism, the *mileu interieur*, experimented on the family dog (a circumstance that alienated him from his wife, who divorced him and was moved to lead an antivivisection movement in France, a family split on more than one level, that Bernard for his own part would ascribe to intellectual philistinism and lack of support for the ideals of science). To this day, medical schools and hospitals are in Bernard's debt for his specific sensitivity *not* to the animals in his charge but to the human researcher. Like any animal, the human animal reacts, viscerally, jarringly to animal cries of pain and this reaction, Bernard recognized, tended to compromise "objectivity." By severing the dog's vocal chords, Bernard was able to reduce the dog's cries to soundlessness. If the dog continued to feel pain, the animal could nevertheless no longer be heard, yielding the now common view in animal experimentation from the side of its practitioners, that the thus prepared animal in fact "feels" nothing like "pain" but only neurological and other physiological effects of the kind observable on the terms of the experiment ["behaviour"]. Bernard's experimental protocol renders animals literally dumb and its intention is manifestly phenomenological for the researcher is to aspire to Bernard's detached ideal:

> the physiologist is not an ordinary man: he is the scientist possessed and absorbed by the scientific idea he pursues. He does not hear the cry of animals, he does not see the flowing of blood; he sees nothing but the idea and is aware of nothing but the organism that conceals from him the problem he is seeking to resolve.[13]

The dissonance of this ideal, as Nietzsche would emphasize for us—if our own experience could not do so—is that we hear and respond to pain across the species barrier. Step, even by accident on a puppy's tail, and we feel the animal's pain as it shrinks away from us, we hear it and feel its pain, as it cries. Not for Descartes, the father of the mind-body distinction of course, a connection that perhaps best illustrated the violence of the Galilean imagery of the *Book of Nature*, a "book" to be "read" by the scientist. But how are these pages to be turned if not by a perfectly careful flaying, a laying out and a laying bare, as in the iconic images that are the legacy of Vesalius?

In an article that uses the example of vivisection to illuminate third world underdevelopment, the Indian social anthropologist and philosopher of science, Shiv Visvanathan cites Descartes' defensive answer to a visitor who faulted him for the paucity of books in his rooms. Descartes pointed to the animals he was then dissecting, identifying them as his "books," using Galileo's metaphor to do so. Descartes' texts were not the pages of tradition, his was what we may call a hermeneutic laying out of nature itself. Hence, as Visvanathan expresses it: "Descartes' texts are alive and the great methodologist believed that the cry of an animal could be compared to the creaking of a wheel."[14]

Extending the ideal of vivisection in science to its systematization in scientific management and its embodiment in the assembly line, its ultimate expression may be found as much in genetic engineering as in the idealization of modernization justifying the oppression of the third world in the name of progress:

> opposition to vivisection has usually been dismissed by scientists as sentimentalist. But one must see it as a paradigm for general scientific activity extending towards wider domains of control, incorporating innumerable sets of violence within the genre of vivisection. . . . One witnesses the violation of the body in the search for "scienticized" production and control. The violation of the body soon leads to the vivisection of the body-politic in theories of scientific-industrial development. And these examples are transforms of one another. The vivisectional code underlies and underwrites the violence implicit in all of them.[15]

Like the project of third world development that has built the infrastructure for today's globalized world economy, like the medical school's cadaver, the silenced dog, or the similarly silenced and immobilized cat, is "used" for medical instruction and demonstration, that is to say, for practicing surgical procedures, in utter inattention to the animal under the knife. Along the way, one learns the ideal of "objectivity," learning to negate "sentimental" responsiveness, sympathy, empathy, an inculcation assured by deliberately discarding the experimental "object." Science is a matter of numbers and practice makes perfect. But this means that the experimental "scene" with all its blood and its literal and metaphorical life-"sacrifice" is to be repeated again and again. For Visvanathan, as for Luce Irigaray who speaks of the scientific "schiz,"[16] there are two "registers" in science: the extant, standard, or "received" view of science as such, as well as that casual accompanying view of practice and everyday assumptions that science has no problem condemning on examination as "pseudo-science"—excluding from reflection but not influence.[17] Limited to the purposes of the current consideration of pain, one can take Irigaray's suggestion further to imagine this same schizophrenic practice on the model of a business that keeps two books. Thus the medical student can find himself in search of suitable animals to complete his studies and take himself to an animal shelter, adopt the animal in the morally conscientious and responsible social mode of one promising to care for the animal as a pet (or companion as we now say to prove our open-minededness),[18] only subsequently to proceed to use the animal in the above fashion.[19]

As the art of healing and care, what is philosophically relevant here, apart from the grievous moral issues with regard to the animals themselves, are the consequences of such learning experiences. The young doctor not only learns the techniques of surgery but the duplicity of vivisection as well: the techniques learned for healing are deployed without empathy and these same techiques repeatedly end by underscoring the precise irrelevance of death from the point of view of the success/ failure of an operation. It is naïve to imagine that he or she might fail to remember this lesson, a lesson in hardening or disattending when it finally comes to the human patient now treated under the terms of an exactly professionalized solicitude.

If it is no accident that Nietzsche could begin with non-Europeans, specifically with Negroes in the aphorism we cited at the start of this chapter, only to end with reference to the *numbers* of animals killed in the name of science, it is also no accident that his conclusion concerns woman in her guise as exaggerating, hysterically intensifying her own *pretended* suffering (hysteria). Much of the advice of both Sade (especially in his philosophic legacy) and the sullen arguments of the rapist (or his legal or journalistic advocate) who insists on the consensuality of an act that cannot be denied in the face of the law, or as it can be heard in the resentment of the abusive lover, has the identical tone. She doesn't really feel pain, she "need" not feel pain: really, she could enjoy it instead, as he does. Even today, for different reasons and following yet another paradigm, we speak of non-Western cultures, or, as in Nietzsche's example, of historical eras, in which pain is not quite "pain."

Just as animals in general are, *per definitionem* and following the Cartesian paradigm, described as "feeling" nothing like "pain" but "stimuli responses" or "behaviors" instead, so too scientific theorists once similarly proposed to reduce the differences between social and cultural expressions of pain and the relevance of similar differences in perception in general between the races: black, white, Asian, and above all native or so-called aboriginal peoples and which races once also, all-too-conspicuously and precisely interior to a "Western" point of view, happened to have included the racist phantasm of the difference between "Aryan" and Jew or Eastern European. Nazi experiments on human pain simply applied the same test of pain thresholds from experiments that had been performed on animals for centuries, the same experiments on animals that continue unchecked after the end of Nazi experimentation to this day. Perhaps the reason is a strange repetition compulsion, but it is more likely that tracking the relation between an electrified or heated cage floor and the agitation and distress of the caged occupant is easy to quantify.

Or, as it continues to be assumed, and it is scientists who still tell us this, women "just" feel less pain than men do, be it the pain of childbirth but also the stress and pain of illness, fatigue, casual injuries, et cetera. Additional examples include the discounting of pain in the circumcision of the newborn, castration of livestock, or, to come closer to home, the dismissal of the pain of ill *and* the terminally ill *and* the elderly by medical practioners who fail to provide adequate pain relief for fear of inducing addiction, and so on.

Pain and the Influence of Hölderlin's *Hyperion* in Nietzsche's *The Birth of Tragedy*

We have already emphasized that Nietzsche's keenly unsparing focus on pain clearly distinguishes him from Hölderlin's more archaically minded Empedoclean comprehension of the interconnection of love (*Liebe*) and suffering (*leiden, Laid*). But, and just as elementally, Nietzsche agrees with Hölderlin on the substance of joy. Nietzsche's struggle with the uncomfortable and demanding insight he calls "tragic knowledge" is thus a Hölderlinian insight, one that not only drives his reading of antiquity[20] but corresponds to the very essence of Nietzsche's Dionysian "invention," greeted as the dangerous festival prince of the art-cult of tragedy itself. Thus if the alchemical transfiguration of the Apollonian aesthetic illusion is understood as "veiling for the course of a tragedy" the power of a "real Dionysian effect" (BT §21), Nietzsche finds that both music and the tragic myth play with the "thorn of displeasure" toward the justification of nothing less than "the existence of even the 'worst' possible world." (BT §25). Nietzsche takes both the notion of dissonance in the world and in life resolved in terms of musical harmony understood from Hölderlin's Empedoclean conception of the concilia-tion that is the lover's tension.[21] The quarrel drives lovers apart, opening both desire and the possibility of reconciliation.

The question of the nature of tragedy is expressed for Hölderlin as the *reconciliation* of individual suffering and the divine nature or the world at the end of Hölderlin's *Hyperion* as he speaks in the voice of the one he elsewhere names "Conciliator" and which we cited at the start: "Living tones, are we, we sound together in thy harmony, Nature! which who can undo? who can part lovers?—." Hölderlin goes on to address the Empedoclean resolution on a cosmic scale: "O Soul! Soul! Beauty of the world! indestructible, ravishing one! with your eternal youth! *you are*; what, then, is death and all the suffering of human beings?" Speaking of delight, of Empedoclean love as the source of everything, we recall that Hölderlin reminds us that "like lover's quarrels are the dissonances of the world. Reconciliation is there, even in the midst of strife, and all things that are parted find one another again."[22]

This is the same question Hölderlin resolved (but, relevantly, did not finish) in brilliant poises in his *The Death of Empedocles*. "There they will open destiny's book for you. Go and fear nothing. Everything recurs. And what is to come is already completed."[23] In this way, what Hölderlin calls the aorgic appears in Nietzsche's *The Birth of Tragedy* in the same Sophoclean epigraph—*already* not to be—a reflection that follows Hölderlin's negative paean to human passion (desire or longing) or the Sophoclean word he likewise repeats, underscoring the strangeness or wonder of the human wanderer between animals and gods, the same strangeness that recurs in Heidegger's *Introduction to Metaphysics*, reprised after Heidegger in Irigaray's *To Be Two*.[24] It is no accident that Irigaray pursues Hegel's question, as much as Heidegger's, inquiring into love by way of the political idea of the uncanny or the strange. As Hölderlin articulates its echoing: "What is man?—so might I begin," the poet has Hyperion write to Bellarmine early in the first book of the novel, "how does it happen that the world contains such a thing, which ferments like a chaos or moulders like a rotten tree, and never grows to ripeness. How can nature tolerate this sour grape among her sweet clusters?"[25] These echoes recur in the pronouncement of Nietzsche's Silenus, illuminating the tenacity of foundational pessimism with Nietzsche's insight into the Dionysian world (BT §3). For Hölderlin the tension is that we "are so utterly in the clutch of the Nothing that governs us, so profoundly aware that we are born for nothing, that we love a nothing, believe in nothing, work ourselves to death for nothing only that little by little we may pass over into nothing. . . ."[26] The reconciliation Hölderlin finds for such a keen sensibility takes him beyond the Romantic to make him one of the most important if still too little adverted to correspondents of Nietzsche's thinking and where Heidegger affirms this same poet's influence so plainly for his own part that we do not need to discover it.

As Nietzsche critically turned his review of the birth of an ancient art form from a forgotten sense of music, in direct contrast with the classical tradition's conventional conviction on the matter (a convention that has continued beyond Goethe and Winckelmann in the neo-Hegelian image of Greece as the "childhood" of mankind, enmired in the mists of primitive superstition and slowly ascending to the sobriety of logic and reason, a dialectial evolutionary process that Nietzsche never failed to challenge throughout his work on the grounds of both logical coherence and epistemic adequacy), the tragic wisdom of the Greeks was a heightened responsiveness to pain as such. Thus, as Hugh Lloyd-Jones reminds us in this context, the Greeks neither "sublimated" nor did they repress (these conventions are too modern) but rather in a fashion alien to us, they set "terrible and irrational forces" in motion for their own distant purposes.[27]

The difference between Nietzsche's view and contemporary, increasingly subtle, or sophisticated readings of such extreme and irrational forces, qua sublimity and transcendence, resides in Nietzsche's insistence that the Greek was superficial, not because of a naïve, primitive, or childish blindness, that is, not because he could not *see* but and very like Hölderlin's Sophoclean Oedipus, much rather because he *could* see and because of what his sight brought him to see out of the depths of his suffering.

In consonance with, for the sake of, life, Nietzsche argued, the Greeks recognized that what would be required for life in the face of pain would be to stop in an abrupt and daring way, to halt "at the surface, the fold, the skin, to adore appearance, to believe in forms, tones, words," to believe "in the whole *Olympus of appearance*! Those Greeks were superficial—*out of profundity*!" (GS §iv) For the Greeks elected to remain "at the surface." In this way they were able to believe in forms, in tones, and in words. It was from such a deeply superficial perspective that Nietzsche could cry: " 'All that exists is just and unjust and equally justified in both.' That is your world! That is a world indeed!" (BT §9; the quote is from Goethe, *Faust* I, 409).

The balance attained by stopping at the surface, the skin of things, is the secret of musical complexity, not the sweetness of simplicity, but complex dissonances and the resolutions only such dissonances make both possible and uncannily beautiful. "The pleasure produced by the tragic myth has the same source as the pleasurable sensation of dissonance in music. The Dionysian, with its original joy, is the shared maternal womb of music and tragic myth" (BT §24). Thus Nietzsche draws the logical consequences of the aesthetic question with which he began: "If one could imagine dissonance in human form—and what else is the human?—then, for the sake of life, this dissonance would need a magnificent illusion, covering itself with a veil of beauty" (BT §25).

9

❧

Nietzsche's Erotic Artist
as Actor/Jew/Woman

In philosophic reviews of the erotic (particularly analytic treatments), abstraction invariably ablates the wings of the god.[1] In what follows, I do not attempt to explore Nietzsche's thinking in terms of the philosophy of sex and love[2] yet I do seek to question the role of Eros in his thinking and to do this, rather than fantasize about the personal life of a man dead now for more than a hundred years, I review his perspective on art: his aesthetics, which he approaches from the perspective of the artist, rather than the spectator, as is traditional in philosophical aesthetics.[3]

In a single, evocative aphorism, "The Problem of the Artist" (GS §361), Nietzsche proposes a concisely phenomenological investigation of the artist. Bracketing, as "dangerous," a direct focus on the artist, the actor is reviewed and then left off in favor of the Jew and, still yielding an epistemic tension with reference to the mask, subsequently given over to the intercalation of "diplomacy," and the pragmatics of rhetoric. Thus the same question recollects the origin of scholarship in general to culminate in the problem of woman outlined against the cultural phantasm of genius, especially as contrasted with the more virulent opposition between philosophy and science.

Given the paradox of Nietzsche's profoundly democratic sensibility (precisely in its emphatically anti-democratic character),[4] this complex register recapitulates and consummates almost the entirety of *The Gay Science*. In the same way, the "problem of the actor" (qua artist, fool, Jew, diplomat, rhetorician, woman) articulates the hysterical sarcasm that represents Nietzsche's ultimate word on the problem as a whole: "Woman is so artistic." The problem of woman, the particularity of the words used to refer to women, is essential here: Nietzsche's language with reference to women repeats the structure of the aphorism as a whole. Indeed, the conclusion of the aphorism tracks the terms in the routinely vulgar but obviously ordinary language used to speak of woman. Starting with *Frau*, he then moves to *Frauenzimmer*, and ends with *Weib*.[5]

This now hysteric resonance articulates a deliberately overwrought determinism: an excess to excess to excess.[6] The critical and dangerous significance of this associative cadence for contemporary reflection[7] is Nietzsche's metonymic transfer of the problem of the Jew to the nineteenth-century image of woman as a coy, fainting, fashion-conscious lie (BGE §§232, 237) and Klaus Theweleit's painstaking deconstruction of the extension of this same metonymy in Nazi imagery and rhetoric shows that it can be broadened to include the generic concept of the Eastern European.[8] It is in this way worth remembering the ordinary reference of the histrionic (to the theatre) and the hysteric in the jokes of everyday life, whereby the apotheosization of the artist becomes the focal point for the question that is the problem of the actor (or the mask), transformed into the question of woman. Commentators have made a good deal of the allusive resonance of this last connection, replaying the music box of Nietzsche's theme in his *Twilight of the Idols*, wherein it becomes, by turns, Platonic truth, taking a Jewish detour to become Christian love, then becoming sufficiently female for Goethe's eternal ideal of woman, to end, via the enlightenment, via Königsberg, and socialist sentimentality aground on its own evolutionary peak—or loss—of values. For Nietzsche, the *evolution* of the ideal is the decay, the decadence of the ideal. It is at once Plato's conversion (as/into Christianity) into the province of popular enlightenment values and as such an inversion; it is also the instrument of Plato's revenge: "what world is left? The apparent world perhaps? . . . But no! *With the real world we have also abolished the apparent world*" (TI, "How the 'Real World' Finally Became a Fable").

Innocence and Becoming: Change, Death, Eros, and God

From the beginning, Nietzsche regarded the modern scientific progress ideal as the optimistic fulfillment of Socrates' invention of modern scientific thinking, that is, a rational inversion of tragic culture characterized by a profound hatred of change or becoming. The same antipathy to process and becoming undergirds the technological enthusiasm of contemporary Western culture. Our horror of the desultory effects endemic to the corruptions of becoming and time means that we want *technological fixes* in our cosmetics and (ideally) in our medicines for aging, sickness, death, and decay. To all appearances—and appearances are all that matter—we want the same *fixes* on the same values in our engineering science for environmental disorders and contamination. In this way, the cult of the new denies (mortal) change. This is the contemporary cult of juvenile perfection: all promise and potential, nothing actual or real—unsullied by quotidian exhaustions or the everyday detours and spiritual stultificaton of procreative investment or the wearing costs of both consummation and growth, not to speak of the desultory transformations of illness and senescence/decadence.

It is capital (it is also extraordinarily difficult) to note that Nietzsche does not simply oppose the optimistic status quo of this Socratic inversion qua life-stasis or cultural stagnation. Instead, Nietzsche opposes the remedial program of Socratic knowing to the life-affirming potency of the artist who would consecrate or immortalize (and so imprint or stamp) not ideal reality but *becoming* in the image of being. The key note will be a pure moment of overflowing abundant joy. Without this excess, without what Nietzsche names abundance or flowing out, his ideal of affirmation: *amor fati* is impossible.

But failing Nietzsche's careful, constant attention to the disagreeable, to pain, suffering, or—equally—to banality or pointlessness, any expression of the affirmative ideal is empty. Without Nietzsche's emphasis on suffering, without pain, anxiety, and despair, that is, failing an oppressive and hard edge in life and love, Nietzsche's teaching of affirmation reduces to cliché-quality therapeutic counseling or television evangelism or new age consolation offered to the victims of cancer or terminal illness. The placebo new age spirituality of popular culture does not merely blame the victim for his or her own condition (caused by lifestyle, drug-abuse, alcohol, cigarettes, etc.) but conspicuously tends to deny the condition itself: there is no suffering.

Although we are, of course, as mortal as we were in Socrates' own time, and although, for all its fanfare, modern medical science has done not a thing to eliminate the ultimate threats of disease and death, it is a commonplace to maintain the opposite. No matter the lack of evidence, in the promissory culture of techno-scientific modernity—Nietzsche called this the culture of Alexandrianism in his first book—the first thing we assert is a triumph over pain and disease and we are sure that a remedy is in the offing for old age, perhaps even for death.

We are committed to a celebration of accomplished permanence— what Heidegger is pleased to tease out of Nietzsche's *Nachlaß* notes as the ideal imprinting of becoming with the still form or image of being.

This means that we celebrate what becomes in a measure that reflects our best and ownmost possibility not according to any tragic accounting of being as/and in time, but as good, little Platonic footnotes. Following in the wake of the inversion of Platonism by way of the Hellenic invention of Judeo-Christianity and the latter's conversion into Western scientific rationality and techno-culture, we today are careful to reserve our enthusiasm not for a tragic affirmation of becoming (i.e., with a choral affirmation of coming undone), but, and instead, we keep our rounds for the latest banausic invention and preservation. Adverting to the ordinary images of consumer culture, we will buy anything that promises to keep us healthy or beautiful and if we might avoid illness, accidents, or age, any one of us could spare a curse for Nietzsche's lonely, moonlight demon arrived to sell the eternal return of the same. The eternal ideal: eternal love, eternal life, eternal youth, yes; but the eternal return, life as it is/was, just as it is/was, **no**.

We want, because we desperately need, a *non-literal* interpretation of Nietzsche's teaching of the Eternal Return of the Same.[9] Yet the basic pattern of eternal recurrence is the ancient Greek insight into the tragic essence of life as the breath or flow of birth and emergence, spontaneous growth, persistence and pain, failure and a wide array of possible deaths. For Nietzsche, the fundamental characteristics of life—growth, procreation, aging, and dying—inherently involve pain. In the exactly Schopenhauerian dynamic of a business that cannot cover its costs, the enterprises of life entail failure.[10] In exactly this connection, we recall the "myth" invented by Plato that gives us the genealogy of Eros, precisely conceived as compensation, exchange, return: a "gift" born of life's poverty [*Penia*] in its calculating concourse with resourcefulness [*Poros*].[11]

We will need poetry to stamp becoming with timeless, inalterable value because "in truth" for Nietzsche—as for Anaximander, Heraclitus/Empedocles,[12] even Parmenides—there "is" only alteration. Science and mathematical logic cannot secure the becoming of what is as perdurant being. Like poetry and like art, both science (including the human or the social as well as the natural sciences) and mathematics *work* as conventions or inventions but lie *about* and most perniciously *to* themselves.[13] Inventing itself, dressing itself to seduce its own expectations of reality, science's unshaken confidence embraces the metaphysical reality of its own invention.

The real—the experienced or lived—world exemplifies nothing but the very unremitting change or becoming Nietzsche celebrates in his most unsettling descriptions of the same world Plato deplores. Contrary to Plato's protest against physical life, the secret of tragic wisdom is the knowledge of ineluctable perdition. Opposing becoming, philosophers seek unchanging truths or logical forms in the same (Lacanian) locus where theologians seek God or purpose, and scientists pursue a unified theory of everything. Nietzsche's project to restore the innocence of becoming, to stamp becoming itself with being, thus affirms neither the scientific mummification of the present moment nor the eschatological dream of the full time of an eternally ultimate life. Such a project plays the music of becoming not only as the native character of the physical or natural world but as the best truth of the world.[14] This is the determinate scheme of erotic benediction—here conceived under the transformative aegis or valencing of art. Speaking of eros, or speaking of art, or, indeed, advocating the renewal of innocence, should not obscure that what is thus transfigured is the tragic character of becoming.

Nietzsche thus returns at the end of his published reflections to his original tragic insight: "All becoming and growing, all that guarantees the future, *postulates* pain" (TI, "What I Owe the Ancients," §4). Affirming subjective pain in every process and needful in every innocence, one is oneself a piece of fate, but—and this is the heart of Nietzsche's insight— not fated by any determining power as a power that might intercede or change anything. Thus everything and anything that happens must be imagined as it is without blame. What is critical in the doctrine of *amor fati* is its unremitting emphasis on what is "disagreeable" or challenging. What is must be as it is not because it follows the law of God or nature (the point of the claim " '*ni Dieu, ni maître*' " (BGE §22), affirms the substitutive logic of secularity where the regularity of the law substitutes for both God as father and master and/as nature), but rather because it is without plan (beyond God or law) and that is also to say without recourse (either in salvation or scientific remedy). If what becomes becomes toward some end, this goal is its reason for being. In this telic projection, it loses all innocence. The event is valued in terms of its mediate good (or evil), that is, its ultimate utility. In order to love the world as Nietzsche's doctrine of *amor fati* proposes, and not merely to *accept* or to *endure* the world as it changes and becomes, one has to deny the concept of ultimate truth or purpose, indeed the concept of God. For "as soon as we *imagine* someone who is responsible for our being thus and thus, etc. (God, nature), and therefore attribute to him the intention that we should exist and be happy or wretched, we corrupt for ourselves the *innocence of becoming*" (KSA 12, 383). Naming God the greatest objection to existence, in an earlier text, in a wholly, melodically related context, Nietzsche invokes Meister Eckhart, to remind us that exactly when one attains to sanctity, transcending illusory and excess attachments, one has still to ask God to be disencumbered of God (cf. GS §292). The erotic domain illuminates this insight as both attained (in ecstasy) and destined to be sacrified (in death).

Nietzsche's teaching of *amor fati* is thus an erotic affirmation. The key to such an affirmation will be consummation, that is, works not faith. As eros, such an affirmation has no part in the resignation endemic either to vulgar nihilism or positivist determinism. Some have maintained that the secret of this teaching is what everyone, including Nietzsche, would call "love."[15] And yet as an erotic, Dionysian affirmation of life, Nietzschean *amor fati* teaches an eros more demanding than *agape* and this is an ideal impossible for the devotees of the cult of sexual distraction.[16] Love, just love, or the idea of sex (the imaginary realm of pornography, an increasingly virtual fantasy domain) is meaningless unless immediately, really affirmed in praxis, declared, enacted in what we do. Whatever one's confessional standpoint on the question of faith and works, it is the working or the practice, that is: the act of love that counts in the real world.

As the work of love that is Empedoclean cosomological power, "love" does not sit and catch an affective emphasis, like the bourgeois vision of the love of the world inspired by a night at the theatre but "lives and acts in the world," like Hölderlin's Napoleon or like the variant forged in the same coin, like Nietzsche's "Roman Caesar with the soul of Christ" (KSA 11, 289).[17] This real eros is the same as the Nietzschean program of reconstrued or restored innocence, or *amor fati*, which teaches the musical necessity of every individual and every event.

The idea of restoring the innocence of becoming is difficult because it is every bit as counter-intuitive and as implausible (or pointless) a notion as the restitution of virginity. And in reference to love in particular, it is likewise essential to emphasize the contextual reference to the pre-Platonic, pre-Socratic understanding of erotic love, particularly Empedoclean love, as a physical not a psycho-sociological dynamic innocent of the constructions of both the anti-materialist Platonic Eros and the Pauline eristic. Becoming is the crime or fault of change, aging, and death. Thus the innocence of becoming, as Nietzsche conceives it, is an erotic innocence and the purity in question, wholly innocent and wholly erotic, is the incarnate chastity of *true* love (cf. BGE §142). To regard becoming in such erotic innocence presupposes *nothing* like a passive tolerance but much rather an unconditional passion for the world, where the impossible impetuosity of real love is a prerequisite for attaining an affirmative disposition toward the world as it is, where affirmation means desire and not resignation. In a *Nachlaß* note from 1883, Nietzsche proposes the "most important viewpoint: *to attain the* **innocence** *of becoming, by means* *of excluding* **purposes** [or ends]" (KSA 10, 245). Denying God—the ideal of perfect being and constancy—we forswear blame: attributing guilt and responsibility neither to our intentions nor to the world of natural determinate causes nor to a supernatural God. Likewise, for love of the world of flux and becoming, "we deny accountability" and restore the passing of things to innocence. Renouncing the dream of salvific compensation, by denying accountability in the purity of love, "we redeem the world" (TI, "The Four Great Errors," §8).

By excluding the concept of God or of truth, excluding the ideal of unchanging Being as of ordinal laws of nature, Nietzsche affirms the lack of ultimate purpose, apart from our own dreams: "*We* invented the concept." Life becomes, in all its becoming, transformations, its decaying in sickness, age, and death, very like the cherubinic rose—without why. Pure blooming: not only buzzing confusion as James's pragmatism winces, but also pure gift. Really to see this, even once, really to catch the aspect of life as affirmable *excess*, desired as *growth and decay, joy and pain inextricably mixed*, requires at least one good day. You "have" as casual language puts it, "to be there" and, in a passage entitled "*Vita femina*" in *The Gay Science*, Nietzsche reminds us in his most rueful tonality, that the raw odds against any such revelation are extraordinarily high (GS §339). Even then: the mischief will be to fight the fade.

The sour note here, as it is this that has produced the world-altering contours of slave morality and culture, is that for the most part, for most of us, there are few moments that remain or *can* stay present as such a divine moment of consecration and blessing: *amor fati*. For this reason, what Nietzsche recommends remains impossible or inconceivable for us until we catch what is given on such a needful day as may still come to pass. Indeed, such a transformational (not salvific) day of neediness is nothing other than the day of longing: real desire (even Lacanian desire will do), that is the temptation to the expression of passionate love. And here we are thinking exactly of actors, of artists, and particularly of women—and I will add the necessary twist—not romantically but *exactly* as problematic.

Faking It: Nietzsche's View of Woman's Erotic Artistry

For desire to work as the everyday model of the Dionysian intoxication Nietzsche proposes, it must be a sensualist, aesthetic desire, felt and lived in the world—not merely lust played at, and not at all—and this is the *heart of the problem* of the Jew, as it is the problem of woman, of actors: feigned or simulated. Thus we have here to do with the "dangerous conception that is the 'artist.' " For this reason, Nietzsche uses the case of woman (not only in the West but the world over in a diachronic extension) to illustrate the difference between actively felt or creative or manly (artistic) desire or reactively induced, slavish, or womanly desire. The problem of woman, for Nietzsche, is that she is rarely "genuine" but much rather and *always* an actor: a "*Vertreter*" (TI, "Arrows," §38), a stand-in in her own space—playing herself as object, playing herself not for herself but for another, be it her parents, her children, and most paradoxically of all, be it a lover, playing herself for another's desire, but always playing herself in place of herself.

This Kojévian, Lacanian desire—for such a desire cannot be understood on Hegelian terms—is the desire to be the desire of the other's desire, expressed as so many rings in a Lacanian necklace: mapped upon a topological space of repetition and reduction, a reflexive ring in a necklace made of rings. For Simone de Beauvoir, who wrote an entire book in the effort to make this elusive point, the disingenuousness Nietzsche identifies as characteristic of woman (as actor and artist) is endemic to the traditional cultural "situation" (or manner) of literally "becoming" a woman in the act of love. To *affect* desire (which is what it is *to be* the *object* of erotic desire, that is, to effect desire) in the heat of desire is the eternal sexual calling card of "women," Nietzsche claims. No matter (and this should appease gender theorists) whether one speaks of a male or female "woman," the point for Nietzsche is "that she plays at what she does even when she—gives herself" [*Dass sie "sich geben," selbst noch wenn sie—sich geben*] (GS §361). Thus the casually ironic problem with women "in love" is that woman plays at loving precisely in the act of love. (Ibid.). Part of the problem is surely male awkwardness and the socialization of desire (and the erotic sphere) that is not female desire but that is not the whole of it, as Nietzsche argues, and as de Beauvoir, Lacan, and Irigaray also attest.

Nevertheless, what Nietzsche imagines as the spiritualization of sensuality in his ideal description of passionate love is the realization of art. The supposedly certain fact (how do we know this? A book has told us so?) that he had so little experience of sexual love in his own life is immaterial to this insight. Indeed a lack of "experience" may well have been what enabled him to hold to it not because one must be naïve to love (nor does naïveté help) but rather because the work and the working of love is hard. If, as is likely enough, Nietzsche lacked experience, it would mean that he might have escaped the compromise, and compensation, the *negotium* of disappointed, misappointed love—where what one so often learns in the experience of love is not how to love but how *not* to love: the art of compromise, that is, what Lacan, again, has very seductively described as "giving up" on one's "desire." Thus Nietzsche too, like the Napoleon he imagined himself to be (with the soul of Christ), might have imagined himself the martyr of love's ideal.

Artistic Affirmation and *Ressentiment*

What the artist realizes in art—this is its erotic valence—is the external in himself, "the eternal joy of becoming." And every one of us can and every one of us does do just this impossible thing in those moments of sexual arousal and intoxication that are not cancelled by nihilation and fear. The mischief is that it does not stay and the evil is that we rarely mark it as such. In such abandon—and I am not saying it is not so rare that it were not almost as if one never has and may never yet experience such a possibility—one realizes what Nietzsche calls the "joy encompassing joy in destruction" (EH, *BT* §3)—a joy with nothing to do with violence, a cruelty that is also a rueful name for sadness. Such a tragic joy is the affirmation of life because no affirmation, and no love, can choose any one part, such as life and not also death, or ecstasy and not also longing, disappointment, and consummate sadness, or joy and not also suffering, or being and not much rather and also becoming. "*Joy* in tragedy characterizes *strong* ages and natures. . . . It is the *heroic* spirits who say Yes to themselves in tragic cruelty: they are hard enough to experience suffering as a *joy*" (KSA 12, 556). Thus for Nietzsche, "Those imposing artists who let a *harmony* sound forth from every conflict are those who bestow upon things their own power and self-redemption: they express their innermost experience in the symbolism of every work of art they produce—their creativity is gratitude for their existence" (Ibid.). To have such an artist's joy encompassing "a joy in destruction" would be at once to realize and to love both *pain* and pleasure, affirming the inherent *deception* in all seduction, the consonance of Rilke's terror that is the meaning of beauty as *violence*, which the French poets of the last century saw in the Hellenic smile and the face of dreaming stone.[18]

It is because the erotic is that species of consummately, irredeemably *wrong* feeling—*glukupikron*, as one haunting antique voice sings the song of erotic, bodily love—that a *tragically* erotic aesthetics necessarily avoids the focus on "right feeling" so prominent in recent readings of the politics of Nietzsche's eternal return. Against this radically wrong feeling, more than one specialist has proffered the same profoundly simplistic solution to the irreducible danger of thinking Nietzsche's thought of the eternal return of the same as affirmation.

Nietzsche, as he tells us, sought to teach the will to will backward. He wanted to effect a retooling of the will on the level of memory and the valences of desire. That is the meaning of *amor fati*, as it is expressed in the thought-question of the Eternal Return of the Same. Yet from a moral point of view, as we have seen in chapter 5, scholars have asked if the ambition of the Eternal Return is justifiable, in the pure spirit of the counter-factual that inspires so much contemporary philosophy. Why not affirm as desired certain changes to the past as it was? Why not say of the past (as we do say, all the time) that it would have been better had it only been otherwise? Would one *have* to be able to will exactly everything—great and, what was Nietzsche's word? *unutterably* small—or could one not limit one's affirmation to the "good parts"?

We note here the precision of Nietzsche's understanding of the interwoven necessity of time and process. What popular science writers and novelists call the "butterfly effect" illuminates the vanity of our backward-working wishes to change an undesired aspect of the past while yet supposing that everything else might remain as it is. For Nietzsche, the best way to understand the whole cloth of physical, real temporality, as opposed to our fantasies of what might have been, expresses the question in almost mathematical terms. Thus his Zarathustra poses the question in a cosmological if clearly ecstatic tonality: "Have you ever said yes to one joy? O my friends, then you also said yes to every woe. All things are linked, interlaced, and in love—Have you ever wanted one time two times, have you ever said, 'you please me, Happiness! Instant! Blink of an eye!' You thus wanted everything to come back again.—All new again, all eternal, all enchained, interlaced, and in love. O so did you love the world—You eternal ones, you love it eternally and for all time: and also to woe do you say: pass away yet return. For all joys want—eternity" (Z, IV, "The Drunken Song," §10). This is the question of the "eternal return": "the question in each and every thing: 'Do you desire this once more and innumerable times more?'" (GS §341). The doctrine of the eternal return entails a question that turns on the desire of eternity. This is a recurrence raised to infinity, it is a recurrence of desire—of delight and joy—to eternity.

For Nietzsche as well as for other contemporary philosophers otherwise unrelated to him, like Levinas and Theunissen but also like Theodor Adorno, who knew how to read Nietzsche critically but who also went far beyond him on just this question, philosophy can hardly do better than to begin (and to end) with the problem of suffering exactly as this is related to joy. We overlook Nietzsche's Schopenhauerian care for the suffering of animals and his developed sensitivity to pain when we take the course of easy or unthinking prejudice, pronouncing Nietzsche a philosopher of joyful cruelty, the heartless philosopher of the will to power as the will to oppress others. Such is the associative metonymy of misinterpretation and it is by far the most common error otherwise competent scholars make with respect to Nietzsche.

For it is absolutely crucial to recognize that Nietzsche's diagnostic reading of the will to power neither celebrates nor does it prescribe power over *other people*. Much rather, Nietzsche articulates the genealogy of the ubiquity of power, as power appears everywhere—most perniciously of all in the will to power of the offended or injured spirit that becomes the sole consciousness of the physically as of the psychically offended or injured. This is the will to power that burns as moral outrage. Finding an alliance between Nietzsche and Hobbes (or Callicles) is the most enduring beginner's mistake.

Beyond Hobbes, Nietzsche points to the long memory of the disaffected and the disadvantaged contra the impossibly short, *because* unsustainable, tenure of any brute state of nature in the life of any fantasized blond beast in the prime moment (and I do mean moment) of bodily strength and health. The physical condition of the powerful is inherently impermanent: expressive by nature, it *cannot* be preserved. By exact contrast, weakness, sickness, impotence enjoy undying staying power because the drive to power of the weak is the conservative, acquisitive drive of lack itself. It is for the same reason that Nietzsche argues that the will to power of slave morality is the driving force of cultural development. Physical power, the strength of a Goliath, as we have heard it told in the Old Testament, was not and will never be a match for any David who comes to compete, whirling a slingshot to down his opponent at a safe distance. And we have had thousands of years of advancement in the technologies of rendering irrelevant our inadequacies as "the *not yet determined animal*" (BGE §162), the naked, tool-*needing* animal. The will to power must also be seen, as Heidegger has emphasized, as the will to overcome the lack of power, not to get beyond power, not as so many techniques of *Gelassenheit* or peace, but for the sake of the acquisition of or cultivation of power. Self-overcoming (self-discipline, asceticism) is thus of the essence of religious as well as techno-scientific calculation, as Nietzsche perceives it, and it is that same part of being human that Zarathustra intends when he speaks of overcoming the way of human being in his doctrine of the *Übermensch*.

As we seek to redress injustice, Nietzsche teaches us to remember that demands for justice and redemption are desperately complex. The will to power as the will of democratic politics is the engine of slave morality. Far from expressing the will to power of the masters, the age of modernity in its ultimate consequentiality is the age of slave morality. In this way, National Socialism as well as Soviet Stalinism but also the currently ongoing U.S. ventures of global imperialism in the name of democracy may *all* be regarded as instantiations of slave morality to the extent that these represent intrinsically reactive moral cultures rather than "master" moralities. What is important to understand in this claim that the weak can (and do) have dominion (or does one really believe that the power elites of this world correspond to what Nietzsche meant by the "noble" or the "strong"?) concerns the extraordinary, world-building, and culture-creating force of *ressentiment*. And yet, and this is Nietzsche's subtlest insight, because *ressentiment*, because what he calls slave morality is reactive it never attains to nobility, it never *becomes* active even at the moment of success or supremacy. Because it remains a morality of implacable resentment, it continues to resent even in a position of dominion, going so far, when it finds itself without an external obstacle, as to turn upon itself. Thus we do well to consider, as Nietzsche sought to remind us, that the victim of any kind of violence, not only physical but also psychological and emotional, that is, in whatever register at all, to use Lacan's canonic terminology: imaginary, symbolic, Real, is also seething with the kind of anger that is not only inverted but is of such a valence that it will never, because it can never, burn itself out.

This conception of life highlights the question of every theodicy, reworked in modern terms under the auspices of mass murder, systematic brutality, or as the question of everyday suffering and difficulty in postmodern terms, cruelties unimaginably easy to overlook because our way of life obscures them for us—from slaughterhouses to vivisection in the blanket name of scientific and consumer research to the suffering, starvation, and illness of the poor in our own Western countries as well as elsewhere in the world (this is the testimony of Bourdieu's *The Weight of the World*), to the havoc in the life of the planet wreaked beyond any estimation, and possibly beyond recovery, by industrial fishing and mecha-nized agriculture not to mention oil production, mining, and the "man-agement" of natural "resources" (who "owns" these?), the details and extent of which take place beyond popular representation. And this in-cludes war, devastating and protracted (infinitely protracted if we learn anything at all from Nietzsche's account of the mechanisms of *ressentiment*—for there are many ways, to use Adorno's expression, of "inventing" other Jews),[19] wars we learn about today by the graceless pity of an increasingly politicized journalism, and so on, and on. In the wake of the death of God (i.e., in modern, postmodern times), Nietzsche turns his appeal to the artists rather than to the theologians.

To teach the love of the world, to teach the love of life, *amor fati*, one must first learn how to love, as Nietzsche reminds us. And loving, loving anything at all, is an acquired art. To love the past and to call it good is to see that everything of what was is wholly necessary, is equally needful, and that one is not apart from but a part of, an intrinsic piece of the whole. This love of fate does not make tragic suffering any less tragic.

As Nietzsche means to teach this, the task is to *learn* to love everything nearest to you, the love of one's neighbor. And it is that affection for what lies closest to us, in Nietzsche's telling of the Syrian gospel, that remains hard to gain, not automatic, and not already accomplished. What Christianity's teachers remanded to the paradisiacal heights of the afterlife, Nietzsche returns to the realm that is mortal immortality: the heaven all about us. That is: immediacy and memory, the spare domain between blessing and curse in the human heart.

We recall that if Nietzsche advocated music as the ultimate redemption from the perception of life as error, he also distinguished between the music of the theatre (or mass culture)—the hysteric or melodramatic music of high society—and the heart's music. In this way, Nietzsche's listener was to be (to become) an active musician. This answering resonance is the esoteric key to Nietzsche's resolution of the problem of the artist, and it is also key to the problem of the other as such, the problem of the actor, the Jew, and the problem of woman. What is now transformed is nothing but the reactive spirit, now rendered, and for the first time, to use Nietzsche's word for felt affinities: *in artibus,* echoing the song of life in its own desire.

Every advance consists in coming to own what one is, in winning every best and worst future.[20] But in order to "become what you are," to use the friendly encomium Nietzsche borrows from Pindar, there remains the challenge of consummation. Not already accomplished, becoming the one you are always entails that something is to be done. So far from a comfortable self-acceptance, such becoming entails that you lose your convictions about the self (or subject) you take yourself to be. We are to seek ourselves but this seeking can only be accomplished by forgetting ourselves. Thus Nietzsche reminds those who are inspired to follow his Zarathustra (in the first book of *Thus Spoke Zarathustra,* "On the Bestowing Virtues," and again to close his Preface to his *Ecce Homo*): "Now I say unto you, lose me and find yourselves and only when all of you have denied me, will I return to you." The point, for us, of course, as modern, self-absorbed as we are, is that the ancient philosophic word reported from Delphi holds true today. We have never sought ourselves (BGE §i). Finding ourselves, like following Zarathustra, can be accomplished only if we begin by losing ourselves. "Only then." This is not a paradox: looking directly within, we ourselves block the way and there is no one who can jump over his own shadow. We need the oblique, the indirect, the reflected, or as Hölderlin teaches us, we need the stranger, the other—that is for Christians, Jews, for Jews, Christians, that is, for men, women, for women, men, and for slaves, masters, for masters, slaves, and so on—all in order to begin to teach us who we are.

To understand this literal obliquity, it will not do to redeem Nietzsche's "errors," neither the wrongness of his feeling (the erotic as royally wrong) nor the wrongness of his doctrine of *amor fati* or the eternal return of the same, nor indeed the timely wrongness of his examples. This is not only because it involves an injustice to Nietzsche's thinking but because what is of lasting importance in his thinking turns exactly on the redemption not of *right* but *wrong* feeling and the transformative power of art in the reply to the question "how can we make things beautiful, attractive, desirable for us when they are not" (GS §299) as what is best learnt from artists. As we shall see later, Nietzsche's aesthetic sensibility is both astonishingly Christian as well as exquisitely antagonistic to this same ideal. This is the meaning of what we name Nietzsche's aesthetic gnomon as it is variously expressed: "Art is worth more than truth" (KSA 13, 522) or, "*We have art* so that we do not perish of the truth" (Ibid., 500) or, as Nietzsche writes in the last of his *Untimely Meditations,* where Wagner's Schopenhauerian Bayreuth is rendered beyond itself with a quintessentially and sweetly Hölderlinian insight—"Art exists *so that the bow shall not break*" (UM, "Richard Wagner in Bayreuth," §4).

Bent by life, alive as we are, we are the bow—we are life—lancing forth. This is Heraclitus's profoundly ambiguous paradox: "the work of life (the bow [βιος]) is death," transformed as it is by Hölderlin, who understood the meaning of inclination better than anyone—before or since—expressed in the figure of the holy sobriety of the swan, swimming head curved into water, in the sight of the poet's tower looking across the Neckar to the *Platanenallee* and thence to Greece itself. Echoing the poet's reflections on Oedipus, Nietzsche explains the meaning of tragedy: "The individual must be consecrated to something higher than himself . . . he must be free of the terrible anxiety death and time evoke in the individual: for at any moment, in the briefest atom of his life's course he may encounter something holy that endlessly outweighs all his struggle and all his distress—this is what it means to have a *sense of the tragic.*" Or, "There is only one hope and one guarantee for the future of humanity: it consists in his *retention of the sense for the tragic*" (UM, "Richard Wagner in Bayreuth," §4).

The Problem of the Actor-Artist

The problem of the actor, the problem of the artist is yoked to the problem of art and life. Because the problem of the artist (and the problem of art) exceeds the artist—if only via the actor, Jew, diplomat, woman—more is at stake than a turn to an active, or virile, or creative aesthetics in Nietzsche's artist's aesthetics. More than a matter of understanding the provenance of the rare or exceptional or consummate human being—which is the nineteenth-century and still ordinal vision of the artist as genius—the problem of the artist for Nietzsche is much rather the problem of education or culture, and the problem of culture is again the problem of mass culture. And for a good many cultures, Nietzsche argues, there will simply be no way to see the difference between the artist, genius, or criminal.

If Nietzsche defines the problem of the actor as "falseness with a good conscience" he does not simply excoriate deceit from the moral standpoint of truth and lie. That is, contrary to current analytic unreadings of the cogency of Nietzsche's "cognitive" claims, Nietzsche does not merely praise the lie of art as an honest lie (it is that, to be sure, but that is only the beginning). Instead where the truth of truth and its value is in question, illusion (the mask or the appearance), takes on a different character: "—But no! *With the real world we have also abolished the apparent world*" (TI, "How the 'Real World' Finally Became a Fable"). To explain this point, as the challenge of art for Nietzsche, it is not because Punch and Judy are puppets or because the actors in a tragedy are "only players," that the violence represented is ameliorated or redeemed: Nietzsche's philosophy of art is not a theory of cathartic, Aristotelian discharge or relief nor indeed Freudian therapy. Not *Schadenfreude*—the pleasure in the pain of another, the thought that it is not me!—Nietzsche understands the pleasure of tragedy on the model of musical dissonance, rendered in human terms. Nietzsche's aesthetics is a creative, artist's aesthetics in this fashion. As the art of illusion, art is the quintessential achievement of human intuition and only from its origins in sense perception can it move to the free invention of the imagination or of cognition.

Reducing the claims of truth to the conventions of art hardly suffices to make every human perspective the achievement of a poet. For the most part, the human artist is less an inspired genius than a dreaming savage, incapable of naming the dream as such, and ultimately unequal to it, even where the course of therapy (or philosophic insight) can lay claim to the dream in words: the "lying truth" as Lacan names it. "That one becomes what one is presupposes that one does not have the remotest idea *what* one is" (EH, "Why I Am So Clever," §9). With a word of praise for "even the blunders of life," for its wrong turns and its "wastes of time," Nietzsche speaks of the "great sagacity" below the "surface" of consciousness itself. "One is," Nietzsche explains, "much more of an artist than one knows" (BGE §192). The archaic pathos of Nietzsche's reminder that "we are *neither as proud nor as happy* as we might be" (GS §301) suggests that lacking consciousness of ourselves as

artists, Nietzsche's programmatic teaching is meant to recall us to ourselves in our strangeness, as other than we take ourselves to be.

For Nietzsche, the other is the artist, the actor, the Jew, and,
perhaps above all the other is woman herself. Starting with the actor and
the artist to get to woman and including the Jew along the way, Nietzsche
traces the excluded grouping of disenfranchised others, both as disenfranchised and in terms of the power of that same exclusion. All coyness,
flirtation, dissembling, delight in the mask, like the depths of all love,
must be understood in terms of its origins. As psychologist, using the
biological metaphor of pulsion, Nietzsche always traces the genealogy of
need. But Nietzsche never traces a genealogy just to leave it there and
here he uncovers the *frisson* at the heart of every basic need. In the same
fashion and in the same locus he captures the desperation of a god.

In a reading that is anything but anti-Christian, Nietzsche reads
the stories told of the life of Jesus as "one of the most painful cases of
the martyrdom, of *knowledge about love*" (BGE §269, cf. 270). To ne-
gotiate the inadequacy of human love and the deiform infinity of desire
(Cartesian, Augustinian "will"), Nietzsche dares a painful series of
reflections concerning what a God of love would have had to come to
know, to learn about love (BGE §269). Posed here in this question is a
sensitivity to the son of man as forsaken and as abandoned in the world.
Nietzsche has all the insight into the vulnerability of the divine that
characterizes the Cherubinic Wanderer, with none of the mystic's esoteric generosity. Given the infinitely self-reflected demands of human
need, Nietzsche is rarely attuned to the uncountenanced and uncountenanceable need of divinity itself. Here too we see again that Nietzsche's
reflections approximate the same Meister Eckhart he is inclined to cite in
an ascetic mode, as we noted earlier.

As the non-erotic god of love, the anti-Dionysus *par excellence*
(Nietzsche does not have Hölderlin's syncretistic temperament), the sky
God of the Jews fell from nomadic jealousy and a thunder-god's vengeance to become the cloying god, the god of nuzzling, Judeo-Christian
neediness (See GS §§135, 137, 141). In this way, love becomes the supreme characteristic of God and the *need* for love becomes the supreme
passion, the agony, or the suffering *of* the divine (BGE §§269, 140). And
because—this is key—the banal and ordinary run of humanity is anything
but divine, anything but pure, but only and all-too human when it comes
to love, human love inevitably falls short of the name. The divinity of love
works in love because it is a reflection of our humanity in the gamut that
runs from the carnal profundity of eros (the body redeemed by the soul,
as Nietzsche expresses it) to the purest height of the love that transforms
the human into the divine, giving the soul wings, in Plato's words. In the

economy of seduction omnipresent in love, human and divine, the infinitesimal mite of human love must be transfigured as the measure of redemptive potential or salvation. Thus the somehow always embarassing sentiment of the sixties' generation ideal—and this will be the key to Milton's twist on the same Hesiodic eros, from Lucifer's light to God's deep blue sea, moving over the waters of Genesis—is the claim that the world *needs* love. This is a foregoing and foregone point of departure for Nietzsche and for every theogony—and for every story of love.

Everyone needs love. But the need is key. Quite literally and just as a *woman* might long to be loved or as a child demands to be loved, every (male) porter, Nietzsche cheerfully reminds us, confidently expects an admirer (TL §1, KSA 1, 875). To teach us this lesson about the nature of Christian love, we needed this pastor's son, famous for reminding us, as every pastor has ever done, that God is dead and that we ourselves have killed him. Protestations of love turn out to be little more than the cries of a child, a need for, a demand for love. For Nietzsche, even God's love is such a demand, a claim for affection, like the Christian's own demand for exchange, or requital, a chit for being as such. The human ideal of love is the ideal of just desserts: purely deserved love or "free" love but the law of love, the compact between the human and the divine, Old and New Testament, is the exchange of justice *as* love.

The Judeo-Christian qua Enlightenment qua Smith-Weberian (or Protestant) ideal of love is the infinite (disinterested) favor that would be the love of the world as a free choice to love everyone as one's nearest and dearest just as one is oneself unconditionally—unaccountably—loved (and this too will be a demand for the sake of the self). Like Kant, Nietzsche uncovers the self-seeking core that lies as the grain of corruption in the gold of this enlightenment fantasy. Raising the question of love in Christianity, Nietzsche also poses the problem of the neediness of human desire in our own lives.

The dialectic of love requires love and a neediness that extends to the God of love. And beyond the need to be well-paid, redeemed, saved, Nietzsche turns to nobility and sacrifice, the erotic ideal of consummate expenditure, without reserve. This is the erotic point at issue in the valence of art.

The context of the satyr dance that framed the development of the play of tragedy, suggests a connection between the Eros of antiquity and Christian love in the excess eroticism of ritual. Beyond Christian and Greek, beyond ancient and modern, experience affirms that in passion, particularly (if not exactly) orgiastic passion—which Nietzsche toward the end of his creative life reads as the key to the Dionysian transformation of the tragic—one simply does love the world, without the least self-denial and yet without self-absorption, if we presume, for the moment, a sufficient measure of ecstasy. But the problem as we now see it in terms of not only of the artist and the Jew but in terms of woman is that in order for such a passionate moment to count as such, one *has* really to be beside oneself.

The problem here for the artist, Jew, woman (as Nietzsche sets these questions together as "the problem of the actor"), is that ecstasy excludes the hysteric's pose, that is, the "falseness" with which we began. We can also call this the problem of the orgasm if we want to go back to the metaphor of woman (via Lacan's art historical reaction to Bernini's *St. Theresa* or else via Irigaray's dryly scientific confutation of Lacan's interpretation).[21] Thus the answer to Nietzsche's transfiguring question will depend upon the intoxication of desire or the framed veiling of artistry. It is to be emphasized once again that the Nietzschean question of transfiguration is not a Christian question if only because the question for Nietzsche is not how to love the unlovable, that is, what Alasdair MacIntyre calls the signally Christian (precisely because unmerited) love for the sinner, but rather for Nietzsche, the question becomes the transfiguratively artistic or creative cultural problem of rendering the unlovable lovable so that our love is positive or in Nietzsche's words: active rather than reactive. But how can this be done, given Nietzsche's terms as we have seen them?

The clear contrast here to the joy of intoxicated desire or masculine artistry is reactive desire, that is to say, womanly desire. Reactive, that is to say, lacking power, the slave's desire to be loved turns into the calculation of semblance: feigning love, to gain love. As Nietzsche poses his invective: "it is 'the slave' in the blood of the vain person, a residue of the slave's craftiness—and how much 'slave' is still residual in woman for example—that seeks to *seduce* one's neighbor to good opinions about oneself; it is also the slave who afterward immediately prostrates himself before these opinions as if he had not called them forth" (BGE §261). Or as Nietzsche expresses the same point more pithily if no less convolutedly, certainly not less offensively, "Seducing one's neighbor to a good opinion and afterward believing piously in this opinion—who could equal woman in this art?—" (BGE §148). For Nietzsche, for Aristotle, as for all antiquity, including the flattering and whining Catullus and the other Latin love poets, this ambition is not merely ignoble but ultimately impotent: it cannot attain but only mime success. "*Woman is so artistic.*"

Contrary to the simple cult ideal of genius, the artist as such (or more evidently the fool, buffoon, or mime), is not the "noble," as Nietzsche reflects in his genealogical analysis of the noble versus slave origins of moral judgments or in his chapter-long reflections on the nature of nobility in *Beyond Good and Evil.* This too is also the point of Nietzsche's reminder to us as star-struck, artist-struck, genius-struck moderns that no noble-born Greek would have wanted to "be" Phidias, the sculptor, the artist. Pericles, the triumphant statesman, yes; Achilles, the glorious warrior yes. But Phidias? an artisan? Might as well be a fieldworker or slave.[22] For Nietzsche, like his closest relative, the criminal, the artist is hard pressed for everything that he or she becomes and this includes the artist's own survival at the most basic level. Moreover, the womanly ideal of the artist is always an artist who is never an artist by choice, as this ideal includes Nietzsche (as philosopher, poet, author) along with actors and buffoons, rhetoricians, and Jews.

In Nietzsche's unmasking of the masks of seduction, a divine or daemonic and furtive neediness unifies actor, artist, Jew, and woman. The urgency of disguise is predicated upon the lack of a sure or secure place in society except on the conditions and terms of the same dissembling assumption of disguise. And yet, and this can be seen in the passions to which all humans are susceptible (in sexual desire above all), one can be driven to distraction, as we say, and in such a state or compulsion, we are the mask and *no one*, not women, not artists, not Nietzsche himself, *has ever had any choice.* It is Nietzsche's merit to have traced the appearance of the mask/artist back to the need that gave it birth.

If the mask is common, general as it must be, it is so for the success of the ruse. Thus the problem of the theatre is not the a matter of inauthenticity or the lie as such. The problem of Wagner (or Schopenhauer or any one of Nietzsche's "educators") as the problem of the actor is not that the feigning of truth (i.e., illusion) is untrue. Rather the rub is the backward and forward vulgarity of display.

The "dangerous concept" of the artist is a *problem* because the only possible artistic genius lies in vulgar expression: "success has always been the greatest liar—and the 'work' itself is a success; the great statesmen, the conqueror, the discoverer is disguised by his creations, often beyond recognition; the 'work' whether of the artist or the philosopher, invents the man who has created it, who is supposed to have created it; 'great men' as they are venerated are subsequent pieces of wretched minor fiction; in the world of historical values, counterfeit rules" (BGE §269). Hence, Nietzsche writes, for artists, as for higher men, "ruination is the rule" (Ibid.). And he will tell us that, like the impossibility of certain truth, there is nothing to be lamented in this.

Recall the strange cadence of Nietzsche's rendering of the "dangerous" notion of the Artist along the continuum: Actor-Jew-Woman. To use Nietzsche's words, the most "interesting" of these cultural problems turns out to be the problem of the Jew, that is, the problem of the actor ultimately resonant in the problem of woman, the southern metaphor Nietzsche gave to the erotic idea, as he said, of music itself. This is the erotic music Nietzsche prescribes for us, as a cultural physician on the image of the Jew or the actor or the woman. This is what he calls the element of the erotic, the Mediterranean-Adriatic-Aegean, in music. Nietzsche meant to contrast this erotic, southern music to "German music." As the "redemption of music from the north," this more sultry music would only be, and thus the goal is a therapeutic one, a "prelude to a deeper, mightier, perhaps wickeder and more mysterious music" (BGE §255). For Nietzsche claims that he, at least, is able to "imagine a music whose rarest magic would consist in this, that it no longer knew anything of good and evil, except perhaps some sailor's homesickness, some golden shadow and delicate weakness would now and then flit across it" (Ibid.).

This is the music heard by the same heart's ecstatic spirit: "the tempter god and born pied piper of consciences whose voice knows how to descend into the underworld of every soul" (BGE §295). There the poses of Nietzsche's seduction take us beyond our routine pettiness (resentments) redeeming in an almost confessedly Christian mode—and, incidentally enough, in the bravest democratic fugue yet heard—nothing less monumental than every vulgar instinct. It is "the genius of the heart, who makes everything loud and self-satisfied fall silent and teaches it to listen, who smooths rough souls and gives them a new desire to savor—" (Ibid.), teaching the agitations of modernity stillness and superficiality out of profundity: "that the deep sky may mirror itself in them" (Ibid.). Such a genius teaches not the cheap promise of the market and its seduction of still vulgar desire in the curse that is the blessing of the "goods of others" but instead and much rather *forms* the common man so that he is "richer in himself, newer to himself than before, broken open, blown upon, and sounded out by a thawing wind, more uncertain perhaps, more delicate, more fragile, more broken, but full of hopes" (Ibid.).

In the genealogy Nietzsche traces between artistic creativity and artistic culture, both abundance and poverty or neediness can give birth, both can bring forth either immortalization or destruction. And Nietzsche wishes to look less at the fruits or works of the artist as a means to understand the psychology of the artist ("I am one thing, my works are another," (EH, "Why I Write Such Good Books," §1), than the nature of the creative impulse, the expression of overabundance or destitute versatility (cf. KSA 7, 440). Not the child of poverty and inventiveness, as in the stories Plato tells us, Nietzsche's Eros is closer to the god of the Orphic's imagination: among the primordial deities of creation, the golden god of many names, the love that brings everything hidden to the light of birth.

Nietzsche's consciousness of the tragic insight colors both the creatively primordial, affirmative, as well as the reactive dispositions of abundance and need. Whatever is replete with overflowing energy cannot be conserved—this is the economy of expenditure or expression: affirmation. The will to power that is a capacity for expression can only be given out without reserve. The Dionysian instinct that Nietzsche employs as a cipher for the "older Hellenic instinct," is also, Nietzsche writes in praise of Burckhardt, *"explicable only as an excess* of energy." In the "orgy," Nietzsche writes—invoking the naked idea of Greek eroticism, a well-known stumbling block for Winckelmann and Goethe (and as it was for the young author of *The Birth of Tragedy* himself)—conceived in "the mysteries of sexuality," Eros expresses a will to life—"exactly as the triumphant Yes to life beyond death and change" (TI, "What I Owe the Ancients," §4). Knowledge, as contrasted with art, merely seeks to tell itself a story: justifying and enduring its own impotence. In this way, Nietzsche speaks of the gap between "know" and "can" (Ibid.) where what can act necessarily excludes knowledge. The reactive will lacking power is the knowing will to power that does (and can do) nothing but conserve itself in the power it lacks, already played out, already without reserve. If, as Nietzsche tells us again and again, no one can spend more than one has, expenditure remains the point. For in the economic dynamic of life as in erotic love, the mystery is that power, enacted and lived, is continually spent, lost, given away.

The need for an active erotic deed as an expressed, articulated desire corresponds to the importance of what Nietzsche calls benediction, yes-saying. If we can find a theodicy for Nietzsche it will be here. If the God of love is faced with the human incapacity for love that same God still teaches love, and Nietzsche reminds us that love has to be taught because it has to be learned. If the point of the active, creative ideal is expression, opposing both conservation and preservation, the secret to *amor fati*, the secret to loving life will be to bless backward and forward, celebrating both the desultory effects of chaos and the body's failures, "the grapes," as Nietzsche recalled, as he buried his forty-fourth year not long before his final collapse, that were "not the only things turning brown."

The question in love is not, as one might imagine: how can it be kept? How can one hold, preserve, conserve, or keep love? The question is always how can we lose it, *how* can it be given out?

If it is true of everything organic and inorganic that the conditions of life include death, the condition of the artist as the creator of the work of art is also the contextual history of what must be overcome or mastered as what must be emphasized to produce the work. Not only "mud and chaos" but also "the divine spectator and the seventh day" (BGE §225) are absolutely necessary aspects of a holy yes, a wheel rolling out of itself, which Nietzsche's Zarathustra compares first to the child's innocence and poses again with the very same words in the impossible to fulfill (and thus impossibly romantic) ideal of lovers who promise a life to one another.

Nor would Nietzsche ever stop talking of, longing for, arguing about love, which he spoke of as *amor fati*, Dionysus teasing Ariadne. Thus he could charge (much as Wittgenstein similarly observed) that "the degree and kind of a man's sexuality reaches up to the topmost summit of his spirit" (BGE §75). Thus Nietzsche could echo his ideal definition of chastity in love: "Dans le véritable amour, c'est l'âme qui enveloppe le corps" (BGE §142).

The word of love would always be in his mouth, even if as the actor, artist, Jew, or else even as the woman he invented for himself (Nietzsche himself tells us that he makes this up, as every man does), "born of a rib of his own ideal" (TI, "Arrows," §13).[23] And in this way, the Nietzsche who "ventured to paint his 'happiness' on the wall" (GS §56) owes much of what made him "dynamite" to a dying era and to the insight that the eighteenth- and nineteenth-century ideal of eternal delight, as Hölderlin spoke of erotic ecstasy (StA 3, 165), Humboldt's "*energeia*" was and remains a metaphor for what Nietzsche despite his innocence (because of his passion) always knew better than to reduce to sex, particularly lacking illusion or erotic artistry. "Denn alle Lust will—Ewigkeit!"

Art, Nature, Calculation

10

❧

Chaos and Culture

Nietzsche's description of the universe as a "chaos" opposed to any human measure, extending "to all eternity" (GS §109) has the extreme character of Nietzsche's many hyperbolic declarations.[1] Nor has this escaped the notice of those who advert to the inherent contradictions of such a claim and, indeed: for the new enthusiasts of Gilles Deleuze as well as those who follow Alain Badiou, this same conceptual frisson enhances Nietzsche's appeal. But other philosophic readers continue to view Nietzsche's propensity to contradiction as the cardinal obstruction to reading Nietzsche as a philosopher. Compounding matters, Nietzsche adds equivocation to the sum of his logical sins: while the universal essence of "chaos" blocks our ability to square the universe in accord with our knowledge, the source of creative potential in human culture is identified as "chaos." Thus, and Badiou explores this reflection on dance, Nietzsche's Zarathustra proclaims, "I tell you: one must have chaos in one, to give birth to a dancing star" (Z, "Prologue," §v).[2] I argue, in a Hesiodic context, that Nietzsche's chaos is explicitly feminine. But what does it mean when Nietzsche speaks of giving "birth to a dancing star"? Is this a self-referential claim for Nietzsche who regarded Zarathustra as his literary "son" and named, as some have argued, for a golden star?[3]

The definition of chaos as a failure of order corresponds to the meaning of chaos on the scientific terms of Nietzsche's nineteenth-century thermodynamic theory.[4] The cosmos, a seemingly parallel term, would thus correspond to the order of arrangement: the order of order. As the array of order, the cosmos itself is a *derivative* (not causal) ordering set in dynamic motion by a creative force usually imagined as prototypically

171

masculine. This is the prime moment described in Genesis as well as in Plato's *Timaeus*, and, beyond religion and even beyond philosophical fables, such a creative force is identified on a scientific level in the popular cosmological notion of the Big Bang.

But Nietzsche attends to chaos as a word for *nature*, highlighting (this is its Orphic and Hesiodic connotation) the feminine aspect of chaos as primordially creative.[5] As encountered in Hesiod's *Theogony*, chaos represents a broad and obscure Orphic tradition that also identifies it as air, the void, and mother night.[6] In philosophic accounts chaos emerges, especially as Nietzsche reads this history, via Anaximander's expression of *apeiron* and the Heraclitean fluidity of all becoming, a dynamic, infinitely fruitful, infinitely self-contradictory, and eternally concordant flux and which may be distinguished from the "chaos of things," a kind of ontic rather than ontological chaos that is the antipode of *nous* and which Nietzsche distinguishes as "Anaxagorean chaos."[7]

Other scholars allude to differently creative accounts of chaos, with suggestive similarities to certain mathematical (and quasi-mathematical) structures, a reading named "postmodern" by at least some advocates/critics. I concede the powerful appeal of such associative readings, and I am quite confident that one can justifiably go beyond Nietzsche's own concerns in Deleuzian (or other) directions. I nevertheless argue that Nietzsche's own conception of chaos deserves further exploration. This discussion is lacking to date. Furthermore, and, from Nietzsche's point of view, it may be that we lack what is even more pernicious.

The question of chaos must be raised in conjunction with the question of science as Nietzsche raised this question throughout his work. Plainly, as we have already noted, Nietzsche had considerable ambivalence with regard to science,[8] and this is to say that although Nietzsche had a certain predisposition to favor science (if only because he regarded himself as a scientist), this same scientific rigor also meant that he maintained explicit criticisms of science. Like its exemplar (and prelude) religion, Nietzsche argued that science lacked the courage to reflect upon its own convictions. For this reason, science could not carry its own project to completion and this inevitably yielded the nineteenth-century triumph of the ideal of scientific "method" above (in place of) science (KSA 13, 442). Regarding death as a godless, "dreamless sleep," as the other side of a preoccupation with life as this *same* life, taken to eternity, Nietzsche described the modern, scientifically articulated dream of eternal life as *nihilism*. And of course, the point of the frenzy vis-à-vis the genome project, the impatient urgency that currently attends awaited innovations in stem cell research, or the enthusiasm for the prospect of human cloning (despite the untoward details of the life and early death of what was probably the most cosseted and surely the most famous ewe the world has ever known) and its selective offshoot technologies (the old National Socialist vision of race science redone in thoroughly self-pleasing capitalist colors for the twenty-first century as Eugenics for the Free Market: from personal genetic re-engineering to selecting your child's genetic traits) are all about life-everlasting, life eternal, about anything *but* suffering, sickness, fragment, deficiency, and the death that Nietzsche always regarded as not merely part of but the very essence of the human condition as ineliminably *mortal* life.

Greek Chaos versus The Waters of Genesis and Scientific Entropy

Although Nietzsche's Zarathustra quite conscientiously invokes the resonant language of the gospels, it is clear from what has been observed that Nietzsche's vision of chaos as precondition for creative possibility (*chaos sive natura*), does not refer to the image of the first waters presented in Genesis, as these reflect the inert depths of uncreative receptivity, nor does it correspond to contemporary visions of chaos, whether as disordered confusion, in casual terms, or, more formally, as correlated with the scientific notion of entropy. Nietzsche's chaos is prototypically Greek, which is to say that it must be read or heard in Greek as *physis*, as Nietzsche counterposes the Greek *chaos* to the Latin *natura*, that which brings forth of and out of itself.[9]

Nietzsche names Zarathustra in metonymic proximity to the whirling stars[10] of the cosmos itself. The very language of the suggestion that one "give[s] birth to a dancing star" supposes that one has kept the same chaos that exemplifies the world "to all eternity" within oneself as the source for creative invention. As such a creative source, this conception suggests that the language Nietzsche uses to describe one's personal chaos is more than just an endangered potentiality in the modern world but the consummation of nihilism or the postmodern and exactly ordered world.

Nietzsche's chaos is feminine,[11] primordially creative, and above all endangered. This is not just Nietzsche's associative reading or as contrasted with modern decadence. Rather and from its inception, at least in its prototypical Hesiodic schema, chaos *recedes*. Following the first generative appearance of Chaos, first of the gods that came to be, in Hesiod's *Theogony* (v. 116), Chaos is only named again in the context of the battle between Zeus and the Titans, significantly there relegated beneath the sphere of world action in lasting exile at the edge of the world, a locus beyond both Olympian gods and Titans (Th. v. 814). Unlike the contemporary physical notion of entropy, archaic Chaos does

not increase her dominion. Nietzsche's archaic conception of a primordially creative chaos is endangered in today's delimitedly banal culture of
scientific nihilism and leisurely, mediatized decadence. It is for this reason
that the "ultimate" men of today reply to Zarathustra's imperative urging that "one must have chaos in one to give birth to a dancing star"
with blinking incomprehension as they repeat the bleated questions, "What
is love? Creation is what? Longing is what? A star is what?" (Z, "Prologue," §v).

Hesiod's *Theogony* relates the emergence of Chaos as first in what
simply comes to be without antecedent but which, because it first comes
to be,[12] is *expressed in* and, more importantly still: still *expresses* the creative order of generation. Although a neuter form, *Chaos* can for this
reason be treated as it functions, that is: as female.[13] Thus we hear
Hesiod: ἦ τοι μὲν πρώτιστα Χάος γένετ'.[14] After Chaos, arise the un-
bounded gods of the beginning, divinities of aorgic nature—if we may
use the name Hölderlin employs in contrast with the cosmetically orgic
(or organic or cultured) world, on Hesiod's account. The divinities include, beyond the gloom of Chaos, Gaia, or broad-breasted earth, dim
Tartarus, golden-winged Eros. First then of the mothers of being, Chaos
gives birth to the deities of darkness: Erebos and that same Night that,
in the Orphic tradition recounting these same origins, lays the silver egg
in the lap of black darkness, from which is born the god of many names,
golden Eros or Phanes, who brings everything hidden to the light of
birth.[15] The *Theogony* includes this Orphic resonance and it is Night's
incestuous union with Erebos that annuls the character of their respective obscurity, yielding brightest Aether and the day.[16] It is explicitly
chaos and *not* the masculine world-ordering process of cosmological
genesis that functions as generatively primordial,[17] and the only comparable instance of this kind of spontaneous and independently creative
generation is the patently feminine Gaia.

It has been suggested that the Hesiodic meaning of *Chaos* (as
yawning gap, or chasm) can perhaps be traced back to an Orphic account
that names the chasm (or night).[18] And this may be so indeed, but the
names are less important than the consequences.

What is telling, to take up the language of Luce Irigaray's suggestive reminder to us, is the "forgetting" itself.[19] Here we are not as concerned with Irigaray's Heideggerian "air" as much we are concerned with
the forgotten word for *apeiron* (along with *aër* [*khaos*]). This is the oblivion
of what is first named, conceded in the order of becoming, and immediately sacrificed, yielding the primacy of masculine pro-generation.[20] For it
is important that the pattern of spontaneous (self-sufficient *and* feminine)
creativity is immediately quashed, even in such archaic accounts, and from

the start. The repression is specifically, prototypically male, even if also intimately bound with feminine complicity, going back to Gaia and her compulsion to engender a mate, Ouranos, arguably among all masculine primordial principles, the most brutally destructive, even more than Kronos, even more than Zeus.

So far from forgetting, we remember that stories that relate original Hesiodic and Orphic accounts of Chaos go on to qualify any emphasis upon the creative attributes of primordial Chaos. This is the story of ambiguity, here as the story of insurgent male power ordered (or else unhinged) by desire or age-old Eros—and this is the point of Plato's esoteric reminder that Eros, as desire, is both the youngest of the gods *and* the oldest of the gods, a point exemplified in today's Viagra-modified times, an emphatic vision not unknown in the days of ancient Greece, as attested by the comic allusion to the supposed effects of oregano and scallions, and all such epithets for Eros, young/old, are inherently ambivalent. In this same way, in the genesis of the Olympian gods, the creative power that is originally female becomes or, better said, is *made* male. One scholar has traced this same pattern back to the castration of Ouranos, and thus back to Kronos (indeed and quite bodily with the analogue of the belly of Kronos to the womb of Rhea).[21] In this way, like his father, Kronos, with his children before him, son Zeus now having supplanted his father and thus replacing him, engulfs and thus becomes his first wife. Swallowing Mētis, Zeus *incorporates* not only her wisdom— lodged in his belly, her counsel would always be his own—but Zeus also *elides* her story and her name, he functionally appropriates her feminine nature.[22] Thus the Zeus who gives birth to Athena, fully armed, sprung from his forehead, is the same Zeus who can rescue the heart of the dismembered Zagreus from the burnt ashes of his Titanic tormenters blasted by Zeus's thunderbolt, thence transferred by the mediating influence of wine into the womb of Semele, his human lover, to engen- der there the child Dionysus, only to reduce Semele herself to ashes with the same lightning flash of his godly countenance (keeping the promise that is the devastation of love between mortal and immortal), rescuing the not yet fully formed child to sew into his own thigh, finally to give birth to Dionysus of the two gateways, twice reborn in the crucible of ashes both titanic and mortal. Such a Zeus incarnates the ambiguity of the all-father, incidentally like Yahweh, another sky god, a god embody- ing male/female principles. Among his brothers, Zeus *became*, he was not born to be, the first among the Olympians—precisely by means of his visceral, gut, or literally physical incorporation of feminine creativity. Now the father gives birth to the son. Now the sky gods that, again, like Yahweh, are always male, come to form human beings in their own image.

For Nietzsche, what matters is not to pay homage (with his Basel friend Bachofen) to the old story of the primordial goddess, or, with Goethe, to the literally named mothers of being. Instead, Nietzsche encourages us to attend to the powers of wild nature in creative self-genesis, to shape oneself out of oneself and so to become oneself a work of art. To create oneself, giving birth to a dancing star—a wheel rolling out of itself—one needs the "chaos and labyrinth of existence" (GS §322). This imperative holds not because order kills (the letter, the spirit) but because the chaos in creative question is primordial nature itself: that which is older than all other deities, that of which the most darkly aorgic deities are born without mediation, as divinities capable of bringing their own opposites out of themselves. The chaos or nature here described is the wild, untamed, and uncontrollable force (Hölderlin's divine, or aorgic, *apeiron* nature, to be further reviewed in the next chapter). And we, so Nietzsche's Zarathustra tells us, still dispose over this creative power: "I tell you: you still have chaos in you." (Z, "Prologue," §5). And in one of his most ecstatic passages in *Beyond Good and Evil*, Nietzsche writes:

> In man *creature* and *creator* are united: in man there is material, fragment, excess, clay, dirt, nonsense, chaos; but in man there is also creator, form-giver, hammer, hardness, spectator divinity, and seventh day. (BGE §225)

Given this complex balance between the creature and the creator in us, we need Zarathustra's reminder because we are also closest to losing the creative force of chaos through a blindness that is as much a blindness about ourselves as about nature as such.

In this way, chaos is less to be thought on the all-too-Platonizing order of a sheerly open, Timean gap, or receptacle. As self-engendering *physis*, chaos thus corresponds to a generative excess or plenum, like the Anaximandrian *apeiron*.[23] As an unthinkably consummate, self-sufficient creativity, a feminine first principle is common to more than one cosmology. Yet, as we have seen, this very same primordial conception of feminine creative potencies (from the notion of Chaos as the most ancient of deities to the fantasies of the cultures of the goddess or matriarchy) was also eclipsed from the moment it began. All accounts of the genesis of the dark children of Chaos are obscured by the more fertile and various earth (Gaia) who, herself complicit, giving birth to her own lover, sets in supporting motion the dominant account of the succession of masculine progenitors. As the story of the birth of the gods, the theogony becomes a story of genesis (i.e., a story of paternity, another kind of genealogy).

Nor are today's more properly scientific (and it is illusory to think the associative connotations of the scientific mode as differing from Deleuzian) conceptions of chaos any less transient or secondary. A pell-mell representing the failure of order, chaos betrays (and thus presupposes) the ideal of order as such, an order *reduced* to disorder (reflecting the temporal schematism articulated in both the religious tradition of Genesis and the thermodynamic conception of entropy). Derived from an aboriginally masculinist vision, the Judeo-Christian tradition regards the lifeless depths recounted in Genesis as the impotent, and featureless waters of an unreal and feminine abyss prior to the first divine moment of the creation of the world. In this convergence of religious and scientific perspectives, chaos is reduced to an expressly negative concept, of value only to the extent that order can be born of it, as a formed and recognizable day-lit order takes the place of the dark, formless children of old chaos.

Nature as Chaos, Nature as Art

By regarding nature as chaos in its original Greek or primordial significance, Nietzsche repudiates the traditional Western opposition between nature and art. As an absolute will to power, without remainder—"und nichts ausserdem"—the native chaos of the world is a raw, uncountenanceable and untrammeled realm beyond the imposition of order for the same Nietzsche who teaches the rule—and the illusion—of perspective. As it recalls Spinoza's *deus sive natura*, Nietzsche's *"chaos sive natura"* (KSA 9, 515) is a proclamation that works to de-deify nature while, at the same time, stripping nature of its rational ground or foundation,[24] that is, its ultimate concord and commensurability with human reason. Nietzsche's *"chaos sive natura"* thus advances a rare critique of the very possibility of nothing less than the science of nature.

By outlining the history of the illusory, as the history of the true (the "real" world of Platonic fantasy and Aristotelian productivity), Nietzsche raises the key question regarding the rational underpinnings of the ideal real. The scientific order perceived in nature is a reflection of the phantasms of human sensibility and human conceptual power.[25] For Nietzsche, always in the lineage of Kant in matters of knowledge and truth, there is no *reality* or nature knowable apart from a thoroughly "humanized [*vermenschlichte*] nature." Thus Nietzsche criticizes the realist conviction (to cite a passage from *The Gay Science* directed "To the realists") that "the world really is the way it appears" to "sober," realist eyes as inevitably naïve and correspondingly egotistical: "As if reality stood unveiled before you only, and you yourselves were perhaps the best part of it" (GS §57).

For Nietzsche, the whole of natural science is a continuous and effective, successful and consummate process of what he calls a "humanization *in summa*."[26] Nature is a human invention and yet and at the same time Nietzsche also argues that it is nature that works its artistry through us and upon us, so that our inventiveness and our artifices are not unnatural—however much we use this inventiveness for the purposes of the mastery and control of nature in the case of science.[27] With the artistic, inventive expression of such scientific "means," we express our own nature, the same essence that reflects the inherent truth of nature as "will to power" (or chaos) to all eternity.

Yet, we apprehend neither nature's chaos—nor could we ever do so given our perceptual and conceptual apparatus—nor can we recollect any sense of the chaos of impressions within us—this last a necessary consequence of the coordinate limitations of our human psycho-physiology. This is a favorite theme for Nietzsche, who declares that nature threw away the key to the welter of physiological activity within our bodies,[28] and it forms a fundamental component of his pre-Freudian critique of the psychological identity of the human subject. In the more straightforward instance of a face-to-face encounter with the natural world, Nietzsche reflects upon the paradoxical dynamic of chaos and the cultivated, imaginary register of "nature" that is modern "nature" when he notes:

> As I walk about in open country, I am always amazed to think how everything works on us with such a supreme precision: the forest thus and so, and the mountain thus and so, but there reigns within us not the slightest confusion, misapprehension, or stammering referring to the sensation as a whole. And yet the greatest uncertainty and chaotic aspect must abound. . . . (KSA 9, 957)

In the same way as we do not (as we *cannot*) attend to our own range of perceptions, neither do we attend to the full complexity of things as experienceable objects. By invoking the metaphor of reading, Nietzsche points out that we tend to see not what is actually in front of our eyes but we perceive what we *believe*. We see what we already "know" much "rather than registering what is different and new in an impression" (Ibid.).[29] To make this argument, Nietzsche suggests the example of our sense perception of something as obvious and static as a tree. Even with regard to such a routine (and sizeable) object of everyday perception, he argues, and perceptual psychologists of all stripes will concur, if for different reasons, that we manage to misapprehend the tree itself: never seeing it "exactly and completely, with reference to leaves, twigs, color,

and form; it is so very much easier for us to fantasize some approximation of a tree" (BGE §192). Thus whether confronted by routine impressions or "in the midst of the strangest experiences, we still do the
same thing: we make up the major part of the experience . . ." (Ibid.).
For Nietzsche, we overlook, overleap, and so invent our experience in
general. Challenging the convenience of conventional theories of truth,
Nietzsche reminds us that we have become *"accustomed to lying."* And
this circumstance is not ameliorated by adding reference to the complexity of things that are too minor to attract our notice—the wild variety of
insects and spiders and plasmodiæ streaming on the bark of the same tree
or crawling and flying in the jungles at our feet.

As Ryogi Okochi[30] has correctly underlined in his comparison of
Nietzsche's conception of nature and Eastern views, "nature"—just so
and as such—is *not* a correlevant *object* for human comprehension.[31]
Regarding the world as will to power to all eternity, that is, naming
nature chaos, Nietzsche emphasizes both its distance from our capacity
to comprehend nature as it is in itself (this is Nietzsche's routine
Kantianism)[32] and its inherent creativity (again, recalling the archaic Greek
conception of chaos). As chaos, nature itself is itself interpretive. On this
same level, nature itself is invention, replete with multiple subjectivities
and a variety of opposed wills. This subjective force is what Nietzsche
means by speaking of the will to power as a perspective or an interpretation: "every center of force adopts a perspective toward the entire
remainder, i.e., its own particular valuation, mode of action, and mode
of resistance. . . ."[33] In the organic world, more conservatively, Nietzsche
had earlier expressed this point by locating interpretation on the external
side: "the entirety . . . is the interweaving of beings with invented little
worlds about them: inasmuch as they impose upon outer experience their
power, their desire, their habits, as their external world" (KSA 11, 590).
Nature as a whole is constant and thoroughgoing interpretation and this
means that it is inherently and necessarily perspectival, from which it
follows that "every center of force—and not only humanity—construes
all the rest of the world from its own viewpoint, i.e., measures, feels,
forms, according to its own force."[34] Giving measure and giving form,
testing, and reacting, Nietzsche can say and mean that nature is art and
artistry at once.[35]

Indeed, from beginning to end, everything turns on the question
of art for Nietzsche. The difference between the art of the human and
the art of nature is the difference between the *artless* art of nature (which
lacks all purposiveness) and the *artful* art of human invention that is
both artistically consummate (or artful *art*) or else poorly executed or
aesthetically artificial—kitsch, or *far-too-*, *all-too-artful* art. Only cultured—

artful—art, and especially the art of practical, technical, purposiveness or *techne*, is *able* to name itself as art (even if it does not always do so). Everything else, be it God[36] or be it nature, lacks artistic awareness, as artless or *natural art*. But the same natural (or divine) artlessness is the key to the (active) creative process. Hence Nietzsche agrees with Kant's claim that the highest art is the artlessness that is (or appears to be) an unconscious or *natural* art—hence unaware of what it is or does. This Nietzsche names innocence. Nietzsche's goal is to recover this (natural) innocence as a possibility for human creativity. The result would be a renaturalized humanity (itself only possible on the basis of a redeemed nature, liberated to its own chaos or independence from the imaginary order of human control).[37]

For Nietzsche, knowledge begins in error and illusion, and thus Nietzsche pairs knowledge and art. In light of this conjunction, he describes the ideal beauties of perceived "nature," in a word-painting as follows: "It was evening: the air streaming with the smell of evergreen, one's gaze opened upon shimmering snow-topped, grey mountain ranges, against a heaven of calm, blue skies" (KSA 7, 468). Contrary to the straightforward, albeit poetic, descriptiveness of this vista, we note that Nietzsche invokes the senses of smell and sight in an encounter with just the kind of majestic landscape we very romantically identify with Nietzsche's nineteenth–century ideal of "nature"—think of the Caspar David Friedrich painting, *From the Summit: Traveller Looking Over the Sea of Fog*, the one that graces the Penguin edition of the late R. J. Hollingdale's translation of Nietzsche's auto-bibliography *Ecce Homo*. The problems with these associations are too numerous to document in full, but also too influential (and amusing) to fail to mention them.[38]

For Nietzsche, beyond our automatic associations coloring our seemingly immediate perception of the world, we do best to challenge the reality of any such pure or direct perception of nature. Such a refusal of unfiltered or direct sense access to the world around us is the point (Kantian as well as psychological) of his teasing assault upon the sobriety of "realist" perception of the "real" world in *The Gay Science*: "That mountain there! That cloud there! What is 'real' in that?" (GS §57). For Nietzsche in a Schopenhauerian modality, "—A thing of this kind we never see as it is in itself, instead we always film it over with a delicate spirit-membrane—that overlay we see instead. Such natural things rouse inherited sensations, our own feelings. We see something of our own self—to this extent, the world itself is our representation. Forest, mountains, much more than a concept, but our own experience and history: a bit of ourselves" (KSA 8, 468). There is no world apart from what he explicates again and again as the chaos of our sensations and the chaos of nature itself. Such a natural chaos can never be perceived as such (and what would that be?) but must always be ordered. For this reason, ordinary perception is interpretation for Nietzsche. It cannot yield an unmediated or direct truth because it cannot yield the chaotic truth of nature apart from our imposed sense-interpretations, an apart-world, a world of abundance or excess. This knowledge-theoretic impossibility is what Heidegger captures with a seemingly paradoxical formula, asserting that for Nietzsche, "*Truth* is missing the *truth*" ["*Wahrheit* ist Verfehlung der *Wahrheit*"].[39] In saying this, Heidegger underscores the exactly aletheic character of Nietzsche's critique of truth and his phenomenological critique of perception and experience. Heidegger is worlds away from the philosophical accusation that charges Nietzsche with tacit contradiction—where Nietzsche declares (as true) that there is no truth. Instead, for Heidegger, as for Nietzsche, raising the question concerning the truth of the natural world requires a preliminary inquiry into the conditions of possible perception as prerequisite conditions of the very possibility of knowledge (and this knowledge counts as much as the knowledge of nature, or as knowledge of ourselves, that Nietzsche also sets as part of his effort to challenge the legacy of Socrates in philosophy).

Chaos Sive Natura

In the context of a *Nachlaß* sketch for *Also sprach Zarathustra*—"Toward the projection of a new art of life"—Nietzsche's first invocation of *chaos sive natura*—he has only two—occurs in a passage from 1881, parsed with a musical allusion to Beethoven: "First book in the style of the first movement of the Ninth Symphony." Thus the conceptual summary: "*Chaos sive natura*: 'regarding the dehumanization of nature' " (KSA 9, 519), offers an expression of the first movement of this projected new way of life. Nietzsche's perspective here is not to be confused with the enlightenment vision of *de-anthropomorphization* proposing to undo or else to deny the efficacy of the "humanization of nature" (i.e.,"—interpretation [of nature] according to us" (KSA 12, 19).

The enlightenment ideal of a liberation from tutelage (self- or otherwise imposed), extracting the human contribution from the world of both psychological (psychosocial) projection and putatively objective perception, is an impossible dream, as Nietzsche sees it. Unlike Protagoras, who highlighted the inseparable contribution of the human to all epistemic endeavors, Nietzsche neither celebrates nor, like Xenophanes, does he mockingly emphasize (or even seek to subvert as postmodernist *avant la lettre*) the inevitably human contribution that is a part of any and all natural knowing. Instead, Nietzsche's ambition goes back to his earlier expression of an "artist's metaphysics" in his *The Birth of Tragedy Out of the Spirit of Music*.[40] This artistic metaphysics is a metaphysics as conceived from the side of the creative artist. Nietzsche's goal is a stylized, conscious art: "we want to take what we need from [nature], in order to dream above and beyond the human. Something more grandiose than the storm, and the mountain range, and the sea should arise—and yet born from humanity!" (KSA 10, 415).

Nietzsche's artistic vision sees a transformed humanity in the light of art presupposing both the unknowability of nature and its abundant excess: *chaos sive natura*. The form of this last expression parodies Spinoza's *deus sive natura* (criticizing Spinoza's formula as a confession of sensibility) Nietzsche accuses Spinoza and other metaphysicians of being guilty of a literally higher "feeling" (GS §372), a mystic return to nature on the background of "christliche Vertrauensseligkeit" (KSA 12, 129), itself derived from Descartes' equation of God and the things of the world (*Meditation* VI). The core of Nietzsche's *chaos sive natura* is Kantian, echoing Nietzsche's rebuke to the Stoic ideal[41]—yoking Rousseau with Spinoza[42] and Comte with Christianity—in the context of the mechanist's music box that is the eternal repetition of a world that, as he claims, more than concealing a hidden or obscure god, now lacks "even the capacity for eternal novelty" (KSA 11, 556).

When Nietzsche identifies his "project" as "the de-anthropomorphization of nature and the subsequent renaturalization of humanity, after regaining the pure concept of 'nature,' "[43] he proposes art as a means to the redemption of both nature and the part of nature that is the human being. This is more than a matter of describing a parallel between the human (as *homo natura*) and nature (as a dynamic creative chaos of abundance and chance) but rather of undoing the obstacles to recognizing ourselves as what we are (as who we are). Once again we note the generous optimism of Nietzsche's definition of humanity: "The human being is the witness to what gigantic powers can be set in motion through a small being of myriad content . . . *Beings that play with stars*" (KSA 12, 40).

The project of renaturalizing humanity in terms of such stellar playfulness presupposes the redeemed conception of nature that restores its creative abundance as chaos. In this way, the physics Nietzsche praises ("long live physics!"), corresponds to the same "physicists" that Nietzsche urges us to become "in order to be able to be *creators* in this sense"— that is, we are to take up a reflection on natural science, a reflection on what is proper to the physicist, in order "*to become those we are*—human beings who are new, unique, incomparable, who give themselves laws, who create themselves" (GS §335). Looking into the chaos within, like the chaos of nature, Nietzsche emphasizes that "in the great as in the small, there is nothing that lasts" [*Das Bleiben fehlt, im Kleinsten und im Ganzen*] (KSA 9, 528). Hence for the sake of cosmic creativity, for cultural creativity, what is needed is an affirmation of chaos as change, alteration, impermanence, flux. This restored emphasis on unfathomable excess also restores the innocence of becoming.

In this way, *amor fati*, or what Heidegger calls *Gelassenheit* in another context, is the point of Nietzsche's de-anthropomorphization of nature as the naturalization of the human being here reworked as, recreated as, or become a work of art. To give oneself "style," becoming "a work of art," at once artist and artificed (like Spinoza's naturing and natured), aesthetic subject *and* aesthetic object, Nietzsche tells us that one must have the disposition of a chaos within. As the power that can give birth to a dancing star, this resonant chaos is not the power of fractal dynamics, the order of chaos reconceived or reframed as the perspective fantasy of smaller and smaller profiles, but reflects the first Hesiodic chaos that gives birth to night and to darkness. This is a dark or "tragic" chaos, and it is one that can risk going to ground, for the sake of a dancing star.

11

⁓ᴗᴄ⁓

The Ethos of Nature and Art

Hölderlin's Ecological Politics

Both poetic and modernizing technological constructions may be seen as parallel, depicting the concept of "nature" as a human invention. This chapter offers a philosophical reading of Friedrich Hölderlin's poem, "Nature and Art or Saturn and Jupiter," not to resolve to be sure but much rather to sharpen the debate on the relationship between nature and art and the political stakes of ecological thinking.

Nature Pure

As represented in an ethical context, the idea of "nature," pure and untouched, is sometimes presented in romantic contrast to the artifices (and artifacts) of technology and science that we have learned to regard with rather more embarrassment and even more resignation than suspicion. We take technology for granted, counting upon the possibilities of a cyborg rebirth, if indeed as projected upon the desolately flat worlds (or screens) of gaming alter-egos, or, more commonly, in the claustrophobic confines of email or the internet, we contract (if indeed the "we" here refers mostly to men who may be accounted as customers) for cyborg intimacies, and above all, as academics, we subscribe to the ideology and the ideal of the educational enrichments of an internet search program. We take ourselves to be tools, as we take nature, untooled but utterly pliable, open to our incursions. Thus nature is represented both as a world apart from human intervention and the prime site of the same.

By the same token (note the great convenience of dialectics), human praxis is both natural and "non-natural" action, to the extent that humanity considers itself distinct from the natural.

Yet ours is increasingly an era of demythification. And it is as easy to demythify nature as it is to criticize its appropriation and devastation. This may be the reason such *demythifying* critiques are so often—and so very paradoxically—deployed on the Left—although this may simply be due to the residual scientism that was characteristic of Engel's marketing of Marxism.[1] Thus in the sense of "natural" healing alternatives or "natural" health foods, the natural is demystified as a phantasm. "Nature" is as meaningless as the advertising copy "all natural" on a cereal box.

From this perspective, nature is merely a domain apart from human life but also a complementary reserve: very like the backdrop for a television commercial advertising the utility of sport utility vehicles: able to get away from the human, to make a path through unconquered territory. And this also means that nature is replete with possibilities for transformation. No matter whether to be exploited *or* to be stewarded, nature is the infinitely plastic, ultimately available human *resource.*

The critical and rationalist, which is sometimes called the deflationist, critique of the romantic disjunction between nature and science (or technology) has its advocates particularly among those who take an analytic approach to the philosophy of ecology and seek at the same time to sidestep critiques of technology and science. For such readings, what historically minded scholars now speak of as the "invention" of nature works to subvert the very substance of romantic critiques. In this sense, Hölderlin's "construction" of nature responds to the engineered construction of nature in modern times, a more literal construction that must be seen as the invention of nature, scientifically driven, technologized, and industrially capitalized.

Nature as Ecological Construct and the Ethos of Poetry

To the extent that nature is seen only as raw material, the defining schema is that of fabrication and appropriation. To be "exploited" or "preserved," the intentional, orientational dynamic of human appropriation articulates the common convictions between rapacity and conservation—the same fully natural rapacity that has John Gray rename the human species: *homo rapiens.* As it will turn out, conservation has not only the same intentional structure but also the same object as exploitation. Nature is to be preserved for the sake of (deferred) consumption, thus the project is an inherently speculative or capitalist ideal, whatever the politics of its disposition. That nature has this utility (now/later), and that humans have every right to use or appropriate it for human use (be it now or later), is not questioned, and there is no social or political perspective that would challenge this conviction that has a hearing (or might be taken seriously enough to win a hearing) in any country on this earth.

For contemporary sensibilities, no matter how instructed by cultural and intellectual critique, nature represents nothing other than a god-given (or natural) bounty. This righteous account of nature as standing reserve is rendered in nothing like the sense of this originally Heideggerian term, but a manager's sense: nature as natural resource is synonymous with natural right, an essentially human endowment.

As the ideological critique of enlightenment rationalism reminds us, the ideal purity of nature, untouched by human hand, unspoiled by industrial development, has its provenance in a cultural dream. And we ourselves with all our polyester, artificial sweeteners, chemical additives, electronic accoutrements, *bio*-chemical and nuclear wastes are nothing apart from nature, and thus everything human and technological, product or by-product of the same, is as "natural" as anything that may be found on the earth. Whether we read the rationalist or pro-modernist account of nature or the opposed and so-called post-romantic philosophies of thinkers such as Nietzsche and Heidegger, the idea of nature remains a poetic invention in truth. To say that nature is an invention is exactly not to say that nature is manmade, even if it does entail that as a poetic invention, there is and can be no such thing as "nature" in actuality, that is, in "real," unimaginary, non-symbolic, but chaos-nature.[2] As we have seen in our account of Nietzschean chaos, regarded as a kind of Anaximandrian *apeiron*, as the source of what comes to be and passes away, nature may not be set apart from our cosmicizing concerns and deeds. I am critical, then, of the physical (and metaphysical) program built into the conception of nature as a resource, "sustainable" or otherwise (this, I believe, is where humanists, logical rationalists, and Marxists—all alike—err).[3] For all visions of nature, that is, nature perceived as alien to us (and so needing to be mastered and tamed) and nature idealized as original garden (and so needing to be rewritten as our home) are, as Nietzsche says, equally inventions. Both conceptions are "poetic constructs," as is, indeed, the idea of our "difference" from nature. Nor is it an accident that such perspectives conveniently leave nature at our disposal to "dominate" or to "cultivate." But without thoughtful clarification of the meaning of invention or poetic construction, we miss the fundamental issue behind the several convergent views criticizing our estimation of nature.

For Nietzsche, it should be added, the human as an element of nature is neither intrinsically superior (kinder or more humane) nor intrinsically base (crueller or merely, Nietzsche would say, all-too human) in comparison with nature as a whole. The point is not to absolve our guilt but to drive it home. Our humanity can serve either way. Thus Nietzsche poses his question, "When will we complete our de-deification of nature?" (GS §109) in the wake of the Cartesian enlightenment project of rampant demystification.

However ironic it may be, the perspective advocated by the pro-development, rationalist conservative coincides with the Marxian argument for appropriating the whole of nature, for the sake of material human progress or comfort. From such enlightened perspectives, nature simply *cannot* be violated merely by being used or exploited (the very concept is anthropomorphic, they will say) because, in a kind of ideal wholeness or totalizing vision of absolute perspectives there *can* be no "difference" between man and nature. The logical man, capitalist rationalist or Marxist materialist, takes alienated nature as separated or sundered from its original or ideal unity with humanity and proposes a corrective in the appropriation or restoration of unity.

Claiming that there is 'no such thing as nature, that nature is a poetic fancy, a romantic ideal,' theorists are trying less to comprehend the complexities of nature (or poetry) than to end all debate. For his part (this is the great difference between ideology, or demystification, and philosophy) Nietzsche (and in a different way, Heidegger too) could desire no such thing. Thus Nietzsche's question concerning the de-deification of nature goes beyond humanism: "When may we begin to naturalize humanity in terms of a pure, newly discovered, newly redeemed nature?" (GS 109).

Hölderlin's Saturn and Jupiter: Archaic Nature and Technical Art

Nietzsche's notion of a naturalized humanity coordinated with a humanized, de-deified nature entails an affinity between nature and human invention (art). The idea is allegorically mapped in Hölderlin's poem, "Natur und Kunst oder Saturn und Jupiter" [Nature and Art or Saturn and Jupiter]:

> *Du waltest hoch am Tag' und es blühet dein*
> *Gesez, du hältst die Waage, Saturnus Sohn!*
> *Und theilst die Loos' und ruhest froh im*
> *Ruhm der unsterblichen Herrscherkünste.*
> *Doch in den Abgrund, sagen die Sänger sich,*
> *Habst du den heil'gen Vater, den eignen, einst*
> *Verwiesen und es jammre drunten,*
> *Da, wo die Wilden vor dir mit Recht sind,*
> *Schuldlos der Gott der goldenen Zeit schon längst:*
> *Einst mühelos und größer, wie du, wenn schon*

Er kein Gebot aussprach und ihn der
Sterblichen keiner mit Nahmen nannte.
Herab denn! oder schäme des Danks dich nicht!
Und willst du bleiben, diene dem Älteren,
Und gönn' es ihm, daß ihn vor Allen,
Göttern und Menschen, der Sänger nenne!
Denn, wie aus dem Gewölke dein Bliz, so kömmt
Von ihm, was dein ist, siehe! so zeugt von ihm,
Was du gebeutst, und aus Saturnus
Frieden ist jegliche Macht erwachsen.
Und hab' ich erst am Herzen Lebendiges
Gefühlt und dämmert, was du gestaltetest,
Und war in ihrer Wiege mir in
Wonne die wechselnde Zeit entschlummert.
Dann kenn' ich dich, Kronion! dann hör' ich dich,
Den weisen Meister, welcher, wie wir, ein Sohn
Der Zeit, Geseze giebt und, was die
Heilige Dämmerung birgt, verkündet. *⁴

---

*High up in the day you govern, your law prevails,
  You hold the scales of judgment, O Saturn's son,
    Hand out our lots and well-contented
      Rest on the fame of immortal kingship.
Yet, singers know it, down the abyss you hurled
  The holy father once, your own parent, who
    Long now has lain lamenting where the
      Wild ones before you more justly languish,
Quite guiltless he, the god of the golden age:
  Once effortless and greater than you, although
    He uttered no commandment, and no
      Mortal on earth ever named his presence.
So down with you! Or cease to withhold your thanks!
  And if you'll stay, defer to the older god
    And grant him that above all others,
      Gods and great mortals, the singer name him!
For as from clouds your lightening, from him has come
  What you call yours. And, look, the commands you speak
    To him bear witness, and from Saturn's
      Primitive peace every power developed.
And once my heart can feel and contain that life
  Most living, his, and things that you shaped grow dim,
    And in his cradle changing Time has
      Fallen asleep and sweet quiet lulls me:
I'll know you then, Kronion, and hear you then,
  The one wise master, who, like ourselves, a son
    Of Time, gives laws to us, uncovers
      That which lives hidden in holy twilight.

Hölderlin's atypical rendering of the relation between art and nature recalls both the essential necessity of conflict and the transformative, redemptive power of recognition, that is, grace. However much art (Jupiter) necessarily overcomes or subdues nature (Saturn), art grows out of nature, and herein lies the first force of its animation and vitality. But Hölderlin goes beyond Schiller or other Romantic poets. Jupiter, *Kronion* (art), owes Kronos, *Saturn* (nature) an ultimate, abiding acknowledgment, which in turn serves as the condition for and thus inaugurates a new age of harmony. It is important to emphasize that the poet invokes not nature but art. The course of redemption proposed is nothing earth-shattering, but a literal matter of observance and reserve. In this way, Hölderlin addresses the redemption of nature beyond ecology.

Contrary to the modern or even Judeo-Christian ideal of progress exemplified by the concept of the fullness of time, an ideal brought to a certain secular pitch in today's modernist thinking, the Greek course of temporal advance was one of tragic decay. This conception of decay was drawn closer to a certain image of nature than the supernatural focus implicit in either the Judeo-Christian religious tradition or the explicit optimism of the modern project of manipulating nature. Progress, for the Greeks, runs backward, thus the current age is always one of down-going [*Unter-gang*], an age of decay in Nietzschean terms. The modern progress ideal opposes such a nihilistic or decadent image and, in contrast to the Greek perspective, presupposes a future paradise of subordinate delight. This deferred enjoyment is also at the heart of Max Weber's analysis of the presumptuous virtuality of modern rationality. Anticipating Heidegger's later analysis of modern scientific calculation or *Machenschaft* or technological "enframing," Weber does not use the neo-Kantian conventionality of the "as if. " Instead, Weber clearly articulates the still-current (that is enduring) spirit of modern techno-scientific confidence in the powers of our achieved rationality. Rather than the ideology of the Will, the essence of modern techno-science employs an ideology of potential power or virtual potency, conceived as what could, in principle, always be done.[5] The logic of modern reason does not contradict the Western religious perspective but is merely an alternate expression. Opposed to the spirit of this modern myth, Hesiod's construction of a golden age of lost harmony is ordered to an absolute rule. But this is a melancholy invocation, for this era is past, the vanished world of the now-deposed titans.

In this perspective, Jove (or Jehovah or Judea) throws off the yoke of Saturn or Kronos. In an ambiguous play on the phonetic similarity of the names Kronos (the titan) and Chronos (time), Jupiter, the son of time, usurps Chronos, in the order of time, Kronos, the old, titanic order. The names can shift as they do, but the oppositions or figures of opposition are preserved by the play of allegory. Thus we recall that the golden age, immortalized in song by the poets, was anything but an age of peaceful harmony. If the golden age is an age of glory, its titan Lord consumes his own children, fully meaning to include, save for a ruse, the child who would one day exile him to inaugurate the new order of law. This is Zeus or Jupiter, and Jupiter's violently circumscribed law is born from Saturn's "primitive" peace, a peace both pristine (Saturn makes no laws) and inaugurated or first guaranteed by Jupiter's succession. Jehovah/Jupiter, we note, may also be named Dionysus, for resonantly complex references are characteristic of Hölderlin.

The poem begins with praise to Jupiter and the modern order of reason and bright day, the enlightenment. Not only is Jove praised as on high, literally "on top of the day," but his word is law, and righteous law. As the son of Saturn, he allots the just portion to all, resting "happily in the fame of his immortal ruling arts." Following the classical Greek style of reversal, the second and third stanzas do not expound on this glory. Reading Jove in mythic terms, we are confronted with an unexpected critique, and read anti-mythically, we will hear little more than a romantic convention, one part Hellenistic ethos, one part Stoic encomium, urging a return to nature. Thus one traditionally understands the description of poetry as holding a culturally mimetic and thus informative mirror, for the instructive benefit of the current day, *ut pictura poesis*, mirroring nature in its purity. This, the art of art, is to seem artless or natural.

But further reading cannot maintain the direction of the allegory, if only because the connection is drawn too intimately. The accession to art is not the truth of nature but its banishment, its renunciation, so that mortals scarcely know its name. This is intimated by the singers, whose task it is to preserve such knowledge and to call art to account. Broader than poetry itself, art must be understood as the domain of law and order, as rational rule: the science of bold invention and measure.

The fourth and fifth stanzas, recalling the creative reign of art to an original and foundational responsibility to nature, express a filial commandment that once acknowledged must be redeemed, whether by abdication or else with the honest expression of gratitude that is shame. Both rational law and the primordially irrational titanic power belong to the full expression of every power that is or can be. Thus the singer asks that the creative artist or scientist or man of law come to recognize and then to acknowledge that he owes everything that he is to the fettered power of Saturn, now mastered and forgotten in the underworld. Everything that we bear in our hearts is first begotten by this age-old power; again, every power that is grows out of Saturn's same primitive peace.

What the poet asks of the creative artist, the scientist, and every poetic construer of nature is what he asks of Jupiter with respect to Saturn: to be the conscientious son of his father, remembering who he is and thus returning to himself again: Jupiter, that is, as the poet reminds him of his name and origin: *Kronion*.

That what is asked is a matter of right order is plain: it is a matter of the recognition of service befitting the first in the order of time. For the sake of justice, the singers are to name by name the older god of a golden time. (Note here that what is asked is not the liberation of the titan bound in "deepest Orkus." Rather, as a son of time, and like ourselves it is Jupiter—and not Kronos—who is enjoined to come to himself.)

The penultimate and ultimate verses adumbrate the necessary prerequisite for and the value of recognition, that is, honor, or what Nietzsche named "affirmative praise." Thus the poet can anticipate that the poet will affirm or praise Jupiter, if only once filled with the feeling or sentiment of life itself, once granted the waning or softening of the light of pure reason, of creative calculation. But this is to say that as the creative artist, as the artist of poetic construction, the poet will know Jupiter as he "knows" himself, as a son of time. And all of us are mortal, all of us likewise children of time. In the blink of changing, rushing time, held in the poetic cradle of resonant verse, of rhythm suspended between past and future, one sees the gift of law and revelation, a justice otherwise concealed in holy twilight.

The conditions for this recognition, for this affirmation of just measure, turn on the muted voice and suspended process that will be time in the balance for Hölderlin. This poised moment is very like Nietzsche's *Augenblick*, the winking blink of an eye: the moment. But in an ecstatic extension, Hölderlin is not catching the moment in the collision of past and future close to Pindar, close to Anaximander and to Heraclitus, older voices from an archaic age. Hölderlin effectively arches the weighted moment in the cadence of poetry: in the hung power of the word in song. This draws out the moment as a still space, a caesura, which Richard Sieburth defines as "a space in between, an interval of silence in which the 'pure Word' may appear."[6] This achievement is the achievement of all true poetry.

The ultimate verse is crucial perhaps because, as in life, last words often say everything one came to say in the first place. Then! "Dann kenn' ich dich, Kronion!" "Then will I know you, son of Kronos!" And the son of Saturn, that is also, in the play of ambiguous reference, the sons of melancholy, poets, and scientists, echoing their origins, can finally emerge as masters of wisdom, not as pretenders to mastery.

Poetic Construction and the Truth of Nature

Poetic founding or naming is key. What is at issue is nothing less than the literally poetic construal or construction of nature. Nature becomes what the poets say it is. But from the side of law and reason, science too will be found on the side of the naming or constructive power. Nature is the life force of the universe itself. To say all this—manifestly to the poet's ear—words inevitably fail. But ordered in just measure, they serve a function for human beings, ordering the universe, naming the beings of heaven. For Hölderlin, who held that poets install what perdures, one learns from discourse, but such teaching can only be observed or consummated in song:

> *Viel hat von Morgen an,*
> *Seit ein Gespräch wir sind und hören voneinander,*
> *Erfahren der Mensch; bald sind wir aber Gesang.**[7]

All that we are is a result of our discourse with ourselves and with one another—this is thinking and this is language. Our humanity then is not only a result of reason—the ability to theorize—but our humanity requires discursive reflection and conversation: the echoing answer of ourselves to ourselves, of another, confirmation, challenge, struggle, and growth. Thus we come to learn who we are from reflective thinking and from discourse. But reason and language are not without limit. It is exactly the failure of language that it cannot say who we are. It is also the failure of the poets in our desperately needful time—more needful than Hölderlin himself could ever have imagined this need—to observe what Hölderlin regarded as the poet's highest task, this is the task of giving praise to what must be praised above all: the most high. The failure to praise first gods, the failure to sing the titanic powers of nature, relegates us to a time of destitution. And what song promises in our destitution is a redemption of meaning.

The question here of modernity, as a newer time to be ranged after the golden time lost with the titan's passing, is mirrored by the loss of the significance of the gods as such. It is, the romantics saw, not only the ancient gods who have abandoned their temples. Today, as Nietzsche memorably punctuates the same requiem in recent centuries, the Judeo-

---

*Much, from the morning onward,
Since we have been a discourse and have heard from one another
Has humankind learnt; but soon we shall be song.

Christian god has been reduced to a civil signifier. Thus in the second
version of the poem Hölderlin dictates to memory, he first writes,

> *Ein Zeichen sind wir, deutungslos,*
> *Schmerzlos sind wir und haben fast*
> *Die Sprache in der Fremde verloren.**

The problem exceeds human doing. But the key to the divine for
anyone who invokes divinity is to let God himself be, as Angelus Silesius
(Johannes Scheffler) would say, given not as commandment but task:
"Gott aber selbst zulassen."[8] The idea of *Gelassenheit* and the juxtaposition of Hölderlin and Angelus Silesius is familiar to us from Heidegger.
What is not familiar is the referent here. This is an assignment scarcely
to be fathomed, a task to be recalled in the spirit of the *Cherubinic
Wanderer's* better-known expression concerning worldly being: "Die Ros'
ist ohn' Warum, sie blühet weil sie blühet" [The rose is without a why,
it blooms because it blooms]. For Hölderlin, as for Angelus Silesius, the
divine in some sense needs the human even if this same need is for our
very humanity in its mortal essence, that is, its most vulnerable expression, and even if that need is expressed as the helping advantage of the
absence of god.

Such weakness and such negative consolation permit us to stay as
wanderers in the holy night and to keep intent on the possibility of the
divine in its return.

> *Denn nicht vermoegen*
> *Die Himmlischen alles. Nämlich es reichen*
> *Die Sterblichen eh' an den Abgrund. Also wendet*
> *es sich, das Echo*
> *Mit diesen. Lang ist*
> *Die Zeit, es ereignet sich aber*
> *Das Wahre.***[9]

---

* A sign we are, without meaning
  Without pain we are and have nearly
  Lost our language in foreign lands.
**   . . . Not everything
  is in the power of the gods. Mortals would sooner
  Reach toward the abyss. With them
  The echo turns. Though the time
  Be long, truth will come to pass.

Here time, not mortal time but time in its length, is mentioned once again. "Though the time be long," it is also the occasion of truth. Once more, the poet's task is to install the heart or memory of a people, and this works in the happening of truth, permitting truth to come to speech in such a way that it can be heard.

Our modern time may be said to be that of transition, like every time, because such transit refers to the nature of time as it is apart from or beyond us. It is the task of the poet to allow an expression of what cannot be said. This venture into impossible articulation is as old as Homer, where the poem achieves even more than words or syntax have the power to say. Although Hölderlin could agree with almost everything Schiller wrote about the importance of all the elements of an aesthetic education and with Goethe's dynamic plan for poetic mastery, he also felt the tension of nature itself; but the tension of nature, of life, although echoed and mourned as a fading harmony since antiquity, is as an experience now very nearly lost in our day, and likely to be less and less available. The paradox in the power of words to say what a thing is and to bring it into being is thus achieved. We become mere signs to ourselves, meaningless, and as our words lose their weighting force, their old ties to nature, our art, our science, seals us off from all contact with origins. And thus we have "almost lost our language in foreign lands."[10] This awful adventure of the paradox of language is the paradox of invention and convention, expressed for American ears by Thoreau's dictum: "we are the tools of our tools."

We recall that George Steiner once identified this paradox as the "breaking"—for my mind, it is the *shattering*—"of logos in our mouths."[11] Taking up the same puzzle, another commentator has made reference to the "sacred" revealed in the connection to nature: "Hölderlin seeks Nature as sustaining time even in the very moment of its dissolution—a form of being that might stay '*die reissende Zeit*' (time which runs along with violent speed but also tears what it touches)."[12] But we do not need romantic sentimentality (quite apart from the genre detail that excludes Hölderlin from this definition). This ripping, tearing time moves at a speed we moderns all too easily imagine, needing not poetic presentiment regarding the industrialized transformation of the world, but the everyday time of ordinary, contemporary time, especially, indeed, as I write this in such a quintessential city as New York, a tempo that is also felt in Paris, but also in Berlin and London as well as in the energy of the Frankfurt of today that Hölderlin, the son of Lauffen and Nürtingen who once walked its streets, might almost have imagined it—Tübingen, Stuttgart, Jena, these were city towns for Hölderlin, just as they were for Goethe. Small or large, then and now, the time of the city is calculated

time, measured and without justice. This is the city's time that none of
us has, the urgent urban time that tears.

It is this weighted, rending time that is the time of the modern
era—the *Neuzeit* as the Germans name it: the newer time as I have been
calling it. Such tearing novelty is distinguished in Hölderlin's "Natur und
Kunst" from the golden time: the time of rightness, rectitude. Speaking
elsewhere of the course or running path of a lifetime, Hölderlin refers to
Saturn/Kronos, banished to the underworld, and links nature's slumber
as a possibility hidden in the vanquished kingship:

> *Aufwärts oder hinab! herrschet in heil'ger Nacht,*
> *Wo die stumme Natur werdende Tage sinnt,*
> *Herrscht im schiefesten Orkus*
> *Nicht ein Grades, ein Recht noch auch?** [13]

What nature holds out as a possibility to art is the imperative of
balance. The creative power is sprung from both. But the key is naming,
as a task and as a sign of incipient failure. Nature is not a myth, but the
force of life that, like Napoleon, hero of all romantic dreamers, "lives and
stays in the world" [*Er lebt und bleibt in der Welt*]. In any case, our time
remains a time of need—thus even the poet called to serve, as Hölderlin
has it, not the needs of the world but the "highest" things, is called to
serve in a time where

> *Zu lang ist alles Göttliche dienstbar schon*
> *Und alle Himmelskräfte verscherzt verbraucht*
> *Die Gütigen, zur Lust, danklos, ein*
> *Schlaues Geschlecht und zu kennen wähnt es,*
> *Wenn ihnen der Erhabne den Acker baut,*
> *Das Tagslicht und den Donnerer, und es späht*
> *Das Sehrohr wohl sie all und zählt und*
> *Nennet mit Namen des Himmels Sterne.*** [14]

---

* Whether upward or down—does not in holy night
  Where mute Nature thinks out days that are still to come
  Though in crookedst Orkus
  Yet a straightness, a law prevail?

** Too long all things divine have been put to use
   Heavenly powers trifled away, mercies Squandered for sport, thankless, a
   Generation of schemers, and it presumes,
   When the most sublime lord tills their fields,
   To know daylight and the thunderer, all these
   The telescope scans and quantifies
   And names the heaven's stars.

And what the names weaken, is given to the song to say, after an insight Hölderlin sees as his vocation: *"das Heilige sei mein Wort."** Following Hölderlin's word on this holy vocation, from his poem *Wie wenn am Feiertage,* we see that it is called forth by nature's power, broken out and forth with the clash of arms.

> *Den sie, sie selbst, die aelter denn die Zeiten*
> *Und über die Götter des Abends und Orients ist,*
> *Die Natur ist jetzt mit Waffenklang erwacht,*
> *Und hoch vom Aether bis zum Abgrund nieder*
> *Nach festem Gesetze, wie einst, aus heiligem Chaos gezeugt, fühlt*** *[15]

Hölderlin's sight is not lost today. Nietzsche shared this vision as Heidegger did. The question of the meaning of poetry and the poetic invention of nature are questions that have a common origin and destiny. Where poetry has lost its voice—where we cannot all name ourselves poets—one hears in the words the might of poetic resonance, the halt and measure of rhythm and balance. And this poetic weight is the weight of meaning.

What is at stake is far more than merely the loss of the sacred dimension, as if the presence of faith or the observance of Christian or Jewish or Islamic traditions could or would be a solution. Hölderlin did not merely speak of the passing of ancient gods as an allegory for the passing of the Judeo-Christian God but he invokes the flight of the divine as such, where all the gods, ancient and modern, have turned away, and where it belongs to the essence of life to recall the golden age—the age of the titans, the highest gods, father Aether, or Nature. The imperative must be more than allegorical: it speaks to the very loss of the earth itself, the veritable flight of life. If it is possible to hear Hölderlin's warning in this way, then we, sons and daughters of time, like Zeus himself, are called to recall the nature of our kinship to nature, and if we do this, we may find a way that will restore us to the poet's "right measure." But we need to do more than speak the name of God, more than proclaim our sensitivity to suffering. To do this we need to attend to the fate of the earth, not just our all-too-swiftly dwindling oil

---

* the holy—my word shall convey. . . .

** For she, she herself who is older than the age
   And higher than the gods of Orient and Occident,
   Nature has now awoken amid the clang of arms,
   And from high Aether down to the low abyss,
   According to fixed law, begotten, as in the past, on holy Chaos . . .

reserves but the assault on the air that it is to use such fuels and the mechanized slaughter of animals and the systematic destruction of forests and the devastation of the land for mineral "harvests." All these things are the pride of our human race, its violent law, and its powerful achievements. But in our complicity with what is done to the earth, what we claim for our needs, we fail as yet to bring out into the light and so admit and so honor what we have done to the heart of nature "which lives hidden in holy twilight."

12

〜〜〜

The Work of Art and the Museum

Heidegger, Schapiro, Gadamer

*M*eyer Schapiro's critique of Martin Heidegger's interpretation of Van
Gogh's Shoes *can be challenged as lacking hermeneutic adequacy. A
review of the culture of the museum together with Hans-Georg Gadamer's
discussion of the role of the ecstatic public (as illustrated by Christo's and
Jeanne-Claude's installation,* The Gates*) supports a reading of Heidegger's
essay on the working of art, including his discussion of the preserver as co-
creator (striking in its absence in the conservation of the temple of Apollo
Epikourios at Bassae in Arcadia, Greece).*

Gadamer's Hermeneutic Windows and Schapiro's Expert Closure

The contested question of art is on display in the museum and its culture,[1] from the perspectives of art history and the philosophy of art, but,
above all, in the pure ideal of art "for its own sake." Such a perspective
on art "alone" is accomplished by severing art "from its original life-
context." For Hans-Georg Gadamer, this alienation from life ultimately
alienates art from art, "engendering the emancipation of art from all of
its traditional subject matters and leading to the rejection of intelligible
communication itself." Thus, for Gadamer, today's "art has become
problematic in a twofold sense: is it art, still and yet? Indeed, does art
want to be art?"[2]

From its inception in Plato, philosophical thinking on art had sought
to limit art's claim to truth. For Gadamer, the question has shifted from

such traditional disputes regarding the truth of art to the question of "what art is" or, for today's analytic aesthetic philosophers, to the where or the when of art. At the same time, the clear locus of art has never been more patent and any one of us, author and reader alike, knows exactly where to find "art" at any time. This extends, in the cultural sphere, to its archetypically geographical locus in Greece.

Martin Heidegger's philosophical meditation "On the Origin of the Work of Art"[3] has controversial political overtones. As lectures first given in 1936, readers have pointed to its intrinsically nationalist, if not to say National Socialist, tonality. If such insightful readers as Robert Bernasconi and Jacques Taminiaux do so—Bernasconi in his careful and hermeneutically sensitive attention to a people,[4] Taminiaux regarding the exigence of what he names "voluntarist proclamations to the German Dasein"[5]—we can also hear elements of this anxiety in Heidegger's most nuanced defenders, such as the late Jacques Derrida. For his part, Gadamer speaks as a contemporary witness to Heidegger's same lectures, describing the impact of these lectures until their first publication in terms elegantly reflective of the contextual circumstances and substance of the essay itself. For Gadamer, the lectures were part of the same history of "suprises" that characterized Heidegger's early university career in Freiburg.[6] In this epochal sense, Heidegger's lectures on the origin of the work of art amounted to a "philosophical sensation."[7]

Of course, what was sensational about "the language of earth and world"[8] was the Hölderlinian and life-philosophical or very Nietzschean reference to the earth, as viscerally, physical earth, that is: earth as more than *"bloßer Stoff."* Earth in this sense "is in truth not matter but that from out of which everything stems and into which everything goes."[9]

Here, like Heidegger's language of "dwelling," Gadamer's powerful, Platonico-Goethean language of "lingering"—[*Verweilen*]—is articulated with reference to Plato's *Phaedrus* (where, by contrast with the gods, mortal beings can only "cast a momentary, fleeting glance upon this eternal order"),[10] as well as in the lived phenomenological occasion of the encounter with the work of art itself: "When one really undergoes an experience with art, then is the world at once become both lighter and easier."[11] In our all-too human and mortal world, Gadamer recalls the demand such an encounter with that which seems to endure poses for us: "the thing now 'stands' and with that it is 'there' for all time."[12] This same demand may be heard in Rilke's "Archaic Torso of Apollo," as Gadamer takes it to be the philosophical keystone for his essay: "there is no place that fails to see you. You must change your life."[13]

Beyond the traditional aesthetics of Baumgarten and Kant, what is significant in Heidegger's essay is the challenge he poses against the arbiters of expert judgment on the history of art. Heidegger's lecture addressing the origins of the work of art counters not only traditional philosophic but also art historical categories by shifting the question of judgment to that of Heideggerian or aletheic—earth-grounding, world-opening truth—but in consequence he manages to *misjudge* the artwork itself as it is judged on expert terms, as we have heard this art-historical judgment from Meyer Schapiro.[14]

Yet Schapiro's critique turns upon a fetishistic conception of art (and the artist) in addition to suffering from a "failure" of hermeneutics (or a "lack of philology" as Nietzsche would have put it). Derrida, Heidegger's careful if esoteric defender, shares Schapiro's judgment, at least on the question of taste, recoiling from Heidegger's all-too professorial (and all-too Schwarzwald or peasant-style) judgment on art, which seems guilty of every philistine error regarding art. Following Derrida, several commentators have emphasized Heidegger's reference to art as relevant solely to "great" art.[15] We may recall Gadamer's note concerning the historically transfiguring power of contemporary modern and abstract art (and we can extend this to include the similarly backward working power of techno-shock realist art), which now yields a context forever altering any traditional understanding either of greatness or of art as such as it transforms our understanding of the work of art as such. For Gadamer, again, "the naïve assumption that the picture is a view—like that which we have daily in our experience of nature or of nature shaped by man—has clearly been fundamentally destroyed."[16]

Schapiro's critique has been effective because it is an art expert's critique of judgment contra philosophy, representing the claim of art history contra aesthetics as it ranges from the Baumgartian "science of the beautiful" to Kant but also including Heideggerian and Nietzschean post-aesthetic reflections.[17] And, if we note too that Gadamer underscores Heidegger's own essay's specific dependence on the German tradition of aesthetics from Baumgarten to Kant,[18] this same critical vision is no longer to be expressed via the (today hardly unimpeachable) authority of Kant's third critique but only in terms of the claim of expert judgment, that is, once again, the art historian's claim to precision.

Art history (and today: art criticism) is addressed neither to the experience of art (the question of subjective judgment or taste) nor, for Heidegger, the working ἐνέργεια of art as the locus or occasion of world-historical truth nor, indeed, the definition and factive details of art as such, that is, art for art's sake and for the sake of the abstract idea of art. As it expresses the contemporary cultural question of art itself, Gadamer reflects upon this esoteric dimensionality. Hence Gadamer articulates the traditionally subversive function or critical character of art as it acquires an eternally postmodern, that is, reflexive aspect: "Our task is not only to recognize the profound continuity that connects the formal language of the past with the contemporary revolution of artistic form. A new social force is at work in the claim of the modern artist. The confrontation with the bourgeois religion of culture and its ritualistic enjoyment of art leads the contemporary artist to attempt to draw us actively into this claim in various ways."[19] The artwork preoccupied with its own character as art, together with our own art-historical and art-critical concern with this very same "art" character, constitutes the self-referentiality not only emblematic of postmodern art while also presupposing a straightforwardly fetishistic conception of art, a conception that finds its most insightful and creative expression in André Malraux's classic account of the museum in terms of its colonization of the human imaginary.[20] Today, much more than Gadamer had imagined, Malraux's vision is seen in its limiting precision, as it exemplifies the image-driven character of our contemporary media-absorbed and preoccupied world. This literally "token" character of art is thus coordinate with the dominion of the museum even as the museum itself, postmodern and experimental, constituted by changeable collections of inherently transportable, reconfigurable, dispositional gallery space, has increasingly come to stand as its own self-immolating ruination, and therewith and with the same assertion of ruin, the exhibit (and its signifiers) reinstalls the museum's stubborn perpetuation of itself as the privileged locus of art together.[21]

The kind of museum art can vary: from classical to modern art, minimalist art, conceptual art of all kinds, video art, Earth art, or, and increasingly, the so-called shock art of formaldehyde sharks (Damien Hirst, *The Physical Impossibility of Death in the Mind of Someone Living* [1991]), religious images imersed in urine or tarred with excrement (Andrés Serrano's *Piss Christ* [1987] or Chris Ofili's *The Holy Virgin Mary*—the last known for the scandal associated with its 1999 exhibition at the Brooklyn Museum) or the anatomical scientist Gunther von Hagens's duly patented "plastination" of "real bodies."[22] For quite apart from the question of whether von Hagens's anatomical displays of dramatically posed cadavers, in the exhibit, *Körperwelten*, are to be counted as art (or artifacts of science, for instruction, or to be seen as entertainment/desecration), von Hagens's installations could not work at all were it not for the cult venue of "The Museum" itself, no matter whether a museum of natural history or of art.

This last point accords with Arthur Danto's reflections on the museum as the substitute for the church. Just as the great churches of the past were built for the sake of organizing a town or a city toward its god, they also served as gathering spots, if only topographical: the church outlines the space of a marketplace. This is the all-too-worldly reason that Nietzsche's madman can find an audience standing by in the marketplace when he cries, "I seek God! I seek God!" and it is the reason they can laugh at him, asking "Has he got lost?" a question more obvious than mocking given the proximity of the nearby church. And it is the same locus of the village church that offers the convenient proximity permitting Nietzsche's madman to break into the same churches (the landscape is a Protestant one and Protestant churches are closed on market days) to strike up his *requiem aeternam deo* (GS §125).

Artists and the Museum: Wares and Wherewithal

It is no secret that Heidegger's essay "The Origin of the Work of Art"[23] does not offer a discussion of art as such. Indeed Heidegger would contend that his question with regard to art was a singular question for thought. Heidegger's question is not the question of art but being. Accordingly Heidegger's reference to and his analysis of a painting by an artist no less famous than Van Gogh is not properly referred to in the context of Heidegger's essay as "art" at all, much less art qua art. For Schapiro, the debate will turn on the issue of the identity of the particular painting in question.[24] But Heidegger, as is similarly well known, chooses the painting as an illustration not of painting but of the kind of thing that the artwork is qua manufactured or poietic thing.

For not only does Heidegger discuss the painting as a kind of τέχνη, but he considers the work of art as liable to be stocked as things can be—as Beethoven's musical scores are stored in the same way potatoes in a cellar might be preserved for future use, just as the greater part of a museum collection can be on reserve in the same way. The virtue of Van Gogh's painting is that it can serve, for Heidegger, as representative of what a thing is in order to show what things are in "truth." Rather than an abstract work of art like that of Kandinsky or a nonfigurative work like those of Malevich or Mondrian, Van Gogh's painting is a work of nicely representative, postimpressionist art. Van Gogh's *Shoes* depicts things of an everyday kind, as Heidegger expresses it: a pair of shoes as the artist had seen them, which Heidegger proceeds to read from a hermeneutic perspective as a revelation of *things*, exactly in terms of their thingness as such and in the view of the artist. The painting in question—and this revelation that takes us to the fetishistic dimension proper to art history and to aesthetic theory—is the one, on Schapiro's account as noted above, Heidegger reported seeing in Amsterdam in 1930.

By contrast with Schapiro, Heidegger overleaps the privilege of the museum definition, that is, the art-historical definition and description of art. But we recall that it is the museum today that serves and has always served as the de facto locus of art, whatever, increasingly, wherever "art" may be.[25] And this is the reason we are not presented with "things" (as Heidegger or as anyone else might name them) in a museum but rather with exactly certified works of art.[26] And if Heidegger differs from many professional, particularly, analytically inclined philosophers of art or aesthetics in failing to define art (or even to say "when" art might "be"), as I observed at the start: for most of us, it is clear enough "where" art can be found—at will.

In this fashion, even Christo and Jeanne-Claude have typically made of their installations a movable museum: employing the signifier of the gallery as museum, as exhibit, as display, with the associations and privileges attached to the museum (Figs. 12.1 and 12.2). The real "work" of art is constituted, in Christo's case, not only by the installation as an event but also by the preparatory drawings and collages in addition to other original works, that serve to finance and hence to advance the work in the age of industrial and factory reproduction and mass media interest, thereby institutionalizing, "corporatizing," the "work" of art. In Christo's (and Jeanne-Claude's) case, in addition to such sketches and collages, only on offer to investors (the artists work as their own agents), this will be a draped and temporary easel-cum-gallery space,[27] literally so in the

Figure 12.1. "The Work of Art," "The Gates," Feb. 23, 2005. Author's photograph.

Figure 12.2. Central Park and "The Gates," Feb. 23, 2005. Author's photograph.

case of the so-called wrapped works of art (the *Wrapped Reichstag* [1971–1975], or else what was Christo's perhaps most iconic preparation of the *Pont-Neuf Wrapped* [1975–1985] in Paris), or else it will be *The Gates*, Feb. 12–26, 2005, nearly twenty-three miles of orange drapes, framed as portals to a work of found or already-made art (in this latter instance: Central Park, designed by Frederick Olmsted and Calvert Vaux, [Fig. 12.2]), all the signifiers of the museum calling forth the private realm of the museum (and the special projections of its donors), but, in the case of the installation, also evoking an inevitably ecstatic exhibit that either excludes or defers access. Thus Christo and Jeanne-Claude engender a desire for the space of—and the space beyond—the exhibition, a desire for the space of an imaginary space: fantasies at an exhibition.

I submit that it is likewise relevant that the desire (or captivation) that is the consequence of this same spatial inaccessibility is also a characteristic of Daniel Libeskind's void, as architectural construct in the Jewish Museum in Berlin,[28] an inaccessibility that was the key to the popular architect's triumphant design (as it turns out only temporarily secured) for the projected rebuilding of the locus of the strike against New York City's Twin Towers on September 11, 2001. It is a trivial but

still key detail that this same inaccessibility yielded (among other infelicities in the projected realization of the surprisingly idealized design) the
unusability of the design in a city where usable/salable space is at a
premium—and it is essential to note that this very circumstance does not
apply, by contrast, in a city like Berlin. Given the world-historical context
of its physical location right in the middle of what had been Eastern
Germany, Berlin is not short on "space." Hence (at the initial time of
this writing, and this is currently still in flux), Libeskind's design for
rebuilding the World Trade Center had been passed along to the more
sophisticated powers of a David Childs (familiar with both the bureau-
cratic constraints and claims of New York City regulations but also with
still more important investor's concerns), the same Childs who not so
very incidentally recently recreated the "twin towers" on a single city
block between 59th and 60th Streets, the Time Warner Center, kitty-
corner to the southwest edge of Central Park, the so-called Merchant's
Gate at Columbus Circle, erected on the site of the former locus of the
New York Coliseum (Fig. 12.3). In the case of the Time Warner Build-

Figure 12.3. Time Warner Building at Columbus Circle, with Trump Hotel.
February 23, 2005. Author's photograph.

ing, like an architect's model writ large, Childs' two steel and glass towers are joined with the kind of office space and atrium that marks the confidently conservative architecture of the future (or the mall). The sharp angles of the glass towers are curved to face Central Park across Columbus Circle, less to make an architectural statement than to solve a marketing problem: maximizing the "best view" in New York, vying with Trump Tower on Central Park South to claim the right to this realtor's phrase.

In a not dissimilar fashion, Christo's and Jean-Claude's "The Gates" was designed to cover an open space. The work of art that was the deliberately ephemeral installation project of "The Gates" thus played into but at the same time it also drew upon the lustre of New York's Central Park. If it can be argued that the workers who set up "The Gates" in a frenzy of casual nepotism might also be counted as the "work" of art, if it can be argued that New York City marketed itself, as it hoped, in support of this project, there is also the play of the park itself

Figure 12.4. "The Gates" and people in Central Park. February 23, 2005. Author's photograph.

(Fig. 12.4). Thus the projected "blanketing" of Central Park turned into people-wash portals of orange set at uneven intervals and widths, accessible in its totality for one with the ambition to walk all twenty-odd miles of the scattered frames of "The Gates." But such an ambition would miss the key to "The Gates" as they framed the classic work of landscape art that is the design of Central Park (Fig. 12.5).

Where the work of art, as Heidegger invokes it, is one that has the potential to lose its place in a sustaining world or as situated upon earth, the "art world" is exactly what Heidegger (if not Gadamer) would call a world-poor domain. For this reason, museum art is incapable of losing its world, a point well illustrated by the success of Christo's projects. Art in the museum's context is eminently movable, exactly without auratic fade; this resilience is also the sign of its restriction within the museum context. Out of place in a museum, the work of art may have been stolen or lost to a natural disaster, or else it might be on loan, as a marker in its former locus will indicate. In every case, the work moves from one fetishized locus to another, remaining within the museum even in its absence.[29]

Defining the museum as the place of art is not a practical, Wittgensteinian definition but an effective or pragmatic one: that is, a

Figure 12.5. Central Park landscaped pathway and the paved path of "The Gates." February 23, 2005. Author's photograph.

stipulated or conventional definition. Art is thus whatever appears in a museum or a gallery or else in a public square when defined as an "installation"[30] with a word borrowed from the same aesthetically fetishized locus and not as a monument (although monuments can be designated art—one thinks of the Vietnam Memorial in Washington—they are not always art but retain the quality of the calculated production and craft that is not pure but merely applied and that is to say, not art at all, not even bad art). I note too that this locus, the place of the museum, is also the place where Gadamer, speaking of the Hellenic Museum in Athens, is able to recall to us as the very festive character of special museum exhibitions, brought into being and exemplified by the public's fascinated response, celebrating the latest discovery in Gadamer's hermeneutically expressive terms of a commemoratively "festive silence" [*feierliches Schweigen*].[31]

The Truth of Things: Jacob Taubes, Witness for the Prosecution

Monument, or archaeological discovery, artworks in storage or on display, all are things. And it is to explore the nature of things, the thing-hood of things, that Heidegger speaks of Van Gogh's painting of a pair of shoes. For writers like Paul Crowther, such a review reduces to little more than an extended prelude to the real work of Heidegger's essay—and this is an impatience shared by more than a few Anglo-Saxon readers.[32] By contrast, the reference to thing-hood remains key for Gadamer who takes pains to remind us that in addition to the traditional aesthetic relevance of the science of aesthetic sensibility of the thing as such, Heidegger's reflections on the "Origin of the Work of Art" went beyond neo-Kantian aesthetics and its relativistic contradictions in a scientific age, an age that forbid one to conceptualize either: "the thingness of the thing or the instrumental quality of the instrument."[33] Instructively, Heidegger takes the thing conception of the art work to be its most important correspondence with materiality as such—*Stoff*—and thus and classically in connection with form. Gadamer reminds us that to talk of things, Heidegger will need to discuss equipment, things regarded, as Heidegger tells us in *Being and Time*, in terms of their coordinate, integrated purposiveness with other things—things *um zu*—things in their telic dimensionality, precisely redolent of the Kantian ideal of *"Zweckmässigkeit ohne Zweck."*[34] In his 1960 essay, Gadamer explains that in this context, "for sake of rendering the instrumentality of the instrument conspicuous," Heidegger "accordingly had recourse to an artistic representation, a painting of Van Gogh's that depicted farmer's shoes."[35] With such an account of thing-hood, Van Gogh's painting can be seen as exemplifying the things painting is meant to be painting of.

But if Heidegger's characterization of "great" art unsettles philosophical aesthetics, as scholars from Bernasconi to Crowther attest, it was
Heidegger's example of Van Gogh as a well-known (ordinal) painter and
his depiction of shoes, ordinary things, in their ordinariness, that disturbed the art historian Meyer Schapiro. The present author thus recalls
several conversations she had from 1984 to 1986 with Jacob Taubes, the
eschatological hermeneuticist in Berlin, conversations held between Berlin and Paris. Taubes had been Schapiro's then-colleague at Columbia
University. If today's debate on the Heidegger–Schapiro conflict carries
Derrida's imprimatur, Taubes would claim that Schapiro's critique was
far more devastating than simply a hermeneutic difference of academic
opinion. By declaring Heidegger's interpretation of Van Gogh's painting
a violation of disciplinary boundaries, with a seemingly patent demonstration of expert incompetence on Heidegger's part, Schapiro, as Taubes
pointed out, simply blew Heidegger away.

Nevertheless, Schapiro's "devastating" proof contra Heidegger reduces to nothing more than Schapiro's assertion that, as Taubes recalled
it, "Heidegger had got the shoes wrong." In spite of the dramatically
conclusive success of Schapiro's critique (a success so complete that one
might wonder whether anything at all remains to say on the issue—a
striking conviction in a discipline of eternal questions), it is important to
note the lack of demonstration (or argument) in Schapiro's essay. Only
surmise and subjective preference on Schapiro's own part prevail in the
claims he presented contra Heidegger (quite apart from the critical note
that these claims were never of relevance to the concern of Heidegger's
essay in the first place, as numerous Heidegger scholars have rightly
argued). The contentiousness of Schapiro's 1968 text is impatiently colloquial, and at least this reader misses the art historian's otherwise careful
rigor.[36] Indeed, it seems that Schapiro's 1994 essay, "Further Notes on
Heidegger and van Gogh," betrays something of Schapiro's own "end-
of-the-day" awareness of this very deficiency.[37]

Thus to point out, as Schapiro does, that Van Gogh purchased the
shoes likely to have been painted in the painting to which Heidegger
refers is not to prove Van Gogh's ownership of the shoes as his very *own*
shoes—in the sense required by Schapiro's claim that the painter painted
his own shoes (rather than a peasant's shoes). The only way anyone can
"own" shoes is by wearing them—not once only—and this point is one
Schapiro explains: "to be in someone's shoes is to be in his predica-
ment"[38]—at least for the duration of the American Indian's aphoristic
mile of life understanding. For one wears one's own shoes as an everyday
or habitual matter of course. The owner of a pair of shoes is the one
whose wearing wears them, so that the shoes "wear" that same wearer—

and this is what Heidegger's phenomenological account of the work of art in Van Gogh's case serves to make clear.[39]

Some commentators note that Schapiro's Marxist sensibilities[40] were also at work in his reaction to Heidegger's manifest a-historicism and supposed a-politicism. But if this is so, such sympathies explain Schapiro's criticisms without justifying them. Contrasting the philosopher's account of the work of art in its origin with that of the art historian's account of the same originality, we recall Heidegger's claim that Van Gogh's painting depicts a pair of peasant shoes—to be exact, and to specify the precise words that so irritated Schapiro—the shoes of a *peasant woman*. Perhaps this attribution of ownership inspired Schapiro to see Heidegger's *expropriation* of Van Gogh's artist's shoes in (and thus on the terms of) Heidegger's own Black Forest world as manifest *exploitation*.[41] But the problem with Schapiro's interpretation begins, it does not end, with this explanation.

Contra Heidegger, Schapiro claims that in this case Van Gogh depicts not the shoes of a peasant but the *artist's* own shoes due to the plain matter of fact that Van Gogh (for his *own* personal use, as Schapiro supposes) had purchased these very shoes at a flea market in Paris. Heidegger, so Schapiro contends, projects nothing but his own art-historical ignorance—Heidegger's egregious lack of expert knowledge—into his account of the painting. In his turn, Derrida thus sees the conflict as one between the faculties.

I have been arguing that Schapiro's expert judgment errs in the case of Van Gogh with regard to the function of the shoes Van Gogh purchased (I do not dispute this). Neither do I mean to claim or to dispute the claim that the shoes do not form a pair (either for or contra Derrida) nor indeed do I contest Derrida's expression of Schapiro's claim "nothing proves that they are peasant shoes,"[42] uttered on behalf of city shoes versus country shoes: the shoes of a Parisian intellectual, the shoes of an Allemanic-Suabian rustic. Rather I contend that in the case of Van Gogh's shoes, to claim that he owned them hardly resolves our problem (and with this contention I mean to submit only a more plausible suggestion than Schapiro's vision of the same). For we have to do with shoes that like as not were purchased from the start not for the artist's personal use or wearing (as Schapiro rather uncritically assumes) but precisely as an object: an accoutrement to be painted, an exemplar or thing acquired precisely for the purpose of painting it.

Artists in general—and here I am not revealing anything Schapiro would not have known very well—hire women they do not necessarily seduce, likewise, artists do not necessarily acquire the fruits depicted in a still life to consume them *themselves*. They may even, as Cezanne famously did to excess, record the specific superfluity of doom: letting apples and other fruit go uneaten—and, again, in general, artists select likely objects for the sake of drawing or painting them. The plain fact that Van Gogh purchased the shoes does not justify the conclusion that he bought them as his own shoes, that is: to wear them. Van Gogh, as Heidegger underlines, painted *several* of these still lifes.

To raise the question concerning Van Gogh's shoes, we need to begin by inquiring not, as Derrida does and to whatever coyly fetishistic extreme, into issues concerning the shoes of peasant women, be they from the South of France or Germany, or even Holland, but only, because Schapiro's contention only concerns, Van Gogh's shoes.

Thus we might ask what shoes Van Gogh wore, as the element of biography important for the critical sake of being sure what shoes, qua painted, we are indeed talking about. And we know, from a fellow student's report, that Van Gogh purchased just a such a pair of leather shoes in Paris (exactly for use in a still life). We also know from a letter Van Gogh wrote from Arles in 1888 to his brother—as Schapiro's source, apart from and in unnoted conflict with the letter he himself had from Heidegger—that he had in his possession a pair of old shoes, "une paire de vieux souliers,"[43] and we know too from Gauguin's powerful account that in Van Gogh's "studio was a pair of big hob-nailed boots, all worn and spotted with mud; he had made of it a remarkable still-life painting. . . ."[44] Schapiro quotes this report at great length because of its association with his claim that the shoes were the artist's own, revealing in Knut Hamsun's words as Schapiro quotes them: "a portion of the self."[45] To these heavy, hob-nailed shoes,[46] which Van Gogh had worn and which he described as "caked with mud," there corresponds a painting that can be matched to such a pair of boots, and this would seem indeed to be the painting Gauguin admires as the "remarkable still-life" in question. To be sure, this painting of boots is not the one Heidegger describes—nor indeed does Schapiro claim that that it is.[47]

To identify the shoes in question, given the variety of similar shoes Van Gogh painted, we further need to attend to Van Gogh's paintings and to do that we need to return to the question of the sort of "things" (in Heidegger's sense of the word) Van Gogh painted.[48]

Heidegger's phenomenological hermeneutic account of the painting not only refers to an identifiable painting by a famous artist but it was named as such for the sake of the representative and representational character of the shoes in question as Heidegger describes them. This character conforms with Van Gogh's aesthetic, as an aesthetic some art scholars regard as consecrational, which sacral character is unmitigated by naming this aesthetic that of the *extraordinarily ordinary* kind: the preternaturally ordinary. Such an aesthetic, representing the ordinary *in extremis*, does not mean that the ordinary is made banal but rather that it is made strange, unfamiliar, and so given to be seen for the first time as such as the only way that everyday things, as Heidegger reminds us of their invisibility or withdrawal in use, can be given to be seen. Estranged in angle and dimension or in perspective, and in the thick dissonances of the painter's medium, and in the choice of painted color—this ordinary character is obvious in the choice of things to be painted as in *The Night Cafe*, *The Potato Eaters*, as well as *Crows Over a Wheat Field*, his *Self-Portrait*(s), and his *Bedroom at Arles*. In other paintings, the preternatural aspect appears in the force of their presentation such as in the *Cypresses*, *Starry Night*, *Irises*, and *Sunflowers*. The difference between human subjects and the traditional scenes of nature (still life and landscapes) adumbrates this same focus. None of these paintings shows the perfection or extraordinary precision of everyday things such as the earlier tradition of Dutch painters exemplified by Vermeer, and the difference is more than an encounter between the north and the light and mores of the south in the eyes of Van Gogh, himself a perfectly immortal Dutch master. Emblematic of this representational everydayness, Van Gogh's *Shoes* lack the sharp divinity of detail: they are redolent of the earth which swirls duskily around them, the dullness of worn leather glowing and highlighted against the dark echo and damp of fatigue.

This is the point of materiality as Gadamer catches it, the same point that would occupy Merleau-Ponty's reading of the work of art for his very different part,[49] the same claim that Malraux himself, agonistically deconstructive far in excess of Derrida, has made contra Van Gogh's own self-invention of himself as signator/guarantor of his work and hence as artist.[50] Gadamer thus is able to attend, as Dieter Jähnig shows us with yet more care,[51] to the material of what is shown in the work: a materiality that shows itself as such and in its truth.[52] As if for the first time, Heidegger would say, for the one and only time of such a revelation in truth.

The shoes are as plain and as forcefully centered as Dürer's more rustic drawings[53] that work in the same way to site, situate, institute, or *found* a world as Heidegger describes the standing efficacy of the temple work: opening a world and simultaneously setting "this world back again on earth, which itself only thus emerges as native ground" (O 42). For Gadamer, in addition to the Platonic significance to be heard in the word ἀλήθεια, this is the event of revelation.[54]

What is revealed in the work of art is the character of the world in truth. It is in order to discover the equipmental character of equipment, the nature of equipment, *in truth*, that Heidegger undertakes what must

then be regarded as a properly, if irrecusably hermeneutic, phenomenological analysis of Van Gogh's painting. The point of departure is one of
convenience for Heidegger who had declared his project from the start
in settling upon a pair of shoes as an example for the sake of its very
redundancy. In the context of the lecture course on the origin of the
work of art, the advantage was patently didactic: just as everyone knows
the painting, everyone knows what shoes are, "everyone is acquainted
with them" (O 32). But we know Heidegger too well simply to trust his
didactic preludes or concession of familiarity, particularly where Heidegger
goes on to suggest the fateful "pictorial representation" of a pair of shoes
found in a "well-known painting by Van Gogh who painted such shoes
several times" (33) to present the reader with a familiar painting of
familiar objects: thus Heidegger turns cliché upon cliché. For Heidegger,
the cliché corresponds to the representational equivalent of the obvious-
ness and intimacy of the example. "Everyone knows what shoes consist
of" (Ibid).

The phenomenological continuity of Heidegger's analysis of the
equipmentality of the shoes qua equipment turns upon and into the
same evidential quality of the obvious—what is made manifest not here
by way of cliché but via Heidegger's earlier phenomenological analysis of
things in use in *Being and Time*. Equipment recedes, disappears, with-
draws, vanishes from conscious intrusion in use: this is the intentional
utility of equipment as such (one cannot use a hammer in construction
and contemplate the hammer qua hammer as philosophers like to do: the
preoccupation with hammerness as such would get in the way. And as
Wittgenstein reminds us in this same context, not only philosophical
contemplation but even full grammatical sentences and reports seem
equally intrusive). Only when the peasant wears them (whether woman
or not, whether the shoes were the shoes of the artist—or philosopher—
as aspiring peasant) "are they what they are." That is, shoes "actually
serve" or work only when they are in use, and when in wearing they are
beneath notice, when they do not intrude as such—when they are worn
and when they are wearable—and not when they are contemplated, regarded, or noticed. Until, and of course, the artist represents them and
this very use for the artist does matter, as utensil, like the rough beer
steins Van Gogh also collected (and also in order to paint them), in
painting the *work* of art.

Plainly, given this interpretive phenomenological context, the painting as such, and on Heidegger's account and in the context of Heidegger's
own early equipmental or tool or use analysis, can be read as yielding
manifest access to the equipmental character of a pair of shoes as such.
By regarding the painting, Heidegger is thus able to trace every aspect

of the wearer of the shoe, in the character of wear, in the painting of the leather of the shoe, its look and character, thus retracing the lost person of the wearer, herself, as Heidegger pretends to know her through Van Gogh's painting.

Phenomenological analysis does not proceed as a detective works or as the art historian might do. Anti-Platonic, quintessentially non-theoretical, the phenomenologist adverts to the use character of a tool, an item of equipment for beings like ourselves who have to be, who need to be, shod. For Heidegger the *work* of art is in the place where truth comes to stand. This perspective on art is opposed to the traditional aesthetic view of art and hence opposed to the philosophy of art from Plato onward. On the traditional view, philosophy does not find "truth" in the work of art or in any way coincident with art. Philosophical aesthetics does not dispute this perspective, it simply assumes it and drops the focus to that of the task or rule of judgment. Art and truth are related as negative (art) and positive affirmation (truth). Plato, as a lover of truth condemns art, as illusion thereby opposed to truth. And the philosopher of art follows suit, even going as far, as seems patent in Nietzsche's case, to condemn truth itself for art's sake.

"This Painting Spoke"

As Heidegger reads the painting, the hermeneutic story Heidegger tells reflects Heidegger's Allemanic-Suabian origins—just as Schapiro charges, just as Derrida defends that same phenomenological reading in his oblique appeal to Schapiro's sympathies for Van Gogh-cum-Schapiro, the "city dweller . . . the uprooted emigrant,"[55]—the patently unsymathetic (in Schapiro's view) but all-too-sympathetically appealing (magically, in Heidegger's view) country dweller's character of Van Gogh's *Shoes*. And as Derrida observed, no matter what can be said of the "migrant" life-trajectory of the artist himself, that same artist's sympathies, both as he painted them and as he movingly recounted them in his letters, were not exactly the sympathies of the city: "this migrant never stopped uttering the discourse of rural artisanal and peasant ideology."[56] Derrida emphasizes Van Gogh's migrant character (rather than the emigrant Schapiro) in just the way in which Schapiro identifies himself with Van Gogh (and against Heidegger). The artistry of Van Gogh exemplifies that ideology precisely as it exploits it: all artists are merchants, of their products and of themselves. But the truth of art is not to be reduced to the merchandising impulse that has recently managed to build a Van Gogh Museum to hold what Amsterdam's now-other museum, the Reijksmuseum, can no longer contain—a trend exemplifying what Nathalie Heinich (a social anthropologist of art exploring the limits of Malraux's characterization of the world)[57] analyzes as the "glory" of Van Gogh,"[58] a glorification (or fetishizing) of the artist that continues today as much under negative as positive guises.[59] Rather the truth Heidegger speaks of as the truth that speaks in the work of art, the truth that originates in the work, holds as the earth, *hyle*, or matter of the work of art. It is this, not the form, that speaks in the duskily enshrined leather of the shoes themselves. This holds no matter, I maintain, whether Van Gogh himself painted them, as Schapiro thinks, after wearing them himself, or whether, as Heidegger seems content to think, they were worn by the fieldworkers Van Gogh celebrated so often.

Heidegger sees the "toilsome tread of the worker" (O 34) in the dark interior of the painted shoes precisely because "from Van Gogh's painting we cannot even tell where these shoes stand" (33) and Heidegger descries the honesty and the rigors of peasant life in the darkness of the shoes revealing an entire world and the wholeness of a human lifetime: "Under the soles slides the loneliness of the field-path as evening falls. In the shoes vibrates the silent call of the earth, its quiet gift of ripening grain and its unexplained self-refusal in the fallow desolation of the wintry field" (34).

It is by wearing them that Heidegger's farmer relates to the shoes and it is the way shoes serve throughout such a lifetime: "the peasant woman is made privy to the silent call of the earth; by virtue of the reliability of the equipment she is sure of her world" (34). I have been arguing that what a phenomenological hermeneutic account of the work of art tells us in Heidegger's account, and as expressed in Gadamer's terms, is that to be affected by the description of such a life and the vibrant call of the earth, no kind of specifically Black Forest sentimentality is needed—as some have claimed. Not nostalgic recollection as Schapiro and, if differently, as also Derrida would claim, and not via a phenomenological bracketing of an actual pair of shoes, but only via a hermeneutic encounter with the work of art: "only by bringing ourselves before Van Gogh's painting" can we "read" a life in this way. For—and this is the reason Heidegger's approach to the work of art is an ineliminably hermeneutic aesthetics, unlike Merleau-Ponty's more classically phenomenological aesthetics—as Heidegger calls us to attend to what we thereby encounter in the presence of the work: "This painting *spoke*." And what it says tells us "what shoes are in truth" (35).

Importantly here, we note that Gadamer moves to transform his own original hermeneutic reading of the work of "language"[60]—"reading" art as he does in his first account of the "truth" at work in Heidegger's art work. For if Gadamer observes, "We must realize that we must first decipher every work of art, and then learn to read it, only then does it begin to speak,"[61] he also speaks, with reference to the subversive character of modern art, of what he calls the "language of art" to which one must respond as art's iconographic claim on us.[62] Gadamer's later turn to what Heidegger calls the "spoken" claim of art is articulated not with reference to Van Gogh's painting but rather to Gadamer's reflective and careful account of the voice the poet Rilke gives to his archaic torso of Apollo and, with reference to Plato, the claim of this poem/encounter is such as to require us to transcend the limitations of our humanity toward the tarrying that is a matter of the extraordinary difficulty of place and dwelling, earth and world. "There is no place that fails to see you" [*Da ist keine Stelle, die Dich nicht sieht*]. I have noted that this is the key point of Gadamer's reflections on the imperative relevance of the beautiful, the *plus quam* expressed in terms of beauty's claim on us, which Gadamer expresses with Rilke's ecstatic invocation as we have already invoked it: "Such a thing stood among men."[63] What comes to stand in the eternal presence of the work of art takes Gadamer to the Platonic variation on the word of longing from Hölderlin with which Gadamer closes his reflections on the beautiful: "Dass in der zaudernden Weile einiges Haltbare sei."[64]

As Gadamer speaks of reading and hearing, what is said (this is Heidegger's word) is the work of art. And for Gadamer, this is explained with regard to that which is to be heard and thus to that which belongs to hearing itself and which the "art of listening" alters or transforms as music. This musical illustration exemplifies Gadamer's analysis of modern art's challenge to traditional perception. On the basis of these reflections, Gadamer offers an elegant articulation of the persistence and transformation of tradition. In this way a kind of "fusion of horizons" takes place in Gadamer's comments on the longstanding tactic of smuggling "new" music into the expected horizon of concert-goers.[65]

For his part, Heidegger invokes a world of use and serviceability brought to representation and claiming us in the same way. We are thus brought before what is as such, that is, "Van Gogh's painting is the disclosure of what the equipment, the pair of peasant shoes *is* in truth." For Heidegger, art is "the truth of beings setting itself to work" (O, 34).

This claim concerning the work of art as the work of truth is Heidegger's dynamite of a completely art-philosophical kind. Since Plato and through to Nietzsche, philosophy sets art against truth. For Heidegger: "Truth happens in Van Gogh's painting. This does not mean that something is correctly portrayed, but rather that in the revelation of the equipmental being of the shoes, that which is as a whole—world and earth in their counterplay—attains to unconcealedness" (O, 56).

But Heidegger's gambit contra the philosophical tradition is compounded by an ambiguity. For us, and this is why we wait for the expert judgment, in order to have "value," the work of art must be a genuine or *true* work of art. This truth of art has to do with its authenticity as art, its authentic *identity* as a genuine work of art. To use Heideggerian terms to speak of a non-Heideggerian problem, such a "free occasioning" of a genuine work of art would be its true (i.e., authenticable) derivation from an original (authentic) artist. The modern tradition determining true art is preoccupied with authenticity and authenticity (and correlative value) is determined with reference to authority, accurate representation, and the proper reception of aesthetic value-attributions. The art expert assumes the truth or untruth of the work of art as corresponding to its genuine character, its authenticity or inauthenticity. Yet, like the logical truth of science, the aesthetic truth of modernity turns out to be other than Heidegger's aletheic occasioning of truth, the origin of the work of art.

The Artist and the Truth of Art

Heidegger's challenge to this expert tradition adverts to the mastery of the artwork precisely as it is able of itself to elide factitious detail, precisely as its presence remains "as the happening of truth." In this way, Heidegger's anti- or post-aesthetic perspective offers a hermeneutic phenomenology of art in truth, and may yet yield a more vital experience of art as the working of the work upon us. Thus Heidegger declares the working of the work of art against the fetishizing ethos of the museum itself, as against the preoccupations proper to art history and the auratic concerns of criticism. For Heidegger, just as the poem in its own voice can "deny" its author, *who* the artist "is remains unimportant," the work of art can deny the artist's "person and name."[66]

Van Gogh's shoes are as morosely frozen as the sepia tone of the photographic image and the infinite reproducibility that was already at work in forever altering the face of the working of art. And Gadamer later addresses this same point as it expresses the essence of alienated work: "Someone who has produced a work of art stands before the creation of his hands in the same way that anyone else does. There is a leap between the planning and the executing on the one side and the successful achievement on the other. The thing now 'stands' and thereby is there once and for all, ready to be encountered by anyone who meets it. . . ."[67] This "uniqueness and irreplaceability" corresponds for Gadamer to what "Walter Benjamin named the aura of the work of art."[68]

What Heidegger restores to art as its proper and ownmost state, that is: its truth, is nothing but what Plato sought to withhold in his charge that art trades in illusion or deception, not truth. Even Nietzsche, for whom, and famously for Heidegger, "art is higher than truth," remains, just as Heidegger asserts that he remains, within the Western philosophic perspective on the relation between art and truth.

Heidegger thus attempts a reversal of the refusal of art's truth (which is for the expert nothing but the erring truth and which for the philosopher is what *aletheia* means) from the inception of philosophy. This attempt at restitution does not prevent critics from charging that Heidegger falls within the scope of the *ressentiment*-driven movement of philosophy against art, disenfranchising art, here to repeat Danto's provocative formula: a fantastic denial of art, thought to be poised against its ownmost scope as a realm over and above, but certainly a world *beyond* philosophy. Here there is more than a disciplinary dispute, or battle of the faculties, but an expert crisis, a default of expertise, and a failure on the part of expert judgment, as such public intellectual battles are increasingly all that remain to us as intellectuals.

For critics, art historians, connoisseurs, it is essential that art be worth *more* than philosophy. On Danto's terms, on the terms of the all-too-routine artworld, especially as this is characteristic of New York City's intellectual art scene, the philosophical disenfranchisement of art takes place whenever it is imagined that philosophy seeks to deny this privilege either by censoring the claims of art and denying its value beyond the aesthetic domain of culture or else by converting art to philosophy, whereby art reveals its own (same) concern with being and with truth.

For Heidegger contends that "art lets truth originate. Art, founding preserving, is the spirit that leaps to the truth of what is, in the work" (O, 77). Thus art "by nature [is] an origin," that is, art is "a distinctive way in which truth comes into being," that is to say, "becomes historical." The place of art will be the locus of the composition of the true wherever a work comes to be, wherever creators find their way and preservers find their own place. As much as the artist, qua creator of art, the preserver is co-important, for Heidegger, even the co-originator of the dynamic working of art as such. Heidegger regards "founding preserving" as the veritable origin of the work of art, not only as a correlative counterpart and rather than the part of the spectators or public educed by any one informed with the right/wrong way of "appreciating" a work, that is, not via a program of art education or the training of connoisseur or art historical experts but rather "to each mode of founding there corresponds a mode of preserving" (75). The preserving openness to the work as its co-creative compositional reception is essential to the working manifestation of the work of art. The preserver is not a conservative element but a veritable prerequisite needed in advance and before the work of art can come into being at all.

Here again the reference goes beyond the aletheic space of truth opened up by Van Gogh's shoes. Beyond painting as a locus of truth, for Heidegger the expertly named and certified "Aegina sculptures in the Munich collection, Sophocles' *Antigone* in the best critical edition" (40) also offer us remnants or traces of art. But for Heidegger, although the truth of art can hold true in a historical context, the artwork can only work as such in an unvanished, still real and present world. And to invoke the need for this *real presence*, we see that to note the passing of a world will also be to admit the eclipse of the working power of art otherwise than as a trace. And in our own time, even if we ourselves undertake to journey to the site of the work itself, to meet, as Heidegger did, "the temple in Paestum or the Bamberg cathedral on its own square," what we find and what that same encounter cannot retrieve is a vanished world, emptied out or lost: "—the world of the work that stands there has perished" (Ibid.). The loss of a world can never be undone. And this is Heidegger's lasting challenge to the ethos of the conservation of art— the ideal of preservation in the frame or guardianship of the museum. Bereft of preservers, the works " 'themselves are gone by' " (41). This does not mean that we cannot come to an encounter with works of long past times, as Gadamer festively recounts both the common occasion for and the significance of such encounters for us, but only that if we do come to engage them, we encounter them *as* antique, *as* eclipsed and closed, abandoned and desolate. The phenomenological description of the Greek temple so important for the dramatic expression of the strife between earth and world shows the force of such an eclipsed or vanished world by contrast with the origin of the work of art. It is the working of the temple that "first fits together and at the same time gathers around itself the unity of those paths and relations in which birth and death, disaster and blessing, victory and disgrace, endurance and decline acquire the shape of destiny for human being" (42).

The Architecture of Preservation

The working truth of the temple as art reveals a vanished world. What remains today is a site for travelers and the increasingly destined locus of a museum. This is not merely so in the tacit wake of forgotten cults (mourned in Nietzsche's cry: "2000 years!—and not a single new god!"), but this constraint follows in the wake of the new world cast by the ruined temple as reconstituted and reworked under the aegis of preservation. Gadamer's moment of "feierliches Schweigen," a festive mien that may also have reflected Gadamer's own spirit, now gives way to a tacit isolation not only from the everyday world. In this way, it is far from irrelevant that apart from illustrations of poetry and literature, Gadamer's aesthetic examples are drawn from events of what is called "culture" today: like opera, concerts, and museum exhibits, and including his examples of play, recalling as they do the sport events of European soccer matches—rather than, say, the schematic aesthetics of the example of the game of chess, as the game is invoked by other philosophers of play like Wittgenstein or MacIntyre, or else like the aesthetic play of the world, for philosophers of cosmic play such as Heraclitus, Nietzsche, and Fink.[69]

What characterizes events of culture or sport is their discontinuous punctuation of everyday life. In the case of the gallery or the museum, we have to do with precincts of confined isolation, set apart from the quotidian. As Heidegger describes it, by contrast, for the Greek (like the parallel example of the cathedral at Bamberg), the temple belongs to the life of the people who built it for the sake of the integrative festive character of life, exactly understood in time, as Gadamer describes the festival. For the successes and failures, birth and death, war and peace of such a people, as Heidegger details it, the temple is consecrated. This is a reciprocal consecration, for the temple is deprived of this character when it loses this same central, centering, essentially sacred focus as a temple and as such. Then, although it continues as a trace, a ruin, a remnant of this vanished world, to be visited on special occasion, for tourism or adventure or even for the purposes of research so familiar to academics, the temple has lost its character as a site of life and time: that is the encounter between mortal beings and the divine, earth and sky. Nor indeed do other cultural events, such as concerts nor museum visits, offer the occasion for such an encounter as that lost in the origin of the temple work in question, neither for the highly cultured in the art and customs of the past nor a contemporary enthusiast of the art of the present and the world to come.

The example for this is the temple at Bassae, set against the Arcadian landscape of Greece: huge and looming but hidden—no accidental juxtaposition—by the mountain approach of the road one must follow to find it. That hidden and dominating aspect has been transformed and not by being brought out of the geographical dynamic of its landscape—indeed in such a way that if it is true that in ancient times one approached the temple on its height by means of a different path than today (as scholars have long debated the right approach to the Acropolis to explain the proportionate paradoxes of Ictinus's and Callicrates' Parthenon in perspective and design), today's circumstance is one that renders all temporal debates in perspective or changed landscapes irrelevant. Today one

Figure 12.6. Temple at Bassae. External view. Author's photograph, 1998.

finds the temple completely covered over, blocked over with a huge tenting structure (Figs. 12.6 and 12.7), the massive steel struts of which vie with the mountaintop against the sky, eliding in an ever more dramatic way the world of truth as the world of the temple in truth that Heidegger could invoke.

The tenting over of the temple at Bassae hardly lacks working power. Outlining nothing less than the world of today's preservers, the temple's tent exemplifies the curator's world, the conservationist's world of the archaeological expert of modern Greece, where the prime natural resources for development in this land, however conflictedly regarded in this same modern world, are the remaining structures and objects of Greek antiquity. This is the world of the modern exhibit and this is the world come to distinctive presence on the Arcadian mountaintop where, once upon a time, a people built its temple. A weirdly circus-like structure of ungainly proportions in a strange landscape, the covering tent builds the closed space of modern vanity—a permanent "temporary" scaffolding—around the temple: a mindless gesture of affected protection from the elements, secluding and so refusing them as the elements the temple was first set up to meet and to greet. For prior to such a conservative blockage, occlusive beyond the passing of the antique world itself, the work of the temple had ever been the work of exposure—set up into the elements of the world itself, a place of wrought encounter between earth and sky, that is the mortal and the divine. After so very

Figure 12.7. Interior/external view. Temple at Bassae. Author's photograph, 1998.

much "antiquity," the tented gesture at Bassae now intends to keep the temple safe from the ravages of the light and the air of the industrial world, calculatedly foreclosing the very elemental exposure that the temple builders put all their energy and all their resources to assure.

The example of the temple at Bassae, tented over and shaded from the sky (Fig. 12.6), proves the conservative force of the modern isolation of art in the locus of the museum or the tourist exhibition, duly labeled, properly "illuminated"—not so that it may be seen as what it is, but like an old parlor, in an old-fashioned style, so that it may not "fade." The museum as such, the conserver's impetus, secures and in so doing seals off whatever trace of the temple world had yet remained on earth in the very place and the look itself of the temple beneath the sky.[70]

The temple, for Heidegger—and as Heidegger (many years after he had given his lectures on the work of art) was still able to see it un-guarded by preservative scaffolding or the interventions of modern self-assertion—is not incidentally but essentially the site of world-withdrawal and decay, as a world in abeyance or retreat that only thus can show itself to us in a world without the temple's cult and thus without temples.[71] The withdrawal alone shows us what has been lost. "The temple in its standing there, first gives to things their look and to men their outlook on themselves." And even where the temple still stands in "perfectly preserved" glory, under the open sky, this look of things and this human outlook are foreclosed. The view of the temple only "remains open as long as the work is a work"—that is, as long as the temple is a working or real temple for a real people, only as long as the cult and the life of the cult remains real: that is, and only, "as long as the god has not fled from it" (O 43).

The "festive silence" [*feierliches Schweigen*] surrounding the exhibition of a recovered treasure of Greek antiquity in Gadamer's account of his revelatory visit to the Hellenic Museum testified to an exactly Platonic *aletheic* moment of revelation: the work was shown from out of its long concealment in the depths of the Aegean sea. This once lost sculpture was brought to an encounter with modern eyes. But what is restored is not the statue as it once "stood among men," be they its creators (or its original preservers as Heidegger speaks of these), standing "there" in Gadamer's Rilkean-Heideggerian words, founding and proclaiming "that such a thing stood among men."

Astonished and wondering, what we see in the space of a newly discovered work is a revelation, a discovery, a find. The sheer act of recovery from the sea anticipates the contours of museum conservation: a found artifact, a genuine antiquity. Nor is there any difference between a temple and a coin, a uncovered floor mosaic or a shattered pot that can be restored with the antiquarian skill of the archaeologist. In Heidegger's sense, the gesture of recovery is *the same* as the gesture that covers over but rather than being brought up from the sea, the temple at Bassae is withdrawn from the sky. A similarly revelatory occultation, as the statue is recovered from the sea, the temple is closed off from the heavens and its setting into the Arcadian mountainscape, the institution of an exhibition for the scholar, for the tourist, an image of eternity, "worth seeing" and corresponding to Heidegger's description of the age of the world picture, all under the watchful mediation of expert conservancy.

When we travel to the site of the temple at Bassae, what we encounter is not even the space of disappointment. Left open to the sky and on its original locus, as in Heidegger's examples of "the temple in Paestum or the Bamberg cathedral on its square," if we may recall that even the pristine temple is similarly occluded, if the perfect temple does not open a world in truth for us today, then the object found on the heights at Bassae is anything but the place of an abandoned world. What we meet in Bassae is not an encounter with a world in eclipse, for what its tenting ensures is no more than the withdrawal of occlusion.

In the heights of Arcadia, the struggle between earth and world might have remained, perhaps as the encounter with the elements themselves. The same after thousands of years: there is the wind and the dry air, there are the spare, small trees and their stark purchase on the rocks,

Figure 12.8. Landscape, Arcadia, Greece. Author's photograph, 1998.

there is the earth itself, and above all, there is the sky and the passage of day and night. And all of this still claims the visitor.

In the absence of a world of preservers, consecrated to the cult of the temple built to situate the crossing of the mortal and the divine, the temple work itself, however, does not and cannot speak. In this sense, conservation elides and cannot correspond to what Heidegger would name the preservers' task. Perhaps we should regret that with this effort to save what has been lost, we have sacrificed the ruined testimony that once, at least, "such a thing stood" and drew the space of destiny around it.

Like the lions that for so many millennia stood as silent witnesses to the long military and mythic history of Delos, the same lions which have now been shifted to a more commodious housing in a climate-controlled, duly monitored museum, all under the watch of the expert, the care of the cultural authorities, Bassae has become a tourist's resource, a world-historical resource. And it seems plain that such things ought to be displaced for the good purposes of preservation as well as for the sake of research and indeed the cultural edification of travelers.

But perhaps it is true, as Nietzsche says, that whatever is poised to fall, needs no more than a helping hand. Pondering death, pondering the essence of Christianity and pagan light, the teacher's furor in the painter Poussin would make an enigma of allegory: *et in Arcadia ego.*

There is no mystery that does not turn us on ourselves.

And once in Arcadia, I, too, would also travel great lengths in a mountain landscape, spare and ethereal in contrast with the vision of the pastoral created in its name, a word that captures no aspect of the place. Perhaps this was once otherwise, but perhaps, so I am inclined to think, given the mountains themselves, it was never otherwise. Vico would remind us that this we cannot know, if only as what inevitably remains alien to us today: perhaps the Arcadian ideal was always the sheer starkness of the landscape. Like Nietzsche's chaos taken to eternity, at its height, the harsh turns sublime.

Famous in antiquity, celebrated for its symmetry by Pausanias, recounted to me by others who had detailed the revelations of their visits, I traveled, together with a friend, in search of a temple. Yet, in Arcadia, like the mystery of Poussin's tomb, if I too could only expect to find that what I sought would not, could not be there, it is important to remember that what had to go missing for me had nothing to do with the manifest obscurity of the temple hidden from the sky.

Dreaming Ovid's dream, dreaming the dream of Rome, Arcadia is like nothing one imagines.

Nothing apart from the height of the world.[72]

13

❧

The Ethical Alpha and
Heidegger's Linguistic Omega

On the Inner Affinity Between Germany and Greece

At the extreme limit of suffering [*Leiden*: *pathos*] nothing indeed remains but the conditions of time or space. At this moment, the man forgets himself because he is entirely within the moment; the God forgets himself because he is nothing but time; and both are unfaithful. Time because at such a moment it undergoes a categoric change and beginning and end simply no longer rhyme within it; man because, at this moment, he has to follow the categorical turning away and that thus, as a consequence, he can simply no longer be as he was in the beginning.

—Hölderlin, "Remarks on Oedipus" §3

In the long-ranging debate on Heidegger's ethics, the rhetoric of conscious and unconconscious equivocation decides. This logical ambiguity perpetuates the causes of the politics of suspicion in the case of Heidegger's Nazism, his anti-Semitism, and his silence. The equivocation plays between Heidegger's Nazism (that is: his party membership) and Heidegger's Nazism (that is: his anti-Semitism).

The terms are equivocal because the Nazism in question corresponds to Heidegger's political affiliation with Nazism and the matter of Heidegger's biographical fact as the first Nazi Rector of the University of Freiburg and Nazi party member until the end of World War II. One can argue that these facts of Heidegger's own life imply the different sense of Nazism as an expression of anti-Semitism. Heidegger's political Nazism entails Heidegger's racist Nazism, such an affiliation tacitly condoning the sense of the party line against Jews to the extreme of the mass murder of six million Jews, the Holocaust that resulted, following precisely from that same "party line."

Working neither to validate nor to invalidate such an argument in its possible expression (the points just mentioned outline but do not articulate such an argument), the functioning of equivocation as a rhetorical figure sidesteps argument altogether. In the present chapter, I am not seeking to make formal, logical, or any other points against such a consummately successful rhetorical campaign. Rather I seek to identify the workings of such rhetoric in what is said about Heidegger's Nazism. This is not to say that a formal analysis could not be offered but rather that (and still to date) such an analysis has not been offered just because such a formal argument or proof is not necessary where what is at stake is persuasion on the matter of Heidegger's (political) persuasion and his (political) persuasiveness. All in all, an ethical issue in the realm of logic, a domain traditionally ruled by rhetoric.

On another rhetorical level, to deduce Heidegger's racist Nazism from Heidegger's silence on Nazism (so proving his anti-Semitism) is the enthymeme that supports the same ethical judgment concerning his political and personal or affective orientation. An enthymeme, when not defined as a Ciceronian rhetorical figure ending in two contraries, is a truncated syllogism consisting of two propositions—a syllogism in which one premise is suppressed as presupposed or given. Thus one may conclude, as important contemporary thinkers have already argued, that the connection between Heidegger and National Socialism is not only racist but impenitent, pernicious evil. In this way, the connection between Heidegger and Nazism not only renders the man morally culpable but his philosophy morally corrupt and (where the turns of argument move fast and easy in enthymematic connection) it also renders the study of his philosophy morally corrupting. Secondarily then, it is necessary to consider Heidegger's silence as itself warranting the enthymeme that works in the suspicions of Viktor Farías and almost all of Heidegger's recent commentators, right and left, on this point. These commentators do not suppress what Heidegger simply does not say. A logical or rhetorical figure is not necessarily comprehensive.

By his silence, then, Heidegger gives voice to his guilt, precisely because anything said is also impotent before the tribunal of right. In the end I seek to indicate—but not to prove, because arguments directed to this question can only be rhetorical—the philosophical relevance of the discussion of Heidegger's Nazism and the suspicion of his anti-Semitism and conviction of racism to philosophy and what, appropriating Hölderlin here, may be called the extreme limit of suffering.

The problem of suspicion as we know, when it is not a matter of an ingredient in a recipe, calling for, as the French say, a suspicion of nutmeg, is directed to or *raised against* a person. What is meant by the expression, "the politics of suspicion" is also directed to issues of personality, of persons, and personal circumstances, or, in a word: associations. One can also, of course, name this problem with an old-fashioned term borrowed from scholastic catalogs of formal offenses, offenses against argument, against logic, the chaining of judgments, of words and consequences, as *argumentum ad hominem*. Such an argument violates formal procedures if it also gets its job done, as it were, by rhetorical aspersion.

We are here speaking about the person of Martin Heidegger. Despite the defining prejudices of logic, it is important to underscore that we must consider the personal here, arguing precisely *ad hominem* because Heidegger himself is under attack, suspect, and because in the case of Heidegger, who spoke no less than if also subsequent to Nietzsche against the strictures of school logic, heretofore one had not been permitted to name the person where the question to be thought was being, the task of thinking itself. The Heidegger case has thus released a tender flood of personal reminiscences, retributions, and restitutional accountings of Heidegger's personality and spirit—all rather more than less at the expense of his philosophy. There is a hint, a suspicion of scholarly *Schadenfreude* in all of this. If, in the past commentators have supposed that for the sake of rigor, Heidegger would have liked to have it said of his life as he said of Aristotle's—he was born, he worked, he died—they are no longer bound by this restriction.

The upshot of this "Vermenschlichung" of Martin Heidegger—"The Man" foregrounding and backgrounding "The Thinker"—now allows access to the matter of Heidegger's guilt: the substance, or the *question*—in the best Heideggerian sense—of Heidegger's philosophy, but without the the stuff of thinking getting in the way. Just how this works we may be able to see further on.

But let me emphasize here that the major issue to be discussed is not a matter of what is philosophically relevant or not. What follows is not a discussion of points of philosophy as such. Quite the opposite. Indeed, the rhetorical question of Heidegger's Nazism does not connect Heidegger with a complex historical phenomenon that specialists are fond of discussing with reference to particular years—the years in question being 1927, the date of publication of *Being and Time* and the efforts, for or against, to see Nazi connections or preconditions in that text, 1929, 1933, 1934, 1935, 1937, 1944, and of course, 1945 all which have special value for historically minded specialists, for *Lebensphilo-sophen*, for philosophers with one axe or another to grind, and so on. But instead of such technical details, what is important are colloquial images and personal associations.[1] This rhetorical level is effective in drawing general attention to the political fortunes of a philosopher (where presidential candidates and movie stars have more selling appeal) just because as Heidegger would say, we are (academics included) proximally and for the most part [*zunächst und zumeist*] common and average (a typification Heidegger with uncommon restraint—or else with uncanny kindness—named *uneigentlich*, that is: inauthentic, not truly our own, not truly what we are, except, and this exception turns the claim around again, in what is closest to us and most ordinary in us). Thus and with the best philosophic interest in the world, one informed by Heidegger's own anthropological or hermeneutic concessions to the connections between biography and philosophy we turn to the level of the individual, the man Heidegger, just because unlike Socrates, to recall one reader's analysis, Heidegger was just Suabian (or, perhaps, more specifically, Allemanic, more broadly, German) enough to be reticent about himself and not like a Mediterranean type, not at all like the people Ted Kisiel characterizes as the "loquacious" Greeks. For Kisiel, a former engineer and currently a philosophy professor from Illinois, who in the interim has become much more intrigued with the intricate details of Heidegger's life, *if* one seeks an answer to the question of Heidegger's silence one is compelled "to eavesdrop on the private record which [Heidegger] graciously left behind. Even Heidegger's intimacies now belong to the world."[2]

But what is the meaning of such a suggestion, betraying the reha-bilitation of approaches traditionally damned in philosophic discourse, namely that of the argument *(um) ad hominem*, a rehabilitation now effected to excess in the bibliography growing and proliferating into subsections and research specialties of such a personal history used as a pernicious rhetorical device?

What is problematic here is the rhetorical twist that is in this case a kind of metaphorical swerve, or (to use a term borrowed from a Roman heir to the Greek *physiologoi*) what one might invoke as the *clinamen* at work in the rhetorical scheme of argumentative cause and effect. To be a Nazi, as Heidegger was, is to stand for, in causal and necessary connection, to be: a representation of absolute evil, the dia-bolical, sheer horror, as claimed by more than one commentator on the matter. But, at the same time, and this is the luxury of equivocation, trading on one term to mean something else also signified by the same term—one need not actually maintain that Heidegger, in his own person, was actually evil. Or then again, one can. In any case one now knows what this kind of evil looks like: it writes *Sein und Zeit* and *Zeit und Sein*; leaves us his "contributions" with the subtitle *Vom Ereignis* and speaks of *Gelassenheit* and *Gefahr*, quotes Heraclitus, claims an essential connection between its own philosophy and a poet known to be mad, has a personal history of neurasthenia and general gutlessness, and holds in just this connection, mysticism *can* go so far, that thinking and poetry are the same.

Silence: Heidegger's Racist Humanism and the Name of the Jews

Simply by speaking of "Heidegger's silence" I can be heard to speak—to be speaking—of Heidegger's anti-Semitism. The focus of this rhetorical association means that Heidegger's silence concerns what he did not express and this is the question of anti-Semitism, for in almost every other connection with his Nazism, Heidegger did indeed, more or less, express himself.[3] The culpable silence here is what George Steiner has named a "calculated silence" on the matter of the crimes of Nazism.[4] The silence in question names what can be taken for anti-Semitism even if we had no other evidence, and we do have other evidence. Heidegger's silence refers to his failure[5] to denounce the murder of the Jews, in a complete and sufficient or satisfactory fashion, which murder, which crime is the most resistant, ultimate facticity of the Holocaust.

For all who write and think on this point it must be remembered again and again that those who attempt to write on this topic are very nearly without words for it. If any constellation of events shows the singular violence of a word of naming it is the naming of the kind of thing the Holocaust was. One may not call the Holocaust a *tragedy*, or a *sacrifice*, or a *crime* or employ any other qualifying nomination simply because what was done exceeds naming and must be acknowledged as it exceeds, is in positive negativity *plus quam*: exceedingly violent and horrifying, the more than merely diabolical act of all the very many—and there are indeed very, very many,—horrifying brutalities of this century, crowning three thousand years or so of Western civilization, that is to say, if we begin with the Greeks.

And we do begin with the Greeks, for the problem of anti-Semitism is also the problem of the opposition between Jerusalem and Athens. With Christianity, the problem is Latinized, Romanized to the conflict between duties to Caesar and duties to God or what we in the United States are fond of discussing as the separation between Church and State, but note that even here the opposition is the same. If Heidegger repudiates the translation of Greek into Latin, it is because Heidegger together with a longer German tradition, historically and most notably, the Romantics, who are nevertheless, according to one account, absolved as guiltless in this connection simply by virtue of their earlier birth, finds a special linguistic and spiritual affinity between German and Greek. Hence if Heidegger claims, as he does in the *Spiegel* interview, in reference to his thinking's "essential connection" with Hölderlin, that the Germans have a special world-historical task, his point is that this task is mediated by "the special inner relationship between the German language and the Greeks."[6]

Thus Heidegger assumes that we begin as his philosophy most primordially begins: with the Greeks. One would have to be half-deaf in heart and spirit not to hear the implicit condescension and insult in Heidegger's pronouncement of the impossibility of philosophizing in languages that are not Greek or German.[7] The contest between Athens and Jerusalem is given a different tone, a different resonance—to be heard in the Nietzschean contrast that may be made between *thumos* and *chutzpah* (although, obviously enough, these were not Nietzsche's words). With all his Germanness and his claims for Greek affinities, Heidegger is best characterized by the latter—and *that* merits further attention. Thus as Rudolf Augstein puts it, the boldest assault against speakers and thinkers of other languages was explicit in the claim Heidegger made during his interview with *Der Spiegel*, "Just as little as one can translate a poem, can one translate a thought."[8] Supplying a fuller context to Heidegger's statements,[9] and in the process paralleling Heidegger's alethiology in quasi-juridical fashion,[10] Augstein points out that from the start Heidegger's articulation of the pride of German place in language and the house of Being, is a veritable coup against the French (if also against the English, the Italians, and of course, to Heidegger's everlasting pain, having insulted that "certain" Victor Farías, against the Chileans and thence and thereby, the Spanish and so on).

It is of course significant that to these terms and on these terms even the French surrender, not only *in fact* but *as* a fact that Heidegger takes to full account. In the house not of Being but philosophy, as practiced under the "continental" rubric, that is between contemporary German and French philosophers, Heidegger's coup has been successful. The French, that chauvinistic people *par excellence*, those of Heidegger's personal acquaintance and those who follow his thought today—who in the estimation of many authors so comprise the horizon of French philosophy that the problem of Heidegger is very nearly a "French question"—are given to declare (or to concede?), so Heidegger tells us: "again and again . . . [that] when they begin to think they speak German. They insist that they could not get through with their own language."[11]

As a reflection on this point, it is worth remembering what we have heard not merely from Nietzsche or even Schopenhauer, but in this same connection, from Freud and the subsequent psychoanalytic tradition, that it is part of the thinking of innocents and victims, part of the psychology of violation that offense is rarely rebuked as such but swallowed.

The primordial transference yields the complicity between trauma and the psychopathology that in repression constitutes the everyday—that is, that tells us who we are, proximally and for the most part. It is the negative word, the word of abuse that tells us our own names.

One becomes a victim simply by receiving an insult, where one quite literally—this is the assault of naming—has no other choice than to take the abusive word at its word. But to protest an insult is to repeat and thus to reinforce the full force of the slight.

We are reminded of the irrecusable violence of the name. It is not only Heidegger who cannot by any number of uttered (or unuttered as we see) words defuse the charges made against him, but no Jew, no Black, no woman, no abused child, no insulted scholar (think of Nietzsche here) ever has or will have the power to refuse an insult, to defuse a characterization, a name, or to deflect a hand raised in suspicion against what is suspected. There is no defense against being, against being called a Jew. Nor are the strong immune, and Nietzsche has shown us that if one has a talent that is otherwise than vulgar or common, such strength, such talents are inverted when the claim of being what one is rather than something else is held against one. Thus strength, thus the expression of strength becomes a weakness: what is becomes a defect in being. And this for Heidegger is the essential violence of *logos*, the word.

But let us be clear here, just to keep to the rhetorical track. Heidegger's philosophy includes "A Racist Conception of Humanity,"[12] to use the title of Rainer Marten's essay on the theme. Elsewhere Marten offers a balanced and passionate discussion of the issue. For Marten it is not a matter of prejudice, but what he calls in a deliberate reductive reference to Jacques Derrida, as well as perhaps unconsciously to a rather local, even specifically provincial German sense, "Heideggers Geist." If the atmosphere of Heidegger studies was previously one of trans-human reverence, this circumstance no longer holds. "Heideggerians" are now prepared to take their revenge upon and self-declared anti-Heideggerians their own sweet way with the father.

What this means in a scientific age, the era of technicity, of techno-complicity—if one may coin a word here where so many words have been coined—is that it is ranged under the opposite sign, the sign of regress and indeed of religion. Thus so-called "Heideggerians" have been and will continue to be—if one may predict—attacked and abused in a postmodern but still scientific age by the explicit use of *quasi-religious* terms. To this effect, Heidegger is named "the Master," Heidegger's philosophy "Dogma" or "Dogmatics," his followers "devotees," "acolytes," or quite simply "the faithful." The religiously inclined (the Catholic) or the mystical (here we have the proof of the *catholicity* of scientific anti-religious prejudice) are per se ideological, fanatical, capable of anything and in this then not properly philosophic. This is the rhetorical use of enthymeme and with it we are quite nearly landed back where we started with the traditional analytic philosophic suspicion against Heidegger's philosophy proper. The positivistic ghost of Carnap could not be more (if more perversely) vindicated. It must be noted that there is surely a hagiographic tendency among Heidegger scholars, if it is unclear that such hagiography is missing in studies of Nietzsche or among Rilke or Hölderlin enthusiasts.[13] But one denounces the literal consequences of that sanctity in Heidegger's case, namely his mysticism and of course, this is the point of the attack: his opposition to technology and science. It is this opposition that as some critics have observed, pits Heidegger against the average person. Accordingly, Heidegger is nothing but an elitist mandarin, expressing the privileges and values of the priest at the expense of the ordinary, the average man. After all, isn't it true, the pious pro-modern mind observes, that the common "man" benefits from the intellectually maligned advances of modern technology? How could Heidegger question such a thing? Doesn't this mean that Heidegger's critique of technology betrays his fascism?

For most scholars, Heideggerian or not (and Reiner Schürmann and Dominique Janicaud are among the rare exceptions to this piety), technology, as such, could never be the problem. The problem, and George Steiner puts this complaint most eloquently, is Heidegger's silence, in particular the egregious absence of protest on his part or indeed against him. This is the problem of Protestantism, anticlericalism, antipapism, here to be heard as dissonance or dissidence. The Heidegger case was nothing like the case of Wagner—condemned and censured as much for fascist appropriation of his music as well as for his anti-Semitic writings. Instead, in Heidegger's case it seemed that one had an "unconditional and fervent *for*, without a corresponding *against*."[14] Thus Heidegger could "complain not of opposition but much rather ignorance." Dogma once again. But as Marten has summarized this issue, in the end "the recollected Heidegger case can no longer be handled by way of the to and fro of explicit clarification and inarticulate obfuscation with regard to 'Heidegger, the human being,' but places a question mark after his philosophy instead."[15] This question leads to the issue of racism and thereby to anti-Semitism as such. The issue for Marten is that already named: the connection between Germany and Greece. The fact that Heidegger's spirit is "primordially Greek" means for Marten what it signifies for other philologically sensitive readers. To count the German and the Greek together as a single "spiritual" event or entity is to steal a people's language, claiming their thunder as one's own.

Whether protesting or dogmatic Catholic, the religious impulse seems to be the same. For his part, Marten suggests that with the claim that in Heidegger's *historical* perspective and time "the Greek spirit is at home simply and solely in German blood and on German soil,"[16] an incalculable violence is done to the Greeks as such. Adorno makes a powerfully similar argument as we have seen, and Marten is somewhat, if indirectly in his debt. Thus violence is also done to those who no matter how complicit they may be are excluded from this heritage. For philological sensitivities, the problem is the same as it ever was: Heidegger is wrong. Hence the connections Marten finds are typically tendentious ones, and not just in subtle ways—for Marten, "[w]hat is at stake is major and basic: it concerns the central concepts and positions of the Greek doctrine of being."[17] It is hardly necessary to note that the remedy—more rather than less preoccupation with or study of Greek,[18]—is one that might have been taken from Heidegger.

And in all the general conclusion to be drawn is the one claimed by Heidegger: that we are not yet thinking. And we are indeed not yet thinking, at least not enough, not to the point, not to the philosophy, the philosopher in question. For the issue remains unposed before us. We fail, as ever in Heidegger's regard, to think or to question so long as we fail to pose the question in the proper way. And what belongs to thought, or to questioning Heidegger here?

There are two rhetorical tacks to the equivocal question of the relation between Heidegger, the man and the thinker. The first stylistic approach—and for all his ferocity and thickness vis-à-vis Heidegger's thought, Habermas takes this tack—separates the thought from the thinker, the thinker from the thought, and the sinner and the sin in a move common to both Catholic and Protestant but not, let it be noted, to the Greek, allowing us to condemn the one and embrace, or even love the other. It is remarkable once more that this tack is not the other, the second interpretive turn, sophisticated readers other than Habermas or philologists who flatter the innocence of the same sophisticated readers, are given to take after Heidegger.

For what Heidegger taught his students to do, despite the philologists' fury at the audacity implied by this inversion, made attentive, reflective thinking on a text primary for, made it the preparation for careful, resonant reading. To read Heidegger is not to read a philosophy of Nazism or anything else, but it is to read philosophically. What we have to learn from Heidegger in the phenomenological tradition after Husserl is a dedication to thinking. To prepare for thinking in this way is no matter of mere reading but a task to be undertaken, a doing that must, as it is thought, undertake, or as Nietzsche taught in another sense, overtake us. In this way Heidegger took seriously Nietzsche's own injunction that "thinking has to be learned in the way that dancing has to be learned" just as much as "reading" is to be practiced as an art.

From Heidegger too, following the hermeneutic turn, one read Freud, one read Marx, one read Kierkegaard, one read Schopenhauer, and even Wittgenstein and found cause to confirm Nietzsche's subterranean strategies in the genealogy of reason, the morality, the grammar of science and philosophy. Not merely desire continues to speak in the name of the *logos* but also power, ambiguity, and fear.

What we have from Heidegger is a complex legacy, one addressed only with comparable complexity. In the present context, to advert to the ineluctability of ambiguity admits—in Schürmann's expression, *accuses*—as Nietzsche charges us to see, that it is a compound lie to pretend that all truths are *simple*. Here the problem does continue to be, in the spirit of Heidegger, again, not a matter of opposition or disagreement but still understanding. And of all the many expressions on this topic, Schürmann's efforts to limn the original meaning of ambivalence—the Real as Lacan has it[19]—speaking of the two-edged essence of technology and Western culture and the ethical meaning for life of triple binds, follows a track of utter restraint to the heart of Heidegger's question and to the old tradition of the question, the love of *sophia*, wisdom, and the importance of the thinker's, that is, of the critic's *own* journey in thought. But that said, focusing on the exigence of understanding, we may not forget what it means to understand differently. Our questions to Heidegger's philosophy, to the topics of his questioning, to his affirmations, to his collaboration, our suspicions raised against his silence, his commission, where we note that he gives consent by silence to a crime at the extreme of expression, beyond image and against reason in its most perfect expression. Heidegger's complicity with this crime of abyssal, abysmal, cataclysmal, horribly sublime proportions inaugurated the terms on which this thinking must acquit itself or stand the threat to be quitted. This is the threat behind the question Karl Löwith began to pose in Heidegger's regard and seconded by Adorno, and raised now with far greater venom and vengeance: "Why read Heidegger?" The greatest evil, we say, perpetuated here once again by refusing to name the Jews, that people singled out now not by God but by evil itself, by what was done, and what thereby is perpetually done against the Jews.

In the wake of *Yom Kippur*, as I first wrote this text—years ago now—in the subsiding awe of the Day of Atonement, it is the thought of the horror and the consequences of anti-Semitism that must set the stakes for thinking from now on. As Sander Gilman writes, it "is not the age of 'post-modernism,' it is the post-Holocaust age."[20]

Speaking of the Jews, as Heidegger did not, Heidegger's racism embraces rather more than the violence done to an ambivalently, complicatedly, nuancedly magnificent people, namely the Greeks—as articulated in Marten's catalog of the ambivalent meaning of Greek culture—with Heidegger's ultimately non-Hölderlinian claim that the German captures the spirit the Greeks themselves failed to master and forgot, so that in the predictable formula here: German becomes for Heidegger more Greek than Greek itself. The problem of nuance and complexity is that the thinker is thereby permitted, following his star, to forget the gross and rude matter at hand. I would repeat, we would repeat: Heidegger failed to express significant sensitivity, horror, pain, remorse; Heidegger failed to confess responsibility for and complicity with the Nazi program of exterminating Jews, the murder of the Jews. It is this last awful fact that weighs on us, that gives the equivocal force to the expression of Heidegger's Nazism, as the ultimate meaning of anti-Semitism today. We are not merely talking about Heidegger's "racist" conception of humanity.

Hence although there are expressions of this last issue ruled by little more than a moralizing fury, raising this questioning accusation at this penultimate point now concerns Heidegger's failure to affirm and to speak to and to speak of the pain and horror of the Holocaust as a German crime against other cultures (where the Nazi program was, of course, so hyper-inclusive in its extermination, its exclusion of "others" that it would seem to have made it possible in the post-Nazi, post-Holocaust era to speak, as Adorno and Horkheimer could, of the "invention" of "other Jews"). Heidegger's silence condemned these events to silence. More crucially, what follows from Heidegger's thinking is that by failing to let these events come to word, to use the language Heidegger borrowed from Stefan George, by breaking off not only the word for these events but the very possibility of words for Jews and non-Germans (non-Greeks), Heidegger's silence is not simply an omission. With the claim that thinking is possible only in the language of ancient Greece (and in German as *Nächstverwandte*), one closes off the words for counting certain events as happenings, as things that matter. Turns of expression, clichés, idioms, phraseologies all speak in the hermeneutical space and play of a language. Whether one follows Gadamer, Quine, or Wittgenstein here, the hermeneutic, the experience, the game of learning a language confirms that to learn a language is to learn to catch, to learn to see or to hear what is cast forth by the play of words. To learn Greek then is to learn to catch this same glimmering playing of a phrase, of what is spoken in what can be, what is said by this one in that time and that place. For a Sophocles is not a Plato in word or in the constellation of words offered, and the difference in expression bespeaks more than the difference between tragedy and philosophic literature but a different resonant efficacy. What Heidegger, what Nietzsche, what Hölderlin, what Goethe, and what Milton saw first reading the Greeks is an intimation of a way of being that can be made to speak and in speaking to us be restored as a possibility for us to know and in knowing to share. This flash of recognition, the vestige of humanism, subjective primacy at its best or worst, betrays a "special linguistic and spiritual affinity" not only for the German student of Greek but the English student of Greek (or German). For something like this occurs in every apt scholar of another language and culture just as Nietzsche saw it occurring between cultures of genius. The *nature* of an affinity is not a given: it is no "second-nature" as such and from the start.

Are we to say, following Heidegger in specific reference to the French (may we count the Belgians too?), that a Georges Dumézil, or indeed a Pierre Vernant or a Marcel Detienne or even (now via Hungary) a Gregory Nagy or a Gàbor Betegh possibly lack some kind of "special affinity" for the language of their specific field of scholarship? Surely not and if one were to do so, if one yielded to the presumption of such an essential failing, one sacrifices the very thing that makes any kind of historical and scholarly sense possible. As the art historian Ludwig Curtius wrote long ago, echoing Wilhelm von Humboldt and Friedrich Hölderlin as he did so in a quaintly vituperative review of Oswald Spengler, what makes history possible is continuity between cultures: *Einigung*, here understood musically as consonance.[21]

It is important to question the nature of these "dragon's teeth," that is, to question the meaning of the autochthonous as such and the meaning of related or affine being, to question those who have an affinity with the original, share the same, the autochthonous essence? This is the question of the relation in Heidegger's word of Germany and Greece. Nietzsche saw "genius" as the resonant capacity that alone and in the end expresses the meaning of affinity.[22] The Greek "art of fruitful learning" constitutes genius—like the Spirit that lists where it will and is nowhere limited.

The question of interpretive affinity can only be raised in a liminal way and not elaborated here. But we have seen enough to suggest that a "special spiritual and linguistic" affinity cannot be a given but must be learned. The question for Nietzsche as he posed it, both at the beginning and in the end of his reflections on culture, turns on the matter of hearing, seen again as if for the first time. "[O]ne has to learn to *see*, one has to learn to *think*, one has to learn to *speak* and *write*." Learning to see is for Nietzsche, the philologist, the disciplinarian, and advocate of careful reading, the hardest of all, requiring one to habituate oneself to a veritable *epoché* in the best Husserlian and scientific sense—even where Nietzsche names this the "*first* preliminary schooling in spirituality": "habituating the eye to repose, to patience, to letting things come to it, learning to defer judgment, to investigate and comprehend the individual case in all its aspects" (TI, "What the Germans Lack," §6). Such an eye for details or subtlety is perhaps a "listening" or attuned eye, an eye that would be *able* to see and *able* to hear.

If we would condemn Heidegger it cannot be for his silence where, as the path of another inquiry would show, silence, the still point between tone (caesura) and the breath (diaresis) is the very condition of full speech and best affinity. Rather what is to be continually deplored is only, if this is also, as Marten says it above, very grave, Heidegger's silencing of the significance of the silence of other languages, of other words. Heidegger's crime then is in forgetting the resonant sense or working of affinity. This forgetfulness impelled him in a move that like nothing else in Heidegger is truly reminiscent of Spengler, thus a move marking Heidegger as a writer if not a child of his own time, to condemn other languages to silence. Heidegger's expression fails as a silence that would be like Nietzsche's "strong will," a silence that in the end would finally "hear" and only thus "defer decision."

Heidegger and Nazism: Philosophy and Tragedy

I have sought neither to prove nor to disprove Heidegger's Nazism. As Jürgen Habermas's inimitable word has it: "Martin Heidegger? Nazi, sicher ein Nazi!"[23] And Heidegger himself, in his interview with *Der Spiegel*, expressly acknowledges his then-conviction of "the 'greatness and magnificence' of Hitler as Chancellor of the Reich,"[24] a judgment that easily parallels the infamous passage where Heidegger declares that the works "peddled about nowadays as the philosophy of National Socialism have nothing whatever to do with the inner truth and greatness of this movement."[25] I have suggested that the effect of *acknowledging* what one has done, giving the deed a name naming oneself as the doer, as responsible, ultimately legitimates, recognizes the past and so naming it, sanctions it, defuses its violence, admits it into presence as what was done. This naming, this setting into language, this failure of failure, of the breaking of the word is, we remember, for Heidegger and in the same classic text: the purest heart of violence.

The prime rhetorical effect of linking Heidegger and Nazism, as such and as Farías has done, yields guilt by association much on the order of Gilbert Ryle's reported laconic and very British, very analytic statement uttered in 1960: "Heidegger. Can't be a good philosopher. Wasn't a good man."[26] With this citation, Robert Bernasconi goes on to emphasize Jean-François Lyotard's point: "One should not seek to neutralize the intrinsic inequality of this affair by regulating it through its alternative: if a great thinker, then not a Nazi; if a Nazi, then not a great thinker—the implication being: either negligible Nazism or negligible thought."[27] But as Lyotard had hastened to remind us, it is not merely Heidegger who is on trial here.

The rhetorical English put on the questions puts us, we ourselves, "*we*"—to use Nietzsche's pronoun as Philippe Lacoue-Labarthe likes to use it in connection with nothing less than the final solution (so that we do not forget whose solution it was)—"*good Europeans*" in question. In an appendix to *Heidegger Art and Politics*, Lacoue-Labarthe offers an abject illustration of the impossibility of articulating the demand to express the meaning of Nazism—in spite of his best efforts, where he seeks to express the impossibility of his own expression, and is thereby condemned to condemn himself. It is this neutralizing distinction that is deeply problematic and not just in the directions not quite given voice by Lyotard. For when one begins as we do, as we all tirelessly seek to show that we do begin, from a position of revulsion, a perspective of condemnation, by recognizing, acknowledging, and denying Nazism for what it was and must be, in all that caused it and all that steadily results from it as its constant effect, we find ourselves on the track not of the diabolical but the repressed. We are thereby condemned to the repetition here and elsewhere, to the compulsion to name Nazism as Lacoue-Labarthe does "an *absolutely* vile phenomenon both in its goals and its result—without question the most grave—by a long way—that the West has known (i.e., that it has produced.)"[28] We could analyze the character of this qualification and others like it as the necessary anacoluthon, nay the very series of breaths and hesitations and indirections required to purchase the space for a near consent (*à la* Levinas) to horror or again (with Levinas) for a sanctioned transaction with the diabolical.

The limits of the present question do not permit me to trace the essentially philosophic implications of this question to the anacoluthon that is only a blind aposiopesis, that is an admonishing hesitation that stumbles in its stammering refusal. But I must say that such breaths are far from the caesura, the "pure word" to speak with Hölderlin of a "counter-rhythmic interruption" of a null or turning point of balance and decay so that what appears, what comes to stand in appearance, is finally "representation itself."[29] The key to Reiner Schürmann's discussion of law, to Heidegger's awful privileging of the No, the mortal and god-awful height of the meaning of Heidegger's utterance that higher than actuality stands possibility—like Richardson's deep and enduring concern with the *die Irre*—is found in Hölderlin's titling expression of a fragment from Pindar, as The Law [*Das Gesetz*]. We do not need Lacan's strictures on the meaning of law nor Benjamin's nor indeed Adorno's discussion of mimesis to understand the dynamic between the imaginary of reflective phantasy and the symbolic of mastery and denial in order to understand Hölderlin's expression of the Law of finitude: " 'The immediate as impossible for both mortals and immortals. . . . But rigorous mediateness [*Mittelbarkeit*] is the law.' "

In Lieu of Judgment

By questioning the virtue of our expectations and our questions, one might in the end underline something of Heidegger's own special integrity, his consuming preoccupation with philosophy. What is to be thought can be called Being or truth or the tragic essence of the event or law or destiny but it always speaks to the reader as that which is given, as one's own, to be.

With this one asks as Heidegger does at the start of his *Introduction to Metaphysics,* "Why are there beings rather than nothing?"[30] That is, why is there what is at all, or better still, the one who is, rather than not-being, rather than the higher possibility of nothing? This is the question of possibility as such, of what is mine to be—for me and for any individual as one must always make this Kantian extension with Kant and it may yet take us to the consideration of nonhuman being and the question of one's ownmost never-to-be-outstripped *possibility*, and that is again to say: the tragic essence of being. This is the height of suffering, once grasped as a law, even if the law transgressed is—to the point at which Hölderlin broke off in his reflection on punishment and law— unknown to me. Thus Heidegger ends by observing "the true problem is what we do not know and what insofar as we know it *authentically*, namely as a problem, we know only *questioningly*."[31]

14

❧

Heidegger's *Beiträge* as Will to Power

Nietzsche himself never wrote *The Will to Power*, the book that is arguably his most famous, certainly his most controversially notorious work.[1] To underscore this point, Heidegger opens his 1936 to 1937 lecture course, *The Will to Power as Art*, by setting the word "work" in quotation marks.[2] As is now well known, what was published as Nietzsche's *Will to Power* was cobbled together from his remaining notes, including, as Heidegger writes, "preliminary drafts" and "partial articulations." In this way, Heidegger is able both to advert to the history of the compilation of this non-book at the same time as he lectures on the topic, a practice alienating Nietzsche specialists, especially the more philologically sensitive—indeed perhaps even more than the politically sensitive—among them.

I regard Heidegger's *Beiträge* as his *Will to Power*, so to speak, and in two senses. The first and more important sense is that in these notes Heidegger engages the issue of power [*Macht*] and domination [*Machenschaft*]. This focus is complicatedly political.[3] But the *Beiträge* is also stylistically modeled on Nietzsche's writing, not on Nietzsche's *Thus Spoke Zarathustra*, as has been rather hastily supposed, but *The Will to Power*, the subject matter of Heidegger's not at all incidentally contemporaneous first lecture course on Nietzsche.[4] The support for this claim is critically stylistic. Like *The Will to Power*, the *Beiträge* features short sections—as short as the scholastic Heidegger could make them—numbering them into subparagraphs that vie with those of Bernard Lonergan's *Insight* for enthusiastically numeric excess, but above all, the *Beiträge* features paragraph titles that work as Nietzsche's titles work in his books, such as *The Gay Science* and *The Will to Power*. In what follows, I cite the titles Heidegger employs along with his numbered paragraphs in the *Beiträge*. And just the invocation of these titles should serve to make Heidegger's debts to Nietzsche's *Will to Power* at least preliminarily, superficially, clear.

The idea of power was omnipresent throughout the 1930s, especially in Germany, especially in a world that had already fought itself to an unprecedented level of devastation and abasement and was about to begin another uncountenanceable course in the natural history of destruction.[5]

For Heidegger, then, *Machenschaft* had a distinctively modern expression, later identified in his lectures to the Club of Bremen as the essence of modern technology: the worldview of modern science. This was an essence that cut across political borders, a truly global essence of the kind that he regarded as obliterating the supposed differences between Bolshevism and Capitalism as well as the reigning rule of National Socialism and its conception of science expressed in its practical and very political commitment to all the devices—technical and cybernetic, biological and psychological—of modern science and its totalizing development.

After discussing Heidegger's *Beiträge* as an editorial production like Nietzsche's *Will to Power*, I offer a review of Heidegger's analysis of power as technical, scientific *Machenschaft*. I conclude by noting the continued relevance of Heidegger's reading of modern technological *Machenschaft* as expressed by the background assumptions and ambitions of genetic engineering in general and the human genome project in particular.

Heidegger, Nietzsche, and Modern Technology: *Machenschaft* and Will to Power

Since its first seemingly surprise publication out of the prescribed order for the *Gesamtausgabe*, scholars have read and reread *Beiträge*[6] without coming to anything resembling consensus regarding its reception. Whether today's reader retains a fondness for the Heidegger of *Being and Time* or appreciates the transformations of the turn in itself, or in its resultant effects yielding the complex linguistic resonances and thoughtful endeavors of the "later Heidegger," the *Beiträge* remains a difficult fit in the Heideggerian corpus.

Why so? Superficially, of course, the easy answer ought to be that the publication is too new—too close to us—both in terms of its 1989 publication in German or in the brief decade (by academic standards) until its appearance in English in December of 1999. But this reply seems wrong.[7] For whether or not, as Otto Pöggeler claims, Heidegger "never mentioned" the *Beiträge* to his closest students, Pöggeler's sustained defense of the *Beiträge* as nothing other than Heidegger's "second major work"[8] has played for forty years in German (and English-language) circles, beginning with Pöggler's own early sketch of the text itself, "Sein und Ereignis" (1959, English: 1975). At the very least, the surprise or novelty factor is inexact.

In this final chapter, I propose to explore the relevance of technology and the constitutive role of Nietzsche's thought as aspects of related importance in Heidegger's *Beiträge*. The latter consideration is tactically more important as it concerns the relevance of style in Heidegger's reading of Nietzsche; the former concerns the enduring complexities of Heidegger's critical take on science in the modern world. Without adverting to Nietzsche's influence *and* without raising the question of modern science/technology, as the essence of what Heidegger names *Machenschaft*, the function and meaning of the *Beiträge* in Heidegger's thinking can only elude us.[9]

In this respect, key emphases in the *Beiträge* recur in Heidegger's later *Zollikon Seminars*.[10] To this extent, Heidegger by no means abandons the insights of *Being and Time*. Such an emphasis opposes the tendency to read a readerly construct named "Heidegger I" (or what Ted Kisiel names the "early," pre-*Being and Time* Heidegger) as if one had to do with another thinker entirely, addressing the personality dynamics of the "two Heideggers" William J. Richardson sets into the scholarly habitus of apotheosization in Richardson's recollection of the genesis of this distinction in his recently written preface to the U.S. edition of his Heidegger book.[11] The same periodizing reification exacerbates the tendency toward mystifying readings of the so-called later Heidegger, the "Heidegger II" who comes after the turn or *Kehre*. But, as we recall and as Heidegger himself emphasizes in his original letter to Richardson, Heidegger I and Heidegger II are to be thought together and ineliminably so because II is already, so Heidegger expresses it, to be found in Heidegger I: "Nur von dem unter I Gedachten her wird zunächst das unter II zu Denkende zugänglich. Aber I wird nur möglich, wenn es in II enthalten ist."[12]

To the perplexities of thinking Heidegger I *and* II, early and late, a reference to Nietzsche seems only to compound the challenge. For many readers, Nietzsche's name continues to work as a key signifier for irrationalism.[13] Correspondingly well known is the related assertion that Heidegger's irrationalism (usually articulated in terms of an explicit antipathy to modern science and technology) is what rendered his philosophy vulnerable to or even sets it equivalent to Nazism.[14]

No accidental byproduct of a contamination with Nietzsche's style, I have been arguing that Heidegger composed his manuscript on the model of the publishing phenomenon that in effect constituted what could be called Nietzsche's "Contributions to Philosophy," the same part of Nietzsche's philosophy that remained *Nachlaß*.[15] In this sense, it is directly relevant that in his first lecture course on Nietzsche, Heidegger offers a reflection on what he calls "Ereignis," the subtitle of the *Beiträge*, posed in equivalent Nietzschean terms as "nihilism."[16]

The *Beiträge* as Heidegger's *Will to Power*

In such a deliberately focused context, we may interpret Heidegger's then-involvement as one of the editors for the planned edition of Nietzsche's works. Because Heidegger's prime official engagement with Nietzsche was adumbrated in a literally textual (editorial) fashion, Heidegger was also—consciously or unconsciously—inspired (as almost any reader of Nietzsche's texts can be seduced into seeking) to appropriate Nietzsche's style. But as already noted in the very first chapter above, to raise the question of Heidegger's encounter with Nietzsche's thinking, substance, and style, is also to raise the problematic issue of style in Heidegger's own work. It is striking that philosophical studies of Heidegger's work have almost invariably avoided the question of style in Heidegger's writings, as if somehow, language should clear the way to thought. And, if Heidegger's *Beiträge* is notoriously a stylistically troublesome text (of which the least one might say of it is that it challenges ordinary ways of reading Heidegger, even for experts in his work), it is also a text where Heidegger addresses the question of style as such.[17]

This would serve as the enduring occasion for Heidegger's calamitous engagement with nothing less than the limits of language itself. As we have already seen, Heidegger's own words for this encounter: "Nietzsche hat mich kaputtgemacht," are far from clear. How could Nietzsche be thought to have been, how could Heidegger have imagined that Nietzsche could have caused his downfall? Ruined in what way? Brought down in what sense?

The conditions under which Heidegger accepted Walter F. Otto's 1935 invitation to join the board of directors for the critical edition of Nietzsche's collected works were politically complicated.[18] And, so I argue, this same engagement offered Heidegger a direct experience with the forces that can control an author's works. By specifically and deliberately composing his own *Nachlaß* materials, Heidegger would attempt to avoid Nietzsche's fate at the hands of professional and politically driven editors (and this is not merely to be imagined something that only happens under particular political regimes). Heidegger intended to limit his vulnerability to the same editorial interference by keeping what he expected could count as his own *Nachlaß* under his own control.

Ironically enough Heidegger himself would not escape editorial manipulations—no more than Nietzsche was able to escape them.[19] For although hardly a conglomerate work like Nietzsche's *Will to Power*, selected out according to editorial fiat and arranged from disparate notebooks and disjointed sketches, it has in fact turned out that Heidegger's *Beiträge* is also a similarly (and similarly radical) *editorial production* as published on the basis of the notes preserved throughout Heidegger's life.

If the radicality of this textual "de-rangement" has gone almost completely without remark,[20] the compilation of the *Beiträge* into its currently published form would result in shifting nothing less substantial than an entire chapter. In its finished form, "Das Seyn" is set as the work's conclusion, following what had originally been the final chapter, "The Last God" [*Der Letzte Gott*], a concluding chapter title that also, shades of Nietzsche's *Will to Power-Nachlaß*, corresponds to its place in a list of chapter titles given in the first section, the "Preview." As Friedrich-Wilhelm von Hermann explains in his epilogue, this very radical editorial transposition responded to a note on a loose slip of paper indicating that the division in question was "not correctly ordered."[21]

How is one to read or to interpret such a slip of paper? Was it a direct message for a later editor? Was it an author's remark noting the necessity for a future rearrangement? As it stands, the editor of the published book assumes a positive answer to both these questions. But Heidegger's routine asides and comments on the arrangement of his texts (obviously directed against presumptions readers might have or employed to undercut the apparent ordering of the text as a whole) are far from unusual for the Heidegger who makes similar comments about argumentative array in *Being and Time* or *Introduction to Metaphysics* or *What Is Called Thinking?*—and this Heidegger's readers know all too well.[22] But the inserted note justified the editor's decision to transpose the chapter from its original placement to the very end of the manuscript,[23] "whereby," as the editor explains, "this now no longer makes up the *second* part but the *eighth* instead."[24]

I am far from suggesting that von Hermann's motives were other than well intentioned and indeed, for my part, I find them unimpeachable. At the very least, and like other scholars, translators, and editors, I find it significant that von Hermann's arrangement follows the temporal order of textual composition.[25] But I also note that von Hermann, precisely in his role as editor, was able to secure the determining force of his interpretation of Heidegger's "intentions" by rearranging the order, and hence the effective design, of the *Beiträge*.

I am suggesting that Heidegger planned the *Beiträge* as his *Nachlaß* in order to escape editorial manipulation. But this was, of course, not to be. If Heidegger himself had first ordered and then (and despite his own

comment on the typewritten table of contents), if Heideger also left the
order of his manuscript (and typescript) unaltered from 1939 (the date
of the manuscript gloss to which von Hermann refers) until his death in
1976, if Heidegger in the interim would transmit directions concerning
the dissemination of that same manuscript of 8 divisions and 935 sections to Pöggeler (among others), and, finally, if Heidegger himself was
to spend the last years of his life working on an exactly authorized, final
edition of his works, it would nonethess transpire that Heidegger could
not quite elude the fate of Nietzsche's *Nachlaß*.

Nietzsche as the Last Metaphysician:
On the Last Men and the "Last God"

In an important expression of the question concerning technology and
science, Heidegger declares Nietzsche the last philosopher of the West,
crowning the end of metaphysics with Nietzsche's philosophy of the
will to power as art or *techne*. Although Nietzsche scholars reject
Heidegger's interpretation of Nietzsche as willful and inaccurate, I argue
that, in drawing on the lecture courses on Nietzsche dating from the
same time, Heidegger's engagement with Nietzsche's thought in the
Beiträge sheds important light on Heidegger's singular and woefully
under-analyzed—or even ignored—preoccupation with the logic of science and modern technology.[26]

In the later *Zollikon Seminars*, referrring to the subtitled theme of
the *Beiträge*: *Vom Ereignis*, Heidegger will declare that "as long as one
understands being as presence . . . one cannot understand technology and
surely not the *event of appropriation* [*Ereignis*] at all."[27]

Nietzsche's thinking offers Heidegger the preliminary expression of
the task of thinking at the end of philosophy, corresponding to the
eventuality of *Ereignis* as such in the *Beiträge*.[28] It is noted here that for
Heidegger, the question of *Ereignis* is linked to the question of science
and of art or technology.[29] Thus in the Nietzsche lecture courses Heidegger
emphasizes that the question concerning technology can be illuminated
in terms of Nietzsche's own reflective self-assessment of his own first
work, *The Birth of Tragedy*. As Nietzsche expressed it in his "Attempt at
a Self-Criticism," "the task is to regard science through the lens [*Optik*]
of the artist, but art in that of life" (BT §ii). For Heidegger, what
Nietzsche says here is typically misunderstood: "Half a century," he wrote
in 1936/37, "has passed in Europe since these words were written. In
these decades, this point has been again and again misinterpreted and,
indeed, especially by those who sought to struggle against the increasing
rootlessness and devastations of science" (N1, 218).

Heidegger is here contending that it was not Nietzsche's claim that what we need is to add a bit more sparkle to science, making it more lively, adding a touch of *Lebenskunst* to the scientist's world, nor indeed was he suggesting that we attend to the aesthetic dimension in science. "The phrase demands knowledge of the event of nihilism which knowledge in Nietzsche's view at the same time embraces the will to overcome nihilism, indeed by means of original grounding and questioning" (N1, 220). This same project of overcoming invokes Hölderlin as well as Heidegger himself with his signature project of redoubled questioning: questioning questioning.

Heidegger notoriously reads Nietzsche's challenge to the notion of truth (as a "species of error") as insufficiently radical. Despite, indeed, as he claims, *in order to* grasp the "the degree of originality of the questioning encompassed by Nietzsche's philosophy as a whole," Heidegger repeats that it is critical to recognize that "the question of the essence of truth absent in Nietzsche's thought is an oversight unlike any other" even if it is also true that Nietzsche is hardly the only or the first thinker to fail to see it. For Heidegger it is just this "oversight" that "pervades the entire tradition of Western philosophy since Plato and Aristotle" (N1, 149). Like Nietzsche in this regard, philosophers from Descartes to Hegel "leave the essence of truth itself untouched" (Ibid.).

But Heidegger does not merely install Nietzsche in the pantheon of philosophy (in itself a not irrelevant achievement): "What Nietzsche for the very first time and indeed with reference to Platonism, *recognized* as *nihilism*, is in truth, and seen according to the grounding question that is alien to him, merely the foreground of the far deeper happening of the forgetting of being, which emerges more and more directly in the course of discovering the answer to the guiding question [*Leitfrage*]" (B §55, "Seinsverlassenheit"). With respect to this epochal connection with the eventuality of appropriation, or *Ereignis*, Heidegger emphasizes that the phrase "God is dead" as it is routinely associated with nihilism ultimately obscures the true compass of Nietzsche's claim. "The phrase 'God is dead' is no aesthetic principle but rather the formula for the foundational experience of the event in Western history" (N1, 156). Thus "Seynsverlassenheit," as the basic experience of the eventualizing of Western history is "perhaps the most concealed and denied through Christianity and its secular descendents" (B §55, "Seinsverlassenheit").

I am not here going to read *Seynsverlassenheit* as the abandonment of God beyond Being, of Being beyond God. The tendency to read the talk of abandonment in this way goes back to an even older seduction. We can be lulled, Heidegger reminds us, by Nietzsche's *style* into mistaking the philosophic significance of what Nietzsche says: "Misdirected by the form of Nietzsche's expressive style, one took his 'teaching' of 'nihilism' as an interesting cultural psychology" (B §72, Nihilism). Nietzsche's insight into the growing reign or sway of nihilism is not an insight into the simple oblivion or forgetfulness of Be-ing.[30] It is the same reason that Heidegger's reflections on Nietzsche's core nihilistic proclamation is expressed as a reflection upon the intersection of the essentially calculative conception of truth as it runs from Platonism to positivism.[31]

If reading Nietzsche in terms of nihilism has led to his identification as an atheistic philosopher, the tireless effort to reduce the core concern of Heidegger's thought to a secret theology, as postmodern theological voices have attempted to do, is a tactic to be discovered on both sides of the so-called analytic-continental divide.[32] On either side, such a re-duction works as a dismissal of Heidegger's claims regarding reality and truth (i.e., modern science and modern technology) in the modern world (nor do we fail to champion modernity even as we invoke the postmodern). In today's context, pronouncing Heidegger a "religious" writer—contra Heidegger's interdiction of this interpretive reduction—betrays the hege-mony of analytic philosophy as the legacy of the positivist turn in phi-losophy, i.e., modeled on the image of science and dedicated to defining science on the terms of science and analyzing it accordingly. From this perforce noncritical (Heidegger would say unrigorous) perspective, there is a recognized or received way to offer substantive philosophy concern-ing truth or reality (i.e, the sphere of modern science and technology), addressing matters of knowledge or truth in accord with the standard account of logical analyses and the valuation of the privilege of the methods of natural scientific theory and experimental process. Whether one takes oneself to be doing philosophy in a so-called continental modality, or not, to the degree to which one concedes this analytic assertion, the reduction of Heidegger's thought to religious or mystical thought inevitably excludes Heidegger's reflections on science/technol-ogy. Thus we should perhaps wonder why we absorb our philosophic energies with reading and rereading Heidegger's words on decision and last gods, reading him theistically but along the way, chiding him for his failure to affirm his theism and for inciting the moral danger that has so historically turned out to be a corollary of Judeo-Christian impiety? In the process, and this has long been the point of such a preoccupation, we save ourselves the trouble of having to concern ourselves with what Heidegger has to say with regard to modern science and technology or what he called calculative machination.

As much against Cassirer, the thinker of the philosophy of symbolic form and myth, as more typically contra Carnap,[33] the philosopher of the logical structure of the world who was to assume the mythic stance of Heidegger's nemesis with his analytically incendiary assessment of the logical content of Heidegger's work as reducing to the claim that the "nothing nothings," Nietzsche's insight into the growing reign or sway of nihilism is not an insight into the simple oblivion or forgetfulness of Be-ing. Rather than opening up a need for a return to theology or religious values, Nietzsche's reflections show Heidegger the singularizing event of nihilism as forging into the scientific domain of truth and the logistic domain of proof.

When Heidegger writes: "What furnishes the standard for the whole history of Western philosophy, including Nietzsche, is *being and thinking*" (B §110), he does not thereby convert Nietzsche to terms imagined foreign to him—a common practice still in use to expose Nietzsche's thinking on truth by revealing it to be enmeshed in its own assertions and claiming it in consequence as inherently self-contradictory. This is not only because Heidegger takes over this very critical figure of thought from Nietzsche himself (this structure Nietzsche names genealogy, the key terms of which, as Deleuze emphasized beyond Foucault, are terms of action and reaction in Nietzsche's dynamic economy), but because rather than an insight to be deployed against Nietzsche's attempt to revalue all values, Heidegger reads Nietzsche as a thinker and hence takes him (as Nietzsche is still all-too-rarely taken) seriously. This is the gravitational force Heidegger outlines as the dialectical force of interpretation or *Auseindersetzung*: "all countermovements and counterforces are to a large degree co-determined by *what* they are 'against,' even though in the form of reversing what they are against" (B §92). For Heidegger: "Countermovements become entangled in their own victory" (Ibid.).

In a similar fashion, Heidegger sets his own articulation of truth as ἀλήθεια in opposition to the rationalist confidence of the interchangeability of correctness with truth at every level, especially at the level of the absolute (as patently expressed in Hegel and as realistically, positivistically presupposed in the technological articulation of natural modern science) (cf. B §102 and §104). But Heidegger emphasizes the inadequacy of this absolutizing ambition of modern sciences and it is Nietzsche who shows us how little "such a controversy" as the rationalist project itself "can succeed" (B §102, "Thinking: The Leading Thread of the Leading-Question of Western Philosophy"). Thus Nietzsche is able to trace the transformative history of the idea (as Platonic or purely ideal, as positivistic or effectively pragmatic) of truth reduced to illusion. For Nietzsche, understanding truth as error meant in turn that truth decays into necessary illusion, into an unavoidable solidification, entangled in beings themselves [here we recognize Heidegger's challenge to the ontic metaphysics of Western technical rationality], comes to be determined as 'will to power' " (B §102). This degenerative course is the point of Nietzsche's "History of an Illusion" in *Twilight of the Idols*, the same six-point historical outline and pattern that Heidegger appropriates again and again in the *Beiträge* (which is not to say that he is able to limit himself to six points, much less to a single page).

For Heidegger, Nietzsche represents both the culmination of and at the same time the overcoming of Western metaphysics. For Heidegger, "Western metaphysics at its end is at its furthest distance from the question of the truth of *Seyn*, as well as closest to this truth—in that this metaphysics prepares the crossing to this truth as end" (Ibid.). Heidegger's challenge to Western techno-scientitic rationality is manifest in this declaration of the closure and turning point of metaphysics. But he expressed his claim by way of a Nietzschean troping: "Truth as correctness is not capable of recognizing and that means grounding its own full scope. It aids itself by attaining to the unconditional, ordering everything so that it is not itself (so it appears) in need of a foundation" (Ibid.).

Heidegger's *Beiträge* as Political Critique

In a stark contrast with the sociopolitical skepticism of the Frankfurt School, Heidegger makes the calculated claim—a claim that would have been subversive and exactly dangerous to its author, had the *Beiträge* been a public work, as it quite decisively was not[34]—that our own world is anything but a disenchanted domain. We live in a perfectly if illusorily and today literally *virtually* enchanted world of technological power and ever-braver new and oh-so American possibilities for what we imagine the future to be. Obsessed, our "bewitchment through technology and its constantly self-surpassing progress is merely *one* sign of this enchantment consequently compelling everything into calculability, utility, productivity, convenience, and regulation. Even 'taste' has now become an object of this regulation and everything depends on 'high-end' quality." (B §59, "The Age of Complete Questionlessness and Enchantment"). But so far from arguing the perspective of nostalgia, Heidegger at the time means to argue that the postmodern/modern, technical/new age world is enchanted on the terms of and by means of "the unlimited dominion of *Machenschaft*."

Machenschaft, as Heidegger articulates it, here refers to the organized shouting of party gatherings. In distinction to the thoughtful ideal of what he calls "reticence" [*Verlegenheit*] or the more obscure notion of "awe" [*Scheue*], one had installed in then-contemporary life "exaggeration and shouting down [*Überschreiung*] and the blind and empty screaming in which one screams at oneself and deceives oneself about the hollowing out of beings" (B §66, "Machination and Lived-Experience"). Thus, Heidegger understands the immediacy of radio broadcasts[35] as Rudolf Arnheim also analyzes radio broadcasts on the basis of the same inter-wartime experience in Germany. In the same way, one may invoke the yet more immediate "ventriloquism"[36] of the loudspeakers used to "energize" party rallies but also working in the fashion of the "streaming media" of today's wired and wireless connections. Heidegger's analysis remains germane to every kind of media, not just the journalism that Heidegger, like Nietzsche for his own part, characterizes dismissively as ersatz knowledge responding to yet more ersatz concerns, but also personal communications of all kinds and their respective and relevantly objective devices: email, beeper, and cell phone technologies. Both the loudspeaker-driven, organized mass politics of National Socialism and the far more subtle public omnipresence of today's cell phones know nothing like an inherent or fundamental limit: just as inherently they lack both "reticence" and any kind of respect or "awe." This lack of restraint unifies the ideal of "Erlebnis"—what we speak of today as participatory or performatively real (or even as virtual, on-line) life, it may also explain the growing appeal of reality TV shows—and machination.

This, as Heidegger reads the anticipatory character of intentional conception/praxis, is more than the fact that what he calls the coincidence of machination and lived experience work to deprive living or real or genuine power of the possibility of any place or postition in the postmodern world. "The projection of re-presentation in the sense of a reaching-ahead-planning-and-arranging *grasping* of everything, even before it is comprehended as particular and singular, such a re-presentation finds no limits in the given and wants to find no limit" (B §70, "The Gigantic.") In this way, echoing Max Weber on modernity and possibility, Heidegger emphasizes that in its essence modern technical praxis must be interpreted otherwise than Aristotelian *techne*: "there is, in principle, no 'impossible'; one 'hates' this word" (Ibid.). The same impatience with limit (and finitude) continues as the capitalist watchword of our own technological "optimism" and information-age technical ambition, which Ivan Illich names "hubris," but here, some sixty-five years ago, Heidegger attributes to the ruling utiliarian logic of fascism: "Everything is humanly possible, if only everything is taken into account in advance, in every regard, and along with the relevant conditions" (Ibid).

Regarded from the terms of and within the scheme of modern techno-science, everything may be taken as given or as known in advance: there is "nothing that is question-worthy" (B §51, "Der Anklang"). Presented as the era of the world spectacle, the scientific viewpoint or technological vision of modern times makes the very immediacy of mediate experience possible in the first place. Eliminating in a perfectly dramatic way everything questionable by transforming what is worth questioning into merely technical problems, the question-worthy becomes no more than so many potential questions to be resolved, no more than a solution waiting to be found. The optimistic result is experientially rendered— "Erlebnis"—now accessible in the form of scientifically knowable and potentially universally available or articulable results. Such results have a single interpretation on the single road toward the increase of progress and prosperity, that anyone can acquire, available to everyone for excitement, entertainment, distraction, et cetera.

Writing on the title subject of "needfulness," Heidegger ponders the question of the late modern ethos of leisure or comfort as Nietzsche had earlier raised it—questioning the contemporary value placed upon freedom from need as an unqualified "good." In this, the echo of Nietzsche's reflections in *Beyond Good and Evil,* along with the third section of *On the Genealogy of Morals,* recalls what Nietzsche named Socratic (Alexandrian) optimism in *The Birth of Tragedy* and recalled again (in the name of Socrates and Plato, and indeed the entire tradition of philosophy) in *Twilight of the Idols* (§53 and §55). More than a focus upon leisure and cultural ease, and more than the capitalist spectacle of media distraction or advertising at every turn, Heidegger finds the abandonment of Being. This dereliction leads beyond "the derangement of the West" to what Heidegger names "the flight of the gods . . ." (B §56, "The Lingering of the Abandonment of Being in the Concealed Manner of Forgottenness of Being"; cf. §13).

This abandonment now expressed in the limitless ambition of the West (and which we accordingly call globalism today) is reflected in terms of the gigantic ideal of totalization, this is what Heidegger would emphasize in the lectures that later became essays condensing in and around his *The Question Concerning Technology*—and what is apparent even in this early text is nothing but our confidence. This corresponds to what the Heidegger of the *Beiträge* calls "Questionlessness" in an unquestioning time. For then, as now, we remain unquestioningly oriented toward both the machinations of our time and our technology, ends and means. This confidence has endured numerous transformations (and any number of refutations), nevertheless—and this is what it means to fail to question—we continue to be sure that we very nearly have our technology under control. If anything can save us, it will not be anything so paltry as a "god,"[37] but our technology. And if technology threatens to cause problems, this too can be guarded against (like the antivirus software developed to protect our cyber-antennae, that is, our internet connections, against the "trojan" or spy software we unknowingly but automatically download whenever we surf the internet). Technological as we are (all the way down), we want to manage the costs and "sustain" the benefits of the power at our disposal—understood ecologically as the "environment," understood as "nature," and ultimately understood as the means of self-expression or the development of the world and ourselves in our own image.[38]

Heidegger, Technology, and the Devastation of Style: Nietzsche's Style and Heidegger's Undoing

What I have been calling Heidegger's *Will to Power* is Heidegger's appropriation not only of the idea of Nietzsche's *Nachlaß* (the very idea), remaking the *Nachlaß* as Heidegger reconceived this project as his own legacy in the exact language of a text set by his "final hand" [*letzter Hand*], but also in the wake of the seductive allure of a thinker who could summon the kind of readership Nietzsche commanded and do the kinds of things with words that Nietzsche could achieve by his writing style.

Heidegger succeeded, at least until his death, with his first ambition: he guarded the finished work that would be his *Will to Power*, precisely as a legacy for his heirs. He would be destroyed, in his own expression of it [*kaputtgemacht*], by the effort to engage and to follow Nietzsche's style and it is in this language-stylized sense that I have been arguing that we should take his confession that Nietzsche had destroyed him. This is Nietzsche's stylized direction of his texts to certain readers (always an achievement of some doing in a published—and therefore, as Nietzsche would remark, a public and consequently all-too-common [cf. BGE §30]—work). But Nietzsche intended his stylistic achievement esoterically, that means, as any Straussian or any Platonist knows, Nietzsche intended to *exclude* readers, exoterically by drawing them in and giving them something to take away from the text in place of a meaning, and to protect that meaning.

For Heidegger, Nietzsche's esoteric distinction concerns his own very esoteric conception of the nature of questioning as the still-awkward elusiveness of his ultimate call "Für die Wenigen—Für die Seltenen" and this stylistic restraint that continues in Heidegger's own (and unremittingly problematic) expression of silence. "The word breaks for us . . . originarily," Heidegger writes, "the word fails to come even to word" (B §13, "Reticence and Concern"). Reflecting on "Keeping Silence and Questioning," he will claim that in seeking, both questioning *and* restrained silence maintain an intimate even essential relationship, as Heidegger explains, "Seeking as questioning and still and yet as keeping silent."

Where Heidegger sets questioning in its guiding modality, that is authentic or genuine questioning (as opposed to the kind of questioning that, as Heidegger emphasizes by contrast in the *Beiträge*, corresponds to "curiosity" and which, we can add, likewise corresponds to investigative research), Heidegger further details the nature of questioning in the Nietzsche lectures.[39] The style of questioning to be opposed is scientific inquiry: answer-bound or problem-directed inquiry. For Heidegger, such inquiry stops short of genuine questioning. And contra received logic,[40] Heidegger proposes the radicality of thinking itself.

Heidegger criticizes modern science in its totalizing logic, which is also to say its technological essence. Read through the express invocation of Nietzsche's history of nihilism and in tacit correspondence with both Cassirer and Carnap, Heidegger's *Beiträge* reflects the concentrated specificity of his engagement with what was then called positivism but which continues today as the veritably working efficacy of modern science and technology as *Machenschaft*, that is: the *dealings* of technology. Heidegger sets authentic or genuine questioning in opposition to the kind of questioning that corresponds to "curiosity" and investigative research. For Heidegger, answer-bound or problem-directed inquiry stops short of genuine questioning. Contra received logic, or better said, the received convictions concerning logic, what Heidegger proposes is the radical poverty of reflective thinking, what Richardson calls the indigence of *thought*. The minimal achievement that is the modesty of open reflection, or reticent questioning is perhaps a great deal more than we are used to regarding as thinking, if only because we might thereby find a way out of calculative thought: "the poverty of reflection is the promise of a wealth whose treasures glow in the resplendence of that uselessness which can never be included in any reckoning."[41]

Whether it is modest or not, this proposal still strikes us as wrong-headed, and this is because it is critical. In Nietzsche's spirit, Heidegger will later go on to affirm the logic of scientific totalization in its subversion of any alternative: "Science *is* the new religion."[42] To take up a position against science, to advert to the limits of logic and language, or to clarify the respective roles of philosophy and science, seems anti-scientific and even science-incompetent.[43] And the charge of incompetence has been raised against Heidegger, indeed, even from the start and in spite of being inaccurate in fact. Heidegger's problem was not that he didn't know logic nor was it that he did not know science nor indeed that the science he knew was insufficiently up to date.

Only as ancilla to theology, and that for impeccably metaphysical reasons, philosophy for Heidegger was the very origin of the sciences: "in the scientific attitude of the sciences, the document of their birth from philosophy still speaks."[44] And almost thirty years before in his Nietzsche lectures, Heidegger emphasizes that "science is only scientific, that is to say partaking of genuine knowledge . . . to the extent that it is philosophical."[45] Thus Heidegger's argument in *Being and Time* has called upon us to make similar distinctions: "Laying the foundations of science" is what Heidegger names "a productive logic"—not "limping after" but much rather "leaping ahead" of science, thus disclosing the constitution of its subject matter or its concern and making these structures "available to the positive sciences as transparent assignments for their inquiry."[46]

In the spirit of the genuine knowing Heidegger always believed to correspond to scientific thought as such, the ascription of antagonism to science mistakes the critical point he had learnt so early in his own life from Aristotle's specification of what we may name "methodological" *phronesis*. Much of Heidegger's enthusiasm for Nietzsche's claim concerning the victory of scientific method over science itself derives from just this critical distinction—and indeed the philosophical importance of *the* qualifying philosophical ability to *make* distinctions. As Heidegger cites Aristotle's account of such judgment in "The End of Philosophy and the Task of Thinking" as well as throughout the *Zollikon Seminars* (following a lifetime of such references): "For not to know of what things we may demand proof, and of what one may not, argues simply a want of education" (Meta. 1006a, cf. N. Eth. 1094b, etc.). In Heidegger's review of the propositions on science offered in the *Beiträge*, he also adverts to the same charge of being "anti-science."[47] Heidegger contends that his summary "characterization of 'science' doesn't correspond to a hostility to science because a hostility of the kind is altogether impossible" (B §76, "Propositions on 'Science,' " §21). The disposition between philosophy and science, as the position of reflection and the object of such reflection excludes the very idea of "hostility" as affect. As Heidegger explains: "Philosophy is neither for nor against science" (Ibid.).[48]

Heidegger's emphasis on the modern (and technological) scientific worldview takes us to what is arguably Heidegger's most reviled textual locus. For the *Beiträge* repeats what Heidegger declares in his better-known passage in *An Introduction to Metaphysics*. Regarded in terms of the calculative, technological-rational ideal of modernity, regarded as a triumphalist, or "logical" ideal, Heidegger claims that both "America" and "Russia" are effectively identical or "the same." In context (or, at least, in his own mind), Heidegger's comment becomes a reproof: critiquing the then-current regime as representing the same dynamic politicizing, technologizing order and ordering momentum as other (and otherwise different) imperial cultures. In consequence, the impetus

Heidegger calls *Machenschaft* would be as common to "Bolshevik" Russia as to "Capitalist" America, and such technological machination would also be, and this indeed was Heidegger's point here, common to "National Socialist" Germany as well.[49] So, Heidegger argues, "the 'folk' [i.e., National Socialist or "German"] 'organization' 'of' science moves on the same track as the 'American.'" (B §76, "Propositions on 'Science,'" §10) We can argue—if it remains a touchy political claim—that this very same globalizing ideal, that is, technological machination as such, continues unabated in the monotonic, more totalized than monopolistic capitalist-cum-consumerist ethos of our own day.

This totalizing parallel however may be seen to lend a different cast to the significance of the so-called inner truth and greatness of National Socialism, precisely in the context of his parenthetical explication of it, "namely with the movement of planetary determined technology and modern humanity."[50] It now corresponds to Heidegger's assertion that the modern or techno-rationalist worldview of Nazism would in essence be the same as (or *not other than* or not *importantly different* from) American or Russian alternatives. We note that Herbert Marcuse makes a similar argument with regard to the bifurcation of reason into critical and objective or scientific (and non-critical) reason.[51] Marcuse's point is that modern technology tends to eliminate the critical in favor of an authoritarian, that is, absolute, that is, objective ideal of reason. In Heidegger's case, and thus different from the insights of his more politically (and dialectically) refined student, it seems clear that precisely Heidegger's least redeeming political values accord with his conviction here in opposition to the essence of modern science. For it is his skepticism regarding the redemptive potential of democracy that puts him on the other side of National Socialism *and* its far-from unique political enthusiasm for science.[52] Heidegger's claim is chillingly prescient to the point of globalization as such. The newest market economies include Russia *and* America, they will eventually include, one can be certain of this when the dust of political conflict has settled, Afghanistan *and* Iraq, all of Korea, Pakistan, et cetera, all economies will be brought under the one umbrella of world commerce, constituting the totalized meaning of the idea of the global per se, now to be understood both in a calculatively economic as well as in a productively rationalist sense (qua the global market and qua that non-locus we call the internet). If the real market economy of the globalized world continues to be beset by old-fashioned political issues, by borders and sociocultural values (so-called)—Jihad (or "olive tree values") versus McWorld (or "Lexus economies")[53]—we now know this global future better than Heidegger (however prescient he was) could possibly have imagined it to be: we know what a totalized, globalized world would look like in praxical theory, that is, we know it "virtually."

In the wake of the attack on the United States on the 11th of September, 2001, perhaps still more in light of the subsequent attacks on Afghanistan and now more brutally and protractedly in our U.S. occupation of Iraq, what had formerly been a debate concerning the autonomy of technology of interest only to specialists has become all-too exact an insight. This is Heidegger's inquiry into the totalizing mechanization of democratically user-specific/user-appropriated technology and the impossible but all-too-real demonstration of the non-masterability of technology even when (perhaps just when) *appropriated* by users only underscores his original insight.

Heidegger warns us that we are most in thrall to technology not when it astonishes us but exactly when we take it for granted, when we assume that we are control, that is, when it is ubiquitous enough that we presume upon its anthropological and instrumental character, convinced that "[e]verything depends upon getting technology as an intrument in hand in the appropriate way. One will, as it is said, get technology spiritually in hand."[54] This is the point of Heidegger's critique of the enchantment of disenchantment in the *Beiträge*. If critics of technology like Marcuse, or like Langdon Winner could raise concerns about the potential for the loss of certain freedoms, formerly presumed inalienable, at least for Americans in their own land, such worries are exactly not empty: they constitute the inescapable ground rules required for American national security.

The rationalist ideal Heidegger named logic, well beyond the dominion of the imaginary sublime now consummate as the virtual image of modern technology, the modern scientific worldview that rages today ever more unencumbered by any "possible"[55] or (imaginable) alternative, is the rule that remains. Neither pluralism nor a "return" to traditional societies can alter the monotonic play of technique. Neither the modern world nor pre-modern societies (as, using an outdated ideology, one insists on regarding fundamentalist Islamic societies) may be thought as other than technological. There is only modernity, liberal or not, as we choose to claim it, and it is what Heidegger in this text names *Machenschaft*.

From this perspective, as Pöggeler also emphasizes, all reflections following in the wake of metaphysics become inescapably "transitional."[56] Modelled on Nietzsche's seemingly fragmentary form of the aphorism and the truncated outline, "contributions" are all that remain of Heidegger's legacy—as his *Will to Power*. This is also because, in the keenest transition from Heidegger I to Heidegger II, paraphrasing Hölderlin's *The Death of Empedocles* and in equally patent reference to

Nietzsche, Heidegger writes, referring as much to philosophy as to his own first book: "The time for 'systems' is over . . ." (B §1, "*Contributions*: Questioning upon a Track . . .").[57] If Hölderlin's Empedocles, resisting popular acclamation as king, declares the time of lordship past, the allusion for Hölderlin himself referred to the French Revolution.[58]

The problems of today's modern technology are not merely the problems of nations and dictators, of politicizing and of war. Today, our problems are in the food we eat, the air we breathe, and very soon our problems will take on the aspect of our very own human flesh: technology is hell-bent on gaining a human face in the new millennium. This is not a kinder, softer technology—this is the technology that sells rice and grains to farmers to grow the kind of rice and grains that offer special features against disease, bugs, weeds (i.e., resistance to special herbicides), but (very conveniently for Monsanto) cannot grow again. Like the activation programs for a certain kind of operating software, these new seeds are one-way seeds, and if you want to continue as a farmer, you'll need to go back to the manufacturer for the new and improved version. The techniques are simple ones, very like the kind of grafting (on a cellular level) farmers and gardeners have always done.

Reworking the cellular mechanisms of genetically altered but still all-too-natural bacteria as readymade technologies (we are far from having invented artificial life with all our genetic modifications of life processes), our mechanisms only imagine operators like nucleotide transcriptions, the uptake of modified genes as therapies or as remodeling transformations. Already patented, already at work are the modified one-celled organisms, readymade for the work at hand precisely because the mechanism needed (infection/ingestion) is already extant even if quite beyond the limitations of what our technologies can currently make. Using modified bacteria and viruses as vectors, as today's researchers do, the technized animal is itself reconceived as the viral vector for profitable mutations, the bacterial plasmid likewise, and Monsanto already imagines the day when it can rule the world.

If Heidegger describes the transition from the human to the technized animal, the image he employs articulates an organic technicity in advance of any available in his own era. Not a representation of Shelley's Frankenstein, a human made in the image not of god, but man, of cobbled together body parts, not even the robot fantasy that still charms us in images of illusory androids, illusions that have given way to the similarly imaginary cyborg of fantasy and indistinct interfaces between virtual and real, today, in the new language of genes, this means that we human beings, not just rice and soybeans and corn will find *our own selves* named in our essence.[59]

What is betrayed in today's digitalized ideal is no longer the warning *threat* that humanity itself, not just the "natural" world of "natural resources," may come to be taken in the image of Heidegger's standing reserve. The past fifty years has made this danger trivially real. In theory, the entire population of Iceland; in practice, let us name only the fertility clinics as veritable banks of human beings, potential and actual. So many ova, so many vials of sperm, so many embryos, not to mention stem cells and cloned cell-lines, the basis of genetic research and cultivated in some cases now already for more than fifty years. All of this is *already* stock on hand and nothing at all compared with the virtual promise of the same technology. If the genome project has proven to be as anticlimactic as it has, the genetic code, the sheer molecular idea of a registered and accessible essence of humanity allures us as a signifier we very complicitly hope to take for granted in place of the lived complexities of human life.

Conclusion, In a Double Sense

I began by reviewing Heidegger's *Beiträge* as his self-composed *Will to Power*, presented under the rubric of academic vanity and publishing markets. I spoke of real politics—in the domain of the world historical as well as the everyday. Beyond the fate of a book left to the kindness of one's editors, beyond the vulnerability of any author's intentions, no matter how venal or genial (a fate linked to the public destiny of an author's words no matter how the author imagines he has protected them), what is most important are the questions I have just concluded: this is the substance of Nietzsche's and Heidegger's philosophical reflections on will and power. Teaching the omnipresence of the will to power in the world of the living and the dead, in organic and inorganic life, but especially common to both the machinations of the mighty and the calculations of the oppressed, Nietzsche's philosophical legacy to us points to the astonishing capacity of the weak, the success of slavish morality, in his all-too-accurate but uncannily counterintuitive reading of the biblical teaching that tells us in different tones, in both Old and New Testaments, that the chosen destiny of the weak—that is, to be very clear as I conclude, the destiny of reactive and slavish will to power—will be to inherit the earth. And that means to dispossess every other living being, animal and plant, in the sea and in the air and on the land. This is not a future conclusion I paint in order to underline the seriousness of our plight. It is already done, to more of a degree and in more ways than can be imagined—where the greatest of our problems is that we hide the works we do from common perception and suppose thereby that nothing is that bad, after all. For we remain, despite all our enlightenment, the children of superstition and make-believe, as Nietzsche always lamented, we believe that where nothing is seen (or heard, or felt), there is nothing. Thus the chemicals in our food and in our water don't really wind up in *our* body fat, even if they can be found detected and measured in the fat reserves of fish and wild animals, we are different (we are higher, whispered Nietzsche's birds). There are no toxins, no need for "de-toxification," we are assured. The meat slaughtered in abysmal cruelty leaves no traces of the hormones of terror unto death for us to absorb, let alone the growth hormones, steroids and plentiful antibiotics that bring our food animals in record time from the desolate sorrow of birth through their wretchedly impoverished lives to their literally agonizing deaths (we hack and bleed our animals to death: slaughter is no word for what we do), nor do we absorb the same steroid cocktail, with a chaser of antibiotics, in our milk. For the human body is unique in the animal world, any medical doctor or clinical nutrionist will tell you so. We take the "nutrition" and our miraculous bodies brilliantly filter out all the rest. Eat properly and exercise, and get regular checkups.

Or, then again, maybe it is time to think about what we do. Not what we eat and what world we live in but what we do to that world and to the beings we raise in order to live off their lives, from their suffering, consuming and shod by and dressed in the products of the same. For we have inherited the earth, literally have dominion over it, over all the animals that crawl, fly, swim. And be it by hunting, poisoning, neutering, genetic modification, or ordinary sacrifice (all the many unsung, extinct equivalents of the snail darter, like the dodo, which we named for its stunning vulnerability to human rapacity, like the last Galapagos tortoise of its kind), we have proven ourselves East and West, North and South to be consummate masters at emptying the world of as many species as we can, and at break-neck speed.

The ecologists have been telling us that such a process cannot be sustained. The thing that upsets us is neither the enormity of our temerity nor the efficiency of our destruction of species or land or water or our veritable alteration of the air. What upsets us, as it would upset a small child, is the thought that the things we do might not be doable for all time. That it cannot be sustained is what galls us, not what we do. That is the challenge to be solved by science and technology. Other questions of right and prerogative remain the province of politicians and social and cultural analysts.

The philosopher must ask the question of real justice in all its complexity. For all the philosopher's questions as Kant summarized them: what can I know? what must I do? what can I hope for? are interwoven questions. When we imagine that we can separate them, finding that

Nietzsche, for example, has much to say on morality or culture but little or nothing to say about knowledge or truth, thus calling him to account for the moral but not the cosmological content of a theory like the eternal return, we fail thereby to understand even his moral theory. The same holds for Heidegger. If we leave the poets out of such remonstrations, it is because the poet has already found his own way to include himself in the scope of philosophy (as Pindar did) by raising the question of tragedy, tying it to the most philosophical question of all, transfigured as the poet's praise and exultation even in mourning, tragic joy as Hölderlin saw it: "das freudigste freudig zu sagen."

Notes

Preface, pages vii–xii

1. Friedrich Hölderlin, *Sämtliche Werke* (Stuttgart: Kohlhammer, 1957), Vol. 3, p. 89. In addition to Dieter Henrich, see, for current philosophical readings of Hölderlin, the books by Veronique Foti, Annette Hornbacher, Dennis Schmidt, and Peter Trawny.

2. *. . . Lesend, aber gleichsam wie/ In einer Schrift, die Unendlichkeit nachahmen und den Reichtum/ Menschen. Ist der einfältige Himmel/ Denn reich? Wie Blüthen sind ja/ Silberne Wolken. Es regnet aber von daher/ Der Thau und das Feuchte. Wenn aber/ Das Blau ist ausgelöschet, das Einfältige scheint/ das Matte, das dem Marmelstein gleichet, wie Erz,/ Anzeige des Reichtums.* Hölderlin, "Was ist der Menschen Leben . . ." StA vol. 2, p. 209.

3. *An euch den neuen Lebenstag erkenne.*

4. *Du musst es wissen, dir gehör ich nicht/ Und du nicht mir, und deine Pfade sind/ Die meinen nicht; mir blüht es anderswo.*

5. *Sieh auf und wags! Was Eines ist, zerbricht,/ Die Liebe stirbt in ihrer Knospe nicht/ Und überall in freier Freude theilt/ des Lebens luftger Baum sich auseinander.*

6. *Ich bin nicht, der ich bin, Pausanias,/ Und meines Bleibens ist auf Jahre nicht,/ Ein Schimmer nur, der bald vorüber muß,/ Im Saitenspiel ein Ton —*

7. *Geh! Fürchte nichts! Es kehret alles wieder./ Und was geschehen soll, ist schon vollendet.*

8. *laß mich izt, wenn dort der Tag/ Hinunter ist, so siehest du mich wieder.*

Chapter One, p. 3

1. This is the context in which I read Gadamer's invocation of Heidegger's expressed regret at the end of his life, "Nietzsche ruined me!" [*Nietzsche hat mich kaputtgemacht!*] Although I have also heard this from Gadamer himself—as have many others—Gadamer did not hear this from Heidegger himself but from his son, as he tells us in a published transcription from 1996 on the occasion of a conference on the twentieth anniversary of Heidegger's death. In the opening remarks of a discussion on Heidegger and Nietzsche (Gadamer's own lecture was on Heidegger and Hegel), Gadamer reflected on the meaning of the formula of "the end of the history of metaphysics" in order to clarify the

sense of transition. What is key, Gadamer emphasized, is Heidegger's conception of the *Übergang* (both in philosophy and a "going beyond" in Nietzsche's thinking): "I believe, however, that Heidegger was correct in this: it was not with a conscious 'I've made it' that Nietzsche effected the crossover. And there is a quote I now repeatedly invoke, ever since I first heard it from Heidegger's son, that in the last months of his life, Heidegger repeated constantly, 'Nietzsche ruined me.' One could hear that on a regular basis from him in conversation, acknowledging his own failure. What Nietzsche had tried to do, he likewise failed to achieve." Gadamer, "Heidegger und Nietzsche. Zu Nietzsche hat mich kaputtgemacht." *Aletheia* 9/10 (1996): 19.

   2. Reading Nietzsche philosophically is still more or less practiced under the sign of qualified disaffection, from the neo-Kantian Hans Vaihinger *(Nietzsche als Philosoph)* to Arthur Danto to today's analytic recuperation of Nietzsche. See here Martin Heidegger, *What Is Called Thinking*, trans. J. Glenn Gray (New York: Harper & Row, 1968), p. 41. Hereafter cited as WT, followed by page number in the text.

   3. See for a discussion, Friedrich Wilhelm von Hermann, "Heidegger und Nietzsche: Der andere Anfang," *Aletheia* 9/10 (1996): 20–21. For a contemporary overview of the very idea of the "other beginning" in Nietzsche and Heidegger, see Harald Seubert, *Zwischem erstem und anderen Anfang: Heideggers Auseinandersetzung mit Nietzsche und die Sache seines Denkens* (Köln: Böhlau, 2000).

   4. Heidegger, "Logos (Heraclitus, Fragment 50)" in Heidegger, *Early Greek Thinking*, trans. David Farrell Krell and Frank A. Capuzzi (San Francisco: Harper & Row, 1975), p. 78.

   5. Heidegger, *Nietzsche: Volume I: The Will to Power as Art*, trans. David Farrell Krell (San Francisco: Harper & Row, 1979), p. 4. Hereafter cited as N1, followed by page number in the text.

   6. Hannah Arendt uses the same convention in her *Homo laborans*. See Arendt, *The Human Condition: A Study of the Central Dilemma Facing Modern Man* (Chicago: University of Chicago Press, 1998).

   7. Heidegger, *Einführung in die Metaphysik* (Tübingen: Niemeyer, 1953), p. 117. The English language translation, *An Introduction to Metaphysics*, trans. Ralph C. Manheim (New Haven: Yale University Press, 1976 [1959]) does not include Heidegger's mention of thinkers in this locus, but Heidegger's roster of what makes the *polis* as such political (and the very "site of history") includes "the gods, the temples, the priests, the festivals, the games, the poets, the thinkers, the ruler, the council of elders, the assembly of the people, the army, and the fleet," (152). This entire array, an array of complexity Nietzsche emphasizes in his reflection on the origins of the tragic work of art not only in *The Birth of Tragedy* but also in "Schopenhauer as Educator," as Heidegger invokes this to explore what he calls the role of the preservers in the work of art, is a notion that also has a precedent in the second of Nietzsche's *Untimely Meditations*.

   8. Heidegger, *What Is Philosophy?*, bilingual edition, trans. Jean T. Wilde and William Kluback (New Haven: College and University Press, 1958), p. 47. Heidegger's text is of a lecture first presented in August, 1955 at Cerisy-la-Salle and subsequently published in Tübingen in 1956. Heidegger importantly draws

the conclusion that the fact that Heraclitus came to coin this term for a man who loved wisdom presupposes "that for Heraclitus *philosophia* did not yet exist" (Ibid.).

9. Ibid.

10. Ibid.

11. Ibid., p. 49.

12. This is the title of aphorism §223 in Nietzsche's *The Gay Science.* One may well bracket the question of the identity of the old "confessor" [*Beichtvater*] "who became deaf" but I take this to be a reference to Friedrich Ritschl for multiple reasons, including Nietzsche's disappointment in Ritschl's non-response to his first book but also where Ritschl's profound physical decline was a painfully tragic characteristic of Ritschl's later life. Without such complex references the reference to sensual compensation can be misunderstood and limited to Nietzsche's Helmholtzian enthusiasms. This would be a mistake (of the kind that can be characteristic for source criticism) because a preoccupation with the senses, from light and sound and the metaphors associated with the same to the idea of hearing as a kind of seeing, absorbed Nietzsche from his earliest student days.

13. Heidegger, *What Is Philosophy?*, p. 51.

14. Heidegger, N1, p. 194, cf. p. 167.

15. »*Warum huldigest du, heiliger Sokrates,/ »Diesem Jünglinge stets? Kennest du Größeres nicht? / »Warum siehet mit Liebe, / »Wie auf Götter, dein Aug' auf ihn? // Wer das Tiefste gedacht, liebt das Lebendigste, / Hohe Jugend versteht, wer in die Welt geblikt, / Und es neigen die Weisen / Oft am Ende zu Schönem sich.* Friedrich Hölderlin, "Sokrates und Alkibiades."

16. WT, 20–21. Cf., for the German here, Heidegger, *Was heißt Denken?* (Tübingen: Niemeyer, 1984), p. 9.

17. Heidegger, "Logos (Heraclitus, Fragment 50)," p. 78.

18. George Steiner, *Lessons of the Masters* (Cambridge: Harvard University Press, 2003).

19. But more skeptical scholars may wish to consider, for a start, Heidegger's discussion of the erotic dimensionality of philosophy in *What Is Philosophy?* as well as his lecture courses on Nietzsche and so on.

20. Giorgio Agamben, *Potentialities: Collected Essays in Philosophy*, trans. David Heller-Roazen (Stanford: Stanford University Press, 1999), p. 185. Agamben cites Karl Jaspers, *Notizen zu Martin Heidegger* (Munich: Piper, 1978), p. 34.

21. Steiner does not refer to Irigaray in *Lessons of the Masters*, although he might well have done so. See Luce Irigaray, *An Ethics of Sexual Difference*, trans. Carolyn Burke and Gillian C. Gill (Ithaca: Cornell University Press, 1993).

22. "Ah this lack of love in these philosophers, who always only think on the chosen ones and do not have so much faith in their wisdom. Wisdom must shine like the sun, on everyone: and a pale ray has to be able to penetrate even into the lowest soul" (KSA 7, 720–721; cf. Nietzsche's discussion of the sun in GS §337). I return to the question of Nietzsche and love in chapter 9.

23. Manifestly, this is not universally or necessarily so but it is just as manifestly true that, to date, such reflections issue from men, from Denis de Rougemont to Hermann Schmitz or Niklas Lühmann or Roger Scruton, et cetera.

24. René Descartes, *Discourse on Method*, Part I.

25. Thus Heidegger writes in "The Anaximander Fragment" that "the collapse of thinking into the sciences and into faith is the baneful destiny of Being." In Heidegger, *Early Greek Thinking*, p. 40. Heidegger reflects further: "This tone is more than familiar to us all in the standard appraisals of the present time. A generation ago, it was 'The Decline of the West.' Today we speak of the 'loss of the center.' People everywhere track and record the decay, the destruction, the imminent annihilation of the world," (p. 29). Indeed, we still have the same concerns, with the journalistic shift to the more universal phenomenon of the "environment." Here it is important to note, if only to distinguish Heidegger's concerns from those of today's ecological/environmental philosophy, that Heidegger's point here distinguishes his discussion from common usage (later in the text, Heidegger specifically denigrates this recourse to Spengler, cf. p. 38). Thus Heidegger sets up a discussion of Nietzsche and prepares the way for his effort to explore what belongs to thinking as such.

26. See Frederick Love, *Young Nietzsche and the Wagnerian Experience* (Chapel Hill: The University of North Carolina Press, 1963). See too Roger Hollinrake, *Nietzsche, Wagner, and the Philosophy of Pessimism* (London: George Allen & Unwin, 1982), as well as Curt Paul Janz, *Friedrich Nietzsche: Biographie* (Frankfurt am Main: Zwei Tausend Eins, 1999), and more recently, if still more Wagnerian, Georges Liébert's *Nietzsche and Music*, trans. David Pelletier (Chicago: University of Chicago Press, 2003). For his own part, Nietzsche was preternaturally conscious of the range of his own talents and the complex interworking of these gifts in terms of their breadth: KSA 8, p. 287, if he also opposed the nineteenth-century culture of "genius."

27. Although for the sake of an understanding of Nietzsche's musical practice as player, Curt Paul Janz's biography is indispensable, it is also hard to exceed Ernst Bertram's rich *Nietzsche: Versuch einer Mythologie* (Berlin: Helmut Küpper, 1918) and David B. Allison, *Reading the New Nietzsche* (Lanham, MD: Rowman & Littlefield, 2001) clarifies this background in terms of Nietzsche's affective responsiveness to music. While repeating, as noted above, the standard and petty account of Nietzsche's limitations as composer, Liébert's *Nietzsche and Music* nevertheless underscores the relevance of Nietzsche's improvisational abilities as a performer. We will return to this interpretive question throughout and especially in the next two chapters.

28. This reviewer of *Beyond Good and Evil* was Josef Viktor Widmann. See Widmann, "Nietzsche's Dangerous Book," trans. Lysanne Fauvel and Tim Hyde, *New Nietzsche Studies* 4 1/2 (2000): 195–200; here p. 195.

29. See further in chapter 4.

30. In particular, the metonymic frame of night and the stars that characterize the atmosphere of Heidegger's poem form the backdrop for the astonishingly beautiful spoken presentation—this was not a written text—that was one of the high points of the scholar's session on William J. Richardson's philosophical work at the Society for Phenomenology and Existential Philosophy meeting in Boston, November 2003.

31. Robert Bernasconi, *The Question of Language in Heidegger's History of Being* (Atlantic Highlands: Humanities Press, 1985), p. 95. Bernasconi alludes to the Anglo-American poet T. S. Eliot's "Burnt Norton"—"Words strain, / Crack and sometimes break, under the burden, / Under the tension, slip, slide, perish, / Decay with imprecision, will not stay in place, / Will not stay still." Cited as the epigraph for his first book on Heidegger, this attention to the breaking of the word echoes Heidegger's reflection on Stefan George's poem "Words" [*Das Wort*] and the phrase Heidegger makes into the refrain for his own essay of the same title "*Kein ding sei wo das wort gebricht.*" ("Words" in Heidegger, *On the Way to Language*, trans. Joan Stambaugh (San Francisco: Harper, 1971), pp. 139–156. Text originally included in *Unterwegs zur Sprache* (Pfullingen: Neske, 1959), pp. 219–238; the poem is given in full on p. 220, cf. p. 221.

32. On this theme, see Babich, "Heidegger's Silence: Towards a Post-Modern Topology," in *Ethics and Danger: Currents in Continental Thought*, eds. Charles Scott and Arleen Dallery (Albany: State University of New York Press, 1992), pp. 83–106. Like Bernasconi, Steiner has also emphasized what he names a "failure" or the "shattering" of language in Heidegger, thetically and tacitly. See Steiner's introduction to his *Martin Heidegger*, "Heidegger: In 1991" (Chicago: University of Chicago Press, 1991) and chapter 13 in this volume.

33. Beyond Stefan George, we can also think of Gottfried Benn and René Char.

34. Bernasconi, *The Question of Language in Heidegger's History of Being*, p. 63.

35. Ibid.

36. And as most English speakers have already learned, more or less to their pain, reading German tends to be a lifelong and nearly futile task, indeed quasi "fatal"—as the Anglo-American poet Randall Jarrell only half humorously implies in his poem to the German language: "Deutsch durch Freud."

37. Later we will have occasion to return to a further discussion of Nietzsche and Hölderlin with regard to von Humboldt.

38. Reiner Schürmann, letter to the author.

39. Heidegger, "The Word of Nietzsche: God Is Dead" in *The Question Concerning Technology and Other Essays*, trans. William Lovitt (New York: Harper & Row, 1977), p. 54–55.

40. This gives a more-than-rhetorical tone to the citation. Beyond rhetoric, but without denying its significance in Nietzsche's writing, Heidegger is thus able to suggest that everything enigmatic in Nietzsche might correspond to Nietzsche's own sense of himself as "a precursor, a transition, pointing before and behind, leading and rebuffing, and therefore everywhere ambiguous, even in the same manner and in the sense of a transition?" (Ibid., p. 55).

41. Heidegger continues to clarify (seemingly to avoid one common misreading): "in the *same*, note well, not the *identical* manner" (70–71). It is also true that Heidegger offers what can seem to be an ironic comment, and this is not the only locus where he has done so (though elsewhere the reference is to Lotze. Here he writes: "It is therefore advisable that you postpone reading Nietzsche for the time being, and first study Aristotle for ten to fifteen years"

(73). If it is obvious that a reading of Aristotle would require no lesser time devoted to it, Heidegger's point is that to read Nietzsche quite literally presupposes the former: "From all that has been suggested, it should be clear that one cannot read Nietzsche in a haphazard way; that each one of his writings has its own character and limits and that the most important works and labors of his thought, which are contained in his *Nachlaß* make demands on us to which we are [still] not equal" (Ibid.).

42. Hölderlin's word is from the poem (and associative reference) "Patmos"— Wo aber Gefahr ist, wächst / das Rettende auch . . ." [Hamburger's translation reads: "But where danger is, grows / The saving power also."]

43. See Heidegger, *The Question Concerning Technology* as well as Heidegger, *Bremer und Freiburger Vorträge*, GA 79 (Frankfurt am Main: Klostermann, 1994).

44. Heidegger's meaning here thus echoes Nietzsche rather than Hegel. See Heidegger, "On the End of Philosophy" in *On Time and Being*, p. 59.

45. The characterization of a thinker as unclear, like the contention that an author is lacking or mediocre or deficient (in the sense of "bad" vs. "good" philosophy), is all the critique that needs to be offered when uttered from the side of today's dominant modality of analytic philosophy. In the analytic philosophical world, the claim that one finds a statement unclear or "confused" is effectively and efficiently to refute the statement. Further discussion does not take place. This instance of scholarly *ressentiment* (to use Nietzsche's word where it belongs) assigns the blame for one's own failure to understand an author to the author one fails to understand. See Babich, "On the Analytic-Continental Divide in Philosophy: Nietzsche's Lying Truth, Heidegger's Speaking Language, and Philosophy," in *A House Divided: Comparing Analytic and Continental Philosophy*, ed. C. G. Prado (Amherst, NY: Humanity Books, 2003), pp. 63–103.

46. Steiner, *Martin Heidegger*, p. xxi.

47. Ibid., p. xiii.

48. Ibid., p. xv.

49. Heidegger, "The Way to Language" in *On the Way to Language*, trans. Peter D. Hertz (New York: Harper, 1982), p. 124. Hereafter cited as WL, followed by page numbers in the text.

50. Heidegger, "Language," *Poetry, Language, Thought*, trans. Albert Hofstadter (New York: Harper, 1971), p. 190. Heidegger, „Die Sprache," *Unterwegs zur Sprache*, p. 12. Hereafter cited as L, followed by page numbers in the text.

51. Heidegger, *Introduction to Metaphysics*, p. 12 [*bei der Philosophie kommt nichts heraus*]. Compare with Nietzsche's twilight reflections on the judgmental wisdom of the ages: "*es taugt nichts*" TI, "The Problem of Socrates," §1).

52. See William J. Richardson's discussion of finitude and negativity retracing the early Heidegger's concept of *Ruinanz* through falleness and errancy in his *Through Phenomenology to Thought* (New York: Fordham University Press, 2003), pp. 32ff. I am, again, indebted to Richardson's recent intervention at the 2005 Heidegger Conference in Baltimore, for this constellation bridging the early and the later Heidegger, Heidegger I and Heidegger II.

53. In the context of several notes dedicated to Descartes and the logic of the conclusions afforded by consciousness vis-à-vis the subject, Nietzsche de-

clares (in quotes in his notes), " 'Es muß besser gezweifelt werden als Descartes!' " (KSA 11, 641), and this is, of course, what Nietzsche means by going beyond Descartes: it is his understanding of the same Heideggerian *Übergang* with which we began this chapter.

54.This, once again, is the context of Gadamer's citation of Heidegger's "Nietzsche hat mich kaputtgemacht!" cited in note 1.

Chapter Two

1. Paul Ricoeur echoes Nietzsche's language when he names him as a "master of suspicion" along with Marx and Freud. Ricoeur uses this formula almost as a mantra (and it has certainly inspired French thought in this way) on a number of occasions. See for example, "Consciousness and the Unconscious," where Ricoeur offers a reflection on the "mood of suspicion" in *The Conflict of Interpretations* (Chicago: Northwestern University Press, 1974), pp. 99–121, see also pp. 18, 143, 149–151, 159, 237 (where Ricoeur aligns Nietzsche with la Rochefoucauld, Jacques Lacan only echoes this reference when he invokes Nietzsche; see further my discussion of Nietzsche and Lacan in Babich, "On the Order of the Real: Nietzsche and Lacan," in *Disseminating Lacan*, eds. D. Pettigrew and F. Raffoul [Albany: State University of New York Press, 1996], pp. 48–63). Ricoeur appropriates Nietzsche's own convention with reference to his work in the later-written Preface to *Human, All Too Human*, where Nietzsche writes, "My writings have been called a schooling in suspicion [*eine Schule des Verdachts*], even more in contempt, but fortunately also in courage, indeed in audacity" (HH §i). If Ricoeur is not the only one to borrow Nietzsche's language, the dependency is surprising when one encounters it, as one often does, *without comment* in the context of Nietzsche commentary.

2. David B. Allison, *Reading the New Nietzsche* (Lanham, MD: Rowman & Littlefield, 2001), p. 1.

3. Part of the point to be made in what follows is that the assumption that Nietzsche models his own work exclusively or even predominantly on the Bible may be a bit overstated. Even Nietzsche's most atheistically inclined readers tend to be all-too-Christian.

4. The surprise here, to be sure, is only for Nietzsche specialists who tend to take Nietzsche as a "compleat" *anti-Christian* to the point of hearing only his shorter (more popular) judgment in *Beyond Good and Evil* §271.

5. The late Jacques Derrida is surely the most famous of these, and see as well, as a commentary in this direct connection, Paul van Tongeren, "Politics, Friendship and Solitude in Nietzsche," *South African Journal of Philosophy* 19/3 (2000): 209–222. Such an attention to the theme of Nietzsche and friendship grows out of a very classical concern with Nietzsche's *agon*. David Allison's analysis throughout his recent book likewise depends on his acute reading of Nietzsche's voice as that of an intimate, indeed a tacitly closest, friend. This same reflection also includes an explicit discussion of both the importance of the friend in Nietzsche's thought and the importance of Nietzsche's friendships with Rohde, Rée, Malwida von Meysenberg, both Richard and Cosima Wagner, Heinrich von

Stein, and indeed the complex "friendship" that was his love affair with Lou, unrequited, despite ambiguities, as Nietzsche ultimately experienced it in his own life and as Lou herself would immortalize it later in her life.

6. In two short *Nachlaß* notes we hear, "Mein Styl hat eine gewisse wollüstige Gedrängtheit" (KSA 8, 291). And "Der Dichter muss ein Ding erst genau sehen und es nachher wieder ungenau sehen: es absichtlich verschleiern. Manche versuchen dies direkt, aber da gelingt's nicht (wie bei Schiller). Die Natur muss durch das Gewand durchleuchten" (Ibid.).

7. Nietzsche, *The Wanderer and His Shadow*, §140, in *Human, All Too Human*. Here, Nietzsche's reference is not to the Latin stylistic tradition but to the Greek and the era of Demosthenes, where he calls for concision as a cultural prophylactic: "Rigorous reflection, terseness, coldness, simplicity, deliberately constrained to their furthest limits, self-containment of the sentiments and silence in general—that alone aids us" HH I §195. See too Nietzsche's reflections a few sections later on "The Revolution in Poetry" (HH I §221). For a recent discussion of Nietzsche's rhetorical style in the context of the philological tradition and philosophical hermeneutics, see Adrian del Caro, "Nietzsche's Rhetoric on the Grounds of Philology and Hermeneutics," *Philosophy and Rhetoric* 37/ 2 (2004): 101–122.

8. Nietzsche writes, "a sense of style, for the epigram as style, was awoken almost instantaneously," in *Twilight of the Idols*, "on coming into contact with Sallust." As Nietzsche continues to emphasize: "I have not forgotten the astonishment of my honored teacher Corssen when he had to give top marks to his worst Latin scholar—I had done all in a single blow" (TI, "What I Owe to the Ancients," §1). Nietzsche also invokes Horace to describe style in words he also meant to claim for his own compositions: "Dies Mosaik von Worten, wo jedes Wort, als Klang, als Ort, als Begriff, nach rechts links und über das Ganze hin seine Kraft ausströmt, dies minimum von Umfang der Zeichen, dies damit erreichte maximum von Energie des Zeichens—das Alles ist römisch und, wenn man mir glauben will, vornehm par excellence: der ganze Rest von Poesie wird dagegen eine Gefühls-Geschwätzigkeit. Ich möchte am wenigsten den Reiz vergessen, der im Contrast dieser granitnen Form und der anmuthigsten Libertinage liegt:—mein Ohr ist entzückt über diesen Widerspruch von Form und Sinn" (KSA 13, 624–625).

9. I elsewhere offer a lengthier discussion of this reader-directed, self-deconstructive style, see Babich, "Nietzsche's Self-Deconstruction: Philosophy as Style," *Soundings* 73 (Spring, 1990): 50–12 and "On Nietzsche's Concinnity: An Analysis of Style," *Nietzsche-Studien* 19 (1990): 59–80.

10. As one can see on the basis of his transmitted letters, Nietzsche regularly wrote the same letter to each of his friends, which did not mean that he did not vary it to address each person individually: composing a draft and then rewriting it in appropriate variations on the same base theme to his different correspondents.

11. In this context, and contra the recent textual tempest as it first appeared and is increasingly more in evidence in the *Nietzsche-Studien* (see later notes for selected references), the relevance of Nietzsche's reading of Gustav

Gerber's *Die Sprache als Kunst*, 2 vols. (Bromberg: Mittler'sche Buchhandlung, 1871), so much of which would find its way into Nietzsche's own (unpublished) "Truth and Lie in an Extra-Moral Sense," turns out, on my reading to be far less a case of suppressed influence (much less plagiarism) than the relevance (or routine influence) of a taken for granted handbook, especially in the era of non-mechanical (non-photocopiable) means of reproduction.

12. I discuss just this extra-moral epistemology in the context of the significance of Nietzsche's critique of truth for the philosophy of science in Babich, *Nietzsche's Philosophy of Science* (Albany: State University of New York Press, 1994).

13. Yet Gerber may be traced to his own predecessors and to the language philosopher Wilhelm von Humboldt in particular. Additionally, Martin Stingelin has explored Nietzsche's relationship to Georg Christian Lichtenberg in his *"Unsere ganze Philosophie ist Berichtigung des Sprachgebrauchs": Friedrich Nietzsches Lichtenberg Rezeption im Spannungsfeld zwischen Sprachkritik (Rhetorik) und historischer Kritik (Genealogie)* (Munich: Fink, 1996). As would have been standard practice for the author of a literary handbook, Gerber's protocol was to illuminate the "art of language" by means of common references. That the scope of such references, be they sources in general philosophy of language or philology, are liable to become dated and eventually obscure to later readers is clear. A comparable fade may be demonstrated for (Anglophone) readers in (Henry Watson and Francis George) Fowler's *The King's English*, a handbook, like Gerber's, first published in 1906. The reference is instructive as Fowler's illustrations are more accessible to the English-speaking reader and they do not (for the most part) involve examples (as Gerber's illustrations did provide) from Greek, Latin, Hebrew, Sanskrit, texts.

14. Gerber, *Die Sprache als Kunst*, see note 13.

15. See my editor's notes to Ulrich Wilamowitz-Möllendorff, "Future Philology," trans. Gertrude Pöstl, Babette E. Babich, and Holger Schmid, *New Nietzsche Studies*, 4:1/2 (2000): 1–32.

16. Gerber, *Die Sprache und das Erkennen* (Berlin: R. Gaertners Verlagsbuchhandlung, 1884).

17. I have already offered a preliminary discussion of Heidegger's image of how philosophy (and language) might work on us in the preceding chapter. Heidegger emphasizes that language always works on us in this way, and thus an openness to language is different from an openness for philosophy. See, further, Babich, "On the Analytic-Continental Divide in Philosophy: Nietzsche's Lying Truth, Heidegger's Speaking Language, and Philosophy," in Prado, ed., *A House Divided: Comparing Analytic and Continental Philosophy*, ed. C. G. Prado (Amherst, NY: Humanity Books/Prometheus, 2003), pp. 63–103.

18. See Josef Simon, "Grammar and Truth: On Nietzsche's Relationship to the Speculative Sentential Grammar of the Metaphysical Tradition," trans. Leo J. Lipis, Babette E. Babich, and Holger Schmid in *Nietzsche, Theories of Knowledge, and Critical Theory: Nietzsche and Science I*, ed. Babich (Dordrecht: Kluwer, 1999), pp. 129–151.

19. The tradition of authors who have reviewed Nietzsche's reception of Kant is extensive but remarkably uneven (as contrasted, say, with the tradition of scholarship on Nietzsche and Hegel or Nietzsche and Schopenhauer). The question of Nietzsche's direct lineage (as opposed to an influence via Schopenhauer) is a necessarily foamy one (how will one prove that Nietzsche "really" read Kant—as contrasted, say, with really reading Schopenhauer or Wagner?), but those scholars who advert to "the" Kantian dimension of Nietzsche's thought include, classically, Hans Vaihinger (see his *Die Philosophie des Als Ob: System der theoretischen, praktischen und religiösen Fiktionen der Menschheit auf Grund eines idealistischen Positivismus: mit einem Anhang über Kant und Nietzsche* [Leipzig: F. Meiner, 1911]) as well as Georg Simmel, Martin Heidegger, and Theodor Adorno. In addition, contemporary scholars include Josef Simon, as noted previously, as well as Alexis Philonenko, Olivier Reboul (see in particular Reboul's *Nietzsches critique de Kant* [Paris: Presses Universitaires de France, 1974]) as well as Gerd-Günther Grau, Volker Gerhardt, and Werner Hamacher (who has more than one contribution in this direction, but see in particular Hamacher, "Das Versprechen der Auslegung: Überlegungen zum hermeneutischen Imperativ bei Kant und Nietzsche," in *Spiegel und Gleichnis*, eds. Norbert Bolz and W. Hübener [Würzburg: Königshausen and Neumann, 1983], pp. 252–387), as well as Friedrich Kaulbach, and Beatrix Himmelman. Other names include George Stack, albeit via Lange, among others. It is to be assumed that in addition to the recent focus on Nietzsche in Douglas Burnham's *Kant's Philosophies of Judgement* (Edinburgh: University of Edinburgh, 2004), R. Kevin Hill's *Nietzsche's Critiques* (Oxford: Oxford University Press, 2003) will encourage further English language research into the relevance of Kant for Nietzsche's philosophy if it must also be said, in all fairness, that these newer English language inquiries take no account of the broader international research tradition.

20. See Gregory Moore, *Nietzsche's Biology and Metaphor* (Cambridge: Cambridge University Press, 2001) for an overview of this topic.

21. See here Alexander Nehamas, *Nietzsche: Life as Literature* (Cambridge, MA: Harvard University Press, 1985) in addition to the many studies that have responded to the impetus of this seminal work.

22. See Tilman Borsche, "Nietzsches Erfindung der Vorsokratiker," in *Nietzsche und die philosophische Tradition*, ed. Josef Simon (Würzburg: Königshausen & Neumann, 1985), pp. 62–87. Borsche offers just one illustration of this argumentative convention, still another of which has found expression in James Porter's studies on Nietzsche and classical philology, (see next note).

23. See James Porter, *The Invention of Dionysus* and *Nietzsche and the Philology of the Future* (Stanford: Stanford University Press, 2000).

24. Declaring the prime principle of science to be the greatest possible (or all-too-deliberate) "stupidity," Nietzsche writes that the triumph of the ever more mechanistic account of world process presupposes just such a (calculated) stupidity and not a little complicity with one's own assumptions (his point here compares to his memorable image of Tübingen theologians busily diving into the bushes in pursuit of "faculties" (BGE §11): "Jedermann kennt diese Prozeduren:

man läßt die 'Vernunft' und die 'Zwecke,' " and in the *Nachlaß*, Nietzsche writes: "so gut es gehen will, aus dem Spiele, man zeigt, daß, bei gehöriger Zeitdauer, Alles aus Allem werden kann, man verbirgt ein schadenfrohes Schmunzeln nicht, wenn wieder einmal die Anscheinende Absichtlichkeit im Schicksale einer Pflanze oder eines Eidotters auf Druck und Stoß zurückgeführt ist: kurz, man huldigt von ganzem Herzen, wenn in einer so ernsten Angelegenheit ein scherzhafter Ausdruck erlaubt ist, dem Principe der größtmöglichen Dummheit" (KSA 11, 564). See also *Schopenhauer as Educator* §6.

25. On Nietzsche in the context of the biology of his day, see Gregory Moore's *Nietzsche, Biology, and Metaphor* (Cambridge: Cambridge University Press, 2002). Particularly revealing are the assumptions of the day regarding diet and health in Moore's discussion of Degeneration. See also Dan Stone's *Breeding Superman: Nietzsche, Race and Eugenics in Edwardian and Literary Britain* (Liverpool: Liverpool University Press, 2002), as well as Marc A. Weiner's informatively balanced chapter on Nietzsche, "Laws of Degeneration" in his *Wagner and the Anti-Semitic Imagination* (Lincoln: University of Nebraska Press, 1995), as well as Janz's biography and Allison's *Reading the New Nietzsche.*

26. See for the classic discussion of this term, Herbert Butterfield, *The Whig Interpretation of History* (London: Bell, 1931). Whiggishness corresponds to the still dominant historical tendency of "presentism," that is, Butterfield has it, "to write on the side of Protestants and Whigs, to praise revolutions provided they have been successful, to emphasize certain principles of progress in the past and to produce a story which is the ratification if not the glorification of the present," p. v. This Butterfield took in an exactly radical direction in his book on the history and philosophy of science *The Origins of Modern Science: 1300–1800* (New York: Free Press, 1965; 1957).

27. This characteristic tends to mark so-called analytic approaches to Nietzsche. For references and further discussion of just this question, see Babich, "On the Analytic-Continental Divide in Philosophy."

28. I refer to the current proliferation of encyclopedias, dictionaries, or handbooks throughout research scholarship in general. In many and sometimes incendiary cases, often countering expectations presuming Nietzsche's innovative modernity, recent research details the common sources from whence Nietzsche drew the ideas he is supposed to have "invented." Such source research increasingly justifies the derivative assessment of the same ideas. Although corresponding to what Nietzsche provocatively characterized as a "lack" of philology, the same convention has become ever more dominant. Main instantiations include Anthonie Meijers and Martin Stingelin, "Konkordanz zu den wörtlichen Abschriften und Übernahmen von Beispielen und Zitaten aus Gustav Gerber: *Die Sprache als Kunst* (Bromberg: Mittler'sche Buchhandlun, 1871) in Nietzsches Rhetorik-Vorlesungen und in *Über Wahrheit und Lüge im außermoralischen Sinne,*" *Nietzsche-Studien* 19 (1988): 350–368 along with their accompanying interpretive essays (Stingelin, "Nietzsches Wortspiel als Reflexion auf poet (olog)ische Verfahren," *Nietzsche-Studien* 19 [1988]: 336–349 and Meijers, "Gustav Gerber und Friedrich Nietzsche: Zum historischen Hintergrund der sprachphilosophischen Auffassungen des frühen

Nietzsche," 369–390). See further Joseph Kopperschmidt and Helmut Schanze, *Nietzsche oder 'Die Sprache ist Rhetorik'* (Munich: Fink, 1994). For philosophical applications, see Hans-Gerald Hödl, *Nietzsches frühe Sprachkritik: Lektüren zu «Ueber Wahrheit und Lüge im aussermoralischen Sinne»* (Vienna: WUV-Universitätsverlag, 1997) and Adrian del Caro, "Nietzsche's Rhetoric on the Grounds of Philology and Hermeneutics." *Philosophy and Rhetoric* 37/2 (2004): 101–122.

29. Hippocrates, *Volume III*, trans. W. H. S. Jones (Cambridge: Harvard University Press [Loeb]: 1995 [1923]). It is Seneca's elaboration of the first two points made in the first line (cited by Seneca from the "most famed physician"): "vitam brevem esse, longam arte" that has ensured its survival. See Seneca, *De brevitate vitae/Von der Kürze des Lebens*, trans. Josef Feix (Stuttgart: Reclam, 1977).

30. The aphorism is a particular literary form, like a motto or an epigraph. Significantly, and more than one commentator has noted this, the aphorism has an inherently philosophical component. See for one example, Heinz Krüger's *Studien über den Aphorismus als philosophische Form* (Frankfurt: Nest Verlag, 1956). Krüger's book is articulated in opposition to Kurt Besser's more properly philological *Die Problematik der aphoristischer Form bei Lichtenberg, Schlegel, Novalis, und Nietzsche* (Leipzig: 1935). For a more recent (and very comprehensive) general discussion: Detlef Otto, *Wendungen der Metapher. Zur Übertragung in poetologischer, rhetorischer, und erkenntnistheoretischer Hinsicht bei Aristoteles und Nietzsche* (Munich: Fink Verlag, 1998). See also on the aphorism, Robin Small's *Nietzsche and Rée: A Star Friendship* (Oxford: Oxford University Press, 2005), pp. 57–65, in addition to further references in the notes below.

31. See, for a discussion of these problems as they have haunted the analytic as well as the literary tradition of philosophic scholarship, and the particular matter of mistaking an epigraph for an aphorism (never a good idea with a scholar of rhetoric such as Nietzsche was), John T. Wilcox, "What Aphorism Does Nietzsche Explicate in *Genealogy of Morals* Essay III?" and Maudemarie Clark, "From Nietzsche Archive: Concerning the Aphorism Explicated in *Genealogy* III," both in *Journal of the History of Philosophy* 35/4 (1997): 593–633. See, further, Wilcox, "That Exegesis of an Aphorism in 'Genealogy III': Reflections on the Scholarship," *Nietzsche-Studien*, 28 (1998): 448–462. See also Paul Miklowitz's reply to Wilcox in *Nietzsche-Studien*, 29 (1999): 267–269. The issue is not yet settled, even for analysts, and Christoph Cox repeats the identification of the epigraph for the aphorism in question at the start of his *Nietzsche: Naturalism and Interpretation* (Berkeley: University of California Press, 1999), p. 15. Jill Marsden likewise identifies the aphorism in question with the epigraph in "Nietzsche and the Art of the Aphorism," in *A Companion to Nietzsche*, ed. Keith Ansell Pearson (Oxford: Blackwell, 2006), pp. 22–38; see in particular, pp. 32–37. Marsden follows Kelly Oliver in this reading. See Oliver, *Womanizing Nietzsche: Philosophy's Relation to the 'Feminine'* (London: Routledge, 1995).

32. *On the Genealogy of Morals* carries the subtitle—as Nietzsche never fails to warn the reader—*A Polemic*. This device has done nothing to hinder scholars intent on reading it as a kind of *Tractatus* for Nietzsche's moral philosophy. See by contrast, KSA 11, p. 579.

33. Again, note Nietzsche's antagonism to Aristotle who for his part had originally located the responsibility for being understood on the plain side of the author and the lucidity of prose.

34. There are other, most notably Augustinian, loci for this image. But my favorite reference for this textual sensibility, precisely because of the comprehension of the full range of the incarnate sensuality of the letter and the book, is Ivan Illich, *In the Vineyard of the Text: A Commentary on Hugh's* Didascalicon (Chicago: University of Chicago Press, 1993), chapter 3, particularly pp. 54ff.

35. This is the point of departure for Jacques Derrida's discussion of style, using the (gallically stylistic conceit of "woman") in *Éperons: Les Styles de Nietzsche* **Spurs**: *Nietzsche's Styles*, trans. Barbara Johnson (Chicago: University of Chicago Press, 1979). I raise this question from another perspective in terms of Nietzsche's question of the problem of the artist in chapter 9 as well as, yet more directly, in Babich, "The Logic of Woman in Nietzsche: The Dogmatist's Story," *New Political Science* 36 (1996): 7–17.

36. Krüger, *Studien über den Aphorismos als philosophischer Form*, p. 26.

37. Apart from the example of readerly anti-Semitism, I elsewhere follow the dynamic of this writing as it engages prejudicial convictions or persuasions in reviewing the functioning of Nietzsche's critique of ascetic ideals in terms not only of religion anterior to morality but science. Babich, *Nietzsche's Philosophy of Science: Reflecting Science on the Ground of Art and Life* (Albany: State University of New York Press, 1994), see chapter 4 and, in particular, chapter 5.

38. See Manfred Riedel, *Hören auf die Sprache: Die akroamatische Dimension der Hermeneutik* (Frankfurt am Main: Suhrkamp, 1989) as well as Holger Schmid, *Kunst des Hörens: Orte und Grenzen philosophische Spracherfahrung* (Cologne: Böhlau, 1999). Giovanni Boniolo has called attention to the role of this kind of reading (in terms of rationality and scientific-logical explanation in Kant's *Critique of Pure Reason*, explaining that Kant distinguishes between philosophy and science not only in terms of the role of mathematics (for Kant this is reserved for the sciences), but in terms of demonstration that, so Boniolo shows, Kant reserves to mathematics alone. "In philosophy, Kant argues there is 'acroamatic' (discursive) proof' (KdrV 591, B763)." That is, Boniolo explains, "in philosophy there is no room for demonstration but only for argumentation. . . . the acromatic leads to proofs that may be discussed and that do not always follow the rules of deductive inference." See Boniolo, "Kant's Explication and Carnap's Explication: The *Redde Rationem*," *International Philosophical Quarterly* 43 3/171 (2003): 289–298, here p. 298.

39. Jacques Rancière, *The Philosopher and his Poor*, trans. John Drury, Corinne Oster, and Andrew Parker, trans. (Durham: Duke University Press, 2003). See further KSA 9, p. 213. See also, *The Weight of the World: Social Suffering in Contemporary Society*, ed. Pierre Bourdieu, et al. (Stanford: Stanford University Press, 1999).

40. See, for an example, the contributions to Jacob Golomb and Robert S. Wistrich, eds., *Nietzsche, Godfather of Fascism: On the Uses and Abuses of Philosophy* (Princeton: Princeton University Press, 2002).

Chapter Three

1. For a start, see Babich, "Nietzsche, Classic Philology and Ancient Philosophy: A Research Bibliography," *New Nietzsche Studies* 4:1/2 (Summer/ Fall 2000): 171–191, in addition to more recent contributions in this direction, only some of which are given below. Although philological controversies associated with Nietzsche go unaddressed, Nietzsche is the prime interlocutor in Pascale Hummel, *Philologus auctor: Le philologue et son œuvre* (Bern: Peter Lang, 2003).

2. Bertram Schmidt points out that Nietzsche's invocation of the architectonic form in music echoes an earlier use already to be found in Eduard Hanslick *(Vom Musikalisch-Schönen,*1854), suggesting that this is Nietzsche's reference when he invokes this same formula. See Schmidt, *Der ethische Aspekte der Musik: Nietzsches "Geburt der Tragödie" und die Wiener klassische Musik* (Würzburg: Königshausen & Neumann, 1991), p. 15.

3. See, for a discussion, J. W. Halporn, "Nietzsche: On the the Theory of Quantitative Rhythm," *Arion* 6 (1967): 233–243; Viktor Pöschl, "Nietzsche und die klassische Philologie" in Hellmut Flashar et al., eds., *Philologie und Hermeneutik im 19: Jahrhundert: Zur Geschichte und Methodologie der Geisteswissenschaften* (Göttingen: Vandenhoeck and Ruprecht, 1979), pp. 141–155, particularly pp. 154–155; Fritz Bornmann, "Nietzsches metrische Studien," *Nietzsche-Studien* 18 (1989): 472–489, and James I. Porter, "Being on Time: The Studies in Ancient Rhythm and Meter (1870–72)," in Porter's *Nietzsche and the Philology of the Future* (Stanford: Stanford University Press, 2000), pp. 127–166.

4. See Nietzsche's letter to Rohde dated 23 November 1870, in *Sämtliche Briefe: Kritische Studienausgabe* 3 April 1869–May 1872 (Berlin: de Gruyter, 1986), p. 159. See also his public lectures of the time, beginning with his inaugural lecture, "Homer und die klassische Philologie" (1869, KSA 1), "Das griechische Musikdrama" (1870, KSA 1, pp. 513–532), "Sokrates und die Tragödie" (1870, KSA 1, 533–549), as well as his unpublished "Die dionysische Weltanschauung" (1870, KSA 1, 551–577), "Wir Philologen" (1874–75, KSA 8, 11–130), and most crucially perhaps his university lecture courses on "Die griechischen Lyrik" (1869, FS 5; KGW II/2, pp. 105–182), "Griechische Rhythmik" (1870/71, KGW II/3, pp. 199–201), and his "Encyclopedie der klassischen Philologie" (1871, KGW II/3, 339–437). See Barbara von Reibnitz, *Ein Kommentar zu Nietzsche "Die Geburt der Tragödie aus dem Geiste der Musik" (Kapitel 1–12)* (Stuttgart: Metzler, 1992) for an overview of the historical philological background of Nietzsche's text and a bibliography for further research.

5. See, again, Pöschl and Bornmann as well as Rudolf Fietz, *Medienphilosphie: Musik, Sprache, und Schrift bei Friedrich Nietzsche* (Würzburg: Königshausen & Neumann, 1992); Marcello Gigante, "Nietzsche nella storia della filologia classica," *Rendiconti dell' Accademia di Archeologia, Letter e Belle Arti di Napoli* LIX (1984): 5–46; as well as Porter, who observes that the currently received authoritative study by A. Devine and L. Stephens, *The Prosody of Greek Speech* (Oxford: Oxford University Press, 1994), seems not to refute Nietzsche's arguments.

6. James Porter notes that Nietzsche's "findings were quietly absorbed into the mainstream of classical philology," *Nietzsche and the Philology of the Future*, p. 129. Porter for his part notes that it was Paul Maas, Wilamowitz's

student, who took over Nietzsche's discovery in his *Griechische Metrik*, first published in 1923 and translated by Hugh Lloyd-Jones as *Greek Metre* (Oxford: Oxford University Press, 1962).

7. See Devine and Stephens, *The Prosody of Greek Speech*, p. 213.

8. Porter emphasizes this distinction in *Nietzsche and the Philology of the Future*, pp. 127–166.

9. See, again, Porter, *Nietzsche and the Philology of the Future*, p. 135. There is debate on the role (presence or absence) of the so-called ictus in Latin. The general view (Nietzsche's view as much as Heidegger's) is that Latin is more akin to related European languages than to Greek.

10. There are books, like Devine and Stephens's, among others, that tell us how to pronounce ancient Greek, and we have recently seen a wealth of realizations or reconstructions of ancient Greek music, in nicely modern musical form, on perfectly listenable, professionally marketed music recordings. Porter invokes Cage (who in turn invokes Satie and Webern) and Reich, and much of this resonates well with the sound of such reconstructions, and concludes his third chapter with a section entitled: "Dionysian Music: A Modern Phenomenon?" in *Nietzsche and the Philology of the Future*, pp. 160–166. The question of such comparisons is both ticklish and circular. Are such musicians as John Cage and Steve Reich (never mind Stravinksky or Schoenberg, both of whom were conscious of just such a resonance with reconstructions of ancient Greek musical performance practice) genuinely useful exemplars of a timeless "sound" in music itself or do the musicians who interpret such ancient music "recognize" what appear to be modern serialist constructions (one is reminded of Nietzsche's musing on the word *Armbrust*), thereby producing recordings of the one that are similar to recordings of the other? If liner notes in the case of Ancient Greek music CDs duly invoke artistic freedom and the spontaneous dimension of feeling (in part to circumvent such questions) the same "realizations for the ear" (in Kepler's sense of such realizations: Kepler composed musical realizations for the proportional relations between planetary orbits) are relevant, as such references to modern minimalist music indicate. A disquiet regarding Nietzsche's reflections (as these challenge such reconstructive endeavors) thus qualifies Porter's otherwise sympathetic analysis.

11. Nietzsche speaks of tragedy in terms of marriage, sexual union, progeny, et cetera. I discuss this further using an alchemical metaphor in Babich, "Nietzsche's *göttliche Eidechse*: 'Divine Lizards,' 'Greene Lyons' and Music," in *Nietzsche's Bestiary*, eds. Ralph and Christa Davis Acampora (Lanham: Rowman & Littlefield, 2004), pp. 264–283.

12. I return to this question of metaphorical preoccupation in the context of Nietzsche's engagement with Pindar (for whom such crossovers were also emblematic) in chapter 7.

13. In addition to Nietzsche's own (very enthusiastic) reading of Lange, see the background offered by Robin Small's indispensable *Nietzsche in Context* (Aldershot: Avebury, 2001) as well as, in the current context, Sören Reuter, "Reiz-Bild-Unbewusste Anschauung: Nietzsches Auseinandersetzung mit Hermann Helmholtz' Theorie der unbewussten Schlüsse in *Über Wahrheit und Lüge im aussermoralischen Sinne*," *Nietzsche-Studien* 34 (2004): 351–372.

14. See for this discussion, Nietzsche's examples quoted and discussed in chapter 7.

15. This formula clearly echoes Kant's Third Critique but the associations are more complex than one might conclude reading only Burnham and Hill (see references in chapter 2, this volume). If one can argue that Robert Zimmerman's *Geschichte der Æsthetik als philosophischer Wissenschaft* (Vienna: Bräumüller, 1858) had a perhaps still more direct influence on the framing of this first line in Nietzsche's *The Birth of Tragedy*, this genesis too must be traced back to Kant and the tradition before him, including Baumgarten. Once again, if I think it reasonable to grant that Nietzsche had read Kant—all by himself—not only as every other German academic of his day was able to do, but directly so as Nietzsche was convinced of the importance of philosophy from the start and included Kant by name in his prescribed educational program for classicists. But contemporary scholars have been so traumatized by the critical specter of Nietzsche's Kant that they contend (when they do not merely take it for granted) that Nietzsche *could not have read* Kant. After source scholarship has been taken to exhaustion on this question (what would be needed to show that he *could have done so?*), scholarly literature is due to be deluged with studies seeking to prove what should have been an obvious point.

16. By contrast, Nietzsche could say, "One should be warned against taking these concepts 'pure' and 'impure' too seriously or broadly, not to say symbolically. . . . The 'pure' is from the beginning merely a man who washes himself, who forbids himself certain foods that produce skin ailments, who does not sleep with the dirty women of the lower classes—not much more, hardly any more!" (GM I §6).

17. See Philippe Lacoue-Labarthe, "Le détour (Nietzsche et la rhétorique)," *Poétique* 5 (1971): 53–76. The fact that this is unlikely (most unlikely—given Nietzsche's all too classical formation not only at Schulpforta but in Bonn and Leipzig) has proven no obstacle to the successful proliferation of the notion. See, further, Philippe Lacoue-Labarthe and Jean-Luc Nancy, "Friedrich Nietzsche: Rhétorique et langage: Textes traduits, présentés et annotés," *Poétique* 5 (1971): 99–142; Paul de Man, "Nietzsche's Theory of Rhetoric," *Symposium: A Quarterly Journal in Modern Foreign Languages* (1974): 33–51; and "Rhetoric of Tropes (Nietzsche)" in de Man, *Allegories of Reading: Figural Language in Rousseau, Nietzsche, Rilke, Freud* (New Haven: Yale University Press, 1976). For a summary (and more conservative account), see Ernst Behler, "Nietzsche's Study of Greek Rhetoric," *Research in Phenomenology* 25 (1995): 3–26. A list of further readings would also include analytic philosophical approaches.

18. Nietzsche, UWL 1, KSA 1, p. 879. In this context, as scholars like Dan Breazeale might confirm, and with his invocation of the formula "A = A," Nietzsche refers here to Fichte's *Wissenschaftslehre*.

19. See Babich, *Nietzsche's Philosophy of Science* as well as my "Nietzsche's Critique of Scientific Reason and Scientific Culture: On 'Science as a Problem' and 'Nature as Chaos' " in *Nietzsche and Science*, eds. G. M. Moore and T. Brobjer (Aldershot: Ashgate, 2004), pp. 133–153.

20. This is a preliminary discussion, to be offered at greater length in chapter 6.

21. Thrasybulos Georgiades, *Music and Language*, trans. Mary Louse Göllner (Cambridge: Cambridge University Press, 1982), pp. 4–5.

22. Ibid. See also Georgiades, *Musik und Rhythmus bei den Griechen: Zum Ursprung der abendländischen Musik* (Hamburg: Rowohlt, 1958), pp. 26ff.

23. Georgiades, *Music and Language*, pp. 4–5.

24. Ibid.

25. In general terms, this conception of music functions only within the complex of ancient Greek culture. See again, chapter 6.

26. Nietzsche, *Thus Spoke Zarathustra*, Prologue 5. Nietzsche here offers us an inversion of Aristotle's reference to the use of proportional metaphor in his *Rhetoric* for helping one's hearers "see" (Rhet. Bk. III: 10, 11).

27. Awkward as it is, one might translate *Augenmensch* as "eye-person," on the model of a "people-person" (if one can forgive the awkward idiom in ordinary spoken English) or a "hands-on" person or an "ear-person." Nietzsche refers to a schizophrenia that is endemic to the very notion of absolute music, and speaks of our appreciation, "bald als Ohrenmenschen, bald als Augenmenschen," in this same inevitably sundered modern context (KSA 1, 518). See further, Thomas Böning, " 'Das Buch eines Musikers ist eben nicht das Buch eines Augenmenschen,' Metaphysik und Sprache beim frühen Nietzsche," *Nietzsche-Studien* 15 (1986): 72–106.

28. Gustav Gerber, *Die Sprache als Kunst*, 2 vols. (Bromberg: Mittler'sche Buchhandlung, 1871).

29. To this same degree, it is dangerous to speak of an early, or a middle, or a late period Nietzsche (as if Nietzsche "overcame" his *early* views or "dallied" with the positivism of his nineteenth-century age in the *middle* interval before the *later* Nietzsche waged a war on values, only to collapse in madness). The problem is not at all that Nietzsche's thinking experienced nothing like development but rather that such interpretations inevitably impose a particular narrative schema on Nietzsche's person in order to rediscover such details in his work (in the process conveniently permitting the interpreter to dispense with "irrelevant" aspects of these same details). I will later argue that Nietzsche had an unusually subtle but unmistakable manner of retaining his concerns from start to finish, returning to such issues long after his teachers, friends, and readers had lost the thread. See, for just one example, my discussion of Niezsche's (protracted) response to the critical comments his teacher, August Koberstein made on his essay on Hölderlin in chapter 7.

30. Nietzsche invokes the formula at the start of his 1878/79 lecture, "*Griechische Lyriker*": "*Wir lesen mit den Augen,*" "We read with the eyes," to mark a contrast to the acoustic directionality of ancient Greek lyric poetry, which was presumably read "with the ears" instead (FS 5, 369).

31. In this reference to the exemplary role of the dance in the rhythmic meter of the text, Nietzsche is preceded by August Boeckh, *De metris Pindari*, Leipzig, 1811 and Wilhelm von Humboldt.

32. In just as many words Nietzsche declared that he had discovered the art of "hearing" with one's eyes (BT §6). See further, "*Das griechische Musikdrama*," KSA 1, pp. 515ff. Cf. *The Birth of Tragedy*, p. 17.

33. One might then say, that although we still have antiquity's letter, we lack its musical spirit. This opposition contrasts oral and written culture and

reflects a distinction that may be found in (the late) Ivan Illich and Barry Sanders, *ABC: The Alphabetization of the Popular Mind* (San Francisco: North Point Press, 1968); see too Walter Ong, *Orality and Literacy: The Technologizing of the Word* (London: Methuen, 1982). Illich's important and beautiful *In the Vineyard of the Text* offers a way to mediate contemporary culture and antiquity, via the medieval text culture and cultivation of Hugh of St. Victor. But in the case of Nietzsche, it is important to emphasize the advances made by the signal discoveries of Milman Parry and Albert Lord in the early part of the twentieth century, see Albert Lord, *A Singer of Tales* (Cambridge: Belknap Press, 1960) and Adam Parry, ed., *The Making of Homeric Verse: The Collected Papers of Milman Parry* (Oxford: Clarendon Press, 1971), see Milman Parry, *L'épithète traditionelle des Homère* (Paris, 1928) as well as Eric Havelock, *Preface to Plato* (Cambridge: Harvard University Press, 1963), et cetera. One can see further, in a different direction, the pioneering work of Alexander Luria to trace out the cognitive consequences of a literate culture. The critics of the technology of writing, in all its manifestations, from reed to stylus to feather quill to computer keyboard, have observed that as one writes, one apparently, and in a very Nietzschean way, *writes* oneself.

34. Raymond Geuss contends that "pure or absolute Dionysian music [. . .] would have to be purely instrumental music with no accompanying words" in his introduction to Ronald Speirs translation of Nietzsche, *The Birth of Tragedy and Other Writings* (Cambridge: Cambridge University Press, 1999), p. xxi.

35. If commentators continue to find this paradoxical, Nietzsche makes the point of his explication of the decadence of ancient tragedy in terms of its original genesis equally explicit: "as tragedy goes to ground with the evanescence of the spirit of music, it is only from this spirit that it can be reborn" (BT §16).

36. For a digest of the relevant qualities of Wagner's scholarly (and even philological) endeavors, see M. Owen Lee, *Athena Sings: Wagner and the Greeks* (Toronto: University of Toronto Press, 2003).

37. I make this point against such casual prejudices in Babich, "Habermas, Nietzsche, and the Future of Critique: Irrationality, *The Will to Power*, and War" in Babich, *Habermas, Nietzsche, and Critical Theory* (Amherst, New York: Humanity Books, 2004), pp. 13–46, here pp. 16–19.

38. Pierre-Daniel Huet (with Jacques Bénigne Bossuet) directed the classical *Ad Usum Delphini (1673–1991)*. See also, a recent collection directed by Catherine Valpilhac-Augen, *La collection Ad Usum Delphini. L'Antiquité au miroir du Grand Siecle* (Paris: Eilug, 2000), as well as Puget de Saint-Pierre, *Histoire de Charles de Sainte-Maure, duc de Montausier* (Genève, Paris: Guillot, 1784). See also: Jacques Bénigne Bossuet, *Politique tirée des propres paroles de l'Ecriture sainte* (Paris: P. Cot, 1709) and Géraud de Cordemoy, *De la nécessité de l'histoire, de son usage & de la manière dont il faut mêler les autres sciences, en la faisant lire à un prince*, dans *Divers traités de métaphysique, d'histoire et de politique* (Paris: 1691). Examples of the project include Jean Doujat, *Abrégé de l'histoire romaine et grecque, en partie traduit de Velleius Paterculus, et en partie tiré des meilleurs auteurs de l'Antiquité* (Paris: 1671) and Esprit Fléchier, *Histoire de Théodose le Grand* (Paris: S. Mabre-Cramoisy, 1679).

39. It is for this reason that William Arrowsmith felt compelled to translate Nietzsche's "We Philologists" in the old series of the journal he edited,

Arion. Arrowsmith regarded this as a kind of call to arms, as gadfly inspiration for the future of the profession.

40. Catherine Osborne makes this point with respect to fragment and scholarly context or gloss in her *Rethinking Early Greek Philosophy: Hippolytus of Rome and the Presocratics* (Ithaca: Cornell University Press, 1987). Osborne's study has been relatively unreceived, at least within philosophy. Yet Osborne's reflections can be taken together with Nietzsche's arguments regarding the so-called pre-Socratics as an imperative call for further critical reflection on the sources themselves. One obvious and contemporary locus for such reflection is the Derveni Papyrus, first transcribed anonymously as "Der orphische Papyrus von Derveni," *Zeitschrift für Papyrologie und Epigraphik*, 47 (1982): 1–12. For an English translation and (unphilosophically minded) commentary, see Gábor Betegh, *The Derveni Papyrus: Cosmology, Theology and Interpretation* (Cambridge: Cambridge University Press, 2004) and André Laks and Glenn W. Most, "A Provisional Translation of the Derveni Papyrus" in *Studies on the Derveni Papyrus*, eds. Laks and Most (Oxford: Oxford University Press, 1997), pp. 9–22.

41. Nietzsche's most extreme exemplification of this manufactured or idealized representation of antiquity is evident in the citational methods he employed in his *Philosophy in the Tragic Age of the Greeks*, with its notoriously creative variations on the received versions of the pre-Platonic "fragments"). Beyond the reactionary or indeed the counterreactionary moves of today's classics experts, it is important to reflect upon the implications of Nietzsche's project for ancient philosophy. In addition to scholars like Marcel Detienne and Luc Brisson, see too the recent work of Pierre Hadot and indeed, if also more traditionally, Charles Kahn's seminal study of Anaximander.

42. "Unsere Augen hören feiner als unsere Ohren: wir verstehen und schmecken lesend besser als hörend—bei Büchern wie bei Musik" (KSA 10, 103).

43. The image of ears and its biblical allusions recurs in (and is perhaps best known from) Nietzsche's *Thus Spoke Zarathustra*, in the third book, in the section entitled "Of the Vision and the Riddle." There Nietzsche invites his readers to identify themselves with bold adventurers, relating Zarathustra's friendship to those who like to see themselves as living dangerously: "to you who are intoxicated by riddles, who take pleasure in twilight, whose soul is lured with flutes to every treacherous abyss." Advocate of courage, Zarathustra offers a litany of what courage can do, it attacks, its overcomes, it destroys dizziness in the face of the abyss, and invites the eternal return: "and where does man not stand at an abyss? Is seeing itself not—seeing abysses? . . . as deeply as man looks into life, so deeply does he look also into suffering. . . . Courage, however, is the best destroyer, courage that attacks: it destroys even death, for it says: 'Was *that* life? Well then! Once more.' . . . He who has ears to hear, let him hear." And again in of "Old and New Law Tablets" (17) we hear Zarathustra declare, "And you should first *learn* from me even how to listen, how to listen well—He who has ears to hear, let him hear." Finally it appears in "The Case of Wagner," section 10: regarding Wagner's cleverness [*Klugheit*], "The system of procedures that Wagner handles is applicable to a hundred other cases: let him who has ears, hear." See for the phrase in the Bible: Mt 13:9; 13:43 and Mk 4:9, et cetera.

Chapter Four

1. This text was originally written in response to Keith Ansell-Pearson's invitation to write on the Chladni sound patterns in *The Gay Science* for the Blackwell *Companion to Nietzsche* (and I do address this theme: see pp. 61ff. and associated context). Beyond patterns in vibrating sand, the visual evidence or transference of sound, I here attend to the fundamental question of the role of the song tradition throughout Nietzsche's work, in particular, the literally "gay science" or poetic song craft of the troubadours.

2. The title plays off many things, most obviously Wagner's *Meistersinger*, and it alludes to Walther von der Vogelweide—Nietzsche had heard a course on his poetry during his student years in Bonn.

3. That one should take this "chaste" character rather lightly seems advisable. See Pierre Bec, *Le comte de Poitiers, premiers troubadour, à l'aube d'un verbe et d'une érotique* (Montpellier: Université Paul Valery "Collection lo gatros," 2003) as well as Arnaud de la Croix, *L'éroticisme au Moyen Âge: le corps le désir l'amour* (Paris: Tallandier, 1999). Nietzsche himself corroborates this erotic dimensionality in a note where he affirms the "Provençale" as a "highpoint" in European culture just because they were "not ashamed of their drives" (KSA 10, 256). Despite the appeal of identifying Nietzsche's "immortal beloved" with Lou (and the question of Nietzsche's love affair with Lou is something else again) or else for tracing his passions for the boys of southern Italy (as some have speculated), it is more likely that the addressee of the love songs of Nietzsche's "gay science" would have been Cosima Wagner. I say this last not because I am personally especially persuaded of Cosima's charms as such but because of the very nature of the gay science. The ambiguous coding of the troubadour's message was exoteric, specifically for public display: a love song in the direct presence of the beloved's husband, who, for good measure, would also be one's own patron. See for a study of this coding, Paul Zumthor, *Langue, texte, énigme* (Paris: Editions du Seuil, 1975).

4. In Nietzsche's notes we find the variant titling: "Studies of every kind/to 'the gay science'/ *(la gaya scienza)*" (KSA 9, 681).

5. Goethe's *Singspiel* from 1784 was originally set to music by Goethe himself in collaboration with the composer Philipp Christoph Kayser in 1785 but never performed in Goethe's day. The title was suggested to Nietzsche by Paul Rée. Heinrich Köselitz, who had promised to dedicate any publication to Rée, finished a comic opera of the same name at the time of Nietzsche's own writing. Beyond Rée, the theme was quite popular. Thus although E. T. A. Hoffman wrote stage music for Goethe's *Singspiel* in 1799, I find it more significant that in 1858, Max Bruch had composed one of his first compositions, music for a comic opera with the same title, using Ludwig Bischoff's abridged version of Goethe. Wagner for his part, composed music for Goethe's *Faust* and this is perhaps relevant to (but hardly the reason for) Nietzsche's allusions to *Faust* in *The Gay Science* and elsewhere.

6. KSA 12, 150. See BGE, §260 and KSA 11, 547 and 551.

7. KSA 11, 547; cf. GS, *Songs of Prince Vogelfrei*; EH, *GS*.

8. For a discussion of this secrecy, see the discussion of *trobar clos* in Elizabeth Aubrey et al.,"Les troubadours," *Guide de la Musique du Moyen Âge*, dir., Françoise Ferrand (Paris: Fayard 1999), p. 263. For a Lacanian interpretation of this coding, see Alexandre Leupin, "L'événement littérature: note sur la poétique des troubadours," in *What is Literature?* eds. F. Cornilliat et al. (Lexington, KY: French Forum, 1993), pp. 53–68.

9. Aubrey, "Les troubadours," p. 259. Due to its non-subjective quality, the same anti-lyrical (i.e., a-personal) lyricism absorbed Nietzsche's interest in *The Birth of Tragedy*. See BT §5.

10. The *tenso* is regarded as the model for scholastic reasoning. See Aubrey et al., "Les Formes" in Ferrand, *Guide de la Musique du Moyen Âge*, p. 335. Part of the justification for this association is Peter Abelard's compositions, compositions that Heloise recalls to him as seductively enchanting and that, as he himself tells us in his own reflections on his "calamities," were channeled into philosophy. Although Abelard's secular songs have been lost, apart from his own allusions and Heloise's recollection of them to us, his sacred songs have been transmitted.

11. The character of nobility is a primordial one for Nietzsche: as inventors of the ideal of love as "passion," Europe "almost" owes its very being (BGE §260) to these "knight-poets."

12. As listed in translation: *"Albas*—Morningsongs; *Serenas*—Evensong; *Tenzoni*—Battlesongs; *Sirventes*—Songs of praise and rebuke; *Sontas*—Songs of Joy; *Laïs*—Songs of Sorrow" (KSA 9, 574).

13. There was thus a medieval tradition of stylized joy (Monty Python gives as good a sense of this as any), and it may be compared to Nietzsche's characterization of Greek (and Germanic) cheerfulness in his notes. Invoking this medieval tradition as animating the art of the troubadour at least since the eleventh century, Roger Dragonetti defines "the spirit of '*jonglerie*' " as that "which makes poetic language into the magic instrument of all the mirrors reflecting its myth." For Dragonetti, the energy of the common people's tongue is expressed in this tradition: "the development of the common language, the flowering of which is accomplished by rhythm and music accompanied by a kind of gleefulness where laughter moves from bantering to sniggering, even including mockery without language ever losing its rights to the sovereignty of play and the pleasure that it secures." Dragonetti, *Le gai savoir dans la rhétorique courtoise: Flamenca et Joufroi de Poitiers* (Paris: Éditions du Seuil, 1982), p. 13. Dragonetti reads the "*gai savoir*" (the orthography of which he continuously varies in his text) via an association with Nietzsche, explicitly invoking Dionysian revelry: "It is absolutely clear that in the concept of *gay saber*, transported by the Dionysian basis of '*joy*,' the courtly poet celebrates in jubiliation and rapture [*ravissement*], assuming an consummately playful, facetious, and pleasing dimension, for which abundant proof may be found in courtly poetry. It has thus seemed necessary for us to insist on these aspects of the *gaya sciensa*, qualities which have for at least two centuries governed an entire rhetorical tradition of lyric as well as narrative literature, the language of which is essentially expressed by the rhythm of contradiction" (Ibid., 15). There is much to be explored here with regard to Nietzsche's conception of rhetoric and metaphor but also parodic form.

14. Marcel Decremps suggests this associative connection in his *De Herder et de Nietzsche à Mistral* (Toulon: L'astrado, 1974).

15. Joachim Köhler, among others, has made the case for this claim, but it is complicated because, as David B. Allison and Marc Weiner have also shown, another argument for a similarly shameful eroticism, namely autoeroticism, can also be made, indeed Nietzsche's couplet joke about the physiology of masculine life seems to allude to this (nor is it not irrelevant that tales of Kant's sex life play upon the same physiological fact of life): "Steh ich erst auf Einem Beine/Steh ich balde auch auf zweien" (KSA 9, 686). See Köhler, *Zarathustra's Secret: The Interior Life of Friedrich Nietzsche*, trans. Ronald Taylor (New Haven: Yale University Press, 2002), Allison, *Reading the New Nietzsche* (Lanham, MD: Rowman & Littlefield 2001), Weiner, "The Eyes of the Onanist or the Philosopher Who Masturbated" in *Wagner and the Anti-Semitic Imagination* (Lincoln: University of Nebraska Press, 1995), pp. 335–347.

16. See for context, Allison, *Reading the New Nietzsche*, p. 154, citing Nietzsche's EH, Z, §7.

17. Nietzsche's letter to Overbeck: Christmas Day, 1882. See Allison, *Reading the New Nietzsche*, p. 115.

18. Despite Nietzsche's clear specification of the intrinsic desires and motivations of knowledge, it is hard to imagine a stronger denunciation of the usual financial motivations of research scholarship than Nietzsche's, although Weber and Heidegger come close. Gold in *The Gay Science*, lightly and *gaily* enough, turns out to be a metaphor for the sun: shining rippling gold on the water (GS §337; GS §339) but it also has other resonances for Nietzsche as we encounter it in the parodic and presaging image of Zarathustra's morning song, as an overflowing vessel: "Bless the cup that wants to overflow in order that the water may flow golden from it and everywhere carry the reflection of your bliss. Behold, this cup wants to become empty again" (GS §342). Readers intrigued by this imagery may wish to read Richard Perkins, "A Giant and Some Dwarves: Nietzsche's Unpublished Märchen on the Exception and the Rule," *Marvels and Fairy-Tales: Journal of Fairy Tale Studies*, 11/1–2 (1997): 61–73.

19. Martin Heidegger, *Nietzsche, Volume II: The Eternal Recurrence of the Same*, trans. David Farrell Krell (San Francisco: Harper & Row, 1982), p. 20. Hereafter cited as N2 in the text. See the following for further discussion.

20. I use the term "grey science" for reasons of acoustic contrast. Nietzsche refers to the color grey, even silver grey, as one among his many declared preferred colors and in particular does so in the context of overextended (and limited) scholarship. Thus we hear him in BGE 14 as well as in his color of preference for the dawn of positivism. And he invokes the same color of almost Hegelian darkness or grey in order to challenge the limitations of neo-Kantianism with regard to the very limits of reason itself built upon the most superficial preconceptions, calling it a philosophy of grey conceptualizing. But Nietzsche can also invoke a grey of context and differentiation, what may be called a hermeneutic grey, as he remarks in an arch reference to Paul Rée in his preface to *On the Genealogy of Morals*, serves to outline "the whole, long hieroglyphic text, so difficult to decipher of humanity's moral past!" (GM §v). This grey of

shades and differentiations makes a pencil sketch or pen and ink drawing more precise than the most colorful photograph for scientists concerned with pragmatic details, as in a medical handbook.

21. Nietzsche's *Thus Spoke Zarathustra* begins with a dawn song *(Albas)* exemplifying another of Nietzsche's master song cycles, in addition to the instantiation of, and ironic variation upon, the more typical troubadour's dawn song (which was traditionally more a song sung less to greet the new day than to mourn the close of the alliances of the night, as the hours steal into the claims of the day) in the *Songs of Prince Vogelfrei*, "Song of a Theocritical Goatherd."

22. "Anyone who recalls the immediate effects produced by this restlessly advancing spirit of science will recognize how myth was destroyed by it, and how this destruction drove poetry from its natural, ideal soil, so that it became homeless from that point onward" (BT §17).

23. "If we are correct in ascribing to music the power to give birth to myth once more, we must also expect to see the spirit of science advancing on a hostile course toward the myth-creating force of music" (Ibid.).

24. This refers to the *Leys d'Amor*—laws of love—a work compiled in Toulouse by seven troubadours who established the *Académie littéraire de Toulouse ou Consistoire du Gai Savoir*, a group that transmitted the poetic code of the *Gay Saber (gay saber/ gai saber/gaia scienza*—the orthography varies as Dragonetti has illustrated in *le gai savoir dans la rhétorique courtoise*). See Olivier Cullen's entry in Ferrand, *La Musique du Moyen Âge*, p. 279. On the relation to law, see Peter Goodrich, "Gay Science and Law," in *Rhetoric and Law in Early Modern Europe*, eds. Victoria Kahn and L. Hutson (New Haven: Yale University Press, 2001), pp 95–125.

25. See previously noted references regarding the troubadours as well as, more broadly, Leo Treitler, *With Voice and Pen: Coming to Know Medieval Song and How It Was Made* (Oxford: Oxford University Press, 2003). See too Elizabeth Aubrey, *The Music of the Troubadours* (Indianapolis: Indiana University Press, 1996) and, for a discussion of the distinction between vocal and unaccompanied song in the context of the tradition of musical accompaniment, Christopher Page, *Voices and Instruments of the Middle Ages* (Berkeley: University of California Press, 1976), as well as, again, Zumthor, *Langue, texte, énigme*.

26. Eugen Fink, *Nietzsche's Philosophy*, trans. Goetz Richter (Athlone: Aldershot, 2003) offers one overview of Nietzsche's "artist's metaphysics." See for further discussion in English as well as additional references, Babich, "Nietzsche's 'Artist's Metaphysics' and Fink's Ontological 'World-Play,' " *International Journal of Philosophy*. In press.

27. Nietzsche attempts several articulations of this, for example, where he writes one variation upon the same expression in *The Birth of Tragedy*. "Logic as artistic conception: biting itself in its own tail thus it opens a portal to the world of myth. Mechanism, the way science turns into art 1: at the periphery of knowledge, 2: beyond the pale of logic" (KSA 7, 224; cf. BT §15).

28. Nietzsche reflects on the ancient and the churchly consilience—to use E. O. Wilson's insulating term—of the thought of science or knowledge as a mere means. The idea of science (or knowledge) as an intrinsic good is, Nietzsche writes, very specific to modernity. See on this point, GS §123.

29. Nietzsche continues to explain this passion as the passion of one "who steadfastly lives, must live, in the thundercloud of the highest problems and the weightiest responsibilities (and thus in no way an observer, outside, indifferent, secure, objective . . .)" (GS §351). The passion of this quite Nietzschean vocational ideal influenced not only Max Weber, who is usually associated with it, but Martin Heidegger as well.

30. Heidegger emphasizes that Nietzsche's "gay science" is not casually "gay," but a passionately cheerful knowing, "invigorated" rather than destroyed by the most "questionable matters" (N2, 22). Heidegger thus reads the thought of the eternal return as Nietzsche's most terrifying or questionable thought, placing it at the heart of *The Gay Science*.

31. And thus numerous commentators tell us that Nietzsche was a fan of "real" science, even if, as they also hasten to inform us, he was ignorant of much of it, an ignorance commentators take to be standard. New research, especially Robin Small's *Nietzsche in Context* (Aldershot: Ashgate, 2001), should change this assessment. See too the contributions featured in Gregory Moore and Thomas Brobjer, eds., *Nietzsche and the Sciences* (Aldershot: Ashgate, 2004).

32. See Aubrey et al., "Les Troubadours," pp. 277–279.

33. See Deborah Steiner, *The Crown of Song: Metaphor in Pindar* (Oxford: Oxford University Press, 1986), pp. 35–36ff.

34. The *planh* is the troubadour song sung to lament the death of the singer's "master" or protector (see Ferrand, *La Musique du Moyen Âge*, pp. 351–352 for a definition of this song and an account of its usually political, and satirical, transformations). In this way, although the setting of Nietzsche's Venice poem in his *Ecce Homo*, "On the Bridge . . ." is twilight and thus would seem to be a plain evening song, it may also be regarded as a lament for Wagner, who died in 1883. The 1886 poem, "My Happiness" [*Mein Glück!*], included in the *Songs of Prince Vogelfrei* would also seem to make reference to this death. The poem begins, citing Kaufmann's translation here: "The pigeons of San Marco I descry / Again: Calm is the square, still signs of dew. / It's mild and cool, Like swarms of pigeons, I / Send up my songs into the blue—. . ." and concludes "Begone, O Music! Give the shadows time / To grow into a brown, mild night and doze! / It is too early in the day to chime: / The golden ornaments have not turned rose, / The day is not holding back: Still time to prowl, talk to oneself, and rhyme—My happiness! My luck!" I offer a further discussion of Nietzsche's Venice poem in chapter 7, including its association with Wagner and internal to the context of Nietzsche's recollection of Hölderlin.

35. An interest in the science of the "future" likewise constituted Nietzsche's abiding concern throughout his creative life.

36. As noted previously, R. Kevin Hill has rightly called attention to the presentist confidence that speaks in all speculation upon Nietzsche's reading of Kant. See Hill, *Nietzsche's Critiques: The Kantian Foundations of His Thought* (Oxford: Oxford University Press, 2003). As Hill notes, such claims depend upon the coincidence of Nietzsche's reading with the critic's own. Hill does not develop this point further and this author wishes that he had. For the assumption that Nietzsche was familiar with Kant's critical philosophy turns out to be no less

grounded than the assumption, as I have emphasized this, that he "could not have been" so acquainted. The present author remains convinced that such familiarity on Nietzsche's part would have been no less taxing than, say, his reading of Schopenhauer or Diogenes Laertius, or, for that matter, Heraclitus. Once more: one does not need to claim that Nietzsche could not possibly have read Kant just because he does not come to the same conclusions as, for example, Jerry Schneewind. If I myself do not agree with the things Schneewind says about Kant, my disagreement does not give me license, although it may tempt me to do so, to conclude that Schneewind could not have read Kant nor even that Schneewind fails to understand him. By instructive contast, David B. Allison addresses the substantive issues common to both Nietzsche and Kant while steering clear of speculation on whether Nietzsche read or did not read Kant. See Allison, "Nietzsche Knows No Noumenon," in *Why Nietzsche Now? Boundary Two*, ed. Daniel O'Hara (Bloomington: Indiana University Press, 1985), pp. 294–310.

37. These critical roots, derived from Kant, are the very critical spirit of critical theory especially as found in the work of Adorno and Horkheimer but also Slavoj Žižek. See too, in connection with Paul Reé, Robin Small, *Nietzsche and Reé: A Star Friendship* (Oxford: Oxford University Press, 2005).

38. For Nietzsche, Kant's critical philosophy, conceiving "space, time and causality as entirely unconditioned laws of the most universal validity," demonstrated that these same concepts "really served only to elevate the mere phenomenon . . . to the position of the sole and highest reality, as if it were the true essence of things" (BT §18).

39. See for a further elaboration of this thematic discussion, Babich, "Nietzsche's Critique of Scientific Reason and Scientific Culture: On 'Science as a Problem' and 'Nature as Chaos' " in Moore and Brobjer, eds., *Nietzsche and Science*, pp. 133–153. See also Babich, *Nietzsche's Philosophy of Science*.

40. See Hume, "Of the Standard of Taste" in *Hume's Essays: Moral, Political, and Literary* (Oxford: Oxford University Press, 1965), pp. 231–255.

41. The collective or systematic dimension of *Wissenschaft* distinguishes it from science in English usage.

42. And still further from the collective ideal of a unified coordinate science of everything as Heidegger invoked it and as German ears can hear it, we note, at least in English but increasingly in all languages, the singularizing paradigm, as it were, of the natural sciences, particularly physics, as prototypical for the meaning of "science" as such.

43. Nietzsche argues that "the sole causality of which we are conscious is that between willing and doing—we transfer this to all things and signify for ourselves the relationship of two alterations that always happen simultaneously. The *noun* is the resultant of the intention or will, the *verb* of the doing. The animal as the creature that wills—that is its essence." (KSA 7, 482). See also GS §112.

44. Digitalization, the engineering of a digital musical reproduction, would have been endlessly fascinating to Nietzsche's Helmholtzian sensibilities, as perhaps still more so would be the new marketing techniques and the engineering design field of "sonic branding." For the latter, see Daniel Jackson, ed., *Sonic*

Branding (London: Macmillan, 2004) and, for the former, Freeman Dyson, "When is the Ear Pierced," in *Immersed in Technology*, eds. Mary Anne Moser and Douglas MacLeod (Bloomington: Indiana University Press, 1999), pp. 73–101.

45. Like the problem of the "music" of ancient tragedy (as argued in chapters 2 and 3 above, this is Nietzsche's ruling problem throughout his life), the problem of the "gay science" thus turns out to be the problem of the "music" of the troubadours' songs. The performative parallel to the Homeric problem is clear. There are thousands of preserved songs—and this is only part of the originally greater song tradition, recorded centuries after its heyday—and only a fraction of these preserved songs have written indications of musical melodies. An intriguing application of digital analysis offers some support for Nietzsche's own conviction that the words themselves constitute the "music." See Ineke Hardy and Elizabeth Brodovitch, "Tracking the Anagram: Preparing a Phonetic Blueprint of Troubadour Poetry," in *The Court Reconvenes: Courtly Literature Across the Disciplines*, eds. Barbara A. Altman and Carleton W. Carroll (D. S. Brewer, 2003), pp. 199–211. The authors use the computer's capacity for phonetic analysis not by relying on transcription into modern linguistic phonetic conventions but invoke instead Robert Taylor's observation that "Old Occitan is largely phonetic; that is, in most cases, the spelling reflects the actual pronunciation" (in T. J. McGee et al., eds., *Singing Early Music: The Pronunciation of European Languages in the Late Middle Ages and Renaissance* [Bloomington: Indiana University Press, 1996], pp. 103–118, here p. 105). The literally phonetic quality of Provençal (as opposed to modern French) makes it possible to teach computers "to 'hear.'" Note that Nietzsche's usage in *Thus Spoke Zarathustra*, Prologue 5 inverts Aristotle's reference to the use of proportional metaphor in his *Rhetoric* for helping one's hearers "see" (Rhet. B III: 10, 11).

46. Nietzsche's sensibility here is intriguingly in accord with Paul Feyerabend's reflection on Galileo and his historical context. See Feyerabend, "Galileo and the Tyranny of Truth," in *A Farewell to Reason* (London: Verso, 1987), pp. 247–264.

47. For this etymology, see pp. 12–13 in Paul Zumthor, "Why the Troubadours?" in *A Handbook of the Troubadours*, eds. F. R. P. Akehurst and J. Davis (Berkeley: University of California Press, 1995), pp. 11–18.

48. See also Nietzsche's early *Nachlaß* note: "We speak as if there were *existent things* and our science speaks only of such things. But an existing thing exists only in terms of the *human perspective*: which we cannot dispense with. Something becoming, movement as such, is *utterly* incomprehensible for us. We move *only existent things*—out of this our worldview is formed in the mirror. If we think the things away, the movement goes too. A moved force makes no sense—for us" (KSA 9, 309; cf. GS §110).

49. "The body is a great reason, a multiplicity with one sense, a war and a peace" (KSA 4, p. 39). Thomas Common uses "sagacity" to render *Vernunft*, R. J. Hollingdale has "intelligence" and Walter Kaufmann, perfectly correctly in this case, translates *Vernunft* as "reason" in its exactly philosophical sense, where Nietzsche continues: "The tool of your body is also your little reason, my brother,

which you call 'spirit,' a little tool and play toy of your great reason." With even more Kantian clarity, we hear: "There is more reason in your body than in your reason" (KSA 10, 4[240]). Nietzsche thus sets the body in contrast to the intellect, our "four-square little human reason" [*viereckigen kleinen Menschenvernunft*] in the materialist context of empirical science (GS §373).

50. Thus and exactly where Nietzsche speaks of a joyful science he is also careful to avoid the simple opposition between science and art, by insisting on a new kind of art: "another kind of art—a mocking, light, fleeting, divinely untroubled, divinely artificial art, that like a bright flame, blazes into an unclouded sky! Above all: an art for artists, only for artists!" (GS §iv).

Chapter Five

1. This chapter takes up but also departs from (as a tribute to the suggestive force of) Alexander's Nehamas's "How One Becomes What One Is," *The Philosophical Review* 92/3 (July 1983): 385–417. For Nehamas, his own essay also developed beyond its original contours into his pathbreaking and highly influential *Life as Literature* (Cambridge: Harvard University Press, 1985). This essay was originally conceived as a lecture given at a meeting of the Friedrich Nietzsche Society in Great Britain. For an earlier version of this essay, foregrounding translation in addition to ethical questions, see "Nietzsche's Imperative as a Friend's Encomium: On Becoming the One You Are, Ethics, and Blessing," *Nietzsche-Studien* 33 (2003): 29–58.

2. Pindar, *Olympian Odes; Pythian Odes*, ed. and trans. William H. Race (Cambridge: Harvard University Press, 1997).

3. See Glenn Most, *The Measures of Praise: Structure and Function in Pindar's Second Pythian and Seventh Nemean Odes* (Göttingen: Vandenhoeck & Ruprecht, 1985) but see also any other discussion of Nietzsche and Pindar. Subsequent reviews seem to follow Most's interpretation (whether directly or coincidentally is unclear to me) but it is important to add that in this text, Most, for his own part, has almost nothing to do with Nietzsche.

4. There is in fact more than one elision that one might worry about and on more than one level. Thus scholars have noted (and I mention it only in passing, as it cannot be here addressed), a second and separate problem regarding the rendering of γένοιο as *become*. In the drama of elision it is thus relevant that this very phrase is missing from Michael Theunissen's study of Pindar and time—this in a book of 989 pages. Theunissen includes a footnote suggesting that the omission was intended to deflect the history and the literature that has centered around this one, detached phrase at more than one contextual remove. See Theunissen, *Pindar* (Munich: C. H. Beck, 2000), p. 12, note 13. This anxiety would seem to be due to those who read Pindar in Foucault's voice as a command to realize one's fullest potentiality for the self (if not, of course, for being): expressed in literary terms as the art of living, the art of life itself. See Wilhelm Schmid, *Philosophie der Lebenskunst* (Frankfurt am Main: Suhrkamp, 1998) and for the classical roots of this ideal, Pierre Hadot,

Philosophy as a Way of Life, trans. Michael Chase (Chicago: University of Chicago Press, 1995).

5. See Race's translation of Pindar, *Olympian Odes; Pythian Odes*, p. 239.

6. J. E. Sandys' earlier Loeb translation of Pindar, originating in 1915, reprinted in 1978, although less pithy than Race's version, also captures the complex meaning of Pindar's Greek.

7. *Archaic Greek Poetry: An Anthology*, selected and trans. Barbara Fowler (Madison: The University of Wisconsin Press, 1992), p. 279.

8. R.W.B. Burton, *Pindar's Pythian Odes: Essays in Interpretation* (Oxford: Oxford University Press, 1962), p. 121.

9. Burton emphasizes the ambiguity of reading the supposed Castor song as a "free offering, and uncommisioned ode," or "merchandise ordered by the king." By contrast, Most highlights the "expensive" quality of Pindar's poems, mirroring Burton's emphasis on Pindar's own expression: "like Phoenician merchandise." See Burton, *Pindar's Pythian Odes*, p. 122. A review of the metaphorical *value* of "cheap" poetry/prose is here at stake and I am aware of several studies that make a general attempt to parse these distinctions. To begin with, see Deborah Steiner's study of Pindar, The *Crown of Song: Metaphor in Pindar* (Oxford: Oxford University Press, 1986). On the philosophical significance of this "value judgment," see Marcel Hénaff, *Le Prix de la vérité: Le don, l'argent, la philosophie* (Paris: Le Seuil, 2002), as well as, and closer to antiquity, Richard Seaford, *Money and the Early Greek Mind: Homer, Philosophy, Tragedy* (Cambridge: Cambridge University Press, 2004).

10. Burton, *Pindar's Pythian Odes*, p. 121. Burton is careful, after following his own excursus justifying the line as beginning a didactic supplement, to note that Pindar's maxim requires still further reflection. Thus he claims (in order to oppose an alternative translation option, "discover and live up to your values," which Burton hears as closer to Polonius and Laertes and in which we can hear the late Allan Bloom and Michel Foucault), "It is safer to suppose that the words mean, quite literally, 'be what you are having learnt what you are.' " Burton, *Pindar's Pythian Odes*, p. 125.

11. Nehamas, *The Art of Living: Socratic Reflections from Plato to Foucault* (Berkeley: University of California Press, 1998), p. 128.

12. We have already seen certain elements of this rhetorical dimensionality in the preceding chapters. The theme is complicated not only in terms of Nietzsche's original reflections on the nature of ancient rhetoric in his teaching and thinking, but also in terms of the history of ideas. See, for one overview of this issue, Heinrich Niehus-Pröbsting, "Ästhetik und Rhetorik in der 'Geburt der Tragödie,' " in *Nietzsche oder «Die Sprache ist Rhetorik»*, eds. J. Kopperschmidt and H. Schanze (Munich: Fink, 1994), pp. 93–107. It is important to keep in mind that Douglas Thomas, *Reading Nietzsche Rhetorically* (New York: The Guilford Press, 1999) takes a distinctively contemporary rather than classicist's approach to the question of Nietzsche's rhetoric. For a contrast, see Silk and Stern's complementary emphasis on Nietzsche's antique contextuality in *Nietzsche on Tragedy* (Cambridge: Cambridge University Press, 1981), an emphasis also on

offer in Sandor Gilman, David Parent, and Carol Blair in their introduction to their selection of Nietzsche's writings on ancient rhetoric, *Nietzsche on Rhetoric and Language* (Oxford: Oxford University Press, 1989). In addition to Sarah Kofman's *Nietzsche and Metaphor*, trans. Duncan Large (Stanford: Stanford University Press, 1994), see also in this same direction as conscientiously representative of this antique tradition, Angele Kremer-Marietti's books, especially her *Nietzsche et la rhétorique* (Paris: Presses Universitaires de France, 1994) and Adrian del Caro, "Nietzsche's Rhetoric on the Grounds of Philology and Hermeneutics" *Philosophy and Rhetoric* 37/2 (2004): 101–122.

13. See Stanley Rosen for an example. Glenn Most likewise alludes to this attributed misreading but engages Nietzsche only indirectly.

14. Ulrich Wilamowitz-Möllendorff, "Zukunfts-Philologie!" in *Der Streit um Nietzsches «Geburt der Tragödie»*, ed. Karlfried Gründer (Olms [Reprint Edition]: Hildesheim, 1989), in English as "Future Philology," trans. Gertrude Pöstl, Babette E. Babich, and Holger Schmid, *New Nietzsche Studies* 4:1/2 (2000):1–32.

15. James Porter's *Nietzsche and the Philology of the Future* is more carefully or reflectively provocative in tone and substance than his *The Invention of Dionysus*. Originally part of the same manuscript, both volumes were published in 2000 by Stanford University Press.

16. I have detailed the relevant distinctions between the word "science" in English (and French) and Nietzsche's use of *Wissenschaft* in the preceding chapter. For further discussion of the difference such a reflection on Nietzsche's understanding of science inevitably makes for any approach to Nietzsche's philosophy of science as such, see the first chapter and throughout, Babich, *Nietzsche's Philosophy of Science: Reflecting Science on the Ground of Art and Life* (Albany: State University of New York Press, 1994).

17. Nietzsche seems to allude to Wilamowitz when he writes, "As I lay sleeping, a sheep grazed upon the ivy wreath on my brow—grazed and said 'Zarathustra is a scholar no more.' Said it and strutted proudly away. A child told it to me." *Z*, "On the Scholars."

18. See my discussion of Heidegger's language in the context of the internal disputes of contemporary philosophy: Babich, "On the Analytic-Continental Divide in Philosophy: Nietzsche's Lying Truth, Heidegger's Speaking Language, and Philosophy," in *A House Divided: Analytic and Continental Philosophy*, ed. C. G. Prado (Amherst, NY: Humanity Books, 2003), pp. 63–103.

19. The tradition of obscurity is a complicated one (as one finds it not only in Pindar but most notoriously in ancient philosophy in thinkers such as Heraclitus or Empedocles). Glenn Most in his *The Measures of Praise* advances the case for an enlightened perspective that shakes off such epithets in their literal rendering by means of what was at the time of its publication (1985) still the latest mode of structuralist textual analysis. From the side of comparative literature, however, this discussion proceeds apace in John T. Hamilton's *Soliciting Darkness: Pindar, Obscurity, and the Classical Tradition* (Cambridge, MA: Harvard University Press, 2003).

20. See, for a preliminary discussion, Race's introductory comments on his translation of Pindar, *Olympian Odes, Pythian Odes,* citation previously given in note 2, pp. 26ff. as well as his "Negative Expressions and Pindaric ΠΟΙΚΙΛΙΑ," *Transactions of the American Philological Association* 113 (1983): 95–122.

21. Charlie Louth, *Hölderlin and the Dynamics of Translation* (Oxford: Legenda, European Humanities Research Centre, 1998), p. 135.

22. See Heidegger, *Hölderlin's Hymn "The Ister,"* trans. William McNeill and Julia Davis (Bloomington: Indiana University Press, 1996), pp. 63. [*Hölderlin's Hymne "Der Ister," Gesamtausgabe 53* (Frankfurt am Main: Vittorio Klostermann, 1984), p. 76.] Heidegger's comment is made in the course of a recollection of his long-standing hermeneutic reflections on translation (as interpretation) and vice versa: "every interpretation, and everything that stands in its service, is a translation." Patently, Heidegger continues a tradition that includes both Nietzsche and Hölderlin.

23. Louth, *Hölderlin and the Dynamics of Translation,* p. 8. Emphasis added.

24. Louth cites the original phrasing as follows, "jeder Uebersetzer muss immer an einer der beiden Klippen scheitern, sich entweder auf Kosten des Geschmacks und der Sprache seiner Nation zu genau an sein Original, oder auf Kosten seines Originals zu sehr an die Eigenthümlichkeit seiner Nation zu halten"—Letter from Wilhelm von Humboldt to August Wilhem Schlegel, 23 July 1796. In Louth, *Hölderlin and the Dynamics of Translation,* pp. 5–6.

25. " 'Ein Räthsel ist Reinentsprungenes. Auch / Der Gesang kaum darf es enthüllen. Denn / Wie du anfingst, wirst du bleiben, / So viel auch wirket die Noth / Und die Zucht, das Meiste nämlich / Vermag die Geburt / Und der Lichtstrahl, der / Dem Neugebornen begegnet.' Hölderlin" (KSA 7, 711). Nietzsche cites Hölderlin, *Der Rhein.* StA 2, p. 143. Given in translation in Friedrich Hölderlin, *Poems and Fragments,* trans. Michael Hamburger (Cambridge: Cambridge University Press, 1980 [1966]), pp. 410–411.

26. In addition to *Sonnenuntergang* (see preceding note), Nietzsche also cites "Sokrates und Alkibiades," "Wer das Tiefste gedacht, liebt das Lebendigste."

27. Hölderlin, *Sämtlicher Werke,* D. E. Sattler (Frankfurt am Main: Roter Stern, 1975), P2, p. 130.

28. See Hölderlin's poem, "Lebenslauf."

29. Nehamas, "How One Becomes What One Is," p. 411.

30. Ibid., p. 416.

31. Yet the self-aggrandizing image of Nietzsche is a staple for a popular and literary tradition of reading (or better still, merely invoking) Nietzsche. Nor is this a postwar phenomenon: Heidegger too takes his point of departure contra Nietzsche's subjectivism. And recent instances abound. I argue for greater nuance in my essay, "Habermas, Nietzsche, and the Future of Critical Theory: Irrationality, Will to Power, and War," in Babich, ed., *Habermas, Nietzsche, and Critical Theory* (Amherst, NY: Humanity Books, 2004), pp. 13–40.

32. The full text on the gravestone runs, "FROG NIT NOCH MIR / WER ICH BIN GEWE / SEN GEDENCH WER / DU BIST UND AUCH / WIRST WERDEN" and is signed "DER EDELL UND VEST RUODOLPH VON RUOST MDCVI."

33. Janz tells us that Nietzsche had failed to join the battalion in Berlin that would have been his first choice, and was accordingly stationed in Naumberg where, as Janz reminds us in his biographical account, Nietzsche had already learned to ride as an adolescent. See C. P. Janz, *Friedrich Nietzsche*, Volume I (Hanser: Munich, 1995/Zweitausendeins, 1999), pp. 223–223.

34. From a letter Nietzsche writes to Rohde in Hamburg on the 3 November 1867. Nietzsche, *Sämtliche Briefe: Kritische Studienausgabe* (Berlin: de Gruyter, 1986), Bd. 2 September 1864–April 1869. Janz comments on this point as a sign of Nietzsche's affirmative claim of friendship for Rohde as the "Freund seines Lebens." Janz, *Friedrich Nietzsche*, Volume 1, p. 227. A similar notion appears in Nietzsche's *Thus Spoke Zarathustra*, "On Marriage," where Nietzsche asks "Bist du der Siegreiche, der Selbstbezwinger, der Gebieter der Sinne, der Herr deiner Tugenden?"

35. " 'Werde der, der du bist': das ist ein Zuruf, welcher *immer* nur bei wenig Menschen erlaubt, aber bei den allerwenigsten dieser Wenigen überflüssig ist" (KSA 8, 340).

36. It is relevant that Nietzsche writes this note to himself following a scathingly scornful comment on nationalist sentiment: "Wer das fremde Blut haßt oder verachtet, ist noch kein Individuum, sondern eine Art menschliches Protoplasma" (KSA 9, 555).

37. As a welcome contribution to the now substantial literature that has grown up around the idea of Nietzsche and "the friend," David Allison's discussion in his *Reading the New Nietzsche* (Lanham, MD: Rowman & Littlefield, 2001) sidesteps the reification of the notion of "the" friend. See for a broader reading (in addition to Curt Paul Janz's biographical contextualization), Hubert Treiber, "Wahlverwandtschaften zwischen Nietzsches Idee eines 'Klosters für freiere Geister' und Webers Idealtypus der puritanischen Sekte: Mit einem Streifzug durch Nietzsches 'ideale Bibliothek,' " *Nietzsche-Studien* 21 (1992): 326–362. See too, in connection with Paul Rée, Robin Small, *Nietzsche and Rée: A Star Friendship* (Oxford: Oxford University Press, 2005).

38. Wilhem Schmid has recently taken a Foucaultian interpretation of this trope to this extent in his recent, *Mit sich selbst befreundet sein* (Frankfurt am Main: Surkamp, 2004).

39. This is one of the unimpeachable insights of Alasdair MacIntyre's discussion of the theme of virtue in *After Virtue* (Notre Dame, IN: Notre Dame University Press, 1972) and his *A Short Introduction to Ethics* (London: Macmillan, 1966).

40. I again emphasize the influence of MacIntyre's analysis of virtue on my reading of Nietzsche. This acknowledgment does not mean that my interpretation coincides with MacIntyre's but it does mean that I find MacIntyre's emphases complex in important ways (far beyond and apart from what would appear to be straightforward criticisms—or misprisions?—of Nietzsche).

41. For an alternative reading and for the important emphatic reminder that the Overman makes no such appearance and serves no such function in Nietzsche's *Thus Spoke Zarathustra*, see Allison, *Reading the New Nietzsche*, chapter 3.

42. Plato used this opposition to create ideal being—the true world beyond all becoming. More recently, after the true world, as Nietzsche recounts it, had become a fable, existential perspectives played with the same opposition to articulate the ambiguity of (latterly existentialist) being: you are not what you are (as becoming) and you are what you are not (as becoming).

43. See Allison's discussion of this recollective contrast in his section entitled "Memories" in *Reading the New Nietzsche*, pp. 150–153.

44. Sarah Kofman, *Explosion I: De l' «Ecce Homo» de Nietzsche* (Paris: Galilée, 1992), pp. 26ff.

45. Nietzsche's words are: "Meine Lehre sagt: so leben, daß du wünschen mußt, wieder zu leben ist die Aufgabe—du wirst es jedenfalls! . . . Es gilt die Ewigkeit!" (KSA 9, 504).

46. I develop these points later in chapter 9.

47. And from the first moment of creation, benediction is a song of blessing or naming or calling things good. Yet what remains as the often unacknowledged stumbling block in all such arts of living and writing the self is the need for love. That is the need to learn love, which is also to say to learn to see that things are good, the necessary art or science of joy, in order to love life itself, that is, with respect to one's own life in its immediacy—"here and now and in little things" as Heidegger expresses it.

48. The ground condition *par excellence* for all genuine creation is the consciousness of creative limit and impotence. I hear this (and as Erich Heller has also affirmed) in Nietzsche's note from 1884–85 where he declares that "die Ehrfurcht vor Gott ist die Ehrfurcht vor dem Zusammenhang aller Dinge und Überzeugung von höheren Wesen als der der Mensch ist . . . Der Künstler ist Götter-Bildner . . ." (KSA 11, 341).

49. This is Nietzsche's key insight into the meaning of the doctrine of "redemption," or Salvation, as anti-life: "The principle of Christian love: it wants to be well *paid*" (AC §45).

50. Wilamowitz first challenges Nietzsche's account of the Greeks and their relation to nature (and to sexuality) with a crude allusion to impotence in the epigraph from Aristophanes affixed to his review and explicitly thematized in his conclusion: "thus the phallus is no phallus: 'the unconcealed and vigorously magnificent characters of nature' (8, 61/58), neither do the Greeks, the eternal children, laugh at grotesque obscenities. No: 'the Greeks used to contemplate with reverent wonder (the sexual omnipotence of nature).' " Wilamowitz, "Future Philology," *New Nietzsche Studies* 4:1/2 (2000): 20. See the translation of this epigraph on p. 1 (and see also my editor's note ii).

Chapter Six

1. See especially Martin L. West, *Ancient Greek Music* (Oxford: Clarendon Press, 1992), as well as Warren D. Anderson, *Music and Musicians in Ancient*

Greece (Ithaca: Cornell University Press, 1994) and for a perspective including the culture of ancient Rome: Giovani Comotti, *Music in Greek and Roman Culture*, trans. Rosaria V. Munson (Baltimore: The Johns Hopkins University Press, 1977). In addition, see Lewis Rowell, *Thinking About Music: An Introduction to the Philosophy of Music* (Amherst: The University of Massachusetts Press, 1983); Wesley Trimpi, *Muses of One Mind: The Literary Analysis of Experience and Its Continuity* (Princeton: Princeton University Press, 1983); and, rather more rigorously, A. M. Dale, "Words, Music and Dance," in Dale, *Collected Papers* (Cambridge: Cambridge University Press, 1969), pp. 156–169.

2. Peter Kingsley does not quite make this identification, but Kingsley is also past express statements to the exoteric beyond the esoteric (that is, even beyond the Straussian). See Kingsley, *In the Dark Places of Wisdom* (Inverness: Golden Sufi Press, 1999). See chapter 10 in this volume for Nietzsche's use of chaos, and for a study of Parmenides, see P. A. Meijer's, *Parmenides Beyond the Gates: The Divine Revelation on Being, Thinking, and the Doxa* (Amsterdam: Gieben, 1997).

3. This dialogical hermeneutics is attendant upon the reader's capacity to hear for Nietzsche, as for Leibniz, Kant, Hegel, Wilhelm von Humboldt, Hölderlin, and so on. The notion of concinnity that is in evidence in Nietzsche's writing presupposes nothing less than a responsive voice on the reader's part, as the one for whom the text is written, as the one who can hear what is said. I understand the oral tradition of philosophy, the so-called acroamatic tradition in this sense.

4. Definitions and source references quoted here from *An Intermediate Greek-English Lexicon, Founded Upon the Seventh Edition of Liddell and Scott's Greek-English Lexicon* (Oxford: Clarendon Press, 1889), p. 520.

5. Ibid.

6. Giovanni Comotti, *Music in Greek and Roman Culture*, trans. Rosaria V. Munson (Baltimore: The Johns Hopkins University Press, 1977), p. 5.

7. Again, I have appropriated Thrasybulos Georgiades' German orthography. Georgiades, *Musik und Rhythmus bei den Griechen: Zum Ursprung der abendländischen Musik* (Hamburg: Rowohlt, 1958), pp. 52–53.

8. Georgiades, *Musik und Rhythmus bei den Griechen*, p. 45. Note that as Anderson is contrasted with Georgiades, Anderson refers to "heard" music in his *Music and Musicians in Ancient Greece*, opposing the "amateur musician" (qua performer) to the theorist or philosopher.

9. This Nietzschean ideal is also Georgiades' practical ideal. See Georgiades, *Musik und Rhythmus bei den Griechen*, p. 45. See Nietzsche's lectures on Greek Rhetoric as well as those on Greek music-drama in addition to his didactic reflections on the "future" of educational institutions.

10. Georgiades, *Music and Language: The Rise of Western Music as Exemplified in the Settings*, trans. Marie Louise Göllner (Cambridge: Cambridge University Press, 1982 [1974]), p. 133–134.

11. For Georgiades in *Music and Language*, "The art of the Western World presupposes something which lies outside its own boundaries. . . . Similarly, the poetry of the Western World presupposes simple prose as its ultimate source . . . ," (134). Gadamer echoes this distinction in his *The Relevance of the Beautiful*.

12. Georgiades, Ibid. Earlier in the same text, Georgiades had introduced this translator's problem as a seductive compound (which he nonetheless identifies as an unbridgable "gulf" between foreign antiquity and the intimately known conventionality of modernity: "It is inaccurate to translate *musiké* as *music*, for these two terms designate two different things. *Musiké* cannot be translated; and yet the word lives on its Western transformation as music," (6–7).

13. Ibid., p. 134. Georgiades' point here is not dissimilar to claims that may be heard (with the same content albeit articulate from the opposite direction) in Arthur Danto's discussion of the "end" of art, see in particular Danto's own retrospective reflections in *After The End of Art* (Princeton: Princeton University Press, 1997). See for a specific discussion of the applicability of the notion of art in antiquity, Lawrence E. Shiner, *The Invention of Art: A Cultural History* (University of Chicago Press, 2001), chapter 1.

14. Anderson, *Music and Musicians in Ancient Greece*, p. 143.

15. In general terms, we can say that μουσική, what Georgiades call *musiké* for the sake of our Anglo-Saxon, is indefinable precisely because it functions only within the complex of ancient Greek culture. For this reason Dale could write that "Classical Greek needed no Wolfian doctrine of 'poetic supremacy' because song, with its dance, [i.e., music] was a function of the words themselves when they were alive—that is in a performance." To say this is not to make music a Hanslickian reserve. For Dale, the performance as such, itself an epiphany of Greek culture and its communal foundation, demanded everything society had to offer it. As a performance, the musical event, the event of "words, music and dance," required a staging and a consummate celebration: "one great occasion in all its bright splendour, its ἀγλαΐα, round an altar, or in the orchestra, or processionally. . . . With the passing of the kind of society which required and supported public performances of this kind, the living art of this supple polymetry soon perished; it shrank and petrified into the words on paper, so unskillfully preserved that even the proper ordering of the phrases quickly faded from memory." Dale, "Words, Music, Dance," p. 168.

16. Egert Pöhlmann and Martin L. West, eds., *Documents of Ancient Greek Music, The Extant Melodies and Fragments Edited and Transcribed with Commentary* (Oxford: Clarendon, 2001).

17. West, *Ancient Greek Music*, pp. 1–7, particularly p. 7.

18. See Babich, "Postmodern Musicology," in *Routledge Encylopedia of Postmodernism*, eds. V. E. Taylor and C. Winquist (London: Routledge, 2001), pp. 153–159.

19. Georgiades, *Music and Language*, pp. 4–5.

20. Ibid.

21. See chapter 1 in this volume. For this reason, Nietzsche challenges the ideal of the subordination of words to music as decadence in both antiquity (post-Euripides) and modernity.

22. Georgiades, *Musik und Rhythmus bei den Griechen*, p. 48. The political question that can be posed against any philosophical text after the unspeakable (now: in the antique Greek sense) experience of the Second World War—or whether on its basis a Hitler could or could not be countenanced—as the ethical

touchstone that rates a Levinas above a Heidegger, becomes a somewhat more fruitless one on this reading. Ernst Bertram confirms this ethical dimension in his study, *Nietzsche: Versuch einer Mythologie*, pp. 106–116, but also p. 43.

23. According to Theon of Smyrna, the Pythagoreans called "music the harmonization of opposites, the unification of disparate things, and the conciliation of warring elements. . . . Music, as they say, is the basis of agreement among things in nature and of the best government in the universe" *(Mathematica* I). Theon in *Greek Mathematical Works, II: From Aristarchus to Pappus*, trans. Ivor Thomas (Harvard, MA: Loeb, 1941).

24. "Damon," as Rowell writes, "one of Socrates' teachers [a distinction he shared with Pericles as Plutarch tells us], was one of the earliest authors to suggest a specific conception between music and the formation of the human character." Rowell, *Thinking About Music*, p. 51.

25. See for a contemporary discussion of the issues at stake, beyond the likewise relevant current debate on performance practice, Lydia Goehr, *The Imaginary Museum of Musical Works: An Essay in the Philosophy of Music* (Oxford: Oxford University Press, 1992).

26. Socrates' literary "silence" is also what saves him from stasis. As Adorno writes, "music and literature alike are reduced to immobility by writing." Theodor Adorno, *Quasi una Fantasia*, trans. Rodney Livingstone (London: Verso, 1992), p. 295.

27. The gentleman's club or (male) biased conviction that Socrates' marriage to Xanthippe was nugatory is opposed to circumstances: Socrates, once a student of the priestess of love and hetaira, Diotima, was, even at his age, married and, likewise at his age, blessed with *young* sons—the very ones referred to in the *Apology* under the guise of not mentioning their vulnerability or their youth. (If his marriage was doubtless a hardship, the trouble would have been largely on Xanthippe's side, given the breadless pursuit that occupied his time. From the Greek perspective, a marriage limited to the expression of intimate relations was routine. The fantasies of conversation had to wait for George Bernard Shaw's arch allusions to Shakespeare.)

28. The command was literal enough: "O Socrates, make and practice music" *(Phaedo* 60e). We may assume that the god of the dream could be named Apollo, as we are justified in so doing by way of metaphor (as the dream-god par excellence) or else metonymy (the Apollo who held state-executions in abeyance for the duration of his feast).

29. The ironic point is that in a Platonic scheme, such a routine rendering of "real" music or poetic composition necessarily limits the poet to the unreal world of myth or fable. The joke equates Aesop with Apollo. In a standard (and musical) joke, we are told that Socrates resembles Marsyas, the Satyr paired with Apollo in musical contests.

30. See Ernest G. McClain, *The Pythagorean Plato* (York Beach, Maine: Nicolas Hays, 1984).

31. West, *Ancient Greek Music*, p. 14. West refers to Socrates' tutelage in the lyre on p. 26, citing Plato, *Euthydemus* 272c.

32. Richmond Y. Hathorn, *Greek Mythology* (Lebanon: American University of Beirut, 1977), p. 162.

33. The contrast between the world of images and the world of ideas, between pious petition in the face of bodily sickness (Asklepius) and the new program of scientific theoretical medicine represented by the followers of Hippocrates deserves further investigation.

34. Curt Paul Janz, "Nietzsche Verhältnis zur Musik seiner Zeit," *Nietzsche-Studien* 7 (1978): 308–26.

35. See, for example, Paul Loeb, "The Dwarf, The Dragon, and the Ring of Recurrence: A Wagnerian Key to the Riddle of Nietzsche's Zarathustra," *Nietzsche-Studien* (2003): 91–113.

36. I have elsewhere spoken of *concinnity* to explore Nietzsche's reader-directed compositional or writing style in music and, more generally, see Jan La Rue, *Guidelines for Style Analysis* (Michigan: Harmonie Park Press, 1992, 1997). Concinnity is a rhetorical term employed by Cicero *(Orator* 19.65; 24.81; 25.82) and Seneca and by Alberti in a musico-architectural context (see note 37 in this chapter). Concinnity is also used as a term for facilitating concourse in urban transportation studies and has been utilized in descriptions of Hindu ethics. In a mechanical extension, Graeme Nicholson uses the term concinnity in a tooled sense to express the fitting and jointure of Heidegger's use of the German *Fug* or *Fügung*, as in the joiner's mortise and tenon but also in terms of the fitting of the organs of human sexual expression, Nicholson, *Illustrations of Being* (Atlantic Highlands: Humanities Press, 1992), pp. 272–273. The explication of the Derveni Papyrus likewise finds a musical or harmonious sense in sexual intercourse: "Aphrodite and Zeus (and to aphrodise and to jump) and Persuasion and Harmony are established as name for the same god. A man mingling with a woman is said by common usage to aphrodise. For when the things that are now were mixed with one another, it was called Aphrodite. And persuasion because the things that are yielded to one another: and 'yield' and 'persuade' are the same. And Harmony because . . . she fitted together . . . to each of the things that are" (Col. XXI). Laks and Most, "A Translation of the Derveni Papyrus," in *Studies on the Derveni Papyrus*, eds. Laks and Most (Oxford: Clarendon Press, 1997), p. 19. Compare with Gabor Betegh's religiously minded translation in his *Derveni Papyrus*.

37. According to Vitruvius, music was among the essential formational requisites for the practice of architecture, and listed the following desiderata: "Let him be educated, have skill with a pencil, . . . have followed the philosophers with attention, understand music . . ." (1.1.3). Such a knowledge of music was useful for practical (mostly military) reasons, "Music, also, the architect ought to understand so that he may have knowledge of the canonical and mathematical theory, and besides be able to tune *balistae, catapultae,* and *scorpiones* to the proper key" (1.1.8), where the "correct note" heard by the skilled workman served as a kind of acoustic level. The same understanding would ensure the sounding proportions of theatres together with the "bronze vessels (in Greek ἠχεῖα) which are placed in niches under the seats in accordance with the musical intervals on mathematical principles. These vessels are arranged with a view to musical concords or harmony . . ." (1.1.9), where such an arrangement evidently served to amplify the actor's voice. Vitruvius's assumption of the importance of music for architecure is echoed in Alberti's claim that the intellectual edification

is inspired by "lines and figures pertaining to music and geometry," *(De re aedificatoria*, VII, chap. 10, cited in Rudolf Wittkower, *Architectural Principles in the Age of Humanism,* [New York: Norton, 1971], p. 9). Wittkower explores the role of "Harmonic Proportion in Architecture" and Palladio's conventions in particular at critical length. For Wittkower, Alberti's claim can only be understood if we recall that for Alberti, "music and geometry are fundamentally one and the same; music is geometry translated into sound, and that in music the very same harmonies are audible which inform the geometry of the building" (Ibid.). Robin Maconie, a music critic captivated by the literal interpretation of such a notion, is more emphatic than Wittkower when he declares that "the Palladian interior can be considered in precisely the same terms as a recording studio" (save that the studio designer generally seeks to avoid the very eigentones Palladio sought to generate). Maconie, *The Concept of Music* (Oxford: Clarendon, 1990), pp. 160ff. Wittkower however notes that such resonant notions for the theory of proportional design is out of style, where he cites the substance of Julien Guadet's critical reserve in *Eléments et théorie de l'architecture,* concerning "je ne sais quelles propriétés mystérieuses des nombres ou, encore, des rapports comme la musique on trouve entre les nombres de vibrations qui déterminent les accords." For Witttkower, if Guadet's sobriety is beyond reproach, the problem remains: " *'Les proportions, c'est l'infini'*—this terse statement is still indicative of our approach. That is the reason why we view researches into the theory of proportion [*that is: musical or harmonic proportion*—BB] with suspicion and awe. But the subject is again very much alive in the minds of young architects today, and they may well evolve new and unexpected solutions to this ancient problem." Wittkower, p. 154.

   38. Alberti writes: "Atque est quidem concinnitas munus et paratio partes, quae alioquin inter se natura destinctae sunt, perfecta quadam ratione constituere, ita ut mutuo ad speciem correspondabat." *De re aedificatori libri decem* IX/5 (1962, 815). Cited by Paul von Naredi-Rainer, *Architektur & Harmonie, Zahl, Maß und Proportion in der abendländischen Baukunst* (Köln: Dumont, 1982), p. 23. In this same context, beyond the reference to urban transport and Hindu ethics (note 36), Naredi-Rainer refers to Luigi Vagnetti's comprehensive investigation of the word *concinnitas* and its verbal affinities, which apparently may be taken as far as the word *cocktail.* See Vagnetti, "Concinnitas, riflessioni sul significato di un termine albertiano," *Studi e documenti di architetura* 2 (1973): 139–161.

   39. I illustrate this point with regard to the philosophy of science and the epistemic and methodological significance of Nietzsche's thought for this tradition in Babich, *Nietzsche's Philosophy of Science.* By contrast, I here attempt to illustrate the musical (philosophical) reading of an aphorism in opposition to a "flat" or literal approach, one that—as we have seen in the previous chapter—Nietzsche would likely have dubbed all-too "grey."

   40. See Augustine, *Confessions,* Book XI.

   41. Archilochus, *Elegies,* 5. See M. L. West, *Iambi et Elegi Graeci* (Oxford: Oxford University Press, 1955) and, for the English translation cited, M. L. West, *Greek Lyric Poetry* (Oxford: Oxford University Press, 1994), p. 14.

   42. Archilochus, *Elegies,* 6.

43. Although this is not Eduardo Marx's conclusion, see his *Heidegger und der Ort der Musik* (Würzburg: Königshausen & Neumann, 1998).

44. George Steiner, *Heidegger, Heidegger* (The University of Chicago Press: Chicago, 1987 [1978]) p. 10, cf. p. xiii.

45. Steiner, *Heidegger*, p. 10.

46. Ibid., p. 43.

47. Ibid.

48. Ibid., p. 44. Here, the conclusion Steiner reaches is dependent on Heidegger—"We take the being of music for granted as we do that of the being of being. We forget to be astonished," p. 45.

49. See further, Babich, "A Musical Retrieve of Heidegger, Nietzsche, and Technology: Cadence, Concinnity, and Playing Brass," *Man and World* 26 (1993): 239–260.

50. Heidegger does not live the "life" of a musician as Nietzsche may be said to have lived it but this has been used against Nietzsche and industrious Wagnerians have other offerings in addition to the nicely resentful, Manfred Eger, *"Wenn ich Wagnern den Krieg mache": Der Fall Nietzsche und das Menschliche, Allzumenschliche* (München: Knaur, 1991).

51. Heidegger, "Language," in *Poetry, Language, Thought*, trans. Albert Hofstadter (New York: Harper & Row, 1971), p. 198. Subsequently cited in the text as L, followed by the page numbers.

52. Heidegger, *Being and Time*, trans. John Macquarrie and Edward Robinson (New York: Harper & Row, 1962). Subsequently cited in the text as SZ, followed by the page numbers.

53. Heidegger, WT, p. 85.

54. Adorno, *Gesammelte Werke*, ed. R. Tiedemann (Frankfurt: Suhrkamp, 1970–86 [20 volumes]), vol. 11, p. 57. Translation as cited in Rolf Wiggershaus, *The Frankfurt School: Its History, Theories, and Political Significance*, trans. M. Robertson (Cambridge, MA: MIT Press, 1994), p. 528.

Chapter Seven

1. Friedrich Nietzsche, *Frühe Schriften*, vol. 2, ed. Hans Joachim Mette (Munich: Verlag C. H. Beck, 1994), p. 398. (April/May 1864). Cf. Sophocles, *Oedipus Tyrannus,* ed. Sir Richard Jebb (Cambridge: Harvard University Press, 1887), ll. 185–187.

2. Nietzsche writes, "Auch die Sage von dem Tönen der Memnonssäule mag wohl im Grund nichts anders bedeuten. Das Umgekehrte, daß die Wirkung des Tones durch eine Lichtwirkung bezeichnet wird, ist vollständig durchgeführt in unsrer jetzigen musikalischen Terminologie. Sei es daß unsre Sprache [zu] arm ist, um Schattirungen der Toneffekte auszudrücken, sei es überhaupt, daß wir, um die Wirkung von Schällen auf uns einem anderen vor die Seele zu führen, die faßlicheren und beschreibbareren Wirkungen des Lichtes als Medium gebrauchen müssen wir reden von glänzenden, düstern, verschwommenen Harmonien,

während wir in der Malerei von dem Tone des Gemäldes, von seiner Harmonie sprechen." *Frühe Schriften* 2, p. 398 (April/May 1864).

    3. Hölderlin, *Sonnenuntergang* in *Sämtliche Werke: Große Stuttgarter Ausgabe* [StA], F. Beißner, ed., (Vols. I–V) & Adolf Beck (Vols. VI–VII, Vol. VIII with U. Oelmann) (Stuttgart: Cotta, 1943–1985), Vol. 1, p. 259. In English in Friedrich Hölderlin, *Poems & Fragments*, trans. Michael Hamburger (Cambridge: Cambridge University Press, 1966), pp. 64–65.

    4. Ibid. Nietzsche cites Ariel, *Faust II*, l. 4666–4667. Translation from Johann Wolfgang von Goethe, *Faust*, trans. Walter Arndt (New York: W. W. Norton, 1976), p. 119.

    5. Goethe's influence on Nietzsche is an influence shared with every German writer of Nietzsche's own generation, an influence that began during Goethe's own life (including, most famously, the poet Friedrich Schiller). With respect to Goethe's literary importance for Nietzsche, see Erich Heller's insightful account, among the many other studies currently on offer.

    6. Nietzsche traces the metaphor of "brilliant" sound (like hymns that "ring clear") in musical reference as proof of the poverty of language. "Unsre Sprach <zu> arm ist, um Schattirungen der Tonaffekte auszudrücken sei es überhaupt, daß wir, um die Wirkung von Schallen auf uns einem anderen vor die Seele zu führen . . ." (see complete citation in note 2 from FS 2, 398). Nietzsche refers to the same *"correspondenz von Tönen und Farbe . . . Auge und Ohr. . ."* in an earlier note "Ueber das Wesen der Musik" (FS 2, 171–172). Cf. *Die Geburt der Tragödie*, §6 (KSA 1, 48); *Morgenröte*, §426. "Das Scheinende, das Leuchtende, das Licht, die Farbe. . . . Der Ton stammt aus der Nacht.: Die Welt des Scheins hält die Individuation fest. Die Welt des Tons knüpft aneinander: sie muß dem Willen verwandter sein" (KSA 7, 70). "Verstärkung der Miene und Geberde durch den Ton" (KSA 7, 66). See too Nietzsche's short poem from *Songs of Prince Vogelfrei*: "Fort, fort, Musik! Lass erst die Schatten dunkeln / Und wachsen bis zur braunen lauen Nacht! / Zum Tone ist's zu früh am Tag, noch funkeln / Die Gold-Zieraten nicht in Rosen-Pracht, / Noch blieb viel Tag zurück, / Viel Tag für Dichten, Schleichen, Einsam-Munkeln / —mein Glück! Mein Glück!" (KSA 3, 648).

    7. Hölderlin's related poem "Dem Sonnengott" makes this connection clearer: "Und unsre Trauer wandelt, wie Kinderschmerz, / In Schlummer sich, und wie die Winde / Flattern und flüstern im Saitenspiele, // Bis ihm des Meisters Finger den schönern Tön / Entlockt, so spielen Nebel und Träum' um uns / . . ." Hölderlin, StA, vol. 1, p. 258.

    8. Nietzsche's poem has inspired an extremely rich range of commentary. See Ernst Bertram's chapter on Venice in his *Nietzsche: Versuch einer Mythologie* (Berlin: Helmut Küpper, 1918), pp. 286–295 as itself the enduring background context for an ongoing discussion of this poem in the literature, including Sandor Gilman, " 'Braune Nacht': Fr. Nietzsche's Venetian Poems," *Nietzsche-Studien* 1 (1972): 247–270; Wolfram Groddeck, "Ein Andres Wort für Musik: Zu Fr. Nietzsches Venedig-Gedicht," in *Gedichte und Interpretationen*, ed. Hartmut Hartung, bd. 5, pp. 18–32; Roger Hollinrake, "A Note on Nietzsche's 'Gondellied,'

Nietzsche-Studien 4 (1975): 139–143; Kai Kauffman, " 'Gondeln, Lichter, Musik': Fr. Nietzsches 'Venedig'-Gedichte und sein Metaphorischer Umfeld,' *Nietzsche-Studien* 17 (1988): 158–178, see as well Holger Schmid, " 'Nacht ist es': Zum philosophischen Ort von Nietzsches Venedig Gedicht," in *Nietzsche und Italien: Ein Weg von Logos zum Mythos?* (Tübingen: Stauffenberg, 1999). Vivetta Vivarelli, "Empedokles und Zarathustra: Verschwendeter Reichtum und Wollust am Untergang," *Nietzsche-Studien* 18 (1989): 509–536 cites Jürgen Söring's "*Incipit Zarathustra*—Vom Abgrund der Zukunft," [*Nietzsche-Studien* 8 (1979)] as overlooking the parallel between Hölderlin's Empedocles and Nietzsche's Zarathustra ("es entgeht ihm jedoch die Parallele zu Hölderlin, obwohl er ihn mehrmals zitiert" in Vivarelli's note 19, p. 522). Vivarelli's exigent tone is ironic as she herself, although noting Nietzsche's citation of Hölderlin's *Sonnenuntergang* and referring it to the context of Apollo as such, does not raise the question of the relevance of this poem for Nietzsche's own later poem.

9. Hölderlin's poem includes the following two lines: "Doch fern ist er zu frommen Völkern, / Die ihn noch ehren, hinweggegangen" (StA, vol. 1, p. 259).

10. Note Nietzsche's use of the same color in his poem, "Mein Glück, Mein Glück."

11. Nietzsche repeats this emphasis on sounding beams of light or the rays of the sun. It is important to note that in spite of the relevance of Goethe for Nietzsche's thinking, Nietzsche's quotation of Goethe's lines on the clang of sunset would not have the same effect on his thinking in the context of the current reflective resonant response to the poetic word, even taking into account the image employed in Nietzsche's later reference to the *Rig Veda* as prelude to an entire book on the subject of the rising sun or the dawning day in *Morgenröte*.

12. Gilman has an extended reflection on this terminus/concept that Kauffman (see citation for both in note 8) cites by way of an opposing contrast with Groddeck and with further reference to an earlier study by Kai Vietor, "Die Barockformel 'Braune Nacht,' " *Zeitschrift für Philologie* 63 (1938): 284–298. This is the same happiness Nietzsche evokes in a letter to Erwin Rohde and this burnished or "brown gold-wine" or "gold wine grapes" is often associated with fully ripe fruit as we hear in the epigraph to *Ecce Homo*, or the "glowing brown" that is the color of death in *Dionysos Dithyrambs* (KSA 6, 406). This brown appears in Nietzsche's *Thus Spoke Zarathustra* (in the sections "On the Great Longing," "At Midday," or crossing the visual senses with the olfactory as expressed in "The Drunken Song": "A perfume and odor of eternity, a rose-blessed, brown, wine-gold odor of old happiness"), as well as in the poem "Mein Glück" in his *Songs of Prince Vogelfrei* and BGE 255. And, like Hölderlin, Nietzsche also uses the color in connection with women. Also a Wagnerian reference, it may be noteworthy that the brown of the night, in addition to its violet and amethyst overtonality of twilight, recurs, as noted in the OED, in the English compound *brown study*, "a state of mental abstraction or musing; *esp.* reverie."

13. See Ernst Bertram, *Nietzsche: Versuch einer Mythologie* (Berlin: Bondi, 1918), pp. 289–290ff. for a discussion of the complex array of references to Wagner.

14. Cosima Wagner's notes betray an obvious anxiety of influence upon the energies and thoughts of a house philosophy professor.

15. See Hans Werner Bertallot, *Hölderlin–Nietzsche: Untersuchungen zum hymnischen stil in prosa und vers* (Berlin: E. Ebering, 1933; Nendeln/Liechtenstein, Kraus Reprint, 1967).

16. Thus Thomas Brobjer, whose carefulness I admire, nevertheless managed after an early version of this article had appeared in the *Nietzsche-Studien* 2000, to conclude at the end of his own 2001 essay on Hölderlin's influence on Nietzsche that it was not Hölderlin himself or Nietzsche's reading of the poet but rather (and this is by now no surprise) his reading of William Neumann's handbook on Hölderlin. As the considerations suggested here are what can be called an artistic influence, in this case, of an acoustic kind and hence only a matter of recollection or memory, the sources of such influences cannot be localized, pro or con. And yet, as an analogy, it is instructive to reflect that in litigation on creative musical influence, when one composer of popular songs just happens to compose a tune he has heard from another, less well-known songwriter (when one cites well-known songs the citation is obvious and so falls into a different category), judges routinely decide in favor of the first author provided only that one can show that the later author had had occasion to have encountered the first. Nietzsche's verbatim citation of Hölderlin in his notes returns in the echoes of that same poem in his later Venice poem.

17. Henning Bothe likewise overlooks the complexity of Nietzsche's relationship to his own "influences" in his book *«Ein Zeichen sind wir, deutungslos»: Die Rezeption Hölderlins von ihren Anfangen bis zu Stefan George* (Stuttgart: Metzler, 1992). Thus although noting Nietzsche's importance in Hölderlin's literary reception, the influence is reduced to a typically romantic one.

18. Both references are evidenced by later verbatim references in *Thus Spoke Zarathustra*, itself a text recalling Hölderlin in its best tonalities, especially the elevated or transfigured tone to be heard at the end of the second part of Hölderlin's *Hyperion*, see also, Bertallot, *Hölderlin–Nietzsche*.

19. Beyond those authors already cited, I discuss some (but hardly *all*) of these additional studies later.

20. Nietzsche's strategic critique here is usually ascribed to his youth. Commentators are quick to claim Nietzsche's own voice on the side of a necessary sense of humor as a prelude to his ultimate provocative and insouciant image as the "laughing philosopher." But, and contra such a typical conviction of today's enthusiastic Nietzsche scholars, Nietzsche promised less to teach us to laugh (this isn't even Archilochus's promise) than he proposed to his readers the very different challenge of learning to laugh at oneself—"as one would have to laugh," if one were to laugh out of the "whole truth" (GS 1). Nietzsche's laughter is as serious as his reflections on play, that is on music and tragedy. See, a bit later in *Beyond Good and Evil*, Nietzsche's provocative definition of maturity: "Mature manhood: that means to have rediscovered the seriousness one had as a child at play" [*Reife des Mannes: das heisst den Ernst wiedergefunden haben, den man als Kind hatte, beim Spiel*] (BGE 94). Here the emphasis is less on

playfulness or the adult fantasy of the lightness lost in childhood than the ex-traordinarily earnest quality of childhood and its unremitting lack of irony.

21. Names can be generated almost at random (and see also the reflection on the possible motivation for this conviction in the preceding note).

22. Cf. Peter Uwe Hohendahl, ed., *Geschichte der deutschen Literaturkritik (1730–1980)* (Stuttgart: Metzler, 1985). Cf. Bernard Böschenstein, *Leuchttürme: Von Hölderlin zu Celan* (Frankfurt: Insel, 1977); Alessandro Pellegrini, *Friedrich Hölderlin: Sein Bild in der Forschung* (Berlin: de Gruyter, 1965) as well as Ingo Seidler's review " 'Stifter einer weiteren Ahnenreihe': Hölderlin's Influence on Ger-man Poets of the Twentieth Century" in *Friedrich Hölderlin: An Early Modern*, ed. Emery E. George (Ann Arbor: The University of Michigan Press), pp. 64–86.

23. Norbert von Hellingrath, "Hölderlins Wahnsinn" in *Hölderlin: Zwei Vorträge: Hölderlin und die Deutschen: Hölderlins Wahnsinn*" (München: Hugo Bruckmann, 1921).

24. Thus, Gordon A. Craig's *The Politics of the Unpolitical: German Writ-ers and the Problem of Power 1770–1871* (Oxford: Oxford University Press, 1995) repeats David Constantine's claim that in quoting "*Germanien,*" the word "wehrlos" is deleted "in the penultimate line," p. 110. Constantine himself notes that "one specific instance of Nazi abuse of Hölderlin is Hermann Binder's quoting the last lines of this poem with the word '*wehrlos*' omitted." *Hölderlin*, p. 257. In a note to this, Constantine cites Binder's 1940 *Deutschland: Heilig Herz der Völker: Lebenswerte in deutscher Dichtung* while taking care to observe that he himself was acquainted with no edition of Hölderlin's poems doctored in the same way and that in the context of the times such alteration was hardly required.

25. In this way, Craig can express his horror at what he calls the Scylla and Charybdis of the contemplation of Hölderlin as "interpreted by Martin Heidegger and protected by Josef Goebbels." Craig, *The Politics of the Unpolitical*, p. 110.

26. Geerd Lernout reviewing Hölderlin's reception in the nineteenth and twentieth centuries, rightly reminds us that at the time of his own writing, Nietzsche was himself "only a marginal figure" thus the reception of Nietzsche's "comments on Hölderlin would only gain importance after Nietzsche's death"— that is, only after a similarly blocked set of obsctacles to undertanding Nietzsche had themselves been overcome. Lernout, *The Poet as Thinker: Hölderlin in France* (South Carolina: Camden House, 1994), p. 4. Lernout cites Allessandro Pellegrini's not uninsightful claim that the key to Nietzsche's reception of Hölderlin lies in his broader cultural program, the ideal of a return to Greece, betraying what has been called the nostalgia of Germany for Greece (Taminiaux) or the tyranny of Greece over Germany. See also Jacques Taminiaux, *Le nostalgie de la Grèce à l'aube de l'idéalisme allemand* (The Hague: Nijhoff, 1967) and Eliza May Butler's classic *The Tyranny of Greece Over Germany* (London: Macmillan, 1935). For a contem-porary statement, see Suzanne S. Marchand, *Down from Olympus: Archaeology and Philhellenism in Germany* (Princeton: Princeton University Press, 2003).

27. Referring to begin with to Romano Guardini's study of Hölderlin and to Walter F. Otto (more in Hölderlin's own spirit), Hans-Georg Gadamer none-theless claims Heidegger's reading as decisive: indeed, literally so, as Heidegger

"forces us to decide." Gadamer, "Von der Wahrheit des Wortes," in *Dichten und Denken bei Martin Heidegger, Jahresausgabe der Martin-Heidegger-Gesellschaft, 1988*, pp. 7–22. "Thinking and Poetizing in Heidegger's and Hölderlin's *Andenken*," trans. Richard Palmer, ed. James Risser, *Towards the Turn*. (Albany: State University of New York Press, 1999), pp. 145–162. See also Lernout's declaration that "Heidegger's influence on Hölderlin criticism in the fifties and sixties in West Germany cannot be exagerated." *The Poet as Thinker*, p. 13.

28. This in a distant way is responsible for the caution with which scholars refer to Hölderlin *editions*, just because, they tell us, like Beissner's edition, new editions of Hölderlin seem regularly underway—just as Nietzsche's works themselves underwent several different instaurations according to particular visions, and some might argue for yet another editorial venture, or at least a complete edition of the current edition of Nietzsche, in this same spirit.

29. Eckhart Förster, "Preface," Dieter Henrich, *The Course of Remembrance and other Essays on Hölderlin* (Stanford: Stanford University Press, 1997), p. 2.

30. Cited in Förster, "Preface" to Henrich, *The Course of Remembrance*, p. 4.

31. Nietzsche, "wie der Wellenschlag der erregten Meeres" (FS, 2, 2). See, further, Stefan Zweig, *Kampf mit dem Dämon: Hölderlin. Kleist. Nietzsche* (Leipzig: Insel-Verlag, 1925).

32. Förster, Preface to Henrich, *The Course of Remembrance*, p. 4.

33. See, again, Taminiaux, *Le nostalgie de la Grèce à l'aube de l'idéalisme allemand* as well as his recent *Le théâtre des philosophes* (Grenoble: Jérôme Millon, 1995) where Taminiaux discusses in three successive chapters, Nietzsche, Heidegger, Sophocles, and the pre-Socratics, and the shadows of Aristotle in Hölderlin. And, again, see too Butler, *The Tyranny of Greece*.

34. I have earlier discussed the relevance of Golomb and Wistrich's recent collection, *Nietzsche Godfather of Fascism: On the Uses and Abuses of a Philosophy* (Princeton: Princeton University Press, 2002), as the editors situate their selection of essays on Nietzsche, Hölderlin, and Nazism in this ongoing political context. See too their very balanced overview, "Nietzsche's Politics, Fascism, and the Jews," *Nietzsche-Studien* 30 (2001): 305–321. But complexities attend this question, as I emphasize in Babich,"Habermas, Nietzsche, and the Future of Critique: Irrationality, *The Will to Power*, and War," in Babich, ed., *Habermas, Nietzsche, and Critical Theory* (Amherst, NY: Humanity Books, 2004), pp. 13–39.

35. Cf. Reinhard May, *Ex oriente lux: Heideggers Werk unter ostasiatischen Einfluß* (Stuttgart: Steiner Verlag Wiesbaden, 1989), translated into English as *Hidden Sources: East Asian Influences on His Work*, trans. G. Parkes (London: Routledge, 1996).

36. See, again, Golomb and Wistrich, eds., *Nietzsche: Godfather of Fascism*.

37. Like the previous question of Nietzsche's fascism, this issue too is an enduring one, despite Mary Lefkowitz's efforts to bring peace to the politically, disciplinarily intransigent debate that has grown up in the wake of and now settled into a cliché regarding Martin Bernal's controversial *Black Athena* in its postmodern instaurations. In earlier chapters, we have had recourse to Nietzsche's

trope of the "art of fruitful learning" as opposed to the all-too-modern image of the "new."

38. This can lead to a concern with racism adumbrated with reference, of all things, to the "brown" woman of the Garonne—one imagines a similar darkness should be ascribed to the sweet, low woman Nietzsche evokes in speaking of the the kind of woman who reminds him of the music of the south, and the name of Venice (EH, "Why I Am So Clever," 7).

39. As Nietzsche's Zarathustra asks of words and tones: "sind nicht Worte und Töne Regenbogen und Scheinbrücken zwischen ewig Geschiedenem?" And then "Wie lieblich ist alles Reden und alle Lüge der Töne! Mit Tönen tanzt unsre Liebe auf bunten Regenbögen" (Z III, "Der Genesende" 2; KSA 4, 272).

40. Hölderlin, "Letter to Böhlendorff."

41. Heidegger's word is expressed in *Being and Time* as self-appropriation, whereby what Da-sein recovers for the sake of authentic being itself is its own past for the sake of its own possibility. Heidegger's best Hölderlinian expression of the need for such a retrieve is his claim, "That which is ontically closest and well known, is ontologically the farthest and not known at all" (SZ 9).

42. Hence Nietzsche even uses this language for Hölderlin's "Hyperion," "dies Prosa ist *Musik*" (FS 2, 3) contra the "Junonian sobriety" that is supposedly the purest nature of, and so unapproachably nearest nature of, the Germans.

43. "nie treff ich, wie ich wünsche, / Das Maas" Hölderlin, "Der Einzige." It should not be thought that this measure is calculative, be it calculative thinking or some other logical stricture, but commentators have made this claim exactly concerning Heidegger, compelling what should be a manifest qualification.

44. See Philippe Lacoue-Labarthe, *Typography: Mimesis Philosophy Politics* (Cambridge, MA: Harvard University Press, 1989) for this double reflex, which Lacoue-Labarthe, with Reiner Schurmann, names a double bind and traces to Gregory Bateson, and which I call a reflex because it catches the more dynamic structure of the German relation to Greece.

45. Lacoue-Labarthe, "Hölderlin and the Greeks," *Typography*, p. 244.

46. Eugen Fink, *Nietzsches Philosophie*. (Stuttgart: Kohlhammer, 1960).

47. Fink's focus on scientific rigor is crucial. Apart from its debt to Heidegger related understanding of science, Fink's understanding accords with Walter Kaufmann's defense of his own translation of Nietzsche's *Die Fröhliche Wissenschaft*. Kaufmann concentrates on his rendering of *Wissenschaft* not as *wisdom* (as an earlier English translation had done) but *science*, to capture Nietzsche's own Provençal subtitle but also to exemplify the meaning of *Wissenschaft* as such. Yet as we have seen the problem is a persistent one for the Anglo-Saxon reader, especially in the dominant context not only of analytic philosophy but the (real) scientific ideal of (natural) science as such and other translators have recourse to terms like *scholarship*. But the point for Nietzsche, and for Kaufmann, a native speaker struggling with the same problem, is not that philology and physics are both kinds of scholarship but that they are both sciences and in the same scientific fashion.

48. Although James Porter seeks to read Nietzsche from within the classics, he also emphasizes Nietzsche's errors. See especially, Porter, *The Invention of Dionysus* (Stanford: Stanford University Press, 2000).

49. In addition to Wilhelm Dilthey, *Das Erlebnis und die Dichtung* (16. Aufl., Göttingen, 1985) and David B. Allison, *Reading the New Nietzsche*, see too Édouard Gaède, "Figures d'Empédocle" in Gaède, ed., *Nietzsche, Hölderlin, et la Grèce* (Paris: Societé d'Édition «Les Belles Lettres», 1985), pp. 33–40.

50. Nietzsche, "Schopenhauer als Erzieher," §3; KSA 1, p. 350. Later, in his five prefaces to five unwritten books, Nietzsche further describes Empedocles (and Pythagoras) in terms drawn from Hölderlin. Cf. KSA 1, p. 755.

51. Again, there is a clear resonance with Hölderlin.

52. KSA 7, p. 161. It is astonishing but regrettably understandable (given his analytic philosophical or U.K. formation), that the classicist, Peter Kingsley, in his emphasis upon reading Empedocles (in the Apollonian lineage of Parmenides) as a "healer" (like Parmenides for Kingsley), does *not* make reference to Nietzsche's Zarathustra, even in his recent book *In the Dark Places of Wisdom* (Golden Sufi Press) where the story he tells of esoteric healing, secret teachings concerning eternal life, indeed, even including the goddess of life (as Nietzsche calls her) or Persephone as Kinglsey names her, goes so far as to explain the initiate's experience in passages that mirror Zarathustra (laying as one dead, as convalescent, as healer, etc.). Likewise absent is any engagement, and this is more grievous, with Marcel Detienne's reading of Apollo, likewise contra traditional readings, in *Apollo, le couteau à la main*.

53. Cf. Nietzsche, KSA 7, pp. 398, 547, 573, 757, and so on.

54. Thus Karl Reinhardt assesses the common judgment of his profession when he observes drily that "the history of philology has no place for Nietzsche. Moreover, his positive achievements are too few for that . . ."* Jackson P. Hershbell and Stephen Nimis offer the same judgment, if also without irony. See Hershbell and Nimis. "Nietzsche and Heraclitus," *Nietzsche-Studien* 8 (1979): 17–38. See too James Porter, cited previously.

55. If and despite what might appear to be a patent thematic connection, A. W. Pickard Cambridge's 1927 *Dithyramb Tragedy and Comedy* (Oxford: Oxford University Press [1927] 1997) made no reference to Nietzsche, this omission is finally made good and given a plausible and sophisticated, indeed almost postmodern, parsing in Porter's *The Invention of Dionysus*. Reinhardt's more carefully philosophical reflections, although an exception, have proven difficult to incorporate even into the German literature. See Hubert Cančik, *Nietzsches Antike* (Stuttgart: Metzler, 2000) for an overall review. Although Cančik refers to Reinhardt's "Nietzsche und die Geschichte," he is not quite sure what to do with

---

*Reinhardt, "Die klassische Philologie und das Klassische," in *Vermächtnis der Antike: Gesammelte Essays zur Philosophie und Geschichtsschreibung* (Göttingen: Vandenhoeck & Ruprecht, 1960/1989), p. 345.

the putatively more philosophical (less patently philological) essay on the very same thematic: "Nietzsches Klage der Ariadne" (both included in *Vermächtnis der Antike*). Manifestly, Henrichs, Kerenyi, Burkert, and others do offer exceptions to the conservative strain Porter illuminates in his *The Invention of Dionysus*. It is significant that this conservative, philosophically negative account is not foregrounded in Porter's larger and more serious companion publication issued by the same publisher, *Nietzsche and the Philology of the Future*. This recurs in modern literary references as well, as Nicholas Martin cites Schadewaldt,"Der Weg Schillers zu den Griechen war nicht—wie bei Winckelmann, Goethe, Hölderlin—der Weg jenes naiv genialen ereignishaften Ergreifens und Ergriffenwerdens der echten Begegnung." Wolfgang Schadewaldt, "Der Weg Schillers zu den Griechen," *JDS* 4 (1960), pp. 96–97 (p. 90). Cited in Martin, *Nietzsche and Schiller*, p. 103.

56. Wilfried Malsch, "The Concept of Enlightenment in Hölderlin's Poetry," pp. 16–37 in Emery George, ed., *Friedrich Hölderlin: An Early Modern*, makes the claim that Lawrence Ryan comes to qualify if not to recant his own path-breaking 1960 study, *Lehre vom Wechsel der Töne* (Stuttgart: Kohlhammer, 1960), in his later work to the great joy of his critical colleagues. That is, rather than reading Hölderlin on his own or intrinsic terms, Ryan now reads him in the "context" of his time. It can be added that this same reference to one's own era or context, just as it means that more than one reading is possible for the inexhaustible industry of critique likewise entails, in any but a Whiggish or presentist reading of history and context, that the word of the poet cannot be usurped. For a recent reading, see Holger Schmid, "Wechsel der Töne," in *Hölderlin Handbuch: Leben—Werk—Wirkung*, ed. Johann Kreuzer (Stuttgart/Weimar: Metzler, 2002), pp. 118–127.

Chapter Eight

1. Hölderlin, *Sophocles*: "Viele versuchten umsonst das Freudigste freudig zu sagen / Hier spricht endlich es mir, hier in der Trauer sich aus." I have used Michael Hamburger's translation from Friedrich Hölderlin, *Poems and Fragments* (Cambridge: Cambridge University Press, 1980), pp. 70–71.

2. From the conclusion of "Die Heimath": Hölderlin, *Poems and Fragments*, pp. 142–143. See also the second half of "Hälfte des Lebens," ". . . wo nehm' ich, wenn / Es Winter ist. Die Blume, und wo / Dem Sonnenschein / Und Schatten der Erde."

3. Friedrich Hölderlin, *Hyperion and Selected Poems*, ed. Eric L. Santner, trans. Willard Trask (New York: Continuum, 1990), p. 75 (StA 3, 92).

4. Ernest McClain has explored similar metaphors, speaking of brothers and mother in music, with the creative generosity of a musicologist in "A Priestly View of Biblical Arithmetic: Deity's Regulative Aesthetic Activity Within Davidic Musicology," in Babich, ed., *Hermeneutic Philosophy of Science, Van Gogh's Eyes, and God: Essays in Honor of Patrick A. Heelan, S. J.* (Dordrecht: Kluwer, 2002),

p. 429–443. See too McClain's *The Myth of Invariance: The Origins of the Gods, Mathematics and Music from the Rg Veda* (York Beach: Nicolas Hays, 1976).

5. See Nietzsche, BT §3; KSA 7, p. 10 and p. 22; and in general the comment from the notes precising "Sophokles der Dichter der Leiden des agonalen Individuums." See on Nietzsche's physiology of pain, Abraham Olivier's discussion, "Nietzsche and Neurology" in *Nietzsche-Studien* 32 (2003): 125–141. This study is part of Olivier's larger monograph on pain.

6. The insight that put natural philosophers or scientists "on the path of certain progress" for Immanuel Kant was the discovery "that reason only perceives that which it produces after its own design; that it must not be content to follow, as it were, in the leading-strings of nature, but must proceed in advance with principles of judgment according to unvarying laws, and compel nature to reply its questions. . . . Reason must approach nature with the view, indeed, of receiving information from it, not, however, in the character of a pupil, who listens to all that his master chooses to tell him, but in that of a judge, who compels the witnesses to reply to those questions which he himself thinks fit to propose." Kant, KdrV, Preface to the second edition.

7. Simone de Beauvoir, *Second Sex* (New York: Random House, 1989 [1949]), p. ix. De Beauvoir's first chapter began with "The Data of Biology." For this same reason, the publishing house contracted with H. M. Parshley, a biologist, to prepare the translation.

8. According to Gail Eisnitz, *Slaughterhouse: The Shocking Story of Greed, Neglect, and Inhumane Treatment Inside the U.S. Meat Industry* (Amherst, NY: Prometheus, 1997), 400 cattle are slaughtered every hour in every "meat processing plant," 1,100 pigs per hour—150, 000 per week, et cetera. Charles Patterson documents the technological mechanisms required in order to attain such numbers and points out that in the last twenty-five years of the twentieth century, the "number of animals killed rose from four billion to 9.4 billion . . . (more than twenty-five million per day)." *Eternal Treblinka: Our Treatment of Animals and the Holocaust* (New York: Lantern Books, 2002), p. 71.

9. Eisnitz tells us that workers consistently report that animals *cry* on the path to slaughter, that they seek to flee, and scream in the process of slaughter, particularly young ones. See Eisnitz, *Slaughterhouse*. See also, again, the historian Charles Patterson's *Eternal Treblinka*. Patterson takes his title from "The Letter Writer," the short story by Isaac Bashevis Singer: "In relation to them, all people are Nazis; for the animals it is an eternal Treblinka."

10. For a methodic discussion of this theme, see Noelle Viales, *Animal to Edible*, trans. J. A Underwood (Cambridge: Cambridge University Press, 1994).

11. See, again, Eisnitz.

12. The comprehensive character of this involvement even more than the point of complicity is the reason Emerson writes in the section "Fate" of his *The Conduct of Life*, "You have just dined, and however scrupulously the slaughterhouse is concealed in the graceful distance of miles, there is complicity—expensive races,—race living at the expense of race." *The Complete Works of Ralph Waldo Emerson*, vol. 6 (New York: Houghton & Mifflin, 1888 [1860]), p. 534.

13. I quote Claude Bernard here from another context precisely for the sake of its broader philosophic referentiality. See Shiv Visvanathan, "On the Annals of the Laboratory State," in Ashis Nandy, ed., *Science, Hegemony, and Violence: A Requiem for Modernity* (Delhi: Oxford University Press, United Nations University, 1990 [1988]), pp. 257–290.

14. Visvanathan, "On the Annals of the Laboratory State," p. 265.

15. Ibid., p. 266.

16. Luce Irigaray uses this Lacanian convention in her discussion of the question in her essay, "In Science, Is the Subject Sexed?" included in Gary Gutting's collection, *Continental Philosophy of Science* (Oxford: Blackwell, 2005), p. 283–292, here p. 284ff.

17. Here one might look for Visvanathan's *A Carnival for Science: Essays on Science, Technology and Development* (Oxford: Oxford University Press, 2005).

18. Marjorie Spiegel, *The Dreaded Comparison: Human and Animal Slavery* (New York: Mirror Books, 1996).

19. Occasionally such cases find their way to today's headlines (William Frist) but this is hardly the only such example. And of course, "pound seizure" laws that permit animal supply companies to claim rescued animals for the same purposes are only more institutionalized versions of the same thing.

20. Hölderlin, *Hyperion, Sämmtliche Werke*, iii, p. 92. See Beißner's editorial note, p. 469.

21. This is to be seen in the conclusion to both books, culminating in the conclusion cited previously from the second book. For a discussion of musical metaphoricity, see references in note 4 in this chapter.

22. Ibid., *Hyperion*, p. 133.

23. Hölderlin, *The Death of Empedocles*, third version, trans. Michael Hamburger (Cambridge: Cambridge University Press, 1980 [1960]), p. 349. [Geh! fürchte nichts! Es kehret alles wieder. Und was geschehen soll, ist schon vollendet.]

24. Luce Irigaray, *To Be Two*, trans. Monique M. Rhodes and Marco F. Cocito-Monoc (New York: Routledge, 2001), pp. 68ff.

25. Hölderlin, *Hyperion*, p. 35.

26. Ibid.

27. Hugh Lloyd-Jones, "Nietzsche and the Study of the Ancient World," in *Studies in Nietzsche and the Classical Tradition*, eds. James C. O'Flaherty et al. (Chapel Hill: University of North Carolina Press), pp. 1–15; here p. 3.

Chapter Nine

1. One can, for examples, consider the great majority of contributions to analytically styled philosophy of love (or sex for that matter). Such accounts of love and sex are typically written by men. This also may be said of continental approaches to these questions Luce Irigaray in her *To Be Two* [trans. M. Rhodes and M. Cocito-Monoc (New York: Routledge, 2001)]. Luce Irigaray names Jean-Paul Sartre and Maurice Merleau-Ponty and others in her reading of the

difference it makes to write on the matter of eros and love (as indeed on the body and perception) as a woman and by contrast with the perspectives that predominate in the literature. Irigaray's writing (substance and style) illustrates that difference, highlighting the presumption of the male perspective in most accounts. In a Nov. 21, 2004 interview in the *New York Times,* the author Elfriede Jelinek, whose novels explore aspects of the differences between male/ female expectations of love, points out that the sexual difference continues to be one that can be described as "a Hegelian relationship between master and slave." She argues that "as long as men are able to increase their sexual value through work, fame, or wealth, while women are only powerful through their body, beauty and youth, nothing will change." Answering her surprised female interviewer's protests that surely the same would not hold for famous women such as Jelinek, "A woman who becomes famous through her work reduces her erotic value. A woman is permitted to chat or to babble but speaking in public is still the greatest transgression. . . . A woman's artistic output makes her monstrous to men if she does not know how to make herself small at the same time and present herself as a commodity. At best people are afraid of her." And as we shall see later, although I also make reference to Howard Caygill and Tracy Strong, the best reflection on love, in my view, remains Gillian Rose's complex and beautiful *Love's Work* (New York: Shocken, 1977).

2. Certainly the so-called philosophy of sex and love excludes what I am here calling the erotic—that domain of desire that would have to include (as it now does not) the male form rather than being dedicated to the female form. A naked woman turns out (very conveniently for the heterosexual male spectator) to be the erotic signifier *par excellence* for both male and female observers in media depictions of the same. When naked men are represented, the stylization of that representation makes it plain that they are objects of homoerotic desire. The closest thing pop culture offers us is photographic celebrations of ordinarily unattractive and not consummately beautiful men. This erotic conviction supposes that, unlike men, women are unconcerned with male beauty, unable to celebrate male bodies (the nauseating repetition of the manifestly false notion that penis size is irrelevant to a woman's pleasure, in whatever direction), unmoved by male youth. And contemporary love stories almost uniformly show that beautiful women passing over beautiful men for the awkward and unattractive but "sensitive" and often self-preoccupied male hero (Woody Allen's films are comic depictions of the allure of the unattractive man [but exactly not the unattractive woman]) and there are many, many others. It should be clear whose fantasy this might be.

3. For further discussion of this distinction, see Babich, "Towards a Post-Modern Hermeneutic Ontology of Art: Nietzschean Style and Heideggerian Truth," *Analecta Husserliana* 32 (1990): 195–209.

4. I owe this insight—as I owe so much else—to David B. Allison. See Allison's more complex discussion of this theme in the concluding chapter of *Reading the New Nietzsche* (Lanham, MD: Rowman and Littlefield, 2001). For a further elaboration, see Babich, "Habermas, Nietzsche, and the Future of

Critique: Irrationality, *The Will to Power*, and War," in Babich, *Nietzsche, Habermas, and Critical Theory* (Amherst, NY: Humanity Books, 2004), pp. 13–46.

5. Nietzsche begins by speaking of "women" [*die Frauen*], then rephrases the reference as "*Frauenzimmer*," to conclude with the open-ended exclamation: "Das Weib ist so artistisch . . ." (GS 361). Some German speakers have claimed to find this transition unremarkable because it is invisible to them in ordinary language use. But those who argue that Nietzsche's use of the offensive term "*Weib*" is either neutral or just characteristic of his era are engaging in a bit of what can only be called (and this is to be kind) "Karl May philology."

6. The problem of the hysteric as the problem of the artist, actor, woman, Jew corresponds to the *vulgar* nihilism specific to contemporary modernity.

7. Nietzsche, BGE 145. See also BGE 148 and 237.

8. This connection between women and Jews is explored in Klaus Theweleit, *Male Fantasies. Volume 1: Women, Floods, Bodies, History*, trans. Stephen Conway (Minneapolis: University of Minnesota Press, 1987) and can be extended. Indeed, the recent photographic and pornographic torture by American and American-allied military personnel at Abu Ghraib shows that the phenomenon of violent and dangerous fantasies, in this case as part of deliberate interrogation (psychosocial and physical torture), is hardly limited to Germany nor has it ended with the politics of the first two World Wars.

9. We are more sophisticated than the Victorian cycles of nineteenth-century thermodynamics, and if we can correct a simplistic reading of Nietzsche, this could be a useful place to begin. See, for example, Larry Hatab, *Nietzsche's Life-Sentence: Coming to Terms with Eternal Recurrence* (New York: Routledge, 2005).

10. See Nietzsche's expression of the negative philosophical judgment concerning the value of life in TI, "The Problem of Socrates," §1.

11. From such a Platonic standpoint, "becoming" regarded in all its aspects, includes growth and procreation as much as death, persisting in an earthly, sullying process of inconsequent beginnings, obscured innocence, fallen ideals. Thus Aristotle's philosophico-bio-anthropology regarded the basic processes of life as vegetative, lower than animal life and even more incidental to the nature of the human. The most basic processes of life are brutalizing and soulless.

12. I have argued above that Nietzsche associates Heraclitus with Empedocles.

13. See Babich, "Nietzsche's Critical Theory: The Culture of Science as Art," in Babich ed., *Nietzsche, Theories of Knowledge and Critical Theory: Nietzsche and the Sciences I* (Dordrecht: Kluwer Academic Publishers, 1999), pp. 1–26.

14. Heidegger takes his quote from Nietzsche's *Nachlaß*, "Dem Werden den Charakter des Seins *aufzuprägen*—das ist der höchste *Wille zur Macht*," Nietzsche, KSA 12, 312. It should be noted here that Heidegger renders the passage in question as a pro-technological expression. See for a related analysis, Babich, "Heidegger's Relation to Nietzsche's Thinking: On Connivance, Nihilism, and Value," *New Nietzsche Studies* 3, 1/2 (1999): 23–52.

15. I here supply the context of Tracy B. Strong's quotation, which he himself cites as a repeated theme in his own work: "what the world needs is

love." Strong, *Friedrich Nietzsche and the Politics of Transfiguration* (Urbana: University of Illinois Press, 2000, 1975), p. xviii. Strong's point is properly political. Here I am more interested in questioning of the work of love (in the sense, as we shall see later, Heidegger speaks of the work of art) as a working, a practical act of being in the world that is exactly without purchase and hence and ineliminably a working power. This is how I understand "*love's work*," in the suggestive and disquieting spirit of Gillian Rose's book. For another account, see Howard Caygill, "The Consolation of Philosophy or 'Neither Dionysus nor the Crucified,' " *Journal of Nietzsche Studies* 7 Spring (1994): 113–140.

16. It is for this reason, though this surprises no psychoanalysts, that neither Casanova nor Don Juan may be said to "love" women (as some reconstructivist interpretations enthusiastically suggest). Yet I would argue, contra psychoanalysis, that their motivation is misunderstood if we speak of it in terms of "fear" of or even hatred of or whatever else of women *in general* or in particular. Instead such men who pose as those who love women (all of them!) offer trivially streamlined versions of the Platonic ideal. These are the patently impotent philosophasters of the imaginary erotic, very like the ordinary fan of pornography and the fashion photograph. In the same way and for the same reasons, we might as well add here, female porn stars are not "empowered" and prostitutes similarly lack power no matter the literary enthusiasm (and life-blindness) of third-wave feminist affirmations of female-objectification and pragmatic sex-marketing. Nor, should it be necessary to add, do bathroom attendants have "power." One is reminded that these are jobs.

17. The love in question is what Caygill insightfully recasts in terms of the traditional concept of *agape*, in the direct spirit of Rose's elusive *Love's Work* and renewed throughout the complex registers of its changing historic context. Popular music is as full of love talk as ever as well as because we are (from a physiological standpoint: quite beyond the possibility of noticing this, just because this is the way sensual or perceptual accommodation works) continually bombarded by images of sex.

18. Beyond Rilke's *Duino Elegies*, here I refer to Baudelaire's reflections on beauty, "comme un rêve de pierre," in his *Les fleurs du mal*.

19. Max Horkheimer and Theodor W. Adorno, "Elements of Anti-Semitism," trans. John W. Cumming, *Dialectic of Enlightenment* (London: Continuum, 1993), esp. pp. 200ff. See further in chapter 13 above.

20. See for further references, chapter 5 below.

21. Very typically, one might say, given the French fascination with Pygmalion, Jacques Lacan undertook to analyze a statue in order to illustrate the transports of feminine desire. Luce Irigaray pointed out, shades of Hans Christian Anderson, that the analysis could have little do with woman's desire not only because the statue was a man's fantasy but because, ah, it was a *statue*.

22. Nietzsche writes, "kein edelgeborner Jüngling werde, wenn er den Zeus in Pisa schaue, das Verlangen haben, selbst ein Phidias, oder wenn er die Hera in Argos sehe, selbst ein Polyklet zu werden: und ebensowenig würde er wünschen, Anakreon Philetas oder Archilochus zu sein, so sehr er sich auch an

ihren Dichtungen ergetze" *(Fünf Vorredern zu Fünf ungeschriebenen Büchern, Der griechische Staat, §3; KSA 1, 764).*
    23. Cf. GS 71, etc.

Chapter Ten

    1. Nietzsche's conception of chaos differs from today's popular science conceptions as well as from the literary conception of chaos. I argue here that although Nietzsche recognizes the disorder of chaos inherent in the contemporary meaning of chaos, his more antique emphasis underlines the fundamental ambiguity of chaos as a primordially abundant (that is, as a prerequisite for) creation rather than a decadent (entropic) state.
    2. Alain Badiou discusses Nietzsche and dancing in his *Handbook of Inaesthetics,* trans. Alberto Toscano (Stanford: Stanford University Press, 2004).
    3. See David B. Allison's discussion of the meaning of the name of Zarathustra in *Reading the New Nietzsche* (Lanham, MD: Rowman & Littlefield, 2001), p. 116 and, further, note 10 in this chapter.
    4. In section 9 of *On the Uses and Disadvantages of History for Life,* Nietzsche mocks the very notion that chaos is supposed to give birth to its opposite, as greatness is ascribed to the masses: "Da soll die Masse aus sich heraus das Grosse, das Chaos also aus sich heraus die Ordnung gebären." Nietzsche likewise, in the same locus, contrasts the scope of ambition with the impotence of human ability: "Freilich kletterst du an den Sonnenstrahlen des Wissens aufwärts zum Himmel, aber auch abwärts zum Chaos" (KSA I, 315), and he will always stress this tension.
    5. Scholars like Martin L. West remind us that "although grammatically neuter, Chaos is treated as female." See West's commentary to his translation of Hesiod, *Theogony* (Oxford: Clarendon Press, 1966), p. 193. Hugh G. Evelyn-White offers the unqualifying account of Chaos, along with Earth and Eros as "primordial beings" but even Evelyn-White does not sidestep the question of gender as he observes the difficulty of placing Eros in just this regard as Chaos is patently implicated here as disposing over a sure if "indefinite reproductive influence." Evelyn-White, "Introduction," in Hesiod, *Homeric Hymns, Epic Cycle, Homerica,* trans. Evelyn-White (Cambridge: Harvard University Press, 1936 [1914]), p. xxi. Others read Chaos as masculine and this textual ambiguity encourages readings such as Robert Mondi's study of Hesiodic cosmogony. Mondi reads chaos as neutral, underscoring as he does its literal or grammatical value. I recommend Mondi's reading to the extent that he reprises other readings linking Chaos to Anaximander's *apeiron* [unbounded, or indefinite] taking Chaos to represent a positive "unbounded formlessness." See Mondi, "ΧΑΟΣ and the Hesiodic Cosmogony," *Harvard Studies in Classical Philology* 92 (1989): 1–41; here p. 35. In his *The Anger of Achilles: Mēnis in Greek Epic* (Ithaca: Cornell University Press, 1996), Leonard Muellner emphasizes the "indeterminate" or "undifferentiated" sex of Chaos but, and it should go without saying, that gender ambiguity is not the same as the neuter form. Mondi himself adverts to the problem with his own neutered assumption. For Chaos gives birth (indeed in the

arch-female fashion, via parthenogenesis—even Gaia, as Mondi remarks, does not do this beyond the singular [and singularly necessary] genesis of a consort); see pp. 30ff. Mondi may be taking the feminine as the counterpart of the masculine, which male counterpart cannot be found in Chaos, unless Mondi would agree to find that counterpart in the *Aether*, with chaos as misty *Aër*. For a discussion of the elemental complexity of the nature or identification of air (with respect here to Empedocles), see the chapter on "Aether" (and only then the following chapter on "Aer") in Peter Kingsley, *Ancient Philosophy, Mystery, and Magic: Empedocles and Pythagorean Tradition* (Oxford: Clarendon Press, 1995). Note here that although this reference to air is not an overt reference to Luce Irigaray, *The Forgetting of Air in Martin Heidegger*, trans. Mary Beth Madder (Austin: University of Texas Press, 1999), the classical reference to Empedocles offers an essential and only elliptically expressed supplement to Irigaray's own text (if also, indeed, a necessary supplement to Heidegger's pre-Platonic studies). Although Tilman Borsche omits reference to Empedocles in Borsche, "Nietzsches Erfindung der Vorsokratiker," in *Nietzsche und die Philosophische Tradition*, ed. Josef Simon (Würzburg: Königshausen & Neumann, 1985), pp. 62–87, Borsche nevertheless insightfully sets up the rationale for Nietzsche's insistance on regarding the philosophers of the "tragic age" of Greece as pre-Platonic (rather than pre-Socratic) thinkers. For Borsche, the key lies in the conjunction of "philosopher and reformer" (84) and Empedocles, we may recall, played both roles, thus one almost sees his presence in a discussion of Socrates' role against this same legislative conjunction, a political conjunction that found fruit, however decadent and impotent, in Plato.

   6. Although textual evidence is lacking in this same famously sparse Orphic tradition, evidence for reading chaos as the chasm is straightforward, but all scholars advert to the importance of taking it as air; note, for example, the paradigmatic instance for such a reading that wonderful image that first gives us the"messenger of wide-ruling, loud roaring Zeus" the eagle "cleaving the deep aether," then taking flight into chaos: that is, "in the limitless void [*khaos*], he plies with breath of the west wind, his plumage." Bacchylides, *Epinician 5*. Translation modified on the basis of Barbara Fowler's *Archaic Greek Poetry* (Madison: The University of Wisconsin Press, 1992). I note, although it hardly makes matters simpler that the same chasm/chaos is described as the point to which the goddess takes the speaker in Peter Kingsley's mythico-topographical reading of Parmenides' Proem. See Kingsley, *In the Dark Places of Wisdom* (Inverness: Golden Sufi Center, 1999).

   7. This is the reading proposed in Nietzsche's elliptical account of the pre-Platonic philosophers in his unpublished *Philosophy in the Tragic Age of the Greeks*, see in particular section 16 (the very first line), as well as sections 17 and 19.

   8. I note that both Heidegger and Nietzsche regarded such categorizations as symptomatic of what they both called philosophical journalism, as if the designations *pro* or *con* had any place in the philosopher's lexicon.

   9. See Pierre Hadot, *Le voile d'Isis: Essai sur l'histoire de l'idée de Nature* (Paris: Gallimard, 2004). Erwin Chargaff, the late physician and biochemist, drew upon a classical German education to play with this etymology of "nature" in his

book *Voices in the Labyrinth: Nature, Man, and Science* (New York: Seabury Press, 1977), p. 1. In the same context, not unrelated to the theme of Hadot's study, Chargaff also teased us for our modern "belief" in certain scientific progress: "But can we really believe that if we keep on plodding for another 200 years or so, suddenly submicroscopic angels will be seen carrying a sign, 'Now you know all about nature'? Actually, knowledge of nature is an expanding universe, continually creating ever greater circumferences of ignorance, a concept that can be expressed in the words, 'the more we know, the less we know' " (Ibid., p. 5).

10. Scholars dispute the accuracy of this etymology, but it was current in Nietzsche's day and hence it is fairly clear that this etymology is the one Nietzsche had in mind, if it remains tempting to think that he was not unaware of rival etymology of Zarathustra as "herder of many camels," or as himself a camel (the Persian name Zarathustra seems to mean yellow or golden camel).

11. See note 5.

12. Chaos here is uncountenanceable nature and it is significant that Chaos retains an association with blackness, a link that also suggests the Orphic accounting of night as primordial being. See the reference to Aristotle in note 18.

13. See note 5.

14. Hesiod, *Theogony*, 116.

15. Carl Kerenyi, *The Gods of the Ancient Greeks* (London: Thames and Hudson, 1951), pp. 16–17.

16. For references, see, again, note 5.

17. This generatively primordial character is unique. Reviewing the notion of "cosmogonic myth," Walter Burkert distinguishes between *biomorphic* and *technomorphic* models, but both of these are creative models—that is, requiring either reproductive generation (on the analogy Burkert draws, complete with "couples of different sex, insemination and birth" [94–95]) or demiurgic/divine creation. To be sure, Burkert does not distinguish the Greek (although largely characterized by the former) and the biblical tradition (although principally characterized by the latter). Yet the emergence of chaos, appearing as it does at a "time which was the 'first' of all, the one beginning from which everthing else is about to arise" (91), turns out for Burkert to be beyond such "narrative options" (94). "Hesiod asks 'Which of these came into being first?" and then starts: 'First of all . . . ' " (92). See Burkert, "The Logic of Cosmogony" in *From Myth to Reason: Studies in the Development of Greek Thought*, ed. Richard Buxton (Oxford: Oxford University Press, 1999), pp. 87–106. Most accounts of this Hesiodic beginning start (or finish) with this inceptive "abruption."

18. Evidence for this is given by Aristotle, Meta. 1071b 27, who implies that Night is an alternative name for Chaos. See preceding note and compare Burkert's discussion on the same for a different (but not opposed) emphasis.

19. See Luce Irigaray, *The Forgetting of Air in Martin Heidegger*, trans. Mary Beth Madder (Austin: University of Texas Press, 1999).

20. Irigaray's "il y'a" is an unspoken, inexplicit reference to Hesiod in *The Forgetting of Air in Martin Heidegger*. See pp. 17ff. This is a reference insinuated in her almost Lacanianly elusive reference to the substitutive "place of this forgetting. A certain void" (28) or: "She gives—first—air." "She gives first." (28)

Later, one sees an incipient parallel between the mythic account of care *(Cura)* and Chaos: pp. 100ff.

21. See Muellner, *The Anger of Achilles*, pp. 69ff.

22. The fact that Mētis also appears under the sign of androgyny testifies less to the gender fluidity of times past (though it surely does this as well) than it confirms the enduring horror of a primary or coequal female principle. The androgyne is the male who takes over and thus who thereby possesses the qualities of the female, without however, consider Tiresias, being reduced to these.

23. One tends to hear in this an associative reference to the combining hollow of Plato's Timaean *khora* but although the Pythagorean tradition may justify this association, the very conception of a hollow dependent upon the working influence of the demiurge *already* testifies to a condition that is underway to the latter conception of a disordered *order* in need of a restoration of order.

24. Cf. Nietzsche's reflections on reason and rationality in *The Gay Science*. For Nietzsche, philosophy has had a long habit of deifying reason. But Nietzsche is so far from this danger (a Thomistic as much as a Platonico-Aristotelian liability) that he always names reason with belittling appellations, such as "unsrer viereckigen kleinen Menschenvernunft" (GS 373), and he liked to use the most unflattering comparisons—gnats and frogs as companion perspectives to human foci—to make the same point. In a move similar to Augustinian piety, Nietzsche declares that desire (the belly) is the body, is the best antidote to our conviction that we are, or might be, divine. This same move opposes Augustine because, of course, for Augustine (as for Descartes), qua will, it is (of course) desire that proves to constitute our dei-formity. Nor does Nietzsche disagree, if it is true that he changes the deifying emphasis and thereby the reference.

25. Hence Nietzsche declares that the world's manifest congruence with perception evidenced by the overwhelming concord between sensations from person to person proves the congruence of the perceptual and conceptual apparatus from one human being to another as a veritable *sensus communis*. Thus Nietzsche invokes "Der ungeheure Consensus der Menschen über die Dinge beweist die volle Gleichartigkeit ihres Perceptionsapparates" (KSA 7, 468).

26. "Genug," Nietzsche writes, "auch die Wissenschaft thut, was der Mensch immer gethan: *etwas* von sich, das ihm als verständlich, als wahr gilt, zur Erklärung benutzen alles Anderen—*Vermenschlichung in summa*" (KSA 11, 191).

27. "Wissenschaft—Umwandlung der Natur in Begriffe zum Zweck der Beherrschung der Natur—das gehört in die Rubrik 'Mittel' " (KSA 9, 194).

28. Consider Nietzsche's well-known comment in "On Truth and Lie in an Extra-Moral Sense": "What does the human really know of himself! Indeed, he is even once able to perceive himself whole, laid out as if in an illuminate glass case? Doesn't nature conceal from him almost everything, even with regard to his own body, in order to ban and fix him within a proud, fraudulent consciousness, distant from the sinuosity of the bowels, the rapid flood of the bloodstream, the snarl of vibrating fibers! She threw the key away! . . ." (KSA 1, 875; cf. 755).

29. Here, as Nietzsche says, it is important to emphasize that the text does not merely disappear in the reading or beneath the interpretation, but the reader

instead "picks about five words at random out of twenty and 'guesses' at the meaning that probably belongs to these five words" (BGE §192).

30. Ryogi Okochi, "Nietzsches Naturbegriff aus östlicher Sicht," *Nietzsche-Studien* 17 (1988): 108–124.

31. There is a superficial concord between this assertion and Parmenidean presumption, but, contra Parmenides, for Nietzsche, it is the unthinkability of nature that compels the philosopher's attention. More critical than Kant, Nietzsche contends that Nature is neither the coordinate nor the correspondent object of human knowing.

32. Hans Vaihinger's *Nietzsche als Philosoph* (Berlin: Meiner, 1902) or else the appendix to his *Die Philosophie des Als-Ob. System der theoretischen, praktischen und religiösen Fiktionen der Menschheit aus Grund eine idealistische Positivismus: mit einem Anhang über Kant und Nietzsche* (Leipzig: Meiner, 1911) remains, along with Friedrich Kaulbach's *Nietzsches Idee einer Experimentalphilosophie* (Cologne: Böhlau, 1980) the best first approach to a review of such "routine" or standard (which is to say: radical) Kantianism. In addition to Olivier Reboul, *Nietzsche, Critique de Kant* (Paris: Presses Universitaires de France, 1974), see also, R. Kevin Hill, *Nietzsche's Critiques: The Kantian Foundations of His Thought* (Oxford: Oxford University Press, 2003) as well as *Kant und Nietzsche in Widerstreit,* ed. Beatrix Himmelmann (Berlin: de Gruyter, 2005).

33. Nietzsche, KSA 13, p. 371. Cf. Nietzsche's earlier remark as well: "Als ob eine Welt noch übrig bliebe, wenn man das Perspektivische abrechnete! Damit hätte man ja die Relativität abgerechnet, das—" (Ibid.).

34. Nietzsche, KSA 13, p. 373. Nietzsche writes further: "Meine Vorstellung ist, daß jeder spezifische Körper darnach strebt, über den ganzen Raum Herr zu werden und seine Kraft auszudehnen (—sein Wille zur Macht:) und Alles das zurückzustoßen, was seiner Ausdehnung widerstrebt. Aber er stößt fortwährend auf gleiche Bestrebungen anderer Körper und endet, sich mit denen zu arrangiren ('vereinigen'), welche ihm verwandt genug sind:—so conspiriren sie dann zusammen zur Macht. Und der Prozeß geht weiter . . ." (Ibid., 373–374).

35. This aesthetic coincidence Nietzsche names his "Artisten-Metaphysik" (BT §1). See further in this volume, pp. 181ff.

36. I note that God is both more present *and* more absent from today's sensibilities than Nietzsche could have imagined in his announcement of (and for) the Death of God in the requiem composed in *The Gay Science* or parodied in *Thus Spoke Zarathustra* or else as mourned in *Beyond Good and Evil* or even in *The Antichrist.*

37. But, Nietzsche makes this his goal because most perniciously · or exactly nihilistically in the human case, another genre of artlessness betrays a singularly bad conscience, a thoughtless *méconnaissance,* lacking all innocence: as the reactive will that seeks to arrogate the right of interpretation for itself alone and to impose that scheme upon all others, by the expedient of calling its interpretation (its ideal, its vision of God) truth.

38. Viewers have taken the Friedrich painting on his book covers as an actual rendering of Nietzsche himself. This metonymic identification is anything

but a beginner's mistake and this same associative vision of Nietzsche's encounter with nature, represented as a mountain traveler, inspired the producers of a video introduction to Nietzsche's works (alas: more in terms of its incendiary rather than its philosophic dimensions) to begin with a series of aerial shots of mountain climbers on the heights, plodding through the snow. See the BBC video, *Nietzsche: Beyond Good and Evil*, part two of the three part series, *Human, All Too Human* (1999).

39. The citation continues *"In der unzweideutigen Wesensbestimmung der Wahrheit als Irrtum wird die Wahrheit notwendig zweimal und jedesmal anders, also zweideutig gemacht: einmal als Festmachung des Beständigen und zum andern als Einstimmigkeit mit dem Wirklichen. Nur unter Zugrundelegung dieses Wesens der Wahrheit als Einstimmigkeit kann die Wahrheit als Beständigkeit ein Irrtum sein . . . als Angleichung an das Wirkliche und als Einstimmigkeit mit ihm, als ὁμοίωσις bestimmt. . . ."* Heidegger, *Nietzsche I* (Pfullingen: Neske, 1960), pp. 621–620.

40. See, for the classic discussion of Nietzsche's "Artistenmetaphysik," Eugen Fink, *Nietzsches Philosophie* (Stuttgart: Kohlhammer, 1979 [1960]), translated into English by Goetz Richter, *Nietzsche's Philosophy* (Aldershot: Avebury, 2003). Tilman Borsche (previously cited in note 5) also discusses Nietzsche's "Metaphysik der Kunst" (67).

41. Nietzsche writes, "Mit welcher Wucht der Ueberzeugung glaubte dagegen der antike Stoiker an das All und an die Vernünftigkeit des Alls!" (KSA 1, 208).

42. "Rückkehr zur Natur" 1. seine Stationen: Hintergrund christliche Vertrauensseligkeit (ungefähr schon Spinoza 'deus sive natura'!)" (KSA 12, 129).

43. Nietzsche, KSA 9, p. 525; cf. GS III.

Chapter Eleven

1. Pro-modern critiques of nature include C. Alford and Marshall Berman as well as the techno-identified/enthusiast's trends following the Krokers' reading of Donna Haraway, Jean Baudrillard, and indeed—and for better or worse—Paul Virilio and even Bruno Latour. For a critique from the side of political theory, one needs the work of Langdon Winner, *The Whale and the Reactor* (Chicago: University of Chicago Press, 1986). See also Aidan Davison, the Australian environmental philosopher. His book features the advantages of the author's wide-ranging formation, *Technology and the Contested Meaning of Sustainability* (Albany: State University of New York Press, 2001). Davison foregrounds his debts to Val Plumwood, *Feminism and the Mastery of Nature* (London: Routledge, 1993), and some part of Davison's otherwise analytic formation in philosophy may account for the limits in his reading of Heidegger. But Heidegger's reflections on technology are famously difficult and hence this last qualification expresses only a minor regret given the achievements of Davison's book. See also, for a sociologically minded reading, Zygmunt Bauman's *Wasted Lives: Modernity and Its Outcasts* (London: Polity, 2004) and, for biologically informed political reflection (though suspiciously weak

on Heidegger and Nietzsche, which the author apparently takes on the word of his colleagues), John Gray's *Straw Dogs: Thoughts on Humans and Animals* (London: Granta Publications, 2002).

2. As seen in the previous chapter, this conception of chaos follows Nietzsche's own.

3. I explore this question in Babich, "The Essence of Questioning After Technology: *Techne* as Constraint and Saving Power." *British Journal of Phenomenology*. 30/1 (January 1999): 106–124, and, more recently in Babich, "Heidegger *Beiträge zur Philosophie* als Ethik. Phronesis und die Frage nach der Technik im naturwissenschaftlichen Zeitalter," trans. Heidi Byrnes, in *Eugenik und die Zukunft*, eds. Stefan Lorenz Sorger, James Birx, and Nikolaus Knoepffler (Freiburg: Alber, 2006).

4. Hölderlin, "Nature and Art or Saturn and Jupiter." In *Friedrich Hölderlin: Poem and Fragments,* trans. Michael Hamburger, bilingual edition (Cambridge: Cambridge University Press, 1966), pp. 165–167.

5. See for this calculative emphasis, Max Weber's expression of the technological confidence of the modern era in his *Science as Vocation*: "das Wissen davon oder den Glauben daran: Daß man, wenn man *nur wollte*, es jederzeit erfahren *könnte*, daß also prinzipiell keine geheimnisvollen unberechnenbare Mächte gebe . . . die da hineinspielen, daß man vielmehr alle Dinge—im Prinzip—durch Berechnnen beherrschen könne. Das aber bedeutet: Entzauberung der Welt." Weber, *Wissenschaft als Beruf 1917/19: Politik als Beruf,* Wolfgang J. Mommsen and Wolfgang Schluchter with Birgitt Morgenbrod (Tübingen: Mohr, 1992). Heidegger's opposition to the claim that we live in a disenchanted world in his recently published *Beiträge* owes its form to Weber here, and one might be inclined to argue that Heidegger owes his account of modern science in terms of calculation to Weber in these terms.

6. Richard Sieburth, trans., "Introduction," *Hymns and Fragments by Friedrich Hölderlin* (Princeton: Princeton University Press, 1984), p. 17.

7. Hölderlin, "Friedensfeier," in *Friedrich Hölderlin: Poem and Fragments,* pp. 438–439.

8. "*Die Geheimste Gelassenheit.* Gelassenheit fäht GOtt, GOtt aber selbst zulassen / ist ein Galassenheit / die wenig Menschen fassen." Angelus Silesius, *Cherubinischer Wandersmann: Kritische Ausgabe*, ed. Louise Gnädinger (Reclam: Stuttgart, 1982), "Andertes Buch," p. 92.

9. Hölderlin, "Mnemosyne," in Sieburth, ed., *Hymns and Fragments by Friedrich Hölderlin*, pp. 116–117.

10. Ibid. In "Die Titanen" (Sieburth, p. 144). Hölderlin also speaks to the question of interpretation quite directly by speaking to the occasion of inspiration as he speaks to the power of poetic song, and to our dependence on it. ". . . Manche helfen / Dem Himmel. Dieses siehet / Der Dichter. Gut ist es, an andern sich / Zu halten. Denn keiner traegt das Leben allein. ["... Some come to heaven's help. These The poet sees. It is good to lean On others. No one can bear life alone."]

11. "We know now that if the Word 'was in the beginning,' it can also be in at the end: that there is a vocabulary and a grammar of the death camps. . . . It

were as if the quintessential, the identifying attribute of man—the *Logos*, the organon of language—had broken in our mouths." George Steiner, *Le sens du sens: Présences Réeles, Real Presences, Realpräsenz* (Paris: Vrin, 1988), p. 174. Steiner's qualified subjunctive fails the sharpness of his own insight. To say "it were as if" is an error: the *Logos is* so broken and that is what it means to acknowledge a grammar of death. See my discussion in chapter 13 and in Babich, "Questioning Heidegger's Silence," in *Ethics and Danger*, eds. Arleen Dallery and Charles Scott, with P. Holley Roberts (Albany: State University of New York Press, 1992), pp. 83–106..

     12. Stanley Corngold, *The Fate of the Self* (New York: Columbia University Press, 1986), p. 29.

     13. Hölderlin, "Lebenslauf," in Hamburger, ed., *Friedrich Hölderlin: Poems and Fragments*, pp. 148–149.

     14. Hölderlin, "Dichterberuf," Christophe Middleton, trans., in *Hölderlin: "Hyperion" and Selected Poems*, ed. Eric L. Santner (New York: Continuum, 1990), pp. 154–155.

     15. Hölderlin, "Wie wenn am Feiertage," in *Friedrich Hölderlin: Poems and Fragments*, pp. 372–373.

Chapter Twelve

     1. See, for some examples, Andrew McClellan, *Inventing the Louvre: Art, Politics, and the Origins of the Modern Museum in Eighteenth-Century Paris* (Berkeley: University of California Press, 1999), Douglas Crimp, *On the Museum's Ruins* (Cambridge: Harvard University Press, 1993) or Didier Maleuve, *Museum Memories: History, Technology, Art* (Stanford: Stanford University Press, 1999), and Susan MacDonald, ed., *The Politics of Display: Museums, Science, Culture* (London: Routledge, 1998). In connection with aesthetics and the philosophy of art, see Günther Seubold, *Das Ende der Kunst und der Paradigmenwechsel der Ästhetik* (Munich: Fink, 1998), Arthur Danto, *After the End of Art: Contemporary Art and the Pale of History* (Princeton: Princeton University Press, 1997), especially chapters 9 and 10, as well as a recent book by Larry Shiner, *The Invention of Art: A Cultural History* (Chicago: University of Chicago Press, 2001), chapters 6 and 9.

     2. Hans-Georg Gadamer, *The Relevance of the Beautiful and Other Essays*, trans. Nicholas Walker (Cambridge: Cambridge University Press, 1986), p. 19. Hereafter cited as RB.

     3. Martin Heidegger, *Ursprung des Kunstwerkes* (Stuttgart: Reclam, 1960), and in: *Holzwege* (Frankfurt am Main: Klostermann). "The Origin of the Work of Art," trans. Albert Hofstadter, *Poetry, Language, Thought* (New York: Harper & Row, 1971). For a review of the political controversy, see the succeeding references and the further associative context in note 15.

     4. See Robert Bernasconi, "The Greatness of the Work of Art," in *Heidegger in Question: The Art of Existing* (Atlantic Highlands: Humanties Press, 1993), pp. 99–116, where Bernasconi ties the concept of what he cites in English as *Volk* (if a bit solecistically because in an acoustic syncretism expressed as "the *Volk*") explicitly to Gadamer and the now almost fashionable notion of Nazi

misuse: "The notion of the Volk has tended to play only a minor part in the interpretation of 'The Origin of the Work of Art' " (102). For Bernasconi, Heidegger himself is to be counted among those who occlude such references. "In the closing pages of 'The Question Concerning Technology' Heidegger continued the task of withdrawing the politically charged vocabulary that had marked the draft of 'The Origin of the Work of Art' and which he had already begun to sanitize in the Freiburg and Frankfurt versions. He omitted all reference to the Volk, to decision, and to 'great art' as such" (115–116).

    5. Jacques Taminiaux, "The Origin of 'The Origin of the Work of Art,' " in *Reading Heidegger: Commemorations*, ed. John Sallis (Bloomington: Indiana University Press, 1993), pp. 392–404; p. 403. Taminiaux's dissection of the rhetoric of self-assertion and the retrospective work of self-rehabilitation (this is not read positively), offers the background context for Bernasconi's reading, and indeed begins with a recollective identification of the same references to Freiburg (13 November 1935) and Frankfurt (November/December 1936), see p. 392.

    6. Gadamer, "Die Wahrheit des Kunstwerkes (1960)," in Hans-Georg Gadamer, *Gesammelte Werke 3: Neuere Philosophie 1* (Tübingen: Mohr Siebeck, 1987), p. 250.

    7. Gadamer, "Die Wahrheit des Kunstwerkes" [hereafter GW3], p. 252.

    8. Ibid.

    9. Ibid., p. 257.

    10. Gadamer, RB, p. 15. Translation modified.

    11. Ibid., p. 26.

    12. Ibid., pp. 33–34.

    13. "Da ist keine Stelle, die dich nicht sieht. Du mußt dein Leben ändern." Rilke, "Archaische Torso Apollons," cited in Gadamer, GS 8, 125, RB, p. 34.

    14. See for a further discussion, Babich, "From Nietzsche's Artist to Heidegger's World: The Post-Aesthetic Perspective," *Man and World* 22 (1989): 3–23. Derrida demurs from this contention as he claims precisely in the measure to which he praises "the strong necessity" of Heidegger's "questioning," noting however that he nonetheless "*repeats* here, in the worst as well as the best sense of the word, the traditional philosophy of art." "Restitutions" in Derrida, *The Truth in Painting*, trans. Geoff Bennington and Ian McLeod (Chicago: University of Chicago Press, 1987), p. 262. Originally published in the context of a series of readings of Heidegger's essay as "Restitutions de la verité en pointure," *Macula*, 3–4 (1978): 11–37. Apart from the Derrida-inspired literature (as it inspires the greater part of the textual reception of this debate), see Karsten Harries, "Poetry as Response: Heidegger's Step Beyond Aestheticism," *Midwest Stud. Phil.* 16 (1991): 73–88. See too Otto Pöggeler, "Heidegger on Art," in *Martin Heidegger: Politics, Art, and Technology*, eds. Karsten Harries and Christoph Jamme (New York: Holmes & Meier, 1994), 106–153. Pöggeler emphasizes Heidegger's attention to Van Gogh's letters, as well as to the paintings of Klee and Cezanne. It goes without saying that Heidegger does not say what—or even, in Nelson Goodman's expression "when"—art is.

    15. This infamous reference is offered in the context of Heidegger's *Introduction to Metaphysics*, trans. Ralph Manheim (New Haven: Yale University

Press, 1959), p. 199. At least for Derrida's interpreters, one may thus condemn Heidegger's judgment on art as singularly guilty of philistinism (a Mandarin specialty): particularly as Heidegger talks of greatness, speaking of the greatness of "great works of art"—in the same voice that may be heard in his lamentable language endorsing the "inner truth and greatness" of National Socialism.

16. Gadamer, RB, p. 8.

17. See again, Babich, "From Nietzsche's Artist to Heidegger's World."

18. Cf. Gadamer, GW3, p. 253ff.

19. Gadamer, RB, pp. 13–21.

20. André Malraux, "Le musée imaginaire," *Les voix du silence* (Paris: Gallimard, 1951).

21. Although it is hard to better the initial insights of Theodor Adorno's *The Culture Industry*, see for the inception of this foundational conception of the museum, Charles Jencks's canonic reflections on the broader concept of the "postmodern," using the museum itself as instantiation. From a somewhat different perspective, see Andrew McClellan, *Inventing the Louvre*. Thus Douglas Crimp, in his book *On the Museum's Ruins*, above all in the chapter on the postmodern museum as such (speaking with reference to James Stirling's *Neue Staatsgalerie* in Stuttgart, Germany), asserts that the museum both installs or institutes art as something "autonomous, alienated, something apart, referring only to its own internal history and dynamics" as well as serving as the literal venue for Benjamin's de-auraticized "working" of art in the age of technological reproduction that was once exemplified by the photograph and is now digitalized and increasingly virtual, alluding to André Malraux's *Museum Without Walls* as "an imaginary museum, a history of art." *On the Museum's Ruins*, p. 13. See Walter Benjamin, "The Work of Art in the Age of Mechanical Reproduduction," in Benjamin, *Illuminations*, trans. Harry Zohn (New York: Schocken Books, 1969).

22. Gunther von Hagens, a medical anatomist, is the author of the patent in question, which recreates (it does not replicate) the lost art of preservation discovered and guarded so carefully by the eighteenth-century veterinary surgeon, Honoré Fragonard (a relative of the artist Fragonard) that the technique was lost with the surgeon's death. In both cases, the technique depends on the replacement of surfaces and not less on the effect achieved by seeing contours otherwise unseen (and hence to which no comparison—or judgment—between the way they look in life and the way they look in death can be made). Thus von Hagens's "plastinated" cadavers are denuded of skin to expose the striations of muscle and nerve and displayed in startling tableaus of inevitably high pathos in the installations *Körperwelten / Body-worlds*. Originally donated for the ideal purposes of medical research, von Hagens's reenactment of Fragonard's specimen exhibitions is an automatically (if not intentionally) postmodern conceit. See H. Mayer, "Stockendes Blut," *Neue Zürcher Zeitung*, Feb. 22 (2003): 2/14 and, more generally Deanna Petherbridge and Ludmilla Jordanova, *The Quick and the Dead: Artists and Anatomy* (Berkeley: University of California Press, 1997).

23. Heidegger, "The Origin of the Work of Art" [hereafter cited in the body of the text as O], pp. 17–81. Originally published as the lead essay in the collection *Holzwege* (Frankfurt am Main-Klostermann 1980 [1950]), "Der

Ursprung des Kunstwerkes (1935/36)," pp. 1–72. References here are given to the English translation by Albert Hofstadter in Heidegger, *Poetry, Language, Thought* (New York: Harper, 1970), pp. 17–82, including addendum.

24. The identity of the painting was settled to Meyer Schapiro's satisfaction after he solved the problem of speculation by writing to Heidegger himself to ask him, thereby identifying the painting as Vincent Van Gogh's *Pair of Shoes*, painted in Paris in 1885 (F255). The painting is currently on display in the Vincent Van Gogh Museum in Amsterdam. Intriguingly, however, Walter Biemel, himself trained as an art historian, reproduces an entirely different (and less striking) painting of another of Van Gogh's *Shoes* in his book, *Martin Heidegger* (Hamburg: Rowohlt, 2002).

25. See Brian O'Doherty, *Inside the White Cube: The Ideology of the Gallery Space* (Santa Monica, CA: The Lapis Press, 1986) as well as Didier Maleuve, *Museum Memories: History, Technology, Art* (Stanford: Stanford University Press, 1999) and Gottfried Korff, *Museumsdinge: Deponieren—Exponieren* (Cologne: Böhlau, 2002). See too Crimp's account in *On the Museum's Ruins* of the postmodern efflorescence of museum construction using Stirling's *Neuestaatsgalerie Stuttgart* in conjunction with Karl Friedrich Schinkel's museum in Berlin, in Crimp's *On the Museum's Ruins*, pp. 282–325, esp. pp. 290ff. For an account of the aura that is both preserved and volatized in the museum, see these and other authors speculating on the museum and its fortunes as well as, writing on Walter Benjamin's canonical "The Work of Art in the Age of Mechanical Reproduction," in Benjamin, *Illuminations: Essays and Reflections*, ed. Hannah Arendt (New York: Schocken Books, 1969), pp. 217–251. Andrew Benjamin, Rebecca Comay, Susan Buck-Morss, et al. For a recent and comprehensive study, see Howard Caygill, *Walter Benjamin: The Colour of Experience* (London: Routledge, 1998).

26. On the matter of such certification, it is worth noting that many art historians aspire to the role of consultant, whether for the museum as curator (directing acquisition) or indeed, for investors. See, to begin with, Horst Wagenführ, *Kunst als Kapitalanlage* (Stuttgart: Forkel, 1965) and note 59 below.

27. Thomas Puttfarken at the beginning of his wonderful art-scholar's reading of *The Invention of Pictorial Composition* (New Haven: Yale University Press, 2000) muses that the age of easel art is said to be at an end—a judgment, manifestly enough, he himself suggests only facetiously.

28. See Daniel Libeskind's *The Space of an Encounter* (New York: Rizzoli, 2000) as well as Bernhard Schneider, *Daniel Libeskind, Jewish Museum Berlin* (Munich: Prestel, 1999).

29. This is partly the achievement of the photograph as Benjamin and Malraux argue (yielding the analyses offered by Crimp and others) but it is largely the legacy of the museum catalog that specifies certain works as properly to be found in or as the property of the particular museum. Hence following a much publicized theft, the Isabella Stewart Gardener Museum in Boston continued to reserve the place of the stolen pictures rather than substitute from its collection. This same circumstance yields the mischief of multiple instances of the same "Rembrandt" precisely as a problem of property rights and hence the

importance of expert attribution—and the impotence of the same: matching expert against expert, which is not always to say art historian against art historian, for in these cases, it is capital rather than academic reputations or convictions that are at stake.

30. Duchamp did not invent this but made it permanently plain to the art theorist's mind as he gave it a name and associated a conceptual catenna to what was already the reigning convention of the thing that is not only art but the *art-world* (which has, patently, nothing to do with the world-abundance or world-emptiness of what Heidegger speaks of as the work of art.)

31. Gadamer, RB, p. 40.

32. Paul Crowther, "Heidegger and the Question of Aesthetics," *Journal of the British Society for Phenomenology* 19/1 (1988): 51–63. See pp. 53ff.

33. Gadamer, GW3, p. 256.

34. And Gadamer invokes this phrase with reference to Kant in his later essay, RB, p. 19.

35. Gadamer, GW3, p. 256.

36. In 1968, Schapiro writes, "They are clearly pictures of the artist's own shoes, not the shoes of a peasant." In Schapiro, "The Still-Life as a Personal Object: A Note on Heidegger and van Gogh," in *The Reach of Mind: Essays in Memory of Kurt Goldstein*, ed. M. L. Simmel (New York: Springer Publishing, 1968), pp. 203–209, here p. 205. Schapiro modifies the passage in reprinting this essay in his *Theory and Philosophy of Art: Style, Artist, and Society* (New York: Braziller, 1994), pp. 135–141. Here he qualifies his claim: "They are more likely pictures of the artist's own shoes, not the shoes of a peasant," p. 136. Shapiro's later book collection includes an additional essay from 1994, "Further Notes on Heidegger and van Gogh," pp. 142–151. Citations to follow refer to Schapiro's *Theory and Philosophy of Art*.

37. This is less a matter of Schapiro's contention than belied by the mere fact of offering such "Further Notes on Heidegger and van Gogh." Although Schapiro mentions defenses of Heidegger's reading from Hans-Georg Gadamer and indeed Heidegger's own marginal corrections, Schapiro reasserts his original interpretation. To say that he could not however have regarded his first interpretation as his last word on the issue is only to advert to his need to offer a further essay.

38. Schapiro, "The Still-Life as a Personal Object," p. 140.

39. Schapiro reacted powerfully and negatively to precisely this moving account. But it is significant that he was inspired to forget the detail that only fairly recently have shoes come to be purchased ready to wear, whether new or used. Until fairly recently, shoes, like clothes, were made for one: that is what cobblers did, even for relatively indigent but still bourgeois artists like Van Gogh.

40. For an account, see Andrew Hemmingway, "Meyer Schapiro and Marxism in the 1930s," *Oxford Art Journal* 17/1 (1994): 13–29. See also Marshall Berman, "Meyer Schapiro: The Presence of the Subject," in Berman's *Adventures in Marxism* (London: Verso, 1999), pp. 221–236.

41. This is the difference Derrida makes of Schapiro's reference to the necessity of a distinction between the shoes of peasant and city dweller—hence the distinction that Derrida claims identifies Heidegger "with the peasant and

Schapiro with the city dweller." *The Truth in Painting,* p. 260—and Derrida's appeal to ideological sympathies evident in this set of associations.

42. Derrida, *The Truth in Painting,* p. 364.

43. Vincent van Gogh, letter no. 529, cited in Schapiro, "The Still-Life as a Personal Object, p. 136.

44. J. de Rotonchamp, *Paul Gauguin 1898–1903* (Paris: C. Cres, 1925), 33 and Paul Gauguin, "Natures mortes," *Essais d'art libre,* 1894, 4, 273–275. Cited in Schapiro, "The Still-Life as a Personal Object," p. 140.

45. Ibid.

46. These are the shoes François Gauzi evidently refers to in a letter Schapiro translates in his "Further Notes on Heidegger and Van Gogh," p. 146, and which Schapiro confidently maintains as confirming his original view. It is this claim that I here dispute.

47. For illustrations of the Van Gogh paintings here discussed, see the earlier version of this chapter, published as "From Van Gogh's Museum to the Temple at Bassae: Heidegger's Truth of Art and Schapiro's Art History," *Culture, Theory, Critique* 44/2 (2003): 151–169. For a phenomenological counter-reading of Schapiro's criticism of Van Gogh's *Leather Clogs,* see especially pp. 158–159. I am indebted to the creative efforts of Carlos Eduardo Sanabria who translated this essay as "La veridad del arte en Heidegger. Salvar el museo entre Schapiro y Gadamer" in his edited collection, *Estética: Miradas contemporáneas* (Bogota, Columbia: Fondation Universidad de Bogotá, 2004), pp. 183–230. Sanabria's translation includes illustrations of every work mentioned in the text, enhancing its phenomenological efficacy.

48. For an illuminating array of the same, it is useful to visit the least-visited level of the new Vincent van Gogh Museum in Amsterdam, where the basement and the research materials of curators and art historians have been brought together to offer a valuable and informative display not only of Van Gogh's paintings but many of his models and associated tools for the same, including the perspective frame that Patrick A. Heelan adverts to in his phenomenological analysis of the painted or pictorial space of the artist's *Bedroom at Arles.* Heelan, *Space-Perception in the Philosophy of Science* (Berkeley: University of California Press, 1983), pp. 114–128.

49. Maurice Merleau-Ponty, "Indirect Language and the Voices of Silence," in Merleau-Ponty, *Signs,* trans. Richard McCleary (Chicago: Northwest University Press, 1964), pp. 39–83.

50. See, again, Malraux, "Le musée imaginaire."

51. Dieter Jähnig has underscored Heidegger's affinity for the modern sculptural art of Alberto Giacometti and offers a particularly compelling account of Brancusi's *Bird in Flight.* See Jähnig, "Die Kunst und der Raum," in *Erinnerung an Martin Heidegger,* ed. G. Neske (Pfullingen: Neske, 1977), pp. 131–148.

52. Cf. Gadamer, GW3, p. 257.

53. See Bernasconi's very fine discussion of Dürer (and Heidegger and Schapiro) in " '*Ne sutor ultra crepidam*': Dürer and Erasmus at the Hands of Panofsky and Heidegger," in *Heidegger in Question: The Art of Existing* (Atlantic Highlands: Humanities Press, 1993), pp. 117–134.

54. Thus Gadamer explains, "In einem ursprünglicheren Sinne »geschieht« Unverborgenheit und diese Geschehen ist etwas, was überhaupt erst möglich macht, daß Seiendes unverborgen ist und richtig erkannt wird" (GW3, 259). Corresponding to Heraclitus's insight into the self-concealment of nature, "hinsichtlich 'ihrem sein nach,' sie 'ist nicht nur das Aufgehen ins Licht, sondern ebensosehr das Sichbergen ins Dunkle, die Entfaltung der Blüte der Sonne ebenso wie das Sichverwurzeln in der Erdtiefe' " (Ibid.).

55. Derrida, *The Truth in Painting*, p. 260.

56. Ibid., p. 273.

57. Again, I refer, as Gadamer does, to Malraux.

58. Cf., for an account of the almost more than literally "fetish" character of Van Gogh (an art conceptual industry that has produced nothing less than a museum and transported Van Gogh's works from the Reijksmuseum to the eponymous VAN GOGH Museum in Amsterdam) as a concept in culture on almost every level, the art critical sociologist Nathalie Heinich, *The Glory of VAN GOGH: An Anthropology of Admiration*, trans. Paul Leduc Browne (Princeton: Princeton University Press, 1996).

59. The *via negativa* of such glorification may be found in Stefan Koldehoff's recent *Van Gogh Mythos und Wirklichkeit: Die Wahrheit über den teuersten Maler der Welt* (Dumont: Köln, 2003). The same 150th commemorative event was also celebrated with a collection of art-historical essays reviewing Van Gogh's contemporaries and historical context of his own reflections on his work: *Mit den Augen von Vincent van Gogh: Seine Wahlverwandtschaften und sein Kunstempfinden* (Amsterdam: Belser/Van Gogh Museum, 2003).

60. Gadamer, GW3, 261.

61. Gadamer, RB, p. 48. Translation altered.

62. See, after Gombrich, for a non-Gadamerian but Lacanian expression of such a "language," Norman Bryson, *Word and Image: French Painting of the Ancien Regime* (Cambridge: Cambridge University Press, 1981) and *Vision and Painting: The Logic of the Gaze* (New Haven: Yale University Press, 1983). But see too James Elkins, *Why Are Our Pictures Puzzles? On the Modern Origins of Pictorial Complexity* (London: Routledge, 1999) and W.J.T. Mitchell, *Iconology: Image, Text, Ideology* (Chicago: University of Chicago Press, 1987).

63. Gadamer, RB, pp. 8ff.

64. Ibid. See notes 12 and 13 in this chapter.

65. Ibid., p. 7.

66. Heidegger, "Language," in *Poetry, Language, Thought*, p. 135. Cf. Gadamer, GW8, 124.

67. Gadamer, RB, pp. 33–34.

68. Ibid.

69. I discuss this further in Babich, "Nietzsche's 'Artists' Metaphysics' and Fink's Ontological 'World-Play,' " *International Studies in Philosophy*. In press.

70. According to the report of the "United Nations Educational, Scientific and Cultural Organization Convention Concerning the Protection of the World Cultural and Natural Heritage Bureau of the World Heritage Committee, Twelfth Session, Unesco Headquarters, Paris. 14–17 June 1988," it may be that at least

part of the justification for the tent apparatus serves to protect the technological devices that are also in evidence at the site. The report confirms the purchase of "two portable micro-earthquake systems and a micro-climato-logical device for the Temple of Apollo Epicurius at Bassae (Greece): **$30,000.**" Bold emphasis in the original.

71. For a discussion of such an aesthetic indigence, see Babich, "On Malls, Museums, and the Art World: Postmodernism and the Vicissitudes of Consumer Culture," *Art Criticism*. 9/1 (Fall 1993): 1–16 and, more specifically with respect to Heidegger, once again, Babich, "From Nietzsche's Artist to Heidegger's World."

72. This chapter was presented as an invited seminar in Fall of 2003 at the Graduate Faculty of the New School. I thank the students and faculty there for their questions and interventions. In its present form, this chapter is a revised version of a text that appears in German translation,"Die Wahrheit des Kunstwerkes: Gadamers Hermeneutik zwischen Martin Heidegger und Meyer Shapiro" in Günter Figal, ed., *Internationales Jahrbuch für Hermeneutik*, trans. Holger Schmid and Heidi Byrnes, vol. 3. (Tübingen: Mohr Siebeck, 2004), pp. 55–80. Among others, I am grateful to Patrick A. Heelan, Holger Schmid, Heidi Byrnes, Robert Bernasconi, and William J. Richardson for encouragement and helpful suggestions.

Chapter Thirteen

1. The late Dominique Janicaud dedicates a key chapter in the first volume of his *Heidegger en France* (Paris: A. Michel, 2001) to reviewing the complexities of critique and partisan defense. Apart from a French context, illuminating as that is given the traditional enmity between Germany and France as it is this that adumbrates the terms of the debate for Janicaud, we may here find it useful to review the exchange between Paul Hühnerfeld (who may be considered as a kind of forerunner of Farías) and Heidegger. In a typically pompous and just as typically professorial or "mandarin" expression of smugness and intellectual distance, Heidegger refused to cooperate with Hühnerfeld's request for biographical information, saying that his life was "totally uninteresting." Annoyed, Hühnerfeld responded to his own query with a book, *Im Sachen Heidegger: Versuch über ein deutsches Genie* (Hamburg: Hoffmann and Campe, 1959). Guido Schneeberger's later *Nachlese zu Heidegger* (Bern: Suhr, 1962), is better known. For Heidegger's account of his correspondence with and reaction to Hühnerfeld, see Heinrich Petzet, *Auf einen Stern zugehen: Begegnungen und Gespräche mit Martin Heidegger, 1929–1976* (Frankfurt: Societäts-Verlag, 1983), pp. 9 and 91.

2. Theodore Kisiel, "Heidegger's Apology: Biography as Philosophy and Ideology," *Graduate Faculty Philosophy Journal*, 14:2/ 15:1 (1991): 363–404, here p. 398.

3. This now notorious silence was a silence in connection not with the well-publicized *Rektoratsrede* (Heidegger himself oversaw the publication of that text and referred to it both at the post-war "clean-up" hearings, and indirectly in other texts as well as directly in a 1945 reflection, "Facts and Thoughts"

published by Hermann Heidegger in 1983, timed either to memorialize the fiftieth anniversary of the rectorial address itself, or else, as Joseph Margolis and Tom Rockmore suggest in their introduction to the English language edition of Farías's *Heidegger and Nazism*, trans. P. Burrell, et al. [Philadelphia: Temple University Press, 1989], its publication was timed "possibly . . . to coincide" [xi] with the anniversary of Hitler's rise to power nor does it concern the sheer fact of Heidegger's being named rector, and thus the fact of his collaboration as such with National Socialism (this too Heidegger himself discussed, referring to it not only through the patent and notoriously unaltered references in his *Introduction to Metaphysics* but also in the posthumously published interview with *Der Spiegel*).

4. For Heidegger's "calculated" silence, see George Steiner's several studies of Heidegger and his concluding remarks in the video, *Heidegger: Design for Living* (BBC, VHS, 1999).

5. Though one must ask what could count as "satisfactory" where the stakes in question are increased with every decade that sees the issue of Heidegger's political involvement emerge once again, and there have already been a number of such decades.

6. Heidegger writes, "die besondere innere Verwandtschaft der deutschen Sprache mit der Sprache der Griechen und ihrem Denken." "Spiegel-Gespräch," p. 107 in Günther Neske and E. Kettering, eds., *Antwort: Martin Heidegger im Gespräch* (Pfüllingen: Neske, 1988). See for the English: G. Neske and E. Kettering, eds., *Martin Heidegger and National Socialism: Questions and Answers* (New York: Paragon House, 1990).

7. Heidegger writes in *Hölderlins Hymne "Der Ister," Gesamtausgabe* 53 (Frankfurt: Klostermann, 1984), "Tell me what you think about translation and I will tell you who you are." p. 76.

8. Heidegger, "So wenig, wie man Gedichte übersetzen kann, kann man ein Denken übersetzen." "Das Spiegel-Interview," *Antwort*, p. 108. Cited by Augstein, p. 189.

9. Rudolph Augstein furnishes what Heidegger specifically admits with the fuller context of the putatively unsaid. Thus, for one illuminating example in a suggestive series, Augstein repeats the query concerning the strain in Heidegger's relations with Jaspers because Jaspers's wife was Jewish and with Heidegger's assertion that Jaspers sent him all his publications with warm greetings, but adds "however that from 1937 Jaspers received no acknowledgment from Heidegger." Augstein, "Aber bitte nicht philosophieren," p. 194 in J. Altwegg, ed., *Die Heidegger Kontroverse*, (Athenaeum: Frankfurt am Main, 1988).

10. At the very least such a casual and literal tour de force proves if nothing else that Augstein has more than outgrown his youthful fear of the "famous thinker"—on Heinrich Petzet's report. See Petzet, "Nachdenkliches zum Spiegel-Gespräch," in *Antwort*, p. 11ff. "Afterthoughts on the Spiegel-Interview," *Martin Heidegger and National Socialism*, p. 67ff.

11. Heidegger famously declares: "Das bestätigen mir heute immer wieder die Franzosen. Wenn sie zu denken anfangen, sprechen sie Deutsch; sie versichern, sie kämmen mit ihrer Sprache nicht durch." *Antwort*, pp. 107–108.

12. Rainer Marten, "Ein rassistisches Konzept von Humanität," *Badische Zeitung*, December 19–20, 1987.

13. A quasi-worshiping reverence can be detected at every level in the university where a residual clericalism or basic medievalism inherently belongs to the academic way of life.

14. Marten, "Heideggers Geist," in Altwegg, ed., *Die Heidegger Kontroverse*, p. 226. As Marten reflects, "So beklagte sich Heidegger auch weniger über Gegnerschaft als vielmehr über Ignoranz." For Marten this will be one ironic sense of *Seinsvergessenheit*: the oblivion or ignorance of Being as the failure to properly receive the "word" from Heidegger.

15. Marten, "Heideggers Geist," p. 226.

16. "ist der griechische Geist einzig und allein im deutschen Blut und auf der deutschen Erde daheim" (Ibid., 228).

17. "Es geht um Grosses und Grobes: um die zentralen Begriffe und Positionien griechischer Seinslehre" (Ibid., 229).

18. Marten observes, "Andernfalls hatte ihm Sappho am Ende geistig dazu verführt, über menschliches Lieben ein Wort mehr zu sagen als dies, dass es ein Mögen sei, und Aischylos, dem Hassen der Fremden eine dem Lieben der Eigenen korrespondiere, machtstabilisierende Funktion zuzutrauen: 'Und auch hassen eines Sinns / Das ist's, was viel Leid dem Menschen heilt.' ('Eumeniden' v. 986ff.)" (Ibid., 228).

19. I read Lacan's Real in alliance with Nietzsche's understanding of nature. See Babich, "On the Order of the Real: Nietzsche and Lacan," in *Disseminating Lacan*, eds. David Pettigrew and François Raffoul (Albany: State University of New York Press, 1996), pp. 48–63.

20. Gilman, *Inscribing the Other*, p. 17.

21. "Geschichte [ist nicht] . . . ein Speicher nebeneinander aufgeschichteter Produkte des Geschehens und Leitens, Geschichte ist unauflöslich weitergestaltende Kraft des Menschen. . . . Geschichte ist nicht Trennung, sondern Einigung, nicht Auflösung, sondern Band, nicht blosser Verlauf, sondern unsterbliche Wirkung, die Fuge im Goethes grossem Wort. Die Einigung aber, das ist ihre Tradition durch die Rezeption ihrer Kulturgestalten." Ludwig Curtius, "Morphologie der antiken Kunst," *Logos* 9/2 (1920/21): 195–221; p. 217. Curtius's style (characteristic of reviews of the time) is bombastic and tends to be overwhelmed by the great minds of the day (kindly disposed toward Troeltsch while chiding his life-antipode in Riegl) and today most readers would so concur with his judgment of Spengler as to find it overstated. Nonetheless Curtius's expression of *Wirkungsgeschichte* as "Einigung" is worth recalling here.

22. As already cited at the start of this book, Nietzsche writes in his early *Philosophy in the Tragic Age of the Greeks*, "nothing would be more foolish than to claim an autochthonous development for the Greeks. To the contrary, they invariably absorbed other cultures. The very reason they were able to advance as much as they did is because they understood how to pick up the spear where others had left it and throw it further" (KSA 1, 806).

23. In "Ein Gespräch mit Jürgen Habermas," in Altwegg, ed., *Die Heidegger Kontroverse*, pp. 172–175.

24. Heidegger, "The Spiegel Interview," p. 44.

25. Here, again, the German is useful: "Was heute vollends als Philosophie des Nationalsozialismus herumgeboten wird, aber mit der inneren Wahrheit und Grösse dieser Bewegung nicht das Geringste zu tun hat." Heidegger, *Einführung in die Metaphysik* (Tubingen: Niemeyer, 1976 [1953]), p. 152. *Introduction to Metaphysics*, trans. Ralph Manheim (New Haven: Yale University Press, 1959), p. 199.

26. In the *Times Higher Educational Supplement*, No. 850, February 17, 1989, p. 12. Cited by Robert Bernasconi, "Habermas and Arendt on the Philosopher's 'Error': Tracking the Diabolical in Heidegger," *Graduate Faculty Philosophy Journal* 14:2/15:1 (1991): 4.

27. Jean-Francois Lyotard, *Heidegger et "les juifs"* (Paris: Galilee, 1989), p. 90; *Heidegger and "the jews,"* trans. A. Michel and M. S. Roberts (Minneapolis: University of Minnesota Press, 1990), p. 52. Cited by Bernasconi, "Habermas and Arendt on the Philosopher's 'Error,' " p. 4.

28. Philippe Lacoue-Labarthe, "Victor Farías's Heidegger et le Nazism," in *Heidegger: Art and Politics* (Oxford: Basil Blackwell, 1990), p. 127.

29. Hölderlin, "Remarks on Oedipus" §1. For Hölderlin further: "The (re)presentation of the tragic rests, principally, on the fact that the monstrous [*das Ungeheure*]—how god and man join together and the power of nature and the innermost being of man boundlessly become as one in the fury—is to be understood through the boundless becoming-one purified by boundless separation." "Remarks on Oedipus" §3.

30. "Warum ist überhaupt Seiendes und nicht vielmehr Nichts ?" in *Einführung in die Metaphysik*, p. 1. In the English translation, Manheim uses majuscule letters in order to convey the sense of this: "WHY ARE THERE ESSENTS rather than nothing?" *An Introduction to Metaphysics*, p. 1.

31. Heidegger, *An Introduction to Metaphysics*, p. 206.

Chapter Fourteen

1. The notes for *Der Wille zur Macht: Versuch einer Umwertung aller Werte* (Leipzig: C. G. Naumann, 1901) were published as volume 15 in the *Großoktavausgabe* of Nietzsche's works initiated by his sister, Elisabeth Förster Nietzsche. This edition was published in 1894 during the time of Nietzsche's paralysis and appeared subsequent to his death. This first edition included 483 sections, selected and edited by Heinrich Köselitz and Ernst and August Horneffer. The second edition in 1906, edited by Köselitz, was expanded to 1,067 sections. A third, 1911 edition was edited by Otto Weiss but was fundamentally unchanged from the 1906 version.

2. At lectures on *The Will to Power as Art*, Heidegger repeatedly emphasizes that the plan of *The Will to Power* corresponds to an extant plan in Nietzsche's notes, while emphasizing that just as it is the question of Being that remains fundamental to his own *Being and Time*, what is essential to Nietzsche's *Will to Power* is not "the sequences of particular fragments . . . collected and subsumed into a book . . . where such an ordering is arbitrary and inessential, but what is

telling is to inquire in, with, and through Nietzsche." Heidegger, *Nietzsche I* (Pfullingen: Neske, 1961), p. 4. Heidegger is not simply telling us to read Nietzsche's *Nachlaß* at the expense of the published works, rather he is talking about how to make sense of the *Will to Power* as part of Nietzsche's *Nachlaß*.

    3. For a thoughtful overview, see Fred Dallmayr's "Heidegger on *Macht* and *Machenschaft*," *Continental Philosophical Review* 34 (2001): 247–267. See for another approach, Stuart Elden, "Taking the Measure of the *Beiträge*: Heidegger, National Socialism and the Calculation of the Political," *European Journal of Political Theory* 2/1 (2003): 35–56. And for an elusive but important reading, Reiner Schürmann, "A Brutal Awakening to the Tragic Condition of Being: On Heidegger's *Beiträge zur Philosophie*," trans. Kathleen Blamey in *Heidegger: Politics, Art, and Technology*, eds. Karsten Harries and Christoph Jamme (New York: Holmes and Meier, 1994), pp. 89–105.

    4. This same involvement also clarifies Heidegger's engagement in his lectures (by name, a specificity fairly rare for Heidegger) with Ludwig Klages, Arthur Baeumler, Karl Jaspers, as names that can be taken as standing for an entire tradition of Nietzsche interpretation and publication.

    5. The title of Winfried Georg Sebald's *The Natural History of Destruction*, trans Anthea Bell (New York: Modern Library, 2003) is due to Lord Solly Zuckerman, who promised to (but never did) write about his experience of the aftermath of the bombing (of which Zuckerman had been one of Britain's most zealous architects).

    6. Martin Heidegger, *Beiträge zur Philosophie (Vom Ereignis), Gesamtausgabe 65*, Friedrich-Wilhelm von Herrmann, ed. (Frankfurt am Main: Vittorio Klostermann, 1989). Throughout I cite the *Beiträge* in my own translation. The text is available as Heidegger, *Contributions to Philosophy (From Enowning)*, trans. Parvis Emad and Kenneth Maly (Bloomington/Indianapolis: Indiana University Press, 1999).

    7. Pre-publication typescripts of the *Beiträge* seem to have been fairly well distributed among Heidegger's other students in addition to Pöggeler.

    8. Pöggeler ascribes the *Beiträge* to a meditative aftereffect of the events of 1933—"Als er sich auf seine philosophische Arbeit zurückgeworfen sah, schrieb Heidegger in den Jahren 1936–1938 sein zweites Hauptwerk." *Neue Wege mit Heidegger* (Freiburg: Alber, 1992), p. 11. Pöggeler first articulates the substance of the *Beiträge* (and in the same vein, it may be said that he simultaneously begins a manifestly public campaign to disseminate what seems to be nothing less than an outline of its place in Heidegger's thought) in the text (appropriately enough) entitled "Sein als Ereignis," *Zeitschrift für philosophischer Forschung*, 13/4 (1959): 599–632. Translated into English by R. H. Grimm as "Being as Appropriation," in *Philosophy Today* 19 2/4 (1975): 152–178. Scholars such as Elizabeth Hirsch and others refer to the *Beiträge* and Pöggeler's representation of its nature, especially with reference to his discussion of it in his book, *Der Denkweg Martin Heideggers* (Freiburg: Alber, 1963), p. 115.

    9. Although Heidegger's relationship to Nietzsche is well marked in Heidegger's writings, beginning with but especially after his *Being and Time*, it

is patent in the *Beiträge*. But in recent discussions of the *Beiträge* this connection can go without remark, and it does not appear even in a collection that aspires to some kind of comprehensiveness such as *Companion to Heidegger's Contributions to Philosophy*, eds. Charles E. Scott et al. (Bloomington: Indiana University Press, 2001). The question of Nietzsche is even less significant than the fact that a review of the relevance of science and technology is absent from most discussions of the *Beiträge* to date (with the important exceptions of Patricia Glazebrook and Stuart Elden). See Glazebrook, "The Role of the *Beiträge* in Heidegger's Critique of Science, Philosophy Today (2001), pp. 24–32 and Elden, "Taking the Measure of the *Beiträge*: Heidegger, National Socialism, and the Calculation of the Political," *Theory* 2 (2003): 35–56.

   10. See Heidegger, *Zollikoner Seminare, Protokolle—Gespräche—Briefe*, ed., Medard Boss (Frankfurt am Main: Klostermann, 1987); translated as *Heidegger, Zollikon Seminars: Protocols—Conversations—Letters*, ed. Medard Boss, trans. Fanz Mayr and Richard Askay (Evanston: Northwestern University Press, 2001).

   11. William J. Richardson makes this reference in his recounting of a comment made by Charles Sherover (I only subsequently learned this from the author as Richardson does not name him here), as the colleague who convivially offered to concur with Richardson's (exactly original) assessment of "two Heideggers' " in Richardson, "Preface to the U.S. Edition," *Through Phenomenology to Thought* (New York: Fordham University Press, 2003), p. xxxv.

   12. Heidegger, "Letter to Father Richardson" in Richardson's *Through Phenomenology to Thought*. (Nijmegen: Nijhoff, 1965), p. xxii. The letter is dated "Anfang April 1962."

   13. This is a classical association that begins with Georg Lukàcs, *Die Zerstörung der Vernunft: Der Weg des Irrationalismus von Schelling zu Hitler* (Berlin: Aufbau Verlag, 1953) translated by Peter Palmer as *The Destruction of Reason: Irrationalism from Schelling to Nietzsche* (Atlantic Highlands: Humanities Press, 1981). See too Lukàcs, *Von Nietzsche bis Hitler oder Der Irrationalismus in der deutschen Politik* (Frankfurt: Fischer, 1966).

   14. As already observed, these names can be multiplied almost at will. See also Babich, "Habermas, Nietzsche, and the Future of Critique: Irrationality, *The Will to Power*, and War" in *Nietzsche, Habermas, and Critical Theory*, ed. Babich (Amherst, NY: Humanity Books, 2004), pp. 13–46.

   15. Heidegger notoriously also declares Nietzsche's unpublished philosophy the locus of his "genuine" philosophy. See Heidegger, *Nietzsche* (Pfullingen: Neske, 1961), in two volumes, references throughout, especially volume 1.

   16. Heidegger, *Nietzsche: Volume I: The Will to Power as Art*, trans. David Farrell Krell (San Francisco: Harper & Row 1979), p. 158. Krell points out that Heidegger's invocation of "the 'event' of nihilism," cited four times in this and the following paragraphs, occasions perhaps the earliest "terminological use of the word *Ereignis* in Heidegger's published writing." Krell goes on to conclude with what this reader reads as a reference to the *Beiträge* made by Heidegger and published in 1969. Krell is referring to the important protocol made by Alfredo Guzzoni to the lecture "Zeit und Sein," dated 11–13 September 1962. See *Zur*

Sache des Denkens (Tübingen: Niemeyer, 1969), p. 46; this protocol is also translated in *On Time and Being*, trans. Joan Stambaugh (New York: Harper and Row, 1972), p. 43. See the prior reference to the context of this reference in *The Letter on Humanism* and *Identity and Difference*, p. 36. Krell cites as follows " 'The relationships and contexts which constitute the essential structure of *Ereignis* were worked out between 1936 and 1938,' which is to say, precisely at the time of the first two Nietzsche lecture courses." Heidegger, *Nietzsche, Volume I*, trans. David Farrell Krell (San Francisco: Harper & Row 1979), p. 156. Krell's helpful gloss is characteristic of his interventionist style in Heidegger's text throughout and, it is worth remarking, in the context of the present reflection on the players in any work's paleography, that Krell's notes (and appended commentary) were expansive enough that they would render the publisher the bookseller's service of turning two volumes into four.

17. As we saw from the very beginning of this book: to raise the question of Heidegger's encounter with Nietzsche's style is also to raise the question of style in Heidegger's own work. Up till now, most Heidegger scholars have tended to avoid the question of style in Heidegger's writings (apart from what can seem to be the obligatory references to obscurity). Although Heidegger's *Beiträge* is a stylistically troublesome text (at least to the extent to which it challenges ordinary ways of reading Heidegger, even for experts in his work), Heidegger here poses the question of style as such and that is relevant.

18. Otto himself had been a member of the board of directors since 1933 and invited Heidegger as well as Heyse and Max Oehler in 1935. For a schematic listing of this involvement, see David Marc Hoffman, *Zur Geschichte des Nietzsche-Archivs* (Berlin: Walter de Gruyter, 1993), p. 115.

19. In addition to *The Will to Power* itself, other editorial productions of Nietzsche's drafts or notes or otherwise unpublished aphorisms were published, sometimes as a kind of "glimpse"—Erich Podach's collection would use the term: *Ein Blick in die Notizbücher Nietzsches: Ewige Wiederkunft. Wille zur Macht. Ariadne. Eine schaffensanalytische Studie* (Heidelberg: Rothe, 1963)—into the workshop of Nietzsche's ideas, sometimes as simply "timely" collections and even sometimes named "breviaries." Such compilations of Nietzsche's notes continue to be popular today, especially in Germany but can also be found in English-language editions.

20. Without posing the question I am raising here, Silvio Vietta has called attention to this factual detail in order to advert to questions of date in his book, *Heideggers Kritik am Nationalsozialismus und an der Technik* (Tübingen: Niemayer, 1989), pp. 70ff.

21. In a note dated 8 May 1939 Heidegger writes, as von Hermann duly undersores as justifying his ultimate ordering of the published text, that " '*Seyn*' as section II [part II] is not correctly arranged; as an attempt to grasp the whole once again, it does not belong at this juncture." See von Hermann's "Editor's Epilogue: *Contributions to Philosophy*," p. 365/514. Von Hermann takes Heidegger's note to support his rearrangement of the manuscript order, shifting "*Seyn*" to the end of the manuscript: "rearranging this part of the manuscript whereby it no longer makes up the second part but the eighth part instead: from

section 50 onward the ordinal number changes. For the preview has 49 sections: the fiftieth section, in both the manuscript as well as the typescript begins with Be-ing" whereas now, after rearranging, section 50 begins with '*Anklang*.' " In other words the entire text has been renumbered thenceforth. In its original ordering, "*Anklang*" would have been section 75, following the section entitled "Language (Its Origins)," currently section 281, and so on.

22. I have noted that it is not uncommon to find Heidegger drawing attention to an apparent ordering dissonance in his published texts but as we have also seen in discussing Heidegger's musical style of writing, he also offered anticipatory and retrospective reviews—in good scholastic style—throughout his texts and not merely at the conclusion of the same: indeed a study of Heidegger's specific manner of coming to end, the "problem of ending" as Nietzsche spoke of it, remains to be offered. For this reason it remains relevant for the current author that throughout all the years that would pass to his death, and even as he himself supervised the ordering of the final publication of his works, published and unpublished, Heidegger himself left the note at that, and made no alteration to the manuscript. Nor did Heidegger simply ignore the manuscript of the *Beiträge*. So far from that we are told that Heidegger himself authorized its representation as a second main work (a depiction that also accords with the current assessment I offer of Heidegger's *Beiträge* as modeled on Nietzsche's *Will to Power*).

23. In keeping with Heidegger's textual order, Pöggeler himself originally cites the *Beiträge*'s introductory "Overview" where Heidegger outlines the order of the text, explicitly beginning with *Seyn*. See Pöggeler, *Martin Heidegger's Path of Thinking*, p. 116.

24. It is perhaps more intriguing still to note that von Hermann's transposition also changes the conclusion, originally planned as "The Last God," which is now positioned in advance of "*Seyn*," as the new concluding division of the *Beiträge*. The manuscript section first addressed to "*Seyn*" is thus moved from a recollective point of departure to become, shades of Heidegger II, a postscript to the published text.

25. To be sure, Heidegger was at the time also engaged with his essay "On the Origin of the Work of Art." Furthermore as the author of a substantive commentary on Heidegger's Art-Work essay, in addition to ongoing seminar courses on the same theme over the course of many recent years, von Hermann emphasizes similarities between the two manuscripts.

26. Today's philosophers and sociologists of technology increasingly speak of techno-science and testify, as they do so, to Heidegger's prevailing concern with the specifically modern expressions of both science and technology. For an overview of the field called STS, Science, Technology, and Society studies, see Stephen H. Cutcliffe, *Ideas, Machines, and Values: An Introduction to Science, Technology, and Value Studies* (Lanham, MD: Rowman & Littlefield, 2000).

27. Heidegger, *Zollikon Seminars*, p. 182.

28. See, as already cited, Heidegger's comment on *Ereignis*, and also as already noted, Krell's footnote gloss in Heidegger, *Nietzsche: Volume I*, p. 156. Dallmayr has rightly emphasized the need to distinguish between the routine

understanding of technology and Heidegger's more Greek conceptualization, a conceptualization that takes us from *techne* (art) to *poiesis*.

29. See Dallmayr, "Heidegger on *Macht* and *Machenschaft*," cited previously. My question is whether the poietic can be the end of the story or whether we do not in the end need to return to a regard for aletheic nature itself.

30. This claim is posed against Heidegger's apparent argument and I discuss this further in my reflections on Heidegger and Nietzsche in my essay, "Dichtung, Eros, und Denken in Nietzsche und Heidegger: Heideggers Nietzsche Interpretation und die heutigen Nietzsche-Lektüre," *Heidegger-Jahrbuch II* (Freiburg: Karl Alber Verlag, 2005), pp. 239–264.

31. It is no accident that both the first Nietzsche lecture, *The Will to Power as Art*, and the *Beiträge* include a section entitled "Truth in Platonism and Positivism." Both count for Heidegger as a kind of calculative thinking, the one supersensuous, the other empiricist, but both assume that "knowing is approximation to what is to be known" (N1, 151).

32. Dominique Janicaud's was a tireless voice against this tendency.

33. This was not different in Heidegger's day—and we can read Michael Friedman's account of the historical circumstances of Heidegger's debate with Carnap and Cassirer with profit here. See Michael Friedman, *Reconsidering Logical Positivism* (Cambridge: Cambridge University Press, 1999) and *Parting of the Ways: Carnap, Cassirer, Heidegger* (Chicago, IL: Open Court, 2000).

34. To the extent that this text is unpublished it patently demonstrates "resistance" of no kind apart from a fantasy substitution for the same. At the very best, it might be accounted as a "mental reservation" in place of action. In Heidegger's lecture courses on Hölderlin as in those on Nietzsche we do find plain and even parallel pronouncements that may be counted (as these statements cannot be counted) as articulations of such resistance.

35. See Rudolf Arnheim's phenomenological reflection on the sacral power of transmitted sound: "The physical fact that the normal distance between the sound source and microphone is inconsiderable, implies as a normal condition of the art of broadcasting a *spiritual* and *atmospheric* nearness of broadcaster and listener." Arnheim, *Radio* (New York: Da Capo Press, 1972), pp. 77–78. For Arnheim who is offering a phenomenological analysis of auditory perception, and he emphasizes in this locus that the primary characteristic of broadcast sound, voice, and music is the "absence of direction," pp. 55–57. Later Arnheim emphasizes that it is not within the capacity of radio per se to "fire" a "huge mass meeting with enthusiasm" (82), yet the use (or as Arnheim analyzes it: the abuse) of a loudspeaker is exactly suited to this same task because the deformation caused by the microphone now explodes with an intimacy focused on the visual speaker.

36. The term is used in the psychology of perception. I am extending it in the direction of a phenomenology of the same in this political context (a recent study extends the same perceptual phenomenon to advertising and brand: *Sonic Branding*. It is worth noting here that, due to another characteristic of sense perception, called "accommodation" by the same theorists, we no longer respond to loudspeakers or radios as we once did, as preserved for our reflection

and most dramatically not in the images of the rallies at Nuremberg, but in an American newsreel showing a family gathered around a large old-fashioned radio set, listening—and I am indebted to Tracy Strong for this reminder—to Franklin Roosevelt's "Day of Infamy" speech. See further, for the language of "broadcasting" and "voice-boxing," as well as "ventriloquism," in the context of the digital representation of acoustic experience: Freeman Dyson, "When Is the Ear Pierced," in *Immersed in Technology*, eds. Mary Anne Moser and Douglas MacLeod (Bloomington: Indiana University Press, 1999), pp. 73–101.

37. I refer of course to Heidegger's strange insistence in his interview with *Der Speigel*: "Nur noch ein Gott, kann uns retten."

38. There are few books that address this complexity. But for a beginning, discussion of the ambivalence of "sustainable development/ecology" may be found in Aidan Davison, *Technology and the Contested Meanings of Sustainability* (Albany: State University of New York Press, 2002). Davison cites a number of relevant texts in the course of contextualizing the issue in terms of technology development and planning, politics, and theory in terms of north-south and European (or Global) economics and political practice and empowerment.

39. Heidegger, *Nietzsche 1*, p. 142; cf. *Beiträge* §5.

40. This received logic would not merely be the logical positivists (the logic that was to become Carnap's intellectual capital) but would have more generic proponents of another less rigorous kind in the journalistic self-importance and correspondingly cavalier self-confidence of the critics of *Being and Time* that would take Heidegger's musing to more bitter reflections in other contexts. I refer here to Heidegger's comments on death and what he called the "journalistic" (and "philistine") interpretations of his *Being and Time*, in which, when it was not presented as an anthropology (evolving into the terms of existentialism) was presented as a philosophy of death. See *Beiträge* §§162, 163.

41. Heidegger, "Science and Reflection," p. 181.

42. Heidegger, *Zollikon Seminars*, p. 18. See Paul Valadier's essay on the same theme, "Science as New Religion," in Babich, ed., *Nietzsche, Epistemology, and Philosophy of Science: Nietzsche and the Sciences II* (Dordrecht: Kluwer, 1999), pp. 241–252.

43. If today's philosophy of science is no longer dominated by scholastic philosophy or, as in Heidegger's day, by neo-Kantianism, it continues to be dominated by the still enduring analytic approach to conceiving the very scientific problem of science on the terms of the modern worldview (this is what Heidegger means by speaking as he does of "science as worldview," that is, contra the idea and ethos of Heidegger's thinking of science in the *Beiträge* and beyond).

44. Heidegger,"The End of Philosophy," p. 59.

45. Heidegger, *Nietzsche, Volume II*, p. 112.

46. Heidegger, *Being and Time*, trans. Macquarrie and Robinson (New York: Harper & Row, 1962), Int. I, (BT, 31/SZ, p. 11). See also §I.1, (BT, 75/S. 50); I.6, §44 (BT, 256–273/SZ S. 212–230).

47. The anti-science charge would dog Heidegger beginning with the earliest reviews of *Being and Time*, then directed to claims he makes there

concerning truth and especially concerning physics itself, BT, p. 269/S. 226–227. See also his characterization of Galileo, "als Physiker Philosoph." *Logik: Die Frage nach der Wahrheit* (1925–26), GA 21, S. 97. Later his direct comments on science and thinking drew greater fire. I have detailed this elsewhere, see, in particular Babich, "Die Wissenschaftsbegriff bei Martin Heidegger und Medard Boss: Philosophisches Denken und *Daseinsanalyse*" in *Heidegger und Daseinsanalyse,* ed. Harald Seubert (Köln: Böhlau, 2003), pp. 249–268 as well as "Heidegger's Philosophy of Science: Calculation, Thought, and *Gelassenheit"* in Babich, ed., *From Phenomenology to Thought, Errancy, and Desire,* pp. 589–599.

48. I hardly need to repeat that Heidegger's critics have been unpersuaded by this claim. If his critics charge that his philosophy is anti-science and therefore irrational, the judgment has proven to endure Heidegger's own efforts to answer such critique directly. In the age of science, under the rational aegis of science, *any* criticism of science is assumed to be irrational, and all Heidegger's training in logic and mathematics, and in spite of his painstaking references to Aristotle, the first master of scientific logic, and to the development of that logic into the organon of precisely modern science in Descartes (and Galileo) and in Kant (and Leibniz), does nothing to abrogate the charge of irrationality. I attempt to oppose this reading on Heidegger and logic. But see Michael Friedman (cited earlier) and on Aristotle, see Patricia Glazebrook's *Heidegger's Philosophy of Science* (New York: Fordham University Press, 1999) and for a still more focused reading from a similar perspective: William McNeill, *The Glance of the Eye* (Albany: State University of New York Press, 1999).

49. Heidegger's conviction concerning the sameness of both Russian and American regimes (for the longest time both were imagined as patently antithetical) is at once absurd (it is tacitly or immediately rejected as naïve or wrong) and it is also, given the tactically, politically unexpected events of recent history, exactly accurate.

50. Heidegger, *Introduction to Metaphysics,* p. 152.

51. Herbert Marcuse, "Some Social Implications of Modern Technology," *Technology, War and Fascism: Collected Papers of Herbert Macuse, Volume One,* ed. Douglas Kellner (London: Routledge, 1998), p. 49 and following.

52. In addition to National Socialism's enthusiastically pro-research science and policy we have also to include its dependency upon and engagement with democracy (we ought not forget, and the popularity of Daniel Goldhagen's controversial book makes the oblique case, that National Socialism was exactly a popular "movement" with broad political, i.e., democratic support). This is one point that Peter Schneider's recent essay on "The Good Germans" in the *New York Times Sunday Magazine* (13 February 2000) seeks to make in his account of the non-heroic or exactly everyday and very small-time generosity of the one hundred or so Germans who were instrumental in saving Konrad Latte throughout the Nazi regime. Yet the trouble with his argument as with all such nuanced readings is that they cannot but run counter to the simpler contours of the politically correct and the black- and white-hat accounts of good and evil.

53. See on these issues Benjamin R. Barber, *Jihad Versus McWorld* (New York: Times Books, 2001 [1995]) and Thomas L. Friedmann, *The Lexus and the*

Olive Tree: Understanding Globalization (New York: Farrar, Straus and Giroux, 2000). The nuances of Barber's perspective are easy to lose and the more straightforward but regrettably oversimplified perspective of a contra-modernity continues to dominate. Thus despite the ubiquity of both technology *and* scientific rationality on *all* sides, and seemingly to advance a simplified agenda, many analysts eagerly paint any opponent of Western culture with the Luddite colors of a putatively anti-rationalism. But a pro-science dogma reigns supreme in our world, permeating even creationist ideology on the conservative side of American politics.

54. This is Heidegger's point in his "Die Frage nach der Technik," *Vorträge und Aifsätze* (Pfullingen: Neske, 1978), p. 11.

55. Heidegger's observation that modernity is opposed to very idea of das »Un-mögliche«; (which our own regime of freedom »haßt« in principle (§70; cf. §51, §58) as much as the Nazi regime he indicted [all-too-pointlessly because all-too-silently] in the *Beiträge*) is exemplified in the one global world all of us have "already" (at least ideally) become.

56. Pöggeler, *Martin Heidegger's Path of Thinking*, p. 115.

57. This reference to Hölderlin's *Empedocles* was important in much the same way for Nietzsche's Zarathustra. This is a complex point of reference and interconnection, already invoked earlier in chapter 7. See also David B. Allison's related discussion of Zarathustra in his *Reading the New Nietzsche* (Lanham, MD: Rowman & Littlefield, 2001). See here also B §43 where Heidegger cites Nietzsche's *Twilight of the Idols*: "Der Wille zum System ist ein Mangel an Rechtschaffenheit."

58. In addition to the points just noted, see Pierre Bertaux, *Hölderlin und die Französiche Revolution* (Frankfurt am Main: Suhrkamp, 1969) for the significance of this event for an understanding of Hölderlin's life story (most particularly, most incendiarily, Hölderlin's madness) and see any number of extant historical accounts of the political involvement of Hölderlin's writing for an understanding of the allusion.

59. The image plays on Heisenberg's original pronouncement. In the *Zollikon Seminars*, Heidegger had argued, with some ironic humor, against the reductive claim of the cybernetic definition of the human offered by the inventor himself, Norbert Wiener. "Von der Methode des Zuganges als einer Naturwissenschaft her bestimmt sich, was der Mensch ist." Wiener, *Mensch und Menschmachine. Kybernetik und Gesellschaft* (Frankfurt am Main: Suhrkamp, 1964), p. 124. But, and of course, as the debacle over the implications (far more than the content) of Peter Sloterdijk's *Rules for the Human Zoo* makes clear, as a consideration of the current tendency to take it for granted that humanity can indeed be reduced to DNA, the point here can no be longer an ironic one.

Bibliography

FRIEDRICH HÖLDERLIN
Primary sources

Sämtliche Werke. Friedrich Beißner et al. ed., Große Stuttgarter Ausgabe. Eight volumes. Stuttgart: Kohlhammer, 1943–85.
Sämtliche Werke, D. E. Sattler, ed., Frankfurt am Main: Roter Stern, 1975.
Sämmtliche Gedichte. Wiesbaden: Aula, 1989.

English translations

Friedrich Hölderlin, Poems and Fragments. Translated by Michael Hamburger. Cambridge: Cambridge University Press, 1980.
Hyperion and Selected Poems. Edited by Eric I. Santner. New York: Continuum, 1990.
Hymns and Fragments by Friedrich Hölderlin. Translated by Richard Sieburth. Princeton: Princeton University Press, 1984.

FRIEDRICH NIETZSCHE
Primary sources

Kritische Gesamtausgabe. Edited by Giorgio Colli and Mazzino Montinari. Berlin: Walter de Gruyter, 1967–.
Nietzsche Werke: Kritische Studienausgabe. Edited by Giorgio Colli and Mazzino Montinari. Fifteen volumes. Berlin: Walter de Gruyter, 1980.
Nietzsche Briefwechsel. Kritische Gesamtausgabe. Edited by Giorgio Colli and Mazzino Montinari. Berlin: Walter de Gruyter, 1975ff.
Sämtliche Briefe: Kritische Studienausgabe. Eight volumes. Berlin: de Gruyter, 1986.
Frühe Schriften. Edited by Hans Joachim Mette. Five volumes. Munich: Verlag C. H. Beck, 1994.
Der Wille zur Macht: Versuch einer Umwertung aller Werte. Leipzig: C. G. Naumann, 1901.

343

English translations

Beyond Good and Evil. Translated by R. J. Hollingdale. Harmondsworth: Penguin, 1967.
The Birth of Tragedy and the Case of Wagner. Translated by Walter Kaufmann. New York: Random House, 1967.
Ecce Homo. Translated by R. J. Hollingdale. Harmondsworth: Penguin, 1993.
The Gay Science. Translated by Josefine Nauckhoff. Cambridge: Cambridge University Press, 2001. Also translated by Walter Kaufmann. New York: Random House, 1974.
Human, All Too Human: A Book for Free Spirits. Translated by R. J. Hollingdale. Cambridge: Cambridge University Press, 1986.
Philosophy and Truth: Selections from Nietzsche's Notebooks of the Early 1870's. Translated by Daniel J. Breazeale. Atlantic Highlands, NJ: Humanities Press, 1979.
On the Genealogy of Morals and *Ecce Homo.* Translated by Walter Kaufmann. New York: Vintage Books, 1969.
Twilight of the Idols. Translated by R. J. Hollingdale. Harmondsworth: Penguin, 1968.
Untimely Meditations. Translated by R. J. Hollingdale. Cambridge: Cambridge University Press, 1983.
Friedrich Nietzsche on Rhetoric and Language. Edited and translated by Sander L. Gilman, Carole Blair, and David J. Parent. New York: Oxford University Press, 1989.
Selected Letters of Friedrich Nietzsche. Translated by Christopher Middleton. Chicago: University of Chicago Press, 1969.

MARTIN HEIDEGGER
Primary Sources

Beiträge zur Philosophie (Vom Ereignis), Gesamtausgabe. Edited by Friedrich-Wilhelm von Herrmann. Frankfurt am Main: Vittorio Klostermann, 1989. GA 65.
Bremer und Freiburger Vorträge. [1949] Frankfurt am Main: Klostermann, 1994. GA 79.
"Brief über dem Humanismus." [1947] *Wegmarken.* Frankfurt am Main: Vittorio Klostermann, 1978. GA 9.
"Die Sprache." In: *Unterwegs zur Sprache.* GA 12.
"Die Frage nach der Technik." In: *Vorträge und Aufsätze.* Pfullingen: Neske, 1978. GA 7.
Einführung in die Metaphysik. [1935] Tübingen: Niemeyer, 1953.
Gelassenheit. Pfullingen: Neske, 1959. GA 16.
Hölderlin und das Wesen der Dichtung, 1936. GA 4.
Hölderlin's Hymne "Der Ister." Frankfurt am Main: Vittorio Klostermann, 1984. GA 53.
Holzwege. Frankfurt am Main: Klostermann, 1950. GA 5.
Nietzsche. 2 Volumes. Pfullingen: Neske, 1961. GA 6.

Sein und Zeit. Tübingen: Niemeyer, 1933. [1927] GA 2.

"Spiegel-Gespräch." In: Günther Neske and E. Kettering, eds., *Antwort. Martin Heidegger im Gespräch.* Pfüllingen: Neske, 1988.

Unterwegs zur Sprache. Pfüllingen: Neske, 1959. GA 12.

Ursprung des Kunstwerkes. Stuttgart: Reclam, 1960. GA 5.

Vorträge und Aufsätze. Pfüllingen: Neske, 1954. GA 7.

Was heist Denken? Tübingen: Niemeyer, 1971; 1984. [1954] GA 8.

Wegmarken. Frankfurt am Main: Klostermann, 1967. GA 9.

Zollikoner Seminare, Protokolle–Gespräche–Briefe. Edited by Medard Boss. Frankfurt am Main: Klostermann, 1987. GA 89.

Zur Sache des Denkens. Tübingen: Niemayer, 1969. GA 16.

English translations

"The Anaximander Fragment." In: *Early Greek Thinking.*

Being and Time. Translated by John Macquarrie and Edward Robinson. New York: Harper & Row, 1962. [SZ]

Being and Time. Translated by Joan Stambaugh. New York: State University of New York Press, 1996.

Contributions to Philosophy (From Enowning). Translated by Parvis Emad and Kenneth Maly. Bloomington/Indianapolis: Indiana University Press, 1999.

Discourse on Thinking. Translated by John Anderson and E. H. Freund. New York: Harper & Row, 1966.

Early Greek Thinking. Translated by David Farrell Krell and Frank Capuzzi. New York: Harper & Row, 1975.

Hölderlin's Hymn "The Ister." Translated by William McNeill and Julia Davis. Bloomington: Indiana University Press, 1996.

Introduction to Metaphysics. Translated by Ralph Manheim. New Haven: Yale University Press, 1959.

"Language." In: Heidegger, *Poetry, Language Thought.*

"Letter to Father Richardson." In William J. Richardson. *Through Phenomenology to Thought.* Nijmegen: Nijhoff, 1965. [2000]

"Logos (Heraclitus, Fragment 50)." In Heidegger, *Early Greek Thinking.*

Nietzsche, Volume 1: The Will to Power as Art. Translated by David Farrell Krell. San Francisco: Harper & Row, 1979.

Nietzsche, Volume 2: The Eternal Recurrence of the Same. Translated by David Farrell Krell. San Francisco: Harper & Row, 1982.

Nietzsche, Volume 4: Nihilism, ed. David Farrell Krell. San Francisco: Harper & Row, 1982.

"Nihilism as Determined by the History of Being." Translated by Frank A. Capuzzi. In: *Nietzsche, Volume 4.* Pp. 197–250.

" 'Only a God Can Save Us': The *Spiegel* Interview (1966)." Translated by William J. Richardson. In: Thomas Sheehan, ed., *Heidegger. The Man and the Thinker.* Chicago: Precedent, 1981. Pp. 45–67. Also in: Gunter Neske & Emil Kettering, eds., *Martin Heidegger and National Socialism: Questions and Answers.* New York: Paragon House, 1990.

Poetry, Language Thought. Translated by Albert Hofstadter. New York: Harper, 1971

The Question Concerning Technology and Other Essays. Translated by William Lovitt. New York: Harper & Row, 1977.

"On the Essence of Truth." Translated by John Sallis. In: David Farrell Krell, ed., *Basic Writings.* New York: Harper & Row, 1977. Pp. 117–41.

"On the Nature of Language." In: *On the Way to Language.*

On Time and Being. Translated by Joan Stambaugh. New York: Harper & Row, 1972.

On the Way to Language. Translated by Peter D. Hertz et al. San Francisco: Harper, 1971.

"The Question Concerning Technology." In: Heidegger, *The Question Concerning Technology.* New York: Harper & Row, 1977. Pp. 3–35.

"The Word of Nietzsche: God is Dead." In: *The Question Concerning Technology.* Pp. 54–55.

"The Thinker as Poet." In: Heidegger, *Poetry, Language Thought.*

"The Turning." In: *The Question Concerning Technology.* Pp. 36–49.

"The Origin of the Work of Art." Translated by Albert Hofstadter. In: *Poetry, Language, Thought.* New York: Harper & Row, 1971. Pp. 17–81.

What is Called Thinking. Translated by J. Glenn Gray. New York: Harper, 1968.

What is Philosophy. Translated by Jean T. Wilde and William Kluback. New Haven: College and University Press. No date. Bilingual edition.

"Words." Translated by Joan Stambaugh. In: *On the Way to Language*, p. 139ff.

Zollikon Seminars. Protocols—Conversations—Letters. Translated by Franz Mayr and Richard Askay. Evanston: Northwestern University Press, 2001.

Research literature and commentary

Adorno, Theodor. *The Culture Industry.* London: Routledge, 2000.

———. *Gesammelte Werke.* Edited by Rolf Tiedemann. Frankfurt: Suhrkamp, 1970–86 [20 volumes.]

———. *Quasi una Fantasia.* Translated by Rodney Livingstone. London: Verso, 1992.

——— and Max Horkheimer. *Dialectic of Enlightenment.* Translated by J. Cumming. New York: Herder & Herder, 1972.

Agamben, Giorgio. *Potentialities: Collected Essays in Philosophy.* Translated by David Heller-Roazen. Stanford: Stanford University Press, 1999.

———. "The Passion of Facticity: Heidegger and the Problem of Love." In: Agamben, *Potentialities. Collected Essays in Philosophy.* Stanford, CA: Stanford University Press, 1999.

Alberti. *De re aedificatori libri decem.* IX/5. 1962.

Allen, Barry. *Truth in Philosophy.* Cambridge: Harvard University Press, 1996.

Allison, David B. "Nietzsche Knows No Noumenon." In: Daniel O'Hara, ed., *Why Nietzsche Now? Boundary 2.* Bloomington: Indiana University Press, 1985. Pp. 294–310.

————. *Reading the New Nietzsche*. Lanham, MD: Rowman & Littlefield, 2001.

Altwegg, Jürg. "Ein Gespräch mit Jürgen Habermas." In: Altwegg, ed.: *Die Heidegger Kontroverse*. Athenaeum: Frankfurt am Main, 1988. Pp. 172–175.

Anderson, Warren D. *Music and Musicians in Ancient Greece*. Ithaca: Cornell University Press, 1994.

Andreae, Bernard. *Laokoon und die Gründung Roms*. Mainz am Rhein: Philipp von Zabern, 1988.

Angelus Silesius, [Johannes Scheffler]. *Cherubinischer Wandersmann: Kritische Ausgabe*. Ed., Loiuse Gnädinger. Reclam: Stuttgart, 1982.

Anon., trans. "Der orphische Papyrus von Derveni." *Zeitschrift für Papyrologie und Epigraphik*, 47 (1982): 1–12.

Arendt, Hannah. "Martin Heidegger at Eighty." In: Michael Murray ed., *Heidegger and Modern Philosophy: Critical Essays*. New Haven: Yale, 1978. Pp. 293–303.

————. *The Human Condition: A Study of the Central Dilemma Facing Modern Man*. Chicago: University of Chicago Press, 1998.

Arnheim, Rudolf. *Radio*. New York: Da Capo Press, 1972.

Aubrey, Elizabeth et. al. "Les Formes." In: Françoise Ferrand, dir.: *Guide de la Musique du Moyen Âge*. Paris: Fayard 1999. Pp. 313–337.

————. "Les troubadours." In: Ferrand, *Guide de la Musique du Moyen Âge*. Pp. 259–267.

————. *The Music of the Troubadours*. Indianapolis: Indiana University Press, 1996.

Augstein, Rudolph. "Aber bitte nicht philosophieren." In: Altwegg, ed.: *Die Heidegger Kontroverse*.

Babbit, Irving. *Rousseau and Romanticism*. New York: Meridian, 1919.

Babich, Babette E. "A Musical Retrieve of Heidegger, Nietzsche, and Technology: Cadence, Concinnity, and Playing Brass." *Man and World*. 26 (1993): 239–260.

————. "Dichtung, Eros, und Denken in Nietzsche und Heidegger: Heideggers Nietzsche Interpretation und die heutigen Nietzsche-Lektüre." *Heidegger-Jahrbuch II*. Freiburg: Karl Alber Verlag, 2005. Pp. 239–264.

————. "Die Wissenschaftsbegriff zwischen Martin Heidegger und Medard Boss." In: Harald Seubert, ed., *Philosophie und Daseinsanalyse*. Köln: Böhlau, 2004. Pp. 249–268.

————. "From Nietzsche's Artist to Heidegger's World: The Post-Aesthetic Perspective." *Man and World*. 22 (1989): 3–23.

————. "From Van Gogh's Museum to the Temple at Bassae: Heidegger's Truth of Art and Schapiro's Art History," *Culture, Theory, Critique* 44/2 (2003): 151–169.

————. "Habermas, Nietzsche, and the Future of Critique: Irrationality, *The Will to Power*, and War." In: Babich, ed.: *Habermas, Nietzsche, and Critical Theory*. Pp. 13–46.

————. "Heideggers Beiträge zur Philosophie als Ethik. *Phronesis* und die Frage nach der Technik im naturwissenschaftlichen Zeitalter." In: Stefan Lorenz Sorgner, et al., eds., *Eugenik und die Zukunft*. Freiburg: Alber, 2006.

———. "Heidegger's Philosophy of Science: Calculation, Thought, and *Gelassenheit.*" In: Babich, ed., *From Phenomenology to Thought, Errancy, and Desire.* Pp. 589–599.

———. "Heidegger's Relation to Nietzsche's Thinking: On Connivance, Nihilism, and Value." *New Nietzsche Studies,* 3: 1/2 (1999): 23–52.

———. "La veridad del arte en Heidegger. Salvar el museo entre Schapiro y Gadamer." In: Carlos Eduardo Sanabria, ed., *Estética: Miradas contemporáneas.* Bogotá, Columbia: Fondation Universidad de Bogotá, 2004. Pp. 183–230.

———. "Nietzsche, Classic Philology and Ancient Philosophy: A Research Bibliography." *New Nietzsche Studies,* 4:1/2 (Summer/Fall 2000): 171–191.

———. "Nietzsche and Music: A Partial Bibliography," *New Nietzsche Studies,* 1: 1/2 (1996): 64–78.

———. "Nietzsche's 'Artist's Metaphysics' and Fink's Ontological 'World-Play.' " *International Studies in Philosophy.* In press.

———. "Nietzsche's Critical Theory: The Culture of Science as Art." In: Babich, ed., *Nietzsche, Theories of Knowledge and Critical Theory: Nietzsche and the Sciences I.* Dordrecht: Kluwer Academic Publishers, 1999. Pp. 1–26.

———. "Nietzsche's Critique of Scientific Reason and Culture: On 'Science as a Problem' and 'Chaos as Nature.' " In: Gregory M. Moore and Thomas Brobjer, eds., *Nietzsche and Science.* Aldershot: Ashgate, 2004. Pp. 133–153.

———. "Nietzsche's *göttliche Eidechse*: 'Divine Lizards,' 'Greene Lyons' and Music." In: Christa Davis Acampora and Ralph Acampora, eds., *Nietzsche's Bestiary.* Lanham: Rowman & Littlefield, 2004. Pp. 264–283.

———. *Nietzsche's Philosophy of Science: Reflecting Science on the Ground of Art and Life.* Albany: State University of New York Press, 1994.

———. "Nietzsche's Self-Deconstruction: Philosophy as Style." *Soundings,* 73 (Spring, 1990): 50–12.

———. "On the Analytic-Continental Divide in Philosophy: Nietzsche's Lying Truth, Heidegger's Speaking Language, and Philosophy." In: C. G. Prado, ed., *A Dubious Estrangement: Analytic and Continental Philosophy.* Amherst, New York: Humanities Press, 2003. Pp. 63–103.

———. "On Malls, Museums, and the Art World: Postmodernism and the Vicissitudes of Consumer Culture." *Art Criticism,* IX/1 (Fall 1993): 1–16.

———. "On Nietzsche's Concinnity: An Analysis of Style." *Nietzsche-Studien,* 19 (1990): 59–80.

———. "On the Order of the Real: Nietzsche and Lacan." In: David Pettigrew and François Raffoul, eds.: *Disseminating Lacan.* Albany: State University of New York Press, 1996. Pp. 48–63.

———. "Postmodern Musicology." In: Victor E. Taylor and Charles E. Winquist, eds., *Encylopedia of Postmodernism.* London: Routledge, 2001. Pp. 255–259.

———. "Questioning Heidegger's Silence: Towards a Post-Modern Topology." In: Charles Scott and Arleen Dallery, eds., *Ethics and Danger: Currents in Continental Thought.* Albany: State University of New York Press, 1992. Pp. 83–106.

————. "The Logic of Woman in Nietzsche: The Dogmatist's Story." *New Political Science*, 36 (1996): 7–17.

Badiou, Alain. *Handbook of Inaesthetics.* Translated by Alberto Toscano. Stanford: Stanford University Press, 2004.

Barber, Benjamin R. *Jihad Versus Mcworld.* New York: Times Books, 2001 [1995].

Bauman, Zygmunt. *Wasted Lives: Modernity and Its Outcasts.* London: Polity, 2004.

Bec, Pierre. *Le comte de Poitiers, premier troubadour. À l'aube d'un verbe et d'une érotique.* Montpellier: Université Paul Valery "Collection lo gatros," 2003.

Behler, Ernst. "Nietzsche's Study of Greek Rhetoric," *Research in Phenomenology,* 25 (1995): 3–26.

Bellermann, J.F. *Die Tonleitern und Musiknoten der Griechen.* Wiesbaden: Sändig, 1969 [1847].

Benjamin, Walter. "Theses on the Philosophy of History." In: Benjamin, *Illuminations,* translated by Harry Zohn, edited by Hannah Arendt. New York: Schocken Books, 1969. Pp. 253–64.

————. "The Work of Art in the Age of Mechanical Reproduduction." In: *Illuminations.*

Benn, Gottfried. "Nietzsche After 50 Years." Translated by Matthew Lund. *New Nietzsche Studies,* 4: 3/4 (2000–2001): 125–135.

Berman, Marshall. "Meyer Schapiro: The Presence of the Subject." In: Berman, *Adventures in Marxism.* London: Verso, 1999. Pp. 221–236.

Berman, Russell and Paul Piccone. "Hidden Agendas: The Young Heidegger and the Post-Modern Debate," *Telos* 17 (1988): 117–25.

Bernasconi, Robert. "The Greatness of the Work of Art." In: Bernasconi, *Heidegger in Question: The Art of Existing.* Atlantic Highlands: Humanties Press, 1993. Pp. 99–116.

————. " 'Ne sutor ultra crepidam:' Dürer and Erasmus at the Hands of Panofsky and Heidegger." In: Bernasconi. *Heidegger in Question.* Pp. 117–134.

————. "Habermas and Arendt on the Philosopher's 'Error': Tracking the Diabolical in Heidegger." *Graduate Faculty Philosophy Journal,* 14:2/15:1 (1991): 1–23.

————. *The Question of Language in Heidegger's History of Being.* Atlantic Highlands: Humanities Press, 1985.

Bertallot, Hans Werner. *Hölderlin-Nietzsche: Untersuchungen zum hymnischen stil in prosa und vers.* Berlin: E. Ebering, 1933; Nendeln/Liechtenstein, Kraus Reprint, 1967.

Bertaux, Pierre. *Hölderlin und die Französiche Revolution.* Frankfurt am Main: Suhrkamp, 1969.

Bertram, Ernst. *Nietzsche. Versuch einer Mythologie.* Berlin: Helmut Küpper, 1918.

Besser, Kurt. *Die Problematik der aphoristischer Form bei Lichtenberg, Schlegel, Novalis, und Nietzsche.* Leibzig, 1935.

Betegh, Gabor. *The Derveni Papyrus: Cosmology, Theology and Interpretation.* Cambridge: Cambridge University Press, 2004.

Binder, Hermann. *Deutschland. Heilig Herz der Völker. Lebenswerte in deutscher Dichtung.* Stuttgart/Berlin: Deutsche Verlagsanstalt, 1940.

Boehme, Gernot. *Für eine Ökologische Naturästhetik.* Suhrkamp: Frankfurt am Main, 1989.

Boeckh, August. *De metris Pindari.* Leipzig, 1811.

Böning, Thomas. " 'Das Buch eines Musikers ist eben nicht das buch eines Augenmenschen,' Metaphysik und Sprache beim frühen Nietzsche." *Nietzsche-Studien,* 15 (1986): 72–106.

Böschenstein, Bernard. *Leuchttürme: Von Hölderlin zu Celan.* Frankfurt: Insel, 1977.

Boniolo, Giovanni. "Kant's Explication and Carnap's Explication: The *Redde Rationem.*" *International Philosophical Quarterly,* 43, 3, 171 (2003): 289–298.

Bornmann, Fritz. "Nietzsches metrische Studien," *Nietzsche-Studien,* 18 (1989): 472–489.

Borsche, Tilman. "Nietzsches Erfindung der Vorsokratiker." In: Josef Simon, ed., *Nietzsche und die philosophische Tradition.* Würzburg: Königshausen & Neumann, 1985. Pp. 62–87.

Boss, Medard. Preface. Pp. xv–xxii. In Heidegger, *Zollikon Seminars.*

Bossuet. *Politique tirée des propres paroles de l'Ecriture sainte.* Paris: P. Cot, 1709.

Bothe, Henning. *«Ein Zeichen sind wir, deutungslos».* Die Rezeption Hölderlins von ihren Anfangen bis zu Stefan George. Stuttgart: Metzler, 1992.

Bourdieu, Pierre, et al., eds. *The Weight of the World: Social Suffering in Contemporary Society,* ed. trans. Priscilla Parkhurst Ferguson, et al. Stanford: Stanford University Press, 1999.

Brambaugh, Robert. *Plato's Mathematical Imagination.* Bloomington: Indiana University Press, 1954.

Brobjer, Thomas. "A Discussion and Source of Hölderlin's Influence on Nietzsche." *Nietzsche-Studien* 30 (2001): 148–152.

Bryson, Norman. *Vision and Painting: The Logic of the Gaze.* New Haven: Yale University Press, 1983.

———. *Word and Image: French Painting of the Ancien Regime.* Cambridge: Cambridge University Press, 1981.

Burkert, Walter. "The Logic of Cosmogony." In: Richard Buxton, ed.: *From Myth to Reason: Studies in the Development of Greek Thought.* Oxford: Oxford University Press, 1999. Pp. 87–106.

Burnham, Douglas. "Nietzsche, Sensibility and Difference." In: Burnham, *Kant's Philosophies of Judgement.* Edinburgh: Edinburgh University Press, 2004.

Burton, R. W. B. *Pindar's Pythian Odes: Essays in Interpretation.* Oxford: Oxford University Press, 1962.

Butler, Eliza May. *The Tyranny of Greece Over Germany.* London: Macmillan, 1935.

Butterfield, Herbert. *The Origins of Modern Science: 1300–1800.* New York: Free Press, 1965; 1957.

———. *The Whig Interpretation of History.* London: Bell, 1931.

Cambridge, A. W. Pickard. *Dithyramb Tragedy and Comedy.* Oxford: Oxford University Press 1997. [1927]

Campbell, Moody. "Nietzsche-Wagner to January, 1872." *PMLA,* 56 (1941), 544–577.

Cančik, Hubert. *Nietzsches Antike.* Stuttgart: Metzler, 2000.

Caygill, Howard. "Nietzsche's Atomism." In: Babich, ed.: *Nietzsche, Theories of Knowledge, and Critical Theory.* Nietzsche and the Sciences I, Dordrecht: Kluwer, 1999. Pp. 27–36.

———. "The Consolation of Philosophy or 'Neither Dionysus nor the Crucified,' " *Journal of Nietzsche Studies,* 7 Spring (1994): 113–140.

———. "The Return of Nietzsche and Marx." In: Babich, ed.: *Habermas, Nietzsche, and Critical Theory.* Pp. 195–209.

———. *Walter Benjamin: The Colour of Experience.* London: Routledge, 1998.

Chanan, Michael. *Musica Practica: The Social Practice of Western Music from Gregorian Chant to Postmodernism.* London: Verso, 1994.

Chargaff, Erwin. *Voices in the Labyrinth: Nature, Man, and Science.* New York: Seabury Press, 1977.

Charles, Daniel. "Heidegger on Hermeneutics and Music Today." *Acta Philosophica Fenica.* 43 (1988): 154–166.

Clark, Maudemarie. "From the Nietzsche Archive: Concerning the Aphorism Explicated in Genealogy III." *Journal of the History of Philosophy,* 35/4 (1997): 593–633.

Comotti, Giovanni. *Music in Greek and Roman Culture.* Translated by. Rosaria V. Munson. Baltimore: The Johns Hopkins University Press, 1977.

Constantine, David. *Hölderlin.* Oxford: Oxford University Press, 1988.

Cordemoy, Géraud de. "De la nécessité de l'histoire, de son usage & de la manière dont il faut mêler les autres sciences, en la faisant lire à un prince." In: Cordemoy, *Divers traités de métaphysique, d'histoire et de politique.* Paris, 1691.

Corngold, Stanley. *The Fate of the Self.* New York: Columbia University Press, 1986.

——— and Geoffrey Waite, "A Question of Responsibility: Nietzsche with Hölderlin at War, 1914–1946." In Golomb and Wistrich, eds.: *Nietzsche Godfather of Fascism.* Pp. 196–214.

Cox, Christoph. *Nietzsche: Naturalism and Interpretation.* Berkeley: University of California Press, 1999.

Craig, Gordon A. *The Politics of the Unpolitical: German Writers and the Problem of Power 1770–1871.* Oxford: Oxford University Press, 1995.

Crimp, Douglas. *On the Museum's Ruins.* Cambridge: Harvard University Press, 1993.

Crowther, Paul. "Heidegger and the Question of Aesthetics." *Journal of the British Society for Phenomenology.* 19/1 (1988): 51–63.

Cullen, Olivier. "Leys d'Amor." In: Ferrand, dir., *La Musique du Moyen Âge.* P. 279.

Curtius, Ludwig. "Morphologie der antiken Kunst." *Logos,* IX: 2 (1920/21): 195–221.

Cutcliffe, Stephen H. *Ideas, Machines, and Values: An Introduction to Science, Technology, and Value Studies.* Lanham, MD: Rowman & Littlefield, 2000.

Dallmayr, Fred. "Habermas's Discourse of Modernity: Nietzsche as Turntable," In: Babich, ed.: *Habermas, Nietzsche, and Critical Theory.* Amherst, NY: Humanity Books, 2004.

————. "Heidegger on *Macht* and *Machenschaft*." *Continental Philosophical Review*, 34 (2001): 247–267.

————. *Margins of Political Discourse*. Albany: State University of New York Press,1989.

Dale, A. M. *Collected Papers*. Cambridge: Cambridge University Press, 1969.

————. *The Lyric Metres of Greek Drama*. Cambridge: Cambridge University Press,1968.

Danto, Arthur. *After the End of Art: Contemporary Art and the Pale of History*. Princeton: Princeton University Press, 1997.

————. *The Philosophical Disenfranchisement of Art*. New York: Columbia University Press, 1986.

Davidson, Arnold. "Questions concerning Heidegger: Opening the Debate, *Critical Inquiry* 15 (1988–89): 407–26.

Davison, Aidan. *Technology and the Contested Meaning of Sustainability*. Albany: State University of New York Press, 2001.

de Beauvoir, Simone. Translated by H. M. Parshley. *The Second Sex*. New York: Random House, 1989 [1949].

de Rotonchamp, J. *Paul Gauguin 1898–1903*. Paris: C. Cres, 1925.

de la Croix, Arnaud. *L'éroticisme au Moyen Âge. Le corps le désir l'amour*. Paris: Tallandier, 1999.

del Caro, Adrian. "Nietzsche's Rhetoric on the Grounds of Philology and Hermeneutics." *Philosophy and Rhetoric*. 37: 2 (2004): 101–122.

————. "Symbolizing Philosophy: Ariadne and the Labyrinth." *Nietzsche-Studien*. 17 (1988): 125–57.

————. "Nietzschean Self-Transformation and the Transformation of the Dionysian." In: Salim Kemal, et al, eds.: *Nietzsche, Philosophy and the Arts*, Cambridge: Cambridge University Press, 1998. Pp. 79–91.

de Man, Paul. *Allegories of Reading: Figural Language in Rousseau, Nietzsche, Rilke, Freud*. New Haven: Yale University Press, 1976.

————. "Rhetoric of Tropes (Nietzsche)." In: de Man, *Allegories of Reading*.

————. "Nietzsche's Theory of Rhetoric," *Symposium: A Quarterly Journal in Modern Foreign Languages* (1974): 33–51.

Decremps, Marcel. *De Herder et de Nietzsche B Mistral*. Toulon: L'astrado, 1974.

Derrida, Jacques. *Éperons: Les Styles de Nietzsche. Spurs: Nietzsche's Styles*. Translated by Barbara Johnson. Chicago: University of Chicago, 1979.

————. "Guter Wille zur Macht: Drei Fragen an Hans-Georg Gadamer." In: Philippe Forget, ed., *Text und Interpretationen*. Munich: Fink, 1984. Pp. 56–58.

————. "Heidegger's Ear: Philopolemology." In: John Sallis, ed., *Reading Heidegger*. Bloomington: Indiana University Press, 1993. Pp. 163–218.

————. "Heidegger's Silence: Excerpts from a Talk Given on 5 February 1988," trans. L. Harries and J. Neugroschel. In: G. Neske and E. Kettering, eds., *Martin Heidegger and National Socialism: Questions and Answers*. New York: Paragon House, 1990. Pp. 145–48.

————. *Otobiographies. L'enseignement de Nietzsche et la politique du nom propre*. Paris: éditions galilée, 1984.

————. *Politics of Friendship.* Translated by George Collins. London: Verso, 1997.

————. "Restitutions." In: Derrida, *The Truth in Painting.* Translated by Geoff Bennington and Ian McLeod. Chicago: University of Chicago Press, 1987.

————. "Restitututions de la verité en pointure," *Macula*, nos. 3–4 (1978): 11–37.

Detienne, Marcel. *Apollon, le couteau à la main.* Paris: Gallimard, 1998.

Devine, Andrew and Lawrence Stephens. *The Prosody of Greek Speech.* Oxford: Oxford University Press, 1994.

Dilthey, Wilhelm. *Das Erlebnis und die Dichtung.* 16. Aufl., Göttingen: Vandenhoeck und Ruprecht, 1985.

Doujat, Jean. *Abrégé de l'histoire romaine et grecque, en partie traduit de Velleius Paterculus, et en partie tiré des meilleurs auteurs de l'Antiquité.* Paris, 1671.

Dragonetti, Roger. *Le gai savoir dans la rhétorique courtoise. Flamenca et Joufroi de Poitiers.* Paris: Éditions du Seuil, 1982.

Dyson, Freeman. "When is the Ear Pierced." In: Mary Anne Moser and Douglas MacLeod, eds, *Immersed in Technology.* Bloomington: Indiana University Press, 1999. Pp. 73–101.

Eger, Manfred. *"Wenn ich Wagnern den Krieg mache." Der Fall Nietzsche und das Menschliche, Allzumenschliche.* München: Knaur, 1991.

Eisnitz, Gail. *Slaughterhouse: The Shocking Story of Greed, Neglect, and Inhumane Treatment Inside the U.S. Meat Industry.* Amherst, NY: Prometheus, 1997.

Elden, Stuart. "Taking the Measure of the *Beiträge*: Heidegger, National Socialism and the Calculation of the Political." *European Journal of Political Theory.* 2/1(2003): 35–56.

Elkins, James. *Why Are Our Pictures Puzzles? On the Modern Origins of Pictorial Complexity.* London: Routledge, 1999.

Else, Gerald. *The Origin and Early Form of Greek Tragedy.* Cambridge, MA: Harvard University Press, 1987.

Emerson, Ralph Waldo. "The Conduct of Life." In: *The Complete Works of Ralph Waldo Emerson* Volume VI. New York: Houghton & Mifflin, 1888 [1860].

Evelyn-White, Hugh. "Introduction." In: *Hesiod.Homeric Hymns.Epic Cycle. Homerica.* Translated by Evelyn-White. Cambridge: Harvard University Press, 1936 [1914].

Ferrand, Françoise, ed. *La Musique du Moyen Âge.* Paris: Fayard, 1999.

Ferry, Luc and Alain Renaut. *Heidegger and Modernity.* Translated by F. Philip. Chicago: University of Chicago Press, 1990.

————. *Heidegger et les Modernes.* Paris: Grasset, 1988.

————. eds., *Why We are Not Nietzscheans.* Chicago: University of Chicago, 1997.

Feyerabend, Paul. "Galileo and the Tyranny of Truth." In: Feyerabend, *A Farewell to Reason.* London: Verso, 1987. Pp. 247–264.

Fichte, Johann Gottlieb. *Grundlage der gesamten Wissenschaftslehre als Handschrift für seine Zuhörer (1794).* Hamburg: Fritz Meiner, 1997.

Fietz, Rudolf. *Medienphilosphie: Musik, Sprache, und Schrift bei Friedrich Nietzsche.* Würzburg: Königshausen & Neumann, 1992.

Fink, Eugen. *Nietzsches Philosophie*. Stuttgart: Kohlhammer, 1979 [1960].
———. *Nietzsche's Philosophy*. Translated by Goetz Richter. Athlone: Aldershot, 2003.
Fléchier, Esprit. *Histoire de Théodose le Grand*. Paris: S. Mabre-Cramoisy, 1679.
Fleschig, Hartmut. "Anstöße Heideggers Musikwissenschaft." *Musikforschung*. 30/1 (1970): 26–30.
Förster, Eckart. "Preface." In: Henrich, Dieter. *The Course of Remembrance and other Essays on Hölderlin*. Stanford: Stanford University Press, 1997.
Fóti, Veronique. *Heidegger and the Poets: Poiesis, Sophia, Techne*. Amherst, NY: Prometheus Books, 1992.
Foucault, Michel. *The Order of Things*. New York: Random House, 1971.
Fowler, Barbara, editor and translator. *Archaic Greek Poetry: An Anthology*. Madison: The University of Wisconsin Press, 1992.
Fowler, H.W and F.G. *The King's English: An Essential Guide to Written English*. Oxford Oxford University Press, 1973 [1906].
Friedmann, Michael. *Parting of the Ways: Carnap, Cassirer, Heidegger*. Chicago, IL: Open Court, 2000.
———. *Reconsidering Logical Positivism*. Cambridge: Cambridge University Press, 1999.
Friedmann, Thomas L. *The Lexus and the Olive Tree: Understanding Globalization*. New York: Farrar, Straus and Giroux, 2000.
Gadamer, Hans-Georg. (Commentary.) *Aletheia* 9/10 (1996): 19.
———. "Die Wahrheit des Kunstwerkes (1960)." In: Gadamer, *Gesammelte Werke 3. Neuere Philosophie 1*. Tübingen: Mohr Siebeck, 1987. Pp. 249–261.
———. "Thinking and Poetizing in Heidegger's and Hölderlin's *Andenken*." Translated by Richard A. Palmer. In: James Risser, ed., *Towards the Turn*. Albany: State University of New York Press, 1999. Pp. 145–162. Originally published as "Von der Wahrheit des Wortes." In: *Dichten und Denken bei Martin Heidegger*, Jahresausgabe der Martin-Heidegger-Gesellschaft, 1988. Pp. 7–22.
———. *The Relevance of the Beautiful and other Essays*. Translated by Nicholas Walker. Cambridge: Cambridge University Press, 1986. [Original in: Gadamer, *Gesammelte Werke 8. Ästhetik und Poetik 1*. Tübingen: Mohr Siebeck, 1999. Pp. 94–142.]
———. "Und dennoch: Macht des guten Willens." In: Philippe Forget, *Text und Interpretationen*. Munich: Fink, 1984. Pp. 59–61.
———. "Von der Wahrheit des Wortes," *Dichten und Denken bei Martin Heidegger*, Jahresausgabe der Martin-Heidegger-Gesellschaft, 1988. Pp. 7–22 [Translated by Richard A. Palmer as "Thinking and Poetizing in Heidegger's and Hölderlin's *Andenken*." In: James Risser, ed.: *Towards the Turn*. Albany: State University of New York Press, 1999. Pp. 145–162.
Gaède, Édouard. "Figures d'Empédocle." In: Gaède, ed., *Nietzsche, Hölderlin, et la Grèce*. Paris: Societé d'Édition «Les Belles Lettres», 1985. Pp. 33–40.
———. ed., *Nietzsche, Hölderlin, et la Grèce*. Paris: Societé d'Édition «Les Belles Lettres», 1985.
Gauguin, Paul. "Natures mortes." *Essais d'art libre*, 1894, 4. Pp. 273–275.

George, Emery E., ed., *Friedrich Hölderlin: An Early Modern*. Ann Arbor: The University of Michigan Press.

Georgiades, Thrasybulos. *Music and Language: The Rise of Western Music as Exemplified in the Settings*. Translated by Marie Louise Göllner. Cambridge: Cambridge University Press, 1982.

———. *Musik und Rhythmus bei den Griechen. Zum Ursprung der abendländischen Musik*. Hamburg: Rowohlt, 1958.

Gerber, Gustav. *Die Sprache als Kunst*. 2 Volumes. Bromberg: Mittler'sche Buchhandlung, 1871.

———. *Die Sprache und das Erkennen*. Berlin: R. Gaertners Verlagsbuchhandlung, 1884.

Geuss, Raymond. "Introduction." In: Nietzsche, *The Birth of Tragedy and other Writings*. Translated by Ronald Speirs. Cambridge: Cambridge University Press, 1999.

Gigante, Marcello. "Nietzsche nella storia della filologia classica," *Rendiconti dell' Accademia di Archeologia, Letter e Belle Arti di Napoli*, LIX (1984): 5–46.

———. "Nietzsche und die Klassik." In Manfred Riedel, ed., *Ein Jedes Wort ist ein Vorurtheile* Köln: Bölau, 2001.

Gilman, Sander. " 'Braune Nacht.' Fr. Nietzsche's Venetian Poems." *Nietzsche-Studien* 1 (1972): 247–270.

———. *Inscribing the Other*. Lincoln: University of Nebraska Press, 1991.

——— and David Parent and Carol Blair, eds., *Nietzsche on Rhetoric and Language*, Oxford: Oxford University Press, 1989.

Glazebrook, Patricia. "The Role of the *Beiträge* in Heidegger's Critique of Science." *Philosophy Today* (2001): 24–32.

———. *Heidegger's Philosophy of Science*. New York: Fordham University Press, 1999.

Goehr, Lydia. *The Imaginary Museum of Musical Works: An Essay in the Philosophy of Music*. Oxford: Oxford University Press, 1992.

Golomb, Jacob and Robert Wistrich, eds. *Nietzsche Godfather of Fascism: On the Uses and Abuses of a Philosophy*. Princeton: Princeton University Press, 2002.

———. "Nietzsche's Politics, Fascism, and the Jews." *Nietzsche-Studien*, 30 (2001): 305–321.

Goodrich, Peter. "Gay Science and Law." In: Victoria Kahn and L. Hutson eds., *Rhetoric and Law in Early Modern Europe*. New Haven: Yale University Press, 2001. Pp. 95–125.

Grau, Gerd-Günther. *Kritik des absoluten Anspruchs. Nietzsche-Kierkegaard-Kant*. Würzburg: Königshausen & Neumann, 1993.

Gray, John. *Straw Dogs: Thoughts on Humans and Animals*. London: Granta Publications, 2002.

Guck, Marion. "Two Types of Metaphoric Transpher." In: Jamie C. Kassler, ed., *Metaphor: A Musical Dimension*. Basel: Gordon and Beacon, 1994.

Groddeck, Wolfram. "Ein Andres Wort für Musik. Zu Fr. Nietzsches Venedig-Gedicht." In: Hartmut Hartung, ed., *Gedichte und Interpretationen*. Stuttgart: Reclam, 1893. Vol. 5, Pp. 18–32.

Guadet, Julien. *Eléments et théorie de l'architecture. Cours professé à l'École nationale et spéciale des beaux-arts*. 3 vols. Paris: Aulanier et Cie, 1901–1903.

Guanti, Giovanni. *Romanticismo e musica. L'estetica musicale da Kant a Nietzsche.* Turin: EDT musica, 1981.

Gustafsson, Lars. *Sprach und Lüge –Drei sprachphilosophische Extremisten: Friedrich Nietzsche. A. B. Johnson, Fritz Mauthner.* München: Hanser, 1980.

Habermas, Jürgen. "Work and *Weltanschauung*: The Heidegger Controversy from a German Perspective." *Critical Inquiry* 15 (1988–89): 431–56.

Hadot, Pierre. *Le voile d'Isis. Essai sur l'histoire de l'idée de Nature.* Paris: Gallimard, 2004.

———. *Philosophy as a Way of Life.* Translated by Michael Chase. Chicago: University of Chicago Press, 1995.

Halporn, J. W. "Nietzsche: On the Theory of Quantitative Rhythm." *Arion* 6 (1967): 233–243.

Halliburton, David. *Poetic Thinking: An Approach to Heidegger.* Chicago, University of Chicago Press, 1981.

Hamacher, Werner. "Das Versprechen der Auslegung. Überlegungen zum hermeneutischen Imperativ bei Kant und Nietzsche." In: Norbert Bolz and W. Hübener, eds.: *Spiegel und Gleichnis. Festschrift für Jacob Taubes.* Würzburg: Königshausen and Neumann, 1983. Pp. 252–387.

Hamilton, John T. *Soliciting Darkness. Pindar, Obscurity, and the Classical Tradition.* Cambridge, MA: Harvard University Press, 2003.

Hanslick, Eduard. *Vom Musikalisch-Schönen.* Wiesbaden: Breitkopf & Härtel, 1989 [1854].

Hardy, Ineke and Elizabeth Brodovitch. "Tracking the Anagram: Preparing a Phonetic Blueprint of Troubadour Poetry." In: Barbara A. Altman and Carleton W. Carroll, eds.: *The Court Reconvenes: Courtly Literature Across the Disciplines.* Woodbridge: D. S. Brewer, 2003. Pp. 199–211.

Harries, Karsten. "Poetry as Response: Heidegger's Step Beyond Aestheticism." *Midwest Stud. Phil.* 16 (1991): 73–88.

Hatab, Larry. *Nietzsche's Life-Sentence: Coming to Terms with Eternal Recurrence.* New York: Routledge, 2005.

Hathorn, Richmond Y. *Greek Mythology.* Lebanon: American University of Beirut, 1977.

Havelock, Eric. *Preface to Plato.* Harvard University Press: Belknap, 1963.

Heelan, Patrick A. *Space-Perception in the Philosophy of Science.* Berkeley: University of California Press, 1983.

Heftrich, Urs. "Nietzsches Auseinandersetzung mit der 'Kritik der Ästhetischen Urteilskraft.'" *Nietzsche-Studien*, 20 (1991): 238–266.

Heinich, Nathalie. *The Glory of VAN GOGH: An Anthropology of Admiration.* Translated by Paul Leduc Browne. Princeton: Princeton University Press, 1996.

Heller, Agnes. *An Ethics of Personality.* London: Blackwell, 1996.

Heller, Erich. *The Importance of Nietzsche. Ten Essays.* Chicago: University of Chicago Press, 1988.

Helsloot, Niels. "*Gaya Scienza*: Nietzsche as a Friend." *New Nietzsche Studies*, Vols. 5 3/4 & 6 1/2 (Winter 2003/ Spring 2004): 89–104.

Hellingrath, Norbert von. *Hölderlins Wahnsinn*, Munich: Bruckmann, 1921.

Hemmingway, Andrew. "Meyer Schapiro and Marxism in the 1930's." *Oxford Art Journal*, 17/1 (1994):13–29.

Hénaff, Marcel. *Le Prix de la vérité. Le don, l'argent, la philosophie.* Paris: Le Seuil, 2002.

Henrich, Dieter. *The Course of Remembrance and other Essays on Hölderlin.* Stanford: Stanford University Press, 1997.

Henrichs, Albert. "Loss of Self, Suffering, Violence: The Modern View of Dionysus from Nietzsche to Girard." *Harvard Studies in Classical Philology*, 88 (1984): 205–240.

Hershbell, Jackson P. and Stephen Nimis. "Nietzsche and Heraclitus." *Nietzsche-Studien*, 8 (1979): 17–38.

Hill, R. Kevin. *Nietzsche's Critiques: The Kantian Foundations of His Thought.* Oxford: Oxford University Press, 2003.

Higgins, Kathleen Marie. *Comic Relief: Nietzsche's Gay Science.* Oxford: Oxford University Press, 1999.

———. "Musical Idiosyncrasy and Perspectival Listening." In: Jenefer Robinson, ed., *Music and Meaning.* Ithaca: Cornell University Press, 1997. Pp. 83–102.

Himmelfarb, Gertrude. *On Looking Into the Abyss.* New York: Knopf, 1994.

Himmelmann, Beatrix, ed., *Kant und Nietzsche im Widerstreit*, Berlin: de Gruyter, 2005.

Hippocrates, *Volume III.* Translated by W.H.S. Jones. Cambridge: Harvard University Press, 1995. [1923]

Hödl, Hans-Gerald. *Nietzsches frühe Sprachkritik. Lektüren zu «Ueber Wahrheit und Lüge im aussermoralischen Sinne».* Vienna: WUV-Universitätsverlag, 1997.

Hohendahl, Peter Uwe, ed., *Geschichte der deutschen Literaturkritik (1730–1980).* Stuttgart: Metzler, 1985.

Hoffman, David Marc. *Zur Geschichte des Nietzsche-Archivs.* Berlin: Walter de Gruyter, 1993.

Hollinrake, Roger. *Nietzsche, Wagner, and the Philosophy of Pessimism.* London: George Allen & Unwin, 1982.

———. "A Note on Nietzsche's 'Gondellied.' " *Nietzsche-Studien*, 4 (1975): 139–143.

Hornbacher, Annette. *Die Blume des Mundes. Zu Hölderlins Poetologisch-Poetischem Sprachdenken.* Wurzbach: Königshausen and Neumann, 2000.

Houlgate, Stephen. "Kant, Nietzsche, and the 'Thing in Itself.' " *Nietzsche-Studien*, 22 (1993):115–157.

Hühnerfeld, Paul. *Im Sachen Heidegger: Versuch über ein deutsches Genie.* Hamburg: Hoffmann and Campe, 1959.

Huet, P. D., dir., collection de classiques latins *Ad usum Delphini (1674–1691)*, *67 volumes, dont 39 auteurs, 5 dictionnaires.*

Hume, David. "Of the Standard of Taste." In: *Hume's Essays: Moral, Political, and Literary* Oxford: Oxford University Press, 1965. Pp. 231–255.

Hummel, Pascale. *Philologus auctor: Le philologue et son Œuvre.* Bern: Peter Lang, 2003.

Ihde, Don. *Bodies in Technology.* Minneapolis: University of Minnesota Press, 2002.

———. *Philosophy of Technology.* New York: Paragon House, 1993.

Illich, Ivan. *In the Vineyard of the Text: A Commentary on Hugh's* Didascalicon. Chicago: University of Chicago Press, 1993.

———— and Barry Sanders, *ABC: The Alphabetization of the Popular Mind* (San Francisco: North Point Press, 1968.

Irigaray, Luce. *An Ethics of Sexual Difference.* Translated by Carolyn Burke and Gillian C. Gill, Ithaca: Cornell Univ. Press, 1993.

————. "In Science, Is the Subject Sexed?" In: Gary Gutting, ed., *Continental Philosophy of Science* Oxford: Blackwell, 2005.

————. *The Forgetting of Air in Martin Heidegger.* Translated by Mary Beth Madder. Austin: University of Texas Press, 1999.

————. *To be Two.* Translated by Monique M. Rhodes and Marco F. Cocito-Monoc. New York: Routledge, 2001.

Jackson, Daniel, ed., *Sonic Branding.* London: Macmillan, 2004.

Jähnig, Dieter. "Die Kunst und der Raum." In: Gunther Neske, ed., *Erinnerung an Martin Heidegger.* Pfullingen: Neske, 1977. Pp. 131–148.

————. "The Liberation of the Knowledge of Art from Metaphysics in Nietzsche's *Birth of Tragedy.*" Translated by Babette E. Babich and Holger Schmid, *New Nietzsche Studies,* 3:3/4 (Summer/Fall 1999): 197–221.

————. *Welt-Geschichte: Kunst Geschichte. Zum Verhältnis von Vergangenheitserkenntnis und Veränderung.* Köln: DuMont Schauberg, 1975.

Jameson, Fredric. "Postmodernism, Or The Cultural Logic of Late Capitalism," *New Left Review* 146 (1984): 53–92.

Janicaud, Dominique. *Heidegger en France.* Paris: A. Michel, 2001.

Janz, Curt Paul. *Friedrich Nietzsche. Biographie.* Frankfurt: Zwei Tausend Eins, 1999.

————. "Nietzsche Verhältnis zur Musik seiner Zeit." *Nietzsche-Studien,* 7 (1978): 308–26.

Jarrell, Randall. *Complete Poems.* New York: Farar, Straus & Giroux, 1981 [1969].

Jaspers, Karl. *Notizen zu Martin Heidegger.* Munich: Piper, 1978.

Kant, Immanuel. *Critique of Pure Reason.* Translated by Norman Kemp Smith. London: Palgrave MacMillan, 2003.

Kassler, Jamie C., ed., *Metaphor: A Musical Dimension.* Basel: Gordon and Beacon, 1994.

Kauffman, Kai. " 'Gondeln, Lichter, Musik.' Fr. Nietzsches 'Venedig'-Gedichte und sein Metaphorischer Umfeld." *Nietzsche-Studien,* 17 (1988): 158–178.

Kaulbach, Friedrich. *Philosophie des Perpektivismus. I. Teil: Wahrheit und Perspektive bei Kant, Hegel und Nietzsche.* Tübingen: J. C. B. Mohr, 1990.

————. "Kant und Nietzsche im Zeichen der Kopernikanischen Wendung: Ein Beitrag zum Problem der Modernität." *Zeitschrift für philosophische Forschung.* 41 (1987): 349–372.

————. *Nietzsches Idee einer Experimentalphilosophie.* Cologne: Böhlau, 1980.

Kerenyi, Carl. *The Gods of the Ancient Greeks.* London: Thames and Hudson, 1951.

Keulartz, Jozef. *The Struggle for Nature: A Critique of Radical Ecology.* Routledge: New York, 1998.

Kingsley, Peter. *Ancient Philosophy, Mystery, and Magic: Empedocles and Pythagorean Tradition.* Oxford: Clarendon Press, 1995.

———. *In the Dark Places of Wisdom*. Inverness: Golden Sufi Press, 1999.

Kisiel, Theodore. "Heidegger's Apology: Biography as Philosophy and Ideology." *Graduate Faculty Philosophy Journal*. XIV:2–XV:1 (1991): 363–404.

Köhler, Joachim. *Zarathustra's Secret: The Interior Life of Friedrich Nietzsche*. Translated by Ronald Taylor. New Haven: Yale University Press, 2002.

Kofman, Sarah. *Explosion I. De l' «Ecce Homo» de Nietzsche*. Paris: galilée, 1992.

———. *Nietzsche and Metaphor*. Translated by Duncan Large. Stanford: Stanford University Press, 1994.

Koldehoff, Stefan. *Van Gogh Mythos und Wirklichkeit. Die Wahrheit über den teuersten Maler der Welt*. Dumont: Köln, 2003.

Kopperschmidt, Joseph and Helmut Schanze, eds., *Nietzsche oder 'Die Sprache ist Rhetorik.'* Munich: Fink, 1994.

Korff, Gottfried. *Museumsdinge: Deponieren – Exponieren*. Cologne: Böhlau, 2002.

Kovacs, George. "On Heidegger's Silence," *Heidegger Studies*, 5 (1989): 135–51.

Kremer-Marietti, Angèle. *L'homme et ses labyrinthes. Essai sur Friedrich Nietzsche*. Paris: Union géneral Éditions, 1972.

———. *Nietzsche et la rhétorique*. Paris, Presses Universitaires de France, 1994.

———. "Rhétorique et rythmique chez Nietzsche" in *Rythmes et philosophie*, sous la direction de P. Sauvanet et de J.-J. Wunenburger. Paris: Kimé, 1996. Pp. 181–194.

———. *Thèmes et structures dans l'oeuvre de Nietzsche*. Paris: Lettres Modernes, 1957.

Krüger, Heinz. *Studien über den Aphorismos als philosophischer Form*. Frankfurt: Nest Verlag, 1956.

Kunas, Tarmo. *Nietzsches Lachen. Ein Studie über das Komische in Nietzsches Werken* Munich: Edition Wissenschft und Literatur. Hg. Frido Flako, 1982.

Lacan, Jacques. "Of the Network of Signifiers." In *The Four Fundamental Concepts of Psychoanalysis*. Translated by Alan Sheridan. New York: W.W. Norton, 1978.

Lacoue-Labarthe, Philippe. "Le détour (Nietzsche et la rhétorique)," *Poétique*, 5 (1971): 53–76.

———. "Neither an Accident nor a Mistake." Translated by Paula Wissing. *Critical Inquiry* 15 (1988–89): 481–84.

———. *Typography: Mimesis Philosophy Politics*. Cambridge, Mass: Harvard University Press, 1989.

———. "Victor Farías's Heidegger et le Nazisme." In *Heidegger: Art and Politics*, trans. C. Turner, Oxford: Basil Blackwell, 1990.

——— and Jean-Luc Nancy, "Friedrich Nietzsche: Rhétorique et langage. Textes traduits, présentés et annotés," *Poétique*, 5 (1971): 99–142.

Laks, André and Glenn W. Most. "A Translation of the Derveni Papyrus," in *Studies on the Derveni Papyrus*, eds. Laks and Most. Oxford: Oxford University Press, 1997. Pp. 9–22.

La Rue, Jan. *Guidelines for Style Analysis*. Michigan: Harmonie Park Press, 1997.

Lee, M. Owen. *Athena Sings: Wagner and the Greeks*. Toronto: University of Toronto Press, 2003.

Leupin, Alexandre. "L'événement littérature: note sur la poétique des troubadours." In: F. Cornilliat et al., eds., *What is Literature?* Lexington, KY: French Forum, 1993. Pp. 53–68.

Leiner, George. "On Wagner and Bizet." *Journal of Nietzsche Studies.* 1:1/2 (Fall, 1995).

Lernout, Geerd. *The Poet as Thinker: Hölderlin in France.* South Carolina: Camden House, 1994.

Libeskind, Daniel. *The Space of an Encounter.* New York: Rizzoli, 2000.

Liébert, Georges. *Nietzsche et la musique.* Paris: Presses Universitaires de France. 1995.

Lippett, John, ed., *Nietzsche's Futures.* London: Macmillan, 1999.

Lloyd-Jones, Hugh. "Nietzsche and the Study of the Ancient World." In: James C. O'Flaherty, et al., eds.: *Studies in Nietzsche and the Classical Tradition.* Chapel Hill: University of North Carolina Press. Pp. 1–15.

Loeb, Paul. "The Dwarf, The Dragon, and the Ring of Recurrence: A Wagnerian Key to the Riddle of Nietzsche's Zarathustra." *Nietzsche-Studien* (2003): 91–113.

Lord, Albert B. *The Singer of Tales.* Cambridge, MA: Harvard University Press, 1960.

Louth, Charlie. *Hölderlin and the Dynamics of Translation.* Oxford: Legenda, European Humanities Research Centre, 1998.

Love, Frederick. *Young Nietzsche and the Wagnerian Experience.* Chapel Hill: The University of North Carolina Press, 1963.

Löwith, Karl. *Nietzsche's Philosophy of the Eternal Recurrence of the Same.* Translated by J. Harvey Lomax. Berkeley: University of California Press, 1997.

Lukàcs, Georg. *Die Zerstörung der Vernunft: Der Weg des Irrationalismus von Schelling zu Hitler.* Berlin: Aufbau Verlag, 1953.

———. *The Destruction of Reason: Irrationalism from Schelling to Nietzsche.* Translated by Peter Palmer. Atlantic Highlands, NJ: Humanities Press, 1981.

———. *Von Nietzsche bis Hitler oder Der Irrationalismus in der deutschen Politik.* Frankfurt: Fischer, 1966.

Lyotard, Jean-François. *Heidegger and "the Jews."* Translated by A. Michel and Mark S. Roberts. Minneapolis: Univ. of Minnesota Press, 1990. Pp. 40–41. [*Heidegger et "les juifs,"* Paris: Galilee, 1989.]

MacDonald, Susan, ed., *The Politics of Display: Museums, Science, Culture.* London: Routledge, 1998.

MacIntyre, Alasdair. "Preface." In: Babich, ed., *Nietzsche, Epistemology and Philosophy of Science: Nietzsche and the Sciences II.* Dordrecht: Kluwer, 1999. P. xvii.

———. *After Virtue.* Notre Dame, IN: University of Indiana Press, 1972.

———. *A Short Introduction to Ethics.* London: Macmillan, 1966.

Maconie, Robin. *The Concept of Music.* Oxford: Clarendon, 1990.

Maleuve, Didier. *Museum Memories: History, Technology, Art.* Stanford: Stanford University Press, 1999.

Malraux, André. "Le musée imaginaire," in: Malraux, *Les voix du silence.* Paris: Nouvelle Revue Française, Gallimard, 1951.

Malsch, Wilfried. "The Concept of Enlightenment in Hölderlin's Poetry." In: George, ed.: *Friedrich Hölderlin: An Early Modern.* Pp. 16–37.

Marchand, Suzanne S. *Down from Olympus: Archaeology and Philhellenism in Germany.* Princeton: Princeton University Press, 2003.

Marcuse, Herbert. "Some Social Implications of Modern Technology," *Technology, War and Fascism: Collected Papers of Herbert Marcuse, Volume One.* London: Routledge, 1998.

Margolis, Joseph and Tom Rockmore. "Introduction." In: Viktor Farías. *Heidegger and Nazism*, Translated by P. Burrell, et al. Philadelphia: Temple University Press, 1989.

Martin, Nicolas. *Nietzsche and Schiller: Untimely Aesthetics.* Clarendon Press: Oxford, 1996.

Marten, Rainer. "Heideggers Geist" In: Altweg, ed.: *Die Heidegger Kontroverse.* Pp. 226–229.

———. "Ein rassistisches Konzept von Humanität." *Badische Zeitung.* December 19/20, 1987.

Marx, Eduardo. *Heidegger und der Ort der Musik.* Würzburg: Königshausen & Neumann, 1998.

Mathiesen, Thomas J. *Apollo's Lyre: Greek Music and Music Theory in Antiquity and the Middle Ages.* Lincoln: University of Nebraska Press, 1999.

Maas, Paul. *Greek Meter.* Translated by Hugh Lloyd-Jones. Oxford: Oxford University Press, 1962.

———. *Griechische Metrik.* Leipzig: Teubner, 1923.

May, Reinhard. *Hidden Sources: East Asian Influences on His Work.* Translated by Graham Parkes. London: Routledge, 1996.

———. *Ex oriente lux: Heideggers Werk unter ostasiatischen Einfluß.* Stuttgart: Steiner Verlag Wiesbaden, 1989.

Mayer, H. "Stockendes Blut," *Neue Zürcher Zeitung,* Feb. 22 (2003): 2/14.

McClain, Ernest G. "A Priestly View of Biblical Arithmetic: Deity's Regulative Aesthetic Activity Within Davidic Musicology." In: Babich, ed.: *Hermeneutic Philosophy of Science, Van Gogh's Eyes, and God: Essays in Honor of Patrick A Heelan, S.J.* Dordrecht: Kluwer, 2002. Pp. 429–443.

———. *The Pythagorean Plato: Prelude to the Song Itself.* Nicolas Hays: York Beach, Maine, 1978.

———. *The Myth of Invariance: The Origins of the Gods, Mathematics and Music from the Rg Veda.* York Beach: Nicolas Hays, 1976.

McClellan, Andrew. *Inventing the Louvre: Art, Politics, and the Origins of the Modern Museum in Eighteenth Century Paris.* Berkeley: University of California Press, 1999.

McNeill, William. *The Glance of the Eye.* Albany: State University of New York Press, 1999.

Meijer, P. A. *Parmenides Beyond the Gates: The Divine Revelation on Being, Thinking, and the Doxa.* Amsterdam: Gieben, 1997.

Meijers, Anthonie. "Gustav Gerber und Friedrich Nietzsche. Zum historischen Hintergrund der sprachphilosophischen Auffassungen des frühen Nietzsche." *Nietzsche-Studien* 19 (1988): 369–390.

——— and Martin Stingelin,"Konkordanz zu den wörtlichen Abschriften und Übernahmen von Beispielen und Zitaten aus Gustav Gerber: *Die Sprache als Kunst* (Bromberg, 1871) in Nietzsches Rhetorik-Vorlesungen und in *Über Wahrheit und Lüge im außermoralischen Sinne*," *Nietzsche-Studien* 19 (1988): 350–368.

Merleau-Ponty, Maurice. "Indirect Language and the Voices of Silence." In: Merleau-Ponty, *Signs*. Translated by Richard McCleary. Chicago: Northwest University Press, 1964. Pp. 39–83.

Merchant, Carolyn. *Death of Nature: Woman, Ecology, and the Scientific Revolution*. San Francisco, Harper, 1990.

Miklowitz, Paul. "Reply to Wilcox, 'That Exegesis of an Aphorism in 'Genealogy III'." *Nietzsche-Studien*, 29 (1999): 267–269.

Mitchell, W. J. T. *Iconology: Image Text Ideology*. Chicago: University of Chicago Press, 1987.

Mondi, Robert. "ΧΑΟΣ and the Hesiodic Cosmogony." *Harvard Studies in Classical Philology*, 92 (1989): 1–41.

Moore, Gregory. *Nietzsche, Biology, and Metaphor*. Cambridge: Cambridge University Press, 2002.

——— and Thomas Brobjer, eds., *Nietzsche and the Sciences*. Aldershot: Ashgate, 2004.

Most, Glenn W. *The Measures of Praise: Structure and Function in Pindar's Second Pythian and Seventh Nemean Odes*. Göttingen: Vandenoeck & Ruprecht, 1985.

Mosser, Kurt. "Nietzsche, Kant, and the Thing in Itself." *International Studies in Philosophy*. 25 (1993): 67–78.

Müller-Lauter, Wolfgang. *Nietzsche's Philosophy of Contradiction and the Contradiction of His Philosophy*. Translated by David Parent. Bloomington: Illinois University Press, 1999. Originally published in German as *Nietzsches Philophie der Gegensätze und die Gegensätze seiner Philosophie*. Locus: Verlag, Date.

———. "On Judging in a World of Becoming." In Babich, ed., *Nietzsche, Theories of Knowledge, and Critical Theory: Nietzsche and the Sciences I*. Dordrecht: Kluwer, 1999. Pp. 165–185.

Muellner, Leonard. *The Anger of Achilles: Mēnis in Greek Epic*. Ithaca: Cornell University Press, 1996.

Nagy, Gregory. *Poetry as Performance: Homer and Beyond*. Cambridge: Cambridge University Press, 1996.

Nancy, Jean-Luc. "Friedrich Nietzsche: Rhétorique et langage. Textes traduits, présentés et annotés," *Poétique* 5 (1971): 99–142.

Nehamas, Alexander. *Nietzsche: Life as Literature*. Cambridge, MA: Harvard University Press, 1985.

———. "How One Becomes What One Is," *The Philosophical Review* XCII, No. 3 (July 1983): 385–417.

———. *The Art of Living: Socratic Reflections from Plato to Foucault*. Berkeley: University of California Press, 1998.

Neske, Gunter and Emil Kettering, eds., *Martin Heidegger and National Socialism: Questions and Answers*. New York: Paragon House, 1990.

Neumann, Günther. *Die phänomenologische Frage nach dem Ursprung der mathematisch-naturwissenschaftlichen Raumauffassung bei Husserl und Heidegger*. Berlin: Duncker & Humblot, 1999.

Nicholson, Graeme. *Illustrations of Being*. Atlantic Highlands: Humanities Press, 1992.

————. "The Politics of Heidegger's Rectoral Address." *Man and World*, 20 (1987):171–87.

Niehus-Pröbsting, Heinrich. "Ästhetik und Rhetorik in der 'Geburt der Tragödie.' " In: J. Kopperschmidt & H. Schanze, eds.: *Nietzsche oder «Die Sprache ist Rhetorik»*. Munich: Fink, 1994. Pp. 93–107.

O'Doherty, Brian. *Inside the White Cube:The Ideology of the Gallery Space*. Santa Monica, CA: The Lapis Press, 1986.

O'Flaherty, James C. et al., eds. *Studies in Nietzsche and the Classical Tradition*. Chapel Hill: The University of North Carolina Press, 1976.

Okochi, Ryogi. "Nietzsches Naturbegriff aus östlicher Sicht." *Nietzsche-Studien*, 17 (1988): 108–124.

Olivier, Abraham. "Nietzsche and Neurology." *Nietzsche-Studien*, 32 (2003): 125–141.

Oliveira, Nythamar Fernandez de. *On the Genealogy of Modernity: Foucault's Social Philosophy*. New York: Nova Scientific Publishers, 2003.

Ong, Walter. *Orality and Literacy: The Technologizing of the Word*. London: Methuen, 1982.

Osborne, Catherine. *Rethinking Early Greek Philosophy: Hippolytus of Rome and the Presocratics*. Ithaca: Cornell University Press, 1987.

Ott, Hugo. *Martin Heidegger: Unterwegs zu seiner Biographie*. Frankfurt am Main: Campus, 1988.

Otto, Detlef. *Wendungen der Metapher. Zur Übertragung in poetologischer, rhetorischer und erkenntnistheoretischer Hinsicht bei Aristoteles und Nietzsche*. Munich: Wilhelm Fink, 1998.

Page, Christopher. *Voices and Instruments of the Middle Ages*. Berkeley: University of California Press, 1976.

Parkes, Graham, ed., *Nietzsche and Asian Thought*. Chicago: The University of Chicago Press, 1991.

Pater, Walter. *The Renaissance: Studies in Art and Poetry*. Oxford: Oxford University Press, 1998.

Patt, Walter. *Formen des Anti-Platonismus bei Kant, Nietzsche und Heidegger*. Frankfurt am Main: Klostermann, 1997.

Patterson, Charles. *Eternal Treblinka: Our Treatment of Animals and the Holocaust*. New York: Lantern Books, 2002.

Parry, Adam, ed., *The Making of Homeric Verse: The Collected Papers of Milman Parry*. Oxford: Clarendon Press, 1987 [1971].

Parry, Milman. *L'Epithète traditionelle des Homère*. Paris, Les belles lettres, 1928.

Pelligrini, Alessandro. *Friedrich Hölderlin: Sein Bild in der Forschung*. Berlin: de Gruyter, 1965.

Perkins, Richard. "A Giant and Some Dwarves: Nietzsche's Unpublished Märchen on the Exception and the Rule." *Marvels and Fairy-Tales: Journal of Fairy Tale Studies*. 11/1–2 (1997): 61–73.

Petherbridge, Deanna and Ludmilla Jordanova. *The Quick and the Dead: Artists and Anatomy*. Berkeley: University of California Press, 1997.

Petzet, Heinrich. *Auf einen Stern zugehen. Begegnungen und Gespräche mit Martin Heidegger, 1929–1976*. Frankfurt: Societäts-Verlag, 1983.

————. "Nachdenkliches zum Spiegel-Gespräch." In: Neske & Kettering, eds., *Antwort.* Pp. 11ff; "Afterthoughts on the Spiegel-Interview." In: Neske & Kettering, eds., *Martin Heidegger and National Socialism.* Pp. 67ff.

Philipse, Herman. "Heidegger's Question of Being: A Critical Interpretation." In: Smith, Barry, ed.: *European Philosophy and the American Academy.* Monist Library of Philosophy: Hegeler Institute, La Salle, Illinois, 1994. Pp. 99–122.

Philonenko, Alexis. *Nietzsche. Le rire et le tragique.* Paris: le livre de Poche, 1995.

Pindar, *Olympian Odes; Pythian Odes.* Translated and edited by William H. Race. Cambridge: Harvard University Press, 1997.

————. *The Odes of Pindar.* Translated by J. E. Sandys. Cambridge: Harvard University Press, 1978 [1915].

Pliny, *Natural History.* Translated by Frank Justus Miller. Cambridge: Loeb, 1977.

Plumwood, Val. *Feminism and the Mastery of Nature.* London: Routledge, 1993.

Podach, Erich. *Ein Blick in die Notizbücher Nietzsches. Ewige Wiederkunft.Wille zur Macht. Ariadne. Eine schaffensanalytische Studie.* Heidelberg: Rothe, 1963.

Pöggeler, Otto."Heidegger on Art." In: Karsten Harries and Christoph Jamme, eds.: *Martin Heidegger: Politics, Art, and Technology.* New York: Holmes & Meier, 1994. Pp. 106–153.

————. *Neue Wege mit Heidegger.* Freiburg: Alber, 1992.

————. *Martin Heidegger's Path of Thinking.* Translated by Daniel Magurshak and Sigmund Barber. Atlantic Highlands, N.J.: Humanities Press, 1987.

————. *Der Denkweg Martin Heideggers.* Pfullingen: Neske, 1983.

————. "Being as Appropriation." Translated by R. H. Grimm. *Philosophy Today,* 19, 2/4 (1975): 152–178.

————. "Sein als Ereignis." *Zeitschrift für philosophischer Forschung,* XIII/4 (1959): 599–632.

Pöhlmann, Egert and Martin L. West, eds. *Documents of Ancient Greek Music, The Extant Melodies and Fragments Edited and Transcribed with Commentary.* Oxford: Clarendon, 2001.

Pöschl, Viktor. "Nietzsche und die klassische Philologie." In: Hellmut Flashar, et al., eds., *Philologie und Hermeneutik im 19. Jahrhundert: Zur Geschichte und Methodologie der Geisteswissenschaften.* Göttingen: Vandenhoeck and Ruprecht, 1979. Pp. 141–155.

Pöltner, Günther. "Mozart und Heidegger: Die Musik und der Ursprung des Kunstwerkes." *Heidegger Studies.* 8 (1992): 123–144.

Podach, Erich. *Ein Blick in die Nietzsches Notizbücher. Ewige Wiederkunft. Wille zur Macht. Ariadne. Eine schaffensanalytische Studie.* Heidelberg: W. Rothe, 1963.

Pont, Graham. "Analogy in Music: Origins, Uses, Limitations," in Kassler, ed., *Metaphor: A Musical Dimension.*

Porter, James. *The Invention of Dionysus: An Essay on the Birth of Tragedy.* Stanford, CA: Stanford University Press, 2000.

————. *Nietzsche and the Philology of the Future.* Stanford, CA: Stanford University Press, 2000.

————. "After Philology: Nietzsche and the Reinvention of Antiquity." *New Nietzsche Studies* 4:1/2 (2000): 33–76.

Potts, Alex. *Flesh and the Ideal. Winckelmann and the Origins of Art History.* New Haven: Yale University Press, 1994.

Prado, C. G., ed., *A House Divided: Comparing Analytic and Continental Philosophy.* Amherst, NY: Humanity Books, 2003.

Puttfarken, Thomas. *The Invention of Pictorial Composition.* New Haven: Yale University Press, 2000.

Race, William H. "Negative Expression and Pindaric ΠΟΙΚΙΛΙΑ." In: *Style and Rhetoric in Pindar's Odes* (Atlanta: Scholar's Press, 1990) *American Philological Association. Classical Studies 24.* Pp. 95–122.

Rancière, Jacques. *The Philosopher and his Poor.* Translated by John Drury, Corinne Oster, and Andrew Parker. Durham: Duke University Press, 2003.

Rand, Nicholas. "The Political Truth of Heidegger's 'Logos': Hiding in Translation." *Proceedings of the Modern Language Association,* 105 (1990): 436–447.

Reboul, Olivier. *Nietzsches critique de Kant.* Paris: Presses Universitaires de France, 1974.

Rée, Paul. *Basic Writings.* Translated by Robin Small. Urbana: University of Illinois Press, 2003.

Reinhardt, Karl. *Vermæchtnis der Antike: Gesammelte Essays zur Philosophie und Geschichtsschreibung.* Göttingen: Vandenhoeck & Ruprecht, 1989. [1960.]

Richardson, William J. *Through Phenomenology to Thought.* With a Foreword by Martin Heidegger. Fourth Edition, including a new author's preface. New York: Fordham University Press, 2003.

————. *Through Phenomenology to Thought.* Nijmegen: Nijhoff, 1965.

Richter, Simon. *Laocoon's Body and the Aesthetics of Pain: Winckelmann Lessing Herder Moritz Goethe.* Detroit: Wayne State University Press, 1992.

Ricoeur, Paul. *The Conflict of Interpretations.* Chicago: Northwestern University Press, 1974.

Rie, Robert. "Nietzsche and After." *Journal of the History of Ideas,* Vol 13, no. 3 (June 1952): 349–369.

Riedel, Manfred. "Der Anfang Europas. Nietzsche und die Griechen." In: *Nietzsche und Kessler* Ettersburger Hefte 2, Kuratorium Schloß Ettersburg e.V., Weimar, 1994. Pp. 13–33.

————. *Hören auf die Sprache. Die akroamatische Dimension der Hermeneutik.* Frankfurt am Main: Suhrkamp, 1989.

————. "The Origin of Europe: Nietzsche and the Greeks." *New Nietzsche Studies,* 4 1/2 (Summer/ Fall 2000): 141–155.

Riethmüller, Albrecht and Frider Zaminer, eds. *Die Musik des Altertums: Neues Handbuch der Musikwissenschaft.* Vol. 1. Laaber: Laaber-Verlag, 1989.

Reuter, Sören. "Reiz–Bild–Unbewusste Anschauung. Nietzsches Auseinandersetzung mit Hermann Helmholtz' Theorie der unbewussten Schlüsse in *Über Wahrheit und Lüge im aussermoralischen Sinne.*" *Nietzsche-Studien,* 34 (2004): 351–372.

Rodriguez, M. "Metafisica de la finidad natural. Su metamorfosis en la linea Kant-Schopenhauer-Nietzsche." *Pensamiento,* 50 (1994): 435–455.

Rose, Gillian. *Love's Work*. New York: Schocken, 1977.

Rossbach, August and Rudolf Westphal. *Theorie der musischen Künste der Hellenen.* Olms, 1966. [1886]

Rowell, Lewis. *Thinking About Music: An Introduction to the Philosophy of Music.* Amherst: The University of Massachusetts Press, 1983.

Ruckser, Udo. "Zum Fall Wagner-Nietzsche." *Allgemeine Musik-Zeitung,* 11 (1913): 1481–82.

Ryan Lawrence. *Wechsel der Töne.* Stuttgart: Kohlhammer, 1960.

Sachs, Curt. "Die griechische Gesangsnotenschrift." *Zeitschrift für Musikwissenschaft,* 7 (1924/5): 1–5.

———. "Die griechische Instrumentalnotenschrift." *Zeitschrift für Musikwissenschaft,* 6 (1923/4): 289–301.

Salem-Wiseman, Jonathan. "Nature, Deception, and the Politics of Art: Divisions of Labor in Kant and Nietzsche." *International Studies in Philosophy,* 30 (1998): 107–120.

Said, Edward. *Musical Elaborations.* New York: Columbia University Press, 1991.

Saint-Pierre, Puget de. *Histoire de Charles de Sainte-Maure, duc de Montausier.* Genève, Paris: Guillot, 1784.

Salter, William Mackintire. "Nietzsche and the War," *International Journal of Ethics,* Vol. 27, Issue 3 (April 1917): 357–379.

Schadewaldt, Wolfgang Otto Bernhard. "Der Weg Schillers zu den Griechen." In: Volkmann-Schluck, et al., eds., *Die Gegenwart der Griechen im neueren Denken. Festschrift für Hans-Georg Gadamer zum sechzigsten Geburtstag* Tübingen: Mohr, 1960. Pp. 225–232.

Schapiro, Meyer. "The Still-Life as a Personal Object: A Note on Heidegger and van Gogh." In Schapiro, *Theory and Philosophy of Art: Style, Artist, and Society.* New York: Braziller, 1994. Pp. 135–141. [Originally published in M. L. Simmel, ed., *The Reach of Mind: Essays in Memory of Kurt Goldstein.* New York: Springer Publishing, 1968. Pp. 203–209.]

———. "Further Notes on Heidegger and Van Gogh." In *Theory and Philosophy of Art.* Pp. 142–151.

Scheffler, Johannes. See: Angelus Silesius.

Schmid, Holger. *Kunst des Hörens: Orte und Grenzen philosophische Spracherfahrung.* Cologne: Böhlau, 1999.

———. " 'Nacht ist es.' Zum philosophischen Ort von Nietzsches Venedig Gedicht." In: *Nietzsche und Italien. Ein Weg von Logos zum Mythos?* Tübingen: Stauffenberg, 1999.

———. "Wechsel der Töne." In: Johann Kreuzer, ed., *Hölderlin Handbuch. Leben–Werk–Wirkung.* Stuttgart/Weimar: Metzler, 2002. Pp. 118–127.

Schmid, Wilhelm. *Auf der Suche nach einer neuen Lebenskunst. Die Frage nach dem Grund und die Neubegründung der Ethik bei Foucault.* Frankfurt am Main: Suhrkamp, 1991.

———. *Mit sich selbst befreundet sein.* Frankfurt am Main: Surkamp, 2004.

———. *Philosophie der Lebenskunst.* Frankfurt am Main: Suhrkamp, 1998.

Schmidt, Bertram. *Der ethische Aspekte der Musik: Nietzsches "Geburt der Tragödie" und die Wiener klassische Musik.* Würzburg: Königshausen & Neumann, 1991.

Schmidt, Dennis. *On Germans and Other Greeks: Tragedy and Ethical Life.* Bloomington: Indiana University Press, 2001.
———. "Changing the Subject: Heidegger, 'the' National and the Epochal." *Graduate Faculty Philosophy Journal,* 14/2–15/1 (1991).
Schmidt, Hermann Josef. *Nietzsche Absconditus oder Spurenlese bei Nietzsche.* Aschaffenberg: Alibri, 1991.
Schmidt, Michael. "«Hören mit Schmerzen»." In: Schirmacher, ed., *Zeitkritik nach Heidegger.* Essen: Die blaue Eule, 1989. Pp. 155–158.
Schneeberger, Guido. *Nachlese zu Heidegger.* Bern: Suhr, 1962.
Schneider, Bernhard. *Daniel Libeskind, Jewish Museum Berlin.* Munich: Prestel, 1999.
Schneider, Peter. "The Good Germans." *The New York Times Sunday Magazine* (13 February 2000).
Schürmann, Reiner. *Heidegger on Being and Acting. From Principles to Anarchy.* Translated by Christine-Marie Gros. Bloomington: Indiana University Press, 1987.
———. "A Brutal Awakening to the Tragic Condition of Being: On Heidegger's *Beiträge zur Philosophie.*" Translated by Kathleen Blamey. In: Karsten Harries and Christoph Jamme, eds.: *Martin Heidegger: Politics, Art, and Technology.* New York: Holmes and Meier, 1994. Pp. 89–105.
Schwan, Alexander. "Heidegger's *Beiträge zur Philosophie* and Politics." In: Harries and Jamme, eds., *Martin Heidegger.* London: Holmes & Meier, 1004. Pp. 71–88.
Scott, Charles, et al., eds., *Companion to Heidegger's Contributions to Philosophy.* Bloomington: Indiana University Press, 2001.
Seaford, Richard. *Money and the Early Greek Mind: Homer, Philosophy, Tragedy.* Cambridge: Cambridge University Press, 2004.
Sebald, Winfried Georg. *The Natural History of Destruction.* Translated by Anthea Bell. New York: Modern Library, 2003.
Seidler, Ingo. " 'Stifter einer weiteren Ahnenreihe': Hölderlin's Influence on German Poets of the Twentieth Century." In George, ed., *Friedrich Hölderlin,* pp. 64–86.
Seneca. *De brevitate vitae/Von der Kürze des Lebens,* trans. Josef Feix. Stuttgart: Reclam, 1977.
Seubert, Harald. *Zwischem erstem und anderen Anfang: Heideggers Auseinandersetzung mit Nietzsche und die Sache seines Denkens.* Köln: Böhlau, 2000.
Seubold, Günther. *Das Ende der Kunst und der Paradigmenwechsel der Ästhetik.* Munich: Fink, 1998.
Shiner, Lawrence E. *The Invention of Art: A Cultural History.* Chicago: University of Chicago Press, 2001.
Sieburth, Richard. "Introduction." In: *Hymns and Fragments by Friedrich Hölderlin.* Princeton: Princeton University Press, 1984.
Silk, Joseph and J. P. Stern. *Nietzsche on Tragedy.* Cambridge: Cambridge University Press, 1981.
Simon, Josef. "Grammar and Truth: On Nietzsche's Relationship to the Speculative Sentential Grammar of the Metaphysical Tradition." In: Babich, ed., *Nietzsche, Theories of Knowledge, and Critical Theory.* Pp. 129–151.

———. "Grammatik und Wahrheit: Über das Verhältnis zur metaphysischen Tradition." *Nietzsche-Studien*, 1 (1972): 1–26.

Singer, Isaac Bashevis. "The Slaughterer. " *The Animals' Voice Magazine* 2 (1989): 38–41.

Sloterdijk, Peter. *Regeln für den Menschenpark*. Frankfurt am Main: Suhrkamp, 1999.

Sluga, Hans. *Heidegger's Crisis: Philosophy and Politics in Nazi Germany*. Cambridge: Cambridge University Press, 1993.

Small, Robin. *Nietzsche and Rée: A Star Friendship*. Oxford: Oxford University Press, 2005.

———. *Nietzsche in Context*. Aldershot: Ashgate, 2001.

Sophocles. *Oedipus Tyrannus*. Translated by Sir Richard Jebb. Cambridge: Harvard University Press, 1887.

Söring, Jürgen. "*Incipit Zarathustra*—Vom Abgrund der Zukunft." *Nietzsche-Studien* 8 (1979).

Spiekermann, Klaus. "Nietzsche and Critical Theory." In Babich, ed.: *Nietzsche, Theories of Knowledge, and Critical Theory*. Pp. 225–242.

Spiegel, Marjorie. *The Dreaded Comparison: Human and Animal Slavery*. New York: Mirror Books, 1996.

Stack, George L. *Kant, Lange, and Nietzsche: Critique of Knowledge, Nietzsche and Modern German Thought*. New York: Routledge, 1991.

———. "Kant and Nietzsche's Analysis of Knowledge." *Dialogos*, 22 (1987): 7–40.

Stahl, Gerry. "Attuned to Being: Heideggerian Music in Technological Society." In: William V. Spanos, ed.: *Martin Heidegger and the Question of Literature*. Bloomington: Indiana University Press, 1979. Pp. 297–324.

Stegmaier, Werner. *Nietzsches »Genealogie der Moral«: Werkinterpretationen* (Darmstadt: Wissenschaftliche Buchgesellschaft, 1990.

Steiner, Deborah. *The Crown of Song: Metaphor in Pindar*. Oxford: Oxford University Press, 1986.

Steiner, George. *The Lessons of the Masters*. Cambridge: Harvard University Press, 2003.

———. *Martin Heidegger*. Chicago: University of Chicago Press, 1991.

———. *Le sens du sens: Présences Réeles, Real Presences, Realpräsenz*. Paris: Vrin, 1988.

Stingelin, Martin. "*Unsere ganze Philosophie ist Berichtigung des Sprachgebrauchs.*" *Friedrich Nietzsches Lichtenberg Rezeption im Spannungsfeld zwischen Sprachkritik (Rhetorik) und historischer Kritik (Genealogie)*. Munich: Fink, 1996.

———. "Nietzsches Wortspiel als Reflexion auf poet(olog)ische Verfahren." *Nietzsche-Studien* 19 (1988): 336–349.

Stone, Dan. *Breeding Superman: Nietzsche, Race and Eugenics in Edwardian and Literary Britain*. Liverpool: Liverpool University Press, 2002.

Strong, Tracy B. *Friedrich Nietzsche and the Politics of Transfiguration*. Urbana: University of Illinois Press, 2000.

Szabó, Árpád. *The Beginnings of Greek Mathematics*. Reidel: Dordrecht and Boston, 1978.

Taminiaux, Jacques. *Le nostalgie de la Grèce à l'aube de l'idéalisme allemand.* The Hague: Nijhoff, 1967.

———. *Le théâtre des philosophes.* Grenoble: Jérôme Millon, 1995.

———. "The Origin of "The Origin of the Work of Art." In: John Sallis, ed., *Reading Heidegger: Commemorations.* Bloomington: Indiana University Press, 1993. Pp. 392–404.

Taylor, Robert. "Old French." In: T. J. McGee, et al., eds., *Singing Early Music: The Pronunciation of European Languages in the Late Middle Ages and Renaissance.* Bloomington: Indiana University Press, 1996. Pp. 103–118.

Theunissen, Michael. *Pindar.* Munich: C. H. Beck, 2000.

Theweleit, Klaus. *Male Fantasies. Volume 1: Women Floods Bodies History.* Translated by Stephen Conway. Minneapolis: University of Minnesota Press, 1987.

Thomas, Douglas. *Reading Nietzsche Rhetorically.* New York: The Guilford Press, 1999.

Tomlinson, Gary. *Music in Renaissance Magic: Toward a Historiography of Others.* Chicago: The University of Chicago Press, 1993.

Trawny, Peter. *Heidegger and Hölderlin oder der Europeische Morgen.* Wurzburg: Königshausen & Neumann, 2004.

Treitler, Leo. *With Voice and Pen: Coming to Know Medieval Song and How it Was Made.* Oxford: Oxford University Press, 2003.

Treiber, Hubert. "Wahlverwandtschaften zwischen Nietzsches Idee eines 'Klosters für freiere Geister' und Webers Idealtypus der puritanischen Sekte. Mit einem Streifzug durch Nietzsches 'ideale Bibliothek.' " *Nietzsche-Studien,* 21 (1992): 326–362.

Trimpi, Wesley. *Muses of One Mind: The Literary Analysis of Experience and Its Continuity.* Princeton: Princeton University Press, 1983.

Tomlinson, Gary. *Music in Renaissance Magic: Toward a Historiography of Others.* Chicago: The University of Chicago Press, 1993.

Vagnetti, Luigi. "Concinnitas, riflessioni sul significato di un termine albertiano." *Studi e documenti di architetura,* 2 (1973): 139–161.

Van Gogh Museum. *Mit den Augen von Vincent van Gogh. Seine Wahlverwandtschaften und sein Kunstempfinden.* Amsterdam: Belser, 2003.

van Tongeren, Paul. "Politics, Friendship and Solitude in Nietzsche." *South African Journal of Philosophy,* Vol 19, no. 3 (2000): 209–222.

———. "On the Friend in Nietzsche's Zarathustra." *New Nietzsche Studies* (Vol. 5 3/4 and 6 1/2 Winter 2003/ Spring 2004): 73–88.

Valpilhac-Augen, Catherine, dir. *La collection Ad Usum Delphini. L'Antiquité au miror du Grand Siecle.* Paris: Eilug, 2000.

Vaihinger, Hans. *Die Philosophie des Als Ob. System der theoretischen, praktischen und religiösen Fiktionen der Menschheit auf Grund eines idealistischen Positivismus: mit einem Anhang über Kant und Nietzsche.* Leipzig: F. Meiner, 1911.

———. *Nietzsche als Philosoph.* Berlin: F, Meine, 1902.

Valadier, Paul. *Nietzsche: L'athée de rigeur.* Paris: Desclée de Brower, 1975.

———. *Nietzsche et la critique du christianisme.* Paris: Editions du Cerf, 1974.

———. "Science as New Religion." In: B. Babich, ed., *Nietzsche, Epistemology, and Philosophy of Science: Nietzsche and the Sciences II.* Dordrecht: Kluwer, 1999. Pp. 241–252.

Veyne, Paul. *Did the Greeks Believe their Myths?* Chicago: University of Chicago Press, 1983.

Viales, Noelle. *Animal to Edible.* Translated by J. A Underwood. Cambridge: Cambridge University Press, 1994.

Vietor, Kai. "Die Barockformel 'Braune Nacht,' " *Zeitschrift für Philologie* 63 (1938): 284–298.

Vietta, Silvio. *Heideggers Kritik am Nationalsozialismus und an der Technik.* Tübingen. Niemayer, 1989.

Visker, Rudi. "Dropping: The 'Subject' of Authenticity: *Being and Time* on Disappearing Existentials and True Friendship with Being." *Research in Phenomenology,* XXIV (1994): 133–158.

Visvanathan, Shiv. "On the Annals of the Laboratory State." In: Ashis Nandy, ed., *Science, Hegemony, and Violence: A Requiem for Modernity.* Delhi: Oxford University Press, United Nations University, 1990. [1988] Pp. 257–290.

Vivarelli, Vivetta. "Empedokles und Zarathustra. Verschwendeter Reichtum und Wollust am Untergang," *Nietzsche-Studien,* 18 (1989): 509–536.

von Hellingrath, Norbert. *Hölderlins Wahnsinn.* In: von Hellingrath, *Hölderlin. Zwei Vorträge. Hölderlin und die Deutschen. Hölderlins Wahnsinn.* München: Hugo Bruckmann, 1921.

von Hermann, Friedrich Wilhelm. "Nachwort des Herausgebers," *Beiträge zur Philosophie. (Vom Ereignis). Gesamtausgabe 65.* Edited by Friedrich-Wilhelm von Herrmann. Frankfurt am Main: Vittorio Klostermann, 1989.

———. "Heidegger und Nietzsche: Der andere Anfang." *Aletheia* 9/10 (1996): 20–21.

von Naredi-Rainer, Paul. *Architektur & Harmonie, Zahl, Maß und Proportion in der abendländischen Baukunst.* Köln: Dumont, 1982.

von Reibnitz, Barbara. *Ein Kommentar zu Nietzsche "Die Geburt der Tragödie aus dem Geiste der Musik" (Kapitel 1–12).* Stuttgart: Metzler, 1992.

Wagenführ, Horst. *Kunst als Kapitalanlage.* Stuttgart: Forkel, 1965.

Warminski., Andrej. "Monstrous History: Heidegger Reading Hölderlin." in: Aris Fioretos, ed.: *The Solid Letter: Readings of Hölderlin,* Stanford: Stanford University Press, California, 1999.

Weber, Max. *Wissenschaft als Beruf 1917/19. Politik als Beruf.* Edited by Wolfgang J. Mommsen and Wolfgang Schluchter with Birgitt Morgenbrod. Tübingen: Mohr, 1992.

West, Martin L. *Ancient Greek Music.* Oxford: Clarendon, 1992.

———. *Greek Lyric Poetry.* Oxford, Oxford University Press, 1994.

———. Commentary. In: Hesiod, *Theogony.* Clarendon Press, Oxford, 1966.

———. *Iambi et Elegi Graeci.* Oxford, Oxford University Press, 1955.

Weiner, Marc A. *Wagner and the Anti-Semitic Imagination.* Lincoln: University of Nebraska Press, 1995.

Weiss, Steven D. "Nietzsche and the Thing in Itself: Surviving Modern Kant Scholarship." *International Studies in Philosophy,* 25 (1993): 79–84.

Weizsäcker, Carl Friedrich von. "Nietzsche and Modernity." Translated by Heidi Byrnes. In: Babich, ed., *Nietzsche, Epistemology, and the Philosophy of Sci-*

ence. Pp. 221–240. Originally in *Wahrnehmung der Neuzeit*. Hanser: Munich, 1983. Pp. 70–106.

Widmann, Josef Viktor. "Nietzsche's Dangerous Book." Translated by Lysanne Fauvel and Tim Hyde. *New Nietzsche Studies*, 4 1/2 (2000): 195–200.

Wiggershaus, Rolf. *The Frankfurt School: Its History, Theories, and Political Significance*. Translated by M. Robertson. Cambridge, MA: MIT Press, 1994.

Wilamowitz-Möllendorff, Ulrich. "Future Philology." Translated by Gertrude Pöstl, Babette E. Babich, and Holger Schmid, *New Nietzsche Studies*, 4: 1/2 (2000):1–32.

———. "Zukunfts-Philologie!" In: Karlfried Gründer, ed., *Der Sreit um Nietzsches «Geburt der Tragödie»*. Hildesheim: Olms [Reprint Edition], 1989. Originally published as a pamphlet: *Zukunfts-Philologie! eine erwiderung auf Friderich Nietzsches ord. professors der classicschen philologie zu Basel "geburt der tragödie*." Berlin: Gebrüder Borntraeger, 1872.

Wilcox, John T. "What Aphorism Does Nietzsche Explicate in Genealogy of Morals Essay III?" *Journal of the History of Philosophy* 35/4 (1997): 593–603.

———. "That Exegesis of an Aphorism in 'Genealogy III': Reflections on the Scholarship," *Nietzsche-Studien*, 28 (1998): 448–462.

Winner, Langdon. *Autonomous Technology: Technics-Out-of-Control as a Theme in Political Thought*. Cambridge: MIT Press, 1977.

———. *The Whale and the Reactor*. Chicago: University of Chicago Press, 1986.

Wittkower, Rudolf. *Architectural Principles in the Age of Humanism*. New York: Norton, 1971.

Wohlfart, Günther. *Der Augenblick. Zeit und ästhetische Erfahrung bei Kant, Hegel, Nietzsche und Heidegger*. Freiburg/München: Alber, 1982.

Wolin, Richard. *The Politics of Being: The Political Thought of Martin Heidegger*. New York: Columbia University Press, 1990.

Wooster, Donald. *Nature's Economy: A History of Ecological Ideas*. Cambridge: Cambridge University Press, 1992.

Zimmermann, Robert. *Geschichte der Æsthetik als philosophischer Wissenschaft*. Vienna: Braumüller, 1858.

Zumthor, Paul. *Langue, texte, énigme*. Paris: Editions du Seuil, 1975.

———. "Why the Troubadours?" In: F. R. P. Akehurst and J. Davis, eds.: *A Handbook of the Troubadours*. Berkeley: University of California Press, 1995. Pp. 11–18.

Zweig, Stefan. *Kampf mit dem Dämon. Hölderlin. Kleist. Nietzsche*. Leipzig: Insel-Verlag, 1925.

Name Index

200–201, 209, 241, 262, 274n 19, 277n 38, 280n 15, 288–289nn 36, 38, 311n 6, 320n 32
Kaufmann, Walter, 50, 65, 288n 34, 308n 47
Kaulbach, Friedrich, 274n 19, 320n 32
Keats, John, 4
Kerenyi, Carl, 310n 55, 318n 15
Kierkegaard, Søren, 236
Kingsley, Peter, 97, 297n 2, 309n 52, 317n 6
Kisiel, Theodore, 230, 245
Klossowski, Pierre, 93
Koberstein, August, 124, 281n 29
Köhler, Joachim, 286n 15
Kofman, Sarah, 88, 293n 12
Kojéve, Alexandre, 154
Koldehoff, Stefan, 329n 59
Kopperschmidt, Joseph, and Helmut Schanze, 276n 28
Krell, David F., 125–126, 335–336n 16
Kremer-Marietti, Angèle, 293n 12
Kronos, 175, 190–192, *see also* Saturn
Kronion, 132, 176, 190, 192, *see* Jupiter
Krüger, Heinz, 276n 30
Kuhn, Thomas, 69

Lacan, Jacques, 7, 76, 91, 112, 125, 152–154, 158, 161, 164, 236, 241, 271n 1, 315n 21, 332n 19
Lacoue-Labarthe, Philippe, 40, 130, 240, 280n 17, 308nn 44, 45
Laks, André and Glenn W. Most, 283n 40
Lange, Frederick Albert, 27, 125, 274n 19, 279n 13
Laplanche, Jean, 125
La Rue, Jan, 300n 36
Lee, M. Owen, 282n 36
Lefkowitz, Mary, 307n 37
Leibniz, Gottfried Wilhelm, 59, 340n 48
Lernout, Geerd, 306–307nn 26, 27
Lessing, Gotthold Ephraim, 39–40

Leupin, Alexandre, 285n 8
Levinas, Emanuel, 91, 140, 156, 240, 299n 22
Libeskind, Daniel, 205–206
Lichtenberg, Georg Christian, 27, 273n 13
Liébert, Georges, 9, 268n 26
Lincoln, Abraham, 109
Lloyd-Jones, Hugh, 146, 312n 27
Loeb, Paul, 300n 35
Löwith, Karl, 110, 236
Lonergan, Bernard, 243
Lord, Albert B., 282n 33
Lotze, Rudolf Hermann, 269n 41
Louth, Charlie, 77, 294nn 21, 24
Love, Frederick, 268n 26
Lucifer, 163
Lukàcs, Georg, 125, 335n 13
Luria, Alexander, 282n 33
Luther, Martin, 19, 21, 77
Lyotard, Jean-François, 240

Machiavelli, Nicolò, 65
MacIntyre, Alasdair, 84, 164, 221, 295nn 39, 40
Maconie, Robin, 301n 37
Mahler, Gustave, 110
Maimon, Solomon, 127
Maleuve, Didier, 323n 1, 326n 25
Malevich, Kasimir, 203
Malraux, André, 202, 213, 216, 325nn 20, 21, 326n 29
Malsch, Wilfried, 310n 56
Marchand, Suzanne S., 306n 26
Marcuse, Herbert, 258–259
Martin, Nicolas, 310n 55
Marsden, Jill, 276n 31
Marten, Rainer, 233–235, 237, 239, 332nn 14–18
Marx, Eduardo, 302n 43
Marx, Karl, 66, 186–187, 236
Maas, Paul, 278–279n 6
May, Karl, 314n 5
McClain, Ernest G., 104, 299n 30, 310–311n 4
McClellan, Andrew, 323n 1, 325n 21

Subject Index

acroamatic, 35, 277n 38, 297n 3, *see also* concinnity, hearing

actor, problem of, 147, 160–162, 164–165, *see* artist, Jew, woman
as falseness with a good conscience, 161

aesthetics, 39–40, 200–201, *see* art
as distinguished from Heidegger's philosophy of art, 201–204, 209–215, 218–220, 324n 17, 330n 71
authenticity of art, 218
disinterest, Kantian, 209
education, Schiller's, 195
science of, 39–40
Nietzsche's, practical, 94, post-, 161, *see also* artist

affirmation, 89–94, 110, 296nn 47, 48; artistic, 149–150, 155–160
and the indispensability of pain and suffering for *amor fati*, 149
and style, 19, 88
as response to Schopenhauer, 109, 132
erotic, 152, 155, 163–164, 166–168, 296n 50, *see amor fati*
expenditure, 165–168

allusions, 26, *see* source scholarship, plagiarism

amor fati, 78, 81, 86, 92–94, 149, 158
as erotic affirmation, 151–152, 155, 186
as the love of the world, 151, 152, 158, *see also* innocence of becoming

analogy, and the problem of metaphor, 42

analytic-continental divide, 27, 250–251, 270n 44, 273n 17, 275n 27 (20), 293n 18

anti-science, Heidegger as, 257, 339–340n 47, 340n 48, *see*: for and against/pro and con

anti-Semitism,
Heidegger's, 227, 231, *see* Nazism, race, silence
readerly, 33–35
and Nietzsche's style, 33–36, 277n 37, *see* style

aphorism, as philosophical form, 33, 276n 30
and commentary, 31, *see* aphorism, Nietzsche's, identifying/locating, interpreting
and epigraph, 30
as phenomenological, 33
composing, 31
Hippocrates, 29
musical character of, 106–110, 301n 39
Nietzsche's, 19, 29–36, 70, 276nn 30, 31
as author-absolving, 30
as model for Heidegger's *Beiträge*, 259
as musical, 98, 105–110, *see* reading, musical
as reading themselves into the reader, 19, 33–36, 106–110, 277n 37, *see* fish-hooks

as irredeemably wrong, 155–156, 160
as nature of philosophy, 4–6, 267n 19
carnal profundity of, 153–154,
  162, 163–164, *see* love
erotic
  idea of music, 166
  Socrates as, 6, 8, 103
errancy, 241, 270n 52
error and knowledge, 43–44, 71–72,
  77
esoteric Protestantism, 108
eternal return, 84–89, 91–94, 155–156,
  314n 9
  and the problem of suffering, 150
  as desire of eternity, desire raised
    to eternity, 156
  "du wirst es jedenfalls," 296, n 45
  ethics of, 85–86, 91–92
  Goethe's expression of, 90–91
  Empedoclean expression in
    Hölderlin, ix–xii, 145
  mathematical literality of, 156
  scholarly aversion to a literal
    account of, 150
etymology, 49, *see* genealogy,
  Nietzsche's
exoteric/esoteric, 13, 26, 50, 53,
  132, 255, 297n 2, 309n 52, *see*
  writerly-readerly reciprocity
exhibition, 202, 204–209, 321n 22,
  see also museum, installation
expression, as going to ground, 157
eyes, hearing with, 46, 239

fish-hooks, 33, 83, *see* aphorisms,
  Nietzsche's, *see* style, Nietzsche's
  selective
for and against, as journalistic rubric,
  72, 257, 339–340n 47, *see* anti-
  science, pro and con
foreign, and native, 11, 25, 78, 127–
  130, 159, 308n 42, 332n 18
forgetting, 174
fragment
  in philosophy, 283nn 40, 41

friend,
  in Nietzsche, 21–22, 62, 82–83,
    271–272n 5, 295nn 34, 37, 38

Gates, The, 199, 203–208
Gay Science, The, 9–10
"gay" science, 56
  as art of poetry, 56–63
  as dedicated science, 58
  as passion, 58, 59, 63–64, 69–72
  music of, 65–69
Gedankenstrich, Nietzsche's, 12, 30
Gelassenheit, 16–17, 194
  as peace, 157
genealogy, 78–79
  as active and reactive, 251
  of mythic to rational thought, 43–
    44, *see* origin of truth in
    untruth
  of science, out of religion, 70
  Nietzsche's, 49
genius
  artistic, in vulgar expression, 165
  cult of, 164–165, 268n 26
German
  and ancient Greek, 4, 12, 127–
    130, 238, 306n 26
  more Greek than Greek, 237
  as language of philosophy for
    Heidegger, 232–233
  as spoken, sound of, 11, 16, 44
  between Hölderlin and Nietzsche,
    117–127, *see* influence
  tradition of translation, 77–84, *see*
    also translation
Greece and Germany, 127–130, 227–
  232, 238, 306nn 26, 33
Greek, ancient, 12
  stressed or accent-based, 38
  meter and rhythm, Nietzsche's
    theory of, 37–49, *see also* ictus
  poetry of, 45
  prosody, 38, 99, 279n 10, *see*
    sound of

Heidegger and, 16, 269nn 31, 38, 273n 17
reason and, 193
speaks, 16
laughter
and Nietzsche, 56–57, 136, 305–306nn 20, 21
playful art of, 55–57, 136
learning, art of
and the Greeks, 24, 123–124
and language,. 237–238
to read, 47, 50, 52, 239, *see* reading, 239
how to love, 89, 158–160, 239
literary scholarship
and philosophy, 134
love, 3, 7–9, 12, 152, 168, 267nn 22, 23, 312–313nn 1, 2
as the art of compromise, 154, *see* desire, giving up on
and eros, 5, 162–3, 313n 2
divine, 9, 162
God's knowledge of, 162–163, *see* neediness, divine
harmony and dissonance, xii
learning to, 64, 167
love-affairs, 6, 8, 70
Abelard and Heloise, 8
Heidegger and Hannah Arendt, 6–8
Nietzsche and Lou Salomé, 7–8, 168, 272n 5
living, art of, 291–292n 4

Machenschaft, 190, 243–246, 250–252, 256, 258–261, *see* calculation
as essence of modern technology, 244–246
political, 252–255, 257–260
mask, 162
masturbation, Nietzsche's, 28, *see* autoeroticism, onanism
measure, 197, *see* poetic balance
media, modern, 202, *see* virtual
medicine, and the practice of pain, 142, 144, 300n 33, *see* pain

melancholy, 192, *see* scientists
Memnon's Column, 118, 303n 6
mental reservation, Heidegger's, as political resistance (pointless), 253, 257, 338n 34
metaphor, 40–44, 46–47, 61, 117–122
and consciousness, 42
and philology, 40–41, 49–55, 279n 11
and sensual compensation, 267n 12, 302n 2, 303n 6, 304n 4
as active leaping over, 41, 279n 12, *see* crossover, energeia
sound figures as exemplification of, 61, 70, *see* Chladni
in analytic readings in Nietzsche, 40
in literary readings of Nietzsche, 40
crossover, 39, 117–122, 279n 12, 303n 6, 304nn 11, 12, 305n 16
hermeneutic of, 40
as genealogy, 49–53
lovers as musical, xii, 310n 4
method, scientific, 58–61, 172
modernity, 193
as time of transition, 195
museum
and exhibition halls, 202, 204–209
as locus of art, 202–209, 220–224
as definition of art, 209
conservation, 220–226
and world-withdrawal, 223–226
culture of, 199, 323n 1, 325nn 21, 22, 326nn 25, 26, 326–327n 29
in the age of mechanical reproduction, 202, 325n 21
signifiers of, 205, 221–237
music
ancient, as opposed to modern, 44, 99–101, 296–298nn 1, 8–24
ancient, and ethics, 102
and architecture, 106, 300n 36, 301nn 37, 38
and tragedy, 38–44
dance, as measure of , 47, 102, *see* dance